Thomas Collett Sandars

**The Institutes of Justinian**

Thomas Collett Sandars

**The Institutes of Justinian**

ISBN/EAN: 9783742831682

Manufactured in Europe, USA, Canada, Australia, Japa

Cover: Foto ©Thomas Meinert / pixelio.de

Manufactured and distributed by brebook publishing software
(www.brebook.com)

Thomas Collett Sandars

**The Institutes of Justinian**

# THE INSTITUTES

## OF

# JUSTINIAN

WITH

## ENGLISH INTRODUCTION, TRANSLATION, AND NOTES

BY

## THOMAS COLLETT SANDARS, M.A.

BARRISTER-AT-LAW

LATE FELLOW OF ORIEL COLLEGE, OXFORD

*FOURTH EDITION*

LONDON
LONGMANS, GREEN, AND CO.
1869

# PREFACE

———◆———

IN PREPARING the second edition of this volume for
the press, I have made some slight changes both in the
Introduction and in the Notes. These changes consist
almost entirely in the removal of passages embodying
theories on the history or interpretation of Roman law
which are not sufficiently supported by evidence to
require notice in a commentary on an elementary treatise. I have endeavoured, in a work which is only
intended for those who are unacquainted with Roman
law, to state nothing but what a beginner can understand, and to avoid as much as possible all difficult and
controverted points.

I must repeat what I stated in the Preface to the
first edition, that in preparing this volume I have been
under obligations to the French edition by Ortolan so
great as to call for the amplest acknowledgment. I
have also derived great assistance from the edition by
Ducaurroy, and from the 'Manuel du Droit romain'
of Lagrange, as well as from the 'Commentaries' of
Warnkœnig, and the 'Institutes' of Puchta. In the

Introduction I have embodied much that was suggested by the 'Histoire de la Législation romaine' and the 'Généralisation du Droit romain' of Ortolan, and by the first volume of the 'Institutes' of Puchta. In the translation I have been greatly assisted by the French translations of Ortolan and Ducaurroy, as well as by the translations in English of Harris and Cooper.

Under each paragraph of the text I have placed references to the parallel passages of the 'Institutes' of Gaius, of the 'Digest' and the 'Code.' These references are nearly the same as those given in the 'Juris Civilis Enchiridium.' The text is almost the same throughout as that given in the 'Corpus Juris,' edited by the Kriegels, Leipsic, 1848.

T. C. S.

## ADVERTISEMENT

### TO

## THE THIRD EDITION.

In this edition no alteration has been made except the correction of typographical errors.

# INTRODUCTION.

1. THE legislation of Justinian belongs to the latest period of the history of Roman law. During the long *Object of the* space of preceding centuries the law had under- *Introduction.* gone as many changes as the State itself. The Institutes of Justinian embody principles and ideas of law which had been the slow growth of ages, and which, dating their first origin back to the first beginning of the Roman people, had been only gradually unfolded, modified, and matured. It is as impossible to understand the Institutes, without having a slight knowledge of the position the work occupies in the history of Roman law, as it is to understand the history of the Eastern Empire without having studied that of the Western Empire and of the Republic. Many, also, of the leading principles of Roman law contained in the Institutes are unfamiliar to the English reader, and though they may be learnt by a perusal of the work itself, the reader, to whom the subject is new, may be glad to anticipate the study of details by having placed before him a general sketch of the part of law on which he is about to enter. It is proposed, therefore, in this Introduction, to give first an outline of the history of Roman law, and then an outline of Roman private law. Each, however, will only be given with the very moderate degree of fulness proper to a sketch intended to be merely a preliminary to the study of the Institutes.

B

# HISTORY OF ROMAN LAW.

*History of early Rome. The Populus.*  
2. However obscure may be the history of early Rome, we cannot doubt that Roman citizens were, from a very early period, composed of two distinct bodies, the *populus* and the *plebs*, of which the first alone originally possessed all political power, and the members of which were bound together by peculiar religious ties. Nor can we have any reasonable doubt about the general features of the constitution of the *populus*. Whatever may have been their origin, it consisted of three tribes. The tribe was divided into ten *curiæ*, and each *curia* into ten *decuriæ*; another name for a *decuria* was a *gens*, and it included a great number of distinct families, united by having common sacred rites, and bearing a common name. It was not necessary that there should be any tie of blood between these different families, in order that they should form part of the same *gens*; but a pure unspotted pedigree, ancient enough to have no known beginning, was claimed by every member of a *gens*,* and there was a theoretical equality among all the members of the whole tribe. The heads of the different families in these hundred *gentes* met together in a great council, called the council of the curies (*comitia curiata*). A smaller body of one hundred, answering in number to the *gentes*, and called the senate, was charged with the office of initiating the more important questions submitted to the great council; and a king, nominated by the senate, but chosen by the curies, presided over the whole body, and was charged with the functions of executive government.

---

* *Gentiles sunt, qui inter se eodem nomine sunt; non est satis: qui ab ingenuis oriundi sunt; ne id quidem satis est: quorum majorum nemo servitutem servivit: absit etiam nunc qui capite non sunt deminuti.*—CICERO, *Topic.* 6.

3. The *populus* was also bound together by strong religious ties. What was most peculiar in the religion of Rome was its intimate connection with *Religious system.* the civil polity. The heads of religion were not a priestly caste, but were citizens, in all other respects like their fellows, except that they were invested with peculiar sacred offices. The king was at the head of the religious body; and beneath him were augurs and other functionaries of the ceremonies of religion. The whole body of the *populus* had a place in the religious system of the State. The mere fact of birth in one of the *familiæ* forming part of a *gens* gave admittance to a sacred circle which was closed to all besides. Those in this circle were surrounded by religious ceremonies from their cradle to their grave. Every important act of their life was sanctioned by solemn rites. Every division and subdivision of the State to which they belonged had its own peculiar sacred ceremonies. The individual, the family, the *gens*, were all under the guardianship of their respective tutelary deities. Every locality with which they were familiar was sacred to some patron god. The calendar was marked out by the services of religion : the pleasure of the gods arranged the times of business and leisure, and a constantly-superintending Providence watched over the counsels of the State, and showed, by signs which the wise could understand, approval or displeasure at all that was undertaken.

4. By the side of this associated body there was another element of the State, occupying a position very *The Plebs.* different from that which was occupied by this privileged community. The *plebs* was probably formed by the inhabitants of conquered towns being brought to Rome; perhaps also by the influx of voluntary settlers. These new-comers, or, if we are to suppose that the *plebs* was coeval with the *populus*, these strangers, remained without the political circle which included the *populus*. They belonged to no *gens*,* had no place

---

* The position of the plebeian families included in the *gentes* was so exceptional, and is so obscure, that we need not qualify the general

in the *comitia*, no share in the legislative or executive government; as little had they any share in the *jus sacrum*. They were as much excluded from the pale of the peculiar divine law as from that of the peculiar public law of the ruling body. Even the Servian constitution, and the formation of the thirty tribes, laid the foundation of future change, rather than altered in early times the basis on which existing institutions were founded. The centuries opened to the *plebs* a door to political power by making the two orders meet on the common ground of a graduated scale of property; and the constitution of the thirty tribes marked off the inhabitants of the town and country into small local divisions, in the *comitia* of which the *plebs* had of course the preponderance. But though the *comitia centuriata* took away ultimately almost all political power from the *comitia curiata*, and the *comitia tributa* formed a rallying point for a plebeian party, still the old relations of the different members of the body politic remained, in theory at least, long unimpaired. The curies alone could give the religious sanction which was indispensable to the validity of the resolutions of the centuries, and the *plebs* was as much as ever excluded from admission into the body of the *populus*, fenced round with its impassable wall of religious privileges.

5. There could be very little direct law-making except to meet temporary emergencies, in such a community as early Rome. What laws were made, were first proposed, arranged, and determined on by the senate, under the guidance of its chief magistrate, the king, and then submitted to the highest source of power, the *comitia curiata*. After the institution of the centuries, the *comitia centuriata* gradually succeeded to the political power of the *curiata*, and the curies only met to give a formal religious sanction to the resolutions of the centuries. The king published regulations on matters that fell exclusively within his province as *pontifex maximus*, and a collection of those *leges regiae*, which were probably nothing more than by-laws for the

*Legislation in early Rome.*

---

statement that the *plebs* did not belong to a *gens*, especially if the expression in the text is considered as referring to the early times of Rome.

conduct of religious ceremonies, was made, or said to be made, by Papirius, who lived in the time of Tarquinius Superbus.*

6. The king was the supreme judge in all causes. But if, in a criminal trial, the accused were a member *Judges.* of the *populus*, he could appeal from the king to the *comitia curiata*. If the accused were a plebeian, he had no tribunal to which he could appeal, until, shortly after the expulsion of the kings, the Valerian laws gave an appeal to a *comitia* of which the *plebs* formed a part. Civil causes were decided by the king in his quality of *pontifex maximus*, or by the subordinate *pontifices* acting under him, as all the private law of the *populus* was so mixed up with the sacred law, that it was part of the duty of a *pontifex* to know and guard its provisions.†

7. After the expulsion of the kings, the struggle between the *plebs* and the *populus* became gradually more and more serious. Besides the the right of appeal *Position of the Plebs after the* to the centuries secured by the *lex Valeria* in *expulsion of the Kings.* every case when a citizen was condemned to death, the secession to the Aventine in 260 A.U.C. wrung from the *patres* a cancelment of existing debts, and the creation of tribunes, at first two in number, and afterwards ten, to defend the *plebs*. These champions of the lower order of the State gave great additional importance and strength to the *comitia tributa*, as having to elect magistrates, protected themselves by a sacred character, and specially commissioned to maintain the interest of so large a body of their fellow-citizens. But the *plebs* had to struggle with an evil which no partial remedies could meet. There was no body of laws to which they could appeal in case they were wronged. The whole administration of the laws was in the hands of the patricians, and there was no appeal from the decision of the

---

* There is no reason to doubt that Papirius was a real person (DIONYS. iii. 36.) But when Pomponius speaks of his collection as the *jus civile papirianum* (D. i. 2. 2. 2), he probably uses the term not with reference to the real work of Papirius, but to a work composed towards the end of the republic by Granius Flaccus, *De Jure Papiriano* (D. i. 16. 144).

† D. i. 2. 2. 6.

magistrate except in cases where life was at stake, or unless the injury, inflicted by wilful perversion of the law, was great enough, as in the memorable instance of Virginia, to rouse the wronged to the redress of physical force. Many of the rights which theoretically belonged to the plebeians as having the same private law with the *populus*, were practically denied them. At last, a successful revolution enabled the *plebs* to insist on a changed form of political government, which might open the door of power and office to the members of their own body, and supply a machinery for the preparation of a fixed and permanent body of law. The Decemvirate, superseding and incorporating into itself every other magistracy, and composed of an equal number of patricians and plebeians, was formed for the purpose of collecting and embodying in the shape of written law all those portions of the customary law which it was most essential for the due administration of justice to place on an indisputable footing, and publish for the benefit of the whole body of citizens.

8. The lavish praises bestowed on the laws of the Twelve

*The Twelve Tables.*

Tables by the later writers of Rome, and the story of the deputation sent to learn the laws of Greece, would give us an idea of a very different body of laws from that which these Tables actually presented. We should expect to find a systematic exposition of Roman public and private law as it existed in the times previous to the Gallic invasion; and to find, also, that the whole body of law was at least coloured by the infusion of a foreign element. We should naturally think that there was something new and original in a legislation which Cicero considers as almost the perfection of human wisdom.* The fragments of the Twelve Tables which remain to us show how erroneous are these conceptions of their contents. There is nothing whatsoever which we can decidedly pronounce to be borrowed from a foreign origin, except some provisions respecting the law of funerals, taken from the laws of Solon. These Tables contained, for the most part, short enunciations of those points of law which the conduct of

---

* See especially *De Orat.* i. 43, 44.

the affairs of daily life required to be settled and publicly announced. The law had existed before, but in a floating, vague, traditionary shape, only some very few laws having been engraved on tablets and publicly displayed. The Twelve Tables left to the decision of the magistrates, and the interpretation of those skilled in law, the application and exposition of these principles ; they also left many parts of the customary law wholly untouched on. But what the exigencies of the time required deciding, they decided, and they laid a firm foundation on which the structure of private law would rest for the future. It is not difficult to understand how this was esteemed so great a gain to the large body of the citizens, that these laws were spoken of by the ancients as the creations of a new legislation.

9. The Decemvirate was nominally intended to be a means of removing, as far as was then thought possible, the political distinction between the orders. *The attainment of political equality by the Plebs.* How little the object was really accomplished is notorious. Although half the decemvirs were plebeians, the suppression of the meetings of the *comitia tributa*, and the loss of tribunes, was poorly compensated by the presence of magistrates who acted in conjunction with patricians, and readily yielded deference to their colleagues. Besides, the Two Tables added in the year of the second Decemvirate contained provisions which later writers considered manifestly unjust ;* and we know that, among other things, they expressly refused the *connubium* to the *plebs.* The Twelve Tables, as fixing and proclaiming the law, were undoubtedly a source of great strength to the plebeians, and enabled them to maintain a much more secure position in their future struggles ; but the Decemvirate, regarded as a crisis in their political history, was certainly unfavourable to them. Nothing shows more completely that this was so than the progress they made immediately after the downfall of Appius Claudius and his colleagues. The laws of Horatius and Valerius not only forbad the constitution of any magistracy

---

* Cic. *De Rep.* ii. 37.

from which there should be no appeal, but provided that the
ordinances of the *comitia tributa* should, if sanctioned by
the senate and the curies, be binding on all Roman citizens;
and in 309, only four years after the abolition of the Decemvirate, the Canuleian law gave the *connubium* to the *plebs*,
and the marriage of a patrician with a plebeian was no longer
forbidden by law. This change was important, not only as
removing a distinction mortifying to many individuals and
embarrassing many of the relations of private life, but as
breaking through one of the barriers which the *jus sacrum*
had hitherto interposed in the way of the *plebs*.* The obstacle of a religious disqualification was the reason generally
assigned by the *populus* for the exclusion of plebeians from
public offices;† and it was a great step towards political
equality that the objection urged to marriages between the two
orders—that it would disturb the *sacra* of the *gentes*—should
be overcome. The advance of the *plebs* to political equality
was, however, very slow; and it was not until a century and a
half had elapsed from the passing of the Canuleian law that
the two orders were placed on an equal footing. We may take
the year 467 A.U.C., the date of the *lex Hortensia*, as the
period when we can first pronounce that the distinction of
the two orders was really done away. When that law had
been passed, the plebeian had a full share in the *jus publicum*
and the *jus sacrum*. The ordinances of the *comitia tributa*
required no confirmation of the curies, no sanction of the
Senate; they were binding on the whole Roman people directly
they were passed. The equality between the two orders was so
complete that the plebeian could become consul, censor, praetor, curule aedile; he could enter the senate, he could administer justice; he was excluded from none of the privileges of the
*jus sacrum*; he could become pontifex and augur; and though
he could not of course take part in any of the *sacra* belonging
to particular *gentes*, go through certain religious ceremonies,

---

* *Ideoque decemviros connubium dirimiss, ne incertâ prole auspicia*
*turbarentur.*—Liv. iv. 6.

† *Interroganti tribuno, cur plebeium consulem fieri non oporteret? re-*
*spondit, quòd nemo plebeius auspicia haberet.*—Liv. iv. 6.

or be engaged in the service of particular gods, these exceptions did not lower his political position. As far as the history of law is concerned, we may henceforward lose sight of the distinction between plebeian and patrician.

10. From the writings of the latter jurists, and especially from those of Gaius and Cicero, and from the fragments of the Twelve Tables that have come *The jus civile.* down to us, we can collect the essential features of the private law of Rome in its earliest period, before a general advance in civilization had modified it. This early law, which rested on custom as its foundation, and the elements of which, except so far as appeared in the laws of the Twelve Tables, were only known by tradition, was called in subsequent times the *jus civile*, the peculiar law of the Roman State. The history of Roman law is the history of the changes introduced into this law, of the additions made to it, and of the method adopted in the process. The notion of a body of customary law, mainly unwritten, which was not abrogated, but was evaded or amplified by persons acting under the ideas of later times, is the notion which, above all others, must be embraced clearly by any one who wishes to understand Roman law. The *jus civile* must always be taken as the standing point, and in tracing the history of the later law, we have always to trace how, while the *jus civile* still remained in force, the law was made to suit the requirements of different periods by evading or adding to the *jus civile*. It was only in the later days of the Empire that the *jus civile* began to be swept away. When we come to speak of the contents of Roman private law, we shall have occasion to notice what were the leading features of the *jus civile*. We need not at present do more than say that, when a student of Roman law has made himself acquainted with the elementary doctrines, he will find that the chief of these peculiar principles, dating from an unknown antiquity, and affecting the whole body of later jurisprudence, are those which determine the position of a father of a family, the succession to his estate, and the contracts and actions relating to the chief possessions of an agricultural proprietor.

11. The conquest of Italy and the gradual spread of Roman conquest materially altered the character of the legal system. A branch of law almost entirely new

*Conquest of Italy.*

sprang up, which determined the different relations in which the conquered cities and nations were to stand with reference to Rome itself. As a general rule, and as compared with other nations of antiquity, Rome governed those whom she had vanquished with wisdom and moderation. Particular governors, indeed, abused their power; but the policy of the State was not a severe one, and Rome connected itself with her subject allies by conceding them privileges proportionate to their importance, or their services. The *jus Latinum* and the *jus Italicum* are terms familiar to all readers of Roman history ; the first expressed that, with various degrees of completeness, the rights of Roman citizenship were accorded to the inhabitants of different towns, some having the *commercium* only, some also the *connubium*. Towards the end of the republic, after the Social War (A.U.C. 663), the distinction of the *Latinitas*, as a partial right of citizenship attached to the inhabitants of particular places, disappeared among the people of Italy. The *lex Junia* (A.U.C. 664) and the *lex Plautia* (A.U.C. 663) gave the full rights of citizenship to almost the whole of Italy, and the Italians were distributed among the thirty-five tribes. The *jus Italicum* expressed a certain amount of municipal independence and exemption from taxation, attached to the different places on which the right was bestowed. The citizens of some particular places in the provinces possessed the *jus Latinum*, and the *jus Italicum* was attached to certain privileged cities; but the provinces generally had no participation in either right. They were subject to a proconsul or propraetor, paid taxes to the treasury of Rome, and had as much of the law of Rome imposed upon them, and were made to conform as nearly to Roman political notions, as their conquerors considered expedient.*

* See WARNKÖNIG, *Hist. du droit romain externe*, p. 70. SAVIGNY, *Geschichte Röm. Rechts*, vol. i. ch. 2.

12. But the contact of Rome with foreign nations produced a much more remarkable effect on Roman law than the introduction of a new branch of law regulating the position of subject nations. It wrought, or at least contributed *Change in* largely to work, a revolution in the legal notions *Roman law* of the Roman people. It forced them to compare *under the* other systems with their own. In the language of *Prætors.* the jurists, it brought the *jus gentium*, that is, the law ascertained to obtain generally in other nations, side by side with the *jus civile*, the old law of Rome. The *prætor peregrinus*, who was appointed to adjudge suits in which persons who were not citizens were parties, could not bind strangers within the narrow and technical limits in which Romans were accustomed to move. Many of the most important parts of Roman law were such that their provisions could not be extended to any but citizens. No one, for instance, except a citizen, could have the peculiar ownership termed *dominium ex jure Quiritium*. But when justice and reason pronounced a stranger to be an owner, it was impossible for a *prætor* not to recognize an ownership different from that which a citizen would claim; and what magistrates were obliged to do in the case of strangers, the requirements of advancing civilization soon induced them to do in the case of citizens. They recognized and gave effect to principles different from those of the municipal law of Rome. This municipal law remained in force wherever its provisions could give all that was required to do substantial justice; but when they could not, the prætor appealed to a wider law, and sought in the principles of equity a remedy for the deficiencies of the *jus civile*. He pronounced decrees (*edicta*), laying down the law as he conceived it ought to be, if it was to regulate aright the case before him. In process of time it became the custom for the prætor to collect into one *edictum* the rules on which he intended to act during his tenure of office, and to publish them on a tablet (*in albo*) at the commencement of his official year. These edicts, put forward at the beginning of the year of office, were termed *edicta perpetua*. How much the prætor was aided in the

formation of a broader and more comprehensive system of
law by a change in the form of actions, will appear when we
come to speak of the system of civil process. By degrees
such a system was introduced and fully established, and the
*jus honorarium*, the law of the prætors * (*qui honores gere-
bant*), was spoken of as having a distinct place by the side,
and as the complement, of the *jus civile*.

13. The progress of law was also much facilitated by the
growth of a body of men termed *juris consulti*
or *juris prudentes*, men who studied the forms,
and, in time, the principles of law, and expounded

*The juris prudentes.*

them for the benefit of their friends and dependents. They
were generally among the first men of the State, and the employment was considered one of the most dignified that could
occupy the evening of a life of public service and magisterial
honours. In the earlier times of the republic the patricians
alone knew the days on which it was or was not lawful to
transact legal business, and the forms in which actions were
to be brought. The story of the publishing of a collection of
these forms, and of a list of the days on which business could
be transacted, by Caius Flavius, is familiar to all readers of
Livy.† But although to a certain extent the study of the law
became open to all, yet it does not seem to have been ever
undertaken except by men of eminence. Such men used to
instruct and protect the persons who sought their advice, explain the steps necessary for the successful conduct of an action,
and write out the necessary forms.‡ They gave answers when
asked as to the law on a particular point; and though they pro-
fessed only to interpret the Twelve Tables, not to make laws,
their notion of interpretation was so wide that it included
whatever could be brought within the spirit of anything which
the Twelve Tables enacted. Such answers (*responsa*) were of

---

* The term also included the edicts of the ædiles who issued decrees
in matters that came specially within their province.

† Liv. ix. 46.

‡ The duty of a jurisprudent was *respondere, cavere, agere, scribere.* —
Cic. *De Orat.* i. 48.

course of no legal authority; but as the sage would frequently accompany his client* (as the questioner was called) before the magistrate, and announce his opinion, it had frequently all the effect upon the magistrate which a positive enactment would have had, and thus the *responsa prudentum* came to be enumerated among the direct sources of law. The names of some of these sages have been handed down to us. Cato the censor, and Severus Sulpicius, the cotemporary of Cicero, are those otherwise best known to us.† In the latter days of the republic the *juris prudentes* were men acquainted with some portion at least of Greek philosophy, men of learning and general cultivation; and it is not difficult to understand how powerfully their authority, acting almost directly on judicial decisions, must have contributed to the change which the law underwent towards the end of the republic.

14. By far the most important addition to the system of Roman law which the jurists introduced from Greek philosophy, was the conception of the *lex naturæ*. We learn from the writings of Cicero whence this conception came, and what was understood by it.‡ It came from the Stoics, and especially from Chrysippus. By *natura*, for which Cicero sometimes substitutes *mundus*, was meant the universe of things, and this universe the Stoics declared to be guided by reason. But as reason is thus a directive power, forbidding and enjoining, it is called law (*lex est ratio summa insita in natura, quæ jubet ea quæ facienda sunt, prohibetque contraria*). But nature is with the Stoics both an active and a passive principle, and there is no source of the law of nature beyond nature itself. By *lex naturæ*, therefore, was meant primarily the determining force of the universe, a force inherent in the universe by its constitution (*lex est naturæ vis*). But man has reason, and as

> The law of nature.

---

* *Clienti promere jura.*—Hor. *Epis.* ii. 104.

† Gibbon, viii. 31.

‡ The most important passages in Cicero, with reference to the *lex naturæ*, are *De Leg.* i. 6–12; *De Nat. Deor.* i. 14, ii. 14, 31; *De Fin.* iv. 7. The expressions used in the text are from *De Leg.* i. 6.

reason cannot be twofold, the *ratio* of the universe must be the
same as the *ratio* of man, and the *lex naturæ* will be the law
by which the actions of man are to be guided, as well as the
law directing the universe. Virtue, or moral excellence, may
be described as living either in accordance with reason, or
with the law of the universe. These notions worked themselves into Roman law, and the practical shape they took was
that morality, so far as it could come within the scope of
judges, was regarded as enjoined by law. The jurists did not
draw any sharp line between law and morality. As the *lex
naturæ* was a *lex*, it must have a place in the law of Rome.
The prætor considered himself bound to arrange his decisions
so that no strong moral claims should be disregarded. He had
to give effect to the *lex naturæ*, not only because it was morally
right to do so, but also because the *lex naturæ* was *lex*.
When a rigid adherence to the doctrines of the *jus civile*
threatened to do a moral wrong, and produce a result that was
not equitable, there the *lex naturæ* was supposed to operate,
and the prætor, in accordance with its dictates, provided a
remedy by means of the pliant forms of the prætorian actions.
Gradually the cases, as well as the modes in which he would
thus interfere, grew more and more certain and recognized,
and thus a body of equitable principles was introduced into
Roman law. The two great agents in modifying and extending
the old, rigid, narrow system of the *jus civile* were thus the *jus
gentium* and the *lex naturæ*; that is, generalizations from the
legal systems of other nations, and morality looked on according to the philosophy of the Stoics as sanctioned by a law.
But as, on the one hand, the generalizations from experience
had in themselves no binding force, and as, on the other, the
best index to ascertain what morality commanded was to examine the contents of other legal systems, the *jus gentium*
and the *lex naturæ* were each the complement of the other,
and were often looked on by the jurists as making one whole,
to which the term *jus gentium* was generally applied.*

---

* See AUSTIN, *Province of Jurisprudence determined.* Appendix,
page xii.

15. The centuries met to decide questions of war and peace, and to choose the higher magistrates; but *Source of legislation.* the laws which, after the *lex Hortensia*, were passed to effect any real change in the body of Roman law, were almost all *plebiscita*. The *comitia tributa* were recognized as almost the exclusive centre of legislative power; but in the later times of the republic a con- *Plebiscita.* tinually-increasing importance was attached to the ordinances of the senate. Gaius says that it had been questioned whether the *senatus-consulta* had the force of law.* Perhaps they had not exactly the force of law at any time under the republic, excepting when they related to matters which it was the peculiar province of the senate to regulate; but they were probably of little less weight than enactments recognized as constitutionally binding. The senate successfully main- *The Senate.* tained a claim† to exercise a dispensing power, and to release individuals from obedience to particular laws. It was generally able to reject a law, either wholly or partly, by calling in the aid of religious scruples; and if it added a clause to a law, the new portion of the law was as binding as the old.‡ In the shape of directions to particular magistrates, it issued injunctions, of which the force was felt by all those who were subject to the magistrate's power, and it made, we have reason to think, independent enactments in matters belonging to religion, police, and civil administration, and perhaps even in matters of private law.§ The senate comprised the richest and most influential men in the State; the disruption of society attending the civil wars strengthened their influence; and the Romans of the days of Cicero were quite prepared for the place which the senate held, as a legislative body, under the early Cæsars.

16. The first emperors were only the chief magistrates of the republic. Augustus and his immediate suc- *The Emperor.* cessors united in their own persons all the highest

---

* Cicero mentions them among the sources of law.—*Topic* 5.
† Ascon. *Argum. in Cornel.* (Orell. p. 57).
‡ Ascon. *Argum. in Cornel.* (Orell. p. 67).
§ Puchta, *Instit.* i. 298.

offices of the State. The *imperium*, or supreme command,
was conferred on them by the *lex regia* passed as a matter of
form at the beginning of their reign, and by which the later
jurists supposed that the people devolved on the emperor all
their own right to govern and to legislate.* The assumption
of despotism was veiled under an adherence to republican
forms ; and, at any rate during the first century of our era,
the emperor always affected to consider himself as nothing
more than the *princeps reipublicæ*. Although we have instances, even in the time of Augustus, of edicts intended to be
binding by the mere authority of the emperor, yet the people
at first, and the senate afterwards, was recognized as the primary source of law. By degrees the emperor usurped the sole
legislative authority, either dictating to the senate what it was
to enact, or in later times, enacting it himself. The will of
the prince came to have the force of law.† Sometimes this
will decided what the law should be by the publication of
*edicta* pronounced by the emperor in his magisterial capacity,
or *mandata*, orders directed to particular officers ; sometimes
by *decreta*, or judicial sentences given by the emperor, which
served as precedents ; at other times by *rescripta*, that is,
answers given by the emperor to magistrates who requested
his assistance in the decision of doubtful points.

17. The people did not cease to make laws for a considerable time after the commencement of the empire.‡
These laws were of course really the creations of
the emperor's will. Augustus, for instance, procured the sanction of legislation to a series of measures which made a considerable innovation in private law. These measures were designed to repress and discourage the excesses and corruption
of a demoralized society. The *lex Julia et Papia Poppæa*, and
others of a similar character, attempted to restore virtue to
private life by a system of rewards and penalties, attached to

*Laws.*

---

* D. i. 4. 1.
† *Inst.* i. 2. 8. *quod principi placuit, legis habet vigorem.*
‡ Gaius mentions a *lex Claudia.*—Gaius, i. 157.

the fulfilment or neglect of family duties. They failed in their object, but the portion of law to which they belonged was considerably modified by their provisions.

18. After the middle of the first century of our era, all legislative enactments of which we know are *senatus-consulta*. The election of magistrates was transferred to the senate from the *comitia*,* and the senate was intrusted with the cognizance of offences against the emperor and the State, and the decision of appeals from inferior tribunals.† The later jurists said that the senate was made to represent the whole people, because the number of the citizens became too great to permit of their acting as a political body.‡ However historically false this may be, it yet is so far true that the senate was, in the earlier times of the empire, a body distinct from, and, in a certain very limited degree, opposed to, the emperor. We have some few memorable instances in Tacitus of senators who dared to speak what they thought,§ and who showed that the senate was, in more than name, a remnant of the republic. Gradually the very notion of independent action died away, and the senate met merely to adopt the will of its master.

*The Senate.*

19. The *edictum perpetuum*, the annual edict of the praetor, as being the written exposition of the *jus honorarium*, was the subject of many of the treatises of the Roman jurists. In the time of Hadrian, a jurist of great eminence, Salvius Julianus, was appointed by the emperor to draw up an edict, partly from existing edicts, partly according to his own opinion of what was necessary, which should serve as the guide and rule of all succeeding praetors. The edict which he drew up and to which the sanction of Hadrian gave the force of law was itself termed the *edictum perpetuum*, the word *perpetuum*,

*The Praetor's edict.*

---

* Tacit. *Annal.* i. 15.
† Suet. *Calig.* 2; *Nero*, 17. Tacit. *Annal.* xiii. 44.
‡ *Inst.* i. 2. 5. Pomponics in *Dig.* i. 2. 9.
§ Tacit. *Hist.* iv. 8. Puchta, *Inst.* i. 512.

c

instead of meaning, as before, that the edict ran on from year to year, being used to express that the edict was permanent and unchangeable. The different magistrates, who had to apply the edict, would thenceforward use their own discretion only when the edict drawn up by Julianus did not serve as an express authority.

20. The writings of the jurists, the authority attached to

*The jurists.*

their decisions, and the admirable manner in which they developed and arranged the law, formed the most marked feature of the legal history of this period. Augustus found the position which the great sages of the law held in public opinion too important a one to be overlooked in his scheme of government. He formally gave to their decisions the weight which usage had in many instances given them already; and it was enacted that their answers should be solicited and announced in a formal manner, and given under the sanction of the emperor. Hadrian decided that they should have the force of law, provided the respondents all agreed in their answers; but, if they differed, the judge was at liberty to adhere to whichever opinion he preferred.* Two jurists of eminence, Antistius Labeo and

*Schools of
Labeo and
Capito.*

Ateius Capito, represented in the days of Augustus two opposite modes of regarding law, and were the founders of schools which maintained and handed down their respective opinions. Labeo, in whom a wider culture had instilled a love of general principles, did not hesitate to make such innovations as he conceived reason and philosophy to require: Capito was distinguished by the fidelity with which he adhered to the law as he had himself received it.† A succession of jurists of greater or less renown divided themselves under the banners of these rival authorities. But the schools of which Labeo and Capito were the first authors

---

* GAIUS, i. 7.

† *Labeo ingenii qualitate et fiducia doctrinæ, qui et in cæteris sapientiæ partibus operam dederat, plurima innovare statuit. Ateius Capito, in his quæ ei tradita erant, perseverabat.—Dig.* i. 2. 2. 47.

did not derive their names from their founders. The one school was termed Proculians, after Proculus a distinguished follower of Labeo; the other Sabinians after Sabinus, a follower of Capito. Gaius, who informs us that he was a Sabinian, gives the differing opinions of the two schools on many subtle questions of law. By the labours of this succession of jurists, the law was moulded and prepared until it came into the hands of the five great luminaries of Roman jurisprudence—Gaius, Papinian, Paul, Ulpian, and Modestinus.

21. Gaius, or Caius, as the name is sometimes written, was probably born in the time of Hadrian, and wrote under the Antonines. Of his personal history *Gaius.* nothing is known. He himself tells us that he was an adherent of the school of Sabinus. Besides other works which he is known or supposed to have written, he composed a treatise on the *edictum provinciale* (the edict of the proconsul in the provinces) and a commentary on the Twelve Tables. But the work by which he is best known to us is his Institutes. The discovery of the manuscript of this work by Niebuhr in 1816 has contributed greatly to the modern knowledge of Roman law. The manuscript had been written over with the letters of St. Jerome, and its existence was almost entirely unknown until Niebuhr brought it to light while examining the contents of the library of the Chapter at Verona. The institutes of Gaius formed the basis of those of Justinian, who has followed the order in which Gaius treats his subject, and adopted his exposition of law, so far as it was applicable to the times in which the Institutes of Justinian were composed. The work of Gaius, therefore, showing us what was common to the two periods, and also, where the law had changed, enables us to understand what the change was, and what the law had really been at the time when its system was most perfect.

22. Æmilianus Papinianus was the intimate friend of the emperor Septimius Severus, and held under him the office of prætorian præfect, which had now *Papinian.* become equivalent to that of supreme judge. He probably

accompanied Severus into Britain, and was present at the emperor's death at York in A.D. 211. Severus commended his two sons, Geta and Caracalla, to his care. Caracalla dismissed Papinian from his office; and, after his murder of Geta, is said to have required Papinian to compose his vindication. Papinian refused, and was executed by the orders of Caracalla. He was considered the first and greatest of jurists, and every epithet which succeeding writers could devise to express wisdom, learning, and eloquence was heaped on him in profusion. We know, from the Digest, of his Books of Questions, Books of Answers, and Books of Definitions. The fragments of his works which we possess amply justify his eminent reputation.

23. Paul, Ulpian, and Modestinus are all said to have been

*Paul*  pupils of Papinian. Julius Paulus was a member of the imperial council and prætorian præfect under Alexander Severus (A.D. 222). Besides numerous fragments in the Digest, we possess his *Receptæ Sententiæ*, which was long the chief source of law among the Visigoths in Spain. The most celebrated of his works, which were very numerous,* was that *Ad Edictum* in 80 books.

24. Domitius Ulpianus derived his origin, as he himself

*Ulpian.*  tells us, from Tyre in Phœnicia.† He wrote several works during the reigns of Septimius Severus and Caracalla, and perished (A.D. 228) by the hands of the soldiers, who killed him in the presence of the emperor, Alexander Severus. He was prætorian præfect at the time of his death, but the exact time when he first was appointed to the office is unknown. The Digest contains a greater number of extracts from his writings than from those of any jurist. Besides these extracts, we also possess fragments of his composition in twenty-nine titles, known by the name of the *Fragmenta Ulpiani.*

---

* We know the names of more than 70, embracing an extraordinary variety of subjects.

† D. 1. 1. 1.

25. Herennius Modestinus was the pupil of Ulpian as well as of Papinian. He was a member of the imperial council in the time of Alexander Severus, *Modestinus.* but hardly anything is known of his history. One of the best known of his writings is the *Excusationum Libri*. We have nothing remaining of his composition except the extracts from his works given in the Digests.

26. The influence of Christianity on Roman law was partly direct, partly indirect. The establishment of a hierarchical rank, the power granted to religious *Influence of Christianity.* corporations to hold property, the distinction between Christians and heretics, affecting the civil position of the latter, the creation of episcopal courts, and many other similar innovations, gave rise to direct specific changes in the law. But its influence is even more remarkable in the changes which were suggested by its spirit, rather than introduced as a necessary part of its system. To the community which citizenship had bound together * succeeded another bound by the ties of a common religion. The tendency of the change was to remove the barriers which had formed a part of the older condition of society. If we compare the Institutes of Justinian with those of Gaius, we find changes in the law of marriage, in that of succession, and in many other branches of law, in which it is not difficult to recognize the spirit of humanity and reverence for natural ties, which Christianity had inspired. The disposition to get rid of many of the more peculiar features of the old Roman law, observable in the later legislation, was partly indeed the fruit of secular causes; but it was also in a great measure due to the alteration of thought and feeling to which the new religion had given birth.

27. Before we pass to the legislation of Justinian, we must bestow a cursory notice on the efforts made by *Theodosius II.*

---

* The tie of citizenship was really done away with by the recklessness with which it was extended. Caracalla (A.D. 212) made all persons citizens who were subjects of the empire.

Theodosius II. to determine and arrange the law, and to
promote its study. With a view to keep alive and increase
the knowledge of law, he founded (in A.D. 425) a school of
jurisprudence at Constantinople. He also constituted the
works of the five great writers, Gaius, Papinian, Ulpian, Paul,
and Modestinus into a source of law of the highest authority,
enacting by a constitution, published A.D. 426, that the judge
should always be bound by the opinion expressed by the
majority of these writers; if those among them who expressed an opinion on the point were equally divided, the
opinion of Papinian was to prevail: if he was silent, the
judge could use his own discretion. In A.D. 438, Theodosius published his Code, containing a collection of the
constitutions of the emperors from the time of Constantine.
It was made on the model of two earlier collections compiled
by the jurists Gregorianus (A.D. 306) and Hermogenianus
(A.D. 365).

28. The Emperor Justinian was of Sclavonic origin. His
*Justinian.* native name was Upranda, a word said to mean
upright, and thus to have found an equivalent in
the Latin Justinianus. He was born at Taurisium in Bulgaria,
about the year A.D. 482, and having been adopted by his uncle,
the Emperor Justin, succeeded him as sole emperor in the
year A.D. 527. He died in A.D. 565, after an eventful reign of
thirty-eight years. Procopius, the secretary of his general
Belisarius, has left us a secret memoir of the times, which, if
we may rely upon his accuracy, would make us believe Justinian to have been a weak, avaricious, rapacious tyrant.
His court, wholly under the influence of his wife Theodora,
a degraded woman, whom he had raised from the theatre to
share his throne, was as corrupt as was customary in the empire
of the East. Justinian would never have been distinguished
from among the long list of Eastern emperors had it not been
for the victories of his generals and the legislation to which
he gave his name. The successes of Belisarius and Narses
have shed the splendour of military glory over his reign. But
his principal claim to be remembered by posterity is his having

directed the execution of an undertaking, which gave to Roman law a form that fitted it to descend to the modern world.

29. In the year A.D. 528, Justinian issued instructions for the compilation of a new code, which, founded on that of Theodosius, and on the earlier codes *The first Code.* on which that code was based,* should embrace the imperial constitutions down to the date of its promulgation. The task was entrusted to a body of ten commissioners, who completed their labours in the following year, and in the month of April, A.D. 529, the emperor gave it his sanction, and abolished all preceding collections.

30. In the December of the following year, Tribonian, who had been one of the commission appointed to draw up the code, and who had recommended him- *The Digest.* self to the emperor by the energy and ability he had shown, was instructed, in conjunction with a body of coadjutors whom he selected to the number of sixteen, to make a selection from the writings of the elder jurists, which should comprehend all that was most valuable in them, and should form a compendious exposition of the law. In spite of the foundation of schools of jurisprudence, of which those of Rome, Constantinople, and Berytus were the most famous, the knowledge which the lawyers of the time had of the writings of the old jurists was exceedingly limited. Justinian wished not only to promulgate a body of law which should not be too bulky and voluminous for general use, but also to provide a work, the study of which should form a necessary part of legal education. The commissioners performed their task in the short space of three years, and on the 30th of December, A.D. 533, the

---

* Shortly before the time of Justinian, three attempts had been made to draw up a body of law for the use of the western barbarians and their Roman subjects. These were—the edict of Theodoric, king of the Ostrogoths (A.D. 500); the *Lex Romana Burgundiorum* (A.D. 500); and the *Lex Romana Visigothorum* (A.D. 506). These names are so well known that it is perhaps hardly proper to pass them over altogether: but, as their assistance was not employed in the construction of Justinian's legislation, a detailed account of them is unnecessary here.

emperor gave to the result of their labours the force of law. The compilation, termed Digesta, or Pandectæ, from its comprehensive character, was divided into fifty books, and was arranged on the model of the perpetual edict. Ulpian's work on the edict had been a text-book in the schools of jurisprudence, and probably it was this that determined the commissioners to adopt a model,* which has prevented their work having anything like a scientific arrangement. There are thirty-nine jurists from whose writings the Digest contains literal extracts, those from Ulpian and Paul constituting about one-half of the whole work.

31. The Digest was too vast a work, and also required for its comprehension too great a previous knowledge *The Institutes.* of law to admit of its being made the opening of a course of legal study. Justinian, therefore, determined to have an elementary work composed. He had declared his intention in the constitution of Dec. A.D. 530, in which he directed the compilation of the Digest; and Tribonian, in conjunction with Theophilus and Dorotheus, respectively professors in the schools of Constantinople and Berytus, were appointed to draw it up. This elementary work is the Institutes. It was formed on the basis of the Institutes of Gaius, alterations being made to bring it into harmony with the Digest and Code.

32. There were still some points which had been debated by the old jurists, and to which the legislation of *The Fifty De-* Justinian did not as yet furnish any answer. To *cisions.* determine these, Justinian published a book of Fifty Decisions; and as the Code of the year A.D. 529 was a very imperfect work, it was determined to revise that Code, and to incorporate the Fifty Decisions in the re- *The second* vised edition. Tribonian was appointed to super- *Code.* intend the undertaking, and in Nov. A.D. 534 the new code, called the code repetitæ prælectionis received the force of law. This is the code we now have; the former code,

---

* WARNKŒNIG, *Hist. du droit romain*, p. 182.

that of A.D. 529, having been carefully suppressed, and no trace of it remaining. The Code, which is divided into twelve books, is arranged nearly in the same manner as the Digest.

33. But Justinian could not endure that his having systematized the law should exclude him from lawmaking. He announced in the Code* that any *The Novels.* legislative reforms he might at any future time see fit to make should be published in the form of *Novellæ Constitutiones*. Many such *Novellæ* were afterwards published; the first in January, A.D. 535, the last in November, A.D. 564. Altogether they amount to 165; but no collection of them seems to have been made in the lifetime of Justinian. Few of them bear a later date than A.D. 545, the year of Tribonian's death.

34. The Institutes of Justinian, after a few general observations on the nature, the divisions, and the *Arrangement* sources of law, proceed to treat, first of persons, *of the Institutes.* then of things, then of successions to deceased persons, then of obligations, and lastly of actions. An arrangement as nearly similar as possible will be observed in the following outline of Roman private law.

---

## ROMAN PRIVATE LAW.

THE reader of Mr. Austin's Treatise on the Province of Jurisprudence will remember that he proposes, in the outline given in the Appendix, to treat the subject of Law by examining, first, the science of General Jurisprudence, that is of the legal notions and principles which enter into every system of law; and secondly, the science of Particular Law, that is, as he explains it, 'The science of any such system of Positive law as now actually obtains, or once actually obtained in a specifically determined nation;' and he carefully distinguishes between the sciences of general and particular jurisprudence and

---

* *Const. de Emend. Cod. 4.*

the science or sciences which would tell us, not what law is,
but what law ought to be.

The Roman jurists made no approach to a division of the
subject so accurate and so exhaustive. It is their great merit,
the real source of their value to modern Europe, that they
apprehended and elucidated the great leading principles and
notions of general jurisprudence; but they did not clearly
distinguish between general jurisprudence and the municipal
law of Rome, or between law and morality. As we have said
before, they assumed, on the authority of Greek philosophy,
that there was a *lex naturæ* binding on them because it was
a *lex*, and they endeavoured to work up the dictates of this
law and of the *jus gentium* together with the provisions of
the old *jus civile* into a whole. The institutes of Gaius open
with a declaration that every system of law must contain
the two elements of general and municipal law; but in the
Institutes of Justinian there are prefixed two definitions

*Definitions of justice and jurisprudence.*
taken from the writings of Ulpian; and, while
the definitions themselves illustrate the inex-
actness with which the jurists determined the
province of jurisprudence, the place assigned to them in
this compilation shows the utter want of anything like
philosophy in the age when the Institutes were written.
The first definition defines the moral virtue of justice by reference to a legal term (*jus*), which it leaves unexplained:
the second pronounces jurisprudence to be the 'science of
things human and divine,' a phrase which has no meaning
except as a summary of the philosophy which thought that
law was the expression of a reason common to the universe
and to man. We can only treat the Roman notions of law
and jurisprudence historically, and ascertain what they were
and whence they came: we cannot make them fit into the
more accurate shapes assigned to these general terms by the
modern philosophy of law.

35. The preceding historical sketch will have sufficed to show

*Sources of law.*
what were the sources of Roman law: (1) There
was the old *jus civile*, which mainly depended on

custom as its basis. (2) There were the judicial decisions of the *prætors*, and the opinion of the *juris prudentes*, supplementing the *jus civile* from the dictates of the *lex naturæ* and the *jus gentium*; and (3) There were positive enactments, which may be divided into *leges, plebiscita, senatus-consulta*, and announcements of the will of the emperor.

36. The main legal term with which we have to start in approaching Roman law is *jus*. The word is *Jus, jura.* used to signify both the sum of rights and their corresponding duties sanctioned by law, and also any single one of these rights. The law prescribes different relations in which the members of a State are to stand to things and to each other. The claim, protected by legal remedies, which each man has to have any of these relations ob- *Rights.* served in his own case is a right; and as the right must be conceived to belong to, or reside in a person, we speak of a right being the right of a person, e.g. my right to have that book, your right to have that house (*jus meum, jus tuum*). When we examine the different rights established by law in a State, we find some of a public character, affecting individuals as members of a body politic; others of a private character, affecting individuals directly. It is only of the private rights established by Roman law that we now propose to speak; and as rights are either rights which persons have over things, or rights which persons have against *Division of* some other person or persons, we shall treat, *the subject.* first, of the mode in which the Roman law regarded persons, then of the mode in which it regarded things; then of the rights it gave to persons over things; then of the rights it gave to persons against persons; and, lastly, of the method by which the State enforced private rights when disputed or disregarded, that is, the system of civil process.

## I. PERSONS.

37. The word *persona* had, in the usage of Roman law, a

*Meaning of the word per-sona.* different meaning from that which we ordinarily attach to the word person. It was employed to denote any being capable of having, and being subject to, rights. All men possessing a reasonable will would naturally be *personæ*; but not all those who were physically speaking, men, were *personæ*. Slaves, for instance, were not in a position to exercise their reason and will, and the law, therefore, refused to treat them as *personæ*. On the other hand, many *personæ* had no physical existence. The law clothed certain abstract conceptions with an existence, and attached to them the capability of having and being subject to rights. The law, for instance, spoke of the State as a *persona*. It was treated as being capable of having rights, and of being subject to them. These rights really belonged to the men who composed the State, and they flowed from the constitution and position of associated individuals. But, in the theory and language of law, the rights of the whole community were referred to the State, to an abstract conception interposed between these rights and the individual members of the society. So, a corporation, or an ecclesiastical institution, was a *persona*, quite apart from the individual *personæ* who formed the one and administered the other. Even the *fiscus*, or imperial treasury, as being the symbol of the abstract conception of the emperor's claims, was spoken of as a *persona*.

38. The technical term for the position of an individual

*Status.* regarded as a legal person was *status*, and the constitutive elements of his *status* were liberty, citizenship, and membership in a family. First, he must be

*Freedom.* free. A slave had no rights. In the earlier days of Roman law, no one would have conceived this to be unnatural. But philosophy, and the study of morality, taught the latter jurists that the condition of a slave was a violation of natural law. It was not, however, necessary that the person should have been born free (*ingenuus*); for the process of manumission placed the slave in some degree on a level with the freedman (*libertinus*, or if spoken of with reference to his master, *libertus* \*). It depended on the mode and circumstance of his manumission whether he became at once a Roman citizen; but in whatever way he was enfranchised he still owed certain duties to his patron, and in certain cases his patron was his heir.

39. The second element of the *status* was citizenship. The Roman notion of the State was that of a compact privileged body separated off from the rest *Citizenship.* of the world by the exclusive possession of certain public and private rights. In the early times of Rome the *cives*, or members of the State, were divided into the two bodies of *patres* and plebeians, the former of whom had a public and sacred law peculiar to themselves, while they shared with the latter the system of private law. Beyond the State all were *hostes* and *barbari*. But as civilization progressed, the number of foreigners who resorted to Rome for trade, or were otherwise brought into friendly relations with citizens, was so great that they were looked upon as a distinct class, that of *peregrini*. To be a citizen was thenceforward not to be a *peregrinus*, the force of the one idea being brought out by the prominence of its opposite. A *peregrinus* was subject only to the *jus gentium*; citizens alone could claim the privileges of the *jus Quiritium*. But when her conquest placed Rome in new and varying relations with the nations of Italy, an intermediate position between the citizen and the *peregrinus* was accorded to the more privileged of the vanquished. Some of the rights of the citizen were given to them, and some were withheld. These peculiar rights of the citizen were summed up in the familiar term *suffragium et honores*, the right of voting and the capacity of holding magisterial offices, and in the terms *connubium* and *commercium*. *Connubium* is a term which

---

\* The Latin for a freedman was *libertinus*: but *libertus Titii* is the Latin for the freedman of Titius.

explains itself. The foundation of the Roman family was a marriage according to the *jus Quiritium*, and not to have the *connubium* was to be incapable of entering into the Roman family system. In the word *commercium* were included the power of holding property and making contracts according to the Roman law, and also the *testamenti factio*, or power to make a will, and to accept property under one. By the *jus Latinum* and the *jus Italicum* various modifications of the different rights implied in the *civitas* were granted. The *jus Latinum* gave private rights to individuals, the *jus Italicum* gave public rights to towns. In some cases the *jus Latinum* gave the *connubium* and *commercium*; in some only the latter, in many only a portion of the latter; the *testamenti factio*, the power of making, or taking under, a testament being withheld. The *jus Italicum* gave certain favoured towns a municipal constitution more or less connected with the supreme power of Rome. In the course of time other shades between the *civis* and the *peregrinus* were introduced, but all distinction between them was gradually swept away, by the increasing recklessness with which the rights of citizenship were bestowed. Until at last Caracalla made all the free subjects of the empire citizens; and thenceforward the class of *peregrini*, properly speaking, ceased to exist. All the free inhabitants of the civilized world were *cives*, and beyond were nothing but *barbari* and *hostes*.

40. The Roman family, in the peculiar shape it assumed under the *jus Quiritium*, was modelled on a civil rather than on a natural basis. The tie which bound members of the same family was not that of blood; it was their common position in the midst of an artificial system. For the formation of such a family, a legal marriage was an indispensable preliminary; but it was only a preliminary, and the peculiar character of the family did not in any way flow from the tie. The head of the family was all in all. He did not so much represent as absorb in himself the subordinate members. He alone was *sui juris*, i. e. had an independent

*The family.*

will; all the other members were *alieni juris*, their wills were not independent, but were only expressed through their chief. The *paterfamilias*, the head of the family, was said to have all the other members of his family in his power; and this power (*patria potestas*) was the foundation of all that peculiarly characterized the Roman family. At the head of the family stood the *paterfamilias* alone. Beneath him came his children, sons and daughters, and his wife, who, in order to preserve the symmetry of the system, was treated by law as a daughter.* If a daughter married, she left this family, and passed into the family of her husband; but if a son married, all his children were as much in the power of the *paterfamilias* as the son himself. Thus all the descendants through the male line were in the power of the same person. And it was this that constituted the link of family relationship between them, not the natural tie of blood. When the *paterfamilias* died, each of the sons became in his turn a *paterfamilias*; he was now *sui juris*, and all his own descendants through the male line were in his power. Each of the daughters, as long as she remained unmarried, was also *sui juris*; but directly she formed a legal marriage, and thereby entered into her husband's family, she passed into the power of another. Hence it was said that a woman was at once the beginning and end of her family, *caput et finis familiæ suæ*, for directly she attempted to continue it, she passed into another family.

41. Persons who were under the power of another could not hold or acquire any property of their own. All belonged to the *paterfamilias*; and whatever the son acquired was acquired for the father. In matters of public law the *filiusfamilias* laboured under no incapacities; he could vote or hold a magistracy, but in all the relations of private law he was absolutely in his father's power. He could not make a will, for he had no

*Position of persons in potestate.*

---

* She was technically said to be in the *manus* of her husband; and perhaps *manus* is the old word signifying the power of the *paterfamilias*, and *potestas* is only an expression of later Latin.

property to dispose of; nor bring an action, for nothing was
owing to him. But in all public relations, whenever this incapability of possessing property was not in question, the
*filiusfamilias* had all the privileges of a citizen; he had, for
instance, the *connubium*, and could contract a legal marriage;
and the *commercium*, and could, therefore, be a witness in
sale by mancipation, to which none except citizens could be
witnesses. The indulgence of later times permitted the
*filiusfamilias* to hold certain property apart from the *paterfamilias*, an indulgence first accorded as an encouragement
to military service. But even over a portion of this property
the head of the family possessed certain rights; and, so far
as it went, it was a departure from the strict theory of law.

42. The distinction between the legal and the natural

*Emancipation.*  marriage is illustrated by its being possible for a
member of the legal family to quit it and become
an entire stranger to it, and for an entire stranger to be admitted to it, and be as completely a member as if he were a
son of the *paterfamilias*. The mode by which the change in
either case was accomplished was by a fictitious sale. Every
Roman citizen could sell himself to another by the peculiar
form of sale called *mancipatio*; and as the father possessed
over the son the rights which a person *sui juris* possessed
over himself, he sold the *filiusfamilias* to a nominal purchaser, who was supposed to buy the son. It was declared by
the law of the Twelve Tables that a son thrice sold by his
father should be free from his power, and the ceremony was
therefore repeated three times, and the son was then *emancipatus*, or sold out of the family. When a stranger, being
himself *alieni juris*, wished or was compelled to enter a
family, the process was effected by adoption. Here again,
then, was another sale, the *paterfamilias* of the family he
quitted being the seller, and the *paterfamilias* of that he
entered being the purchaser. If the stranger was *sui juris*,
he entered his now family by arrogation, which in ancient
times could only be effected by a vote in the *comitia curiata*,
it being considered a matter of public policy to keep a watch

over such a proceeding, lest the last of his *gens* should arrogate himself, and its *sacra* be lost. Much simpler modes for
effecting arrogation, as well as for effecting emancipation and
adoption, were employed in later times.

40. A person might be *sui juris*, and be in possession of
every right, and yet be unable, through some
imperfection, to exercise the rights he possessed.

*Tutors and Curators.*

A child, for instance, was not only not able to
conduct his affairs with discretion, but he was unable to understand, perhaps to speak, the forms necessary to be expressly
pronounced in almost every legal transaction. A tutor was
therefore appointed, who, until the child attained the age of
puberty, supplied this defect of his ward, or, as he was
called, his pupil. And this is the Roman notion of a tutor:
he was a person who supplied something that was wanting,
who filled up the measure of his pupil's *persona*. He of
course took care of the person and property of the child;
but this was only an accessory of his position; his primary
office was to supply by his *auctoritas** what the pupil fell
short of. So too, in the old law, women, of whatever age,
if *sui juris*, required a tutor, not to control them, but
because women could not go through legal forms. Further,
a person might be *sui juris*, and be of an age to exercise
his rights, and yet it might be necessary to ensure that he
did not hurt himself and his family by the mode in which
he exercised them. In such cases a curator was appointed,
whose duty it was to look after his property. This curator
had a perfectly different office from a tutor; in technical language, the tutor was said to be appointed to the person, the
curator to the property. The curator was only appointed as
a check to prevent pecuniary loss. Curators were, for instance,
appointed to watch over the interests of insane persons, of
persons notoriously prodigal, and of those who had attained
the age of puberty, but were under the age of twenty-five.

---

* The derivation of *auctoritas* should never be lost sight of. When
one person increased, *augebat*, what another had, so as to fill up a deficiency, this increasing or filling up was called *auctoritas*.

D

41. While the head of a family lived, all those who were in
his power were connected together by the tie of
*Agnati.* subjection to the power of the same person. The
tie was called *agnatio*, and the persons so mutually connected
were *agnati* to each other. When the *paterfamilias* died, the
tie of *agnatio* still subsisted. Each of those who, by his death,
became *sui juris*, became the head of a new family; but still
they and their descendants were *agnati* to each other so long
as they did not by emancipation, or, in the case of women,
by marriage, leave their original family. All those, in short,
who would have been *agnati* to each other if the life of the
original *paterfamilias* had been prolonged, were *agnati* at any
distance of time, however great, after his death. A number
of distinct families might thus, when looked on as connected
by *agnatio*, be spoken of as one family: for they were all
portions of the family of the deceased *paterfamilias*.

45. Beyond the circle of the *agnati*, the ancient patrician
had that of the *gens*. They were nearer to him
*Gentiles.* than those who were only related to him by blood.
If a patrician dies intestate, in default of *agnati*, his *gentiles*,
the men of his *gens*, were his heirs. He was placed in the
midst of two artificial circles, shutting out the natural circle
of blood relations; while the plebeian, and when the system
of *gentes* had faded away, the patrician also, acknowledged the
ties of blood as next to that of *agnatio*. All those who were
connected together by the ties of blood were *cognati*.
*Cognati.* It was the tendency of the later Roman legislation
to give greater and greater weight to the ties of blood, and to
substitute a natural for an artificial system of family relationship. Lastly, the *cognati* of each of the parties to a
*Affines.* marriage were said to be *affines* to the other party.

46. We have spoken as if the wife had been always in the
*manus*, or power of her husband. And this was
*Position of the wife.* so, probably, in the strict theory of the Roman
family, and in the practice of early times. The
tie of marriage was formed among the patricians by the ceremony of *confarreatio*, in which none could partake except

those who had the privileges of the *jus sacrum*; and apparently the mere fact of going through the ceremony placed a wife in the *manus* of her husband. The plebeians had no corresponding ceremony; and in order that, when two persons came together in marriage, the wife should be in the power of her husband, she was sold to the husband by the father, a process which was termed *coemptio*, or if she remained with her husband a year, then the power over her was acquired by *usus*, that is, by the uninterrupted lapse of time. If, however, she absented herself for three nights in the year, this prevented her falling into the husband's power. Perhaps, at all times, at least in plebeian families, a woman could so marry as not to fall into the *manus* of her husband; and in later times such marriages formed the rule. It made no difference in other relations of the family whether the wife was in the power of the husband or not. Supposing she and her husband had the *connubium*, that is, were capable of intermarrying, all the usual incidents of a marriage, such as the *patria potestas*, attached to the connection. If a man and a woman entered into a permanent connection without marriage *Concubinage.* (*concubinatus*), their children were *naturales liberi*, and were so far favoured by the later law as to be capable of being placed in the position of children sprung from a legal marriage, by the process of *legitimatio*. After the time of Constantine they were always made legitimate by the subsequent marriage of their parents. In all unions of the sexes, other than a legal marriage, the children followed the condition of their mother: being free, for instance, if she was free, and slaves if she was a slave. The union of slaves was called *contubernium*; but however solemnly entered into, and however faithfully its natural tie acknowledged, it was never in the eye of the law regarded as anything better than promiscuous intercourse.

47. It was possible that any one who possessed a complete *status* should undergo a change of *status*, and this change might happen in any one of the three *Deminutio capitis.* component parts of the *status*. The capability of exercising all those rights implied in a perfect *status* was

frequently spoken of as a man's *caput*, and the change in
each of these component parts were said to be a *deminutio
capitis*, a lessening or impairing of the *caput*. First, a man
might lose his freedom; he might be taken prisoner by an
enemy, or undergo a very severe criminal sentence. The
loss of this element of the *status*, called *capitis deminutio
maxima*, involved the loss of the remaining two, the person
who ceased to be free, ceasing also to have the rights of citizenship or family rights. Secondly, he might lose his rights of
citizenship, and this loss, called the *capitis deminutio media*,
involved the loss of family rights, but still left him free.
Thirdly, by what was called the *capitis deminutio minima*
he might lose his position in his family, by emancipation or
arrogation. In early times there were rights, principally
those forming part of the *jus sacrum*, which a person who
passed out of his family really lost; but in later times, as in
every case the person who underwent this *capitis deminutio*
either entered another family, or became the head of his own
family, his *status* was really not made at all less perfect by the
change. Of course this *capitis deminutio* involved the loss of
neither of the two other component parts of the *status*.

48. When a person was possessed of a perfect *status*, he was
*Existimatio.*    considered to enjoy a high dignity and reputation
              in the eyes of others. This reputation (*existi-
matio*) the Romans considered as one of the chief possessions
of a person. It was even to a certain extent regulated by
law. If a person ceased to be free, his *existimatio* was gone.
Certain offences were treated by law as impairing it. If the
offence was so grave as to impair the *existimatio* very
seriously, its diminution was said to amount to *infamia*; if
the offence was rather less grave, the consequence was
*turpitudo*; and if the person was in some inferior position,
as, for instance, an actor, he was said to be marked with a
*levis nota*, a slight brand of disgrace.

49. It only remains to be observed that, although persons
*End of the*   that were the mere creations of law, as corpora-
*existence of*
*persons.*     tions, ceased to exist when the law in any way

put an end to their existence, as by the dissolution of the
corporation, yet the person of individuals, that is, their legal,
as opposed to their natural being, never became extinct. At
the moment of death it was shifted to those who represented
them. The son was clothed with the person of the father,
the heir with that of the testator. What we mean by saying
that the deceased is represented, that is, again made present
and brought before us, the Roman jurists expressed by
saying that his person had been shifted to those who succeeded in his place.

## II. THINGS.

50. The word thing (*res*) has, in Roman law, a sense as
artificial and as wide as the word person. As *Use of the word res.*
person comprehends every being who has rights
and is subject to them, so thing comprehends all that can be
considered as the object of a right. The object of a right
may be incorporeal, or the pure creation of law, and need
not be limited to things corporeal and visible. The law can
separate the right to possess a field and the right to walk in
it, and the object of each right is called indifferently a thing.
When we attempt to classify these objects of rights, we are
unable to select any one principle of division according to
which we may distribute them. The aspects in which we
may view them are too various to admit of a simple arrangement; we may, however, make a division approximately
accurate by considering, first, those heads of things which
we arrive at by examining the nature of the things themselves; and secondly, those gained by inquiring into the
interest which persons have in them.

51. First, then, things may be corporeal or incorporeal;
or, as the jurists expressed it, *tangi possunt* or
*tangi non possunt*. We see a house or a field; *Division of things.*
we do not see a right to inhabit the one or *Corporeal and Incorporeal.*
reap the fruits of the other. The physical
tangible objects of sense is a corporeal thing; the intangible

abstraction of the mind is an incorporeal thing. Incorporeal things always consist in a right; if we see a stream flowing, or a path winding through a field, the mind sees, as something distinct from the object of sense, the power of using the water or of following the path. This power is, in the language of the law, an incorporeal thing; and a person may have a right to possess it just as he may have a right to possess a house or field. But this power is itself a right if taken cognizance of by the law, and considered as capable of being exercised by one or more persons to the exclusion of all others. When we say that an individual has a right to this right, we merely mean that he has a claim to be the person to exercise exclusively this power.

52. We may again speak of corporeal things as moveable
*Things moveable and immoveable.* and immoveable (*res mobiles, se morentes,* and *res soli, res immobiles*), a distinction so obvious that it needs no other remark than that some moveable things are so incorporated with immoveables, or so constantly associated with their use that the law treats them as immoveables; as for instance a house, each brick of which is a moveable, is itself an immoveable, because attached to the soil.

53. Things are also either divisible or indivisible. We
*Things divisible and indivisible.* cannot divide a slave or a horse so that the several parts have the same value which they had when they were parts of a whole; but if we divide a field into four, we have four small fields.

54. There are also principal or accessory; that is, they
*Things principal and accessory.* are the direct object of rights, or are only so as forming portion of, or being intimately connected with, something that is; thus a tree is a principal thing, its fruit an accessory.

55. Another distinction relating to things familiar to the
*Genus and Species.* Roman jurists was that between the *genus* and the *species.* By the *genus* was meant a whole class of objects, such as horses, or the general name for an object, such as wine, oil, wheat. *Species* was

the particular member of the class, or particular portion of the object comprehended under the *genus*, as *this* horse, or the wine in *this* bottle. If a purchaser bought a horse or a certain quantity of oil, the thing bought was said to be determined *genere*; if he bought a particular horse or the oil in a certain vase, the thing bought was said to be determined *specie*. All things which are included under a general name, such as oil or wheat, are commonly divided by being weighed, numbered, or measured, and were therefore spoken of by the jurists as being those things *quæ pondere, numero, mensurave constant.*

56. We may, lastly, regard things as particular, or as collected under some head, when the whole collection is a thing in law. Thus a sheep is a *Res singularis and rerum universitas.* particular thing (*res singularis*), a flock, composed *ex distantibus uni nomini subjectis*, is a collection of things, or, as the jurists expressed it, is a *rerum universitas* (or simply *universitas*). As also, of course, are such comprehensive things as an inheritance, a dowry, the *peculium* of a slave.

57. In proceeding to the second division of things according to the persons who have rights over them, and to the extent of those rights, we must first notice the distinction in things caused by certain things having a sacred character (*res divini juris*). These were *Res Sacræ.* *res sacræ*, consecrated to the superior gods; or *res religiosæ*, such as tombs or burial grounds, consecrated to the infernal gods; or lastly, *res sanctæ*, things human, but having a sort of sacredness attaching to them, such as the walls and gates of cities.

58. The State, again, impressed on some things a peculiar character. All things which were held by *peregrini* and not by citizens were *peregrina*. The soil which was included in the territories of the early State, the *ager Romanus*, was distinguished from all other land *Ager Romanus.* by being alone capable of being the subject of a sale by mancipation, and being alone held by the especial tenure

of the *jus Quiritium*.* In later times, a greater portion of
the soil of Italy was placed on the same footing with the soil
of the *ager Romanus*, and *solum Italicum* came to be the
name of all soil wherever situated to which the privileges of
the old *ager Romanus* were accorded as opposed to *solum
provinciale*, which always remained, at least in theory, the
property of the State, and of which a perfect ownership
could not be acquired.† Justinian abolished this difference
in the tenure of the soil.

59. In the older law there also prevailed a distinction,
abolished by Justinian, between *res mancipi*
*Res mancipi.* and *res nec mancipi*. We know from a fragment of Ulpian,‡ what things were *res mancipi*. They
were *prædia in Italico solo*, whether in the country or the
city, servitudes (a term to be explained presently) over
these *prædia* when in the country, slaves, and four-footed
animals, as oxen and horses, tamed for the service of man.
All other things were *nec mancipi*. We also know that
property in *res mancipi* could only be transferred by *mancipatio*, that is, by a form of sale, in which the purchaser
took hold with his hand of the thing purchased, and
claiming it to be his tendered a piece of copper to the
seller.§ The list of *res mancipi* is evidently a list of the
possessions of an early agricultural community, and there
can be scarcely any doubt that the form of sale required to
transfer the property in them was the ordinary form of sale
in such a community. At some period, and in some
manner of which we have no knowledge, these possessions of
an early agricultural community were contrasted with other
forms of wealth, and the mode of transfer customary in the
one case was found not to be customary in the other. The
law, sanctioning and embodying the custom, made the form
of *mancipatio* necessary to pass *res mancipi*, and declared

---

* Dion. Halicarn. iv. 13.
† Ulpian. xix. 1 ; Cicero, *Pro Flacco*, i. 32 ; Gaius, i. 20.
‡ Ulp. *Frag.* xix.
§ The form of *mancipatio* will be more fully noticed in sec. 81 of the
Introduction.

it not to be necessary to pass other things. So far is clear;
but the difficulty is to account for the origin of the term.
Why were these things called *res mancipi*? How is the
expression connected with the word *manus*? In order to
arrive at an answer, we must remember, in the first place, that
a wife in the power of her husband was said to be *in manu*,
and a free person, who sold himself, or was sold by the person
in whose power he was, was said to be *in mancipio*. In the
second place, it was an essential feature in the form of transfer mentioned above that the purchaser should take the thing
purchased in his hand. Two theories have been formed out
of these data. The one considers *manus* as signifying
'power,' * to be the root of the phrases *mancipi* and
*mancipatio*. Thus *res mancipi* meant originally things in
the hand, or taken by the hand, of the owner, and the
taking by the hand in the form of transfer was symbolic of
the purchaser holding or acquiring the thing in the way in
which the seller had held or acquired it. The other theory
looks primarily to the form of transfer. In order to show to
the witnesses the fact of the transfer of the property, the
purchaser made use of the expressive gesture of seizing the
thing he bought with his hand, and hence the hand came to be
a symbol of power or ownership. Either of these theories is
plausible, and neither can be conclusively established.

60. If we look at things according to the persons by whom
they are owned, we have a division into *res com-* *Res communes.*
*munes*, as the sea and the air, which cannot be
appropriated by any particular individuals; *res publicæ*
things which belong to the State, as the State *Res publica.*
land (*ager publicus*), navigable rivers, roads, &c.;
*res universitatis*, things which belong to aggregate bodies, as
to corporations; and *res privatæ*, things which *Res privatæ.*
belong to individuals; and which were said to

---

* How *manus* signifies power is a further question; it may be that
the hand is merely a metaphor, as we say 'in the hands' for 'in the
power' of a person; or it may mean the hand of a conqueror or plun-
derer, and thus originally things *manu capta* would be the booty of
plunderers.

be in *nostro patrimonio*, i.e. we could, in one way or another,

*In nostro patrimonio.* have a property in them : whereas things common, or public, or dedicated to the gods, were *extra patrimonium*, i.e. could not become the subject of private property. Lastly, there were *res nullius*, things of which no one has acquired the ownership, as wild animals, or unoccupied islands in the sea.

61. Having now given a sketch of the position of persons in Roman law, as also of the divisions of things,

*Rights.* we now proceed to speak of that connection between persons and things which what are termed rights express. The necessities of his physical position oblige man

to exert his power over the world of things; his *How divided.* special interests prompt each man to claim, as against his fellows, an exclusive interest in particular things. Sometimes such a claim sanctioned by law is urged directly : the owner, as he is said to be, of the thing publishes this claim against all other men, and asserts an indisputable title himself to enjoy all the advantages which the possession of the thing can confer. Sometimes the claim is more indirect; the claimant insists that there are one or more particular individuals who ought to put him in possession of something he wishes to obtain, or do something for him, or fulfil some promise, or repair some damage they have made or caused. Such a claim is primarily urged against particular persons, and not against the world at large. On this distinction between claims to things advanced against all men, and those advanced primarily against particular men, is based the division of rights into real and personal expressed by writers of the middle ages* on the analogy of terms found in the writings of the Roman jurists, by the phrase *jura in re* and *jura ad rem*. A real right, a *jus in re*, or, to use the

---

* The term *jus in re* appears in the summary of law bearing the name of the Brachylogus which belongs to the twelfth century ; both phrases occur in the pontifical constitutions of the thirteenth century. (See *Sarti Decret.* iii. 7, 8, *in quibus jus non erat quæsitum in re, licet ad rem.*)

equivalent phrase preferred by some later commentators, *jus in rem*, is a right to have a thing to the exclusion of all other men. A personal right, *jus ad rem*, or, to use a much more correct expression, *jus in personam*, is a right in which there is a person who is the subject of the right, as well as a thing as its object, a right which gives its possessor a power to oblige another person to give or procure, or do or not do something. It is true that in a real right the notion of persons is involved, for no one could claim a thing if there were no other persons against whom to claim it ; and that in a personal right is involved the notion of a thing, for the object of the right is a thing which the possessor wishes to have given, procured, done or not done. But the leading principle of the distinction is simple and intelligible, and though it has not been formally adopted in the system of the Institutes or of the leading jurists, yet the classifications of the different relations of persons and things which they actually employed, are so capable of being assimilated to that which this distinction suggests that we need not hesitate to adopt it.

## III. RIGHTS OVER THINGS.

62. The most complete real right is of course that possessed by the absolute owner of the thing, the person who has power to dispose of it as he likes, and *Dominium.* who holds it by a title recognized as valid by law. This ownership was in Roman law expressed by the word *dominium*, sometimes by *proprietas*. The *dominus* was entitled to the use of the thing (*usus*), to the perception of all its products (*fructus*), or to consume the thing entirely if it were capable of consumption (*abusus*). He could also dispose of, or alienate it at will. In the ancient system of private law, the owner was said to be owner *ex jure Quiritium*. Nor did the old law recognize any *dominium* other than that which was enjoyed *ex jure Quiritium*. But the *prætors* found occasions when they wished to give all the advantages

of ownership but were prevented by the civil law from giving
the legal *dominium*.  Another kind of *dominium* came
therefore to be spoken of: and the term *in bonis habere* was
used to express an ownership which was practically absolute
because it was protected by the *prætor's* authority, but which
was not technically the same as ownership *ex jure Quiritium*.
Commentators have called this ownership the *dominium
bonitarium*, a term not, however, used by the jurists.  The
distinction between the *dominium bonitarium* and that *ex
jure Quiritium* entirely disappeared under Justinian.

63. To the notion of *dominium* was opposed that of
*Possessio.* *possessio*.  A person might be owner of a thing
and yet not possess it, or possess it without being
the owner.  Possession implied actual physical occupation,
or *detention*, to use the technical term, of the thing; but it
also implied something more in the sense in which it was
used by the Roman lawyers.  It implied not only a fact, but
an intention; not only the fact of the thing being under the
control of the possessor, but also the intention on the part of
the possessor to hold it so as to reap exactly the same benefit
from it as the real owner would, and to exercise the same
rights over it, even though he might be well aware that he
was not the real owner, and had no claim to be so.  The
possessor had no rights over the thing; but he was entitled
to have his possession protected against every one but the
true owner, and length of possession would, under certain
conditions fixed by law, make the possessor really become the
owner of the thing possessed.

64. As the real rights over a thing may be very numerous,
it is perfectly possible to separate them, and to give some to
one person and some to another.  We can, for instance,
separate the right of walking in a field from the right of
digging under the surface, and give the right of doing the one
to this person and of doing the other to that.  In this way
each right that is separated off may be considered as a fragment of the whole *dominium*, capable of being given away
from the proprietor.  These fragmentary rights, these portions

of the whole right comprised in the absolute ownership, were termed *servitutes*, because the thing was under   *Servitutes.* a kind of slavery for the benefit of the person entitled to exercise over it this separate right. In some servitudes, the right over the thing subject to the servitude, *res serviens*, was attached to the ownership of another thing (*res dominans*); the servitudes were then spoken of as *servitutes rerum* or *prædiorum*, and a distinction was made in these servitudes according as the right given by them referred to the soil itself, as the right to go or to drive over it, when the *servitutes* were said to be *rusticorum prædiorum*, or to the soil as supporting some superstructure as a house, when the servitudes were said to be *urbanorum prædiorum*. In other servitudes, the right was given to particular persons; and the servitudes were then termed *servitutes personarum*. The most important of these latter servitudes were *usufructus* and *usus*. *Usufructus* was the right to enjoy a thing belonging to another person so as to reap all the produce derivable from it, as, for instance, all the fruits of the soil; *usus* was the right to use and enjoy a thing belonging to another person, only without reaping any of its produce, or altering its substance. Only immoveable property was subject to the *servitutes prædiorum*; both moveable and immoveable to the *servitutes personarum*.

65. There were two other real rights which had something of the nature of servitudes, but which received   *Emphyteusis* a particular name. These were *Emphyteusis*  *and super-* and *superficies*. The former was an alienation  *ficies.* of all rights except that of the bare ownership for a long term, in consideration of the proprietor receiving a yearly rent (*pensio*); the latter was the alienation by the owner of the surface of the soil of all rights necessary for building on the surface, a yearly rent being generally reserved.

66. Lastly, there was the real right given over a thing by pledge or mortgage *pignus*, *hypotheca*; the   *Jus pignoris.* former term being used to express the case of

the thing, over which the right was given, being placed in the possession of the creditor, the latter to express the case of it being left in the possession of the debtor. The right was given to secure a creditor the payment of his debt; and he had power to sell the thing, and to satisfy his claim out of the proceeds, if he could find no purchaser to have himself made owner of the thing.

67. We may now proceed to speak of the mode in which real rights are acquired. We find at the outset an obvious difference between acquiring rights over a particular thing, and acquiring rights over the entirety of a number of things comprised in such a term as an inheritance, which includes the entirety of the rights belonging to a deceased person, both real and personal.

*Acquisition of rights over things.*

We may thus divide the subject of the acquisition of rights into two parts, the first comprising the modes in which real rights are acquired over particular things, the second comprising the modes in which an entirety (*universitas*) of rights, both real and personal, passed from one person to another.

68. We may mention, as the first of the modes of acquiring particular things, occupation, i. e. the seizing on a thing which is a *res nullius*: land in an unoccupied country is a *res nullius*, so are wild animals; if we seize on, or, as we should say, occupy the land, and catch the wild animal, we gain our right over the soil and the animal by having been the first to seize it.

*Acquisition of right over particular things. Occupatio.*

69. Accession is the general term for the acquisition of rights either over things which are added by the forces of nature to, and become an inseparable part of, another thing regarded as the principal thing, or over things which by the operation of man are united with other things so as to form an indivisible product. The owner of the principal thing, by virtue of his being owner, is the owner also of the accessory thing.

*Accessio.*

70. A contract, by which one person bound himself to give a thing to another, did not make that other *Tradition.* the owner of the thing. A further step was necessary. The thing must be handed over to the person who was, under the terms of the contract, to become, the owner of it. This handing over was called *traditio*; and a perfect *traditio* implied, first, that it was a real absolute owner, capable of alienating the thing, who transferred it, and secondly, that he placed the new proprietor in actual possession of the thing.

71. The above are termed natural modes of acquisition; but there are some which derive their force only *Gifts.* from the civil law. Among these is acquisition by a peculiar kind of gift. An ordinary gift did not make the person, to whom the thing was given, its owner; the gift must be followed by a *traditio*; but a gift given in expectation of death (*mortis causa donatio*), if the death took place, passed, without any *traditio*, the property in the thing given, as also did a gift by legacy.

72. The law also gave the ownership of a thing by *usucapio*, that is, by quiet possession, *bonâ fide*, *Usucapio.* and founded on a good title, which sufficed to transfer the *dominium*, or legal ownership, if maintained during one year over moveable things, or during two years over immoveable. The operation of *usucapio* was of great importance in Roman law; for by it the interest of a person to whom a *res mancipi* was transferred otherwise than by mancipation and the interests of all persons who held things *in bonis* (see sec. 62) was, after a short lapse of *Prescription.* time, converted into full *Quiritarian* ownership. Prescription, before the time of Justinian, was not a means of acquiring rights: it merely gave a means of repelling actions brought to retain rights which had long been held by another than the absolute owner. It was applicable to immoveables in the provinces, they being not affected by *usucapio*, which regarded all moveables, but only such im-

moveables as were in Italy. Justinian makes considerable
alterations in the law with respect to acquisition of ownership by length of possession. The same law was made to
prevail throughout the Empire, and possession during three
years gave the ownership of moveables, and possession
during ten years, if the parties had inhabited the same
province during the time, or possession during twenty years
if they had not, gave the ownership of immoveables.

73. The ownership was also transferred when things were
surrendered by the fictitious process of *in jure
cessio,* that is, a suit in which the defendant
gave up to the plaintiff all he claimed, or when things were
adjudged (*adjudicatio*) in certain actions, such as those for
assigning boundaries, and dividing a family estate, when the
judge had a power to assign the respective portions to the
different parties.

*In jure cessio.*

74. The entirety of rights was acquired when one person
succeeded to the *persona,* or legal existence, of
another, and thereby succeeded to all his rights,
whether over things or against persons. The
cases in which this most naturally occurred were that of arrogation (for when a person was arrogated, he, of course,
transferred all that he had to the person whose
family he entered), and that of succession to the
inheritance of testators and intestates.

*Acquisition of
an entirety of
rights.*

*Arrogation.*

75. Testaments were originally made by being proclaimed
in the *comitia curiata* or by a fictitious sale, in
which testators transferred their property to a
purchaser (*familiæ emptor*), who was himself heir, or who
was, after their death, to distribute it according to their
wishes. In later times, they were made in writing in the
presence of seven witnesses. In order to make a testament,
it was necessary to have the *testamenti factio,* a term implying such a participation in the law of private Roman citizens
as to make a person considered capable of making, taking
under, or being witness to, a testament.

*Testaments.*

76. The testator was obliged to disinherit by name every one who, being among those in his own power, *Disinheriting.* had a natural claim on his property; and if he failed to do so, the whole will was set aside. The great peculiarity of a Roman will was the institution of the heir, that is, of the person who was to succeed to the *Institution of* *the heir.* persona of the testator. Unless there was such a person, no other disposition of the will could take effect, for there was no continuation of the testator's legal existence. The heir was, therefore, appointed at the beginning of the will; in case of the heir accepting, he placed himself exactly in the position of the testator, received all his property, and was answerable for all his debts; in receiving his property he was, however, bound to give effect to the subsequent dispositions of the testament. In order that the testament might not fail because the heir was not willing to enter on the inheritance, it was customary to name one or more persons, to whom in succession it might be open to take upon them the office of heir. And a testator could always secure an heir by naming, as the last of the list, one of his own slaves, whom the law did not permit to refuse the office (*heres necessarius*). When some of the conditions necessary to create an heir, or give a legacy, were wanting in a will, still the expressions of the testator's will were binding as trusts upon the heir under the will, or heir *ab intestato*. Such trusts (*fidei-* *Fideicom-* *commissa*) were first made obligatory by Au- *missa.* gustus, who also first gave effect to codicils, that is, writings purporting to deal with property in the manner of a testamentary disposition, but *Codicils.* not executed with the solemnities which were required to make a testament valid.

77. If there was no testament to determine the succession to the particular property, the law prescribed the order in which it was to devolve. The first *Succession to* *intestato.* claimants were the *sui heredes*, that is, all persons in the power of the deceased, and who, on his death, became

themselves *sui juris.* Thus, a son *in potestate* was a *suus heres* of the deceased, but not a grandson until the son was dead. Why these persons were termed *sui heredes* is doubtful. Probably the term *suus* was merely meant to express that they belonged to the *patrfamalias* as being in his power. If there were no *sui heredes,* the next heirs were the *agnati,* i. e. all members of the same civil family; and then, in default of *agnati,* the law of the Twelve Tables gave the inheritance to the members of the same *gens,* an enactment which could of course only take effect when the deceased was a member of a *gens.* What was the course of devolution beyond the *agnati* under the old civil law, when the deceased was not a member of a *gens,* we do not know. In default of *agnati,* under the Prætorian legislation, the claims of the natural family were attended to, and the *cognati,* or blood-relations, succeeded to the inheritance. In the later times of the Roman law the claims of blood-relations were more and more favoured, and in many important points were gradually preferred to those of merely civil kinmanship.

## IV. RIGHTS AGAINST PERSONS.

78. A personal right is, as we have said before, a right which one person has against another; a right to constrain that other to do something for, or give something to, the possessor of the right. Such a right was generally spoken of in Roman law as an obligation, the notion of an obligation being that of a tie between two parties of such a nature as to confer on the one a power of compelling by action the other to give, do, or furnish something. The obligation did not give any interest in a thing, to get which might be the ultimate object of the proceeding, but only gave a means of acquiring it.

*Rights against persons.*

79. The three words, *dare, facere, præstare,* were used to embrace all the possible duties an obligation could create. Either the person bound by the obligation was obliged, *dare,* i. e. to give the

*Dare, facere, præstare.*

absolute ownership of a thing; or *facere*, that is, to do or not to do some act; or *præstare*, that is, to provide or furnish any advantage or thing, the yielding of which could not be included in the limited sense of the word '*dare*.' Every person who possessed a personal right against another was termed a *creditor*, and every one who owed the satisfaction of a claim, or was the subject of a a personal right, was a *debitor*. The word *creditor*, of course, points to those transactions in which the possessor of the right trusted the person who was the subject of it; but the application of the terms was perfectly general, and must not be confounded with the English usage of the words creditor and debtor.

80. According to the theory of Roman law, all obligations owed their origin either to the consent of the parties (*contractus*), or to injuries (*delicta*) done *Division of obligations.* by one person to another, which gave the injured party a right to recompense. Contracts did not, however, include all cases when an obligation arose from the mutual consent of the parties. The general name for such an obligation was *conventio*, *pactum conventum*. A contract was properly an obligation arising by mutual consent, and made in one of the forms recognized by the civil law; but all obligations arising from mutual consent are spoken of as arising from contracts, because in the old law no other mode of expressing mutual consent was recognized, and mere agreements were not binding.

81. The mode of transferring *res mancipi* was, as we have said in sec. 58, called *mancipatio*. Gaius (i. 119) *Nexum.* thus describes the form of transfer: 'Mancipation is effected in the presence of not less than five witnesses, who must be Roman citizens of the age of puberty, and also in the presence of another person of the same condition, who holds a pair of scales, and hence is called *libripens*. The purchaser, taking hold of the thing, says and affirms that this thing is mine, *ex jure Quiritium*, and it is purchased by me with this piece of copper and these scales. He then strikes

the scales with the piece of money, and gives it to the seller as a symbol of the price.' But the generic term for this mode of sale was not *mancipatio*, but *nexum*,* for this form was used not only when a sale was its real object, but when under the form of a sale the parties intended to effect a contract of deposit or pledge. The purchaser took the thing handed over to him under the condition of restoring it under certain specified circumstances, and thus a form of transfer came to be a form of contract where part of the contract was still to be executed.

82. In the time when the civil law had assumed its full shape, and prior to the alterations it received *Contracts made re.* from the prætorian system, the *nexum* was used chiefly as the mode of transferring *res mancipi*, for contracts of deposit and pledge were ordinarily made, as it was termed, *re*. That is, by the mere delivery of the thing the person to whom it was delivered, and who accepted it, was bound by an obligation to hold it for the purposes for which it had been delivered. There were four heads of contracts recognized by the civil law, and this of contracts made *re* was the first. Under it were classed four kinds of contract, namely, the contracts of *mutuum* when the receiver had to return as much of the thing as he received, *commodatum* when he had to return the specific thing itself, *depositum* when the receiver was bound to keep safe a thing committed to his charge, and *pignus* when the receiver took a thing in pledge.

83. The second head of contract under the civil law *Contracts made verbis.* was that of contracts made *verbis*, of executory contracts, that is, made in a prescribed form of solemn words. One of the parties put to the other a formal question (*stipulatio*), to which the other gave a formal answer (*responsio, promissio*). To the validity of

---

* *Nexum est, quodcumque per as et libram geritur, idque nexi dicitur.*
—FESTUS.

the contract it was necessary that the question should
be couched in the form '*spondes?*' and the answer in
that of '*spondeo.*' Do you engage? I do engage. It
was long before equivalent words, such as *promitto* or
*dabo*, were admitted as substitutes. A contract made by
the pronunciation of these solemn words was said to be made
*verbis.*

84. A third head of contract under the civil law was that of
contracts made *literis*. An engagement having
been made to give a definite amount, the parties *Contracts made literis.*
agreed to make a memorandum of the terms of the
contract. The creditor placed in his book of domestic accounts
(*tabulæ*, or *codex*) the name of the debtor, and the sum as
being *pecunia expensa lata*, weighed out and given to the
debtor; and the debtor entered in his *tabulæ*, the same sum as
*pecunia accepta relata*. Either party could call on the other
to produce his *tabula*, which it was considered so incumbent on
a Roman citizen to keep carefully and accurately, that any
wilful error was discoverable without much difficulty. The
debtor, in fact, furnished the creditor with a means of proving
that the debtor had on a certain day received the money, and
even if the debtor had not set the sum down in his *tabulæ*, the
creditor could show his own *tabulæ* as a proof of the contract.
Sometimes the debt (*nomen*, literally the name of the debtor)
was not entered directly in the *tabulæ*, but in the *adversaria*
or casual memorandum book of the two parties, and then
entered subsequently in the *tabulæ*; when the *nomen* was
spoken of as a *nomen transcriptitium*, i. e. transcribed from
one to the other.

85. There were, also, four particular contracts, for the
formation of which the civil law required no *Contracts made consensu.*
formalities whatever, but which were made
merely *consensu*, by the consent of the parties.
These four contracts were—sale (*emptio-venditio*), hiring
(*locatio-conductio*), partnership (*societas*), and bailment
(*mandatum*). The four modes, then, in which contracts

might be entered into under the civil law were—*re, verbis, literis*, and *consensu*.

86. When, however, the old law of contracts fell under the manipulation of the prætors many changes were *Prætorian innovations.* introduced. The few forms of contract recognized by the civil law, that is, the four heads of contract made *re*, the four heads of contract made *consensu*, and contracts made *verbis* and *literis* still remained the basis of the whole law of contracts; but the prætors, while nominally adhering to the civil law, introduced changes that had a great practical effect. The nature of this change can only be understood by studying the details of the Roman law of contracts, and it would be out of place in a general introduction to attempt to notice them. But there are three ways in which the prætors wrought a change, which were so important that they may be briefly stated here. By an extension of the theory of the civil law contract *re*, the prætors permitted an action to be brought to enforce every contract that was in part executed; secondly, as we have stated above, agreements that would not furnish a cause of action, were permitted to be set up by way of defence, to an action with which they were inconsistent; and thirdly, there were a few specified particular cases in which the prætor permitted pacts to be enforced by action.

87. Obligations might, however, very well arise, without *Obligations quasi ex contractu.* any fault on the part of any one, and yet without having their origin in mutual consent. The mere fact of occupying a certain position will sometimes involve duties, the performance of which may be enforced by an action, and which give rise to a personal right which the person interested in their performance has against the person bound to perform them. An heir, for instance, was by the mere fact of accepting the inheritance, bound to pay the legacies given by the testament. Such obligations were said to be *quasi ex contractu*, not that they really rested on any contract, but there was

an analogy between the obligation thus arising, and that arising from the formation of a contract.*

88. It was not every wrong deed for which compensation could be obtained that gave rise to an obligation *ex delicto*; there were certain particular wrong deeds, such as theft and robbery with violence, which the law expressly characterized as *delicta*, and to procure reparation for which the law provided a special action. It was only when a person suffered by one of these wrong deeds that an obligation *ex delicto* arose. When any wrong deed was done not thus expressly designated by law as a *delictum*, and when no particular and appropriate form of action was provided, the obligation was said to arise *quasi ex delicto*; among the instances given in the Institutes is that of dangerous things being placed so as to fall into a public way. If any one were hurt by the fall, the author of the injury would be bound to make reparation by an obligation *quasi ex delicto*, there being this point of analogy between this obligation, and that in the case of a delict, that the person liable to be sued had done harm to the person or property of another. The division of obligations adopted in the Institutes is therefore into those *ex contractu*, those *quasi ex contractu*, those *ex delicto*, and those *quasi ex delicto*.

*Obligations ex delicto.*

*Obligations quasi ex delicto.*

89. The ancient law considered an obligation as existing until the tie of law, the *vinculum juris*, was loosed by the thing being given, furnished, or done, or by a new tie being formed in place of the old; this loosening of the tie was termed *solutio*. Each mode of forming a contract by the civil law was accompanied by a corresponding mode of dissolving it. When the contract had been formed *re*, it was enough that the thing should be restored; when it had been formed *verbis*, a question and answer again furnished the means of accom-

*Dissolution of obligations.*

---

* See Austin, *Province of Jurisprudence determined*, Appendix, page xl.

plishing the desired object. *Habesne acceptum?* *Habeo,*
sufficed to put an end to the contract. The parties made an
entry of payment in their *codices,* if the contract had been
*literis;* and mutual consent dissolved those contracts which
it had sufficed to form. The *solutio verbis* was most frequently employed, and it was easy to employ it on every
occasion: for in whatever way the contract might originally
have been entered into, its terms could be repeated in the
form of a stipulation, and then this stipulation could be
dissolved by a *solutio verbis.* The stipulation extinguished
the original contract. For contracts were extinguished not

*Novatio.* only by payment, but by what was called *novatio;*
that is, by making a new contract, and substituting it in the place of the original one. The law required
that the new contract should be always made *verbis* or
*literis.* When strict adherence to the rule of law, requiring
a particular mode of payment, would work injustice, the
praetor would always provide a remedy by means of his
equitable jurisdiction.


## V. SYSTEM OF CIVIL PROCESS.

90. An action is the process by which a right is enforced.

*Meaning of the word ac- tion.* Unless a means of enforcing it were provided,
the right would be a mere inoperative abstrac-
tion. Directly it was disputed, it would cease
to have any real existence; but in order that it may have
a real existence, the State uses its powers to ensure a
free exercise of it, as soon as it is made certain to the
magistrate, who is entrusted with the authority of the State,
that the right claimed does really belong to the claimant.
The proceeding by which this is made evident to the
magistrate, and the machinery set in motion by which the
State exerts its power of compulsion, is called an action.
The word action is not, however, always used exactly in this
sense; for it is also employed to mean sometimes the right

to institute such a proceeding: and sometimes the form which the proceeding takes.

91. There are three great epochs in the history of the Roman system of civil process. First, that of the system of the *legis actiones*, certain hard, sharply-defined forms which a rude civilization prescribed for all proceedings. Secondly, that *Epochs in the history of Roman system of civil process.* of the system of *formulæ*, by which the prætor, adopting a most flexible form of organizing the proceedings, was enabled to give a means of enforcing every right which the more enlarged views of an advancing civilization pronounced to be founded on equity; and thirdly, that of the *extraordinaria judicia*, by which, under the later emperors, the supreme authority took the whole conduct of the proceeding into its own hands, and arrived at what seemed to it to be just in as direct and speedy a manner as it found possible.

92. In enforcing rights two very different functions have to be exercised by those to whom the powers of the State are delegated. First, there must be some one invested with magisterial authority, *The magistrate and the judge.* giving the sanction and solemnity of his position to the whole proceeding, who shall represent the law and say what the law is, and who shall have power to employ the force which the State places at the disposal of those it selects to administer justice. Secondly, an inquiry has to be made into particular facts, evidence has to be received and weighed, and an opinion formed and pronounced as to the real merits of the case. The person who exercised the one function was spoken of by the Romans as *magistratus*; the person who exercised the other as *judex*. To the law, represented, pronounced, vindicated, by the magistrate, they applied the term *jus*: to the examination of contested facts by the judge, the term *judicium*. It is perfectly possible that the same person should act as magistrate and judge: but it is also possible that the two provinces should be separated and placed in the hands of different persons. Among

the Romans the *magistratus* was a different person from the *judex*, until the introduction of the system of *extraordinaria judicia*. The two functions were kept almost entirely apart under the system of *formulæ*, and, from a comparatively early period of Roman history, the notion of a judge distinct from the magistrate was familiar to the national mind. After the expulsion of the kings, and during the time of the first period of the system of civil process, first the Consuls, then the *prætor*, and in some cases the *ædiles*, acted as the magistrate. As *judex*, any member of the senatorial body could act who was chosen by the mutual consent of the parties: if they could not agree, the choice was determined by lot. There was also a standing body of judges, the *centumviri*, elected annually by the *comitia*, three from each local tribe, and divided into sections. They had special jurisdiction over questions of *status*, of *dominium ex jure Quiritium*, and of successions. Probably in cases involving any question into which the *centumviri* were the proper persons to inquire, it was not open to the parties to ask for a judge, and the whole proceedings were carried on before the *centumviri*. Lastly, in cases where the interests of *peregrini* were involved, the *recuperatores* furnished the body who were to act the part of the *judex*. It may be added that where the doubtful circumstances of the case

*Arbiters.*    demanded that the judge, in pronouncing his opinion on the facts, should exercise a wider discretion than was ordinarily open to him, he was spoken of as an *arbiter*.

93. All judicial proceedings, whether before a magistrate or a judge, were conducted publicly at Rome.

*Character of judicial proceedings at Rome in early times.* In early times, the magistrate sat in the *forum*, and openly dispensed justice to all comers. Nothing, perhaps, conveys a more correct picture of the ideas and feelings that lay at the bottom of the public life of a Roman citizen, while Rome was still the rival of the Volscians, or the Æquians, than the mode in which the actions of law were conducted. The magistrate and the judge of the patrician order, the distinction of days *fasti* and *nefasti*, the key to which only those, who knew the *jus sacrum*, possessed, the solemn and indispensable form of words by which every stage of the proceeding must be accompanied, would throw over the conduct of the action much of the same character which the existence of a privileged, and partly sacerdotal order, impressed on the whole body politic.

94. The most ancient and most important of the actions of law, the *actio sacramenti*,[*] brings before us, in the most marked manner, the delight in appeals to the external senses, and the use of symbolical acts, sanctioned by long usage and expressive in themselves, which belongs to the early times of so many nations. It was originally the only form of action; and every species of right could be enforced by it. When it was employed to enforce a right over things, the proceedings opened by the thing being brought before the magistrate (*in jure*); the claimants appeared, each touched it with a rod (*vindicta* or *festuca*), and said ' *Hunc ego hominem* (the instance given in Gaius is that of a claim to a slave) *ex jure Quiritium meum esse aio secundum suam causam, sicut dixi. Ecce tibi vindictam imposui.*' His adversary repeated the same words. At the same time that the words were spoken each party seized hold of the thing claimed; this was termed the *manuum consertio*, and the imposing the rod was termed *vindicatio*. If the thing was one that could not be brought into court, a portion of it was brought to represent the whole. A piece of turf, a twig, a brick, or one sheep, stood in place of a field, a house, or a flock.[†]

*First epoch.*
*Actions of law.*
*—actio sacramenti.*

---

[*] Gaius, iv. 13.

[†] If the thing was an immoveable there appears to have been an old ceremony of the parties going to the land or other immoveable thing, and one expelling the other from it, and leading him before a magistrate (*deductio*). See Aulus Gellius, *Noct. Att.* xx. 10; Cicero, *Pro Murena*, c. 6.

When the *vindicatio* and *manuum con#ertio* were over, the
magistrate said to the parties, *mittite ambo hominem*; both
were to place their claims in his hands. Then came the
wager, the *sacramentum*, each party challenging his adversary to deposit a certain sum, which the loser of the cause
was to forfeit to the treasury of the people (*ærarium*), to be
applied to the expenses of sacrifices. The law of the Twelve
Tables fixed the amount of the wager at 500 or 50 asses,
according as the value of the thing contested fell above or
below 1000 asses. The formal words by which this was done
are thus given by Gaius. He who had first gone through the
*vindicatio* asked his adversary why he claimed it. *Postulo
anne dicas, qua ex causa vindicaveris*. The other replied
that it was in conformity with right and law that he had
made his claim. *Jus peregri sicut vindictam imposui*: the
first answered, *Quando tu injuria vindicasti, D. L. æris
sacramento te provoco*; 'I challenge you to a deposit of 500
pounds of copper ;' and the other accepted the challenge by
saying, *Similiter ego te*. The magistrate then awarded the
possession of the thing contested until a decision was pronounced to the party that appeared to have the best right to
it, requiring him to furnish security that it would be forth-
coming at the proper time. These sureties were called
*prædes litis et vindiciarum—lis.* signifying the thing contested itself, and *vindiciæ* the fruits or profits which might
arise from it before the final sentence was given. After a
certain delay, a judge was appointed to examine the facts ;
he informed the magistrate what his decision was, and the
magistrate gave effect to this decision by using the force
placed at his disposal. When the right to be tried was a
personal one, there was of course nothing that could be
claimed by *vindicatio*, and the action began at once with the
wager.

95. The details of the *actio sacramenti* furnish so lively a
picture of the actual working of early Roman
law, that it is worth while to set them fully before us; but the other actions of law may be

*Actio per ju-
dicis postula-
tionem.*

passed over with a much more cursory notice;* indeed, our
knowledge of them is very deficient, as the portion of the
manuscript of Gaius which contained a sketch of the proceedings is imperfect. We know that the action called
*judicis postulatio* was employed with regard to obligations,
the machinery of the *actio sacramenti* being obviously but
very ill adapted for enforcing rights against persons. We
know little more than that the magistrate was asked to allow
the appointment of a judge, or *arbiter*, to decide the matter
in question; and that the form of action was probably adopted,
not where some certain thing was asked for as the fulfilment
of the engagement, but where a greater uncertainty in the
circumstances of the case allowed a greater latitude of opinion,
and where an appearance of good or bad faith would naturally
colour the whole cause.† In the year A.U.C. 510 (as it is
conjectured) the *lex Silia* instituted a new form of action
where the obligation was for the giving a definite
sum of money, and a *lex Calpurnia* (A.U.C. 520)      *Condictio.*
extended the scope of the action to all obligations for any
certain definite thing.‡ This action was called *condictio*,
because the plaintiff gave notice (*condicere*) to the defendant
that he must appear before the magistrate, at an interval of
thirty days, to receive a judge.

96. There were two other actions of law,§ that *per manus
injectionem*, and that *per pignoris capionem.*      *Actio per
manus in-
jectionem.*
These were, however, not really actions so much
as methods of obtaining execution. If it was a
right over a thing that was claimed, then, if the sentence
was in favour of the claimant, the magistrate at once put
the claimant in possession of the thing, having recourse to
force, *manus militaris*, if necessary. But when a right

---

* Gaius. iv. 12.

† *Praeclarum a majoribus accepimus morem rogandi judicis, si ea ro-
garemus quae salva fide facere possit.*—Cicero, *De Off.* iii. 10.

‡ Gaius, iv. 19.

§ Gaius, iv. 21.

against a person had to be enforced, there was nothing which
could be thus handed over; the remedy was against the
person, the liberty of the defeated adversary, and the action
*per manus injectionem* was the means by which the successful litigant exerted his power. He laid hands on him, *manus
injecit*, and brought him before a magistrate, stating that he
had been cast in the previous suit; if this was denied, a *judex*
was appointed, and inquiry made whether judgment had
really been given against him as alleged. If this was found
to be the case, he was *adjudicatus* to the claimant, and then
being brought before the magistrate, was *addictus*, or assigned over to him, and became the slave of his creditor. To
the principle that the person, and not the property, of the
debtor was bound, an exception was made when the debt was
due to the military service, the fund for sacrifices, or the
public treasury.* The creditor, in such cases, might seize on

*Actio per
pignoris
capionem.*
anything belonging to the debtor, and take it as
a pledge for the payment of the debt. This *pignoris capio* was only spoken of as an *actio* because it was conducted with certain solemnities, and accompanied by the repetition of a peculiar form of words.

97. Such forms of action were necessarily replaced by

*Suppression of
the actions of
law.*
others more convenient as Rome advanced in
civilization. They were in a great measure suppressed by the *lex Æbutia* (about A.U.C. 573),
and afterwards, in the time of Augustus, by the *leges Juliæ*.
They were, however, long retained in cases where the
*centumviri* were the proper *judices*, that is, in questions
of Quiritian ownership and disputed succession; and a
fictitious process, termed *in jure cessio*, which was nothing
else than an undefended action at law, in which a disputant
gave up (*cessit*) before the magistrate (*in jure*) the thing in
dispute, was retained as a ready means of many legal changes,
such as manumission or adoption, long after the actions of
law had fallen into disuse.

---

* GAIUS, iv. 26,

98. The changes wrought by intercourse with foreign nations, the new duties of extended dominion, and the stimulus given to the national mind by the long internal struggles which had now sub- *Second epoch; the system of formulæ.* sided, produced a corresponding change in the mode in which justice was administered. A new system succeeded to the old *legis actiones;* the magistrate was more strongly marked off from the *judex,* *Judges in the second period,* and it was the directions which the former gave the latter that constituted the important feature of the now system of procedure. At home the prætors, of whom there were eighteen in the days of Pomponius,* and one or two other magistrates; and in the provinces the *præsides* or præfects, who held *conventus* or assizes in the principal towns at stated intervals, sat as magistrates. As *judices* there were, in certain cases, the *recuperatores,* in others the *centumviri;* but principally those citizens whose names appeared in the yearly list drawn up by the prætor (*judices in albo relati*). The long struggle between the senate and the *equites* for the exclusive right to furnish judges ended in the judges ceasing to be taken entirely either from the senate or the *equites;* and two, at least, out of the five decuries of judges appearing in the *album* were taken from a comparatively humble class.

99. The directions which the magistrate sent to the judge were always conveyed in a formal shape, and the word *formulæ* was used to express the different *Formulæ.* forms in which directions were given. These *formulæ* were preserved and collected, and it became the great object of the contending parties that the right *formula* should be used in their case, the judge not being allowed to depart from the instructions he received. As there was no legal form to bind the magistrate, he could easily vary the formula so as to render substantial justice, and had thus a ready means of availing himself of any equitable doctrine, which a more

_____
* *Dig.* i. 2. 34.

refined jurisprudence or his own sense of what was right
suggested to him. These *formulæ*, so flexible in their general
character, yet couched in terms always precise and simple,
and as little varying from ordinary precedent as possible,
furnish one of the many admirable instances of the power of
the Romans to express correctly the subtlest legal ideas.

100. To show what these *formulæ* were, it will perhaps be
best to give at length one of those we find in
*Example of a formula.*  Gaius, and then to explain its different parts.
One which we may collect from different sections
of the Fourth Book runs thus :—

*Judex esto : Quod Aulus Agerius Numerio Negidio ho-
minem vendidit ; si paret Numerium Negidium Aulo Agerio
sestertium X. millia dare oportere, judex Numerium Negidium Aulo Agerio sestertium X. millia condemnato, si non
paret, absolvito.* \*

*Judex esto* is merely the order for the appointment of the
judge, and is not, strictly speaking, a part of the *formula*.
From ‘*quod*’ to ‘*vendidit*’ is what is called the *demonstratio ;*
from ‘*si paret*’ to ‘*dare oportere*’ is the *intentio ;* and from
‘*judex*’ to the end is the *condemnatio*. The *formula* ordinarily consisted of these three parts—the *demonstratio*,
the *intentio*, and the *condemnatio*.

101. The *demonstratio* is the statement of the fact or facts
which the plaintiff alleges as the ground of his
*Demonstratio.*  case.† Aulus Agerius, the plaintiff, says that
he has sold a slave to Numerius Negidius. The *demonstratio*
varied, of course, with each particular case.

102. The *intentio* was the really important part of the
*formula*. It was a precise statement of the de-
*Intentio.*  mand which the plaintiff made against (*tendebat
in*)‡ his adversary. It was necessary that it should exactly
meet the law which would govern the facts alleged by the
plaintiff, if true. Whether Aulus Agerius has sold this slave
to Numerius Negidius at the price he alleges, and whether

---

\* Gaius, iv. 40–43.        † Gaius, iv. 40        ‡ Gaius, iv. 41.

the debt is still owing, this is what the *judex* has to determine; if the judge thinks he has (*si paret*), then the judge is instructed to pronounce his judgment against him; if he thinks he has not (*si non paret*), he is to be acquitted.

109. The *condemnatio* is the direction to condemn or acquit according to the true circumstances of the case.* The *judex* was only a private citizen, and *Condemnatio.* unless specially authorized by a magistrate, could have no power to pronounce a judicial sentence. It is to be observed that the *condemnatio* was always pecuniary; the judge was always directed to condemn to a payment of money, never to do or give a particular thing. In three particular actions, however, and perhaps in more, the judge was directed to ' adjudicate ' a thing, in the sense of dividing it out among several litigants. These three actions were those brought to divide a family inheritance, to divide the property of partners, and to settle boundaries. In these actions there was an additional part of the *formula* running thus : *quantum adjudicari oportet, judex Titio adjudicato.* This was called the *adjudicatio;* so that in these actions the parts of the *formulae* were four—*demonstratio, intentio, adjudicatio,* and *condemnatio.* Of course when a thing, and not a sum of money, was claimed, it was not possible for the magistrate always to fix a precise sum in which the defendant was to be condemned. Sometimes, therefore, the *condemnatio* merely fixed the maximum as the sum, and ran *duntaxat X. millia condemnato.* Sometimes the direction was still more indefinite, and the sum was left to the discretion of the judge. *Quanti ea res erit, tantam pecuniam, &c., condemnato.* When the object of the suit was to get a thing, as, for instance, to get back a slave whom the defendant kept from the plaintiff, some such words as *nisi restituat* were inserted in the *condemnatio.* The defendant was only to pay the money if he refused to restore the thing.

---

* Gaius, iv. 42.

F

104. The *intentio* sometimes stood quite alone, and was then called a *prejudicialis formula ;* *Prejudicialis formula.* when this was the case, the object of the action was merely to establish a point which it was necessary to have settled with a view to a future action. The decision of such a preliminary point was called a *prejudicium.* Of course the *intentio* took any form that best suited the case; and it was the *intentiones* that were so carefully preserved as precedents, and so keenly debated by the contending parties. Sometimes the grounds of the defence made part of the *intentio.* The defendant might admit the plaintiff's statement, but say that there were special circumstances to take this particular case out of the general rule of law under which it would naturally fall. He might own, for instance, that he had bought a slave at the price alleged, but say that he had been induced to do so by fraud. This plea was called an *exceptio* (i. e. a *Exceptio.* taking out), and was made to form part of the *intentio,* some such words as these being added : *si in ea re nihil dolo malo Auli Agerii factum sit neque fiat.* The plaintiff, again, might have something to urge as an exception in reply to this plea: his answer was *Replicatio.* called *replicatio;* if the defendant had a further answer, it was called a *duplicatio,* the plaintiff's further reply a *triplicatio,* and so on. There was also sometimes an accessory part of the *formula* called the *præscriptio,* placed, as its name denotes, at the beginning of the whole *formula* for the purpose of limiting the enquiry. The plaintiff might, for instance, wish that, in enforcing a security on which payments were due from time to time, the action brought to try whether this security was valid should only affect his claim to payments already due, so that if he failed he might have a further action for future payments. In such a case some such words as *ea res agatur cujus rei dies fuit* (let the enquiry only be made as to the sum for the

---

* Gaius, iv. 44, 133.

payment of which the time has arrived) were prefixed to the *formula*. Gradually, however, the *præscriptio* fell into disuse, and the *intentio* and *exceptio* were so constructed as to serve every purpose for which it had been employed.

105. In the Roman system of civil process the time when a contested right was to be considered as really made the subject of litigation, was very carefully marked. It was very necessary that this should be clearly ascertained. *Litis contestatio.* The claimant in whose favour the ultimate decision was given was entitled to all that accrued to the thing claimed from this moment; and when once a point had been submitted to litigation, it could not be again litigated, both parties surrendering all their interest into the hands of the court, which assigned to the successful claimant such a fresh interest in the thing claimed as might appear to be due to him. This time was marked by each party, at the end of the proceedings before the magistrate, calling bystanders to witness, that they submitted the matter to the decision of the judge.* This was called the *litis contestatio.* In process of time the ceremony might be omitted, or at any rate became a mere form, but the conclusion of the proceedings before the magistrate (*in jure*) still formed the crisis at which the claims of the different parties were considered to be finally submitted to the decision of the law. The *litis contestatio* belongs, of course, to all the three periods of the Roman civil process: but it is so often spoken of with reference to actions under the formulary system, that it is, perhaps, most convenient to notice it here.

106. *Actio* meant, under the system of the actions of law, a particular form of procedure; under that of the *formulæ*, it meant the right granted to a plaintiff by the magistrate to seek what was due to him before a judge. Sometimes, however the *formula* by which the judge was to determine *Meaning of the word action under the system of formulæ.*

---

* Festus, *sub voce Contestari.*—*Dig.* xxviii. 1, 20.

the right, and sometimes the *judicium*, the proceedings by which the judge determined the right, were spoken
of as if *formulæ*, *judicium*, and *actio* were synony-
mous terms.  Under the system of *formulæ* there were
many divisions of actions, according to the form which the
right given by the magistrate assumed.  The most important division, perhaps, was that into actions *in*
*Divisions of* *rem* and *in personam.**  If the object of the
*actions.*
proceedings was to enforce a right to a thing
then the *formula* ran *si paret hominem Auli Agerii esse* ;
if to enforce an obligation, then the *formula* ran *si paret*
*Numerium Negidium Auli Agerii dare oportere* ; and it
was according to this difference in the *intentio* that actions
were said to be *in rem* or *in personam*.  *Vindicatio* came
to be used as a generic term for actions *in rem*, and *condictio*
for actions *in personam*.  Another important division was
that of *actiones in jus conceptæ* and *in factum conceptæ*.†
In the former, the judge had to decide whether the claim of
the plaintiff was legally just ; in the latter, whether a particular fact was true.  If it were true, then the magistrate
directed the judge to pronounce a particular sentence, and
by this means many claims were enforced which by the
letter of the law were not valid.  In an *actio in jus concepta*
the judge was directed to enquire, for instance, whether according to the usual rules of law, a valid contract had been
made.  In an *actio in factum concepta*, he was directed to
enquire whether *Aulus Agerius* did a particular thing ; if
he did, the magistrate making the law for a particular case,
provided what was to be the consequence.  Another division
of action separated those which were established by law or
precedent for the enforcement of some particular right
(*directæ*) from the *utiles*,‡ that is, those which, by an extension of the *directæ*, embraced cases analogous to, but not
among those to which the *directæ* applied.  Sometimes,
again, actions were said to be *stricti juris*,§ when the judge

* Gaius, iv. 1.                      † Gaius, iv. 37, 45, 47.
‡ Gaius, iv. 38.                     § Gaius, iv. 62.

was to decide rigidly according to the letter of the law, as opposed to those *bonæ fidei*, in which he was to allow his decision to be affected by equitable considerations, the nature of the case determining whether one or the other kind of action was appropriate. There are also numberless other divisions of actions, into which it is unnecessary to enter here; one species, however, the *actiones arbitrariæ*,\* deserves a passing notice. In these actions the judge had the power of calling on the defendant to give such compensation to the plaintiff as he might think fit to direct. They were, therefore, especially adapted to secure a plaintiff receiving the particular thing which had been the subject of a contract, and not its money value. The judge made a preliminary order commanding the defendant to give the thing, and only enforced the pecuniary condemnation in case of his refusal or inability to restore the thing itself.

107. In speaking of actions under the system of *formulæ*, it is impossible to pass over without notice the interdicts of the prætor,† though they were only incidentally connected with actions. An interdict was an order issued by the prætor, and was in fact an edict addressed to a particular individual with reference to a particular thing. *Vim fieri veto, exhibeas, restituas,* 'I forbid you to have recourse to violence, you are to produce, you are to restore;' such were the forms in which these commands were couched. Interdicts were granted, generally where some danger was apprehended, or some injury was being done to something to which a public character attached; as, for instance, if a road was stopped up; but they were also granted to protect private interests, if the necessity for the interference of a magistrate was immediate. If the person to whom the interdict was addressed acquiesced and obeyed the prætor's injunction, nothing remained to be done; but if he refused to obey, the magistrate then referred to the decision of a judge, whether the terms of the interdict ought to be complied with. For instance, the interdict *rem restituas* might

*Interdicts.*

---

* Gaius, iv. 47.       | Gaius, iv. 138.

have been issued; but the person to whom it was directed
might deny that by law he was bound to restore the thing.
On his stating this to the magistrate, the magistrate would
give an action to try the question, shaping the terms of the
interdict into the *intentio* of the formula, *si paret A. A.
rem restituero oportere, &c.* And it is thus that interdicts
are connected with actions, as their validity depended on no
action being brought to contest them, or the result of an
action being to support them.

108. There were under the system of *formulæ* certain cases
which the magistrate decided without sending
*Extraordinaria judicia.* to a judge. In these cases the magistrate was
said *extra ordinem cognoscere*, and the pro-
ceedings were termed *extra ordinem cognitiones, judicia*, or
*actiones.* Among the cases in which the magistrate proceeded in a summary way, were *restitutiones in integrum*,
(that is, certain cases in which he restored a person suffering
from something from which he ought not by law to suffer,
to the same position as he had occupied before the injury
was sustained), and cases relating to *fideicommissa.* But he
was called upon most frequently to proceed in this way in
order to give execution to the sentence of a judge. The old
modes of execution, the *manus injectio* and *pignoris capio*,
remained, though under a mitigated form; but a new method
of execution was also permitted by the prætor, and was much
more generally adopted. The creditors were placed in full
possession of all that the debtor had belonging to him; his
*persona* was, in fact, transferred to them. This was termed
the *missio in bonorum possessionem.* After a certain delay,
the creditors sold their interest in the debtor's property to
the person who would offer to pay the largest proportion of
the sums they claimed. He became the purchaser, and this
*emptio bonorum* transferred to him the *persona*, or legal
existence of the debtor, who thereby suffered a *capitis deminutio*, and became, in the language of the law, 'infamous.'
It was in the exercise of his 'extraordinary' jurisdiction that
the magistrate gave this mode of execution.

109. In the third period of the Roman system of civil process, the period of *extraordinaria judicia*, this summary jurisdiction was the only juris- *Third period of the Roman system of civil process.* diction the magistrate exercised. There was no longer any distinction between *jus* and *judi-* *The extraor-dinaria judi-cia.* cium ; the magistrate and the judge were the same person. By a constitution published A.D. 294, Diocletian directed all magistrates in the provinces to decide causes themselves. Tho practice was, in course of time, extended throughout the whole of the empire ; and in the days of Justinian, it was possible to speak of tho *ordinaria judicia* as quite past.*

110. In the days of the later emperors, tho provinces were classed together into præfectures. Over each province was a *præses*, who had a *vicarius*, or *Judges.* vice-president, under him, and who, either himself or by his *vicarius*, tried all cases above a certain amount, fixed by Justinian at 300 *solidi ;* cases below that amount were tried by inferior judges, called *judices pedanei.* The great cities, such as Constantinople and Alexandria, were under a separate jurisdiction. The prætorian prefect was the head judge of appeal ; but a final appeal lay to the emperor himself.

111. In the time of Justinian, an action was begun by the plaintiff announcing to a magistrate that he wished to bring an action, a proceeding which was *Mode of pro-cedure.* termed the *denuntiatio actionis*, and furnishing a short statement of his case ; this statement, called the *libellus conventionis*, the magistrate sent by a bailiff of the court (*executor*) to the defendant. The parties or their procurators appeared before the magistrate, and the magistrate decided the case. *Exceptio* was still used as the term to express the plea of the defendant, which he generally, of course reduced to writing, but apparently not only was he not obliged to do so, but it was not even necessary in all cases for the plaintiff to put his plaint into writing ; if he did not, the *executor*

---

* *Inst.* iv. 15.

would merely tell the defendant, by word of mouth, that an action had been brought against him, perhaps adding a general statement of the object for which it was brought. The *litis contestatio* took place directly the magistrate began to hear the cause. The condemnation was no longer merely a pecuniary one, but the system of execution was not materially different from what it had been under the prætorian system.

# INSTITUTIONUM

## JUSTINIANI

## PROŒMIUM.

---

IN NOMINE DOMINI NOSTRI JESU CHRISTI.

IMPERATOR CÆSAR FLAVIUS JUSTINIANUS, ALAMANICUS, GOTHICUS, FRANCICUS, GERMANICUS, ANTICUS, ALANICUS, VANDALICUS, AFRICANUS, PIUS, FELIX, INCLYTUS, VICTOR AC TRIUMPHATOR, SEMPER AUGUSTUS, CUPIDÆ LEGUM JUVENTUTI.

Imperatoriam majestatem non solum armis decoratam, sed etiam legibus oportet esse armatam, ut utrumque tempus et bellorum et pacis recte possit gubernari: et princeps Romanus victor existat non solum in hostilibus præliis, sed etiam per legitimos tramites calumniantium iniquitates expellens, et fiat tam juris religiosissimus, quam victis hostibus triumphator.

1. Quorum utramque viam cum summis vigiliis summaque providentia, annuente Deo, perfecimus. Et bellicos quidem sudores nostros barbaricæ gentes sub juga nostra deductæ cognoscunt, et tam Africa quam aliæ numerosæ provinciæ post tanta temporum spatia, nostris victoriis a cælesti Numine præstitis, iterum ditioni Romanæ nostroque additæ imperio protestantur; omnes vero populi legibus jam a nobis promulgatis vel compositis reguntur.

IN THE NAME OF OUR LORD JESUS CHRIST.

THE EMPEROR CÆSAR FLAVIUS JUSTINIANUS, VANQUISHER OF THE ALAMANI, GOTHS, FRANCS, GERMANS, ANTES, ALANI, VANDALS, AFRICANS, PIOUS, HAPPY, GLORIOUS, TRIUMPHANT CONQUEROR, EVER AUGUST, TO THE YOUTH DESIROUS OF STUDYING THE LAW, GREETING.

The imperial majesty should be not only made glorious by arms, but also strengthened by laws, that, alike in time of peace and in time of war, the state may be well governed, and that the emperor may not only be victorious in the field of battle, but also may by every legal means repel the iniquities of men who abuse the laws, and may at once religiously uphold justice and triumph over his conquered enemies.

1. By our incessant labours and great care, with the blessing of God, we have attained this double end. The barbarian nations reduced under our yoke know our efforts in war; to which also Africa and very many other provinces bear witness, which, after so long an interval, have been restored to the dominion of Rome and our empire, by our victories gained through the favour of heaven. All nations moreover are governed by laws which we have either promulgated or arranged.

2. Et cum sacratissimas constitutiones antea confusas in luculentam ereximus consonantiam, tunc nostram extendimus curam ad immensa veteris prudentiæ volumina; et opus desperatum, quasi per medium profundum euntes, cœlesti favore jam adimplevimus.

3. Cumque hoc Deo propitio peractum est, Triboniano viro magnifico, magistro et exquæstore meri palatii nostri, nec non Theophilo et Dorotheo viris illustribus, antecessoribus nostris (quorum omnium solertiam et legum scientiam et circa nostras jussiones fidem jam ex multis rerum argumentis accepimus) convocatis, mandavimus specialiter ut nostra auctoritate nostrisque suasionibus Institutiones componerent, ut liceat vobis prima legum cunabula non ab antiquis fabulis discere, sed ab imperiali splendore appetere; et tam aures quam animæ vestræ nihil inutile nihilque perperam positum, sed quod in ipsis rerum obtinet argumentis, accipiant. Et quod priore tempore vix post quadriennium prioribus contingebat, ut tunc constitutiones imperatorias legerent, hoc vos a primordio ingrediamini: digni tanto honore tantaque reperti felicitate, ut et initium vobis et finis legum eruditionis a voce principali procedat.

4. Igitur post libros quinquaginta Digestorum seu Pandectarum, in quibus omne jus antiquum collatum est, quos per eundem virum excelsum Tribonianum nec non ceteros viros illustres et facundissimos confecimus, in hos quatuor libros easdem Institutiones partiri jussimus, ut sint totius legitimæ scientiæ prima elementa.

5. In quibus breviter expositum est et quod antea obtinebat, et quod postea desuetudine inumbratum imperiali remedio illuminatum est.

2. When we had arranged and brought into perfect harmony the hitherto confused mass of imperial constitutions, we then extended our care to the endless volumes of ancient law; and, sailing as it were across the mid ocean, have now completed, through the favour of heaven, a work we once despaired of.

3. When by the blessing of God this task was accomplished, we summoned the most eminent Tribonian, master and ex-quæstor of our palace, together with the illustrious Theophilus and Dorotheus, professors of law, all of whom have on many occasions proved to us their ability, legal knowledge, and obedience to our orders; and we specially charged them to compose, under our authority and advice, Institutes, so that you may no more learn the first elements of law from old and erroneous sources, but apprehend them by the clear light of imperial wisdom; and that your minds and ears may receive nothing that is useless or misplaced, but only what obtains in actual practice. So that, whereas, formerly, the foremost among you could scarcely, after four years' study, read the imperial constitutions, you may now commence your studies by reading them, you who have been thought worthy of an honour and a happiness so great as that the first and last lessons in the knowledge of the law should issue for you from the mouth of the emperor.

4. When therefore, by the assistance of the same eminent person Tribonian and that of other illustrious and learned men, we had compiled the fifty books, called Digests or Pandects, in which is collected the whole ancient law, we directed that these Institutes should be divided into four books, which might serve as the first elements of the whole science of law.

5. In these books a brief exposition is given of the ancient laws, and of those also, which, overshadowed by disuse, have been again brought to light by our imperial authority.

6. Quas ex omnibus antiquorum Institutionibus, et præcipue ex commentariis Gaii nostri tam Institutionum quam rerum cotidianorum, aliisque multis commentariis compositas cum tres prædicti viri prudentes nobis obtulerunt, et legimus et cognovimus et plenissimum nostrarum constitutionum robur eis accommodavimus.

7. Summa itaque ope et alacri studio has leges nostras accipite; et vosmetipsos sic eruditos ostendite, ut spes vos pulcherrima foveat, toto legitimo opere perfecto, posse etiam nostram rempublicam in partibus ejus vobis credendis gubernari.

D. CP. XI. calend. decembris, D. Justiniano PP. A. III. cons.

6. These four books of Institutes thus compiled, from all the Institutes left us by the ancients, and chiefly from the commentaries of our Gaius, both from his Institutes and his Journal, and also from many other commentaries, were presented to us by the three learned men we have above named. We read and examined them, and have accorded to them all the force of our constitutions.

7. Receive, therefore, with eagerness, and study with cheerful diligence, these our laws, and show yourselves persons of such learning that you may conceive the flattering hope of yourselves being able, when your course of legal study is completed, to govern our empire in the different portions that may be entrusted to your care.

Given at Constantinople on the eleventh day of the calends of December, in the third consulate of the Emperor Justinian, ever August.

# LIBER PRIMUS.

## Tit. I. DE JUSTITIA ET JURE.

| | |
|---|---|
| Justitia est constans et perpetua voluntas jus suum cuique tribuendi. | Justice is the constant and perpetual wish to render every one his due. |

D. i. 1. 10.

The term *jus* (*id quod jussum est*), in its most extended sense, was taken by the Roman jurists to include all the commands laid upon men that they are bound to fulfil, both the commands of morality and of law. The distinction between commands which are only enforced by the sanction of public or private opinion, and those enforced by positive legal sanctions, may seem clear to us; but the Roman jurists, in speaking of the elementary principles and divisions of jurisprudence, did not keep law and morality distinct. Celsus defines *jus* as *ars boni et æqui*. (D. i. I. 1.) This extension of the term would sink positive law in morality; that only would be supposed to be commanded which ought to be commanded. The confusion arose principally from the view of the law of nature, borrowed from Greek philosophy by the jurists. (See Introd. sec. 14.)

*Jus*, used in its strictly legal sense, has two principal meanings. It either signifies *law*, that is, the whole mass of rights and duties protected and enforced by legal remedies, or it means any single right, that is, any faculty or privilege accorded by law to one man accompanied by a correlative duty imposed on another man. *Jus itineris*, for instance, is the right given to one man of going through the land of another who is placed under a duty of (*obligatio*) to let him pass. Neither a right nor a duty can exist without the other. (See Introd. sec. 36).

| | |
|---|---|
| 1. Jurisprudentia est divinarum atque humanarum rerum notitia, justi atque injusti scientia. | 1. Jurisprudence is the knowledge of things divine and human; the science of the just and the unjust. |

D. i. 1. 10. 2.

*Jurisprudentia* is the knowledge of what is *jus*, and *jus*, according to the theory of the law of nature, laid down what is commanded by right reason, this right reason being common to nature, or, as the Romans more often said, to the Gods, and to man. The knowledge of divine things was therefore necessary, as well as the knowledge of human things, to say what were the contents of *jus*. Both this and the preceding definition are taken at random out of the writings of Ulpian, are unintelligible unless taken in connection with a philosophical theory from which they are here dissevered, and are quite out of place at the beginning of an elementary treatise on law. (See Introd. sec. 34.)

2. His igitur generaliter cognitis et incipientibus nobis exponere jura populi Romani, ita videntur posse tradi commodissime, si primo levi ac simplici via, post deinde diligentissima atque exactissima interpretatione singula tradantur. Alioquin, si statim ab initio rudem adhuc et infirmum animum studiosi multitudine aut varietate rerum oneraverimus, duorum alterum, aut desertorem studiorum efficiemus, aut cum magno labore, sæpe etiam cum diffidentia quæ plerumque juvenes avertit, serius ad id perducemus, ad quod leviore via ductus sine magno labore et sine ulla diffidentia maturius perduci potuisset.

2. Having explained these general terms, we think we shall commence our exposition of the law of the Roman people most advantageously, if we pursue at first a plain and easy path, and then proceed to explain particular details with the utmost care and exactness. For, if at the outset we overload the mind of the student while yet new to the subject, and unable to bear much, with a multitude and variety of topics, one of two things will happen—we shall either cause him wholly to abandon his studies, or, after great toil, and often after great distrust of himself (the most frequent stumbling-block in the way of youth), we shall at last conduct him to the point, to which, if he had been led by an easier road, he might, without great labour, and without any distrust of his own powers, have been sooner conducted.

3. Juris præcepta sunt hæc: honeste vivere, alterum non lædere, suum cuique tribuere.

4. Hujus studii duæ sunt positiones, publicum et privatum. Publicum jus est, quod ad statum rei Romanæ spectat; privatum, quod ad singulorum utilitatem. Dicendum est igitur de jure privato, quod tripertitum est; collectum est enim ex naturalibus præceptis aut gentium aut civilibus.

3. The maxims of law are these: to live honestly, to hurt no one, to give every one his due.

4. The study of law is divided into two branches; that of public and that of private law. Public law regards the government of the Roman Empire; private law, the interest of individuals. We are now to treat of the latter, which is composed of three elements, and consists of precepts belonging to natural law, to the law of nations, and to the civil law.

D. i. 1. 1. 2.

Both the *jus publicum* and the *jus privatum* fall under municipal law, that is, the law of a particular state. *Publicum*

*jus in sacris, in sacerdotibus, in magistratibus consistit.*
(D. i. 1. 2). Public law regulates religious worship and civil administration ; private law determines the rights and duties of individuals. The threefold division of private law given in the text is discussed in the next section.

## Tit. II. DE JURE NATURALI GENTIUM ET CIVILI.

Jus naturale est, quod natura omnia animalia docuit : nam jus istnd non humani generis proprium est, sed omnium animalium quæ in cœlo, quæ in terra, quæ in mari nascuntor. Hinc descendit maris atque fœminæ conjunctio, quam nos matrimonium appellamus ; hinc liberorum procreatio,hinc educatio. Videmus etenim cetera quoque animalia istius juris peritia censeri.

The law of nature is that law which nature teaches to all animals. For this law does not belong exclusively to the human race, but belongs to all animals, whether of the earth, the air, or the water. Hence proceeds the union of male and female, which we term matrimony ; hence the procreation and bringing up of children. We see, indeed, that all the other animals besides man are considered as having knowledge of this law.

D. i. 1. 1. 3.

In the Introduction (sec. 14) a sketch has been given of what the jurists meant by the *lex naturæ*. It was the expression of right reason inherent in nature and man, and having a binding force as a law. It was contrasted with the *jus civile*, the old strict law of Rome (Introd. sec. 10), and also with the *jus gentium*, the sum, that is, of the law found to obtain in other nations besides the Romans, as well as in Roman law. (Introd. sec. 12.) There thus arose the threefold division of law adopted in the last paragraph of the last title ; but the *jus gentium* and the *jus naturale* were often placed in the same head of division, for the law common to all nations was but the embodiment and indication of what right reason was supposed to command to all men. Thus while the threefold division of law was adopted by some jurists, a twofold division was adopted by others, and is adopted in the next and the last paragraphs of this title, Justinian first borrowing from Ulpian, who adopted the threefold division, and then from Gaius who adopted the twofold.

Unfortunately, in order to give a notion of *jus naturale*, Justinian has borrowed a passage from Ulpian, in which that jurist runs off into a subsidiary and divergent line of thought. It is easy to see that if we begin to make inherent reason the foundation of law, we may find it necessary, to take into account the community of actions which, in some of the primary features of physical life, reason or instinct suggests to man and animals. If *jus* is that which nature commands, nature may be said to command the propagation of the species in animals as much as in man, and thus there would be a *jus* common to animals and to men. A jurist, to whom the theory of the *lex naturæ* was familiar, might easily pursue the subject to a point in which men and animals seemed to meet. But the main theory had nothing to do with animals, as it looked only to the reason inherent in the universe and in man, and in considering what the Roman jurists meant by *jus naturale* this fragment of Ulpian may be almost entirely dismissed from our notice.

1. Jus autem civile vel gentium ita dividitur. Omnes populi qui legibus et moribus reguntur, partim suo proprio, partim communi omnium hominum jure utuntur; nam quod quisque populus ipse sibi jus constituit, id ipsius civitatis, proprium est, vocaturque jus civile, quasi jus proprium ipsius civitatis. Quod vero naturalis ratio inter omnes homines constituit, id apud omnes peræque custoditur, vocaturque jus gentium, quasi quo jure omnes gentes utuntur. Et populus itaque Romanus partim suo proprio, partim communi omnium hominum jure utitur: quæ singula qualia sint, suis locis proponemus.

2. Sed jus quidem civile ex unaquaque civitate appellatur, veluti Atheniensium: nam si quis velit Solonis vel Draconis leges appellare jus civile Atheniensium, non erraverit. Sic enim et jus quo populus Romanus utitur, jus civile Romanorum appellamus, vel jus Quiritium quo Quirites utuntur; Romani enim a Quirino Quirites appellantur. Sed quotiens non addimus nomen cujus sit civitatis, nostrum jus significamus: sicuti cum poetam dicimus nec addimus nomen, subauditur apud Græcos egregius Homerus, apud nos Virgilius. Jus autem gentium omni humano generi commune est: nam usu exigente et humanis necessitatibus, gentes humanæ quædam sibi constituerunt.—Bella etenim orta sunt et captivitates secutæ, et servitutes quæ sunt naturali juri contrariæ; jure enim naturali ab initio omnes homines liberi nascebantur. Et

1. Civil law is thus distinguished from the law of nations. Every community governed by laws and customs, uses partly its own law, partly laws common to all mankind. The law which a people makes for its own government belongs exclusively to that state and is called the civil law as being the law of the particular state. But the law which natural reason appoints for all mankind obtains equally among all nations, and is called the law of nations, because all nations make use of it. The people of Rome, then, are governed partly by their own laws, and partly by the laws which are common to all mankind. We will take notice of this distinction as occasion may arise.

2. Civil law takes its name from the State which it governs, as, for instance, from Athens: for it would be very proper to speak of the laws of Solon or Draco as the civil law of Athens. And thus the law which the Roman people make use of is called the civil law of the Romans, or that of the Quirites, as being used by the Quirites: for the Romans are called Quirites from Quirinus. But whenever we speak of civil law, without adding the name of any state, we mean our own law; just as the Greeks, when 'the poet' is spoken of without any name being expressed, mean the great Homer, and we Romans mean Virgil. The law of nations is common to all mankind, for nations have established certain laws, as occasion and the necessities of human life required. Wars arose and in their train followed captivity and slavery, both which are contrary to the law of nature; for by that law,

ex hoc jure gentium, omnes pene contractus introducti sunt, ut emptio, venditio, locatio, conductio, societas, depositum, mutuum et alii innumerabiles.

all men are originally born free. Further, by the law of nations almost all contracts were at first introduced, as, for instance, buying and selling, letting and hiring, partnerships, deposits, loans, and very many others.

D. i. 4. 5.

The term *jus civile*, as used here, entirely depends for its meaning on the contrast between it and the *jus gentium*. When the jurists came to examine different systems of laws, they found much in each that was common to all. This common part they termed the *jus gentium :* and the residue, the part peculiar to each state, they called *jus civile*. The contracts of sale, hiring, and the others mentioned in the text, were, they found, carried on much in the same way in every country, and they therefore assigned them to the head of *jus gentium*, and contrasted them with forms of contract which were peculiar to the old Roman law, and were therefore considered part of the *jus civile*. In the usual sense of *jus civile*, in which it means the old law of Rome prior to the *jus honorarium* (see Introd. sec. 10), these contracts were part of the *jus civile*, that is, they were part of, and were recognised by, the old law, but they were also part of the general law of nations, no forms peculiar to Roman law being necessary for their creation.

3. Constat autem jus nostrum aut ex scripto aut ex non scripto, ut apud Græcos τῶν νομῶν οἱ μὲν ἔγγραφοι, οἱ δὲ ἄγραφοι. Scriptum jus est lex, plebiscita, senatus-consulta, principium placita, magistratuum edicta, responsa prudentium.

4. Lex est quod populus Romanus, senatorio magistratu interrogante, veluti consule, constituebat. Plebiscitum est quod plebs, plebeio magistratu interrogante, veluti tribuno, constituebat. Plebs autem a populo eo differt, quo species a genere; nam appellatione populi universi cives significantur, connumeratis etiam patriciis et senatoribus. Plebis autem appellatione, sine patriciis et senatoribus, ceteri cives significantur. Sed et plebiscita, lata lege Hortensia, non minus valere quam leges coeperunt.

3. Our law is written and unwritten, just as among the Greeks some of their laws were written and others not written. The written part consists of laws, *plebiscita*, *senatus-consulta*, enactments of emperors, edicts of magistrates, and answers of jurisprudents.

4. A law is that which was enacted by the Roman people on its being proposed by a senatorian magistrate, as a consul. A *plebiscitum* is that which was enacted by the plebs on its being proposed by a plebeian magistrate, as a tribune. The *plebs* differs from the people as a species from its genus; for all the citizens, including patricians and senators, are comprehended in the people; but the *plebs* only includes citizens, not being patricians or senators. *Plebiscita*, after the Hortensian law had been passed, began to have the same force as laws.

A *lex* or *populi scitum*, to use a word made by the commentators on the analogy of *plebiscitum*, was passed originally only in the *comitia curiata*; after the establishment of the *comitia centuriata* in both these *comitia*; but, excepting in the case of conferring the *imperium*, almost always in the *centuriata*. (See Introd. sec. 15.)

The *lex Hortensia*, 467 A.U.C., had been preceded by the *lex Valeria*, 304 A.U.C., and the *lex Publilia*, 414 A.U.C., by both of which it was provided that *plebiscita* should bind the whole people. Either the effect of their provisions had been disputed, or exceptions had been made to them, or perhaps the extension of the authority of the *plebiscitum* which they gave was not so complete as their terms would seem to imply. (Nieb. 2. 366.) The term *lex* is very frequently applied to *plebiscita* as well as to *populi scita*. (See Introd. sec. 9.)

| | |
|---|---|
| 5. Senatus-consultum est quod senatus jubet atque constituit: nam cum auctus esset populus Romanus in eum modum ut difficile esset in unum eum convocari legis sanciendæ causa, æquum visum est senatum vice populi consuli. | 5. A *senatus-consultum* is that which the senate commands and appoints: for, when the Roman people were so increased that it was difficult to assemble it together to pass laws, it seemed right that the senate should be consulted in the place of the people. |

GAL. i. 4; D. i. 2. 2. 9.

*Senatus-consulta* had in some instances the force of a law even in the times of the republic, for we have a few preserved of a date antecedent to the Cæsars, which undoubtedly had the force of law; but they all relate to matters of social administration, such as forbidding burial within the city, or the importation of wild beasts. (See Introd. sec. 17.) But we cannot speak of *senatus-consulta* as a substantial part of the general legislation till the times of the emperors, when they superseded every other except the emperor's enactments. The appeal of the emperor to their authority dwindled down almost immediately into a mere form. (Cod. i. 14. 12. 1., *in præsenti leges condere soli imperatori concessum est*.)

| | |
|---|---|
| 6. Sed et quod principi placuit, legis habet rigorem; cum lege regia quæ de ejus imperio lata est, populus ei et in eum omne imperium suum et potestatem concessit. Quodcumque ergo imperator per epistolam constituit, vel cognoscens decrevit, vel edicto præcepit, legem esse constat; hæ sunt quæ constitutiones appellantur. Plane ex his quædam | 6. That which seems good to the emperor has also the force of law; for the people, by the *lex regia*, which is passed to confer on him his power, make over to him their whole power and authority. Therefore whatever the emperor ordains by rescript, or decides in adjudging a cause, or lays down by edict, is unquestionably law; and it is these enactments of |

...sunt personales, quæ nec ad exemplum trabuntur, quoniam non hoc princeps vult; nam quod alicui ob meritum indulsit, vel si cui pœnam irrogavit, vel si cui sine exemplo subvenit, personam non transgreditur. Aliæ autem cum generales sint, omnes procul dubio tenent.

the emperor that are called constitutions. Of these, some are personal, and are not to be drawn into precedent, such not being the intention of the emperor. Supposing the emperor has granted a favour to any man on account of his merit, or inflicted some punishment, or granted some extraordinary relief, the application of these acts does not extend beyond the particular individual. But the other constitutions, being general, are undoubtedly binding on all.

Gai. i. 5; D. i. 4. 1.

The imperial constitutions, though known in the time of the previous emperors, first attained, under Hadrian, the position of being in reality the only source of law. They were of three kinds; first, *epistolæ*, letters, or answers to letters addressed by the emperor to different individuals or public bodies, or *mandata*, orders given to particular officers, and *rescripta*, answers given by the emperor to magistrates who requested his assistance in the decision of doubtful points; secondly, judicial sentences, *decreta*, given by the emperors (Bk. ii. 15. 4); both these kinds having force only by serving as a precedent in similar cases; and thirdly, *edicta*, or laws binding generally on all the subjects of the emperor. (See Introd. sec. 16.)

It is here said, on the authority of Ulpian (D. i. 4. 1), that the emperor derives his authority from the *lex regia*. This does not refer to any one law of that name; but to the law of the *comitia curiata* by which the *imperium* was conferred. Gaius says, i. 5, *nec unquam dubitatum est quin principis constitutio legis vicem obtineat cum ipse imperator per legem imperium accipiat.* This law was a relic of that by which the king had been invested with the royal authority, intrusted to him by the *curia* representing the *populus*; and it was considered that the emperor was in like manner invested with all the power of the Roman people transferred to him on his receiving the *imperium*. (See Introd. sec. 16.)

7. Prætorum quoque edicta non modicam juris obtinent auctoritatem. Hoc etiam jus honorarium solemus appellare, quod qui honorem gerunt, id est magistratus, auctoritatem huic juri dederunt. Proponebant et ædiles curules edictum de quibusdam causis, quod edictum juris honorarii portio est.

7. The edicts of the prætors are also of great authority. These edicts are called the honorary law, because those who bear honours in the state, that is, the magistrates, have given them their sanction. The curule ædiles also used to publish an edict relative to certain subjects, which edict also became part of the *jus honorárium*.

Gai. i. 6: D. xxi. 1. 1.

Papinian says (D. i. 1. 7), that the *jus prætorium* was introduced by the prætors, *adjuvandi vel supplendi vel corrigendi juris civilis gratia*. New circumstances, new habits of thinking, and, in the case of the *prætor peregrinus*, a new scope for authority, compelled the prætor to use an equitable power, and frequently equitable fictions, to extend the narrow limits of the old civil law. (See Introd. sec. 12.) The decisions by which he did this were called *edicta*. At the beginning of his year of office, the prætor published a list of the rules by which he intended to be bound, and this was called the *edictum perpetuum*, because it was to apply to all cases that might fall under it during the year of office, and was not made, like an *edictum repentinum*, to meet a particular case. Of course each prætor borrowed much from his predecessors, and thus the edict, or rather all that was not new in it, was called the *edictum tralatitium*. (Cic. Ad At. v. 21.) The *lex Cornelia* (B.C. 67) forbad a prætor to depart during his term of office from the edict he had promulgated at its commencement. In the time of Hadrian, a jurist named Salvius Julianus, who filled the office of prætor, systematized and condensed the edicts of preceding prætors into one which he called the *edictum perpetuum*, and thus this term, *edictum perpetuum*, which generally means the edict for the year, is sometimes the name of this work of Julianus, which was intended, no doubt, to serve as the basis for future annual edicts. (See Introd. sec. 19.)

| | |
|---|---|
| 8. Responsa prudentium sunt sententiæ et opiniones eorum quibus permissum erat jura condere. Nam antiquitus institutum erat, ut essent qui jura publice interpretarentur, quibus a Cæsare jus respondendi datum est, qui jurisconsulti appellabantur: quorum omnium sententiæ et opiniones eam auctoritatem tenebant, ut judici recedere a responso eorum non liceret, ut est constitutum. | 8. The answers of the jurisprudents are the decisions and opinions of persons who were authorized to determine the law. For anciently it was provided that there should be persons to interpret publicly the law, who were permitted by the emperor to give answers on questions of law. They were called jurisconsulti; and the authority of their decisions and opinions, when they were all unanimous, was such, that the judge could not, according to the constitution, refuse to be guided by their answers. |

GAI. i. 7.

See Introd. secs. 13. 20.
It is to the change in the position of the jurists effected by Augustus (sec. 20), that allusion is made in the words *quibus a Cæsare jus respondendi datum est*, and it is to the constitutions of Hadrian (sec. 20) and Theodosius (sec. 27), that the words *judici recedere a responso eorum non liceret, ut est constitutum*, refer.

9. Ex non scripto jus venit, quod usus comprobavit: nam diuturni mores consensu utentium comprobati legem imitantur.

9. The unwritten law is that which usage has established; for ancient customs, being sanctioned by the consent of those who adopt them, are like laws.

D. i. 3. 32.

*Quid interest suffragio populus voluntatem suam declaret an rebus ipsis et factis?* (D. i. 3. 32.) The Roman jurists did not trouble themselves to ascertain very accurately whence laws derive their binding force. The vague expression in the text *mores legem imitantur*, and the question asked in these words of the Digest leave undecided the question of the relation of customs to laws. The Roman law held that customs could not only interpret law (*optima legum interpres consuetudo*, D. i. 3. 37), but also abrogate it. In the last section of this title it is said that the enactment of a state may be changed *tacito consensu populi*, and in the Digest (i. 3. 32. 1.) it is expressly stated that *leges tacito consensu omnium per desuetudinem abrogantur*. The Code, certainly, lays down (viii. 53) that the authority of a custom is not so great that it can ' conquer reason or law.' We may escape from the difficulty by supposing the Code to be speaking of particular not general customs. A law fallen into desuetudo might be abrogated by general custom, but a particular custom, opposed to public utility or express enactment, would not be suffered to prevail.

10. Et non ineleganter in duas species jus civile distributum esse videtur: nam origo ejus ab institutis duarum civitatum, Athenarum scilicet et Lacedæmonia fluxisse videtur. In his enim civitatibus ita agi solitum erat, ut Lacedæmonii quidem magis ea quæ pro legibus observarent, memoriæ mandarent; Athenienses vero, ea quæ in legibus scripta comprehendissent, custodirent.

10. The civil law is not improperly divided into two kinds, for the division seems to have had its origin in the customs of the two states Athens and Lacedæmon. For in these states it used to be the case, that the Lacedæmonians rather committed to memory what they observed as law, while the Athenians rather observed as law what they had consigned to writing, and included in the body of their laws.

It is hardly necessary to say, that the distinction between written and unwritten law must always exist where laws are written at all, and where no attempt has been made to express all law in positive terms; and that this Greek origin for the two branches of Roman law is quite imaginary.

11. Sed naturalia quidem jura quæ apud omnes gentes peræque servantur, divina quadam providentia constituta, semper firma atque immutabilia permanent. Ea vero

11. The laws of nature, which all nations observe alike, being established by a divine providence, remain ever fixed and immutable. But the laws which every state has

| | |
|---|---|
| qœ ipsa sibi quæque civitas con-stituit, sæpe mutari solent, vel tacito consensu populi, vel alia ponitea lege lata. | enacted, undergo frequent changes, either by the tacit consent of the people, or by a new law being sub-sequently passed. |

Gai. i. 1; D. i. 3. 02. 1.

Justinian, abandoning the threefold division of Ulpian, which he had adopted in the earlier paragraphs of this chap-ter, now follows the twofold division of Gaius (i. 1), into *jus naturale* and *jus civile*.

## Tit. III. DE JURE PERSONARUM.

| | |
|---|---|
| Omne autem jus quo utimur vel ad personas pertinet, vel ad res, vel ad actiones. Et prius de personis vi-deamus: nam parum est jus nosse, si personæ quarum causa constitu-tum est, ignorentur. Summa itaque divisio de jure personarum hæc est, quod omnes homines aut liberi sunt, aut servi. | All our law relates either to per-sons, or to things, or to actions. Let us first speak of persons; as it is of little purpose to know the law, if we do not know the persons for whose sake the law was made. The chief division in the rights of persons. is this: men are all either free or slaves. |

Gai. i. 8.

In Gaius, and in the Institutes of Justinian, obligations are treated of under the head of things. The division of law which compels them to be so treated is obviously inaccurate, for actions themselves are just as much things as obligations; and if obligations were classed under the head of things be-cause they are a mode of obtaining things, there is the objec-tion to the classification, that the obtaining a thing is only an ultimate and accidental result, not a necessary part, of an obligation.

Every being capable of having and being subject to rights was called in Roman law a *persona*. (See Introd. sec. 37.) Thus not only was the individual citizen, when looked at as having this capacity, a *persona*, but also corporations and public bodies. Slaves, on the contrary, were not *personæ*. They had no rights. (See Introd. 38.) The word *persona* has also another sense. It was used not only for the being who had the capacity of enjoying rights and fulfilling duties, but also for the different characters or parts in which this capacity showed itself; or, to borrow the metaphor suggested by the etymology of the word, for the different masks or faces which the actor wore in playing his part in the drama of civic and social life. Thus, for instance, the same man might have the *persona patris*, or *tutoris*, or *mariti*; that is, might be re-garded in his character of father, tutor, or husband.

*Status* or *caput* (legal standing) is the correlative of *persona*. *Status* is the legal capacity of a *persona*: *persona* is that which has a *status*. In Roman law there were recognised three great heads of this legal capacity: the *status libertatis*, the capacity to have and be subject to the rights of a freeman; the *status civitatis*, the capacity to have and be subject to the rights of a Roman citizen; and the *status familiæ*, the capacity to have and be subject to the rights of a person *sui juris*. The extent and meaning of each of these capacities is to be determined by contrasting it with its corresponding negative, that is, with the absence of the capacity spoken of. In order to determine the capacity of freemen, we must speak of the position of slaves: in order to determine the capacity of a citizen, we must speak of the position of a *peregrinus*: in order to determine the capacity of a person *sui juris*, we must speak of the position of a person not *sui juris*. The discussion of these points occupies the remainder of the first book of the Institutes.

1. Et libertas quidem, ex qua etiam liberi vocantur, est naturalis facultas ejus quod cuique facere libet, nisi si quid vi aut jure prohibetur.

2. Servitus autem est constitutio juris gentium, qua quis dominio alieno contra naturam subjicitur.

1. Freedom, from which men are said to be free, is the natural power of doing what we each please, unless prevented by force or by law.

2. Slavery is an institution of the law of nations, by which one man is made the property of another, contrary to natural right.

D. l. 5. 4. 1.

The institution of slavery was the one thing in which the *jus gentium* seemed to be irreconcilable with the *jus naturale*; and it was this, probably, more than anything else, that made some of the jurists adopt the threefold division of law.

3. Servi autem ex eo appellati sunt, quod imperatores captivos vendere, ac per hoc servare nec occidere solent: qui etiam mancipia dicti sunt, eo quod ab hostibus manu capiuntur.

4. Servi autem aut nascuntur aut fiunt. Nascuntur ex ancillis nostris: fiunt aut jure gentium, id est ex captivitate; aut jure civili, cum liber homo, major viginti annis, ad pretium participandum sese venundari passus est.

3. Slaves are denominated *servi*, because generals order their captives to be sold, and thus preserve them, and do not put them to death. Slaves are also called *mancipia*, because they are taken from the enemy by the strong hand.

4. Slaves either are born or become so. They are born so when their mother is a slave; they become so either by the law of nations, that is, by captivity, or by the civil law, as when a free person, above the age of twenty, suffers himself to be sold that he may share the price given for him.

D. i. 5. 5. L.

Children born out of the pale of lawful marriage always
followed the condition of the mother; and as slaves were incapable of contracting a lawful marriage in the peculiar sense
of 'lawful' adopted by Roman law, the children of a female
slave were necessarily slaves. They were called *vernæ* when
born and reared on the property of the owner of their mother.
(See Introd. sec. 46.)

In order to prevent a fraud, by which a person, having
allowed himself to be sold, turned round on the purchaser
and claimed his liberty as being free-born, a law, perhaps the
*Senatus-consultum Claudianum* (D. xl. 3. 5), enacted that
the perpetrator of the fraud should be bound by his statement,
and be held to be a slave. In the early law of Rome, it may
be observed, a citizen could really sell himself so as to lose his
freedom; but he always retained a right of redemption.

There were other modes by which slavery could arise under
the Roman law, as (1) when a free woman had commerce with
a slave, or (2), when malefactors were condemned to the am-
phitheatre or the mines, the guilty parties were held in law to
be slaves. These latter modes of legal slavery were abolished
by Justinian. (Bk. iii. 12. 1. Nov. 22. cap. 8.) Lastly (3), an
emancipated slave, if guilty of ingratitude towards his master,
might be reclaimed to slavery.   (D. xxv. 3. 6.)

In the older law, *addictio*, that is, delivery of the person to
a creditor by way of execution for a debt, the being detected
in *furtum manifestum*, and omitting to be inscribed in the
tables of the census in order to defraud the revenue, were
each a cause of slavery; but these causes had become obsolete long before the time of Justinian.

| 6. In servorum conditione nulla est differentia, in liberis multæ differentiæ sunt: aut enim sunt ingenui aut libertini. | 6. In the condition of slaves there is no distinction; but there are many distinctions among free persons; for they are either born free, or have been set free. |
|---|---|

D. i. 5. 5. 5.

In the later empire there was introduced what may be almost
termed a difference in the condition of slaves by the institution
of *coloni*, that is, persons attached to the soil, *ascripti glebæ*,
passing with it, and bound to remain on it, but entitled to
retain for their own use all they could gain from it beyond
the value of a yearly payment, which they had to make to
the owner of the soil, and enjoying also all the family rights
of freemen.

## Tit. IV.   DE INGENUIS.

Ingenuus est is qui, statim ut natus est, liber est, sive ex duobus ingenuis matrimonio editus est, sive ex libertinis duobus, sive ex altero libertino et altero ingenuo. Sed etsi quis ex matre nascitur libera, patre servo, ingennus nihilominus nascitur: quemadmodum qui ex matre libera et incerto patre natus est, quoniam vulgo conceptus est. Sufficit autem liberam fuisse matrem eo tempore quo nascitur, licet ancilla conceperit. Et e contrario si libera conceperit, deinde ancilla facta pariat, placuit eum qui nascitur liberum nasci; quia non debet calamitas matris ei nocere, qui in ventre est. Ex his illud quaesitum est, si ancilla praegnans manumissa sit, deinde ancilla postea facta pepererit, liberum an servum pariat? Et Marcellus probat liberum nasci; sufficit enim ei qui in ventre est, liberam matrem vel medio tempore habuisse: quod verum est.

A person is *ingenuus* who is free from the moment of his birth, by being born in matrimony, of parents who have been either both born free, or both made free, or one of whom has been born and the other made free; and when the mother is free, and the father a slave, the child nevertheless is born free: just as he is if his mother is free, and it is uncertain who is his father; for he had then no legal father. And it is sufficient if the mother is free at the time of the birth, although a slave when she conceived; and conversely, if she be free when she conceives, and is a slave when she gives birth to her child, yet the child is held to be born free; for the misfortune of the mother ought not to prejudice her unborn infant. The question hence arose, if a female slave with child is made free, but again becomes a slave before the child is born, whether the child is born free or a slave? Marcellus thinks it is born free, for it is sufficient for the unborn child, if the mother has been free, although only in the intermediate time; and this is true.

Gai. i. 11. 82. 89, 90; D. i. 5. 5.

If a child was born *in matrimonio*, a tie which could only, in the eyes of the civil law, be contracted between two free persons, the child was free from the moment of conception. If it was not born *in matrimonio*, then it followed the condition of the mother; and it was her condition at the time of birth, not at that, of conception, which decided the *status* of the child. It was only by a departure from the strict theory of law that the enjoyment of liberty by the mother before the birth was allowed to make the child free.   (Gai. i. 89.)

1. Cum autem ingenuus aliquis natus sit, non officit illi in servitute fuisse, et postea manumissum esse; saepissime enim constitutum est, natalibus non officere manumissionem.

1. When a man has been born free he does not cease to be *ingenuus*, because he has been in the position of a slave, and has subsequently been enfranchised; for it has been often settled that enfranchisement does not prejudice the rights of birth.

*In servitute fuisse.* This does not mean to have been a

slave, but to have been in the position of one. As if a free-born child were considered erroneously to be a slave, and were manumitted, and then his free birth were discovered, his *status* would be that of an *ingenuus*, and not of a *libertinus*.

## Tit. V. DE LIBERTINIS.

Libertini sunt, qui ex justa servitute manumissi sunt. Manumissio autem est datio libertatis; nam quamdiu quis in servitute est, manui et potestati suppositus est, et manumissus liberatur potestate. Quæ res a jure gentium originem sumpsit, utpote cum jure naturali omnes liberi nascerentur, nec esset nota manumissio, cum servitus esset incognita. Sed posteaquam jure gentium servitus invasit secutum est beneficium manumissionis; et cum uno naturali nomine homines appellarentur, jure gentium tria genera esse cœperunt, liberi et his contrarium servi. et tertium genus libertini, qui desierant esse servi.

Freedmen are those who have been manumitted from just servitude. Manumission is the process of freeing from ' the hand.' For while any one is in slavery, he is under ' the hand ' and power of another, but by manumission he is freed from this power. This institution took its rise from the law of nations; for by the law of nature all men were born free; and manumission was not heard of, as slavery was unknown. But when slavery came in by the law of nations, the boon of manumission followed. And whereas all were denominated by the one natural name of ' men,' the law of nations introduced a division into three kinds of men, namely, freemen, and in opposition to them, slaves; and thirdly, freedmen who had ceased to be slaves.

Gai. i. 11; D. i. 1. 4.

In some few cases a slave could obtain liberty without manumission. Many of these cases are enumerated in the Digest (xl. 8). A slave for instance, who was abandoned by his master on account of disease or infirmity (*ob gravem infirmitatem*), was pronounced free by an edict of Claudius.

1. Multis autem modis manumissio procedit, aut enim ex sacris constitutionibus in sacrosanctis ecclesiis, aut vindicta, aut inter amicos, aut per epistolam, aut per testamentum, aut per aliam quamlibet ultimam voluntatem. Sed et aliis multis modis libertas servo competere potest, qui tam. ex veteribus quam ex nostris constitutionibus introducti sunt.

1. Manumission is effected in various ways; either in the face of the Church, according to the imperial constitutions, or by the *vindicta*, or in the presence of friends, or by letter, or by testament, or by any other expression of a man's last will. And a slave may also gain his freedom in many other ways, introduced by the constitutions of former emperors, and by our own.

Gai. i. 17; D. xl.; C. i. 13; vii. 6. 1. 1.

A *manumissio* was said to be *legitima* when made in one of the three ways recognised by the old law. These three modes of effecting a *legitima manumissio* were *censua, vindicta,* and *testamentum.* A *manumissio* was made ; 1st, *censu*, i.e. by the master and the slave appearing before the censor at the time of the census being taken, and the slave's name being, at the master's desire, enrolled on the census list. This mode was obsolete in the time of the empire (ULP. *Reg.* i. 8. GAI. i. 140). 2nd, *vindicta*, i.e. by means of a fictitious suit called *causa liberalis* (D. xl. 12), in which a person, termed the *assertor libertatis*, that is, a friend of the slave, or in his place a lictor, asserted before the praetor that the slave was free, by touching him on the head with a wand (which represented the *hasta* or symbol of proprietorship), and thus claiming him as against the master. In token of his consent, the master turned him round and then let him go, and the magistrate pronounced him free. 3rd, *testamento* (D. xl. 4), i. e. by testament. Freedom might be given by testament, either as a legacy to the slave himself, in which case the slave was called *orcinus*, because his patron, i. e. the person to whom he owed his liberty, was dead when he gained it ; or the heir might be charged to grant or procure the liberty of the slave. If a slave was made by testament conditionally free, he was said to be *statu liber—statu liber est, qui statutam et destinatam in tempus vel conditionem libertatem habet* (D. xi. 7, 1). The solemnities attached to manumission by the *vindicta* ceased to be strictly observed long before the time of Justinian. Although the magistrate was at his country seat (D. xl. 2. 8), no lictors present, or the master silent, the manumission was still held good. But manumission was not always *legitima.* Usage and the praetor's authority established gradually many other less formal methods of accomplishing the same object, and the imperial constitutions added others. Of those mentioned in the text, that in presence of the Church was established by Constantine, A.D. 316 (C. i. 13). The ceremony was generally performed at some one of the great feasts, and it was necessary it should take place before the bishops. Freedom could also be given by a master writing to a slave (*per epistolam*), or declaring before his friends (*inter amicos*), that he gave the slave liberty, or by his making a codicil to that effect (*per quamlibet aliam ultimam voluntatem*), witnesses, however, being necessary in each of these cases (C. vii. 6. 1 ; C. vii. 6. 2 ; C. vi. 36. 8. 3). Other methods are noticed in the Code (vii. 6. 3–12), all based upon an implied wish of the masters to free the slave.

2. Servi autem a dominis semper manumitti solent, adeo ut vel in transitu manumittantur, veluti cum

2. Slaves may be manumitted by their masters at any time ; even when the magistrate is only passing along,

prætor ant præses ant proconsul in balneum vel in theatrum eant.

3. Libertinorum autem status tripertitus antea fuerat: nam qui manumittebantur, modo majorem et justam libertatem consequebantur, et fiebant cives Romani; modo minorem, et Latini ex lege Junia Norbana fiebant; modo inferiorem, et fiebant ex lege Ælia Sentia dedititiorum numero. Sed dedititiorum quidem pessima conditio jam ex multis temporibus in desuetudinem abiit, Latinorum vero nomen non frequentatur. Ideoque nostra pietas omnia augere et in meliorem statum reducere desiderans, duabus constitutionibus hoc emendavit et in pristinum statum perduxit: quia et a primis urbis Romæ cunabulis una atque simplex libertas competebat, id est, ea quam habebat manumissor; nisi quod scilicet libertinus ait qui manumittitur, licet manumissor ingenuus sit. Et dedititios quidem per constitutionem nostram expulimus, quam promulgavimus inter nostras decisiones, per quas suggerente nobis Triboniano, viro excelso, quæstore antiqui juris altercationes placavimus. Latinos autem Junianos, et omnem quæ circa eos fuerat observantiam, alia constitutione per ejusdem quæstoris suggestionem correximus, quæ inter imperiales radiat sanctiones; et omnes libertos, nullo nec ætatis manumissi, nec dominii manumissoris, nec in manumissionis modo discrimine habito, sicuti antea observabatur, civitate Romana donavimus, multis modis additis per quos possit libertas servis cum civitate Romana, quæ sola est in præsenti, præstari.

as when a prætor, or præses, or proconsul is going to the baths, or the theatre.

3. Freedmen were formerly divided into three classes. For those who were manumitted sometimes obtained a complete liberty, and became Roman citizens; sometimes a less complete, and became Latins under the *lex Junia Norbana*; and sometimes a liberty still inferior, and became *dedititii*, by the *lex Ælia Sentia*. But this lowest class, that of the *dedititii*, has long disappeared, and the title of Latins become less frequent; and so in our benevolence, which leads us to complete and improve everything, we have introduced a great reform by two constitutions, which re-established the ancient usage; for in the infancy of the state there was but one liberty, the same for the enfranchised slave as for the person who manumitted him; excepting, indeed, that the person manumitted was a freedman, while the manumittor was freeborn. We have abolished the class of *dedititii* by a constitution published among our decisions, by which, at the suggestion of the eminent Tribonian, the quæstor, we have put an end to difficulties arising from the ancient law. We have also, at his suggestion, altered the condition of the *Latini Juniani*, and corrected the laws which related to them, by another constitution, one of the most remarkable of our imperial ordinances. We have made all freedmen whatsoever Roman citizens, without distinction in the age of the slave, or the interest of the manumittor, or the mode of manumission. We have also introduced many new methods, by which slaves may become Roman citizens, the only kind of liberty that is now conferred.

GAI. i. 12–17; Cod. vii. 5, 6.

For a complete emancipation it was originally necessary that the owner should have quiritary, i. e. complete ownership (see Introd. sec. 62) of the slave, and that the ceremony should be public. If the ownership were less full, or the ceremony private, the slave lived in a state of freedom, and the prætor forbad the master to exert his strictly legal power of reasserting his right to the services of the slave; but the condition of the slave as regarded the State was not changed, and at his death his master took all his property.

By the *lex Ælia Sentia*, A.D. 4, it was enacted that, to make the emancipation complete, that is, to make the slave a citizen, a third requisite should be added. He was to be thirty years old; or else, if he were under that age, the ceremony was to be performed by *vindicta*, after the reason for the emancipation had been held good by a *consilium*, consisting, at Rome, of five senators and five *equites*; in the provinces of twenty *recuperatores* (GAI. i. 17–20).

The *lex Junia Norbana* was made A.D. 19; and the effect of its provisions, coupled with that of the *lex Ælia Sentia*, was to place those whose emancipation was defective in any one of these three requisites on the footing of the Latini, that is, they might marry and trade with Romans on the footing of Roman citizens, but could not vote at elections or fill public offices. Further, they could not become heirs, legatees, or guardians, except in an indirect mode, and could only make a testament by the cumbrous form of *familiæ emptio* (ULP. *Reg.* 20. 8. See Introd. sec. 75); and at their death their original owner took their property exactly as if they had never ceased to be slaves (see Bk. iii. Tit. 7, sec. 4, *in ipso ultimo spiritu simul animam et libertatem amittebant*). But there were many ways in which a *libertus*, in this position, could attain citizenship; as by an imperial rescript, by proving before a magistrate his marriage and the birth of a child, or by going through the ceremony of emancipation again and fulfilling the three conditions requisite (this was called *iteratio*), or by the modes alluded to by Ulpian (*Reg.* 3. 1) in the words *militia, nave, ædificio, pistrino*, that is, by military service, building a ship and carrying wheat for six years, making a building, or establishing a bakeshop. (GAI. i. 22, 23, 24–28. 31; ii. 275; iii. 56, *et seq.*) The *lex Ælia Sentia* further provided that slaves who had been guilty of a crime for which they had been put in chains, branded, or put to the torture, should, by emancipation, be only raised to the level of *dedititii*, that is, of people vanquished in war. They enjoyed personal liberty, but that was all. They could not trade except on the footing of strangers; could not make a testament; were forbidden to live within a hundred miles of Rome, on pain of being themselves sold, together with all their property; they could never become citizens; and at their death their master took all their property, by right of succession if the emancipation had been complete; and if not, by the right an owner always had to the slave's *peculium*. (GAI. i. 12–15. 25–27; iii. 74–76.)

All these distinctions were abolished by Justinian *nullo nec ætatis manumissi, nec dominii manumittentis, nec in modo manumissionis discrimine habito* (C. vii. 5 and 6); and under his legislation a slave became at once completely free by any act of the owner signifying his intention to bestow liberty. By a Novel (78. 1) Justinian abolished all distinction between *libertini* and *ingenui*, retaining, however, the *jus patronatus*. The *libertus* owed his *patronus* reverence (Dig. xxxvii. 15), and also in many cases had to discharge certain services (Dig. xxxvii. 14) for him; but the chief feature of the *jus patronatus* was the right of the patron to succeed to the inheritance of his *libertus*; for if the *libertus* died childless, the patron succeeded to his whole inheritance, supposing he left no testament; and if he left one, still the patron took a third part of the property. (Bk. iii. Tit. 7. 3.)

## Tit. VI. QUI, QUIBUS EX CAUSIS, MANUMITTERE NON POSSUNT.

| | |
|---|---|
| Non tamen cuicumque volenti manumittere licet. Nam is quis in fraudem creditorum manumittit, nihil agit; quia lex Ælia Sentia impedit libertatem. | It is not, however, every master who wishes that may manumit, for a manumission in fraud of creditors is void, the *lex Ælia Sentia* restraining the power of enfranchisement. |

GAI. i. 37.

A person, as the third section informs us, manumitted his slaves in fraud of creditors, who knew that by doing so he made himself unable or less able to pay his debts; and in such a case, as the Roman law held that liberty once given could not be revoked, the *lex Ælia Sentia* provided that the act of manumission was entirely void (*nihil agit*): the freedom was considered never to have been given. The slave would indeed be treated as free until the creditors attacked the manumission as fraudulent; but directly they did so successfully, he was exactly in the position in which he would have been if never enfranchised. If, however, though the master was insolvent at the time of manumission, his debts were paid before the manumission was attacked, the creditors could no longer impugn the manumission, and the slave was considered to have been free from the date of the manumission. Probably there was a time limited, beyond which creditors were not allowed to attack the manumission. We learn from the Digest that if the manumission were made in fraud of the *fiscus*, it must be impugned within ten years; and it is not probable that the private creditor would have had a longer time allowed him. (Dig. xl. 9. 11.)

1. Licet autem domino qui solvendo non est, in testamento servum suum cum libertate heredem instituere, ut liber fiat heresque ei solus et necessarius; si modo ei nemo alius ex eo testamento heres extiterit, aut quia nemo heres scriptus sit, aut quia is qui scriptus est, qualibet ex causa heres non extiterit. Idque eadem lege Ælia Sentia provisum est, et recte; valde enim prospicieudam erat, ut egentes homines quibus alius heres extiturus non esset, vel servum suum necessarium heredem haberent, qui satisfacturus esset creditoribus; aut hoc eo non faciente, creditores res hereditarias servi nomine vendant, ne injuria defunctus adficiatur.

1. A master, who is insolvent, may, however, by his testament, institute a slave to be his heir, at the same time giving him his liberty, so that the slave becoming free may be his only and necessary heir, provided that there is no other heir under the same testament, which may happen, either because no other person was instituted heir, or because the person instituted, from some reason or other, does not become heir. This was wisely established by the lex Ælia Sentia; for it was very necessary to provide, that men, in insolvent circumstances, who could get no other heir, should have a slave as necessary heir, in order that he might satisfy their creditors; or that if he failed to do so, the creditors might sell the goods of the inheritance in the name of the slave, so as to prevent the deceased suffering disgrace.

GAI. ii. 154.

The heirs under a Roman testament accepted all the liabilities of the deceased. When, therefore, the debts exceeded the value of the inheritance, the heir named in the testament would probably refuse the inheritance; and if no one would accept the heirship, the creditors stepped in and had the estate sold for their benefit. As this was thought a great stigma on the memory of the deceased, a slave was frequently enfranchised by the testator and named heir; and as the slave could not refuse to take the office upon him (being thence called *heres necessarius*), the sale of the effects, if necessary, was made in his name, and not in that of his master. Of course this could only take place when the slave was the only heir. If there were any other heir, the slave would not be heir by necessity, and hence, in the text, the expression *solus et necessarius heres* is used.

2. Idemque juris est, et si sine libertate servus heres institutus est. Quod nostra constitutio non solum in domino qui solvendo non est, sed generaliter constituit nova humanitatis ratione, ut ex ipsa scriptura institutionis etiam libertas ei competere videatur: cum non est veri-

2. The law is the same also when a slave is instituted heir, although his freedom be not expressly given him; for our constitution, in a true spirit of humanity, decides not only with regard to an insolvent master, but, generally, that the mere institution of a slave implies the grant of

simile, enim quem heredem sibi elegit, si prætermiserit libertatis dationem, servum remanere voluisse, et neminem sibi heredem fore.

3. In fraudem autem creditorum manumittere videtur, qui vel jam eo tempore quo manumittit, solvendo non est, vel datis libertatibus desiturus est solvendo esse. Prævaluisse tamen videtur, nisi animum quoque fraudandi manumissor habuerit, non impediri libertatem, quamvis bona ejus creditoribus non sufficiant. Sæpe enim de facultatibus suis amplius quam in his est, sperant homines. Itaque tunc intelligimus impediri libertatem, cum utroque modo fraudantur creditores, id est, et consilio manumittentis et ipsa re, eo quod ejus bona non sunt suffectura creditoribus.

liberty. For it is highly improbable, that a testator, although he has omitted an express gift of freedom, should have wished that the person he has selected as heir should remain a slave, and that he himself should have no heir.

3. A person manumits in fraud of creditors, who is insolvent, at the time that he manumits, or becomes so by the manumission itself. It is, however, the prevailing opinion, that unless the manumittor intended to commit a fraud, the gift of liberty is not invalidated, although his goods are insufficient for the payment of his creditors; for men often hope their circumstances are better than they really are. The gift of liberty is then invalidated only when creditors are defrauded, both by the intention of the manumittor, and in reality; that is to say, by the insufficiency of the effects to meet their claims.

D. al. 9, 10; alii. 8. 15.

*Fraudis interpretatio semper in jure civili non ex eventu duntaxat, sed ex consilio quoque desideratur* (D. l. 17. 79). Gaius informs us (i. 47) that *peregrini* were prevented from enfranchising slaves in fraud of creditors, though the other provisions of the *lex Ælia Sentia* did not affect them.

4. Eadem lege Ælia Sentia domino minori viginti annis non aliter manumittere permittitur, quam si vindicta, apud consilium justa causa manumissionis probata, fuerint manumissi.

4. By the *lex Ælia Sentia*, again, a master, under the age of twenty years, cannot manumit, except by the *vindicta*, and upon some legitimate ground approved of by the council.

Gai. i. 88.

This *consilium* was held on certain days at Rome, and in the provinces sat during a session, on the last day of which cases such as those referred to in the text were decided on. (Gai. i. 20.)

5. Justæ autem manumissionis causæ hæ sunt: veluti si quis patrem aut matrem, filium filiamve, aut fratrem sororemve naturales, aut pædagogum, nutricem, educatorem, aut alumnum alumnamve aut collactaneum manumittat, aut servum procuratoris habendi gratia, aut ancillam matrimonii causa: dum tamen intra sex menses uxor

5. Legitimate grounds for manumission are such as these: that the person to be manumitted is father or mother to the manumittor, his son or daughter, his brother or sister, his preceptor, his nurse, his foster-father, his foster-child, or his foster-brother; that the person is a slave whom he wishes to make his procurator, or female slave whom he intends to marry,

ducatur, nisi Justa causa impediat;
et qui manumittitur procuratoris
babendi gratia, non minor decem
et septem annis manumittitur.

provided the marriage be performed
within six months, unless prevented
by some good reason; and provided
that the slave who is to be made a
procurator, be not manumitted under the age of seventeen years.

GAI. i. 19. 39; D. xl. 2. 11-13.

The most common case of a person emancipating his father
and mother, and other near relations, would be when a slave
was made heir. Theophilus (paraphr. on this paragraph) gives
us an instance of a person enfranchising his brother, the case
of a man having a child by a slave and then a son by a legal
marriage. The former would be the slave of the latter.

If the marriage was in any way impossible, the minor would
not be allowed to enfranchise his female slave; and it was
requisite that it should be he himself who intended to marry
her.

A procurator below the age of seventeen could not represent
his principal in any action (D. iii. 1. 1. 3), and it is this probably that makes Justinian here require that the slave should
be seventeen years of age in order to be emancipated by a
minor.

6. Semel autem causa probata,
sive vera sit sive falsa, non retrac-
tatur.

7. Cum ergo certus modus ma-
numittendi minoribus viginti annis
dominis per legem Æliam Sentiam
constitutus erat, eveniebat ut qui
qualuordecim annos ætatis exple-
verat, licet testamentum facere et
in eo sibi heredem instituere, legata-
que relinquere posset, tamen si adhuc minor esset viginti annis, libertatem servo dare non posset. Quod
non erat ferendum, si is cui totorum
honorum in testamento dispositio
data erat, uni servo dare libertatem
non permittebatur. Quare non
similiter ei, quemadmodum alias
res, ita et servos suos in ultima voluntate disponere quemadmodum
voluerit, permittimus, ut et libertatem eis possit præstare? Sed cum
libertas inæstimabilis est, et propter hoc ante XX ætatis annum
antiquitas libertatem servo dare
probibebat, ideo nos mediam quodammodo viam eligentes, non aliter

6. The approval of a ground of
manumission once given, whether
the reasons on which it is based be
true or false, cannot be retracted.

7. Certain limits being thus assigned by the lex Ælia Sentia, to the
power of persons under the age of
twenty, to manumit slaves, the result
was that anyone, who had completed
his fourteenth year, might make a
testament, institute an heir, and
give legacies, and yet that no person,
under twenty, could give liberty to
a slave. This seemed intolerable;
that a man, permitted to dispose of
all his effects by testament, could
not enfranchise one single slave.
Why should we not, then, give him
the power of disposing, by testament,
of his slaves, as of all his other property, exactly as he pleases, and of
giving them their liberty? But as liberty is of inestimable value, and one
ancient laws, therefore, prohibited
any person under twenty years of
age, to give it to a slave, we adopt a
middle course, and only permit a
person, under twenty years of age, to

H

minori viginti annis libertatem in testamento dare servo suo concedimus nisi septimum et decimum annum impleverit, et octavum decimum annum tetigerit. Cum enim antiquitas hujusmodi ætati et pro aliis postulare concessit, cur non etiam sui judicii stabilitas ita eos adjuvare credatur, ut ad libertates dandas servis suis possint pervenire?

confer freedom on his slaves by testament, if he has completed his seventeenth and entered on his eighteenth year. For since ancient custom permitted persons at eighteen years of age to plead for others, why should not their judgment be considered sound enough to enable them to give liberty to their own slaves?

GAI. 40.

The *Ælia Sentia* required the manumission to be given by the form of *vindicta*. This was held to exclude the minor from giving it by testament. Manumission was something more than the disposal of a piece of property; it was the creation of a citizen, and thus might consistently be denied to minors whose power of disposing of property was unfettered. Justinian, nine years after the Institutes were published, abolished the distinction he establishes in the text by a Novel (119. 2), containing the words *sancimus ut licentia pateat minoribus in ipso tempore, in quo eis de reliqua eorum substantia disponere permittitur, etiam servos suos in ultimis voluntatibus manumittere.*

## Tit. VII.　DE LEGE FUSIA CANINIA SUBLATA.

Lege Fusia Caninia certus modus constitutus erat in servis testamento manumittendis. Quam, quasi libertates impedientem et quodammodo invidam, tollendam esse censuimus; eum satis fuerat inhumanum, vivos quidem licentiam habere totam suam familiam libertate donare, nisi alia causa impediat libertatem, morientibus autem hujusmodi licentiam adimere.

The *lex Fusia Caninia* imposed a limit on manumission by testament; but we have thought right to abolish this law as invidiously placing obstacles in the way of liberty. It seemed very unreasonable, to allow persons, in their lifetime, to manumit all their slaves, if there is no special reason to prevent them, and to deprive the dying of the power of doing the same.

GAI. i. 42–40.

The *lex Fusia Caninia* was made in the year A.D. 8, four years after the *lex Ælia Sentia*. (SUET. *Aug.* 40.) Its object was to prevent the manumission of crowds of slaves enfranchised in order to gratify the vanity of testators, who wished their funeral train to be swollen with these witnesses to their liberality. It provided that the owner of two slaves might enfranchise both; of from two to ten, half; of from ten to thirty, one-third; of from thirty to one hundred, one-fourth; and of a larger number, one-fifth; but in no case was the

number enfranchised to exceed one hundred.  The slaves to
be manumitted were required to be designated by name.
The citizenship was so worthless in the days of Justinian,
that it mattered little how many slaves were made free, but
in the days of Augustus, the distinction made between the
living and the dying master, which Justinian calls *satis inhumanum*, was far from unreasonable.  A master might well be
trusted not to impoverish himself by reckless manumission
during his life, and yet be denied the power of gratifying his
vanity at the expense of his heir.

## Tit. VIII.   DE IIS QUI SUI VEL ALIENI JURIS SUNT.

Sequitur de jure personarum alia divisio; nam quædam personæ sui juris sunt, quædam alieno juri subjectæ.  Rursus earum quæ alieno juri subjectæ sunt, aliæ in potestate parentum, aliæ in potestate dominorum sunt.  Videamus itaque de iis quæ alieno juri subjectæ sunt: nam si cognoverimus quæ istæ personæ sunt, simul intelligemus quæ sui juris sunt.  Ac prius dispiciamus de iis quæ in potestate dominorum sunt.

We now come to another division relative to the rights of persons; for some persons are independent, some are subject to the power of others.  Of those, again, who are subject to others, some are in the power of parents, others in that of masters.  Let us first treat of those who are subject to others; for, when we have ascertained who these are, we shall at the same time discover who are independent.  And first let us consider those who are in the power of masters.

Gai. i. 48. 51.

Justinian now passes to the division of persons as members
of a family.  The head of a Roman family exercised supreme
authority over his wife, his children, his children's children,
and his slaves.  (See Introd. sec. 40.)  He was their owner
as well as their master.  He alone was *sui juris*, and all the
other members of the family were *alieni juris*, for they belonged to him.  The whole group, that is, the head and those
in his power were the *familia*.  The head was the *paterfamilias*, a term not expressive of paternity (D. 1. 16. 195. 2), but
merely signifying a person who was not under the power of
another, and who, consequently, might have others under his
power.  An unmarried woman whose father was dead, was
said to be a *materfamilias*, a term which, in this sense, is only
the feminine form of *paterfamilias*.  She was *sui juris*, and
might have slaves, though of course she could have no power
over persons free-born.  For if she married, her children were
in her husband's power, not in hers. (See Introd. sec. 40.)
    The word *familia* was used in so many different senses, that

H 2

it may be as well to collect them here, before entering on the
subject of family relations.  *Familia* is used to mean,—1.
all persons of the blood of the same ancestor; 2. The head
of the family and all those in his power whether slaves or free;
3. All connected by agnation (see Introd. sec. 45); 4. The
slaves of one man; 5. The property of a *paterfamilias*, of
whatever sort.  The word is fully explained in a fragment of
Ulpian.  (D. 1. 16. 195.)

Gaius, from whom much of this section is borrowed, says,—
*Rursus earum personarum quæ alieno juri subjectæ sunt, aliæ
in potestate, aliæ in manu, aliæ in mancipio sunt* (i. 49).
The persons *in manu* were those wives who passed through
the particular forms of marriage which placed a wife in the
position of a daughter to her own husband: that is, the
religious ceremony of *confarreatio*, the fictitious sale *coemptio*,
and *usus*, or cohabitation unbroken by an absence of three
nights in the year.  (See Introd. sec. 46.)  Persons *in mancipio* were those sold by the head of their family, or by themselves with the form of *mancipatio*.  (See Introd. sec. 42.)
They were said to be *servorum loco* (not *servi*) with reference
to the purchaser.  Such sales were merely fictitious, except
in the early days of Rome.  The subjection *in manu* had
ceased before the time of Justinian, and he did away with
the last traces of that *in mancipio*.  (See Tit. 12.)

| | |
|---|---|
| 1. In potestate itaque dominorum sunt servi.  Quæ quidem potestas Juris gentium est: nam apud omnes peræque gentes animadvertere possumus, dominis in servos vitæ necisque potestatem fuisse; et quodcumque per servum adquiritur, id domino adquiritur. | 1. Slaves are in the power of masters, a power derived from the law of nations: for among all nations it may be remarked that masters have the power of life and death over their slaves, and that everything acquired by the slave is acquired for the master. |

GAI. i. 52.

The power of the master over his slaves was spoken of as
the *dominica potestas*.  The origin of this power has been
already ascribed to the *jus gentium*.  (Tit. 3. 2.)

| | |
|---|---|
| 2. Sed hoc tempore nullis hominibus qui sub imperio nostro sunt, licet sine causa legibus cognita in servos suos supra modum sævire; nam ex constitutione divi Pii Antonini, qui sine causa servum suum occiderit, non minus puniri jubetur, quam qui alienum servum occiderit.  Sed et major asperitas dominorum ejusdem principis constitutione coercetur; nam consultus a quibusdam præsidibus provin- | 2. But at the present day none of our subjects may use unrestrained violence towards their slaves, except for a reason recognized by law.  For, by a constitution of the Emperor Antoninus, he who without any reason kills his own slave, is to be punished equally with one who has killed the slave of another.  The excessive severity of masters is also restrained by another constitution of the same emperor.  For, when consulted by |

ciarum de iis servis qui ad ædem sacram vel ad statuas principum confugiunt, præcepit, ut si intolerabilis videatur sævitia dominorum, cogantur servos suos honis conditionibus vendere, et pretium dominis daretur; et recte. Expedit enim reipublicæ, ne sua re quis male utatur. Cujus rescripti ad Ælium Marcianum emissi verba sunt hæc: ' Dominorum quidem potestatem in servos suos illibatam esse oportet, nec cuiquam hominum jus suum detrahi; sed dominorum interest, ne auxilium contra sævitiam vel famem vel intolerabilem injuriam denegetur iis qui juste deprecantur. Ideoque cognosce de querelis eorum qui ex familia Julii Sabini ad statuam confugerunt; et si vel durius habitos quam æquum est, vel infami injuria affectos cognoveris, veniri jube, ita ut in potestatem domini non revertantur. Qui si meæ constitutioni fraudem fecerit, sciet me admissum severius executurum.'

certain governors of provinces on the subject of slaves who fly for refuge either to temples or the statues of the emperors, he decided that if the severity of masters should appear excessive, they might be compelled to make sale of their slaves upon equitable terms, so that the masters might receive the value, and this was a very wise decision, as it concerns the public good, that no one should misuse his own property. The following are the terms of this rescript of Antoninus, which was sent to Ælius Marcianus. 'The power of masters over their slaves ought to be preserved unimpaired, nor ought any man to be deprived of his just right. But it is for the interest of all masters themselves, that relief prayed on good grounds against cruelty, the denial of sustenance, or any other intolerable injury, should not be refused. Examine therefore, into the complaints of the slaves who have fled from the house of Julius Sabinus, and taken refuge at the statue of the emperor; and, if you find that they have been too harshly treated, or wantonly disgraced, order them to be sold, so that they may not fall again under the power of their master; and if Sabinus attempt to evade my constitution, I would have him know, that I shall severely punish his disobedience.'

GAI. i. 53; D. i. 6. 2.

The *lex Cornelia*, passed by Sylla, B.C. 82, made killing a slave punishable as homicide, with death or exile. (D. ix. 2. 23. 9.) The *lex Petronia* (D. xlviii. 8. 11. 2), passed in the time of one of the early emperors, forbade masters to expose their slaves to contests with wild beasts. Hadrian required the sanction of a magistrate in all cases before death was inflicted. (SPART. in *Hadr.* cap. 18; D. i. 6. 2.) Constantine only permitted moderate corporal chastisement to be inflicted, and Justinian in the Code retains his enactment. (C. ix. 14.)

Justinian does not notice the corresponding changes which the clemency of latter times worked in the control of the master over the slave's property; according to the usage of these times this property, called *peculium*, belonged, in fact, though not in law, to the slave, and he often purchased his liberty with it. (TACIT. *Ann.* xiv. 42; D. xv. i. 53.)

## Tit. IX.　DE PATRIA POTESTATE.

| | |
|---|---|
| In potestate nostra sunt liberi nostri, quos ex justis nuptiis procreaverimus. | Our children, begotten in lawful marriage, are in our power. |

GAI. i. 55.

The *patria potestas* differed originally little, if at all, from the *dominica potestas*. If the sense of ownership was not so complete in the former, it was probably limited more by natural feeling than by law. The father could sell, expose, or put to death his children. Time, however, ameliorated the position of the child, and all that was left was a power to inflict moderate chastisement (Cod. viii. 47. 31), and to sell at the time of birth in cases of extreme necessity. (Cod. iv. 43. 1.) Constantine condemned the father who killed his child to the punishment of a parricide. (C. ix. 17. 1.) The sale of a child was in general fictitious, and only formed the mode by which the child was released from the father's power.

Like that of the slave, the child's property was only a *peculium*, belonging strictly to the father. But under the early emperors an exception to this was made, and the son had complete ownership in property acquired in war (*castrense peculium*); Constantine made a further exception of property acquired in employments about the court (*quasi-castrense peculium*). (See Bk. ii. 9, and Introd. sec. 41.)

The meaning of *justæ nuptiæ* will appear in the next title.

Neither age nor marriage, nor anything except emancipation, terminated the power of a father over his son. If a daughter married *in manu*, she passed from her father's power into that of her husband.

| | |
|---|---|
| 1. Nuptiæ autem sive matrimonium est viri et mulieris conjunctio, individuam vitæ consuetudinem continens. | 1. Marriage, or matrimony, is a binding together of a man and woman to live in an indivisible union. |

D. xxiii. 2. 1.

*Nuptiæ* is properly the ceremonies attending the formation of the legal tie, and *matrimonium* is the tie itself; but the jurists use the two terms quite indifferently, as for instance, Modestinus says, '*nuptiæ sunt conjunctio maris et feminæ.*' (D. xxiii. 2. 1.)

The *individua vitæ consuetudo* implied a community of rank and position, and of sacred and human law, *divini et humani juris communicatio* (D. xxiii. 2. 1), but not necessarily of property. Marriage gave neither party any right over the property of the other, except when the wife passed in *manum*, and then all that she had belonged to the husband.

2. Jus autem potestatis quod in liberos habemus, proprium est civium Romanorum; nulli enim alii sunt homines, qui talem in liberos habeant potestatem, qualem nos habemus.

2. The power which we have over our children is peculiar to the citizens of Rome; for no other people have a power over their children, such as we have over ours.

GAI. i. 55.

Gaius mentions the Galatæ as being reported to have had a similar institution.

3. Qui igitur ex te et uxore tua nascitur, in tua potestate est. Item qui ex filio tuo et uxore ejus nascitur, id est, nepos tuus et neptis, æque in tua sunt potestate, et pronepos et proneptis, et deinceps ceteri. Qui tamen ex filia tua nascitur, in tua potestate non est, sed in patris ejus.

3. The child born to you and your wife, is in your power. And so is the child born to your son of his wife, that is, your grandson or granddaughter; so are your great-grandchildren, and all your other descendants. But a child born of your daughter is not in your power, but in the power of its own father.

If a woman, although she was not in the power of her husband, had children, they were not in her power; and hence, as she could have no descendants in her power, it was said, *mulier familiæ suæ et caput et finis est*, i. e. her family ended with herself. (D. l. 16. 195. 5.)

TIT. X.   DE NUPTIIS.

Justas autem nuptias inter se cives Romani contrahunt, qui secundum præcepta legum coeunt, masculi quidem puberes, feminæ autem viripotentes, sive patresfamilias sint sive filiifamilias: dum tamen, si filiifamilias sint, consensum habeant parentium quorum in potestate sunt. Nam hoc fieri debere et civilis et naturalis ratio suadet, in tantum ut jussum parentis præcedere debeat. Unde quæsitum est an furiosi filia nubere aut furiosi filius uxorem ducere possit? Cumque super filio variabatur, nostra processit decisio, qua permissum est, ad exemplum filiæ furiosi, filium quoque posse et sine patris interventu matrimonium sibi copulare, secundum datum ex nostra constitutione modum.

Roman citizens are bound together in lawful matrimony, when they are united according to law, the males, having attained the age of puberty, and the females a marriageable age, whether they are fathers or sons of a family; but, if the latter, they must first obtain the consent of their parents, in whose power they are. For both natural reason and the law require this consent; so much so, indeed, that it ought to precede the marriage. Hence the question has arisen, whether the daughter of a madman could be married, or his son marry? And as opinions were divided as to the son, we decided that as the daughter of a madman might, so may the son of a madman marry without the intervention of the father, according to the mode established by our constitution.

C. v. 4. 25.

In the earliest times of Roman law there were three modes of forming the tie of marriage; first, *confarreatio*, a religious ceremony, in which none but those to whom the *jus sacrum* was open could take part; secondly, *coemptio*, a fictitious sale, in which the wife was sold to the husband; and lastly, *usus*, i. e. cohabitation with the intention of forming a marriage. All three modes had the same effect on the position of the wife. She always passed *in manum viri*. (See Introd. sec. 46.) This incident of marriage was attached to the marriage by mere cohabitation and lapse of time, on the analogy of the ownership which was acquired in a thing by uninterrupted possession. It was, however, open to the wife to 'break the use,' to prevent, that is, her husband gaining complete power over her by lapse of time : the law of the Twelve Tables declared that, if the wife absented herself from her husband for three nights in the year, the *usus* should be interrupted and she should remain in her own *familia*, and not pass into that of her husband. This was considered so much more advantageous to the wife that, even in the latter days of the republic, almost all marriages were formed without the wife passing into the *manus* of her husband. In the time of Justinian she never did so, and the whole distinction of the effect of different modes of marriage had been long obsolete.

At no time did these different modes of being married form part of the real tie of marriage; they only decided, when the tie of marriage was formed, what should be the position of the wife. Neither were the religious ceremonies nor the nuptial-rites anything more than accessories of that which created the binding relation between the parties. The tie itself was a civil contract, depending upon and formed by the mutual consent of the husband and wife. Whenever two persons, capable of entering into the contract, mutually consented to do so, and evidenced their consent by any mode recognised by law, the legal tie was formed, the *justae nuptiae* were complete. Everything else was only subsidiary. The consent might either be made manifest by being solemnly expressed (Cod. v. 17, 11), or by some act, such as the wife being led to the husband's house and the husband receiving her, which sufficed to make known the intention of the parties.

In order that the contract might be binding, it was necessary that the parties should be capable of forming it. First, they must have the *connubium* ; i. e. so long as there was any distinction of citizenship, both were required to be citizens, or to have had this particular part of citizenship given them (see Introd. sec. 39). Secondly, they must not stand within the prohibited degrees of relationship; what these were is discussed

in the following paragraphs of this Title. Thirdly, they must
have attained the age of puberty, i. e. fourteen for men, and
twelve for women (see Tit. 22); and, lastly, if under the power
of any one, they must have obtained that person's consent.
The husband was obliged, even though in his grandfather's
power, to obtain his father's consent; otherwise the grandfather could have eventually increased the number of the
father's family without consulting him (D. i. 7. 7), which it was
against the spirit of the law to allow, as no one could have a
new suus heres forced on him by agnation against his will.
(See Tit. 11. 7.)

This same reason had caused the doubt adverted to in the
text, whether, even if the father were incapable of giving his
consent, the son could introduce new members into his father's
family.  This did not apply to the daughter, who could not
introduce new members into her father's family.  Justinian,
in the code, proscribed the mode in which marriage might be
validly made either by the son or daughter of a madman.  The
son or daughter of the madman was to submit the proposed
marriage to be approved, and the gift to the wife, or dowry,
to be fixed, by the præfectus urbis at Constantinople, by the
præses or bishop of the city in the provinces, in the presence
of the curator of the madman and his principal relations.
Marcus Aurelius had previously provided for the care of children of imbocile persons, dementes. (C. v. 4. 25.) Where the
rights of the paterfamilias were not in question, as when the
son was emancipated, it was not necessary to have the father's
consent. (D. xxiii. 2. 25.)

If the persons, whose consent was necessary, did not give
it, the marriage was absolutely void, and therefore no subsequent consent could ratify it.  Thus Justinian says here, that
the consent, jussus (a word denoting the authority of the paterfamilias), must precede the marriage.  It was not, however,
necessary that the consent should be expressly given.  If the
paterfamilias knew of the marriage and did not oppose it,
his assent was presumed (C. v. 4. 5); and if he were absent
or a captive for three years, his children might form a marriage, which he could not afterwards disapprove of. (D. xxiii.
2. 9. 10.)

1. Ergo non omnes nobis uxores
ducere licet; nam quarumdam nuptiis abstinendum est. Inter eas enim
personas quæ parentium liberorumve locum inter se obtinent, contrahi
nuptiæ non possunt: veluti inter
patrem et filiam, vel avum et neptem, vel matrem et filium, vel aviam

1. We may not marry every woman without distinction: for with
some, marriage is forbidden.  Marriage cannot be contracted between
persons standing to each other in
the relation of ascendant and descendant, as between a father and
daughter, a grandfather and his

et nepotem. et usque ad infinitum ; et si tales personæ inter se coierint, nefarias atque incestas nuptias contraxisse dicuntur. Et hæc adeo ita sunt, ut quamvis per adoptionem parentium liberorumve loco sibi esse cœperint, non possint inter se matrimonio jungi, in tantum ut etiam dissoluta adoptione idem juris manent. Itaque eam quæ tibi per adoptionem filia vel neptis esse cœperit, non poteris uxorem ducere quamvis eam emancipaveris.

granddaughter, a mother and her son, a grandmother and her grandson ; and so on, ad infinitum. And, if such persons unite together, they only contract a criminal and incestuous marriage ; so much so, that ascendants and descendants, who are only so by adoption, cannot intermarry ; and even after the adoption is dissolved, the prohibition remains. You cannot, therefore, marry a woman who has been either your daughter or granddaughter by adoption, although you may have emancipated her.

Gai. i. 58, 59.

When two persons were related by being *agnati* to each other, they were exactly in the same relative position, so far as regarded the power of marrying, as if they had been related in the same degree by blood. If the tie of *agnatio* was dissolved by emancipation, the tie of blood, if any, would of course remain, and be a bar to marriage, but if there were no tie of blood, that is, if one of the parties had entered the family by adoption, then, if the emancipated person had, while the *agnatio* subsisted, occupied the position of ascendant or descendant to the other person, marriage was forbidden, but if of a collateral, it was allowed.

3. Inter eas quoque personas quæ ex transverso gradu cognationis junguntur, est quædam similis observatio, sed non tanta. Sane enim inter fratrem sororemque nuptiæ prohibitæ sunt. sive ab eodem patre eademque matre nati fuerint, sive ex alterutro eorum ; sed si qua per adoptionem soror tibi esse cœperit, quamdiu quidem constat adoptio, sane inter te et eam nuptiæ consistere non possunt; cum vero per emancipationem adoptio sit dissoluta, poteris eam uxorem ducere. Sed et si tu emancipatus fueris, nihil est impedimento nuptiis. Et ideo constat, si quis generum adoptare velit, debere eum ante filiam emancipare ; et si quis velit nurum adoptare, debere eum ante filium emancipare.

3. There are also restrictions, though not so extensive, on marriage between collateral relations. A brother and sister are forbidden to marry, whether they are the children of the same father and mother, or of one of the two only. And, if a woman becomes your sister by adoption, so long as the adoption subsists, you certainly cannot marry ; but, if the adoption is destroyed by emancipation, you may marry her ; as you may also, if you yourself are emancipated. Hence it is certain, that if a man would adopt his son-in-law, he ought first to emancipate his daughter ; and if he would adopt his daughter-in-law, he ought previously to emancipate his son.

Gai. i. 60, 61 ; D. xxiii. 2. 17. 1.

To adopt a son-in-law would be to make him brother by agnation of his own wife. The bar did not invalidate the previous marriage, but operated to restrain the adoption, until the daughter had been emancipated.

3. Fratris vero vel sororis filiam uxorem ducere non licet. Sed nec neptem fratris vel sororis quis uxorem ducere potest, quamvis quarto gradu sint; cujus enim filiam uxorem ducere non licet, neque ejus neptem permittitur. Ejus vero mulieris quam pater tuus adoptavit, filiam non videris impediri uxorem ducere, quia neque naturali neque civili jure tibi conjungitur.

3. A man may not marry the daughter of a brother, or a sister, nor the granddaughter, although she is in the fourth degree. For, when we may not marry the daughter of any person, neither may we marry the granddaughter. But there does not appear to be any impediment to marrying the daughter of a woman whom your father has adopted; for she is no relation to you, either by natural or civil law.

Gai. i. 62; D. xxiii. 2. 12. 4.

In the direct line every degree represents a generation. The son is in the first degree with respect to his father; the grandson in the second with respect to his grandfather. In the collateral line the generations are taken first up to and then down from, the common ancestors. For instance, first-cousins are in the fourth degree. From either cousin to his father is one degree, from the father to the grandfather is another, from the grandfather to the father of the other cousin is a third, and from that father to that cousin is a fourth.

The marriage of an uncle with a niece had been legalised in favour of Claudius and Agrippina (Suet. in Claud. 26); but prohibited by Constantine. (Cod. Theod. i.)

The children never followed the family of the mother, and therefore, though she was adopted, remained as they were before. But of course a daughter could not have married an adopted son's son.

4. Duorum autem fratrum vel sororum liberi, vel fratris et sororis, jungi possunt.

4. The children of two brothers, or two sisters, or of a brother and sister, may marry together.

D. xxiii. 2. 3.

The marriage of first-cousins, forbidden by preceding emperors, had again been legalised by Arcadius and Honorius. (C. v. 4. 19.)

5. Item amitam, licet adoptivam, ducere uxorem non licet; item nec materteram, quia parentium loco habentur. Qua ratione verum est, magnam quoque amitam et materteram magnam prohiberi uxorem ducere.

5. So, too, a man may not marry his paternal aunt, even though she be so only by adoption; nor his maternal aunt; because they are regarded in the light of ascendants. For the same reason, no person may marry his great-aunt, either paternal or maternal.

Gai. i. 62; D. xxiii. 2. 17. 2.

It was of course only possible to be in the same family with an adopted aunt on the father's side. A mother's sister by adoption would be in the family of the mother, whereas the nephew would be in the family of the father, and therefore *aduptivam* is added to *amitam* only, not to *materteram*.

Every person in the first degree from a common ancestor, was considered, so far as regarded marriage, in the position of that ancestor. Thus an aunt, being in the first degree from the grandfather, the common ancestor, was looked upon as standing in the place of that grandfather (*parentis loco habetur*), and could not therefore marry her nephew. A cousin would be in the second degree from the common ancestor, and therefore proximity would not be a bar to the union.

6. Adfinitatis quoque veneratione quarumdam nuptiis abstinendum est, ut ecce: privignam aut nurum uxorem ducere non licet, quia utræque filiæ loco sunt. Quod ita scilicet accipi debet, si fuit nurus aut privigna tua: nam si adhuc nurus tua est, id est, si adhuc nupta est filio tuo, alia ratione uxorem eam ducere non possis, quia eadem duobus nupta esse non potest. Item si adhuc privigna tua est, id est, si mater ejus tibi nupta est, ideo eam uxorem ducere non poteris, quia duas uxores eodem tempore habere non licet.

6. There are, too, other marriages from which we must abstain, from regard to the ties created by marriage; for example, a man may not marry his wife's daughter, or his son's wife, for they are both in the place of daughters to him; and this must be understood to mean those who have been our step-daughters or daughters-in-law: for if a woman is still your daughter-in-law, that is, if she is still married to your son, you cannot marry her for another reason, as she cannot be the wife of two persons at once. And if your step-daughter is still your step-daughter, that is, if her mother is still married to you, you cannot marry her, because a person cannot have two wives at the same time.

Gai. i. 63.

*Affinitas* is the tie created by marriage between each person of the married pair and the kindred of the other.

7. Socrum quoque et novercam prohibitam est uxorem ducere, quia matris loco sunt. Quod et ipsum dissoluta demum adfinitate procedit: alioquin, si adhuc noverca est, id est, si adhuc patri tuo nupta est, communi jure impeditur tibi nubere, quia eadem duobus nupta esse non potest. Item si adhuc socrus est, id est, si adhuc filia ejus tibi nupta est, ideo impediuntur nuptiæ, quia duas uxores habere non possis.

7. Again, a man is forbidden to marry his wife's mother, and his father's wife, because they hold the place of mothers to him; a prohibition which can only operate when the affinity is dissolved: for if your step-mother is still your step-mother, that is, if she is still married to your father, she would be prohibited from marrying you by the common rule of law, which forbids a woman to have two husbands at the same time. So if your wife's mother is still your

wife's mother, that is, if her daughter is still married to you, you cannot marry her, because you cannot have two wives at the same time.

GAI. i. 63.

The Institutes do not notice the marriage of a brother and sister-in-law. It was permitted up to the time of Constantine, who forbade it. (Cod. Theod. i. 2.) The prohibition was renowed by Valentinian, Theodosius, and Arcadius. (C. v. 5. 5.)

8. Mariti tamen filius ex alia uxore, et uxoris filia ex alio marito, vel contra, matrimonium recte contrahunt, licet habeant fratrem sororemve ex matrimonio postea contracto natos.

8. The son of a husband by a former wife, and the daughter of a wife by a former husband, or the daughter of a husband by a former wife, and the son of a wife by a former husband, may lawfully contract marriage, even though they have a brother or sister born of the second marriage.

9. Si uxor tua post divortium ex alio filiam procreaverit, hæc non est quidem privigna tua, sed Julianus hujusmodi nuptiis abstineri debere ait: nam nec sponsam filii nurum esse, nec patris sponsam novercam esse, rectius tamen et jure facturos eos qui hujusmodi nuptiis abstinuerint.

9. The daughter of a divorced wife by a second husband is not your step-daughter; and yet Julian says we ought to abstain from such a marriage. For the betrothed wife of a son is not your daughter-in-law; nor your betrothed wife your son's stepmother; and yet it is more decent and more in accordance with law to abstain from such marriages.

D. xxiii. 2. 12. 1, and foll.

The sponsalia constituted in no way a binding tie. They were, as far as law went, mutual promises to contract a tie. Sponsalia sunt sponsio et repromissio nuptiarum futurarum. (D. xxiii. 1. 1.) All that was necessary was, that the parties, and their respective patresfamilias, should consent, and that the betrothed should have attained the age of seven years. Either party wishing to renounce the engagement, which by law was always permissible, could do so by announcing the wish in these words—conditione tua non utor. Hence it could only be custom founded on a respect for boni mores that prevented a father marrying his son's betrothed, or a son his father's.

10. Illud certum est, serviles quoque cognationes impedimento nuptiis esse, si forte pater et filia aut frater et soror manumissi fuerint.

10. It is certain that the relationship of slaves is an impediment to marriage, even if the father and daughter, or brother and sister, as the case may be, have been enfranchised.

D. xxiii. 2. 14. 2.

The union of slaves, *contubernium*, was not recognised in law as a marriage, but still the law did not permit natural ties to be violated in the case of slaves any more than in the case of the issue of concubinage, or that of illicit commerce. (C. v. 4. 4.) Of course a manumission must have taken place, or there could be no question of *nuptiæ*, but if slaves were freed, then, although competent to contract a marriage, they were bound by the ties of blood, and could not marry any one connected with them by close natural relationship.

| | |
|---|---|
| 11. Sunt et aliæ personæ quæ propter diversas rationes nuptias contrahere prohibentur, quas in libris Digestorum seu Pandectarum ex veteri jure collectarum enumerari permisimus. | 11. There are other persons, also, between whom marriage is prohibited for different reasons, which we have permitted to be enumerated in the books of the Digest or Pandects, collected from the old law. |

D. xxiii. 2. 44, pr. and 1.

The reasons alluded to are not, like the preceding, founded on nearness of relationship or other tie, but on public or political grounds. The *patres* and *plebs* could not intermarry till the *lex Canuleia*. Nor the freeborn and freedmen till the *lex Julia* and *Papia Poppæa*. (D. xxiii. 2. 23.) These laws prohibited the marriage of senators with *liberti*, but allowed that of other freeborn, forbidding at the same time all freeborn to marry actresses or women of openly bad character. (D. xxiii. 2. 44.) Constantine extended the prohibition to marrying women of the lowest class, *humiles abjectæve personæ*. (C. v. 27. 1.) This was repealed by Justinian. (Nov. 117. 6.) The guardian could not marry his ward before she was twenty-six years of age, unless betrothed or given to him by her father. (D. xxiii. 2. 66.) The governor of a province could not, while he held his office, marry a native of that province (D. xxiii. 2. 38. 57.), lest he should abuse his authority. The ravisher could not marry the woman he violated. (C. ix. 13. 2.) Nor the adulteror his accomplice. (Nov. 134.) Nor a Jew a Christian. (C. i. 9. 6.)

| | |
|---|---|
| 12. Si adversus ea quæ diximus, aliqui coierint, nec vir, nec uxor, nec nuptiæ, nec matrimonium, nec dos intelligitur. Itaque ii qui ex eo coitu nascuntur, in potestate patris non sunt, sed tales sunt (quantum ad patriam potestatem pertinet) quales sunt ii quos mater vulgo concepit : nam nec bi patrem habere intelliguntur, cum his etiam | 12. If persons unite themselves in contravention of the rules thus laid down there is no husband or wife, no nuptials, no marriage, nor marriage portion, and the children born in such a connection are not in the power of the father. For, with regard to the power of a father, they are in the position of children conceived in prostitution, who are looked upon as |

pater incertus est. Unde solent *spurii* appellari, vel a græca voce *quasi σποράδην* concepti; vel quasi sine patre filii. Sequitur ergo, ut dissoluto tali coitu nec dotis exactioni locus sit. Qui autem prohibitas nuptias contrahunt, et alias pœnas patiuntur, quæ sacris constitutionibus continentur.

having no father, because it is uncertain who he is; and are therefore called *spurii*, either from a Greek word *σποράδην*, meaning 'at hazard,' or as being, *sine patre*, without a father. On the dissolution of such a connection there can be no claim made for the demand of a marriage portion. Persons who contract prohibited marriages are liable also to further penalties set forth in our imperial constitutions.

GAI. i. 64; D. i. 5. 23; D. xxiii. 2. 52.

Under the head of *stuprum* the Romans included every union of the sexes forbidden by morality. Different punishments awaited the guilty according to the degree of crime implied in the union. (Cod. v. 5. 4.) But the law recognized and regulated in concubinage (*concubinatus*) a permanent cohabitation, though without the sanction of marriage, between parties to whose marriage there was no legal obstacle. In every case where such an obstacle existed, unless the obstacle was one merely founded on public policy, such as that of being governor of a province, who was not permitted to marry a native of that province, the law inflicted a punishment on parties cohabiting in defiance of law. The chief incident of the Roman *concubinatus*, which was so far restricted that a man could not have two concubines at once, or a wife and a concubine, was, that the children could be legitimatized, and so placed on a footing with the offspring of a legal marriage. Between the formation of such an union, and the contracting a legal marriage, there seems to have been no difference except what rested in the intention of the parties. If two persons lived together, it was the intention with which they did so which decided whether the union was concubinage or marriage. *Concubinam ex sola animi destinatione æstimari oportet.* (D. xxv. 7. 4.) If there was no *affectio maritalis*, no intention to treat the woman as a wife, she was not a wife. Of course, practically, the question of consent was seldom, if ever, left doubtful. Generally speaking, an instrument fixing the amount settled respectively by the husband and wife, was drawn up, and the consent was publicly given in the presence of friends. And as concubinage was a dishonourable state, the presumption in favour of marriage, when the woman was of honest parentage, and of good character, was very strong. To the union of concubinage none of the incidents of marriage attached. No dowry could be asked for, no settlement was made by the man: the children

were not in the power of the father.  But the connection
was separated from that of a temporary intercourse by no
man being allowed to have two concubines, or a wife and a
concubine at the same time, and by the power which was
given to legitimate the children, and place them in the
position of the offspring of a legal marriage.  (See next paragraph.)

In a legal marriage, without *conventio in manum*, the marriage portion of the wife (*dos*) belonged to the husband during
the continuance of the marriage.  In early times his power
over the *dos* was unrestricted, but afterwards successive limitations of this power were introduced.  (See Bk. ii. Tit. 7. 3.
Tit. 8. introd. paragr.)  The settlement on the wife by the
husband (*donatio propter nuptias*) belonged, during the marriage, to the wife, but was managed by the husband.  (See
Bk. ii. Tit. 7. 3.)  When the marriage was dissolved, which it
might be by death, loss of liberty, captivity, or divorce (D.
xxiv. 2. 1), the *dos* was returned to the wife or her father.
Divorce was always permitted if either party ceased to wish
to preserve the tie of marriage, which was only looked on as
a contract resting on mutual consent.  But, unless both parties
consented to a divorce, heavy penalties were attached to its
being insisted on by one alone, unless any of the grounds for
divorce established by law, such as adultery or criminal conduct (Cod. v. 17. 8.), could be shown to exist.  After the
divorce either party might marry again.

13.  Aliquando autem evenit ut
liberi qui, statim ut nati sunt, in
potestate parentum non fiunt, postea autem redigantur in potestatem
parentum.  Qualis est is qui, dum
naturalis fuerat, postea curiæ datus
potestati patris subjicitur: nec non
is qui a muliere libera procreatus,
cujus matrimonium minime legibus interdictum fuerat, sed ad
quam pater consuetudinem habu-
erat, postea ex nostra constitutione
dotalibus instrumentis compositis
in potestate patris efficitur.  Quod
si alii liberi ex eodem matrimonio
fuerint procreati, similiter nostra
constitutio præbuit.

13.  It sometimes happens, that
children who at their birth were not
in the power of their father, are
brought under it afterwards.  Such
is the case of a natural son, who is
given to the *curia*, and then becomes
subject to his father's power.  Again,
a child born of a free woman, with
whom marriage was not prohibited
by any law, but with whom the father
only cohabited, will likewise become
subject to the power of his father if
at any time afterwards instruments
of dowry are drawn up according to
the provisions of our constitution.
And this constitution confers the
same benefits on any children who
may be subsequently born of the
same marriage.

Gai. i. 65;  C. v. 27. 10,

By legitimation the offspring of concubinage were placed
in the position of *liberi legitimi*, and this was effected in three

ways: 1. By oblation to the *curia*; 2. By the subsequent
marriage of the parents; and 3. By a rescript of the emperor,
a mode introduced by Justinian in the 74th Novel. The *curia*
was the class from which, in provincial towns, the magistrates
were eligible. To be a member was a distinction, but an
onerous one, from the expenses and burdens attached to the
position. In order to prevent the order decaying through
unwillingness to incur the expenses attending it, Theodosius
and Valentinian permitted citizens, whether themselves members of the *curia* or not, to present their children born in
concubinage to, and make them members of, the order (Cod.
v. 27. 3), by which they became legitimate, and the heirs of
their father. This mode of legitimation which could, of
course, only be adopted when the parents were rich, did not,
however, make the children complete members of the father's
family. They became his legitimate children, but gained no
new relationship or right of succession to any other member
of his family. (C. v. 27. 9.)

Constantine first established that natural children should
be made legitimate by the subsequent marriage of their
parents. The law required that at the moment of conception
the parents should have been capable of a legal marriage;
that an instrument settling the dowry (*instrumentum dotale*),
or, at least, attesting the marriage (*instrumentum nuptiale*),
should be drawn up, and that the children should ratify the
legitimation, for no one was made legitimate against his will.
(Nov. 89. 11.)

If the mother were dead or had disappeared, and the marriage was thus impossible, the emperor would by a rescript
allow the natural children (if there was no legitimate one) to
be placed in the position they would have held if the marriage had taken place, as he would also if a father by his
testament expressed his wish to that effect.


## Tit. XI.   DE ADOPTIONIBUS.

Non solum autem naturales li-     Not only are our natural children,
beri, secundum ea quæ diximus,   as we have said, in our power, but
in potestate nostra sunt, verum  those also whom we adopt.
etiam ii quos adoptamus.

                       GAI. i. 97.

Before the time of Justinian, the effect of adoption (see
Introd. sec. 42) was to place the person adopted exactly in
the position he would have held had he been born a son of
the person adopting him. All the property of the adoptive

                       I

son belonged to his adoptive father. The adoptive son was heir to his adoptive father, if intestate, bore his name (retaining, however, the name of his own *gens* with the change of *us* into *anus*, as Octavius, Octavianus), and shared the sacred rites of the family he entered.

*Naturales liberi* is here opposed to *adoptivi*, not, as in the last Title, to *legitimi*.

| | |
|---|---|
| 1. Adoptio autem duobus modis fit, aut principali rescripto, aut imperio magistratus. Imperatoris auctoritate adoptare quis potest eos easve qui quæve sui juris sunt: quæ species adoptionis dicitur adrogatio. Imperio magistratus adoptare licet eos easve qui quæve in potestate parentium sunt, sive primum gradum liberorum obtineant qualis filius, filia, sive inferiorem, qualis est nepos neptis, pronepos proneptis. | 1. Adoption takes place in two ways, either by imperial rescript, or by the authority of the magistrate. The imperial rescript gives power to adopt persons of either sex who are *sui juris*; and this species of adoption is called *arrogation*. By the authority of the magistrate we adopt persons in the power of an ascendant, whether in the first degree, as sons and daughters, or in an inferior degree, as grandchildren or great-grandchildren. |

Gai. i. 98, 99.

A public character was always attached in ancient Roman law to so important an alteration in families as adoption. (See Introd. sec. 42.) The sanction of the *curiæ* was probably necessary to its validity, when the family of a member of the *curiæ* was affected. If the person adopted was *sui juris*, his entry into a new family (*arrogatio*) was jealously watched, as the *pontifices* would never allow it where there was any likelihood of the sacred rites of the family he quitted becoming extinct by his departure from it. The form of gaining the consent of the *curiæ* was even continued when the *curiæ* were only represented by thirty lictors, until the rescript of the emperor was substituted as a means of effecting arrogations.

What were the forms of arrogation, when neither the person arrogated nor the person arrogating belonged to the body of the *curiæ*, we have no certain knowledge; but we may guess arrogation was effected by a fictitious suit, in which the person arrogated was claimed as the child of the arrogator, and let judgment go by default.

If the person adopted were under the power of another, the person under whose power he was had to release him from that power, which he did by selling him (*mancipatio*) three several times, which destroyed his own *patria potestas* (see Introd. sec. 42), and then giving him up to the adopting parent by a fictitious process of law, called 'in jure cessio,' in which he was claimed and acknowledged as the child of the person who adopted him, and pronounced to be so by the magistrate before whom the proceeding was held (*imperio magistratus*). The word *adoptio* was common to both processes, both to *arrogatio*, said by Gaius to be derived from *rogo*, because the person arrogated was asked before the *curie* whether he consented (GAI. i. 99), and to *adoptio* in its more limited sense of the adoption of a person not *sui juris*. For the ceremonies previously required for the adoption of a person *alieni juris*, Justinian substituted the simple proceeding of executing, in presence of a magistrate, the deed declaring the fact of the adoption—the parties to the adoption, that is, the person giving, the person given, and the person receiving, being personally present to give their consent. But it was sufficient if the consent of the party adopted were expressed by his not declaring his dissent—*non contradicente*. (C. viii. 48. 11. Tit. 12. 10.)

2. Sed hodie, ex nostra constitutione, cum filiusfamilias a patre naturali extraneæ personæ in adoptionem datur, jura potestatis patris naturalis minime dissolvuntur, nec quicquam ad patrem adoptivum transit, nec in potestate ejus est, licet ab intestato jura successionis ei a nobis tributa sint. Si vero pater naturalis non extraneo, sed avo filii sui materno, vel si ipse pater naturalis fuerit emancipatus, etiam avo paterno vel proavo simili modo paterno vel materno filium suum dederit in adoptionem: in hoc casu, quia concurrent in unam personam et naturalia et adoptionis jura, manet stabile jus patris adoptivi, et naturali vinculo copulatum, et legitimo adoptionis nodo constrictum, ut et in familia et in potestate hujusmodi patris adoptivi sit.

2. But now, by our constitution, when a *filiusfamilias* is given in adoption by his natural father to a stranger, the power of the natural father is not dissolved; no right passes to the adoptive father, nor is the adopted son in his power, although we allow such son the right of succession to his adoptive father dying intestate. But if a natural father should give his son in adoption, not to a stranger, but to the son's maternal grandfather, or, supposing the natural father has been emancipated, if he gives the son in adoption to the son's paternal grandfather, or to the son's paternal or maternal great-grandfather, in this case, as the rights of nature and adoption concur in the same person, the power of the adoptive father, knit by natural ties and strengthened by the legal bond of adoption, is preserved undiminished, so that the adopted son is not only in the family, but in the power of his adoptive father.

C. viii. 48. 10.

The change made by Justinian in the law of adoption (C. viii. 48, 10) completely altered its character. It used sometimes to happen under the old law, that a son lost the succession to his own father by being adopted, and to his adoptive father by a subsequent emancipation. Justinian wished to remedy this effectually. He therefore provided that the son given in adoption to a stranger, that is, any one not an ascendant, should be in the same position to his own father as before, but gain by adoption the succession to his adoptive father, if the adoptive father died intestate. The adoptive father was not, however, bound, like the natural father (lib. ii. Tit. 18), to leave him a share of his property, if he made a will. In this kind of adoption, which commentators have termed the *adoptio minus plena*, the adoptive son still remained in the family of his natural father; and the only change which adoption caused, was, that he acquired a right of succession to his adoptive father, if intestate.

When the person to whom the adoptive son was given, was one of his own ascendants, then the old law was permitted to regulate the effects of the adoption, and the adoption in this case was what the commentators term *adoptio plena*. The adoptive son entered the family of the ascendant, who became his adoptive father. A grandson was not naturally in the same family with his maternal grandfather, and could only enter the family of his maternal grandfather by being adopted. If he had been born after his father had been emancipated, he would not be in the same family with his maternal grandfather, who might therefore wish to adopt him. It was even possible that he might be adopted by his own father; for if born before his father was emancipated, his grandfather might have emancipated his father without emancipating him, and then might afterwards have given him in adoption to his father.

3. Cum autem impubes per principale rescriptum adrogatur, causa cognita adrogatio permittitur, et exquiritur causa adrogationis an honesta sit expediatque pupillo, et eum quibusdam conditionibus adrogatio fit: id est, ut caveat adrogator personæ publicæ, hoc est tabulario, si intra pubertatem pupillus decesserit, restituturum se bona illis qui, si adoptio facta non esset, ad successionem ejus venturi essent. Item non alias emancipare eum potest adrogator, nisi causa cognita dignus emancipatione fuerit, et tunc sua bona ei reddat. Sed etsi decedens pater eum exheredaverit, vel vivus sine justa causa eum emancipaverit, jubetur quartam partem ei bonorum suorum relinquere, videlicet præter bona quæ ad patrem adoptivum transtulit et quorum commodum si postea adquisivit.

3. When any one under the age of puberty, is arrogated by the imperial rescript, the arrogation is only allowed when inquiry has been made into the circumstances of the case. It is asked, what is the motive leading to the arrogation, and whether the arrogation is honourable and expedient for the pupil. And the arrogation is always made under certain conditions; the arrogator is obliged to give security before a public person, that is, before a notary, that if the pupil should die within the age of puberty, he will restore all the property to those who would have succeeded him if no adoption had been made. Nor, again, can the arrogator emancipate the person arrogated, unless, on examination into the case, it appears that the latter is worthy of emancipation: and, even then, the arrogator must restore the property belonging to the person he emanci-

pates. Also, even if the arrogator, on his death-bed, has disinherited his arrogated son, or, during his life, has emancipated him without just cause, he is obliged to leave him the fourth part of all his goods, besides what the son brought to him at the time of arrogation, or acquired for him afterwards.

GAI. i. 102; D. i. 7. 13; D. xxxviii. 5. 13.

Neither women nor children under the age of puberty could be arrogated. Arrogation was first permitted in the case of the latter by Antoninus Pius (ULP. *Reg.* viii. 5. D. i. 7. 21), but only after strict inquiry had been made into the circumstances of the case. Besides the general inquiry which took place in every case of adoption, as to the ages of the parties, and the possible injustice to other members of the family, which the introduction of a new member might give rise to, in this case inquiry was made whether the character and circumstances of the proposed arrogator were such as to make it probable that the arrogation would be beneficial to the person arrogated. Further, certain regulations were made, designed to protect the property of the *impubes*, which were briefly as follows:—1. If the arrogated son died before puberty, the arrogator had to restore the property of the son to that son's natural heirs. 2. If the arrogated son were emancipated or disinherited without good reason before puberty, the arrogator had to restore to the son all the son's property, and give him a fourth of his (the arrogator's) own property, called the *quarta D. Pii*, or *quarta Antonina*, as having been first required by that emperor. 3. If the son were emancipated or disinherited before puberty for a good reason, the son received his own property from the arrogator, but nothing more. 4. Lastly, if the arrogated son, on attaining puberty, wished to rescind the arrogation, he was at liberty to do so, if he could show it was prejudicial to him.

There is some little doubt when arrogation was first made *per rescriptum principis*. However, Ulpian (*Reg.* viii. 5) expresses himself too plainly to admit of a doubt that in his time arrogation was made *per populum* (i. e. by the curies represented by lictors), and not by imperial licence. He further adds, that arrogation was only made at Rome (*Reg.* viii. 4), and, of course, when the system of permitting it by imperial rescript was adopted, place could have nothing to do with arrogation.

The *tabularii* here spoken of were public notaries, who kept public registers (*tabulae*), on which formal acts were recorded.

4. Minorem natu majorem non posse adoptare placet. Adoptio enim naturam imitatur, et pro monstro est ut major sit filius quam pater. Debet itaque is qui sibi filium per adoptionem vel adrogationem facit, plena pubertate, id est, decem et octo annis praecedere.

4. A younger person cannot adopt an older; for adoption imitates nature; and it seems unnatural, that a son should be older than his father. Any one, therefore, who wishes either to adopt or arrogate a son, should be the elder by the term of complete puberty, that is, by eighteen years.

D. i. 7. 15. 3; D. i. 7. 16; D. i. 7. 40. 1.

As long as the required number of years intervened, there was no further positive rule as to age; but it being in the discretion of the emperor to allow adoption or not, there was generally a disposition to refuse it unless the person who wished to adopt was of such an age as to make it improbable he should have children of his own. (D. i. 7. 15.)

The legal age of puberty in males was fourteen; but eighteen was the age at which the body was considered to be fully developed in all cases, *plena pubertas.*

5. Licet autem et in locum nepotis vel pronepotis, vel in locum neptis vel proneptis, vel deinceps adoptare, quamvis filium quis non habeat.

5. A person may adopt another as grandson or granddaughter, great-grandson or great-granddaughter, or any other descendant, although he has no son.

As adoption follows nature, it would have seemed, without express enactment, that none but married persons could have adopted grandsons, and that a person, to have had a grandson, must have had a son. With respect to the degrees of marriage, it sometimes made an important difference whether a person was adopted as a son or grandson. The natural (i. e. non-adoptive) granddaughter, for instance, of the person adopting would be cousin or niece of the person adopted, according as he was adopted as a grandson or son, and might marry him in the one case, and not in the other.

6. Et tam filium alienum quis in locum nepotis adoptare potest, quam nepotem in locum filii.

7. Sed si quis nepotis loco adoptet, vel quasi ex eo filio quem habet jam adoptatum, vel quasi ex illo quem naturalem in sua potestate habet, in eo casu et filius consentire debet, ne ei invito suus heres adgnascatur. Sed ex contrario, si avus ex filio nepotem det in adoptionem, non est necesse filium consentire.

6. A man may adopt the son of another as his grandson, and the grandson of another as his son.

7. If a man adopts a grandson to be the son of a son already adopted, or of a natural son in his power, the consent of his son ought first to be obtained, that he may not have a *suus heres* given him against his will. But, on the contrary, if a grandfather gives his grandson by a son in adoption, the consent of the son is not necessary.

D. i. 7. 6. 10, 11; D. xxiii. 1. 18. 1.

A grandson could be adopted either generally, when he was supposed to be the issue of a deceased son, and so was *sui juris* at the death of the grandfather; or, specially as the son of a particular son, in which case he came under that son's power when the grandfather died. The grandfather could at his pleasure diminish, but could not add to the number of his son's family; because otherwise the son would have had a *suus heres* (see Introd. sec. 77) forced on him against his will, to take a share of his property.

8. In plurimis autem causis adsimilatur is qui adoptatus vel adrogatus est, ei qui ex legitimo matrimonio natus est. Et ideo si quis per Imperatorem, sive apud praetorem vel apud praesidem provinciae non extraneum adoptaverit, potest eumdem alii in adoptionem dare.

8. He who is either adopted or arrogated is assimilated, in many points, to a son born in lawful matrimony; and therefore, if any one adopts another by imperial rescript, or, if the person is not a stranger, before the praetor, or the *praeses* of a province, he can afterwards give in adoption to another the person whom he has adopted.

GAI. i. 105.

The text says that the adoptive son is assimilated to the natural *in plurimis causis*, and not altogether; because, among other differences, if the adoptive son left his adoptive family, he ceased to have any relationship whatever to its members; but the natural son was always *cognatus* to his own blood relations, although, by emancipation or adoption, he might cease to be *agnatus* to them.

Of course, under Justinian's legislation, the adoptive father, if a stranger, had no *patria potestas* at all, and therefore could not exercise such a power as that of giving his adoptive son in adoption to another person.

When once the tie of adoption was dissolved, all the relations created by it were entirely at an end, except that marriage was forbidden between the person adopting and the person adopted. (See Tit. 10. 1.) *In omni fere jure, finita patria adoptivi potestate, nullum ex pristino retinetur vestigium.* (D. i. 7. 13.) But the tie could never again be renewed between the same persons. (D. i. 7. 37. 1.)

9. Sed et illud utriusque adoptionis commune est, quod et ii qui generare non possunt, quales sunt spadones, adoptare possunt; castrati autem non possunt.

9. It is a rule common to both kinds of adoption, that persons, although incapable of procreating, as, for instance, impotent persons, may, but those who are castrated, cannot, adopt.

GAI. i. 103.

The distinction was drawn because it was considered as never perfectly certain that the former (*spadones*) would not at some time or other have children of their own.

| | |
|---|---|
| 10. Feminæ quoque adoptare non possunt, quia nec naturales liberos in sua potestate habent. Sed ex indulgentia principis ad solatium liberorum amissorum adoptare possunt. | 10. Women, also, cannot adopt: for they have not even their own children in their power; but, by the indulgence of the emperor, and as a comfort for the loss of their own children, they are allowed to adopt. |

Gai. i. 104; C. viii. 48. 5.

Women could not adopt, because the meaning of adoption was that the person adopted passed into the *patria potestas* of the person adopting. The adoption mentioned in the text (which was permitted by a constitution of Diocletian and Maximian, C. viii. 48. 5), only placed the adopted children in the same relation to the woman as her own children would have held. She gained nothing like *patria potestas* over them.

| | |
|---|---|
| 11. Illud proprium est adoptionis illius quæ per sacrum oraculum fit, quod is qui liberos in potestate habet, si se adrogandum dederit, non solum ipse potestati alrogatoris subjicitur, sed etiam liberi ejus in ejusdem fiunt potestate, tamquam nepotes. Sic enim et divus Augustus non ante Tiberium adoptavit, quam is Germanicum adoptavit, ut protinus adoptione facta incipiat Germanicus Augusti nepos esse. | 11. Adoption by the rescript of the emperor has this peculiarity. If a person, having children under his power, should give himself in arrogation, not only does he submit himself to the power of the arrogator, but his children are also in the arrogator's power, being considered his grandchildren. It was for this reason that Augustus did not adopt Tiberius until Tiberius had adopted Germanicus; so that directly the adoption was made, Germanicus became the grandson of Augustus. |

Gai. i. 107.

This is said to be an incident of arrogation only, because when a person not *sui juris* was adopted, his children were not in his power, and so he could not transfer them to the power of his adoptive father; into which they only came after the death of the person in whose power their own natural father was.

All the property of the person arrogated became the property of the arrogator. (See Bk. iii. Tit. 10.) The adoptive son, as he was previously in the power of his natural father, had no property to pass.

| | |
|---|---|
| 12. Apud Catonem bene scriptum refert antiquitas, servos, si a domino adoptati sint, ex hoc ipso posse liberari. Unde et nos eruditi in nostra constitutione, etiam eum | 12. Cato, as we learn from the ancients, has with good reason written, that slaves, when adopted by their masters, are thereby made free. In accordance with which opinion, |

servum quem dominus actis intervenientibus filium suum nomina-
verit, liberum esse constituimus,
licet hoc ad jus filii accipiendum
non sufficiat.

we have decided by one of our constitutions, that a slave to whom his
master by a solemn deed gives the
title of son is thereby made free
although he does not acquire thereby the rights of a son.

C. vii. 6. 10.

It is doubtful whether slaves could be adopted, so as to
become members of the family of the person adopting them.
Aulus Gellius (*Noct. Attic.* v. 9) says that the majority of the
ancient jurists, including Sabinus, held they could. Theophilus says Cato was of the contrary opinion. They certainly
became freedmen, and never *ingenui* by adoption ; even a
freedman never became *ingenuus* by adoption ; (D. i. 7. 26),
and he could only be adopted by his patron (D. i. 7. 15), and
on a good ground, such as the patron having no children.
(C. viii. 48.)

## Tit. XII. QUIBUS MODIS JUS POTESTATIS SOLVITUR.

Videamus nunc quibus modis ii
qui alieno Juri sunt subjecti, eo
jure liberantur. Et quidem servi
quemadmodum potestate liberantur,ex iis intelligere possumus quæ
de servis manumittendis superius
exposuimus. Hi vero qui in potestate parentis sunt, mortuo eo sui
juris fiunt ; sed hoc distinctionem
recipit. Nam mortuo patre, sane
omnimodo filii filiæve sui juris
efficiuntur ; mortuo vero avo, non
omnimodo nepotes neptesque sui
juris fiunt, sed ita si post mortem
avi in potestatem patris sui reca-
suri non sunt. Itaque, si moriente
avo pater eorum vivit et in potestate patris sui est, tunc post obitum
avi in potestate patris sui fiunt. Si
vero is quo tempore avus moritur,
aut etiam mortuus est aut exiit de
potestate patris, tunc ii, quia in
potestatem ejus cadere non possunt, sui juris fiunt.

Let us now inquire into the different ways in which persons in the
power of others are freed from it.
How slaves are freed from the power
of their masters may be learnt from
what we have already said with regard to manumission. Those who
are in the power of a parent become
independent at his death ; a rule,
however, which admits of a distinction. For when a father dies, his
sons and daughters become undoubtedly independent ; but when a
grandfather dies, his grandchildren
do not necessarily become independent, but only if on the grandfather's
death they do not fall under the
power of their father. Therefore, if
their father is alive at the death of
their grandfather, and was in his
power, then, on the grandfather's
death, they become subject to the
power of their father. But, if at the
time of the grandfather's death their
father is either dead, or has already
passed out of the grandfather's
power by emancipation, as they do
not fall under the power of their
father, they become independent.

The modes in which the *patria potestas* was ended were—
(1) the death of the parent: (2) the parent or son suffering
loss of freedom or of citizenship; (3) the son attaining certain
dignities; (4) emancipation. All those modes are treated of
in this Title.

| | |
|---|---|
| 1. Cum autem is qui ob aliquod maleficium in insulam deportatur, civitatem amittit, sequitur ut, qui eo modo ex numero civium Romanorum tollitur, perinde ac eo mortuo desinant liberi in potestate ejus esse. Pari ratione, et si is qui in potestate parentis sit, in insulam deportatus fuerit, desinit in potestate parentis esse. Sed si ex indulgentia principali restituti fuerint, per omnia pristinum statum recipiant. | 1. If a man, convicted of some crime, is deported to an island, he loses the rights of a Roman citizen; whence it follows, that the children of a person thus banished cease to be under his power, exactly as if he were dead. Equally, if a son is deported, does he cease to be under the power of his father. But, if by the favour of the emperor any one is restored, he regains his former position in every respect. |

GAI. I. 128.

The *patria potestas* belonging exclusively to citizens, and
being necessarily exercised over citizens, when a parent or
son lost the rights of citizenship, or, as it was termed, underwent a *media capitis deminutio* (see Tit. 16. 2.), the *patria
potestas* was necessarily at an end. (ULP. *Reg.* x. 3.) The
punishment of *deportatio in insulam* consisted in the condemned being confined within certain local bounds, whether
really those of an island, or of some prescribed space of the
mainland, and being considered as civilly dead (*deportatus
pro mortuo habetur* (D. xxxvii. 4. 10. 8), and looked on as
*peregrinus*, not as a *civis*. (ULP. *Reg.* x. 3.) If the condemned
was recalled, and by the pardon of the emperor all the effects
of his punishment were done away, he was said to be *restitutus
in integrum*: he then resumed all his civil rights, and was
placed as exactly as possible in the position which he would
have held, had he never been *deportatus*. (Cod. ix. 51. 1.)
Many texts, instead of reading in this section *restituti
fuerint, per omnia . . . . recipiunt*, read *restituti fuerint
per omnia*, making *restitutio per omnia* equivalent to *restitutio in integrum*. The reading adopted in the text supposes that a *restitutio in integrum* is spoken of in the word
*restituti*.

| | |
|---|---|
| 2. Relegati autem patres in insulam, in potestate sua liberos retinent. Et ex contrario liberi relegati in potestate parentium remanent. | 2. A father who is merely banished by relegation, still retains his children in his power; and a child who is relegated still remains in the power of his father. |

D. xlviii. 22. 4.

The *relegatus* was merely forbidden to leave a certain spot, and his civil *status* was in no way altered. (See OVID, *Trist.* v. 11.)

3. Pœnæ servus effectus filios in potestate habere desinit. Servi autem pœnæ efficiuntur, qui in metallum damnantur, et qui bestiis subjiciuntur.

3. When a man becomes a 'slave of punishment' he ceases to have his sons in his power. Persons become 'slaves of punishment' who are condemned to the mines, or exposed to wild beasts.

D. xlviii. 19. 17. 19.

A slave had no legal power over his children; in whatever way, therefore, a father became a slave, he lost his power over his children. When a person was sentenced to work in the mines, or to contend with wild beasts in the arena, punishments only inflicted for very great crimes, he became, by the mere operation of his sentence, a slave. But as there was no master whose slave he could be considered, it was said that he became the slave of the punishment (*servus pœnæ*).

4. Filiusfamilias, si militaverit vel si senator vel consul fuerit factus, manet in potestate patris; militia enim vel consularis dignitas potestate patris filium non liberat. Sed ex constitutione nostra, summa patriciatus dignitas, illico imperialibus codicillis præstita, filium a patria potestate liberat. Quis enim patiatur, patrem quidem posse per emancipationis modum suæ potestatis nexibus filium relaxare, imperatoriam autem celsitudinem non valere eum quem sibi patrem elegit, ab aliena eximere potestate?

4. A son, though he becomes a soldier, a senator, or a consul, still remains in the power of his father, from which neither military service nor consular dignity can free him. But by our constitution the supreme dignity of the patriciate frees the son from the power of his father immediately on the grant of the imperial patent. It is obviously absurd that a parent could emancipate his son from the tie of his power, and that the majesty of the emperor should not be able to release from the power of another, one whom he had chosen to be a father of the State.

D. i. 7. 3; C. xii. 3. 5.

Under the old Roman law no child was released from a father's power, by having any dignity or office, except that of a *flamen dialis*, or a vestal virgin. Persons holding either of these offices without undergoing any *capitis diminutio*, or ceasing to be members of their father's family, became *sui juris*. Justinian conferred the privilege on those enjoying the dignity of the patriciate, and at a later period of his legislation enlarged the number of dignities to which this incident was attached; and the child was freed from the power of his father by being made a bishop, a consul, quæstor of the palace, prætorian præfect, or master of infantry or cavalry; and, in

general all those whose dignity exempted them from the burdens of the *curia* were freed from the power of their father.
(Nov. 31; C. x. 31. 66.) When under Justinian's legislation
a child was released by attaining a dignity, he still, as in the
older law, remained a member of his father's family, and enjoyed all his rights of succession and agnation. (Nov. 81. 2.)

Constantine changed the meaning of *patricius*, by making
it a title of the highest honour conferred on persons who enjoyed the chief place in the emperor's esteem. The power of
making *patricii* was, in general, used very sparingly by the
emperors, and hence the title became an object of ambition
even to foreign princes.

6. Si ab hostibus captus fuerit parens, quamvis hostium fiat, tamen pendet jus liberorum propter jus postliminii; quia hi qui ab hostibus capti sunt, si reversi fuerint, omnia pristina jura recipiunt. Idcirco reversus etiam liberos habebit in potestate; quia postliminium fingit eum quia captus est, semper in civitate fuisse. Si vero ibi decesserit, exinde ex quo captus est pater, filius sui juris fuisse videtur. Ipse quoque filius nepusve si ab hostibus captus fuerit, similiter dicimus propter jus postliminii, jus quoque potestatis parentis in suspenso esse. Dictum est autem postliminium a LIMINE et POST. Unde eum qui ab hostibus captus in fines nostros postea pervenit, postliminio reversum recte dicimus; nam limina sicut in domibus finem quemdam faciunt, sic et imperii finem limen esse veteres voluerunt. Hinc et limes dictus est, quasi finis quidam et terminus; ab eo postliminium dictum, quia eodem limine revertebatur, quo amissus fuerat. Sed et qui captus victis hostibus recuperatur, postliminio rediisse existimatur.

6. If a parent is taken prisoner, although he becomes the slave of the enemy, yet his paternal power is only suspended, owing to the *jus postliminii*, for captives, when they return, are restored to all their former rights. Thus, on his return, the father will have his children in his power: for the *postliminium* supposes that the captive has never been absent. If, however, a prisoner dies in captivity, the son is considered to have been independent from the time when his father was taken prisoner. So, too, if a son, or grandson, is taken prisoner, the power of the parent, by means of the *jus postliminii*, is only in suspense. The term *postliminium* is derived from *post* and *limen*. We therefore say of a person taken by the enemy, and then returning into our territory, that he is come back by *postliminium*. For, just as the threshold forms the boundary of a house, so the ancients have termed the boundary of the empire a threshold. Whence *limes*, also, is derived, and is used to signify a boundary and limit. Thence comes the word *postliminium*, because the prisoner returned to the same limits whence he had been lost. The prisoner, also, who is retaken on the defeat of the enemy, is considered to return by *postliminium*.

Gai. i. 129; D. xlix. 15. 29. 3; D. xlix. 15. 26.

By the *jus postliminii*, property taken in war, and retaken
from the enemy, was restored to the original owners (see Bk.
ii. Tit. 1. 17); and captives, on their return to their own

country, were re-established in all their former rights. When the captive returned, all the time of his captivity was, in the eye of the law, blotted out, and he was exactly in the position he would have held if he had not been taken captive. (D. xlix. 15. 21. 6.) The manner of his return was quite immaterial. *Nihil interest quomodo captivus revertur est.* (D. xlix. 15. 26.) When the father returned, he resumed all his rights over his property, and his *patria potestas* over his children; when a child returned, he regained his rights of succession and agnation, and at the same time he fell again under the *patria potestas* of his father. (D. xlix. 15. 14.) If the captive did not return from captivity, the law considered him to have died at the moment of his captivity commencing, a point important with regard to testaments (see Bk. ii. Tit. 12, 5); and also as making children *sui juris*, and giving them all property acquired by them, from the time of the parent's captivity. Gaius says that in his time this point in favour of the children was not established (GAI. i. 129); but, at any rate, it was so when Ulpian wrote. (D. xlix. 15. 18.)

6. Præterea emancipatione quoque desinunt liberi in potestate parentium esse. Sed emancipatio antea quidem vel per antiquam legis observationem procedebat, quæ per imaginarias venditiones et intercedentes manumissiones celebrabatur, vel ex imperiali rescripto. Nostra autem providentia et hoc in melius per constitutionem reformavit, ut fictione pristina explosa, recta via ad competentes judices vel magistratus parentes intrent, et sic filios suos vel filias, vel nepotes, vel neptes ac deinceps sua manu demitterent. Et tunc ex edicto prætoris in hujus filii vel filiæ vel nepotis vel neptis bonis, qui vel quæ a parente manumissus vel manumissa fuerit, eadem jura præstantur parenti, quæ tribuuntur patrono in bonis liberti; et præterea, si impubes sit filius vel filia vel ceteri, ipse parens ex manumissione tutelam ejus nanciscitur.

6. Children, also, cease to be under the power of their parents by emancipation. Formerly emancipation was effected, either by adopting the process of the ancient law, consisting of imaginary sales, each followed by a manumission, or by imperial rescript; but we, in our wisdom, have introduced a reform on this point by one of our constitutions. The old fictitious process is now done away with, and parents may now appear directly before a proper judge or magistrate, and free from their power their children, or grandchildren, or other descendants. And then, according to the prætorian edict, the parent has the same rights over the goods of those whom he emancipates, as the patron has over the goods of his freedman. And further, if the child or children emancipated are within the age of puberty, the parent, by the emancipation, becomes their tutor.

GAI. i. 132. 134; D. xxxvii. 12. 1; D. xxvi. 4. 3. 10; C. viii. 49. 5. 6.

We have no trace of any other form of giving freedom, in early times, than that of emancipation. In the law of the Twelve Tables we find it laid down, ' *Si pater filium ter venumduit* (sells) *liber esto.*' The father might sell his son,

and he would then be in the *mancipium* of the purchaser ; but
when the purchaser freed him, the son would fall again under
his father's power.  This might happen over and over again,
but the Twelve Tables, whether making a new enactment, or
sanctioning an old custom, declared that after a third sale the
father's power was extinguished for ever.  This may perhaps
have been originally intended as a kind of check on the father
abusing his power of selling his son ; and have been afterwards used as a means of giving freedom by a fictitious sale ;
or it may have been expressly enacted in the Twelve Tables
to extinguish all doubts whether the custom of freeing from
a father's power by three sales was valid.  In the form the
fictitious sale took in the times of historical certainty, the
father three times sold his son to a fictitious purchaser, who,
between the first and the second sale, and also between the
second and the third, manumitted the son, i.e. discharged him
from his power as a master which he had acquired by the sale.
After the third sale, the son was in the *mancipium* of the
fictitious purchaser, and if this purchaser had manumitted him,
he would have been the son's patron.  But as the father generally wished to be the patron of his son, the relation giving
him, among other things, the right of succeeding to the son if
intestate and childless, the purchaser, instead of manumitting
him, resold (*remancipavit*) him to the father, who then himself manumitted him, and became his patron.  In cases where
the fictitious purchaser manumitted the third time, he was
considered as a trustee for the father of all the rights of
patronage.   Originally, an express contract was made, con-
*tracta fiducia*, to bind the purchaser to remancipate or to
manumit, reserving the rights of patronage to the father, as
the case might be ; but in later times the purchaser was considered bound by an implied contract, and the prætorian edict,
as we learn from the text, secured to the father in all cases
the rights of patronage.

As the law of the Twelve Tables spoke only of a son, it
was considered sufficient, by a strict interpretation of the
term ' son,' that one sale instead of three was sufficient in
the case of a daughter or grandchild. (G. i. 132.)

Anastasius introduced a new mode of freeing the child
from the power of the father.  The emperor issued, in cases
where he thought it proper, a rescript authorising the emancipation ; and this rescript being registered by a magistrate,
the process was complete. (C. viii. 49. 5.)

Justinian, in giving the greatest possible facility to emancipation, preserved all the effects which the process had had

under the old system of fictitious sales.  Both under his system and that of Anastasius, a child could be emancipated in his absence, which was not possible in the times when the old forms of manumission were strictly observed.

7. Admonendi autem sumus, liberum arbitrium esse ei qui filium et ex eo nepotem vel neptem in potestate habebit, filium quidem potestate dimittere, nepotem vero vel neptem retinere; et ex diverso filium quidem in potestate retinere, nepotem vero vel neptem manumittere, vel omnes sui juris efficere. Eadem et de pronepote et pronepte dicta esse intelligantur.

8. Sed et si pater filium quem in potestate habet, avo vel proavo naturali, secundum nostras constitutiones super his habitas, in adoptionem dederit: id est, si hoc ipsum actis intervenientibus apud competentem judicem manifestaverit praesente eo qui adoptatur et non contradicente, nec non eo praesente qui adoptat, solvitur jus potestatis patris naturalis; transit autem in hujusmodi parentem adoptivum, in cujus persona et adoptionem esse plenissimam antea diximus.

7. It is also to be observed, that a parent having in his power a son, and by that son a grandson or granddaughter, may emancipate his son, and retain in his power his grandson or granddaughter; or, conversely, he may emancipate his grandson or granddaughter, and retain his son in his power; or, he may make them all independent. And it is the same in the case of a great-grandson, or a great-granddaughter.

8. If a father has a son in his power, and gives him in adoption to the son's natural grandfather or great-grandfather, in conformity with our constitutions enacted on this subject, that is, if he declares his intention in a formal act before a competent judge, in the presence and without the dissent of the person adopted, and also in the presence of the person who adopts, then the right of paternal power is extinguished as to the natural father, and passes from him to the adoptive father; with regard to whom, as we have before observed, adoption preserves all its effects.

C. viii. 47. 11.

The adoptive father could not acquire any *patria potestas* by fictitious sales; he could only extinguish that of the natural father. In order to gain it himself, he had recourse to another fictitious process, called *in jure cessio*. He claimed the child as his before a magistrate, and the natural father not withstanding the claim, the child was given into the *patria potestas* of the adoptive father. For the change made by Justinian in the law of adoption, see Tit. 11. 1.

9. Illud autem scire oportet, quod si nurus tua ex filio tuo conceperit, et filium postea emancipaveris vel in adoptionem dederis praegnante nuru tua, nihilominus quod ex ea nascitur, in potestate tua nascitur; quod si post emancipationem vel adoptionem conceptus fuerit, patris sui emancipati vel avi adoptivi

9. It must be observed, that, if your daughter-in-law becomes pregnant, and if during her pregnancy you emancipate your son, or give him in adoption, the child will be born in your power; but if the child is conceived subsequently to the emancipation or adoption, he is born in the power of his emancipated father, or

potestati subjicitur; et quod neque naturales liberi neque adoptivi ullo pene modo possunt cogere parentes de potestate sua eos dimittere.

his adoptive grandfather. Children, natural or adoptive, have almost no means of compelling their parents to free them from their power.

GAI. i. 135. 137; D. i. 7. 31. 33.

The rights of a child were always determined by reference to the moment of conception, not of birth, when he was born *in justo matrimonio*, because he then followed the condition of his father. But when he followed the condition of his mother, as he did when he was born out of *justum matrimonium*, reference was had to the time of his birth (G. i. 89), or, in the later law, to the time of his conception, of his birth, or to any intermediate time, as might be most favourable to him. (See Tit. 4. pr.)

The exceptional cases alluded to in the words *neque ullo pene modo* only occurred where the father attempted to make a base use of his power over his children, or abandoned them (C. xi. 40. 6; C. viii. 52. 2); or when a person, adopted under the age of puberty, on attaining that age, compelled his adoptive father to emancipate him. (D. i. 7. 33.).

## TIT. XIII.　DE TUTELIS.

Transeamus nunc ad aliam divisionem personarum; nam ex his personis quæ in potestate non sunt, quædam vel in tutela sunt vel in curatione, quædam neutro jure tenentor. Videamus ergo de his qui in tutela vel curatione sunt: ita enim intelligemus ceteras personas quæ neutro jure tenentor. Ac prius dispiciamus de his quæ in tutela sunt.

Let us now proceed to another division of persons. Of those who are not in the power of a parent, some are under a tutor, some under a curator, some under neither. Let us treat, then, of those persons who are under a tutor or curator; for we shall thus ascertain who are they who are not subject to either. And first of persons under a tutor.

GAI. i. 142. 143.

This is rather a subdivision of persons *sui juris* than another division of persons generally. There were some persons who were exempt from the *patria potestas*, and yet required constant protection and assistance. When this arose from youth, or, in the old law of Rome, from the incapacity supposed always to attach to females (*propter animi levitatem*, GAI. 1. 144), the protector was called a *tutor*; when it arose from mental incapacity, he was called a *curator*. The two offices greatly resembled each other; but there was one leading distinction between them. The tutor was said to be given to the person; he not only administered the property of the pupil, but he also supplied what was wanting to complete the pupil's legal character. The *curator* was said to be given to the property: his duty was exclusively to see that the person under his care did not waste his goods.   (See Introd. sec. 43.)

| | |
|---|---|
| 1. Est autem tutela (ut Servius definivit) vis ac potestas in capite libero, ad tuendum eum qui propter ætatem se defendere nequit, jure civili data ac permissa. | 1. Tutelage, as Servius has defined it, is an authority and power over a free person, given and permitted by the civil law, in order to protect one whose tender years prevent him defending himself. |

D. xxvi. 1. 1.

By a free person is meant here one *sui juris*. The power of a tutor (*vis ac potestas* being merely a redundant expression) was either given (*data*) by the civil law, when it devolved on the next of kin, or allowed (*permissa*) by that law, when it was conferred by testament.

| | |
|---|---|
| 2. Tutores autem sunt, qui eam vim ac potestatem habent, exque ipsa re nomen reperunt. Itaque appellantur tutores, quasi tuitores atque defensores, sicut æditui dicuntur qui ædes tuentur. | 2. Tutors are those who have this authority and power, and they take their name from the nature of their office; for they are called tutors, as being protectors (*tuitores*) and defenders; just as those who have the care of the sacred edifices, are called æditui. |
| 3. Permissum est itaque parentibus, liberis impuberibus quos in potestate habent, testamento tutores dare, et hoc in filios filiasque procedit omnimodo. Nepotibus tamen neptibusque ita demum parentes possunt testamento tutores dare, si post mortem eorum in patris sui potestatem non sunt recasuri. Itaque si filius tuus mortis tuæ tempore in potestate tua sit, nepotes ex eo non poterunt testamento tuo tutorem habere, quamvis in potestate tua fuerint: scilicet, quia mortuo te in potestatem patris sui recasuri sunt. | 3. Parents may give tutors by testament to such of their children as have not attained the age of puberty, and are under their power. And this, without any distinction, in the case of all sons and daughters. But grandfathers can only give tutors to their grandchildren when these will not fall under the power of their father on the death of the grandfather. Hence, if your son is in your power at the time of your death, your grandchildren by that son cannot have a tutor appointed them by your testament, although they were in your power; because, at your decease, they will fall under the power of their father. |

Gai. 1. 144. 146.

The law of the Twelve Tables said, '*Uti legassit super pecunia tutelare suæ rei, ita jus esto.*' None but the head of the family could appoint a tutor by testament, and for none but children, or descendants in his power, who were included in the term *sua res*. Further, he could only appoint a tutor for those who, on his death, became *sui juris*, and were under age.

K

4. Cum autem in compluribus aliis causis postumi pro jam natis habentur, et in hac causa placuit non minus postumis quam natis testamento tutores dari posse: si modo in ea causa sint ut, si vivis parentibus nascerentur, sui et in potestate eorum fierent.

4. Posthumous children, as in many other respects, so also in this respect, are considered as already born before the death of their fathers; and tutors may be given by testament to posthumous children, as well as to children already born, provided that the posthumous children, had they been born in the lifetime of their father, would have been *sui heredes*, and in their father's power.

Gai. i. 147.

It was a maxim of Roman law that nothing could be given by testament to an uncertain person, and a posthumous child was looked on in this light, so much so that he could not be heir, nor take a legacy, nor have a tutor appointed by will; afterwards this was so far modified that, as far as regarded the chief of his family, he was looked on as if born in the father's lifetime (*pro jam nato habebatur*); that is, the ascendant might make him heir, disinherit him, give him a legacy, or appoint a tutor for him.

It was not until the time of Justinian that the posthumous child of a stranger was capable of taking under a testament. (See note on Bk. ii. 20, 28.) The words *compluribus in causis* are extracted from Gaius; Justinian left no point of difference between the posthumous child and the child born in its father's lifetime.

By the term *sui heredes* were meant those persons who, on the death of the head of the family, having no one above them in the line of ascent, became *sui juris*, and were the necessary heirs of the deceased, if intestate. (See Introd. sec. 77.)

5. Sed si emancipato filio tutor a patre testamento datus fuerit, confirmandus est ex sententia præsidis omnimodo, id est, sine inquisitione.

5. But, if a father gives a tutor by testament to his emancipated son, the appointment must be confirmed by the sentence of the *præses* in all cases, that is, without inquiry.

D. xxvi. 3, i.

The emancipated child not being in the power of his father, not being the father's *res*, could not, strictly speaking, be subject to the father's directions as to his tutor; but a magistrate had power to carry out an appointment of a tutor in a testament if there was only this technical objection to be surmounted. The wishes of a father were considered so sure an indication to the magistrate of the fittest person to be tutor, that they were always carried out without examining into the snitability of the appointment (*sine inquisitione*), unless some change in the position of the tutor since the making of the testament made him obviously unfit for the office. (D. xxvi. 111. 8. 9.)

A father could appoint by testament a tutor for his natural children if he left them property; and the mother, the patron, and indeed any one who left property to infants *sui juris*, might appoint a tutor by testament, and the magistrate carried out the appointment, but in these cases not until he had examined all the circumstances of the case. (D. xxvi. 111. 2. 4.)

## Tit. XIV. QUI TESTAMENTO TUTORES DARI POSSUNT.

| | |
|---|---|
| Dari autem potest tutor non solum paterfamilias, sed etiam filiusfamilias. | Not only a father of a family may be appointed a tutor, but also a son of a family. |

The office of tutor was looked on as in some respects a public one, as the tutor supplied what was wanting to the *persona* of a citizen; and a *filiusfamilias* was always capable of holding any public office. (D. i. 6. 9.)

Any one could be made a tutor with whom there was the *testamenti factio* (D. xxvi. 2. 21), or, in other words, any one who had the rights of citizenship sufficiently to enable him to go through the peculiar forms of Roman law.

1. Sed et servus proprius testamento cum libertate recte tutor dari potest. Sed sciendum est cum, et sine libertate tutorem datum, tacite libertalem directam accepisse videri, et per hoc recte tutorem esse. Plane si per errorem quasi liber tutor datus sit, aliud dicendum est. Servus autem alienus pure inutiliter testamento datur tutor; sed ita cum liberterit, utiliter datur. Proprius autem servus inutiliter eo modo tutor datur.

1. A man may also by testament appoint as a tutor his own slave, at the same time giving him his liberty. But it must be observed that if a slave be appointed tutor without an express gift of liberty, he is still held to receive by implication a direct freedom, and thus can legally accept the office of tutor. If, however, it is by mistake, and from the testator supposing him to be free, that he is appointed tutor, the decision would be different. The appointment of a slave belonging to another person as tutor is ineffectual, if unconditional; but is valid when made with this condition 'when he shall be free.' If, however, any one appoints his own slave with such a condition, the appointment is void.

A slave was incapable of holding any legal office.  It was therefore necessary to enfranchise him in order that he might become a tutor.  If the appointment were made without express enfranchisement, it was the opinion of Paul (D. xxvi. 2. 32.) that the appointment implied enfranchisement, and this as if given by the testator himself (*directa*), and not entrusted to his heir to give (*fideicommissaria*).  Valerian and Gallian, however, decided subsequently by a rescript (C. vii. 4. 9), that it was only a *libertas fideicommissaria*) which such an appointment carried with it.  Justinian here restores the authority of the former opinion.

The appointment of the slave of another carried with it the *libertas fideicommissaria*, that is, it was incumbent on the heir to purchase and emancipate the slave, who could then discharge the office of tutor.  (D. xxvi. 2. 10. 4.)  If the heir was not able to purchase the slave, then the slave could not act as tutor until he gained his freedom in some other way.  Even if the testator had not used the words *cum liber erit*, or some corresponding expression, he was presumed to have intended to have used them unless a contrary intention appeared.  (Cod. vii. 4. 9.)  If a testator said of his own slave that he was to be tutor when free, this showed that the testator, who had the power to enfranchise him, did not choose to exercise it; and as he thus voluntarily made his own appointment void the law would not help him.

2. Furiosus vel minor viginti quinque annis tutor testamento datus tutor erit, cum compos mentis aut major viginti quinque annis factus fuerit.

2. If a madman or a person under the age of twenty-five years is by testament appointed tutor, the one is to begin to act when he becomes of sound mind, and the other when he has completed his twenty-fifth year.

D. xxvi. 1. 11 ; xxvi. 2. 32. 2.

Meanwhile the magistrate would appoint another tutor. (See Tit. 20.)

3. Ad certum tempus, seu ex certo tempore, vel sub conditione, vel ante heredis institutionem posse dari tutorem non dubitatur.

3. There is no doubt that a tutor may be appointed either until a certain time, or from a certain time, or conditionally, or before the institution of an heir.

The old law regarded the naming the persons designed to take as heirs under the testament as the base of the testament, and passed over every declaration of the testator's wishes placed before this as out of due order and entirely void.  The Proculians (Gai. ii. 231) thought this ought not to be extended to the appointment of a tutor, and Justinian did away with the doctrine altogether.

4. Certæ autem rei vel causæ tutor dari non potest, quia personæ non causæ vel rei datur.

4. A tutor cannot be appointed for a particular thing or business, as it is to a person, and not for a business or a thing, that a tutor is appointed.

D. xxvi. 2. 12. 14.

The tutor had to take charge of the whole interests of the pupil, and therefore to appoint him to take charge of his interest in any one matter only was inconsistent with the nature of his office, and such an appointment was void. (D. xxvi. 2. 13.) If, however, the property of the pupil was situated in provinces far apart from each other, a separate tutor might be appointed to take care of his interests in each province. (D. xxvi. 2. 15.)

5. Si quis filiabus suis vel filiis tutores dederit, etiam postumæ vel postumo dedisse videtur ; quia filii vel filiæ appellatione postumus vel postuma continetur. Quod si nepotes sint, an appellatione filiorum et ipsis tutores dati sunt ? Dicendum est ut ipsis quoque dati videantur, si modo liberos dixit : ceterum si filios, non continebuntur ; aliter enim filii, aliter nepotes appellantur. Plane si postumis dederit, tam filii postumi quam ceteri liberi continebuntur.

5. If any one appoint a tutor to his sons or daughters, he is held also to appoint him as tutor to his posthumous children; because under the appellation of son or daughter, a posthumous son or daughter is included. But if there are grandchildren, are they included in the appointment of a tutor to sons? We answer, that under an appointment to children, grandchildren are included, but not under an appointment to sons; for son and grandson are quite distinct words. But, if a testator appoints a tutor to his posthumous descendants, the term obviously includes all posthumous children, whether sons or grandsons.

## Tit. XV.   DE LEGITIMA ADGNATORUM TUTELA.

Quibus autem testamento tutor datus non sit, his ex lege duodecim tabularum adgnati sunt tutores, qui vocantur legitimi.

They to whom no tutor has been appointed by testament have their Agnati as tutors, by the law of the Twelve Tables, and such tutors are called ' legal tutors.'

D. xxvi. 4. 1 ; Gai. i. 155.

Tutores legitimi was a general term applied to all tutors appointed by law, and especially by the law of the Twelve Tables, or according to some inference from its provisions, as in the case of patrons.  We do not know the exact terms of the law of the Twelve Tables on this subject.

1. Sunt autem, adgnati, cognati per virilis sexus cognationem conjuncti, quasi a patre cognati; veluti frater eodem patre natus, patris filius neposve ex eo; item patruus et patrui filius, neposve ex eo. At qui per feminini sexus personas cognatione junguntur, non sunt adgnati, sed alias naturali jure cognati. Itaque amitæ tuæ filius non est tibi agnatus, sed cognatus, et invicem scilicet tu illi eodem jure conjungeris; quia qui nascuntur, patris non matris familiam sequuntur.

1. *Agnati* are those who are related to each other through males, that is, as related through the father, as a brother by the same father, or the son of a brother, or the son of such a son; or, again, a father's brother, or a father's brother's son, or the son of such a son.  But those who are related to us through females are not *agnati*, but merely *cognati* by their natural relationship.  Thus the son of a father's sister is related to you not by agnation but by cognation, and you are also related to him by cognation; as children belong to the family of their father, and not to that of their mother.

Gai. i. 156.

The law gave the right of relationship, such as inheritance and appointment as tutors, to the *agnati* only.  All persons, related by ties of blood, were *cognati* to each other.  Within this larger circle the members of any one family were *agnati* to each other.  A family, in this sense, consisted of all persons related to each other, by having a common ancestor, in whose power, if he were alive, they would all be.  A brother and sister, for instance, were *agnati*; and a nephew and aunt, by the father's side.  For if the grandfather were alive, all would be in his power.  But the tie was dissolved by the sister or aunt marrying *in manum* (see Introd. sec. 46); and as the children of females would be in the power of the husband, they could never be *agnati* to their mother's *agnati*, except by adoption; and hence it is here said that *agnati* are related through males only.  By the 118th Nov. Justinian abolished the distinction between *agnati* and *cognati*, and the nearest in blood was thenceforth the *tutor legitimus*.

2. Quod autem lex ab intestato vocat ad tutelam adgnatos, non hanc habet significationem, si omnino non fecerit testamentum is qui poterat tutorem dare; sed si, quantum ad tutelam pertinet, intestatus decesserit; quod tunc quoque accidere intelligitur, cum is qui datus est tutor, vivo testatore decesserit.

2. The law of the Twelve Tables, calling the *agnati* to be tutors in case of intestacy, does not refer merely to the case of a person who might have appointed a tutor, dying without having made any testament at all, but also to that of a person dying intestate only so far as regards the appointment of a tutor, and this includes the case of a tutor nominated by testament, dying in the lifetime of the testator.

D. xxvi. 4. 6.

It was necessary to state expressly that the testament was good, as far as it went, and that the law remedied its deficiency by making the *agnati* tutors, because it was a maxim of Roman law that a man could not die partly testate and partly intestate.

| | |
|---|---|
| 3. Sed adgnationis quidem jus omnibus modis capitis deminutione plerumque perimitur, nam adgnatio juris est nomen. Cognationis vero jus non omnibus modis commutatur; quia civilis ratio civilia quidem jura corrumpere potest, naturalia vero non utique. | 3. The right of agnation is ordinarily taken away by every *capitis deminutio*, or change of *status*, for agnation is a civil right: but the right of cognation is not lost by every kind of *capitis deminutio*, for although civil law may destroy civil rights, it cannot destroy natural rights. |

GAI. i. 158.

The tie of agnation being created by law, could also be dissolved by it: not so that of cognation, which was a tie of nature. But the law could take away the legal rights attaching to the natural tie; and this it did in the case of the *maxima capitis deminutio*. (See next Title, 6.)

## Tit. XVI. DE CAPITIS DEMINUTIONE.

| | |
|---|---|
| Est autem capitis deminutio prioris *status* commutatio, eaque tribus modis accidit: nam aut maxima est capitis deminutio, aut minor quam quidam mediam vocant, aut minima. | The *capitis deminutio* is a change of *status*, which may happen in three ways: for it is either the greatest *capitis deminutio*, the low, also called the middle, or the least. |

GAI. i. 159.

In examining the subject of *status*, we have to consider not only the position of those who have it, and of those who have not it, but also of those who having had it, lose it. By *capitis deminutio* is meant the loss of *status*, the ceasing to have the capacity to hold and be subject to rights. If a freeman lost his liberty or underwent the greatest *capitis deminutio*, he ceased to have any legal capacity at all, and therefore the loss of the *status libertatis* involved the loss of the *status civitatis* and the *status familiæ*. The loss of the *status civitatis* involved the loss of the *status familiæ*, but did not involve the loss of the *status libertatis*.

| | |
|---|---|
| 1. Maxima capitis deminutio est, cum aliquis simul et civitatem et libertatem amittit: quod accidit in his qui servi pœnæ efficiuntur atrocitate sententiæ, vel libertis ut ingratis erga patronos condemnatis, | 1. The greater *capitis deminutio* is, when a man loses both his citizenship and his liberty; as they do who by a terrible sentence are made 'the slaves of punishment;' and freedmen, condemned to slavery for ingratitude |

vel qui se ad pretium participandum  
venumdari passi sunt.    .

towards their patrons; and all those  
who suffer themselves to be sold in  
order to share the price obtained.

Gai. i. 160; D. xxviii. 8. 6. 6; xxv. 3. 7. 1.

For the meaning of *servi pœnæ*, see Tit. 12. sec. 3.

2. Minor sive media capitis demi-  
nutio est, cum civitas quidem amit-  
titur, libertas vero retinetur: quod  
accidit ei cui aqua et igni inter-  
dictum fuerit, vel ei qui in insulam  
deportatus est.

2. The less or middle *capitis demi-*  
*nutio* is, when a man loses his citi-  
zenship, but retains his liberty; as is  
the case when any one is forbidden  
the use of fire and water, or is de-  
ported to an island.

Gai. i. 161.

In this kind of *capitis deminutio*, as well as in the preceding,
the position in the *familia* was lost, its rights belonging only
to citizens.  In this lesser kind, freedom is preserved; but the
person who undergoes the change of *status* becomes a stranger,
*peregrinus fit*. (Ulp. *Reg.* 10. 3.)  It was a maxim of Roman
law, that no one could cease to be a citizen against his will.
*Civitatem nemo unquam ullo populi jussu amittit invitus.*
(Cic. *pro Dom.* 29.)  The condemned was therefore denied the
necessaries of life, until he was driven to withdraw himself
from the city.  *Id autem ut esset faciendum, non ademptione*
*civitatis, sed tecti, et aquæ et ignis interdictione faciebant.* (Cic.
*pro Dom.* 30.)  The *aquæ et ignis interdictio* thus became a
form by which a sentence of perpetual banishment was inflicted.
The *deportatio in insulam* superseded this form. (D. xlviii. 29.
2.)  The person who was banished was confined to certain
limits, out of which he could not stir without rendering himself punishable with death.  This must be kept distinct from
simple *relegatio*, which was also an exile within prescribed
limits, but did not in any way affect the *status*. (D. xlviii.
22. 7.)

3. Minima capitis deminutio est  
cum et civitas et libertas retinetur,  
sed status hominis commutatur;  
quod accidit in his qui, cum sui  
juris fuerint, cœperunt alieno juri  
subjecti esse, vel contra.

3. The least *capitis deminutio* is,  
when a person's *status* is changed  
without forfeiture either of citizen-  
ship or liberty; as when a person *sui*  
*juris* becomes subject to the power  
of another, or a person *alieni juris*  
becomes independent.

Gai. i. 102.

The *status* was not impaired by the change of family, but
the family position of the citizen was altered.  Therefore Ulpian
says the *minima capitis deminutio* takes place *salvo statu*.
(D. xxxviii. 17. 1.)  What is said here of change of family
by arrogation and emancipation must be extended to adoption.

(D. iv. 5. 9.)  In old times, the wife who passed *in manum viri*, or the freeman who was given *in mancipio* underwent this *minima capitis deminutio*. (GAI. 1. 162.)

After the words *vel contra*, at the end of this paragraph, some texts have the following words: *veluti si filiusfamilias a patre emancipatus fuerit, est capite deminutus*. The addition is probably owing to some writer having perceived that it was only in the case of emancipation that it was true that when a person became *sui juris* he was *capite minutus*. There was no change of family when a son became *sui juris* on the death of his father.

| | |
|---|---|
| 4. Servus autem manumissus capite non minuitur, quia nullum caput habuit. | 4. A slave who is manumitted is not said to be *capite minutus*, as he has no '*caput*,' or civil existence. |

D. iv. 8. 3. 1.

| | |
|---|---|
| 5. Quibus autem dignitas magis quam status permutatur, capite non minuuntur; et ideo senatu motum capite non minui constat. | 5. Those whose dignity rather than their *status* is changed, do not suffer a *capitis deminutio*, as those, for instance, who are removed from the senatorial dignity. |

D. i. 9. 9.

| | |
|---|---|
| 6. Quod autem dictum est manere cognationis jus et post capitis deminutionem, hoc ita est, si minima capitis deminutio interveniat; manet enim cognatio. Nam si maxima capitis deminutio currat, jus quoque cognationis perit, ut puta servitute alicujus cognati; et ne quidem si manumissus fuerit, recipit cognationem. Sed et si in insulam quis deportatus sit, cognatio solvitur. | 6. In saying, that the right of cognation remains in spite of a *capitis deminutio*, we were speaking only of the least *deminutio*, after which the cognation subsists. For, by the greater *deminutio*, as, for example, if one of the *cognati* becomes a slave, the right of cognation is wholly destroyed, so as not to be recovered even by manumission. So, too, the right of cognation is lost by the less or middle *deminutio*, as, for example, by deportation to an island. |

D. xxxviii. 8. 5. 7.

A change of the civil family by adoption or arrogation never dissolved the natural tie of *cognatio*, or destroyed its attendant civil rights; but these were destroyed by a sentence which involved the loss of the *civitas*. And if the *civitas* were once lost and then regained, the restored or rather new, *civis*, was in all respects the founder of a new family, excepting when he was *restitutus in integrum*, that is, restored by the emperor to the same position that he had formerly held. (See Tit. 12. 1.)

| | |
|---|---|
| 7. Cum autem ad adgnatos tutela pertineat, non simul ad omnes pertinet, sed ad eos tantum qui proximiore gradu sunt, vel si plures ejus- | 7. The right to be tutor, which belongs to the *agnati*, does not belong to all at the same time, but to the nearest in degree only; or, if |

dem gradus sunt ad omnes: relati si plures fratres sunt qui unam gradum obtinent, ideoque pariter ad tutelam vocantur.

there are many in the same degree, then to all in that degree. Several brothers, for instance, in the same degree, are all equally called to be tutor.

GAI. i. 164.

The principle of the law was, that those persons should have the burden of the tutelage who had the hope of the succession. (Tit. 17. pr.) The nearest in degree of the *agnati* were therefore the tutors in case of intestacy. The nearest in degree might, however, happen to be a woman or an infant, and then, although this person was the next in succession to the inheritance, it was necessary to go a step further off to find the tutor. (D. xxvi. 4. 1. 1.)

## Tit. XVII. DE LEGITIMA PATRONORUM TUTELA.

Ex eadem lege duodecim tabularum, libertorum et libertarum tutela ad patronos liberosque eorum pertinet. Quæ et ipsa legitima tutela vocatur, non quia nominatim in ea lege de hac tutela caveatur, sed quia perinde accepta est per interpretationem, atque si verbis legis introducta esset. Eo enim ipso quod hereditates libertorum libertarumque, si intestati decessissent, jusserat lex ad patronos liberosve eorum pertinere, crediderunt reteres voluisse legem etiam tutelas ad eos pertinere: cum et adgnatos quos ad hereditatem lex vocat, eosdem et tutores esse jussit; quia plerumque ubi successionis est emolumentum, ibi et tutelæ onus esset debet. Ideo autem diximus plerumque, quia si a femina impubes manumittatur, ipsa ad hereditatem vocatur, cum alius sit tutor.

By the same law of the Twelve Tables, the tutelage of freedmen and freedwomen belongs to their patrons, and to the children of their patrons; and this tutelage is called legal tutelage, not that the law contains any express provision on the subject, but because it has been as firmly established by interpretation, as if it had been introduced by the express words of the law. For, as the law had ordered that patrons and their children should succeed to the inheritance of their freedmen or freedwomen who should die intestate, the ancients were of opinion that the intent of the law was that the tutelage also belonged to them; since the law, which calls *agnati* to the inheritance, also appoints them to be tutors, in most cases, where the advantage of the succession is, there also ought to be the burden of the tutelage. We say 'in most cases,' because, if a person below the age of puberty is manumitted by a female, she is called to the inheritance, although another person is tutor.

GAI. I. 165, D. xxvi. 4. 1. 3.

The law gave the patron the right of succession to the inheritance of the freedman; and as the right of succession was connected with the tutelage in the case of the *agnati*, it seemed natural to connect the two in the case of the patron.

## Tit. XVIII. DE LEGITIMA PARENTIUM TUTELA.

Exemplo patronorum recepta est et alia tutela, quæ et ipsa legitima vocatur; nam si quis filium aut filiam, nepotem aut neptem ex filio et deinceps impuberes emancipaverit, legitimus eorum tutor erit.

In imitation of the tutelage of patrons, there is, too, another kind which also is said to be legal; for if a parent emancipate, below the age of puberty, a son, a daughter, a grandson, or a granddaughter, who is the issue of that son, or any other descendant, he is their legal tutor.

GAI. i. 175.

It was not the sales by the father which emancipated the son, but the subsequent enfranchisement after these sales had destroyed the father's power, and made the son a *mancipium* of the fictitious purchaser. Sometimes, probably generally, the purchaser resold (*remancipavit*) the son thus *in mancipio* to the father, who freed him, and thus became his *patronus* and his *tutor legitimus*. If the purchaser did not resell him, but himself emancipated him, he became the *patronus*, and so the *tutor*; but as the whole proceeding was but a form, he became only a *tutor fiduciarius*. (GAI. i. 160. 172. 175: ULP. *Reg.* xi. 5; D. xxvi. 4. 3. 1.)

## Tit. XIX. DE FIDUCIARIA TUTELA.

Est et alia tutela quæ fiduciaria appellatur; nam si parens filium vel filiam, nepotem vel neptem vel deinceps impuberes manumiserit, legitimam nanciscitur eorum tutelam; quo defuncto, si liberi virilis sexus ei extant, fiduciarii tutores filiorum suorum, vel fratris vel sororis et ceterorum efficiuntur. Atqui patrono legitimo tutore mortuo, liberi quoque ejus legitimi sunt tutores. Quoniam filius quidem defuncti, si non esset a vivo patre emancipatus, post obitum ejus sui juris efficeretur, nec in fratrum potestatem recideret, ideoque nec in tutelam; libertus autem, si servus mansisset, utique eodem jure apud liberos domini post mortem ejus futurus esset. Ita tamen hi ad tutelam vocantur, si perfectæ ætatis sunt. Quod nostra constitutio gene-

There is another kind of tutelage called fiduciary; for, if a parent emancipate, below the age of puberty, a son, or a daughter, a grandson or a granddaughter, or any other descendant, he is their legal tutor; but if, at his death, he leave male children, they become the fiduciary tutors of their own sons, or brother, or sister, or other descendants of the deceased. But when a patron, who is a legal tutor, dies, his children also become legal tutors, the reason being that a son, although never emancipated, becomes independent at the death of his father, and does not fall under power of his brother, nor, therefore, under his tutelage. The freedman, on the contrary, had he remained a slave, would also have been, after the death of his master, the slave of his master's children.

| | |
|---|---|
| raliter in omnibus tutelis et cura-tionibus observari præcepit. | These persons, however, are not called to be tutors unless of full age, a rule which by our constitution ap-plies generally to all tutors and cu-rators. |

D. xxvi. 4. 3, 4; C. v. 30. 5.

The person who emancipated the child succeeded to all the rights of a patron over the child; if it was the father, then, as being a patron, he was included in the terms of the law of the Twelve Tables, and was a *tutor legitimus* (GAI. i. 172; D. xxvi. 4. 3–10); if it was not, he was a *tutor fiduciarius* (GAI. i. 166), a tutor bound to the father by a trust. In the case of a slave, the children of a patron succeeded to the rights of patronage; but this did not extend to the case of emancipated children: the children not emancipated were not the patrons of those who were. They were not tutors, therefore, by the law of the Twelve Tables, and the word *fiduciarii* is borrowed from its more proper usage to express their position, and is in this case merely opposed to *legitimi*. (D. xxvi. 4. 4.) The reason given in the text for their being only *tutores fiduciarii*, viz. that the emancipated infant would have been *sui juris* if he had not been emancipated, is mani-festly an imperfect one. For it would not be necessarily true when a grandfather emancipated his grandson, who, if his father were living, would not on the grandfather's death become *sui juris*. If the father of the emancipated child left no other children above the age of puberty, the nearest *agnatus*, as, for instance, the father's brother, was the *tutor*, and he, too, was called the *tutor fiduciarius*. (THEOPH. *Paraph.*)

The *perfecta ætas* was the age of twenty-five years.

## TIT. XX. DE ATILIANO TUTORE ET EO QUI EX LEGE JULIA ET TITIA DABITUR.

| | |
|---|---|
| Si cui nullus omnino tutor fuerit, ei dabatur, in urbe quidem Romaa prætore urbano et majore parte tri-bunorum plebis tutor ex lege Atilia; in provinciis vero, a præsidibus pro-vinciarum ex lege Julia et Titia. | If any one had no tutor at all, one was given him in the city of Rome by the *prætor urbanus*, and a ma-jority of the tribunes of the plebs, under the *lex Atilia*; in the pro-vinces, appointed by the *præsides* under the *lex Julia et Titia*. |

GAI. i. 185.

The date of the *lex Atilia* is unknown, but it must have been in existence in the year of the city 557, when Livy

(xxxix. 9) says of a *liberta*, '*Post patroni mortem, quia nullius in manu esset, tutore a tribunis et prætore petito.*' And as the necessity for some means of appointing a tutor, where one was not appointed by testament or law, must have been early felt, the *lex Atilia*, or one similar to it, must probably have existed long before the time of which Livy speaks. The date of the *lex Julia et Titia* was probably 721 A.U.C.

The term *tutor dativus* was used to express a tutor given by the magistrate; it also included a tutor appointed by testament. (GAI. i. 154; D. xxvi. 4. 5.)

1. Sed et si testamento tutor sub conditione aut die certo datus fuerat, quamdiu conditio aut dies pendebat, ex iisdem legibus tutor dari poterat. Item si pure datus fuerat, quamdiu ex testamento nemo heres existebat, tamdiu ex iisdem legibus tutor, petendus erat: qui detinebat esse tutor, si conditio existeret, aut dies veniret, aut heres existeret.

1. Again, if a testamentary tutor had been appointed conditionally, or from a certain time, until the completion of the condition or arrival of the time fixed, another tutor might be appointed under the same laws. Also, if a tutor had been given unconditionally, yet, as long as no one had accepted the inheritance, as heir by the testament, another tutor might be appointed for the interval. But his office ceased when the condition was accomplished, when the time arrived, or the inheritance was entered upon.

GAI. i. 186; D. xxvi. 2. 11.

If the wishes of the testator were declared to any extent respecting the appointment of a tutor, this entirely excluded the *tutores legitimi* and every deficiency in the declaration was remedied by the interposition of the magistrate. (D. xxvi. 2. 11.)

No testament took effect until an heir entered on the inheritance. If it was known that a testament existed appointing a tutor, this excluded the *agnati* from being tutors; but the tutor under the testament did not commence his *tutela* until the testament took effect. Meantime, then, a tutor appointed by the magistrate took care of the pupil.

2. Ab hostibus quoque tutore capto, ex his legibus tutor petebatur: qui desinebat esse tutor, si is qui captus erat, in civitatem reversus fuerat; nam reversus recipiebat tutelam jure postliminii.

2. If, again, a tutor was taken prisoner by the enemy, application could be made, under the same laws, for another tutor, whose office ceased when the first tutor returned from captivity; for on his return he resumed the tutelage by the *jus postliminii*.

GAI. i. 187.

For an account of the *jus postliminii*, see Title 12. 5.

3. Sed ex his legibus tutores pupillis desierunt dari, postesaquam primo consules pupillis utriusque sexus tutores ex inquisitione dare coeperunt. deinde praetores ex constitutionibus; nam supradictis legibus, neque de cautione a tutoribus exigenda rem salvam pupillis fore, neque de compellendis tutoribus ad tutelae administrationem quicquam cavebatur.

3. But tutors have ceased to be appointed under these laws, since they have been appointed to pupils of either sex, first by the consuls, after inquiry into the case, and afterwards by the praetors under imperial constitutions. For the above-mentioned laws required no security from the tutors for the safety of the pupils' property, nor did they contain any provisions to compel them to accept the office.

The power to appoint tutors was given by Claudius to the consuls (SUET. *in Claud.* 23), and transferred by Antoninus Pius (JUL. CAPIT. *in Vit. M. Anton.* 10) to the praetors.

4. Sed hoc Jure utimur, ut Romae quidem praefectus urbi vel praetor secundum suam jurisdictionem, in provinciis autem praesides ex inquisitione tutores crearent; vel magistratus jussu praesidum, si non sint magnae pupilli facultates.

4. Under our present system tutors are appointed at Rome by the praefect of the city, or the praetor, according to his jurisdiction, and, in the provinces, by the *praesides* after inquiry; or by an inferior magistrate, at the command of the *praeses*, if the property of the pupil is only small.

D. xxvi. 6. 1.

The *praefectus urbi* was, from the time of Augustus, an officer who had the superintendence of the city and its police, with jurisdiction extending one hundred miles from the city, and power to decide on both civil and criminal cases. As he was considered the direct representative of the emperor, much that previously belonged to the *praetor urbanus* fell gradually into his hands. The *praefectus urbi* appointed tutors in cases where pupils of higher rank and larger fortune were concerned; the *praetor*, when the pupils were of humbler station and smaller fortune; and this it is which is alluded to in the words *secundum suam jurisdictionem*.

In the provinces the *praeses* appointed; but until Justinian altered the law (see next paragraph), not only could not municipal magistrates appoint without the authority of the *praeses*, but no one could be authorized by the *praeses* unless he were a magistrate, or some one who, by virtue of his office, could exercise a delegated choice. (D. xxvi. 5. 8.)

5. Nos autem per constitutionem nostram, et hujusmodi difficultates hominum revocantes, nec expectata jussione praesidum, disposuimus, si facultas pupilli vel adulti usque ad quingentos solidos valeat, defensores civitatum una cum ejusdem

5. But by one of our constitutions, to do away with these distinctions of different persons, and to avoid the necessity of waiting for the order of the *praeses*, we have enacted, that if the property of the pupil or adult amount to five hundred *solidi*,

civitatis religiosissimo antistite, vel alias publicas personas, id est, magistratus vel juridicum Alexandrinæ civitatis tutores vel curatores creare, legitima cautela secundum ejusdem constitutionis normam præstanda, videlicet eorum periculo qui eam accipiunt.

tutors shall be appointed by the *defensores* of the city acting in conjunction with the religious head of the place, or by other public persons, that is, by the magistrates, or, in the city of Alexandria, by the judge; and legal security must be given according to the terms of the same constitution, that is to say, at the risk of those who receive it.

Cod. i. 4. 30.

The change made by Justinian was that, where the fortune of the person requiring a tutor or curator did not amount to more than 500 *solidi* (the *aureus*, £1. 1s. 1d. of English money, after the time of Alexander Severus, was called a *solidus*), a local magistrate could appoint, not making a formal examination into the position and character of the tutor or curator (*inquisitio*), but merely taking a money security for his faithful performance of his duties.

The *defensor* was a magistrate appointed for two years out of the *decuriones* of a city. His principal business was to act as a check on the *præses*, and he had besides a limited civil and criminal jurisdiction.

6. Impuberes autem in tutela esse naturali juri conveniens est, ut is qui perfectæ ætatis non sit, alterius tutela regatur.

6. It is agreeable to the law of nature, that persons under the age of puberty should be under tutelage, so that persons of tender years may be under the government of another.

Gai. i. 189.

Gaius, in his Institutes, after the words extracted from him in the text, proceeds to contrast with the tutelage of minors, which is an institution natural and necessary in all communities, the tutelage of women, which he considers founded on no reasonable basis.  The original reason of this tutelage was probably the incapability of women to share in the proceedings of the *curia*, and their being supposed unfit to go through solemn forms.  In default of a testamentary tutor, the nearest *agnatus* was the tutor, women being either *alieni juris*, or else under a tutor all their lives.  The *lex Papia Poppæa* exempted from tutelage women who had three children, and a *lex Claudia* (A.D. 45) suppressed the tutelage of the *agnati* altogether in the case of women of free birth, leaving only the tutelage of ascendants and patrons.  (Gai. i. 157.)  This modified tutelage of women existed in the time of Ulpian (*Reg.* 11. 6), but had fallen into desuetude in the time of Justinian.

7. Cum igitur papillorum pupillarumque tutores negotia gerunt,

7. As tutors administer the affairs of their pupils, they may be com-

post pubertatem tutelæ judicio rationes reddunt.

pelled to account, by the *actio tutelæ*, when their pupils arrive at puberty.

GAI. i. 191.

The modes by which the faithful discharge of his duty by a tutor was insured are given in the 24th Title.

## TIT. XXI.   DE AUCTORITATE TUTORUM.

Auctoritas autem tutoris in quibusdam causis necessaria pupillis est, in quibusdam non est necessaria. Ut ecce, si quid dari sibi stipulentur, non est necessaria tutoris auctoritas; quod si aliis pupilli promittant, necessaria est: namque placuit meliorem quidem suam conditionem licere eis facere, etiam sine tutore auctore, deteriorem vero non aliterquam tutoris auctoritate. Unde in his causis ex quibus obligationes mutuæ nascuntur; ut in emptionibus, venditionibus, locationibus, conductionibus, mandatis, depositis, si tutoris auctoritas non intervenist, ipsi quidem qui cum his contrahunt, obligantur; at invicem pupilli non obligantur.

In some cases it is necessary that the tutor should authorize the acts of the pupil, in others not. When, for instance, the pupil stipulates for something to be given him, the authorization of the tutor is not requisite; but if the pupil makes the promise, it is requisite; for the rule is, that pupils may make their condition better, but may not make it worse, without the authorization of their tutor. And therefore in all cases of reciprocal obligation, as in contracts of buying, selling, letting, hiring, bailment, deposit, if the tutor does not authorize the pupil to enter into the contract, the person who contracts with the pupil is bound, but the pupil is not bound.

D. xix. 1. 13. 29.

There were many things in which the Roman law, in its stricter times, did not allow one person to represent another. Much that to us seems only to belong to private life was bound up with political and public duties and rights. (See Introd. sec. 43.) The law could not contemplate one beneath the age of puberty acting as if he were a member of the *curia*, or any one else coming forward to fill for him his place in the list of citizens. No one else could bring actions of strict law in another name, or go through, for another, the fictitious process of *in jure cessio*, or through the forms of manumission and adoption, or perform for another any of those acts to which a solemn ceremony was attached, such as mancipation or stipulation. (D. xl. 2. 24; D. xlvi. 4. 13. 10.) It was necessary that a minor should himself go through the forms and repeat the words requisite for the validity of such transactions; but it was also necessary that the tutor should be present and give his sanction. The *auctoritas* of the tutor was the complement (*auctoritas* is derived from *augeo*) to the symbolical forms through which the child went. (See Introd. sec. 43.) It re-

presented the intention or the mental act on which those forms
ultimately rested. If the child could not speak, of course no
such forms could be used ; if he could speak, but could not
understand the import of what he said, or, in technical language, if, being still *infanti proximus*, he had as yet little or
no *intellectus* (GAI. iii. 109), the tutor could but very rarely,
by interposing his sanction, give legal validity to words uttered
without understanding. It was only when the act would confer
a very great and very clear benefit on the child, that this was
allowed. (D. xxix. 2. 9.) But when the child had entered on
his eighth year, and was now *pubertati proximus*, he was considered to have *intellectus*, but not *judicium* (THEOPH. *Paraph.*
on Bk iii. 19. 9) ; that is, he understood the meaning of the
form ; but could not decide for himself whether it was to his
advantage to go through the act or not. This want of judgment the tutor supplied ; and in every case where the tutor
gave his sanction, the act was legally valid. In some cases,
such as that of a stipulation (see Introd. sec. 83), or accepting
an inheritance (see next paragraph), the pupil could do nothing
without the authority of the tutor, while the tutor could not
represent the pupil, but both were obliged to act together.
Contracts of a less formal kind could be made by the tutor
alone as the agent of the pupil, and of course could be made
by the pupil if the tutor gave his sanction. Justinian, in the
concluding part of this Title, discusses the effect of the pupil
acting in such cases without this sanction, and states that the
minor, in cases of bilateral contracts, took every benefit, but
sustained no injury from the contract; because, while his tender
years shielded him, the person with whom he contracted, having
by the agreement made a formal expression of his will, must
abide the event. But when it is said that a pupil took every
benefit of the contract, it must not be understood that he
could continue to enjoy at pleasure the advantages of another's
property without giving anything for the enjoyment. The
original owner might reclaim the property ; and if a profit was
being derived from its possession, might take that profit to
himself. (D. xxvi. 8. 5. 1.) Only he could never make the
pupil restore or refund anything that was once gone; and while
a pupil could always disclaim an executory contract made to
his disadvantage, he could always, through the intervention
of his tutor, enforce one that promised to benefit him.

1. Neque tamen hereditatem adi-
ire, neque bonorum possessionem
potere, neque hereditatem ex fideicommisso suscipere aliter possunt,

1. Pupils, however, cannot, without the authorization of the tutor,
enter on an inheritance, demand the
possession of goods, or take an in-

nisi tutoris auctoritate quamvis illis lucrosa sit, nec ullum damnum habeat.

heritance given by a *fideicommissum*, even though to do so would be to their gain, and could involve them in no risk.

D. xxvi. 8. 9. 11.

The *hereditas* was the legal succession to the property of the deceased, the *bonorum possessio* here spoken of was an interest in the property of a deceased person, accorded by the prætor, and the *hereditas ex fideicommisso* was a succession received through the intervention of a trustee appointed by the testator. (See Introd. sec. 76.)

It was not any risk which might attach to accepting the inheritance that originated the rule that the pupil was unable to accept it unless with the authority of his tutor, for the text says, *quamvis lucrosa sit*, but the act of accepting was too formal and solemn a one for a minor to go through.

2. Tutor antem statim, in ipso negotio, præsens debet auctor fieri, si hoc pupillo prodesse existimaverit. Post tempus vero aut per epistolam interposita auctoritas nihil agit.

2. A tutor who wishes to authorize any act, which he esteems advantageous to his pupil, should do so at once while the business is going on, and in person, for his authorisation is of no effect if given afterwards or by letter.

D. xxvi. 8. 9. 5.

3. Si inter tutorem pupillumque judicium agendum sit, quia ipse tutor in re sua auctor esse non potest, non prætorius tutor ut olim constituitur, sed curator in locum ejus datur : quo interveniente judicium peragitur, et eo peracto curator esse desinit.

3. When a suit is to be commenced between a tutor and his pupil, as the tutor cannot authorise anything in a matter pertaining to himself, a curator, and not, as formerly, a prætorian tutor, is appointed, by whose assistance the suit is carried on, and who ceases to be curator when the suit is determined.

Gai. I. 184.

Although the person who assisted the pupil in an action in which the tutor was concerned did exactly what the tutor did for the pupil in any other action, and thus, as having to authorize the proceedings, might be spoken of as a tutor (Ulp. Reg. 11. 24), yet, as he was given for a particular purpose, which tutors were not (see Tit. 14. 4), it was very natural that he should, in preference, receive the name of *curator*.

Subsequently the 72nd Novel (cap. 1) provided that, if the pupil became at any time the debtor of the tutor, another tutor or curator should be added to protect the pupil.

## Tit. XXII. QUIBUS MODIS TUTELA FINITUR.

Pupilli pupillæque cum puberes esse cœperint, tutela liberantur. Pubertatem autem veteres quidem non solum ex annis, sed etiam ex habitu corporis in masculis æstimari volebant. Nostra autem majestas dignum esse castitate nostrorum temporum bene putavit, quod in feminis et antiquis impudicum esse visum est, id est, inspectionem habitudinis corporis, hoc etiam in masculos extendere. Et ideo sancta constitutione promulgata, pubertatem in masculis post quartum decimum annum completum illico initium accipere disposuimus, antiquitatis normam in feminis personis bene positam suo ordine relinquentes, ut post duodecimum annum completum viripotentes esse credantur.

Pupils, both male and female, are freed from tutelage when they attain the age of puberty. The ancients judged of puberty in males, not only by their years, but also by the development of their bodies. But we, from a wish to conform to the purity of the present times, have thought it proper, that what seemed, even to the ancients, to be indecent towards females, namely, the inspection of the body, should be thought no less so towards males: and, therefore, by our sacred constitution, we have enacted, that puberty in males should be considered to commence immediately on the completion of their fourteenth year; while, as to females, we have preserved the wise rule adopted by the ancients, by which they are esteemed fit for marriage on the completion of their twelfth year.

GAI. I. 196; C. v. 60. 3.

We learn from Gaius and Ulpian (*Reg.* 11. 28) that the Proculians were in favour of a particular age being fixed as that of puberty; the Sabinians wished to let it be decided by nature. Justinian here decides in favour of the former.

1. Item finitur tutela, si adrogati sint ad hoc impuberes, vel deportati; item si in servitutem pupillus redigatur ut ingratus a patrono, vel ab hostibus fuerit captus.

1. Tutelage is also determined, if the pupil, before attaining the age of puberty, is either arrogated, or suffers deportation, or is reduced to slavery, or becomes a captive.

D. xxvi. 1. 14.

The *pubertati proximus* was considered liable to criminal punishment (C. ix. 47. 7), and he might be made a slave for ingratitude towards his patron. (ΤΗΕΟΡΗ. *Paraph.*) If he returned from captivity the tutelage would recommence. (See Tit. 20. 2.)

2. Sed et si usque ad certam conditionem datus sit testamento, æque evenit ut desinat esse tutor existente conditione.

2. Again, if a person is appointed by testament to be tutor until a condition is accomplished, he ceases to be tutor on the accomplishment of the condition.

D. xxvi. 1. 14. 5.

3. Simili modo finitur tutela morte vel pupillorum vel tutorum.

3. Tutelage ends also by the death of the tutor, or of the pupil.

D. xxvii. 3. 4.

L 2

4. Sed et capitis deminutione tutoris, per quam libertas vel civitas
ejus amittitur, omnis tutela perit.
Minima autem capitis deminutione
tutoria, veluti si se in adoptionem
dederit, legitima tantum tutela
perit; ceterae non pereunt. Sed
pupilli et pupillae capitis deminutio,
licet minima sit, omnes tutelas
tollit.

4. When a tutor, by a *capitis deminutio*, loses his liberty or his citizenship, his tutelage is in every case at
an end. But, if he undergo only the
least *capitis deminutio*, as when a
tutor gives himself in adoption, then
only legal tutelage is ended, and not
the other kinds; but any *capitis deminutio* of the pupils, even the least,
always puts an end to the tutelage.

D. iv. 5. 7; D. xxvi. 4. 2.

The *tutela legitima* belonged to the nearest of the *agnati*
in right of his position in the family; but a tutor appointed by
testament or by any special means had a charge committed to
him personally, and his change of family could not alter this.
The *minima deminutio capitis* suffered by the pupil
would make him under the power of the arrogator; and as
he would be no longer *sui juris*, he could no longer have a
tutor.

5. Praeterea, qui ad certum tempus testamento dantur tutores,
finito eo deponunt tutelam.

5. A tutor, again, who is appointed
by testament to hold office during a
certain time, lays down his office
when the time is expired.

D. xxvi. 1. 14. 3.

6. Desinunt autem tutores esse,
qui vel removentur a tutela ob id
quod suspecti visi sunt, vel ex justa
causa sese excusant et onus admi-
nistrandae tutelae deponunt, secundum ea quae inferius proponemus.

6. They also cease to be tutors
who are removed from their office on
suspicion, or who excuse themselves
on good grounds from the burden of
the tutelage, and rid themselves of
it according to the rules we will
give hereafter.

D. xxvi. 1. 14. 4.

At the end of the tutelage the pupil could bring an action
to make the tutor account (*actio tutelae directa*); the tutor
could bring one to procure indemnification for all losses he
had sustained (*actio tutelae contraria*). In the same way
there was an action against and in behalf of a curator for
similar purposes (*actio negotiorum gestorum directa vel
contraria*).

## Tit. XXIII.   DE CURATIONIBUS.

Masculi puberes et feminae viripotentes usque ad vicesimum quintum annum completum curatores
accipiunt; quia licet puberes sint,
adhuc tamen ejus aetatis sunt ut sua
negotia tueri non possint.

Males arrived at the age of puberty
and females of a marriageable age,
receive curators, until they have completed their twenty-fifth year: for,
although they have attained the age
of puberty, they are still of an age

which makes them unfit to protect
their own interests.

GAI. i. 107.

The law of the Twelve Tables provided for the appointment of curators in the case of madmen and prodigals, but
did not make any provision for the protection of young persons who had attained the age of puberty.  The first enactment on the subject, of which we have any knowledge, is the
*lex Plætoria*, or, as it was often written, *Lætoria*, passed before
the time of Plautus (*Pseud.* act 1. sc. 3), which, fixing the
age of the *perfecta ætas* at twenty-five years, provided that
any one defrauding a person under that age should be liable
to a criminal prosecution and to infamy (Cic. *de Nat. Deor.*
3. 30; *de Off.* 3. 15); and probably permitted the appointment of curators in cases where a good reason for the appointment was given.  The prætor subsequently provided a
remedy, which was a great protection to persons under twenty-
five years who came before him, by directing, in all cases of
fraud, a *restitutio in integrum*; that is, that the applicant
should be placed exactly in the position in which he would
have been had not the fraud been practised against him.
Finally, Marcus Antoninus ordered that curators should be
given in all cases, without inquiry, on the application of the
*pubes.*  This seems the most probable and consistent account
of the matter, which has been the subject of much dispute
among commentators.  The chief authority is Julius Capito-
linus, in *Vita M. Aurel. Anton.* cap. 10, who says,—'*De
curatoribus vero, quum ante non nisi ex lege Lætoria, vel
propter lasciviam vel propter dementiam darentur, ita statu-
tuit [M. Antoninus], ut omnes adulti curatorem acciperent
non redditis causis.*

1. Dantur autem curatores ab
iisdem magistratibus, a quibus et
tutores.  Sed curator testamento
non datur, sed datus confirmatur
decreto prætoris vel præsidis.

1. Curators are appointed by the
same magistrates who appoint tutors.
A curator cannot be so appointed by
testament, but if appointed, he may
be confirmed in his office by a decree
of the prætor or præses.

GAI. I. 1. 198; D. xxvi. 3. 1. 3.

The magistrates who appointed the curators were, therefore, at Rome, the *præfectus urbi* or the prætor; in the provinces, the *præses*, or municipal magistrate.  (See Tit. 20.
4.)  A curator could not be appointed by testament, because
it was not certain that the *adolescens* would require one.  If
he did require one, it was natural that the person named in
the testament of the father should be selected by the magistrate as the most proper person.

2. Item inviti adolescentes cura- | 2. No adolescent is obliged to re-
tores non accipiunt, praeterquam | ceive a curator against his will, un-
in litem: curator enim et ad certam | less in case of a law-suit, for a curator
causam dari potest. | may be appointed for a particular
special purpose.

D. xxvi. 6. 2. 5.

A person who had attained the age of puberty was not
obliged to have a curator: but, practically, he was almost
sure to apply for one, as it was part of his tutor's duty to
urge him to do so (D. xxvi. 7. 5. 5), and he could not, at the
age of fourteen, be fit to manage his own affairs. There
were two other cases, besides that mentioned in the text, in
which a curator was given against the will of the adolescent
for whom he was appointed. When a debtor wished to pay a
debt owed to the adolescent (D. iv. 4. 72), or the tutor to
settle his accounts with him (C. v. 31. 7), a curator was appointed to watch the interests of the adolescent, and thus to
make the payment and settlement indisputably valid; for if
the adolescent were left to himself, the prætor might, on suspicion of fraud, order a *restitutio in integrum.* The curator,
once appointed, held his office until the adolescent attained
the age of twenty-five; but if an adolescent who had a curator was thought capable of managing his affairs, he might,
by the special grant of the emperor, have a dispensation
(*venia ætatis*) from waiting for the full age; but it was requisite, to obtain this, that a man should be twenty, and a
woman eighteen years of age.   (D. iv. 4. 3; C. ii. 45.)

3. Furiosi quoque et prodigi, | 3. Madmen and prodigals, al-
licet majores viginti quinque annis | though past the age of twenty-five,
sint, tamen in curatione sunt | are yet placed under the curatorship
adgnatorum ex lege duodecim ta- | of their *agnati* by the law of the
bularum: sed solent Romæ præ- | Twelve Tables. But ordinarily, after
fectus urbi vel prætor, et in pro- | inquiry has been made into the cir-
vinciis præsides ex inquisitione his | cumstances, curators are appointed
curatores dare. | for them, at Rome, by the præfect
of the city or the prætor; in the
provinces, by the *præses.*

D. xxvii. 10. 1.

If the father of the person requiring a curator had died
intestate, the nearest *agnatus* was the curator by the law of
the Twelve Tables; but if there was no *agnatus,* or only some
one unfit for the office, the magistrate appointed a curator.
(THEOPH. *Paraph.*) If the person who required the curator
was heir under his father's testament, the *agnati* were excluded from their right of curatorship *ex lege,* and the magistrate appointed. (ULP. *Reg.* 12. 3.) The passage in Ulpian
is too clear to admit a doubt that this was the law in his

time, but it is not easy to see how the *agnati* were interested
in the one case less than in the other, unless we are to suppose that the *paterfamilias* making a testament in favour of
the person requiring a curator was considered as an expression
of his wish to exclude the *agnati* from any concern with the
inheritance.   Probably, except in the case of a testament
made by an ascendant, the distinction did not apply, and an
*agnatus* would be the legal curator of a person who had inherited under the testament of a stranger.

| | |
|---|---|
| 4. Sed et mente captis, et sur- dis, et mutis, et qui perpetuo morbo laborant, quia rebus suis superesse non possunt, curatores dandi sunt. | 4. Persons who are of unsound mind, or who are deaf, mute, or sub- ject to any perpetual malady, since they are unable to manage their own affairs, must be placed under curators. |

D. xxvii. 10. 2.

The word *furiosi*, that is, the mad as opposed to the im-
becile, in the law of the Twelve Tables was taken strictly,
and there was no legal curator for any one suffering under
any other form of mental malady.

| | |
|---|---|
| 5. Interdum autem et pupilli curatores accipiunt: ut puta si legitimus tutor non sit idoneus; quoniam habenti tutorem tutor dari non potest. Item si testamento datus tutor, vel a praetore vel praeside, idoneus non sit ad administrationem, nec tamen frau- dulenter negotia administret, solet ei curator adjungi. Item in locum tutorum qui non in perpetuum, sed ad tempus a tutela excusantur, solent curatores dari. | 5. Sometimes even pupils receive curators; as, for instance, when the legal tutor is unfit for the office; for a person who already has a tutor cannot have another given him; again, if a tutor appointed by testa- ment, or by the praetor or praeses, is unfit to administer the affairs of his pupil, although there is nothing frau- dulent in the way he administers them, it is usual to appoint a curator to act conjointly with him. It is also usual to assign curators in the place of tutors excused for a time only. |

D. xxvi. 1. 13; D. xxvi. 2. 27; D. xxvi. 5. 15 and 16.

| | |
|---|---|
| 6. Quod si tutor adversa vale- tudine vel alia necessitate impe- ditur quominus negotia pupilli administrare possit, et pupillus vel absit vel infans sit, quem velit actorem, periculo ipsius tutoris, praetor vel qui provinciae praeerit, decreto constituet. | 6. If a tutor is prevented by ill- ness or otherwise from administering the affairs of his pupil, and his pupil is absent, or an infant, then the praetor or praeses of the province will, at the tutor's risk, appoint by decree any one whom the tutor selects to be the agent of the pupil. |

D. xxvi. 7. 24.

This agent is to be distinguished from a curator.   He is
merely a person who acts under the tutor, and for whom the
tutor is responsible.   If the pupil were present, and past the
age of infancy, he, with the authorization of the tutor, could
appoint the agent, and there would be no necessity for the

confirmation of a magistrate; hence the words *at pupillus vel absit vel infans sit.*

The uncertain duration of mental incapacity made the person entrusted with the case of one suffering under it be termed a curator, not a tutor; otherwise the sufferer might be as incapable of going through legal forms as an infant.  An adolescent and a *prodigus* could go through all the forms of law, and therefore there was no necessity, in their case, for the curator having an *auctoritas*.  If they went through the prescribed forms, they were legally bound, whether the curator consented or not; but unless the curator consented, the prætor would always interpose and relieve them from any consequences that might be prejudicial; and so they were not really bound, unless with the curator's consent.

## Tit. XXIV.   DE SATISDATIONE TUTORUM VEL CURATORUM.

Ne tamen pupillorum pupillarumve, et eorum qui quæve in curatione sunt, negotia a curatoribus tutoribusve consumantur vel deminuantur, curat prætor ut et tutores et curatores eo nomine satisdent.  Sed hoc non est perpetuum: nam tutores testamento dati satisdare non coguntur, quia fides eorum et diligentia ab ipso testatore probata est.  Item ex inquisitione tutores vel curatores dati satisdatione non onerantur, quia idonei electi sunt.

To prevent the property of pupils and persons placed under curators being wasted or destroyed by tutors or curators, the prætor sees that tutors and curators give security against such conduct.  But this is not always necessary; a testamentary tutor is not compelled to give security, as his fidelity and diligence have been recognized by the testator.  And tutors and curators appointed upon inquiry, are not obliged to give security, because they have been chosen as being proper persons.

Gai. I. 100, 200.

A patron and a father, when tutors, were ordinarily, though not as a matter of right, exempt from the necessity of giving caution.  (D. xxvi. 4. 5. 1.)  This necessity, therefore, only fell on *tutores* or *curatores legitimi*, and those appointed by inferior magistrates; those appointed by higher magistrates being only appointed after inquiry, which rendered the giving of security needless.  (See Tit. 20. 4.)  The persons who became sureties (for the security demanded was always that of the guarantee of third persons) went through the form of *fidejussio*.  The pupil or the person requiring a curator asked the surety whether he guaranteed the safety of the property, *Fide jubisne rem salvam fore.*  And he answered, *Fide jubeo.*  If the pupil or adult could not go through the ceremony, his slave, or, if he had no slave, a person appointed by the magistrate, went through the form for him. (See Bk. iii. Tit. 20.) Besides the guarantee taken for the fidelity of the tutor and curator, and the general liability of the whole of the tutor's or curator's property to make good any losses incurred through their neglect, those entrusted to their care had a further protection in the necessity under which the tutor and curator were to make an inventory of all the property of the pupil or person requiring a curator (C. v. 51. 13); and, after the publication of the 78th Novel, by the tutor or curator being obliged to pledge himself by oath that he would act as a ' *bonus paterfamilias* ' would act.   (Nov. 78, cap. 7.)

1. Sed si ex testamento vel inquisitione duo pluresve dati fuerint, potest unus offerre satis de indemnitate pupilli vel adolescentis, et contutori vel concuratori praeferri ut solus administret, vel ut contutor satis offerens praeponatur ei, et ipse solus administret. Itaque per se non potest petere satis a contutore vel concuratore suo; sed offerre debet, ut electionem det contutori vel concuratori suo, utrum velit satis accipere an satisdare. Quod si nemo eorum satis offerat, si quidem adscriptum fuerit a testatore quis gerat, ille gerere debet; quod si non fuerit adscriptum, quem major pars elegerit, ipse gerere debet, ut edicto praetoris cavetur. Sin autem ipsi tutores dissenserint circa eligendum eum vel eos qui gerere debent, praetor partes suas interponere debet. Idem et in pluribus ex inquisitione datis probandum est, id est, ut major pars eligere possit, per quem administratio fieret.

1. If two or more are appointed by testament, or by a magistrate, after inquiry, as tutors or curators, any of them, by offering security for the indemnification of the pupil or adolescent, may be preferred to his co-tutor or co-curator, so that he may either alone administer the property, or may oblige his co-tutor or co-curator to give security, if he wishes to obtain the preference and become the sole administrator. He cannot directly demand security from his co-tutor or co-curator; he must offer it himself, and so give his co-tutor or co-curator the choice to receive or to give security. If no tutor or curator offers security, the person appointed by the testator to manage the property shall manage it; but if no such person be appointed, then the administration will fall to the person whom a majority of the tutors shall choose, as is provided by the praetorian edict. If the tutors disagree in their choice, the praetor must interpose. And in the same way, when several are appointed after inquiry by a magistrate, a majority is to determine who shall administer.

D. xxvi. 2. 17. 19. 1; D. xxvi. 7. 3. 1. 7, 8, 9.

As it was generally most convenient that one tutor alone should act, although all continued responsible (D. xxvi. 7. 3. 2. 6), it was necessary that the tutor who did act, *tutor onerarius* (opposed to *tutores honorarii*, those who did not act), should give security to the co-tutors. If he did not, he could be compelled by the means described in the text, either to do so or to allow some other co-tutor to take his place. Sometimes the tutelage was apportioned by the magistrate among the different tutors, and each had a separate duty to perform, for which he alone was responsible. (D. xxvi. 7. 3. 9.)

2. Sciendum autem est non solum tutores vel curatores pupillis vel adultis ceterisque personis ex administratione rerum teneri; sed etiam in eos qui satisdationem acceperunt, subsidiariam actionem eam, quæ ultimum eis præsidium possit adferre. Subsidiaria autem actio in eos datur, qui aut omnino a tutoribus vel curatoribus satisdari non curaverunt, aut non idonee passi sunt caveri. Quæ quidem, tam ex prudentium responsis quam ex constitutionibus imperialibus, etiam in heredes eorum extenditur.

2. It should be observed that it is not only tutors and curators who are responsible for their administration to pupils, minors, and the other persons we have mentioned, but, as a last safeguard, a subsidiary action may be brought against the magistrate who has accepted the security as sufficient. The subsidiary action may be brought against a magistrate who has wholly omitted to take security, or has taken insufficient security; and the liability to this action, according to the responses of the jurisprudents, as well as the imperial constitution, extends also to the heirs of the magistrate.

D. xxvii. 8. 1. 11, 12. 4. 6.

The heirs of the magistrate were only liable where the negligence of the magistrate had been very great. (D. xxvii. 8. 6.)

3. Quibus constitutionibus et illud exprimitur, ut nisi caveant tutores vel curatores, pignoribus captis coerceantur.

3. The same constitutions also expressly enact, that tutors and curators who do not give security, may be compelled to do so by seizure of their goods as pledges.

C. v. 35. 2.

The magistrate would order a portion of their property to be seized, and retained until they gave security. (THEOPHIL. Paraphr.)

4. Neque autem præfectus urbi, neque prætor, neque præses provinciæ, neque quis alius cui tutores dandi jus est, hac actione tenebitur; sed hi tantummodo qui satisdationem exigere solent.

4. Neither the prefect of the city, nor the prætor, nor the præses of a province, nor any other magistrate to whom the appointment of tutors belongs, shall be liable to this action, but only those magistrates whose ordinary duty it is to exact the security.

D. xxvii. 8. 1. 1.

The words of the text, which are borrowed from Ulpian, are not strictly correct when applied to the title of Justinian; as under his system the municipal magistrates, whose business it was to take security, could in some cases appoint tutors. (Tit. 20. 5.)

## TIT. XXV.  DE EXCUSATIONIBUS TUTORUM VEL CURATORUM.

Excusantur autem tutores vel curatores variis ex causis, pleramque autem propter liberos, sive in potestate sint, sive emancipati. Si enim tres liberos superstites Romæ quis habeat, vel in Italia quatuor, vel in provinciis quinque, a tutela vel cura potest excusari, exemplo ceterorum munerum; nam et tutelam vel curam placuit publicum munus esse. Sed adoptivi liberi non prosunt, in adoptionem autem dati naturali patri prosunt. Item nepotes ex filio prosunt, ut in locum patris succedant; ex filia non prosunt. Filii autem superstites tantum ad tutelæ vel curæ muneris excusationem prosunt; defuncti non prosunt. Sed si in bello amissi sunt quæsitum est an prosint? Et constat eos solos prodesse, qui in acie amittuntur; hi enim qui pro republica ceciderunt, in perpetuum per gloriam vivere intelliguntur.

Tutors and curators are excused on different grounds; most frequently on account of the number of their children, whether in their power or emancipated. For any one who at Rome has three children living, in Italy four, or in the provinces five, may be excused from being tutor or curator as from other offices, for the office of both a tutor and a curator is considered a public one. Adopted children will not avail the adopter, but though given in adoption are reckoned in favour of their natural father. Grandchildren by a son, when they succeed to the position of their father, may be reckoned in the number, but not grandchildren by a daughter. It is only those children who are living that can be reckoned to excuse any one from being tutor or curator, and not those who are dead. It has been questioned, however, whether those who have perished in war may not be reckoned; and it has been decided, that those who die in battle may, but they only, for glory renders those immortal who have fallen for their country.

D. xxvii. 1. 2. 2, &c.; D. xxvii. 1. 18.

It was considered a matter of public policy that tutors or curators should act when their assistance was necessary, and, therefore, those who were appointed were obliged to accept the office, unless they could establish any valid reason for being excused. This Title gives a number of grounds on which a person appointed tutor or curator was excused from holding the office. These grounds of excuse may be classed with tolerable accuracy under three heads—1. The discharge of some public duty (pr. and paragraphs, 1, 2, 3. 14, 15); 2. Being in a position adverse to the pupil or adult (paragraphs, 4. 9. 11, 12. 19); 3. Being incompetent to sustain the burden of the office (paragraphs 5, 6, 7, 8. 13).

It was the *lex Papia Poppæa* that first introduced exemption on the ground of the number of the children.

Grandchildren by the daughter were not reckoned, as, otherwise, they would have been reckoned by two different persons,

their maternal grandfather and their paternal father or grandfather.

1. Item divus Marcus in seme-
stribus rescripsit, eum qui res fisci
administrat, a tutela vel cura, quamdiu administrat, excusari posse.

1. The Emperor Marcus declared
by rescript in his *Semestria*, that a
person engaged in administering the
property of the fiscal department is
excused from being tutor or curator
while his administration lasts.

D. xxvii. 1. 41.

Augustus and Tiberius held a council of senators every six
months for the discussion of affairs (SUET. *Aug.* 35); and we
gather from the text that the practice was also adopted by
Marcus Aurelius, who published the records of the councils
under the name of *semestria.*

2. Item qui reipublicæ causa absunt, a tutela vel cura excusantur.
Sed et si fuerint tutores vel curatores, deinde reipublicæ causa
absens cœperint, a tutela vel cura
excusantur, quatenus reipublicæ
causa absunt, et interea curator loco
eorum datur. Qui si reversi fuerint,
recipiunt onus tutelæ: nam nec
anni habent vacationem, ut Papinianus libro quinto responsorum
rescripsit; nam hoc spatium habent
ad novas tutelas vocati.

2. Persons absent on the service
of the state are excused from being
tutors or curators; and if those who
have already been appointed either
as tutors or curators, should afterwards be absent on the public service, they are excused during their
absence, and meanwhile curators are
appointed in their place. On their
return, they must again take upon
them the burden of tutelage; and,
according to Papinian's opinion, expressed in the fifth book of his
answers, are not entitled to the privilege of a year's vacation, which is
only allowed them when they are
called to a new tutelage.

D. xxvii. 1. 10. pr. and 2.

The meaning of the text is that, if they had commenced
holding the office of tutor before their absence, they were
obliged to resume it immediately on their return. If, when
they returned, a new tutelage was imposed on them, they
might delay for a year to enter on its duties.·

3. Et qui potestatem habent aliquam, se excusare possunt, ut divus
Marcus rescripsit; sed cœptam tutelam deserere non possunt.

3. By a rescript of the Emperor
Marcus, all persons invested with
magisterial power may excuse themselves; but they cannot abandon the
office of tutor, which they have
already undertaken.

D. xxvii. 1. 17. 6.

*Qui potestatem aliquam habent:* i.e. all magistrates, including local magistrates.

4. Item propter litem quam cum pupillo vel adulto tutor vel curator habet, excusare nemo se potest, nisi forte de omnibus bonis vel hereditate controversia sit.

4. No tutor or curator can excuse himself by alleging a law-suit with the pupil or adult; unless the suit embraces the whole of the goods, or the property, or is for an inheritance.

D. xxvii. I. 21.

Justinian afterwards, in the 72nd Novel (c. 1), decided that no creditor or debtor of the pupil or adult should be allowed to become tutor or curator.

5. Item tria onera tutelæ non adfectatæ vel oure præstant vacationem, quamdiu administrantur: at tamen plurium pupillorum tutela, vel cura eorumdem bonorum, veluti fratrum, pro una computetur.

5. Three tutelages or curatorships, if unsolicited, serve as an excuse from filling any other such office, while the holder continues to discharge the duties. But the tutelage of several pupils, or the curatorship of an undivided property, as where the pupils or adults are brothers, is reckoned as one only.

D. xxvii. 1. 3. 15. 16.

6. Sed et propter paupertatem excusationem tribui tam divi fratres quam præ se divus Marcus rescripsit, si quis imparem se oneri injuncto possit docere.

6. Poverty also is a sufficient excuse, when it can be proved such as to render a man incapable of the burden imposed upon him, according to the rescripts given both by the imperial brothers together, and by the Emperor Marcus singly.

D. xxvii. 1. 7.

Marcus Aurelius Antoninus and Lucius Verus were the *divi fratres.*

7. Item propter adversam valetudinem, propter quam nec suis quidem negotiis interesse potest, excusatio locum habet.

8. Similiter eum qui literas nesciret, excusandum esse divus Pius rescripsit; quamvis et imperiti literarum possunt ad administrationem negotiorum sufficere.

7. Illness also, if it prevent a man from superintending his own affairs, affords a ground of excuse.

8. So, too, a person who cannot read must be excused, according to the rescript of the Emperor Antoninus Pius; but persons who cannot read are sometimes considered capable of administering.

D. xxvii. 1. 6. 19.

The magistrate would have to decide whether the property was so small, and the position of the pupil or adult so humble, that this ignorance would be no bar.

9. Item si propter inimicitias aliquem testamento tutorem pater dederit, hoc ipsum præstat ei excusationem: sicut per contrarium non

9. If it is through enmity that the father appoints by testament any one as tutor, this circumstance itself will afford a sufficient excuse; just as on

excusantur, qui se tutelam adminis- | the other hand, they who have pro-
traturos patri pupillorum promise- | mised the father of the pupils to fill
runt. | the office of tutor, cannot be excused.

D. xxvii. 1. 0. 17.

10. Non esse admittendam excu- | 10. That the tutor was unknown
sationem ejus qui hoc solo utitur, | to the father of a pupil is not of it-
quod ignotus patri pupillorum sit, | self to be admitted as a sufficient
divi fratres rescripserunt. | excuse, as is decided by a rescript of
| the imperial brothers.

D. xxvii. 1. 15. 14.

11. Inimicitiae quas quis cum | 11. Enmity against the father of
patre pupillorum vel adultorum | the pupil or adult, if of a deadly
exercuit, si capitales fuerunt, nec | character, and no reconciliation has
reconciliatio intervenit, a tutela vel | taken place, is usually considered as
cura solent excusare. | an excuse from being tutor or cura-
| tor.

D. xxvii. 1. 6. 17.

12. Item qui status controversiam | 12. So, too, he whose status has
a pupillorum patre passus est, ex- | been called in question by the father
cusatur a tutela. | of the pupil, is excused from the
| office of tutor.

That is, if the deceased has attempted to show that the
person appointed tutor was a slave.

13. Item major septuaginta annis | 13. Persons above seventy years of
a tutela vel cura excusare se potest. | age may be excused from being tutors
Minores autem viginti quinque an- | or curators. Persons under the age
nis olim quidem excusabantur. A | of twenty-five were formerly excused,
nostra autem constitutione prohi- | but, by our constitution, they are
bentur ad tutelam vel curam ad- | now prohibited from aspiring to these
spirare, adeo ut nec excusationis | offices, so that excuses are become
opus fiat. Qua constitutione cave- | unnecessary. This constitution pro-
tur ut nec pupillus ad legitimam | vides that neither pupils nor adults
tutelam vocetur, neo adultus ; cum | shall be called to a legal tutelage.
erat incivile, eos qui alieno auxilio | For it is absurd that persons who
in rebus suis administrandis egere | are themselves governed, and are
noscuntur, et aliis reguntur, aliorum | known to need assistance in the ad-
tutelam vel curam subire. | ministration of their own affairs,
| should become the tutors or curators
| of others.

D. xxvii. 1. 2. 10. 7 : C. v. 30. 5.

14. Idem et in milite observan- | 14. The same rule holds good also
dum est, ut nec volens ad tutelae | as to military persons. They cannot,
onus admittatur. | even though they wish it, be admitted
| to the office of tutor or curator.

15. Item Romae grammatici, rhe- | 15. Grammarians, rhetoricians, and
tores et medici, et qui in patria sua | physicians at Rome, and those also
id exercent et intra numerum sunt, | who exercise such professions in
a tutela vel cura habent vacationem. | their own country, and are within
| the number authorized, are exempted
| from being tutors or curators.

D. xxvii. 1. 6. 1.

It was Antoninus Pius who fixed the number which each city was to have. (D. xxvii. 1. 6. 1.) The largest provincial city was not allowed to have more than ten physicians, five grammarians, and five rhetoricians.

Philosophers were also excepted (D. xxvii. 1. 6. 5); jurisprudents who were members of the council of the emperor (xxvii. 1. 30); and all *clerici*. (C. L. 3. 52.)

16. Qui autem vult se excusare, si plures habeat excusationes et de quibusdam non probaverit, aliis uti intra tempora non prohibetur. Qui autem excusare se volunt, non appellant; sed intra dies quinquaginta continuos ex quo cognoverunt, excusare se debent, cujuscumque generis sint, id est, qualitercumque dati fuerint tutores, si intra centesimum lapidem sunt ab eo loco ubi tutores dati sunt; si vero ultra centesimum habitant, dinumeratione facta viginti millium diurnorum et amplius triginta dierum. Quod tamen, ut Scævola dicebat, sic debet computari ne minus sint quam quinquaginta dies.

16. If a person wishes to excuse himself, and has several excuses, even supposing some are not admitted, there is nothing to prevent his employing others, provided he does so within the prescribed time. Those who wish to excuse themselves are not to appeal, but whatever kind of tutors they may be, that is, however they may have been appointed, must offer their excuses within the fifty days next after they have known of their appointment, if they are within a hundred miles of the place when they were appointed. If they are at a greater distance they are allowed a day for every twenty miles, and thirty days besides; but the time should, as Scævola said, be so calculated as never to be less than fifty days in the whole.

D. xxvii. 1. 21. 1. 13. 1. 0.

If he lived anywhere within four hundred miles, he would, reckoning a day for each twenty miles, and thirty days besides, fall short of fifty days, and therefore the rule was laid down as stated in the concluding sentence of the text. If he did not excuse himself within the appointed time, he could not afterwards escape the charge.

*Dies continui* are opposed to *dies utiles*, the days on which legal business could be done; *dies continui* meaning the next days, of whatever kind.

17. Datus autem tutor ad universum patrimonium datus esse creditur.

17. The tutor who is appointed is considered as appointed for the whole patrimony.

D. xxvii. 1. 21. 2.

The tutor was appointed for the whole patrimony; but if it was situated in very different parts, he might apply to have other tutors appointed to act in the different localities. (D. xxvii. 1. 21. 2.)

18. Qui tutelam alicujus gessit,

18. A person who has discharged

invitus curator ejusdem fieri non compellitur: in tantum ut, licet paterfamilias qui testamento tutorem dedit, adjecerit se eumdem curatorem dare, tamen invitum eum curam suscipere non cogendum divi Severus et Antoninus rescripserunt.

the office of tutor is not compelled against his will to become the curator of the same person; so much so, that although the father, after appointing a tutor by testament, adds that he also appoints the same person to be curator, the person so appointed if unwilling cannot be compelled to take the office of curator; so it has been decided by the rescript of the Emperors Severus and Antoninus.

It is Antoninus Caracalla who is here meant.

19. Iidem rescripserunt, maritum uxori suæ curatorem datum excusare se posse, licet se immiscent.

19. The same emperors have decided by rescript, that a husband appointed as curator to his wife may excuse himself from the office, even after he has intermeddled with her affairs.

D. xxvii. 1. 1. 5.

The husband not only might excuse himself from the curatorship of his wife, but in the time of Justinian he could not fill the office (C. v. 34. 2.); neither could the wife's curator marry her. (C. v. 6.)

It was the general rule that a tutor or curator who intermeddled with the affairs of the pupil or adult renounced the right of offering excuses.

20. Si quis autem falsis allegationibus excusationem tutelæ meruit, non est liberatus onere tutelæ.

20. Anyone who has succeeded by false allegations in getting himself excused from the office of tutor, is not thereby discharged from the burden of the office.

D. xxiii. 2. 00.

## Tit. XXVI. DE SUSPECTIS TUTORIBUS VEL CURATORIBUS.

Sciendum est suspecti crimen ex lege duodecim tabularum descendere.

The right of accusing a suspected tutor or curator is derived from the law of the Twelve Tables.

D. xxvi. 10. 1, 2.

1. Datum est autem jus removendi tutores suspectos Romæ prætori, et in provinciis præsidibus earum et legato proconsulis.

1. The power of removing suspected tutors belongs at Rome to the prætor: in the provinces to the præsides, or to the legate of the proconsul.

D. xxvi. 10. 1. 3, 4.

2. Ostendimus, qui possint de suspecto cognoscere; nunc videamus qui suspecti fieri possint. Et quidem omnes tutores possunt, sive testamentarii sint sive tuti, sed alterius generis tutores; quare et si legitimus sit tutor, accusari poterit. Quid si patronus? Adhuc idem erit dicendum: dummodo meminerimus famæ patroni parcendum, licet ut suspectus remotus fuerit.

2. We have shown what magistrates may take cognisance of suspected persons: let us now inquire, what persons may become suspected. All tutors may become so, whether testamentary, or others; thus even a legal suitor may be accused. But what is the case with a patron? He, too, may be accused; but we must remember, that his reputation must be spared, although he be removed as suspected.

The descendants could not bring an action to which infamy attached against an ascendant. They and the *libertus* could only call for the interference of the law to protect their property, not to punish the tutor with infamy. (D. xxxvii. 15. 5.) And in the case of all legal tutors it was customary, except in very bad cases, not to remove them, but to join a curator with them. (D. xxvi. 10. 9.) By *famæ parcendum* is meant that the grounds of the decision for their removal were not to be expressed.

3. Consequens est ut videamus, qui possunt suspectos postulare. Et sciendum est quasi publicam esse hanc actionem, hoc est, omnibus patere. Quinimo et mulieres admittuntur ex rescripto divorum Severi et Antonini, sed eæ solæ quæ pietatis necessitudine ductæ ad hoc procedunt, ut puta mater; nutrix quoque et avia possunt, potest et soror. Sed et si qua alia mulier fuerit, cujus prætor perpensam pietatem intellexerit non sexus verecundiam egredientem, sed pietate productam non continere injuriam pupillorum, admittet eam ad accusationem.

3. Let us now inquire, by whom suspected persons may be accused. Now an accusation of this sort is in a measure public, that is, it is open to all. Nay, by a rescript of the Emperors Severus and Antoninus, even women are admitted to be accusers; but only those who are induced to do so through feelings of affection, as a mother, a nurse, or a grandmother, or a sister, who may all become accusers. But the prætor will admit any other woman to make the accusation, in whom he recognises a real affection, and who, without overstepping the modesty of her sex, is impelled by this affection not to endure the pupil suffering harm.

D. xxvi. 10. L. 0, 7.

The action is called *quasi publica*, because on the one hand it had the private object of securing the pupil's interests, and on the other had, like public actions, criminal consequences, and might be brought by a person not interested in the private result.

Women, as a general rule, could not institute public actions. (D. xlviii. 2. 1.)

4. Impuberes non possunt tutores suos suspectos postulare; puberes autem curatores suos ex

4. No person below the age of puberty can bring an accusation against his tutor as suspected: but

M

consilio necessariorum suspectos possunt arguere, et ita divi Severus et Antoninus rescripserunt.

those who have attained that age may, under the advice of their near relations, accuse their curators. Such is the decision given in a rescript of the Emperors Severus and Antoninus.

D. xxvi. 10. 7.

5. Suspectus autem est, qui non ex fide tutelam gerit, licet solvendo sit, ut Julianus quoque rescripsit. Sed et antequam incipiat tutelam gerere tutor, posse eum quasi suspectum removeri idem Julianus rescripsit, et secundum eum constitutum est.

5. A tutor is suspected who does not faithfully execute his trust, although perfectly solvent, as Julian writes, who also thinks that even before he enters on his office, a tutor may be removed, as suspected; and a constitution has been made in accordance with this opinion.

D. xxvi. 10. 8.

Ulpian says that a tutor could not be *suspectus* before he entered on his office, and that if there were any reason to think him an improper person beforehand, the magistrate would forbid him to assume the administration. (D. xxvi. 10. 3. 5. and 12.) Justinian decides in opposition to this.

6. Suspectus autem remotus, si quidem ob dolum, famosus est; si ob culpam, non æque.

6. A suspected person, if removed on account of fraud, is infamous, but not if for neglect only.

C. v. 40. 0.

For the meaning of the word *infamia* see Introd. sec. 48.

7. Si quis autem suspectus postulatur, quoad cognitio finiatur, interdicitur ei administratio, ut Papiniano visum est.

7. If an action is brought against any one as suspected, his administration, according to Papinian, is suspended, while the accusation is pending.

D. xlvi. 3. 14. 1.

8. Sed si suspecti cognitio suscepta fuerit, postesque tutor vel curator decesserit, extinguitur suspecti cognitio.

8. If a process is commenced against a tutor or curator, as suspected, and he dies while it is going on, the process is at an end.

D. xxvi. 10. 11.

The action to force the tutor or curator to give in his accounts would be brought against the heirs of the tutor or curator. But the *suspecti cognitio* could not, as its object was to remove the tutor or curator, not to recover money from him.

9. Si quis tutor copiam sui non faciat ut alimenta pupillo decernantur, cavetur epistola divorum

9. If a tutor fails to appear, that a certain amount of maintenance may be fixed on for his pupil, it is

Severi et Antonini, ut in possessionem bonorum ejus pupillus
mittatur; et quæ mora deteriora
futura sunt, dato curatore distrahi
jubentur. Ergo ut suspectus removeri poterit, qui non præstat
alimenta.

provided by a rescript of the Emperors
Severus and Antoninus, that the
pupil shall be put into the possession
of the effects of the tutor, and that
after a curator has been appointed,
those things, which are perishable,
may be sold. Therefore a tutor, who
does not afford maintenance to his
pupil may be removed, as suspected.

D. xxvi. 10. 7. 2.

The prætor generally determined the amount to be annually expended on the maintenance and education of the
pupil (the word *alimenta* must be taken very widely), when
it was not determined by the testament of the father. The
tutor had therefore to attend before the magistrate to state
what amount the fortune of the pupil would bear.

*Dato curatore*, i.e. a curator given for this particular purpose only.

10. Sed si quis præsens urget
propter inopiam alimenta non posse
decerni, si hoc per mendacium
dicat, remittendum eum esse ad
præfectum urbi puniendum placuit: sicut ille remittitur, qui
data pecunia ministerium tutelæ
redemit.

10. But if the tutor appears, and
maintains that no certain amount of
maintenance can be fixed in consequence of the smallness of the pupil's
estate; if he says this falsely, he
shall be handed over to the prefect
of the city, to be punished, just as a
person is handed over who has purchased a tutelage by bribery.

D. xxvi. 10. 3. 15.

The prætor had no criminal jurisdiction, and therefore persons were sent for punishment to the *præfectus urbis*. (D.
i. 12. 1.) In the provinces the *præses* could punish, as well
as remove, the tutor.

11. Libertus quoque, si fraudulenter tutelam filiorum vel nepotum patroni gessisse probetur,
ad præfectum urbis remittitur
puniendus.

11. Also a freedman, who is proved
to have been guilty of fraud, when
acting as tutor to the son or grandson of his patron, is handed over to
the prefect of the city to be punished.

D. xxvi. 10. 2.

12. Novissime sciendum est, eos
qui fraudulenter tutelam vel curam
administrant, etiamsi satis offerant,
removendos a tutela; quia satisdatio tutoris propositum male-
volum non mutat, sed diutius gras-
sandi in re familiari facultatem
præstat.

12. Lastly, it must be known that
they who are guilty of fraud in their
administration, must be removed, although they offer sufficient security.
For giving security makes no change
in the malevolent purpose of the
tutor, but only procures him a longer
opportunity of injuring the estate.

D. xxvi. 10. 5. 6.

M 3

A person is considered thus open to suspicion whose general character and conduct warrant the suspicion.   But a zealous and honest man, as we learn in the next paragraph, is not to be removed on suspicion, because he is poor.

13. Suspectum enim eum putamus, qui moribus talis est ut suspectus sit. Enim vero tutor vel curator, quamvis pauper est, fidelis tamen et diligens removendus non est quasi suspectus.

13. We also deem every man suspected, whose conduct is such that we cannot but suspect him. A tutor or curator who is faithful and diligent, is not to be removed, as a suspected person, merely because he is poor.

D. xxvi. 10. 8.

# LIBER SECUNDUS.

### Tit. I.  DE DIVISIONE RERUM ET QUALITATE.

HAVING treated in the first book of the law of persons, the Institutes now proceed to treat of the law of things—that is, they pass from persons who exercise rights to things over which rights are exercised. Rights may be divided into those which we have in or over things as against all the world, and those which we have against particular persons. (See Introd. sec. 61.) The second book of the Institutes, and the first portion of the third, treat of the former class, and of the mode in which they are acquired.

The most proper mode of treating the law of things would be, perhaps, first to inquire of what divisions things themselves are susceptible; next, to divide rights in things (*jura in re*) according to the extent of the right; and lastly, to treat of the mode in which those rights are acquired. To a certain extent this mode of dividing the subject is adopted in the Institutes, but not very distinctly or expressly. Things themselves may be divided, generally, by making the basis of division either the relation in which they stand to persons, or something inherent in the nature of the things. Things divided in the first way may be subdivided according as they are the subject of the rights of all men or no men on the one hand, and of particular men on the other, the latter class receiving modifications according to the character in which particular men hold them. This division of things is treated of in the first sections of this Title. The most prominent distinction inherent in things is that of things corporeal and things incorporeal, and this is treated of in the second Title. There are other divisions of things (see Introd. secs. 52–60) which are alluded to in the Institutes, but not expressly noticed.

A person may have the whole sum of all rights over a thing when in Roman law he was said to have the *dominium*. These

rights of the *dominus* were summed up in the *jus utendi*, that
is, making use of the thing; the *jus fruendi*, that is, reaping
the fruits and profits; and the *jus abutendi*, that is, consuming
the thing, if capable of consumption. Or any one of the *jura
in rem* may be separated from the rest and enjoyed by different
persons. (See Introd. sec. 64.) These fragments of the *dominium*, called servitudes, are treated of in the third and three
following Titles. Or a person may have a right over a thing
in the ownership of another, limited by the extent to which
he has a claim against the owner, as a creditor has over the
thing given him in pledge as a security for the debt. This
right, generally termed in Roman law the *jus pignoris*, is not
spoken of expressly in the Institutes, but a brief sketch of the
law on the subject will be found in the conclusion of the notes
to the fifth Title.

The Institutes then recur to the modes by which the ownership in things is acquired, and the subject is divided according
as ownership is acquired in a particular thing, or in a *universitas rerum*, that is, the aggregate of rights possessed by a
particular person. Two of the principal modes of acquiring
particular things, occupation, that is, being the first person to
appropriate an unappropriated thing, and tradition, that is, the
owner handing over the thing to another person with the intention of transferring the ownership, and the transferee receiving the thing with the intention of becoming owner of it,
have been treated of in the first Title as also have the subordinate modes of accession, when an inferior thing is acquired by
the owner of a more important thing, and specification, when
a new thing is created, and belongs to the creator. In the sixth
Title, another mode of acquiring particular things is treated
of, that of *usucapion*, the process by which the law attached
the legal ownership after a certain length of possession. The
seventh Title treats of certain cases in which gift might be
looked on as a different mode of conferring ownership from
tradition. This ends the discussion of the modes of acquiring
the ownership in particular things. The eighth and ninth Titles
speak of certain restrictions on alienation, and of one person
acquiring ownership through other persons. In the tenth Title,
the Institutes proceed to discuss the modes of acquiring a
*universitas rerum*. The two chief modes are, the gift of an
*hereditas* by testament, and the succession to an *hereditas* in
case of intestacy. The subject of testaments occupies the
remainder of the second book, and that of succession to an
intestate occupies the first nine Titles of the third book. Three
or four minor modes of acquiring a *universitas rerum*, of

which arrogation is the most important, are then noticed; and
with the twelfth Title of the third book the treatment of *jura
in re*, and of the modes of acquiring ownership in them, is
brought to a conclusion.  This treatment of the modes of
acquisition is subject to the inconvenience noticed by Gaius
(ii. 191), that legacies which are a mode of acquiring specific
things, are treated of as if coming under the acquisition of a
*universitas rerum* by testament.

Previously to the legislation of Justinian, there had been
two other modes of acquisition applicable both in the case of
particular things and in that of a *universitas rerum*, which
are treated of by Gaius at considerable length. (GAI. ii. 18–37.
See also ULPIAN, *Reg.* 19. 2.)   These were, mancipation, the
process by which *res mancipi* were conveyed from one Roman
citizen to another (see Introd. sec. 59), and *in jure cessio*. The
*cessio in jure* was a fictitious suit, in which the person who
was to acquire the thing claimed (*vindicabat*) the thing as his
own, the person who was to transfer it acknowledged the justice
of the claim, and the magistrate pronounced it to be the property (*addicebat*) of the claimant.  Mancipation and *cessiones
in jure* were both abolished by Justinian.

| | |
|---|---|
| Superiore libro de jure persona- rum exposuimus : modo videamus de rebus, quæ vel in nostro patri- monio vel extra patrimonium nos- trum habentur.  Quædam enim naturali jure communia sunt om- nium, quædam publica, quædam universitatis, quædam nullius, ple- raque singulorum, quæ ex variis causis cuique adquiruntur, sicut ex subjectis apparebit. | In the preceding book we have treated of the law of persons.  Let us now speak of things, which either are in our patrimony, or not in our patrimony.  For some things by the law of nature are common to all ; some are public ; some belong to corporate bodies, and some belong to no one.  Most things are the pro- perty of individuals, who acquire them in different ways, as will ap- pear hereafter. |

GAI. ii. 1 ; D. i. 8. 2.

Under the word *res*, thing, is included whatever is capable
of being the subject of a right.  The principal division of
Gaius is into things *divini juris* and *humani juris*.  Here
the principal division is according as things are *in nostro
patrimonio*; that is, belong to individuals ; or *extra nostrum
patrimonium*; that is, belong to all men (*communes*), or no
men (*nullius*), or to bodies of men (*universitatis*).  The
words *bona* and *pecunia*, it may be observed, are only used
of things *in nostro patrimonio*.

| | |
|---|---|
| 1. Et quidem naturali jure com- munia sunt omnium hæc : aer, aqua profluens, et mare et per hoc litora maris.  Nemo igitur ad litus maris | 1. By the law of nature these things are common to mankind—the air, running water, the sea, and con- sequently the shores of the sea.  No |

accedere prohibetur, dum tamen villis et monumentis et ædificiis abstineat: quia non sunt juris gentium, sicut et mare.

one, therefore, is forbidden to approach the sea-shore, provided that he respects habitations, monuments, and buildings, which are not, like the sea, subject only to the law of nations.

D. I. 8. 2. 1; D. I. 8. 4.

Of things that are common to all any one may take such a portion as he pleases. Thus a man may inhale the air, or float his ship on any part of the sea. As long as he occupies any portion, his occupation is respected; but directly his occupation ceases, the thing occupied again becomes common to all. The sea-shore, that is, the shore as far as the waves go at furthest, was considered to belong to all men. For the purposes of self-defence any nation had a right to occupy the shore and to repel strangers. Individuals, if they built on it, by means of piles or otherwise, were secured in exclusive enjoyment of the portion occupied; but if the building was taken away, their occupancy was at an end, and the spot on which the building stood again became common. (D. i. 8. 6.)

2. Flumina autem omnia et portus publica sunt. Ideoque jus piscandi omnibus commune est in portu fluminibusque.

2. All rivers and ports are public; hence the right of fishing in a port, or in rivers, is common to all men.

D. I. 8. 4. 1; D. xlvii. 10. 13. 7.

The word *publicus* is sometimes used as equivalent to *communis*, but is properly used, as here, for what belongs to the people. Things public belong to a particular people, but may be used and enjoyed by all men. Roads, public places and buildings might be added to those mentioned in the text. The particular people or nation in whose territory public things lie may permit all the world to make use of them, but exercise a special jurisdiction to prevent any one injuring them. In this light even the shore of the sea was said, though not very strictly, to be a *res publica*: it is not the property of the particular people whose territory is adjacent to the shore, but it belongs to them to see that none of the uses of the shore are lost by the act of individuals. Celsus says, *Litora in quæ populus Romanus imperium habet populi Romani esse arbitror* (D. xliii. 8. 3), where, if we are to bring this opinion of Celsus into harmony with the opinions of other jurists, we must understand '*populi Romani esse*' to mean 'are subject to the guardianship of the Roman people.'

3. Est autem litus maris, quatenus hybernus fluctus maximus excurrit.

3. The sea-shore extends as far as the greatest winter flood runs up.

D. I. 16. 96.

Celsus ascribes this definition to Cicero, who apparently borrowed it from Aquilius. (Cic. *Top.* 7.)

4. Riparumquoque usus publicus est juris gentium, sicut ipsius fluminis. Itaque navem ad eas adplicare, funes arboribus ibi natis religare, onus aliquod in his reponere cuilibet liberum est, sicut per ipsum flumen navigare; sed proprietas earum illorum est quorum praediis haerent: qua de causa arbores quoque in iisdem natae earumdem sunt.

4. The public use of the banks of a river is part of the law of nations, just as is that of the river itself. All persons therefore are as much at liberty to bring their vessels to the bank, to fasten ropes to the trees growing there, and to place any part of their cargo there, as to navigate the river itself. But the banks of a river are the property of those whose land they adjoin; and consequently the trees growing on them are also the property of the same persons.

D. i. 8. 5.

The banks of rivers belonged to the proprietors of the adjacent lands; but the use of them, for the purposes of navigation or otherwise, was open to all. The proprietors therefore could alone reap the profits of the soil; but if they attempted to exercise their rights so as to hinder the public use of the bank, they would be restrained by an interdict of the praetor. (See Introd. sec. 107.)

5. Litorum quoque usus publicus juris gentium est, sicut ipsius maris: et ob id quibuslibet liberum est casam ibi ponere in quam se recipiant, sicut retia siccare et ex mari reducere. Proprietas autem eorum potest intelligi nullius esse, sed ejusdem juris esse cujus et mare, et quae subjacet mari terra vel arena.

5. The public use of the sea-shore, too, is part of the law of nations, as is that of the sea itself; and therefore any person is at liberty to place on it a cottage, to which he may retreat, or to dry his nets there, and haul them from the sea; for the shores may be said to be the property of no man, but are subject to the same law as the sea itself, and the sand or ground beneath it.

D. i. 8. 5. pr. and 1.

The shores over which the Roman people had power were not the property of the Roman people, although it belonged specially to the Roman people to see that the free use of them was not hindered. (See note to paragraph 2.)

6. Universitatis sunt, non singulorum, veluti quae in civitatibus sunt theatra, stadia et similia, et si qua alia sunt communia civitatum.

6. Among things belonging to a corporate body, not to individuals, are, for instance, buildings in cities, theatres, race-courses, and other similar places belonging in common to a whole city.

D. i. 8. 6. 1.

Universitas is a corporate body, much as the guilds (collegia) of different trades; for instance, the collegium pistorum. Res universitatis are things which can be used by every member of the universitas.

Both the state and corporate bodies had property which they held exactly like individuals; as, for instance, the *agri vectigales*, or slaves and lands belonging to a *collegium*. Such things were not *publicæ* or *universitatis* in the sense in which the words are used here; for every member of the state or corporation could not use and enjoy such things, although the proceeds went to the general purposes of the state or corporation. They were, like the property of individuals, *in nostro patrimonio*, the state or corporation being looked on as any other owner.

7. Nullius autem sunt res sacræ et religiosæ et sanctæ; quod enim divini juris est, id nullius in bonis est.

7. Things sacred, religious, and holy, belong to no one; for that which is subject to divine law is not the property of any one.

GAI. II. 9.

*Res nullius* are either things unappropriated by any one, in which sense things common, or unoccupied lands, or wild animals, are *res nullius*; or they are things to which a religious character prevents any human right of property attaching.

8. Sacræ res sunt, quæ rite et per pontifices Deo consecratæ sunt, veluti ædes sacræ et donaria quæ rite ad ministerium Dei dedicata sunt. Quæ etiam per nostram constitutionem alienari et obligari prohibuimus, excepta causa redemptionis captivorum. Si quis vero auctoritate sua quasi sacrum sibi constituerit, sacrum non est sed profanum. Locus autem in quo ædes sacræ sunt ædificatæ, etiam diruto ædificio sacer adhuc manet, ut et Papinianus rescripsit.

8. Things are sacred which have been duly consecrated by the pontiffs, as sacred buildings and offerings, properly dedicated to the service of God, which we have forbidden by our constitution to be sold or mortgaged, except for the purpose of purchasing the freedom of captives. But, if any one consecrates a building by his own authority, it is not sacred, but profane. But ground on which a sacred edifice has once been erected, even after the building has been destroyed, continues to be sacred, as Papinian also writes.

D. i. 8. 6. 9; C. i. 2. 21.

The distinction between *res sacræ* and *religiosæ*, in the older pagan law, was that the former were things dedicated to the celestial gods, the latter were things abandoned to the infernal—*relictæ diis manibus*. (GAI. ii. 4.) In order that a thing should be *sacra*, it was necessary that it should be dedicated by a pontiff and with the authority of the people, afterwards of the senate, finally of the emperor. (D. i. 8. 6. 1.) Things consecrated were by law inalienable. The support of the poor in a time of famine (C. i. 2. 21), and afterwards the payment of the debts of the church (Nov. 120. 10), sufficed, as well as the release of captives, as reasons for the sale of consecrated moveables; but immoveables were always inalienable.

9. Religiosum locum unusquisque sua voluntate facit, dum mortuum infert in locum suum. In communem autem locum purum invito socio inferre non licet; in commune vero sepulcrum etiam invitis ceteris licet inferre. Item si alienus ususfructus est, proprietarium placet, nisi consentiente usufructuario, locum religiosum non facere. In alienum locum concedente domino licet inferre; et licet postea ratum habuerit quam illatus est mortuus, tamen religiosus fit locus.

9. Any man at his pleasure makes a place religious by burying a dead body in his own ground; but it is not permitted to bury a dead body in land hitherto pure, which is held in common, against the wishes of a coproprietor. But when a sepulchre is held in common, any one coproprietor may bury in it, even against the wishes of the rest. So, too, if another person has the usufruct, the proprietor may not, without the consent of the usufructuary, render the place religious. But a dead body may be laid in a place belonging to another person, with the consent of the owner; and even if the owner only ratifies the act after the dead body has been buried, yet the place is religious.

D. I. 8. 6. 4; D. xi. 7. 2. 7.

Directly the body or bones of a dead person, whether slave or free, were buried, the ground in which they were buried became *religiosus*, although previously pure, that is, neither *sacer*, *religiosus*, nor *sanctus* (D. xi. 7. 2. 4), provided that the person burying the body was the owner of the soil or had the consent of the owner.

Although the place was a *res nullius*, yet there could be a special kind of property in it. There were tombs and burial-places in which none but certain persons, as, for instance, members of the same family, could be buried; and this kind of interest in a *locus religiosus* was transmissible to heirs, or even to purchasers of a property, if the right of burying in a particular place was attached, as it might be, to the ownership of that property. (D. xviii. 1. 24.)

10. Sanctae quoque res, veluti muri et portae, quodammodo divini juris sunt, et ideo nullius in bonis sunt. Ideo autem muros sanctos dicimus, quia poena capitis constituta sit in eos qui aliquid in muros deliquerint. Ideo et legum eas partes quibus poenas constituimus adversus eos qui contra leges fecerint, sanctiones vocamus.

10. Holy things also, as the walls and gates of a city, are to a certain degree subject to divine law, and therefore are not part of the property of any one. The walls of a city are said to be holy, inasmuch as any offence against them is punished capitally; so too those parts of laws by which punishments are established against transgressors, we term sanctions.

Gai. li. 8. 9; D. i. 8. 9; D. i. 8. 0. 3; D. i. 8. 11.

*Res sanctae* are those things which, without being sacred, are protected against the injuries of men (*sanctum est quod ab injuria hominum defensum atque munitum est*) by having a severe penalty attached to the violation of their security.

11. Singulorum autem hominum multis modis res fiunt; quarumdam enim rerum dominium nanciscimur jure naturali quod, sicut diximus, appellatur jus gentium; quarumdam jure civili. Commodius est itaque a vetustiore jure incipere; palam est autem vetustius esse jus naturale, quod cum ipso genere humano rerum natura prodidit. Civilia enim jura tunc esse coeperunt, cum et civitates condi et magistratus creari et leges scribi coeperunt.

11. Things become the property of individuals in various ways; of some we acquire the ownership by natural law, which, as we have observed, is also termed the law of nations; of others by the civil law. It will be most convenient to begin with the more ancient law; and it is very evident that the law of nature, established by nature at the first origin of mankind, is the more ancient, for civil laws could then only begin to exist, when states began to be founded, magistrates to be created, and laws to be written.

**D. xli. 1. 1.**

We now proceed to inquire how property is acquired in particular things. It is acquired either by natural or civil modes. The natural mode first treated of is occupation, of which there are two essential elements; that the thing, the property in which is acquired, should be a *res nullius*, and that the person acquiring it should bring the thing into his possession, that is, into his power, and do so with the intention of holding it as his property (*pro suo habendi*).

12. Ferae igitur bestiae et volucres et pisces, id est, omnia animalia quae mari, coelo et terra nascuntur, simul atque ab aliquo capta fuerint, jure gentium statim illius esse incipiunt: quod enim ante nullius est, id naturali ratione occupanti conceditur. Nec interest, feras bestias et volucres utrum in suo fundo quisque capiat, an in alieno. Plane qui in alienum fundum ingreditur venandi aut aucupandi gratia, potest a domino, si is providerit, prohiberi ne ingrediatur. Quidquid autem eorum ceperis, eo usque tuum esse intelligitur, donec tua custodia coercetur; cum vero evaserit custodiam tuam, et in naturalem libertatem se receperit, tuum esse desinit, et rursus occupantis fit. Naturalem autem libertatem recipere intelligitur, cum vel oculos tuos effugerit, vel ita sit in conspectu tuo, ut difficilis sit ejus persecutio.

12. Wild beasts, birds, fish, and all animals, which live either in the sea, the air, or on the earth, so soon as they are taken by any one, immediately become by the law of nations the property of the captor; for natural reason gives to the first occupant that which had no previous owner. And it is immaterial whether a man take wild beasts or birds upon his own ground, or on that of another. Of course any one who enters the ground of another for the sake of hunting or fowling, may be prohibited by the proprietor, if he perceives his intention of entering. Whatever of this kind you take is regarded as your property, so long as it remains in your power, but when it has escaped and recovered its natural liberty, it ceases to be yours, and again becomes the property of him who captures it. It is considered to have recovered its natural liberty, if it has either escaped out of your sight, or if, although not out of sight, it yet could not be pursued without great difficulty.

Gai. ii. 67.; D. xli. 1. 1. 1; D. xli. 1.3 pr. and 1; D. xli. 1. 3. 2; D. xli. 1. 5.

Directly the thing ceases to be in the power of the occupant, the property in it is lost, and it is exactly as if it had never been seized or occupied. What is meant by being in the power of the occupant must vary according to the nature of the thing occupied. Several examples are given in this and the following paragraphs.

| | |
|---|---|
| 13. Illud quæsitum est, an si fera bestia ita vulnerata sit ut capi possit, statim tua esse intelligatur. Quibusdam placuit statim esse tuam, et eousque tuam videri donec eam persequaris; quod si desieris persequi, desinere tuam esse, et rursus fieri occupantis. Alii non aliter putaverunt tuam esse, quam si eam ceperis. Sed posteriorem sententiam non confirmamus, quia multa accidere possunt ut eam non capias. | 13. It has been asked, whether, if you have wounded a wild beast, so that it could be easily taken, it immediately becomes your property. Some have thought that it does become yours directly you wound it, and that it continues to be yours while you continue to pursue it, but that if you cease to pursue it, it then ceases to be yours, and again becomes the property of the first person who captures it. Others have thought that it does not become your property until you have captured it. We confirm this latter opinion, because many accidents may happen to prevent your capturing it. |

D. xB. 1. 5. 1.

Gaius, in this passage of the Digest, informs us that the former opinion was that of Trebatius.

| | |
|---|---|
| 14. Apium quoque natura fera est. Itaque quæ in arbore tua condederint, antequam a te alveo includantur, non magis tuæ intelliguntur esse, quam volucres quæ in arbore tua nidum fecerint; idenque si alius eas incluserit, is earum dominus erit. Favos quoque si quos effecerint, quilibet eximere potest. Plane integra re, si provideris ingredientem fundum tuum, poteris eum jure prohibere ne ingrediatur. Examen quoque quod ex alveo tuo evolaverit, eousque intelligitur esse tuum, donec in conspectu tuo est, nec difficilis ejus est persecutio: alioquin occupantis fit. | 14. Bees also are wild by nature. Therefore, bees that swarm upon your tree, until you have hived them, are no more considered to be your property than the birds which build their nests on your tree; so, if any one else hive them, he becomes their owner. Any one, too, is at liberty to take the honeycombs the bees may have made. But of course, if, before anything has been taken, you see any one entering on your land, you have a right to prevent his entering. A swarm which has flown from your hive is still considered yours as long as it is in your sight and may easily be pursued, otherwise it becomes the property of the first person that takes it. |

D. xII. 1. 5. 2–4.

It is said that the owner of the land, if he wished to secure the bees for himself, must prevent any one entering *integra re*; because, if the bees are once taken, they belong to the person who takes them, although the owner of the land

may have an action against the person entering against his will.

15. Pavonum et columbarum fera natura est: nec ad rem pertinet, quod ex consuetudine avolare et revolare solent; nam et apes idem faciunt, quarum constat feram esse naturam. Cervos quoque ita quidam mansuetos habent, ut in silvas ire et redire soleant, quorum et ipsorum feram esse naturam nemo negat. In iis autem animalibus quæ ex consuetudine abire et redire solent, talis regula comprobata est, ut eousque tua esse intelligantur, donec animum revertendi habeant; nam si revertendi animum habere desierint, etiam tua esse desinunt, et fiunt occupantium. Revertendi autem animum videntur desinere habere, cum revertendi consuetudinem deseruerint.

GAI. ii. 68;

10. Gallinarum autem et anserum non est fera natura: idque ex eo possumus intelligere, quod aliæ sunt gallinæ quas feras vocamus, item alii anseres quos feros appellamus. Ideoque si anseres tui aut gallinæ tuæ aliquo casu turbati turbatæve evolaverint, licet conspectum tuum effugerint, quocumque tamen loco sint, tui tuæve esse intelliguntur; et qui lucrandi animo ea animalia retinet, furtum committere intelligitur.

D. xli. 1. 6. 6.

17. Item ea quæ ex hostibus capimus, jure gentium statim nostra fiunt, adeo quidem ut et liberi homines in servitutem nostrum deducantur. Qui tamen, si evaserint nostram potestatem et ad suos reversi fuerint, pristinum statum recipiunt.

GAI. II. 69; D. xli. 1. 5. 7; D. xli. 1. 7.

15. Peacocks, too, and pigeons are naturally wild, nor does it make any difference that they are in the habit of flying out and then returning again, for bees, which without doubt are naturally wild, do so too. Some persons have deer so tame, that they will go into the woods, and regularly return again; yet no one denies that deer are naturally wild. But, with respect to animals which are in the habit of going and returning, the rule has been adopted, that they are considered yours as long as they have the intention of returning, but if they cease to have this intention, they cease to be yours, and become the property of the first person that takes them. These animals are supposed to have lost the intention, when they have lost the habit, of returning.

D. xli. 1. 55.

10. But fowls and geese are not naturally wild, which we may learn from there being particular kinds of fowls and geese which we term wild. And, therefore, if your geese or fowls should be frightened, and take flight, they are still regarded as yours wherever they may be, although you may have lost sight of them; and whoever detains such animals with a view to his own profit, commits a theft.

17. The things we take from our enemies become immediately ours by the law of nations, so that even freemen thus become our slaves; but if they afterwards escape from us, and return to their own people, they regain their former condition.

The possessions of an enemy were always looked on as *res nullius*: the first person who took them became the owner. Practically, of course, things taken in war did not belong to the particular soldier who took them, unless in very exceptional cases, because he took them as one of a large body, whose exertions all contributed, directly or indirectly, to the capture. The army, again, did but represent the state; and though moveables were generally given up to the soldiers and divided among them, land taken in war was claimed by the state, whose servants the soldiers were and in whose behalf they fought.

Just as the freeman, who had been made a prisoner and a slave, regained his *status* when he returned to his own country by the *jus postliminii* (see Bk. i. Tit. 12. 5), so everything that returned to its former state of being free from any owner, was said to do so by a process analogous to the *jus postliminii*. Marcian, for example, speaks in the Digest (i. 8. 6.) of a person building on a shore, and after having said that the soil is only his while the building remains, goes on, *alioquin, ædificio dilapso, quasi jure postliminii revertitur locus in pristinam causam*.

We have no mention here, which we might expect to have, of the mode by which things retaken in war returned to their owners, nor what things did so return. We know that the things that did return were said to do so by *postliminium*: Pomponius says, (*duæ species postliminii sunt aut ut ipsi revertamur aut aliquid recipiamus*, D. xlix. 15. 14.) Generally speaking, if the property of individuals was captured by an enemy and retaken, it was *præda*, that is, was part of the spoil of war, and belonged to the state, not to its former owner. But there were certain things to which a *jus postliminii* attached, and which, if retaken, reverted to their original owner, and did not form part of the *præda*. These things, so far as we know them, were land, slaves, horses, mules, and ships used in war. (Cic. *Top.* 8; D. xlix. 15. 2.)

| | |
|---|---|
| 18. Item lapilli et gemmæ et cætera quæ in litore inveniuntur, jure naturali statim inventoris fiunt. | 18. Precious stones, gems, and other things, found upon the sea-shore, become immediately by natural law the property of the finder. |

D. i. 8. 3.

In the next section Justinian leaves the subject of acquisition by occupation, but afterwards speaks of matters that properly belong to it, of islands rising in the sea (paragr. 22), treasures found (paragr. 39), things abandoned by their owner (paragr. 47, 48).

| | |
|---|---|
| 19. Item ea quæ ex animalibus dominio tuo subjectis nata sunt, eodem jure tibi adquiruntur. | 19. All that is born of animals of which you are the owner, becomes by the same law your property. |

D. xli. l. 6.

From the 19th to the 35th paragraph inclusive, may be taken together as bearing more or less on the subject of accession. The Latin word *accessio* always means an increase

or addition to something previously belonging to us, but
commentators have used the word accession not only for the
increase itself, but also for the mode in which the increase
becomes our property.

First, there is the instance given in this section and in the
35th section of the produce of animals, and the fruits of lands
belonging to us. They are really part of that which originally belonged to us. The owner of the wheat-seed is potentially the owner of the blade and the ear, the owner of the
animal is potentially the owner of its young.

Again, a thing may be an *accessio*, an actual gain or increase to our property, which was in theory of law, but not in
fact, ours already. This is the case with an island in a river,
an instance given in sec. 22. The bed of the river becomes
*publicus* by the mere fact of the river flowing over it; if
any portion of the bed is dried so as to form an island, it
ceases to be public, and, becoming private, is presumed to
be a part of the adjacent land. It is something not newly
acquired, but restored to us by nature; we have been tem-
porarily deprived of it, and again resume our rights over it.

Again, a person who uses materials sometimes only gives
them a new form, sometimes makes with them a new thing,
different from the materials themselves. When he does the
latter, the thing he makes, the *nova species*, as the jurists
termed it, becomes his by the fact of his making it. The
thing did not exist, and he has made it to exist, and it belongs to him by a title not dissimilar to that of occupation :
it is a new thing, which he is the first to get into his power.
To take an instance given in paragraph 25, a man who makes
wine out of another's grapes has made something new of a
kind distinct from the grapes themselves, and the wine belongs to him.

Again, when two things belonging to different owners are
united so as to become integral portions of a common whole,
but one portion is subordinate and inferior to the other, we
have to ask whether the owner of the greater became the
owner of the less? The Roman jurists answered this by asking whether the two things could after their union be separated from each other. If this was physically possible each
owner of the respective portions continued to be owner; but
if not, the owner of the more important or principal thing
became the owner of the less important or accessory thing.

20. Præterea quod per alluvionem
agro tuo flumen adjecit, jure gentium tibi adquiritur. Est autem
alluvio incrementum latens; per

20. Moreover, the alluvial soil
added by a river to your land becomes yours by the law of nations.
Alluvion is an imperceptible increase,

alluvionem autem id videtur adjici, quod ita paulatim adjicitur ut intelligere non possis quantum quoquo momento temporis adjiciatur.

and that is added by alluvion, which is added so gradually that no one can perceive how much is added at any one moment of time.

D. xll. 1. 7. 1.

The deposit of earth gradually formed by alluvion upon the bank of a river is inseparable from the native soil of the bank: and the owner of the latter acquires the former by right of accession.

An exception was made in the case of *agri limitati*, that is, lands belonging to the state by right of conquest, and granted or sold in plots. If these plots were enlarged by alluvion, the increase did not become the property of the owner of the plot. (D. xli. 1. 16.) The reason seems to be that the particles deposited by alluvion were considered public as forming portion of the current of the stream, the waters of which were public, and when these particles were deposited by the side of a plot granted or sold by the state, they were not allowed to enlarge the plot of which the state had already determined the proper size.

21. Quod si vis fluminis partem aliquam ex tuo praedio detraxerit, et vicini praedio attulerit, palam est eam tuam permanere. Plane, si longiore tempore fundo vicini tui haeserit, arboresque quas secum traxerit, in eum fundum radices egerint, ex eo tempore videntur vicini fundo adquisitae esse.

21. But if the violence of a river should bear away a portion of your land, and unite it to that of your neighbour, it undoubtedly still continues yours. If, however, it remains for a long time united to your neighbour's land, and the trees, which it swept away with it, take root in his ground, these trees from that time become part of your neighbour's estate.

D. xll. 1. 7. 2.

When a large mass of earth is carried to the side of a river bank, it is quite possible to detach it, and consequently the mass remains the property of its former owner, but if it becomes inseparable in the manner described in the text, then the property in it is changed.

*Videntur acquisitae* is substituted here for *videtur acquisita* in the Digest, to include the trees themselves as well as the soil of the fragment. (See paragr. 31.)

22. Insula quae in mari nata est, quod raro accidit, occupantis fit; nullius enim esse creditur. In flumine nata, quod frequenter accidit, si quidem mediam partem fluminis tenet, communis est eorum qui ab utraque parte fluminis prope ripam praedia possident, pro modo latitu-

22. When an island is formed in the sea, which rarely happens, it is the property of the first occupant: for before occupation, it belongs to no one. But when an island is formed in a river, which frequently happens, if it is placed in the middle of it, it belongs in common to those

N

dinis cujusque fundi, quæ latitudo propo ripam sit. Quod si alteri parti proximior sit, eorum est tantum qui ab ea parte propr ripam prædia possident. Quod si aliqua parte divisum sit flumen, deinde infra unitum, agrum alicujus in formam insulæ redegerit, ejusdem permanet is ager cujus et fuerat.

who possess the lands near the banks on each side of the river, in proportion to the extent of each man's estate adjoining the banks. But, if the island is nearer to one side than the other, it belongs to those persons only who possess lands contiguous to the bank on that side. If a river divides itself and afterwards unites again, thus giving to any one's land the form of an island, the land still continues to belong to the person to whom it belonged before.

D. xli. 1. 7. 3, 4.

An island formed by a stream cutting off a portion of land could not be supposed to belong to any one but its former owner. But if the island was formed by the bed of the river becoming dry in any part, it might be doubtful to whom it belonged. The bed of the river, as long as the river flowed over it, was public. *Ille alveus quem sibi flumen fecit, et si privatus antea fuit, incipit tamen esse publicus* (D. xliii. 12. 1. 7); or rather the use of it was public, while the soil itself was the property of the private individuals to whom the soil of the banks belonged, and therefore when the bed was dried, when it had ceased to be subject to public use, the private owners resumed the rights of ownership over it, *quum exsiccatus esset alveus, proximorum fit, quia jam populus eo non utitur.* (D. lxi. 1. 30. 1.) If the bed was not wholly but partially dried, the island formed would belong to the owner of the nearest bank; if it lay entirely on one side of the stream, or if it lay partly on one side and partly on the other, it would belong to the owners of both banks in such proportion as a line drawn from the middle of the stream would divide it.

22. Quod si naturali alveo in universum derelicto, alia parte fluere cœperit, prior quidem alveus eorum est qui prope ripam ejus prædia possident, pro modo scilicet latitudinis cujusque agri quæ, latitudo prope ripam sit. Novus autem alveus ejus juris esse incipit, cujus et ipsum flumen, id est publicus. Quod si post aliquod tempus ad priorem alveum reversum fuerit flumen, rursus novus alveus eorum esse incipit qui prope ripam ejus prædia possident.

23. If a river, entirely forsaking its natural channel, begins to flow in another direction, the old bed of the river belongs to those who possess the lands adjoining its banks, in proportion to the extent that their respective estates adjoin the banks. The new bed follows the condition of the river, that is, it becomes public. And, if after some time the river returns to its former channel, the new bed again becomes the property of those who possess the lands contiguous to its banks.

D. xli. 1. 7. 5.

It might happen that the soil over which the river flowed was known to have belonged to a different person, and not to the owners of the adjacent banks. If the river changed its channel and left the soil dry, to whom was the recovered land to belong, could its original owner claim it, or was the presumption of law so fixed in favour of the owners of the adjacent banks that nothing was admitted to rebut it? Gaius says that strict law was against the original owner, but adds, *vix est ut id obtineat* (D. xli. 1. 7. 5); equity would hardly allow such strictness to prevail in all cases.

24. Alia sane causa est, si cujus totus ager inundatus fuerit: neque enim inundatio fundi speciem commutat, et ob id si recesserit aqua, palam est eum fundum ejus manere cujus et fuit.

24. The case is quite different if any one's land is completely inundated; for the inundation does not alter the nature of the land, and therefore, when the waters have receded, the land is indisputably the property of its former owner.

D. xli. 1. 7. 6.

An inundation is here contrasted with a change in the course of a river. A field overflowed with water is still a field, and as much belongs to its owner as if it were dry.

25. Cum ex aliena materia speciem aliquam facit sit ab aliquo, quaeri solet quis eorum naturali ratione dominus sit, utrum is qui fecerit, an ille potius qui materiae dominus fuerit. Ut ecce, si quis ex alienis uvis aut olivis aut spicis vinum aut oleum aut frumentum fecerit, aut ex alieno auro vel argento vel aere vas aliquod fecerit, vel ex alieno vino et melle mulsum miscuerit, vel ex medicamentis alienis emplastrum aut collyrium composuerit, vel ex aliena lana vestimentum fecerit, vel ex alienis tabulis navem vel armarium vel subsellium fabricaverit. Et post multas Sabinianorum et Proculianorum ambiguitates placuit media sententia existimantium, si ea species ad materiam reduci possit, eum videri dominum esse, qui materiae dominus fuerit; si non possit reduci, eum potius intelligi dominum, qui fecerit: ut ecce, vas conflatum potest ad rudem massam aeris vel argenti vel auri reduci; vinum autem aut oleum aut frumentum ad uvas et olivas et spicas reverti non potest, ac ne

25. When one man has made anything with materials belonging to another, it is often asked which, according to natural reason, ought to be considered the proprietor, whether he who gave the form, or he rather who owned the materials. For instance, suppose a person has made wine, oil, or wheat, from the grapes, olives, or ears of corn belonging to another; has cast a vessel out of gold, silver, or brass, belonging to another; has made mead with another man's wine and honey; has composed a plaster, or eye-salve, with another man's medicaments; has made a garment with another's wool; or a ship, a chest, or a bench, with another man's timber. After long controversy between the Sabinians and Proculians, a middle opinion has been adopted, based on the following distinction. If the thing made can be reduced to its former rude materials, then the owner of the materials is also considered the owner of the thing made; but, if the thing cannot be so reduced, then he who made it is the owner of it. For

mulsum quidem ad vinum et mel reddi potest. Quod si partim ex sua materia partim ex aliena speciem aliquam fecerit quis, veluti ex suo vino et alieno melle mulsum miscuerit, aut ex suis et alienis medicamentis emplastrum aut collyrium, aut ex sua lana et aliena vestimentum fecerit, dubitandum non est hoc casu eum esse dominum qui fecerit, cum non solum operam suam dedit, sed et partem ejusdem materiae praestavit.

example, a vessel, when cast, can easily be reduced to its rude materials of brass, silver, or gold; but wine, oil, or wheat, cannot be reconverted into grapes, olives, or ears of corn; nor can mead be resolved into wine and honey. But, if a man has made anything, partly with his own materials and partly with the materials of another, as, if he has made mead with his own wine and another man's honey, or a plaster or eye-salve, partly with his own, and partly with another man's medicaments, or a garment with his own and also with another man's wool, then in such cases, he who made the thing is undoubtedly the proprietor; since he not only gave his labour, but furnished also a part of the materials.

GAI. ii. 70; D. xli. 1. 7. 7; D. vi. 1. 5. 1; D. xli. 1. 27. 1.

When materials belonging to different persons were mixed together, or one person bestowed his labour on the materials of another, although one person only might be the owner of the product, yet he did not become so at the expense of others. He was obliged to pay those whose materials or labour had been employed the value of their respective materials or labour, and was liable to a *condictio* or personal action (see Introd. sec. 95) for the enforcement of the payment. He himself could claim the product itself by *vindicatio*, or real action, given only to the owner of a thing. The jurists very commonly speak of a person being able to vindicate a thing as a mode of saying that he is the owner, the test of ownership being whether the supposed owner could or could not claim the thing by *vindicatio*.

Supposing a person formed a thing with materials belonging to another, which was the one that could claim it by a real action, the maker of the thing or the owner of the materials? The Proculians said, the thing is a new thing and its maker is the owner; the Sabinians said, the materials remain, although their form is changed, and their proprietor is the owner of the thing made. The distinction sanctioned by Justinian decided the question according to the fact of there being or not being a really new thing made. If there was, then the reasoning of the Proculians held good, and the maker becomes the owner by a species of occupation, *quia quod factum est, antea nullius fuerat.* If the thing made was only the old materials in a new form, then it belonged to the owner of the materials in accordance with the opinions of the Sabinians. The opinion of each school, therefore, was admitted where the facts were in accordance with it.

In the latter part of the section Justinian says that if the materials were partly the property of the maker, the thing made certainly belonged to him. This must be understood strictly with reference to the case spoken of in the text, that, namely, of materials, none being merely accessory, i.e. subordinate, to the others, being inseparably mixed together. If some of the materials were only accessory, and the thing made was not a new thing, it would not necessarily belong to the maker, but would only belong to him if he were the owner of the principal materials; and if the different materials were separable from each other, they would still belong to their respective owners.

20. Si tamen alienam purpuram vestimento suo quis intexuit, licet pretiosior est purpura, accessionis vice cedit vestimento. Et qui dominus fuit purpurae, adversus eum qui subripuit, habet furti actionem et condictionem, sire ipse sit qui vestimentum fecit, sive alius; nam extinctae res, licet vindicari non possint, condici tamen a furibus et quibusdam aliis possessoribus possunt.

20. If, however, any one has interwoven purple belonging to another into his own vestment, the purple, although the more valuable, attaches to the vestment as an accession, and its former owner has an action of theft, and a condiction against the person who stole it from him, whether it was he or some one else who made the vestment. For although things which have perished cannot be reclaimed by vindication, yet this gives ground for a condiction against the thief, and against many other possessors.

D. x. 4. 7. 9; Gai. ii. 79.

This is an instance of what is termed by commentators *adjunctio*. The owner of a thing in the possession of another could bring an action called *ad exhibendum*, to make the person, in whose possession it was, produce or exhibit it, so that the owner, if he could establish his claim to it by vindication, might be sure that it was not made away with. Ulpian says, in the Digest (x. 4. 7. 2), that a person whose purple was interwoven could bring an action *ad exhibendum* against the owner of the vestment. This, which is as much as to say that the owner of the purple is still its owner, seems at variance with what Justinian says here of the purple acceding to the vestment, and of the person, *qui dominus fuit purpurae*, having only a personal action. Their respective decisions would, however, be right, according as the purple was not or was an inseparable part of the vestment. Supposing the purple was so interwoven that it could be again separated, then its owner, remaining its owner, could bring an action *ad exhibendum*. If it were made an inseparable part of the vestment, if it were an *extincta res*, i. e. could no more have a separate, distinct existence, then, being by its nature accessory to the vestment, it would become the property of the owner of the vestment, and its former owner would only have a personal action to recover its value.

*Quibusdam possessoribus.* The word *quibusdam* is used to exclude *bona fide* possessors of the *res extincta*, who had not done anything to cause it to perish. Against an actual thief an *actio furti* and a *condictio* might be brought, against others only a *condictio.* (THEOPHIL. *Paraphr.*)

27. Si duorum materiae ex voluntate dominorum confusae sint, totum id corpus quod ex confusione fit utriusque commune est; veluti si qui vina sua confuderint, aut massas argenti vel auri conflaverint. Sed etsi diversae materiae sint, et ob id propria species facta sit, forte ex vino et melle mulsum, aut ex auro et argento electrum. idem juris est: nam et eo casu communem esse speciem non dubitatur. Quod si fortuitu et non voluntate dominorum confusae fuerint vel diversae materiae, vel quae ejusdem generis sunt, idem juris esse placuit.

27. If materials belonging to two persons are mixed together by their mutual consent, whatever is thence produced is common to both, as if, for instance, they have intermixed their wines, or melted together their gold or silver. And although the materials are different which are employed in the admixture, and thus a new substance is formed, as when mead is made with wine and honey, or electrum by fusing together gold and silver, the rule is the same; for in this case the new substance is undoubtedly common. And if it is by chance, and not by the intention of the proprietors, that materials, whether similar or different, are mixed together, the rule is still the same.

D. xli. 1. 7-9.

This union of liquids is termed by commentators *confusio.* When the product became common property, then any of the joint proprietors could procure their own share to be given up to them by bringing an action called *communi dividendo.*

28. Quod si frumentum Titii frumento tuo mixtum fuerit, si quidem ex voluntate vestra, commune erit; quia singula corpora, id est, singula grana quae cujusque propria fuerunt, ex consensu vestro communicata sunt. Quod si casu id mixtum fuerit, vel Titius id miscuerit sine tua voluntate, non videtur commune esse, quia singula corpora in sua substantia durant; nec magis istis casibus commune fit frumentum, quam grex intelligitur esse communis, si pecora Titii tuis pecoribus mixta fuerint. Sed si ab alterutro vestrum totum id frumentum retineatur, in rem qui-

28. If the wheat of Titius is mixed with yours, when this takes place by your mutual consent, the mixed heap belongs to you in common; because each body, that is, each grain, which before was the property of one or other of you, has by your mutual consent been made your common property; but, if the intermixture were accidental, or made by Titius without your consent, the mixed wheat does not then belong to you both in common; because the grains still remain distinct, and retain their proper substance. The wheat in such a case no more becomes common to you both, than a flock would be, if

dem actio pro modo frumenti cujusque competit; arbitrio autem
judicis continetur, ut ipse æstimet
quale cujusque frumentum fuerit.

the sheep of Titius were mixed with
yours; but, if either one of you keep
the whole quantity of mixed wheat,
the other has a real action for the
amount of wheat belonging to him,
but it is in the province of the judge
to estimate the quality of the wheat
belonging to each.

D. vi. l. 4. 5.

This mixing together of things not liquid is termed by commentators *commixtio.* If the things mixed, still remaining
the property of their former owners, were easy to separate
again, as for instance, sheep united in one flock, when one
owner brought his claim by *vindicatio,* his property was restored to him without difficulty; but if there was difficulty in
separating the materials from each other, as in dividing the
grains of wheat in a heap, the obvious mode would be to
distribute the whole heap in shares proportionate to the
quantity of wheat belonging to the respective owners.   But it
might happen that the wheat mixed together was not all of
the same quality, and therefore the owner of the better kind
of wheat would lose by having a share determined in amount
only by the quantity of his wheat; and the judge therefore
was permitted to exercise his judgment (*arbitrio continetur*
—see Introd. sec. 106) how great an addition ought to be
made to his share to compensate for the superior quality of
the wheat originally belonging to him.

29. Cum in suo solo aliquis ex
aliena materia ædificaverit, ipse
intelligitur dominus ædificii; quia
omne quod inædificatur solo cedit.
Nec tamen ideo is qui materiæ
dominus fuerat, desinit dominus
ejus esse; sed tantisper neque vindicare eam potest, neque ad exhibendum de ea re agere, propter
legem duodecim tabularum, qua
cavetur ne quis tignum alienum
ædibus suis junctum eximere cogatur, sed duplum pro eo præstet
per actionem quæ vocatur de tigno injuncto. Appellatione autem
tigni omnis materia significatur,
ex qua ædificia fiunt. Quod ideo
provisum est, ne ædificia rescindi
necesse sit; sed si aliqua ex causa
dirutum sit ædificium, poterit materiæ dominus, si non fuerit duplum jam persecutus, tunc eam

29. If a man builds upon his own
ground with the materials of another,
he is considered the proprietor of the
building, because every thing built on
the soil accedes to it.  The owner of
the materials does not, however, cease
to be owner, only while the building
stands he cannot claim the materials,
or demand to have them exhibited, on
account of the law of the Twelve
Tables, providing that no one is to be
compelled to take away the *tignum* of
another which has been made part of
his own building, but that he may be
made, by the action *de tigno injuncto*
to pay double the value: and under
the term *tignum* all materials for
building are comprehended. The object of this provision was to prevent
the necessity of buildings being
pulled down.  But if the building is
destroyed from any cause, then the

vindicare et ad exhibendum de ea re agere.

owner of the materials, if he has not already obtained the double value, may reclaim the materials, and demand to have them exhibited.

Gai. ii. 73; D. xli. 1. 7. 10.

Materials, although forming part of a building belonging to the owner of the ground, were not considered themselves as necessarily belonging to the owner of the building. They were still the property of the person to whom they had belonged before being employed in the building. They were separable from the soil, and, if a special law had not prevented it, could have been claimed by their owner, and their production enforced by an action *ad exhibendum*. The Twelve Tables forbad, however, the needless destruction of buildings, *ne ædificia rescindi necesse sit*. They suspended the right of claiming the materials, or bringing an action *ad exhibendum* until the building was destroyed. When it was destroyed in any way (*aliqua ex causa*) the material might be reclaimed, or an action *ad exhibendum* brought. Meanwhile, by an action termed *de tigno injuncto* their owner might, if he preferred, recover double their value, forfeiting, however, thereby all right of eventually reclaiming them.

Such was the law when the builder employed the materials of another quite innocently. If this conduct was tainted with *mala fides*, as it would be if he knew that the materials did not belong to him, the law of the Twelve Tables still prevented the materials being at once reclaimed by the compulsory destruction of the building; but an action *ad exhibendum* was permitted to be brought as a means of punishing the builder. (D. vi. 1. 23. 6.)  The effect of this action in such a case was that the defendant, not producing the thing demanded, was condemned in such a sum as the judge thought right as a punishment for his having put it out of his power to produce it—*quasi dolo fecerit quominus possideat*. (D. xlvii. 3. 1. 2.)

30. Ex diverso, si quis in alieno solo sua materia domum ædificaverit, illius fit domus cujus et solum est. Sed hoc casu materia dominus proprietatem ejus amittit, quia voluntate ejus intelligitur alienata, utique si non ignorabat se in alieno solo ædificare; et ideo licet diruta sit domus, materiam tamen vindicare non potest. Certe illud constat, si in possessione constituto ædificatore, soli dominus petat domum suam esse, nec solvat

30. On the contrary, if any one builds with his own materials on the ground of another, the building becomes the property of him to whom the ground belongs. But in this case the owner of the materials loses his property, because he is presumed to have voluntarily parted with them, that is, if he knew he was building upon another's land; and, therefore, if the building should be destroyed, he cannot, even then, reclaim the materials. Of course, if the person

pretium materiæ et mercedes fabrorum, posse eum per exceptionem doli mali repelli, utique si bonæ fidei possessor fuerit, qui ædificarit; nam scienti alienum solum casu potest objici culpa, quod ædificaverit temere in eo solo quod intelligeret alienum esse.

who builds is in possession of the soil and the owner of the soil claims the building, but refuses to pay the price of the materials and the wages of the workmen, the owner may be repelled by an exception of *dolus malus*, provided the builder was in possession *bona fide*. For if he knew that he was not the owner of the soil, it might be objected that he was wrong to build on ground which he knew to be the property of another.

D. xli. 1. 7. 12.

If a person used his own materials in building on the land of another, he must have done so either knowing or not knowing that the land was not his own. If he did not know this, then, when the building was destroyed, he could reclaim the materials; or, if he was in possession of the building, could refuse to deliver it to the owner unless he was indemnified for his expenses, at least so far as they had been incurred profitably to the owner of the soil. If he did know that the land was not his own, the text, adopting the words of Gaius (D. xli. 1. 7. 12), says that he entirely lost all property in the materials, and was considered to have voluntarily alienated them. There are passages both in the Digest and Code not quite in accordance with this decision, and which would make it appear that, if the owner of the materials could show that it was not his intention to give them to the owner of the land, he could recover them or their value. (D. v. 3. 38; Cod. iii. 32. 2; C. iii. 32. 5.)

*Dolus malus* (opposed to *dolus bonus*, artifice which the law considers honestly employed) means fraud. When a plaintiff was repelled by an exception of fraud, such words as these were introduced in the *intentio* of the action : *si in ea re nihil dolo malo Auli Agerii factum sit, neque fiat.* (See Introd. sec. 104.)

31. Si Titius alienam plantam in solo suo posuerit, ipsius erit, et ex diverso si Titius suam plantam in Mævii solo posuerit, Mævii planta erit : si modo utroque casu radices egerit ; ante enim quam radices egerit, ejus permanet cujus et fuerat. Adeo autem ex eo tempore quo radices agit planta, proprietas ejus commutatur, ut si vicini arbor ita terram Titii presserit ut in ejus fundum radices egerit, Titii effici arborem dicimus ; rationem enim non per-

31. If Titius places another man's plant in ground belonging to himself, the plant will belong to Titius ; on the contrary, if Titius places his own plant in the ground of Mævius, the plant will belong to Mævius—that is, if, in either case, the plant has taken root ; for, before it has taken root, it remains the property of its former owner. But from the time it has taken root, the property in it is changed ; so much so, that if the tree of a neighbour presses so closely on the ground of Titius as to take root

mittere ut alterius arbor esse intelligatur, quam cujus in fundum radices egisset. Et ideo prope confinium arbor posita, si etiam in vicini fundum radices egerit, communis fit.

In it, we pronounce that the tree becomes the property of Titius. For reason does not permit, that a tree should be considered the property of any one else than of him, in whose ground it has taken root; and therefore, if a tree, planted near a boundary, extends its roots into the lands of a neighbour, it becomes common.

GAI. il. 74; xli. 1. 7. 13.

The tree after it had once taken root, did not belong to its former owner, although it was afterwards severed from the soil. It would seem natural that it should belong to him, because it was separable from the soil, and did not become a part of it more than the materials of a building became part of the soil; but the jurist considered that the nourishment it had drawn from the soil had made it a new tree, *alia facta est* (D. xli. 1. 26. 2), and thus the owner of the soil claimed it by occupation.

When the text says that the tree which strikes root into the soil of Titius belongs to Titius, this is only to be understood of a tree of which all the roots are in the soil of Titius. If only some of the roots were in the soil of Titius, the tree would belong partly to Titius, partly to its former owner.

32. Qua ratione autem plantæ quæ terra coalescunt, solo cedunt, eadem ratione frumenta quoque quæ sata sunt, solo cedere intelliguntur. Ceterum sicut is qui in alieno solo ædificaverit, si ab eo dominus petat ædificium, defendi potest per exceptionem doli mali recundum ea quæ diximus, ita ejusdem exceptionis auxilio tutus esse potest is qui alienum fundum sua impensa bona fide conseruit.

32. As plants rooted in the earth accede to the soil, so, in the same way, grains of wheat which have been sown are considered to accede to the soil. But as he, who has built on the ground of another, may, according to what we have said, defend himself by an exception of *dolus malus*, if the proprietor of the ground claims the building; so also he may protect himself by the aid of the same exception, who, at his own expense and acting *bona fide*, has sown another man's land.

GAI. il. 75, 76; D. xli. 1. 0.

33. Literæ quoque, licet aureæ sint, perinde chartis membranisque cedunt, ac solo cedere solent ea quæ inædificantur aut inseruntur: ideoque si in chartis membranisve tuis carmen vel historiam vel orationem Titius scripserit, hujus corporis non Titius sed tu dominus esse videris. Sed si a Titio petas tuos libros tuasve membranas, nec impensas scripturæ solvere paratus sis, poterit se Titius defendere per exceptionem doli mali, utique si

33. Written characters, although of gold, accede to the paper or parchment on which they are written. Just as whatever is built on, or sown in, the soil, accedes to the soil. And therefore if Titius has written a poem, a history, or an oration, on your paper or parchment, you, and not Titius, are the owner of the written paper. But if you claim your books or parchments from Titius, but refuse to defray the expense of the writing, then Titius can defend him-

rarum chartarum membranarumve
possessionem bona fide nactus est.

self by an exception of *dolus malus*;
that is, if it was *bona fide* that he
obtained possession of the papers or
parchments.

GAL. ii. 77; D. xU. 1. 9. 1.

In this case the letters are inseparable from, and subordinate to, the substance on which they are written, and
become at once the property of the owner of that substance.

34. Si quis in aliena tabula pinx-
erit, quidam putant tabulam picturae cedere; aliis videtur picturam
qualiscumque sit, tabulae cedere.
Sed nobis videtur melius esse tabulam picturae cedere; ridiculum est
enim picturam Apellis vel Par-
rhasii in accessionem vilissimae tabulae cedere. Unde si a domino
tabulae imaginem possidente, is qui
pinxit eam petat, nec solvat pretium
tabulae, poterit per exceptionem
doli mali submoveri. At si is qui
pinxit possideat, consequens est ut
utilis actio domino tabulae adversus
eum detur: quo casu, si non solvat
impensam picturae, poterit per exceptionem doli mali repelli, utique
si bona fide possessor fuerit ille qui
picturam imposuit. Illud enim
palam est quod, sive is qui pinxit
subripuit tabulas, sive alius, competit domino tabularum furti actio.

34. If a person has painted on the
tablet of another, some think that
the tablet accedes to the picture,
others, that the picture, of whatever
quality it may be, accedes to the
tablet. It seems to us the better
opinion, that the tablet should accede
to the picture; for it is ridiculous,
that a painting of Apelles or Par-
rhasius should be but the accessory of
a thoroughly worthless tablet. But
if the owner of the tablet is in possession of the picture, the painter,
should he claim it from him, but refuse to pay the value of the tablet,
may be repelled by an exception of
*dolus malus*. If the painter is in
possession of the picture, it follows
that the owner of the tablet is entitled to a *utilis actio* against him;
and in this case, if the owner of the
tablet does not pay the value of the
picture, be may also be repelled by
an exception of *dolus malus*; that is,
if the painter obtained possession
*bona fide*. If the tablet has been
stolen, whether by the painter or
any one else, the owner of the tablet
may bring an action of theft.

GAI. ii. 78; D. xli. 1. 9. 2.

As written characters belong to the owner of the substance
on which they are written, so it would seem to follow that a
painting also would belong to the owner of the substance on
which it was painted; and Paul (D. vi. 1. 23. 3) decides that
it does, saying that the painting could not exist without the
substance on which it was painted, and therefore acceded to
it. Gaius, whose opinion is adopted in the text, makes the
great value of the painting the reason for an exception to
the rule. But the owner of the tablet or substance, on which
the painting was painted, had in one way something of the
rights of an owner; for if the painter was in possession of the
painting, the owner of the tablet was not left only to a per-

sonal action for the value of the board, but could claim the board itself. The action by which he did so was termed *utilis*, because it was only an equitable method of protecting him. The direct legal power of claiming the tablet (*vindicatio recta*) was in the painter whose property the tablet had become; but the former owner of the tablet was allowed still to treat it as his, in order to compel the painter to pay its value. If, when the *actio utilis* was brought, the painter paid the value of the tablet, the right of action was at an end, and the owner of the tablet could not get possession of the picture by offering to pay its value.

The expression *consequens est ut utilis actio*, &c., must be taken to mean, 'Under the circumstance of the painter possessing, it follows that a *utilis actio* must be given as a remedy to the owner of the tablet.'

35. Si quis a non domino quem dominum esse crediderit, bona fide fundum emerit, vel ex donatione aliave qualibet justa causa æque bona fide acceperit, naturali ratione placuit fructus quos percepit, ejus esse pro cultura et cura; et ideo si postea dominus supervenerit, et fundum vindicet, de fructibus ab eo consumptis agere non potest. Ei vero qui alienum fundum sciens possederit, non idem concessum est: itaque cum fundo etiam fructus, licet consumpti sint, cogitur restituere.

35. If any one has *bona fide* purchased land from another, whom he believed to be the true owner, when in fact he was not, or has *bona fide* acquired it from such a person by gift or by any other good title, natural reason demands that the fruits which he has gathered shall be his in return for his care and culture. And therefore, if the real owner afterwards appears and claims his land, he can have no action for fruits, which the possessor has consumed. But the same allowance is not made to him, who has knowingly been in possession of another's estate; and therefore he is compelled to restore, together with the lands, all the fruits, although they may have been consumed.

D. xll. 1. 48; D. xxil. 1. 15.

Justinian now passes to the interest of a *bona fide* possessor and an usufructuary in the fruits of land, a subject to which he is led by having spoken of other ways in which the interest of the owner of the soil was limited.

A person would be said to possess *bona fide* and *ex justa causa* who had received a thing from a person he believed to be the owner in any method by which ownership could legally pass.

As long as the fruits still adhered to the soil, that is, were still ungathered, they belonged to the owner of the soil. If gathered, but not consumed, they belonged to the *bona fide* possessor as against every one except the owner of the soil.

When the owner of the soil claimed them, they became his, for they had only been the property of the *bona fide* possessor *interim* (D. xli. 1. 48), that is, provisionally; but if they had been consumed, the owner of the soil could not recover their value from the *bona fide* possessor. The *mala fide* possessor, on the contrary, was obliged to give the value even of those that were consumed (*restituere fructus consumptos*).

There seems little doubt that the interest of the *bona fide* possessor extended over all the fruits of the land, and not only over those produced by his cultivation and care (see D. xli. I. 48), although Pomponius (D. xxii. 1. 15) seems to limit it to the latter.

30. Is ad quem ususfructus fundi pertinet, non aliter fructuum dominus efficitur, quam si ipse eos perceperit; et ideo, licet maturis fructibus nondum tamen perceptis decesserit, ad heredem ejus non pertinent, sed domino proprietatis adquiruntur. Eadem fere et de colono dicuntur.

30. The usufructuary of land is not owner of the fruits until he has himself gathered them; and, therefore, if he should die, while the fruits, although ripe, are yet ungathered, they do not belong to his heirs, but are the property of the owner of the soil. And nearly the same may be said of the *colonus*.

The interest of the usufructuary has a special Title (Tit. 4) devoted to it, and all remarks upon it may be reserved till we arrive at that Title.

*Eadem fere.* The heirs of the *colonus* could gather fruits not gathered by him, for his rights did not perish with him; but the heirs of the usufructuary had no rights transmitted to them, and could not therefore gather fruits which he had not gathered.

37. In pecudum fructu etiam foetus est, sicut lac, pili et lana. Itaque agni, hædi et vituli et equuli et suculi statim naturali jure dominji fructuarii sunt. Partus vero ancillæ in fructu non est, itaque ad dominum proprietatis pertinet; absurdum enim videbatur hominem in fructu esse, cum omnes fructus rerum natura gratia hominis comparaverit.

37. In the fruits of animals are included their young, as well as their milk, hair, and wool; and therefore lambs, kids, calves, colts, and young pigs, immediately on their birth become, by the law of nature, the property of the usufructuary; but the offspring of a female slave is not considered a fruit, but belongs to the owner of the property. For it seemed absurd that man should be reckoned a fruit, when it is for man's benefit that all fruits are provided by nature.

D. xxii. 1. 28. pr. and 1.

Ulpian gives, as a reason for the children of slaves not being *in fructu*, that *non temere ancillæ ejus rei causa comparantur ut pariant.* (D. v. 3. 27.) There were, however, many animals, cows or mares for instance, used for

draught, that could not be said to be expressly destined to
bear offspring, and yet their offspring was *in fructu.*

38. Sed si gregis usumfructum
quis habeat, in locum demortuorum
capitum ex foetu fructuarius sum-
mittere debet, ut Juliano visum
est; et in vinearum demortuarum
vel arborum locum alias debet substituere: recte enim colere debet et
quasi bonus paterfamilias.

38. The usufructuary of a flock
ought to replace any of the flock that
may happen to die, by supplying the
deficiency out of the young, as also
Julian was of opinion. So, too, the
usufructuary ought to supply the
place of dead vines or trees. For he
ought to cultivate with care, and to
use everything as a good father of a
family would use it.

This paragraph relates entirely to the subject of Title 4.

39. Thesauros quos quis in loco
suo invenerit, divus Hadrianus naturalem aequitatem secutus ei concessit qui invenerit; Idemque statuit, si quis in sacro aut religioso
loco fortuito casu invenerit. At si
quis in alieno loco, non data ad hoc
opera, sed fortuito invenerit, dimidium inventori, dimidium domino
soli concessit; et convenienter, si
quis in Caesaris loco invenerit, dimidium inventoris, dimidium Caesaris esse statuit. Cui conveniens
est, ut si quis in fiscali loco vel
publico invenerit, dimidium ipsius
esse, dimidium fisci vel civitalis.

39. The Emperor Hadrian, in accordance with natural equity, allowed any treasure found by a man
in his own land to belong to the
finder, as also any treasure found by
chance in a sacred or religious place.
But treasure found without any express search, but by mere chance, in a
place belonging to another, he granted
half to the finder, and half to the
proprietor of the soil. Consequently,
if anything is found in a place belonging to the emperor, half belongs
to the finder, and half to the emperor.
And, hence it follows, that if a man
finds anything in a place belonging
to the *fiscus,* the public, or a city,
half ought to belong to the finder,
and half to the *fiscus* or the city.

D. xII. 1. 63; D. xlix. 14. 3. 10.

*Thesaurus,* says Paul (D. xli. 1. 31. 1), *est vetus quædam
depositio pecuniæ* (that is of anything valuable), *cujus non
extat memoria, ut jam dominium non habeat.* Of course if
it was known who placed it there, it was known to whom it
belonged. But a treasure, though its depositor was unknown,
was not considered exactly as a *res nullius.* The owner of the
land in which it was found had always some interest in it. If
he found it himself, it all belonged to him; if another person
found it, the finder and the owner of the land divided it
equally. When there was no owner of the land, as when the
place was sacred or religious, the finder took it all; but no
one was allowed to make the search for treasures an excuse
for digging up tombs and sacred places, or for digging up
other men's ground; and therefore it was only when the discovery was quite accidental, and the finder had made no
search for it, that the treasure, or the half of it, as the case
might be, was permitted to belong to him.

40. Per traditionem quoqne jure naturali re*nobis adquiruntur: nihil enim tam conveniens est naturali æquitati, quam voluntatem domini volentis rem suam in alium transferre, ratam haberi. Et ideo cujuscunque generis sit corporalis res, tradi potest et a domino tradita alienatur. Itaque stipendiaria quoqueet tributaria prædia eodem modo alienantur: vocanturautem stipendiaria et tributaria prædia, quæ in provinciis sunt: inter quæ nec non et italica prædia ex nostra constitutione nulla est differentia; sed et quidem ex causa donationis aut dotis aut qualibet alia ex causa tradlantur, sine dubio transferuntur.

40. Another mode of acquiring things according to natural law is tradition; for nothing is more conformable to natural equity, than that the wishes of a person, who is desirous to transfer his property to another, should be confirmed; and therefore corporeal things, of whatever kind, may be passed by tradition, and when so passed by their owner, are made the property of another. In this way are alienated stipendiary and tributary lands, that is, lands in the provinces, between which and Italian lands there is now, by our constitution, no difference, so that when tradition is made of them for purpose of a gift, a marriage portion, or any other object, the property in them is undoubtedly transferred.

D. xli. 1. 9. 3; C. vii. 25.

When the property in a thing was to be transferred from one person to another, it was necessary that the process should be complete in four points:—1. The person who transferred it must be the owner; 2. He must place the person to whom he transferred it in legal possession of the thing; 3. He must transfer the thing with intention to pass the property in it; 4. The person to whom it was transferred must receive it with intention to become the owner.

The placing another in legal possession of a thing was termed the *traditio* of that thing. In the simplest case, that of a portable moveable, the owner might really hand over the thing to the person who was to become its possessor; but in no case was it necessary that this should be done; 'what was necessary was that the party, who was to receive it, should have the thing in his power, and that the two parties should express, in any way whatever, the wish of the one to transfer, of the other to accept, the possession. The thing need not be touched; land, for instance, need not be entered on; but the person, who was to be placed in possession, must have the thing before him, so as to be able, by a physical act, to exercise power over it. (See SAVIGNY on *Possession*, Bk. ii. secs. 16 and 17.)

Property could not be transferred by mere agreement. (*Traditionibus et usucapionibus, non nudis pactis dominia transferuntur.* C. ii. 3. 20.) The agreement was but the expression of the intention of the parties; and this was ineffectual unless it was accompanied by the party being placed in possession to whom the thing was to be transferred.

*Prædia stipendiaria* were provincial lands belonging to the people, *tributaria* provincial lands belonging to the emperor. (GAI. ii. 21.) It will be remembered that, until Justinian destroyed all distinction between Italian and provincial land by a constitution (C. vii. 25), the *Italicum solum* was a *res mancipi*, and could only he transferred by the peculiar form of *mancipatio*. (See Introd. sec. 59.)

41. Venditæ vero res et traditæ non aliter emptori adquiruntur, quam si is venditori pretium solverit, vel alio modo ei satisfecerit, veluti expromissore aut pignore dato. Quod cavetur quidem etiam lege duodecim tabularum, tamen recte dicitur et jure gentium, id est, jure naturali id effici. Sed si is qui vendidit, fidem emptoris secutus est, dicendum est statim rem emptoris fieri.

41. But things sold and delivered are not acquired by the buyer until he has paid the seller the price, or satisfied him in some way or other, as by procuring some one to be security, or by giving a pledge. And, although this is provided by a law of the Twelve Tables, yet it may be rightly said to spring from the law of nations, that is, the law of nature. But if the seller has accepted the credit of the buyer, the thing then becomes immediately the property of the buyer.

D. xviii. 1. 19. 53.

The seller would probably not have the intention to transfer the property until he received the price; but sometimes he might be content to receive security for the payment of the price, or he might choose to accept the credit of the buyer instead of the price itself; and if, in either of these latter cases, he intended to pass the property, it would pass at once, irrespectively of the price being paid.

42. Nihil autem interest, utrum ipse dominus tradat alicui rem, an voluntate ejus alius.

42. It is immaterial whether the owner deliver the thing himself, or some one else by his direction.

D. xll. 1. 0. 4.

43. Qua ratione, si cui libera universorum negotiorum administratio a domino permissa fuerit, isque ex his negotiis rem vendiderit et tradiderit, facit eam accipientis.

43. Hence, if any one is intrusted by an owner with the uncontrolled administration of all his goods, and he sells and delivers anything which is a part of these goods, he passes the property in it to the person who receives the thing.

D. xll. 1. 0. 4.

By the will of the owner, the manager of the property is able to deal with it; and if he deals with it, the will of the owner is expressed through him.

44. Interdum etiam sine traditione nuda voluntas domini sufficit ad rem transferendam, veluti si rem

44. Sometimes, too, the mere wish of the owner, without tradition, is sufficient to transfer the property in

quam tibi aliquis commodavit aut locavit aut apud te deposuit, vendiderit tibi aut donaverit; quamvis enim ex ea causa tibi eam non tradiderit, eo tamen ipso quod patitur tuam esse, statim tibi adquiritur proprietas, perinde ac si eo nomine tradita fuisset.

a thing, as when a person has lent, or let to you anything, or deposited anything with you, and then afterwards sells or gives it to you. For, although he has not delivered it to you for the purpose of the sale or gift, yet by the mere fact of his consenting to it becoming yours, you instantly acquire the property in it, as fully as if it had actually been delivered to you for the express purpose of passing the property.

D. xli. 1. 9. 5.

When the person to whom the property in the thing was transferred was already in possession of the thing, then, if the wishes of the parties to give and receive the property in it were added to this, and the person who affected to give the property was the real owner, all the conditions of a transfer were complete. It made no difference what was their respective order in time. Generally the expression of will would precede the placing in possession, but not necessarily. When the person to whom the property in the thing was transferred had only the mere detention of the thing, that is, had it in his keeping and power as a hirer or depositary would have, but had not the possession of it, that is, had not also the intention of dealing with it as an owner, all that was necessary to change this detention into possession was a change in the *animus* with which it was held; and of course the intention to hold it as an owner was sufficiently shown by accepting the transfer of the property. The person, in like manner, who transferred the property, by doing so sufficiently showed his intention of placing the other in possession. Thus the different elements of *traditio* were broken up and separated, not, as usual, united in a single act; and this is what is meant in the text by saying the property passes *sine traditione*.

45. Item si quis merces in horreo deposuit vendiderit, simul atque claves horrei tradiderit emptori, transfert proprietatem mercium ad emptorem.

45. So, too, any one, who has sold goods deposited in a warehouse, as soon as he has handed over the keys of the warehouse to the buyer, transfers to the buyer the property in the goods.

D. xli. 1. 9. 6.

The text does not state all that was necessary to transfer the property in such a case. It was requisite that the key should be given *apud horrea*, at the warehouse (D. xviii. 1. 74). A person who was at the warehouse and had the key

o

in his hand was in a position to exercise immediate power over the contents of the warehouse; the goods were in his custody, and he was thus placed in possession of them. The key was not symbolical, but was the means by which he was enabled to deal with the goods as an owner.

46. Hoc amplius, interdum et in incertam personam collata voluntas domini transfert rei proprietatem: ut ecce, praetores et consules qui missilia jactant in vulgus, ignorant quid eorum quisque sit excepturus, et tamen quia volunt quod quisque exceperit ejus esse, statim eum dominum efficiunt.

46. Nay, more, sometimes the intention of an owner, although directed only towards an uncertain person, transfers the property in a thing. For instance, when the praetors and consuls throw their largesses to the mob, they do not know what each person in the mob will get; but as it is their intention that each should have what he gets, they make what each gets immediately belong to him.

D. xli. 1. 9. 7.

47. Qua ratione verius esse videtur, si rem pro derelicto a domino habitam occupaverit quis, statim eum dominum effici. Pro derelicto autem habetur, quod dominus ea mente abjecerit, ut id rerum suarum esse nollet, ideoque statim dominus esse desinit.

47. Accordingly, it is quite true to say that anything which is seized on, when abandoned by its owner, becomes immediately the property of the person who takes possession of it. And anything is considered as abandoned, which its owner has thrown away with a wish no longer to have it as a part of his property, as it therefore immediately ceases to belong to him.

D. xli. 7. 1.

Pomponius (D. xli. 7. 5) speaks as if the property in things abandoned was transferred, like that in things thrown to the mob, by the wish of the owner to transfer it to the person who should first take possession of it; but it is much more natural to consider, with the text, that the thing becomes a *res nullius* by being abandoned, and the property of the first occupant by being taken possession of.

48. Alia causa est earum rerum quae in tempestate maris, levandae navis causa, ejiciuntur; hae enim dominorum permanent, quia palam est eas non eo animo ejici quod quis eas habere non vult, sed quo magis cum ipsa navi maris periculum effugiat. Qua de causa, si quis eas fluctibus expulsas, vel etiam in ipso mari nactus, lucrandi animo abstulerit, furtum committit; nec longe discedere videntur ab his quae de rheda cur-

48. It is otherwise with respect to things thrown overboard in a storm, to lighten a vessel; for they remain the property of their owners; as it is evident that they were not thrown away through a wish to get rid of them, but that their owners and the ship itself might more easily escape the dangers of the sea. Hence, any one who, with a view to profit himself by them, takes them away when washed on shore, or found at sea, is

rente non intelligentibus dominis cadunt.

guilty of theft. And much the same may be said as to things which drop from a carriage in motion, without the knowledge of their owners.

D. xll. 1. 9. 8; D. xlvii. 43. 4.

A thing could not be considered as abandoned and made a *res nullius* unless its owner intended to cease to be its owner.


## Trt. II. DE REBUS INCORPORALIBUS.

Quædam præterea res corporales sunt, quædam incorporales.

Certain things, again, are corporeal, others incorporeal.

GAI. ii. 12; D. i. 8. 1. 1.

Justinian, after having spoken of the natural modes of acquiring property in things, returns in this Title to the division of things, and adds one more division, that of things corporeal and incorporeal, to the divisions given at the beginning of the last Title. Our senses tell us what things corporeal are: things incorporeal are rights, that is, fixed relations in which men stand to things or to other men, relations giving them power over things or claims against persons. And these rights are themselves the objects of rights, and thus fall under the definition of things. For instance, the right to walk over another man's land is said to be an incorporeal thing; for we may have a claim or right to have this right, exactly as, if the land belonged to us, we should have a right to have the land. These rights over things were termed *jura in re*, and these *jura in re*, some of the more important of which are treated of in this part of the Institutes, were almost exactly on the footing of ' res ' in Roman law, and were the subjects of real actions equally with things corporeal. (See Introd. sec. 50.)

We can hardly speak of the possession of a thing incorporeal, but still the actual exercise of the right so much resembles the occupation and using of a corporeal thing, that the term *quasi-possessio* has been employed to denote the position of a person who exercises the right without opposition, and exercises it as if he were its owner. As little can we speak of the *traditio* or delivery of a right, but just as *quasi-possessio* is used to express a position analogous to that of a *possessor*, so *quasi-traditio* is a term used to signify the placing a person in this position.

u 2

1. Corporales hæ sunt, quæ sui natura tangi possunt: veluti fundus, homo, vestis, aurum, argentum, et denique aliæ res innumerabiles.

1. Corporeal things are those which are by their nature tangible, as land, a slave, a garment, gold, silver, and other things innumerable.

GAI. li. 13; D. i. 8. 1. 1.

2. Incorporales autem sunt, quæ tangi non possunt: qualia sunt ea quæ in jure consistunt, sicut hereditas, ususfructus, usus, obligationes quoquo modo contractæ. Nec ad rem pertinet, quod in hereditate res corporales continentur; nam et fructus qui ex fundo percipiuntur corporales sunt, et id quod ex aliqua obligatione nobis debetur, plerumque corporale est, veluti fundus, homo, pecunia: nam ipsum jus hereditatis, et ipsum jus utendi fruendi, et ipsum jus obligationis incorporale est.

2. Incorporeal things are those which are not tangible, such as are those which consist of a right, as an inheritance, an usufruct, use, or obligations in whatever way contracted. Nor does it make any difference that things corporeal are contained in an inheritance: for fruits, gathered by the usufructuary, are corporeal; and that which is due to us by virtue of an obligation, is generally a corporeal thing, as a field, a slave, or money; while the right of inheritance, the right of usufruct, and the right of obligation, are incorporeal.

GAI. ii. 14; D. i. 8. 1. 1.

3. Eodem numero sunt jura prædiorum urbanorum et rusticorum, quæ etiam servitutes vocantur.

3. Among things incorporeal are the rights over estates, urban and rural, which are also called servitudes.

GAI. ii. 14; D. i. 8. 1. 1.

In the last section it was said that usufruct, a personal servitude, was an incorporeal thing, and the same is now said of real or prædial servitudes. This is intended as an observation preliminary to the three next Titles, which treat of servitudes. By servitudes are meant certain portions or fragments of the right of ownership separated from the rest, and enjoyed by persons other than the owner of the thing itself. When the servitude was given to a particular person, it was said to be a personal servitude; when it was associated with the ownership of another thing, so that whoever was the owner of this other thing was the owner of the servitude, the servitude was said to be a real or prædial servitude; the latter term being used because it was indispensable that there should be an immoveable thing (see paragraph 3 of next Title), in virtue of which, the right given by the servitude was exercised; and the word *prædium* being taken in a general sense, was used to denote this immoveable. The thing over which the prædial servitude was exercised was also always an immoveable. Things over which servitudes, whether personal or prædial, were exercised, were said to *serve* the person to whom or the thing to which the servitude was attached; and hence the terms *servitus, res serviens* were employed, the thing, in right of which the

servitude was enjoyed being, in opposition, termed *res dominans.* (See Introd. sec. 64.)

No one could have a servitude over his own thing, *nulli
res sua servit.* (D. viii. 2. 26.) For as he was the owner of
all the portions into which the right of ownership was separable, he could not have a second right of ownership over any
one portion separated from the rest. Again, as a servitude
was the subtraction of some one portion of ownership, it could
never have the effect of making the owner of the *res serviens*
do any positive act; its force was either to make him undergo
something, as that another should exercise a certain power
over a thing of which he was owner, or to make him abstain
from doing something which as owner of the thing he had
power to do. *Servitutum non ea est natura ut aliquid faciat quis, sed ut aliquid patiatur vel non faciat.* (D. viii.
1. 15. 1.) Lastly, it may be observed that a servitude was
indivisible; the person who enjoyed the servitude could not
break up this fragment of ownership into lesser fragments.
*Servitus servitutis esse non potest.*

## Tit. III.  DE SERVITUTIBUS.

Rusticorum prædiorum jura sunt
hæc: Iter, actus, via, aquæductus.
Iter est jus eundi ambulandi hominis, non etiam jumentum agendi
vel vehiculum. Actus est jus
agendi vel jumentum vel vehiculum: itaque qui habet iter, actum
non habet; qui actum habet, et
iter habet, eoque uti potest etiam
sine jumento. Via est jus eundi et
agendi et ambulandi: nam et iter
et actum in se continet via. Aquæductus est jus aquæ ducendæ per
fundum alienum.

The servitudes of rural immoveables are, the right of passage, the
right of passage for beasts or vehicles,
the right of way, the right of passage
for water. The right of passage is
the right of going or passing for a
man, not of driving beasts or vehicles. The right of passage for beasts
or vehicles is the right of driving
beasts or vehicles over the land of
another. So a man who has the
right of passage simply has not the
right of passage for beasts or vehicles; but if he has the latter right
he has the former, and he may use
the right of passing without having
any beasts with him. The right of
way is the right of going, of driving
beasts or vehicles, and of walking;
for the right of way includes the
right of passage, and the right of
passage for beasts or vehicles. The
right of passage for water is the
right of conducting water through
the land of another.

D. viii. 3. 1.

Prædial servitudes, that is, servitudes possessed over one immoveable in right of having another immoveable, were divided into those of rural and urban immoveables (*prædia rustica vel urbana*). The distinction undoubtedly arose from the one kind being more common in the country, the other in the town. But the distinction, as it was practically understood, soon lost the traces of its origin ; and a servitude was said to be that of a rural immoveable when it was one which affected the soil itself, and that of an urban immoveable when it was one which affected the *superficies*, that is, anything raised upon the soil. *Servitutes prædiorum aliæ in solo, aliæ in superficie consistunt.* (D. viii. 1. 3.)  If the servitude was one which affected the soil, and for the enjoyment of which the soil itself sufficed, as, for instance, the right to traverse another man's land, or to draw water from his spring, it made no difference where the land or the spring was situated.  They might be in the heart of a city, and yet the servitude was one of a rural immoveable. So, too, if the servitude was one which affected something built or placed on the soil, as, for instance, the right to place a beam on another man's building ; although this building was in the country, the servitude was one of an urban immoveable.   In this paragraph and in paragraph 2, instances are given of servitudes of rural immoveables.  The object of the servitude *iter* was the power of passing across land on foot or horseback, *iter est qua quis pedes vel eques commeare potest.*   (D. viii. 3. 12.)   That of the servitude *actus* was the power of driving animals or vehicles across land, *qui actum habet, et plaustrum ducere, et jumenta agere potest.*   (D. viii. 3. 7.)   That of the servitude *via* was the power of using the road in any way whatever, as, for instance, of dragging stones or timber over it, which he could not do if he had only the *actus* (D. viii. 3. 7) ; and of having it, in the absence of special agreement, of the width provided by the law of the Twelve Tables, that is, eight feet where it ran straight, and sixteen feet where it wound round to change its direction, *via latitudo ex lege Duodecim Tabularum in porrectum octo pedes habet ; in anfractum id est ubi flexum est, sedecim.*   (D. viii. 3. 8.)   Of course the larger of these rights comprehended the smaller ; if a person had the right of driving over land he had the right of passing over it.   A special agreement might indeed be made to the contrary ; a person might, for instance, grant the right of driving beasts, but insist that the way should never be used except when beasts were driven.

1. Prædiorum urbanorum servitutes sunt quæ ædificiis inhærent :

1. The servitudes of urban immoveables are those which appertain

Ideo urbanorum prædiorum dictæ quoniam ædificia omnia urbana prædia appellamus, etsi in villa ædificata sint. Item urbanorum prædiorum servitutes sunt hæ: ut vicinus onera vicini sustineat, ut in parietem ejus liceat vicino tignum immittere, ut stillicidium vel flumen recipiat quis in ædes suas vel in aream vel in cloacam, vel non recipiat, et ne altius tollat quis ædes suas, ne luminibus vicini officiat.

to buildings, and they are said to be servitudes of urban immoveables, because we term all edifices urban immoveables, although really built in the country. Among these servitudes are the following: that a person has to support the weight of the adjoining house, that a neighbour should have the right of inserting a beam into his wall, that he has to receive or not to receive the water that drops from the roof, or that runs from the gutter of another man's house on to his building, or into his court or drain; or that he is not to raise his house higher, or not to obstruct his neighbour's lights.

D. viii. 2. 2.

The words quæ ædificiis inhærent in the text, are equivalent to the in superficie consistunt of Paul. (D. viii. 2. 20.) The servitudes attach to some building raised on the soil.

Onera vicini sustineat.—By this servitude a wall or pillar of the res serviens was obliged to support the weight of the res dominans. The owner of this wall or pillar, so long as he remained owner, was bound to keep it in good repair, so as to continue to support the weight safely. (D. viii. 5. 6. 2.) But the owner of the wall, into which a beam was let by the servitude tigni immittendi, was not compelled to repair the wall, in order that the beam might rest there safely. (D. viii. 5. 8. 2.)

It is easy to understand what is meant by the servitudes stillicidii vel fluminis recipiendi and altius non tollendi. By the one the res serviens was made to receive the rain-water of the res dominans, by the other the res serviens was prohibited from being raised above the res dominans. But in the text we have the servitude stillicidii vel fluminis non recipiendi, and in the passage of the Digest (viii. 2. 2.), from which much of the text is borrowed, we read of a servitude altius tollendi; and it is not very easy to understand what these servitudes were. Theophilus, in his paraphrase of this section, thus explains the former. Aut tu jus hujusmodi (i.e. stillicidia tua in meas ædes projiciendi) habebas in ædes meas; et rogavi te ne stillicidia tua aut canales in domum vel aream meam projiceres. Thus it would appear that the servitude non recipiendi was an extinction of a pre-existent servitude recipiendi, made in favour of the owner of the res serviens. So, too, the servitude altius tollendi is explained to mean the allowing the house of a neighbour to be built above ours; so that the neighbour who was previously under a servitude, or,

at any rate, of an obligation *non altius tollendi*, by the creation of what may be called a counter-servitude, does away
with the impediment to his building above our house.   If it
were really a servitude, as we should certainly suppose from
the language of Theophilus, that was extinguished or nullified
by this new counter-servitude, it seems scarcely natural that
this should not be given among the modes of ending a servitude, and still more, that the usual language of the jurists
with respect to the extinction of a servitude should be departed from.   The ordinary phrase was, that the thing affected,
the *res serviens*, was freed, *res liberatur*, and it seems a very
cumbrous mode of effecting the *liberatio rei* to create a new
servitude, when the object would have been at once accomplished by merely surrendering the existing servitude to the
owners of the *res serviens*.   The commentators are therefore
driven to understand that the right previously existing, that,
namely, of having our water flow into our neighbour's house,
or of having our neighbour's house kept at the level of our
own, was not a servitude, but was given by law.   Positive
enactments, such as we read of in Tac. *Annal*. 15. 43; Suet.
*Aug*. 89; D. xxxix. 1. 1. 17, may have decided that adjoining
houses should, in particular places, for the mutual advantage
of the owners, be of the same level, or pour off their water on
to the adjoining house, while those persons who were intended
to be benefited might still forego this advantage, if they pleased
to allow of a servitude being created to do away with the
effect of the enactment.   It must, however, be confessed, that
no one who reads the passages in which enactments for the
regulation of buildings are mentioned, would suppose that
individuals were ever allowed to infringe them by the mere
permission of their neighbours.   All that we can be quite
sure of is, that these servitudes, which were the contraries of
other servitudes, were constituted for the benefit of the owner
of a thing that previously had been under some disadvantage.

It is to be observed that words are sometimes used to express
servitudes which seem proper to the owner of the *res dominans*,
not to the owner of the *res serviens*.   Thus, if the above
explanation is correct, the *servitus tollendi* means the *servitus patiendi vicinum tollere* (see Bk. iv. Tit. 6. 2), and
what is termed in the text, as it would seem more properly,
the *servitus stillicidii recipiendi*, is termed in the Digest
(viii. 2. 2), the *servitus stillicidii avertendi*.

*Ne luminibus officiat*.—There was also a servitude termed
the *jus luminum*, between which and that *ne luminibus officiat* the difference was probably one of degree.  The *jus luminum*

prevented a neighbour blocking up our lights ; the servitude *ne luminibus officiat* prevented his doing anything, whether by building, planting trees, or by any other means, whereby the light was in any way, however slightly, intercepted from our house. (D. viii. 2. 15. 17. 40.)

| 2. In rusticorum prædiorum ser- | 2. Some think that among the ser- |
| vitutes quidam computari recte pu- | vitudes of rural estates are rightly |
| tant aquæ haustum, pecoris ad | included the right of drawing water, |
| aquam adpulsum, jus pascendi, cal- | of watering cattle, of feeding cattle, |
| cis coquendæ, arenæ fodiendæ. | of burning lime, of digging sand. |

D. viii. 3. 1. 1.

There are many servitudes, both of rural and of urban immoveables, mentioned in the Digest, besides those given as examples in the Institutes.

| 3. Ideo autem hæ servitutes præ- | 3. These servitudes are called the |
| diorum appellantur, quoniam sine | servitudes of immoveables, because |
| prædiis constitui non possunt : nemo | they cannot exist without immove- |
| enim potest servitutem adquirere | ables. For no one can acquire or |
| urbani vel rustici prædii, nisi qui | owe a servitude of a rural or urban |
| habet prædium ; nec quisquam de- | immoveable, unless he has an im- |
| bere, nisi qui habet prædium. | moveable belonging to him. |

D. viii. 4. 1. 1.

The nature of most servitudes of urban immoveables demanded that the immoveable over which, and the immoveable in right of which, the servitude was exercised, should be contiguous ; but when the servitude was one of rural immoveables, the *prædia* need not necessarily be near together. Still, however, a servitude was not permitted to exist which was useless to its owner ; and a person could not have a right of way, for instance, over the land of another, if he was prevented from using the way by land, over which he had no servitude, lying between his land and that over which the servitude was to be exercised. (D. viii. 1. 14. 2.)

There was another difference between the servitudes of rural and urban immoveables. The latter were, for the most part, used continuously ; the former only at times. The beam, for instance, always rested in the wall ; there was no moment in which the owner of the *res serviens* was not prohibited from blocking up his neighbour's lights. But the way was not always being used, nor were cattle always being watered (D. viii. 1. 14) ; and this difference was productive of very important results. For instance, servitudes might be lost by not being used ; but as the servitudes of most urban immoveables were by their nature perpetually used, they were preserved without their owner taking any trouble to preserve them, and possessory rights could be acquired in them, which,

with a few exceptions, could not be acquired in servitudes
whose usage was not continuous.   (D. viii. 2. 20.)

4. Si quis velit vicino aliquod jus
constituere, pactionibus atque stipulationibus id efficere debet.  Potest
etiam in testamento quis heredem
suum damnare, ne altius tollat ædes
suas ne luminibus ædium vicini
officiat, vel ut patiatur eum tignum
in parietem immittere vel stillicidium habere, vel ut patiatur eum
per fundum ire, agere, aquamve ex
eo ducere.

4. If any one wishes to create a
right of this sort in favour of his
neighbour, he must effect it by
agreements and stipulations.  A person can, also, by testament, oblige his
heir not to raise his house higher,
not to obstruct a neighbour's lights,
to permit a neighbour to insert a
beam into his wall, or to receive the
water from an adjoining roof; or,
again, he may oblige his heir to
allow a neighbour to go across his
land, or to drive beasts or vehicles,
or to conduct water across it.

Gai. li. 31 ; D. viii. 4. 10.

Gaius tells us (ii. 29), that *servitutes prædiorum rusticorum* were among *res mancipi* (see Introduc. sec. 59), while
*servitutes prædiorum urbanorum* were not, and that the
former were constituted by *mancipatio*; the latter, as well as
personal servitudes, were constituted by the process termed *in
jure cessio*. (See introductory note to this Book.) But these
modes of constituting servitudes were only applicable to the
*solum Italicum*: in the provincial lands, where there was no
legal ownership at all, no ownership of servitudes could be
given. But Gaius says, that if any one wished to create a
servitude over provincial *prædia*, he could effect it *pactionibus et stipulationibus*, using the words of the text. The
parties agreed to constitute the servitude, and this agreement
(*pactio*) was generally, perhaps almost always, followed by
a stipulation or solemn contract (see Introd. sec. 83), by
which the person who permitted the servitude to be constituted over his *prædium*, bound himself to allow of the exercise of the right, by subjecting himself to a penalty in case of
refusal. (See THEOPHIL. *Paraphrase of Text*.) When the
right had been once exercised, and the owner of the servitude
had thus the *quasi-possessio* of the servitude, the prætor
secured him in the enjoyment of his right by granting him
possessory interdicts (see Introd. sec. 107, and note on introductory section of Title 6 of this Book), and also permitted
him, if the servitude afterwards passed out of his *quasi-
possessio*, to bring an action to claim it, called the *actio
publiciana*, by which a *bona fide* possessor was allowed to
represent himself fictitiously as a *dominus*, and to claim
(*vindicare*) a thing as if he were the owner. In all probabi-
lity the same mode of constituting servitudes obtained also

with regard to the *solum Italicum*: although there were proper and peculiar modes of constituting servitudes over *prædia Italica*, yet if an agreement and stipulation were followed by *quasi-possessio*, the prætor would protect the *quasi-possessor*. And hence it was said that servitudes were constituted *jure prætorio* and were maintained *tuitione prætoris*.

Modern writers on Roman law are much divided in opinion whether servitudes were really constituted *pactionibus atque stipulationibus*, by agreements and stipulations alone, or whether we are always to understand that to perfect the title, what is termed *quasi-traditio* was necessary. That is, whether, as *traditio* was necessary to transfer the property in a corporeal thing, so it was necessary in order to transfer the property in an incorporeal thing, that the person to whom it was transferred should be placed in the legal quasi-possession of his right. If the servitude was a positive one, it is very easy to see how this quasi-possession could be established; for directly the right was exercised with the *animus possidendi*, and permitted to be so exercised by the owner of the *res serviens*, the person in favour of whom the servitude was constituted, would have the quasi-possession. But when the servitude was a negative one, when the owner of the *res serviens* was merely bound *not* to do something, the only evident mode by which possession could be said to be gained was, when the owner of the *res dominans* successfully resisted an attempt of the owner of the *res serviens* to do the thing which he was bound by the servitude not to do. But as the exercise of the right given by a positive servitude was an act evident and cognizable by all whom it concerned, it is with regard to positive servitudes that the question is principally debated, whether the exercise of the right was an indispensable part of the right being constituted. On the whole, it seems the better opinion that quasi-tradition was a necessary part of the constitution of a servitude.

Mancipation and *in jure cessio* were quite obsolete in the time of Justinian. We have two modes given in the text by which servitudes might be constituted under his legislation: *pactionibus atque stipulationibus*, i.e. agreements, whether followed or not by a stipulation and *testamento*. When given *testamento*, a servitude might be given directly to the legatee equally well as by condemning the heir to transfer it to him, both modes, in the time of Justinian, having exactly the same effect. To these modes must be added (1) that *adjudicatione*, when a judge awarded the property in a servitude under the actions *familiæ erciscundæ* and *communi dividundo*. (See Introd. sec. 103; D. x. 2. 22. 3.) 2. That of

reserving the servitude in making a *traditio* of the rest of the
property, when it was in fact constituted by having all the
other *jura in re* separated from it, instead of, as usual, being
itself separated from the rest.   3.  Lastly, the possessor who
had had a long quasi-possession of a servitude was protected
in it.   The usucapion of servitudes, which perhaps existed
previously, was forbidden by the *lex Scribonia*.   (A.U.C. 720 ;
D. xli. 3. 4. 29.)  But a long *bona fide* possession was perhaps protected by prætorian actions and interdicts.   Properly
this only applied to servitudes *urbanorum prædiorum*, for
these only were capable of a continuous exercise (*servitutes
quæ in superficie consistunt, possessione retinentur*).   (D.
viii. 2. 20.)  But there were particular servitudes *rusticorum
prædiorum*, long usage of which gave rights which were protected.   Among these were the *jus aquæ ducendæ* (D. viii.
5. 10), the *jus itineris*, and the *jus actus*.   (D. viii. 6. 25.)
The possessor had to show that his possession had been neither
*vi, clam*, or *precario* ; but had not to show any good title for
possession.   (D. viii. 5. 10.)   The length of time requisite
for the possessor to have exercised the right was not fixed.
It has been thought that Justinian fixed this at ten years for
those present and twenty for the absent ; but this opinion is
chiefly based on a passage in the Code (vii. 33. 12 ; see also
C. iii. 34. 2), which it is better to interpret of the length of
time, by non-usage during which a servitude was lost.

## Tit. IV.   DE USUFRUCTU.

| | |
|---|---|
| Ususfructus est jus alienis rebus utendi fruendi, salva rerum substantia: est enim jus in corpore, quo sublato et ipsum tolli necesse est. | Usufruct is the right of using, and reaping the fruits of things belonging to others, without destroying their substance.   It is a right over a corporeal thing, and if this thing perish, the usufruct itself necessarily perishes also. |

### D. vii. 1. 1, 2.

We now pass to personal servitudes, those, namely, which
consist of a *jus in re*, i.e. one portion of the *dominium* being
detached from the rest for the benefit of a person.   Personal
servitudes differed from real in being applicable to moveables
as well as to immoveables; and the personal servitude *ususfructus* was divisible, that is, some of the fruits included in
the servitude might be parted with, although the servitude
*usus* was, like real servitudes, indivisible.

The person to whom the *ususfructus* was given had two
rights united; he had the *jus utendi*, that is, the right of
making every possible use of the thing apart from consuming

it or from taking the fruits of it, as, for instance, the right of
living in a house or employing beasts of burden ; and he had
also the *jus fruendi*, the right of taking all the fruits of the
thing over which the servitude was constituted. The definition of *fructus* is *quicquid in fundo nascitur* (D. vii. 59. 1),
that is, the ordinary produce, but not accidental accessions or
augmentations, such as a treasure found (D. xxiv. 3. 7. 12)
or islands formed in a river.

He might sell, or let, or give his right of taking the fruits
to another, and the profits he thence derived were termed his
*fructus civiles.* (D. vii. 1. 12. 2.) It was only such of the
*fructus* as were actually taken or gathered by him, or those
acting under him that belonged to him ; and no fruits which
were not gathered at the time of his death passed to his heir.
He was obliged to give security, on entering on the exercise
of his right, that he would use his right as a good *paterfamilias*, and give up, at the time when his right expired,
the possession of the thing. (D. vii. 9. 1.) We have had an
instance of what was meant by using his right as a good *paterfamilias* in paragr. 38 of Tit. 1, where it is said that he is
bound to replace dead sheep and dead trees. He was also
bound not to alter the nature of the thing over which the
right extended ; he could not, for instance, build on land un-
built on, or change the use to which land was specially destined. (D. vii. 1. 7. 1.; D. viii. 13. 4.) And it is with reference to this that the words *salva rerum substantia*, in the
text, are sometimes understood, so that the sentence would
mean, usufruct is the right of using and taking the fruits of
things belonging to another, but so as not to alter the substance. Ulpian (*Reg.* 24. 26) certainly uses the words *salva
rerum substantia* in a sense very similar ; but the concluding words of the section make it more natural to understand
*salva rerum substantia* as referring here to the duration of
the usufruct. It lasts as long as the thing over which it is
constituted remains unaltered ; for if the thing perishes, the
usufruct perishes. The two sentences of this section are
taken without alteration from the Digest, but are from different authors, the first being from Paul, the latter from Celsus. (D. vii. 1. 1, 2.) Very probably Paul did not use the
words *salva rerum substantia* with reference to the duration
of the servitudes; but the compilers of the Institutes saw
that, if they were used in this sense, the two sentences would
cohere together.

1. Usufructus a proprietate se-
parationem recipit, idque pluribus
modis accidit: ut ecce, si quis

1. The usufruct is detached from
the property ; and this separation
takes place in many ways; for exam-

usumfructum alicui legaverit, nam heres nudam habet proprietatem, legatarius usumfructum; et contra, si fundum legaverit deducto usufructu, legatarius nudam habet proprietatem, heres vero usumfructum. Item alii usumfructum, alii deducto eo fundum legare potest. Sine testamento vero si quis velit usumfructum alii constituere, pactionibus et stipulationibus id efficere debet. Ne tamen in universum inutiles essent proprietates semper abscedente usufructu, placuit certis modis extingui usumfructum et ad proprietatem reverti.

ple, if the usufruct is given to any one as a legacy; for the heir has then the bare ownership, and the legatee has the usufruct; conversely, if the estate is given as a legacy, subject to the deduction of the usufruct, the legatee has the bare ownership, and the heir has the usufruct. Again, the usufruct may be given as a legacy to one person, and the estate minus this usufruct may be given to another. If any one wishes to constitute a usufruct otherwise than by testament, he must effect it by pacts and stipulations. But, lest the property should be rendered wholly profitless by the usufruct being for ever detached, it has been thought right that there should be certain ways in which the usufruct should become extinguished, and revert to the property.

D. vii. 1. 6; D. xxxii. 2. 10; D. vii. 1, 3, pr. and 2.

We may refer to what we have said in the note to the fourth section of the last Title for the modes in which usufructs were acquired. In the time of Justinian they were constituted, 1, by testament; 2, by agreements followed by quasi-tradition; 3, by being reserved in an alienation of the *nuda proprietas*; 4, by adjudication; and also, lastly, *lege*, by the law, an instance of which we have in the first paragraph of the ninth Title of this Book, where it is said that, under Justinian's legislation, the father acquired the usufruct of his son's *peculium.*

It will be observed that, in putting the third case of gift of usufruct by testament, that, namely, in which the usufruct is given to one legatee, the *nuda proprietas* to another, the gift to the latter is expressed by the words *fundum deducto usufructu.* The Digest (xxxiii. 2. 19) explains why *deducto usufructu* should, in such a case, be carefully added to a gift of the *fundus*; for if they were not, the second legatee would be treated as having the *nuda proprietas*, and also as having a joint interest in the usufruct with the first legatee.

2. Constituitur autem ususfructus non tantum in fundo et aedibus, rerum etiam in servis et jumentis ceterisque rebus, exceptis iis quae ipso usu consumuntur; nam hae res neque naturali ratione neque civili recipiunt usumfructum. Quo numero sunt vinum, oleum, frumentum, vestimenta: quibus proxima est pecunia numerata, namque ipso usu assiduus permutatione quodam-

2. A usufruct may be constituted not only of lands and buildings, but also of slaves, of beasts of burden, and everything else except those which are consumed by being used, for they are susceptible of an usufruct neither by natural nor by civil law. Among these things are wine, oil, garments, and we may almost say coined money; for it, too, is in manner consumed by use, as it continually

modo extinguitur. Sed utilitatis causa senatus censuit posse etiam earum rerum usumfructum constitui, ut tamen eo nomine heredi utiliter caveatur. Itaque si pecuniae ususfructus legatus sit, ita datur legatario ut ejus fiat, et legatarius satisdet heredi de tanta pecunia restituenda, si morietur aut capite minuetur. Ceterae quoque res ita traduntur legatario ut ejus fiant; sed aestimatis his satisdatur, ut si morietur aut capite minuetur, tanta pecunia restituatur quanti hae fuerint aestimatae. Ergo senatus non fecit quidem earum rerum usumfructum (nec enim poterat), sed per cautionem quasi usumfructum constituit.

passes from hand to hand. But the senate, thinking such a measure would be useful, has enacted that a usufruct even of these things may be constituted, if sufficient security be given to the heir; and therefore, if the usufruct of money is given to a legatee, the money is considered to be given to him in complete ownership; but he has to give security to the heir for the repayment of an equal sum in the event of his death or his undergoing a *capitis diminutio*. All other things, too, of the same kind are delivered to the legatee so as to become his property; but their value is estimated and security is given for the payment of the amount at which they are valued, in the event of the legatee dying or undergoing a *capitis diminutio*. The senate has not then, to speak strictly, created a usufruct of these things, for that was impossible, but, by requiring security, has established a right analogous to a usufruct.

D. vii. 1. 3. 1; D. vii. .1. 3; D. vii. 5. 2, pr. and 1; D. vii. 5. 7.

Properly only things *quæ in usu non consumuntur* could be the subject of a servitude which consisted in using things only for a time; but as things *quæ usu consumuntur*, things that perish in the using, are things that may for the most part be easily replaced by similar things of an equal quantity and quality, the *senatus consultum* alluded to in the text (the date of which is uncertain, but is probably not later than Augustus) permitted that things *quæ usu consumuntur* should be made subject to a kind of usufruct by which they might be consumed at once, and then, on an event occurring by which a real usufruct would have expired, that is, the death or *capitis deminutio* of the usufructuary, they were to be replaced by similar things, or, what effected the same object in a different way, their pecuniary value was estimated on the commencement of this quasi-usufruct, as it is termed, and paid at its expiration. Ulpian gives the following as the terms of the *senatus consultum: Ut omnium rerum, quæ in cujusque patrimonio esse consuevit, ususfructus legari possit.* (D. vii. 5. 1.)

It will be observed that the text includes garments, *vestimenta*, among things of which there was only a quasi-usufruct, whereas the Digest twice speaks of them as things of which there was a real usufruct. (D. vii. 1. 15. 4; vii. 9. 9.

3.) They were, in fact, one or the other according as it was the garments or their value, that was to be given to the owner of the *nuda proprietas* at the end of the usufruct, and this might depend on the intention of the parties or the nature of the materials.

*Satisdatur.* The usufructuary not only guaranteed by a stipulation the replacement of the things or the payment of their value, but he procured a surety (*fidejussor*) to guarantee it also.

3. Finitur autem ususfructus morte fructuarii, et duabus capitis deminutionibus, maxima et media, et non utendo per modum et tempus: quæ omnia nostra statuit constitutio. Item finitur ususfructus, si domino proprietatis ab usufructuario cedatur (nam cedendo extraneo nihil agit); vel ex contrario si fructuarius proprietatem rei acquisierit, quæ res consolidatio appellatur. Eo amplius constat, si ædes incendio consumptæ fuerint, vel etiam terræ motu aut vitio suo corruerint, extingui usumfructum, et ne areæ quidem usumfructum deberi.

3. The usufruct terminates by the death of the usufructuary, by two kinds of *capitis deminutio*, namely, the greatest and the middle, and also by not being used, according to the manner, and during the time fixed: all which points have been decided by our constitution. The usufruct is also terminated if the usufructuary surrenders it to the owner of the property (a cession to a stranger would not have this effect); or, again, by the usufructuary acquiring the property, which is called consolidation. Again, if a building is consumed by fire, or thrown down by an earthquake, or falls through decay, the usufruct of it is necessarily destroyed, nor does there remain any usufruct due even of the soil on which it stood.

C. iii. 33. 10, pr. and 1, 2; Gai. ii. 33.

The text points out five ways in which the usufruct would terminate. 1. By the natural or civil death of the usufructuary. If the usufruct belonged to a city or corporation which could not die, it lasted for a hundred years, as being the extreme length of the duration of human life. (D. vii. 1. 56.) Previously to Justinian the *minima capitis deminutio* extinguished a usufruct, because the person who underwent it was not the same person in the eyes of the law after undergoing it as he was before; he commenced a new existence. Justinian altered the law in this respect (C. iii. 33. 16), and he also decided a question which had divided the jurists, whether a usufruct acquired by a slave or a *filiusfamilias* terminated on the death of the slave, or death or *capitis deminutio* of the son, or whether it remained for the benefit of the master or father. He decided that it should remain until the master or father's natural or civil death, and further, that in the case of a *filiusfamilias*, it should also continue for his benefit after his father's death; so that the father had the usufruct for his life, and then the son, if he survived the father, had it for his life. (C. iii. 33. 16. 17.)

*Non utendo per modum et tempus.* Secondly, the usufructuary might lose the usufruct by not using it in the way agreed on by the parties during the time fixed by law. The usufructuary might, for instance, have the use of a *fundus* for the summer, and if he used it only during the winter he would not use the usufruct of the *fundus* in the way it was given him, and this was equivalent to not using it at all; and if he did not exercise his right at any period previous to the time fixed by law, as that when the usufruct became extinct by non-usage, his right was gone. This time was, under the old law, one year when the usufruct affected moveables, and two years when the usufruct affected immoveables. If this period elapsed without the right being exercised, the owner of the *nuda proprietas* gained the usufruct by usucapion. Justinian altered this by fixing three years as the time for moveables, and ten or twenty years for immoveables, according as the person affected was present or absent. (See Tit. 6. 1.) The usufructuary was placed so far in the position of an owner of a thing, that it required the same length of time to make him lose the usufruct as it did to make the owner lose the property. Hence it is said in the Code (iii. 33. 16. 1) that he was not to lose the usufruct unless *talis exceptio* (i.e. of usucapion) *usufructuario opponatur, quæ etiam si dominium vindicabat, poterat eum præsentem vel absentem excludere.*

*Non-usage* and the *minima capitis deminutio* only affected rights already commenced; and in order to avoid their effects the usufruct was often given by legacy *in singulos annos, vel menses, vel dies.* As a new usufruct thus began each year, month, or day, there could be no non-usage for a longer time than the duration of each usufruct, and the *minima capitis deminutio* only affected the usufruct existing at the time it was undergone. (D. vii. 4. 1. 1.)

*Si domino cedatur.* Thirdly, the usufruct was lost if it was surrendered to the owner of the *nuda proprietas.* The words *cedatur,* and *cedendo* belong, in the passage of Gaius from which this part of the section is taken, to the *in jure cessio,* the fictitious suit by which personal servitudes were given up in the time of Gaius. As this mode of giving up servitudes to the *dominus* was obsolete, less technical words would be more appropriate in the text. The usufructuary could not transfer the usufruct to another, because the usufruct attached to him personally, and was to terminate by his

P

death or *capitis deminutio,* and not by that of a stranger. He could allow another to exercise his right of taking the fruits until he himself died or lost the servitude, but this did not make that person the owner of the usufruct.

The two other modes by which a usufruct might be lost, viz. *consolidatio,* when the usufruct was extinguished, *qui res sua nemini servit,* and the thing being consumed, that is, either really perishing, or having its *substantia* altered, need no explanation.

Of course, if a usufruct was made conditionally, or for a limited time, it expired when the condition was accomplished or the time ended.

Servitudes generally were extinguished in much the same way as the particular servitude of usufruct. 1. By the destruction of the thing—the *res dominans* or the *res serviens.* 2. By the same person becoming owner of the *res dominans* and the *res serviens,* or, in case of personal servitudes, of the remainder of the *proprietas* and the servitude. 3. By the owner of the servitude permitting the person affected by it to do something which made the exercise of the right impossible. 4. Lastly, by non-usage, there being, however, a remarkable difference in this respect between servitudes *rusticorum prædiorum* and servitudes *urbanorum prædiorum* : for as the possession of the former was not continuous, that is, the right was not always being exercised, the mere non-usage of the right during the time fixed by law extinguished it; but as the possession of the servitudes *urbanorum prædiorum* was continuous, it was necessary that the owner of the *res serviens* should do something to break the possession, or, as it was termed by the jurist, *usucapere libertatem* (D. viii. 2. 6), i.e. to commence the liberation of the *res serviens,* as, for instance, to turn a *stillicidium* away from his premises; and if this was acquiesced in during the time fixed by law, that is, ten years for persons present and twenty for persons absent, the owner of the *res dominans* could not afterwards claim his servitude.

| | |
|---|---|
| 4. Cum autem finitus fuerit usufructus, revertitur scilicet ad proprietatem, et ex eo tempore nudæ proprietatis dominus incipit plenam in re habere potestatem. | 4. When the usufruct is entirely extinguished, it is reunited to the property; and the person who had the bare ownership, begins thenceforth to have full power over the thing. |

Some texts have *finitus fuerit totus ususfructus;* for as the usufruct was divisible, portions of it might exist, and yet other portions have reverted to the owner of the *nuda proprietas.* It may be remarked that if two persons had a joint interest in the same usufruct, and the usufruct was divided between them, when one died, his share went, not to the owner of the *nuda proprietas*, but to his coproprietor. (D. vii. 2. 1.)

## Tit. V. DE USU ET HABITATIONE.

| | |
|---|---|
| Iisdem istis modis quibus ususfructus constituitur, etiam nudus usus constitui solet; iisdemque illis modis finitur, quibus et ususfructus desinit. | The naked use is constituted by the same means as the usufruct; and is terminated by the same means that make the usufruct to cease. |

D. vii. 1. 3. 3.

The use was a portion of the usufruct. The person to whom this right was given could use the thing, but not take any of its fruits. He had the *nudus usus* (D. vii. 8. 1), the bare use of the thing; and enjoyed all the advantages he could obtain from the use; but he could avail himself of nothing which the thing produced. He could not, like the usufructuary, let, sell, or give the exercise of his right, for he was excluded from taking what were termed *fructus civiles*, as much as from taking *fructus naturales*. The jurists, however, modified in some degree the rigour of this principle; and the owner of the use was allowed, in cases where the right would otherwise have produced no benefit whatever, or where it seemed right to put a favourable interpretation on the wording of a testament, to take as much of certain kinds of produce as was sufficient for his daily wants.

| | |
|---|---|
| 1. Minus autem scilicet juris est in usu quam in usufructu. Namque is qui fundi nudum habet usum, nihil ulterius habere intelligitur quam ut oleribus, pomis, floribus, foeno, stramentis et lignis ad usum quotidianum utatur. In eo quoque fundo hactenus ei morari licet, ut neque domino fundi molestus sit, neque iis per quos opera rustica fiunt, impedimento: nec ulli alii jus quod habet, aut locare aut vendere aut gratis concedere potest: cum is qui usumfructum habet potest haec omnia facere. | 1. The right of use is less extensive than that of usufruct; for he who has the naked use of lands, has nothing more than the right of taking herbs, fruit, flowers, hay, straw, and wood, sufficient for his daily supply. He is permitted to establish himself upon the land, so long as he neither annoys the owner, nor hinders those who are engaged in the cultivation of the soil. He cannot let, or sell, or give gratuitously his right to another, while a usufructuary may. |

D. vii. 8. 10. 4; D. vii. 8. 12. 1; D. vii. 8. 11.

The jurists differed as to the *fructus* of which a certain daily supply might be taken, and as to whether it was necessary that they should be consumed on the spot. (D. vii. 8. 10. 1 : D. vii. 8. 12. 1.) The station of the *usuarius* and the abundance of the fruits would make a difference in particular cases.

The *usuarius* could prevent the owner as well as any one

else from coming on land subject to a *usus*, except for the purpose of cultivating it.

*Aut gratis concedere.* There would be a sort of *fructus* in being able to gratify the wish of giving and of conferring a favour, instead of receiving a price.

2. Item isqui ædium usum habet, hactenus jus habere intelligitur, ut ipse tantum habitet; nec hoc jus ad alium transferre potest, et vix receptum esse videtur ut hospitem ei recipere liceat; sed cum uxore sua liberisque suis, item libertis, nec non aliis liberis personis quibus non minus quam sortis utitur, habitandi jus habet. Et convenienter, si ad mulierem usus ædium pertinent, cum marito ei habitare licet.

2. He who has the use of a house, has nothing more than the right of inhabiting it himself; for he cannot transfer this right to another; and it is not without considerable doubt that it has been thought allowable that he should receive a guest in the house, but he may live in it with his wife and children, and freedmen, and other free persons who may be attached to his service no less than his slaves are. A wife, if it is she who has the use of the house, may live in it with her husband.

D. vii. 8. 2. 1; D. vii. 8. 4. 6. 8.

The *usuarius* had the use of the whole thing, and the owner could not make use of any part not used by the *usuarius*. (D. vii. 8. 22. 1.) So, too, the right of *usus* was indivisible and could not be given in detached portions, as that of usufruct could be, to different persons. (D. vii. 8. 19.) But one person could have the use, and another the usufruct of the same thing. (D. vii. 8. 14. 3.)

3. Item is ad quem servi usus pertinet, ipse tantummodo operis atque ministerio ejus uti potest: ad alium vero nullo modo jus suum transferre ei concessum est. Idem scilicet juris est et in jumentis.

3. So, too, he who has the use of a slave, has only the right of himself using the labour and services of the slave: for he is not permitted in any way to transfer his right to another. And it is the same with regard to beasts of burden.

D. vii. 8. 12. 5, 6.

*Ipse tantummodo uti potest*; but the wife or the husband might use the thing of which the use was given to the other. (D. vii. 8. 8.)

4. Sed si pecorum, veluti ovium, usus legatus sit, neque lacte neque agnis neque lana utetur usuarius, quia ea in fructu sunt. Plane ad stercorandum agrum suum pecoribus uti potest.

4. If the use of a flock or herd, as, for instance, of a flock of sheep, be given as a legacy, the person who has the use cannot take the milk, the lambs, or the wool, for these are among the fruits. But he may certainly make use of the flock to manure his land.

D. vii. 8. 12. 2.

As a flock was hardly of any use if a person might not take

any of the *fructus*, the *usuarius* was allowed to have a little milk (*modicum lac*) when the *usus* had been constituted in a way to admit of a favourable interpretation.   (D. vii. 12. 2.)

5. Sed si cui habitatio legata sive aliquo modo constituta sit, neque usus videtur neque usus-fructus, sed quasi proprium aliquod jus. Quam habitationem haben-tibus, propter rerum utilitatem, secundum Marcelli sententiam nos-tra decisione promulgata, permi-simus non solum in ea degere, sed etiam aliis locare.

5. If the right of habitation is given to any one, either as a legacy or in any other way, this does not seem a use or a usufruct, but a right that stands as it were by itself. From a regard to what is useful, and conformably to an opinion of Mar-cellus, we have published a decision, by which we have permitted those who have this right of habitation, not only themselves to inhabit the place over which the right extends, but also to let to others the right of inhabiting it.

D. vii. 8. 10 ; C. iii. 33.

The jurists had doubted whether *habitatio* was to be con-sidered a distinct servitude (D. iv. 5. 10; D. vii. 8. 10. 2), which Justinian here pronounces it to be.  So far as it dif-fered from the use, or, after Justinian gave the power of let-ting the house, from the usufruct, of the house, it differed by being an occupation allowed as a fact rather than as a right, the creation of the law, to which the incidences of a personal servitude would attach. Modestinus says of it, *potius in facto quam in jure consistit*. (D. iv. 5. 10.)  Thus, it did not cease by non-usage or by the *minima capitis deminutio*. (D. vii. 8. 10.)

6. Haec de servitutibus et usu-fructu et usu et habitatione dizimus sufficiat ; de hereditate autem, et obligationibus, suis locis propo-nemus. Exponuimus summatim quibus modis jure gentium res nobis acquiruntur: modo videamus, quibus modis legitimo et civili jure acquiruntur.

6. Let it suffice to have said thus much concerning servitudes, usu-fruct, use, and habitation. We shall treat of inheritances and obligations in their proper places.  We have al-ready briefly explained how things are acquired by the law of nations ; let us now examine how they are acquired by the civil law.

D. vii. 8. 10.

Before quitting the subject of servitudes it is proper to ob-serve that, besides the possessory interdicts by which the pos-session of servitudes was secured, there were two real actions by which a claim was made with regard to a servitude.  By the one (*actio in rem confessoria*), the owner of the servi-tude claimed to have his servitude protected, and the right to it pronounced to be his, against any one who attempted to disturb him in his quasi-possession, or disputed his right.  By

the other (*actio in rem negatoria*), the owner of a thing
over which another person claimed or exercised a servitude
himself claimed to have this thing pronounced free from the
servitude. It might seem as if this was rather a defence to
an action for the servitude than itself a real action. But it
was considered a substantive and independent action, because
the owner of the *dominium* thereby vindicated his claim to
a portion of it, namely, to the servitude which it was attempted to detach from the ownership.

Justinian now returns to the examination of the modes in
which things are acquired, and the sixth Title would properly
follow the latter part of the first. Before, however, we leave
the subject of *jura in re*, we must notice three other kinds
of *jura in re* besides servitudes, of which the Institutes make
no mention. These are the *jus emphyteuticarium*, the *jus
superficiarium*, and the *jus pignoris*.

The exact time when servitudes first became a part of Roman law is not easy to discover. The Twelve Tables determine the width of a way, but there is nothing to show that
this was intended to regulate the width of a way to which one
person had a right over the land of another, although, probably, the width assigned by the law of the Twelve Tables
was afterwards employed as the standard to regulate private
ways. However, the nature of servitudes makes it almost
certain that they must have very early been recognized by
law; and, at any rate, we learn that they were so long before
the end of the Republic. The period at which the three *jura
in re*, of which we have just spoken, were established as a
part of law, can be ascertained more readily. The first, the
*jus emphyteuticarium*, though based on an institution of the
civil law, yet only assumed its peculiar character in the time
of the Lower Empire; the two others owed their existence to
the praetors.

The *jus emphyteuticarium*, or, as it is more generally
called, *emphyteusis*, was the right of enjoying all the fruits,
and disposing at pleasure, of the thing of another, subject to
the payment of a yearly rent (*pensio*, or *canon*) to the owner.
Formerly the lands of the Roman people of municipalities, or
the college of priests, used to be let for different terms of
years, sometimes for a short term, such as that of five years,
sometimes for a term amounting almost to a perpetuity, under
the name of *agri vectigales*. (GAI. iii. 145.) Afterwards,
the lands of private individuals were let in a similar manner,
and were also comprehended under the term *agri vectigales*.
The emperors let the patrimonial lands in a similar way, and

these lands so let were termed *emphyteuticarii* (C. xi. 5H.
61), a name arising from there being a new ownership, or
what almost amounted to an ownership, engrafted (*hv, φυτεύω*)
on the real *dominium*.  Either shortly before, or in the time
of Justinian, the two rights, that of the *ager vectigales*, and
that of *emphyteusis*, were united under the common name of
*emphyteusis*, and subjected to particular regulations.
Both lands and buildings could be subject to *emphyteusis*.
(Nov. vii. 3. 1. 2.)  The *emphyteuta*, as the person who enjoyed the right was termed, besides enjoying all the rights of
an usufructuary, could dispose of the thing, or rather of his
rights over it, in any way he pleased (Nov. vii. 3. 2); he could
create a servitude over it or mortgage it (D. xiii. 7. 16. 2) ;
he had a real action (which, however, was said to be a *utilis
vindicatio*, because he was not the owner, but only in the
place of one) to defend or assert his rights ; and at his death
his right was transmitted to his heirs.  (Nov. vii. 3.)

He was obliged to pay his *pensio* under any circumstances,
whether he actually benefited by his *emphyteusis* or not, because the payment of rent was an acknowledgment of the
title of the *dominus*.  He was also bound to use the thing
over which his right extended, so that it was not deteriorated
in value at the time his right expired.  (Nov. vii. 3. 2.)

The right of *superficies* was almost identical with that of
*emphyteusis*, but applied only to the *superficies*, that is,
things built on the ground, not to the ground itself.  It was
the right of disposing freely of a building erected on another
man's soil without destroying it, subject to the payment of a
yearly rent.  (D. vi. 1. 74.)  It must have been the creation
of the *jus prætorium* at a time when there was nothing like
the *emphyteusis* of buildings, and when it was only lands
that were let as *agri vectigales*.  The rights and duties of
the *superficiarius*, the person who enjoyed the right, may be
gathered from those of the *emphyteuticarius*.

The *jus pignoris* was the right given to a creditor over a
thing belonging to another, in order to secure the payment of
a debt.  When the thing over which the right was given was
passed into the possession of the creditor, the right of the
creditor was expressed by the word *pignus*; when the thing
remained in the hands of the debtor, the right of the creditor
was expressed by *hypotheca*.  Sometimes only one or more
particular things were under a *hypotheca*, sometimes all the
property of the debtor.  The right of the creditor extended
only to the amount of his debt, but all the thing pledged was
subject to his claim.  The right might be created by the

mere agreement of the parties, without any handing over or
tradition of the thing pledged to the creditor. (C. viii. 17. 2.
0.)  Sometimes the right was created by a magistrate, who
gave execution to a creditor by this means; and in many
cases the law created what was called a *hypotheca tacita* over
the property, as, for instance, over the property of a tutor in
favour of the pupil, and over the property of a husband, that
the dowry of the wife might be restored.

The creditor had the right (1) of selling (D. xx. 5.) or
pledging (C. viii. 24) the thing pledged: (2) of satisfying his
own claim before that of any one else out of the proceeds of
the sale, or of the money obtained by pledging the thing:
(3) of having himself constituted owner of the thing if no
purchaser could be found for the thing: (4) of bringing a real
action (termed the *actio quasi-serviana*) against any one
who unlawfully detained the thing pledged to him.

If the same thing was pledged to different creditors, the
one to whom it was first pledged had generally a preference,
*potior tempore, potior jure.* But there were certain *hypothecæ* which had special privileges attached to them, and
which had a first claim on the property of the debtor, such
as the *hypotheca* of the *fiscus* or imperial treasury for the
payment of taxes (C. iv. 46. 1), and that of a wife for her
dowry (C. viii. 14. 12); and *hypothecæ* which were created
by an instrument publicly registered had a preference over
others by a constitution of Leo.  (C. viii. 18. 11.)

### Tit. VI.  DE USUCAPIONIBUS, ET LONGI
### TEMPORIS POSSESSIONIBUS.

Jure civili constitutum fuerat, ut
qui bona fide ab eo qui dominus
non erat, cum crediderit eum dominum esse, rem emerit vel ex
donatione aliave quavis justa causa
acceperit, is eam rem, si mobilis
erat annoubique, si immobilis bien-
nio tantum in italico solo usuca-
piat, ne rerum dominia in incerto
essent.  Et cum hoc placitum erat
putantibus antiquioribus dominis
sufficere ad inquirendas res suas
præfata tempora, nobis melior sententia sedit, ne domini maturius
suis rebus defraudentur, neque certo loco beneficium hoc concludatur.
Et ideo constitutionem super hoc
promulgavimus, qua cautum est ut
res quidem mobiles per triennium,
immobiles vero per longi temporis

By the civil law it was provided,
that if anyone by purchase, gift, or
any other legal means, had *bona fide*
received a thing from a person who
was not the owner, but whom he
thought to be so, he should acquire
this thing by use if he held it for one
year, if it were a moveable, whereever it might be, or for two years, if
it were an immoveable, but this only
if it were in the *solum Italicum*; the
object of this provision being to prevent the ownership of things remaining in uncertainty.  Such was the
decision of the ancients, who thought
the times we have mentioned sufficient for owners to search for their
property, but we have come to a
much better decision, from a wish
to prevent owners being despoiled of

possessionem (Id est, inter præsentes decennio, inter absentes viginti annis) usucapiantur; et his modis non solum in Italia, sed in omni terra quæ nostro imperio gubernatur, dominis rerum justa causa possessionis præcedente acquirantur.

their property too quickly, and to prevent the benefit of this mode of acquisition being confined to any particular locality. We have accordingly published a constitution providing that moveables shall be acquired by a use extending for three years, and immoveables by the ' possession of long time,' that is, ten years for persons present, and twenty for persons absent; and that by these means, provided a just cause of possession precede, the ownership of things may be acquired, not only in Italy, but in every country subject to our empire.

GAL ii. 42-44; D. xII. 3. 1; C. vII. 35.

The subject of *possessio* is only treated indirectly in the Institutes, and it is necessary to have a general conception of the meaning of the term before proceeding to examine the mode of acquiring property called usucapion.

By *possessio* is meant primarily mere detention, i. e. the physical apprehension of a thing. If the possessor adds the intention (*animus*) of holding the thing as his own and of exercising over it all the rights of an owner, then he has legal possession of it as opposed to the mere physical possession involved in simple detention. When a person had legal possession of a thing he was protected in his possession against any one who had not a better title to possess, and in order to protect him the prætor granted him an interdict. If his possession was not founded on force or fraud, and had been acquired by a legal mode of acquisition, then it ripened, after a length of time laid down by law, into full ownership, and the process by which the change was effected was termed *usucapio*. Thus the meaning of the term legal or juristical possession, the protection of the rights of the possessor by the interdicts, and the transmutation under certain circumstances of *possessio* into ownership by the lapse of time, are the three main points on which attention has to be fixed in examining the subject of *possessio*.

The two requisites of legal possession are briefly summed up in the words ' *apprehensio* ' and *animus*. The apprehension of a corporeal thing means such a dealing with it as enables the person apprehending to deal with the thing at his pleasure. Thus a person who enters on part of a piece of land has possession of the whole because it is at his pleasure to go to any part of it. A person who has the key of a granary has the means of going into the granary. The *animus* means the intention of the possessor to hold the thing possessed as his own, and not as a person to whom a thing has been pledged holds the thing, for he holds it avowedly as belonging to another (*alieno nomine*).

The edict fixed certain cases in which the prætor would himself at once give a decision and pronounce what was to be done without sending the case to be examined by a judex, and the order of the prætor thus given was called an interdict (see Bk. iv. Tit. 16). What was termed an *interdictum retinendæ possessionis* was granted to a person whose possession had been disturbed or threatened with disturbance, and an *interdictum recuperandæ possessionis* was granted to a person who had been forcibly ejected from his possession. Any person in possession was entitled to these interdicts against every one who could not show that he had a better title.

Whenever a person possessed a thing as a matter of fact, with the intention of treating it as if he were the owner, that is, as if it belonged to him, the possessor had a right to the interdicts that protected his possession. But it was only when the possession was *bona fide* and *ex justa causa* that the operation of usucapion would transmute his possession into ownership, that is, the possessor must have commenced his possession, thinking he had a real right to possess, and have acquired it by a recognized legal method of acquiring property. A *possessio* which was commenced under these circumstances was changed into *dominium* by lapse of time, and the time required, as fixed by the law of the Twelve Tables, was two years if the thing possessed was an immoveable, and one year if it were a moveable. The operation of usucapion was of the greatest importance in the system of Roman law. Things that being *res mancipi* ought to have been conveyed by mancipation, but had been conveyed without the necessary ceremony, were not legally passed in ownership to the person to whom they were nominally conveyed. But the very short time requisite for the operation of *usucapion* quickly changed the possession into *dominium*, and thus ended the separation of the legal and beneficial interests. And, generally, when the prætor gave the possession of property where he could not by strict law give the ownership, that is, when he exercised his equitable jurisdiction, the operation of *usucapio* soon converted the *possessor bonorum* into the full legal *dominus*.

In order that the ownership of a thing should be acquired by usucapion it was of course necessary that the thing itself should be susceptible of being held in *dominio*. There was no ownership possible, for instance, in the case of the *solum provinciale*, and, therefore, no usucapion.  The emperor or the people were owners of the soil, and the actual occupier of land in the provinces could not be the owner; he could only be protected in the possession of it; and the prætors protected his possession against the claim of any one asserting himself to be the rightful possessor, by permitting the possessor, when he had held the land for ten years, if he and the claimant had during that time inhabited the same province (*inter præsentes*), or when he had held it for twenty years, if they had not, to repel the action by an exception, which, as being placed at the beginning of the *intentio*, was termed a *præscriptio* (see Introd. sec. 104), and would probably be in this form : *Ea res agatur, cujus non est longi temporis præscriptio*; and this prescription or exception (for the terms may be used indifferently, as it was only in the early times of the construction of the *formula* that such a defence was really placed at the beginning of the *intentio*), if found to be true in fact, made the possessor quite secure.

This prescription, however, had not exactly the same effect as usucapion.  In the first place, it did not make the person owner of the immoveable, for nothing could do that with respect to the *solum provinciale*.  Secondly, if an action was brought by the real owner, the usucapion was not interrupted until judgment had been given against the possessor (D. xli. 4. 2. 21); whereas if an action was brought against the possessor of an immoveable in the *solum provinciale*, the *præscriptio longi temporis* was of no avail unless the time required had expired before the proceeding had reached that stage termed the *litis contestatio*.  (See Introd. sec. 105.)  Lastly, the effect of the *præscriptio longi temporis* was in one way more favourable to the possessor than that of usucapion; for the person who acquired a thing by usucapion acquired it with all its liabilities and charges; whereas the *præscriptio longi temporis* was a good plea to the action of a person who claimed to have a right over the thing, as, for instance, a right of servitude or mortgage, so that the possessor who could use this plea had the thing he possessed quite free from any liability or charge anterior to the commencement of his possession.  (D. xli. 3. 44. 5 ; D. xliv. 3. 12.)

In the time of Justinian all difference between the *solum Italicum* and the *solum provinciale* was done away.  The text furnishes us with a brief statement of the change made in the effect of possession.  Under Justinian possession during three years (called, however, usucapion in this case—see parag. 12 of this Title) gave the ownership of moveables; possession during ten years if the parties were present, or

twenty if they were absent, gave the ownership of immoveables. Thus the length of possession no longer afforded
merely a means of repelling an action, but conferred the *dominium*, although the word *præscriptio* was used to express
the process. See parag. 5, Title 9 of this Book.

1. Sed aliquando, etiamsi maxime
quis bona fide rem possederit, non
tamen illi usucapio ullo tempore
procedit, veluti si quis liberum hominem vel rem sacram vel religiosam vel servum fugitivum possideat.

1. Sometimes, however, although
the thing be possessed with perfect
good faith, yet use, however long,
will never give the property; as, for
instance, when the possession is of a
free person, a thing sacred or religious, or a fugitive slave.

GAI. ii. 45. 48.

The Institutes now proceed to speak of the exceptions to the
rule of acquisition by use. These exceptions arise from two
sources: either the thing which we have possessed is in its
nature incapable of being acquired by use, or there is something in the mode in which it has come into our possession
which prevents length of possession having its ordinary effect.

No incorporeal thing could be acquired by usucapion, but
long quasi-possession was protected by prætorian actions and
interdicts. We have mentioned, in the note to Tit. 3. 4, that
it is a subject of some doubt whether, either before Justinian
or by his legislation, the possession of ten or twenty years
gave the ownership of servitudes. If it did not, then, probably, at no time of Roman law was the property in incorporeal things ever transferred by length of quasi-possession.

The fugitive slave could not be acquired by use, because he
was considered to have robbed his master of his interest in him
by his flight, *sui furtum facere intelligetur*. (D. xlvii. 2. 60.)

2. Furtivæ quoque res, et quæ vi
possessæ sunt, nec si prædicto longo
tempore bona fide possessæ fuerint,
usucapi possunt: nam furtivarum
rerum lex duodecim tabularum et
lex Atinia inhibent usucapionem;
vi possessarum, lex Julia et Plautia.

2. Things stolen, or seized by violence, cannot be acquired by use,
although they have been possessed
*bona fide* during the length of time
above prescribed; for such acquisition is prohibited, as to things stolen,
by the law of the Twelve Tables, and
by the *lex Atinia*; as to things seized
by violence, by the *lex Julia et Plautia*.

GAI. ii. 45; D. xli. 3. 4–6.

The *lex Atinia* was a *plebiscitum* named after its proposer
Atinius Labeo, 557 A.U.C. The *lex Plautia*, proposed by
M. Plautius, was passed 665 A.U.C. We know nothing of the
*lex Julia* here mentioned, except that its name makes it
probable that it was passed in the time of Augustus; it may
possibly be the *lex Julia de vi publica seu privata* referred
to in Book iv. Tit. 18. 8.

3. Quod autem dictum est, furtivarum et vi possessarum rerum usucapionem per leges prohibitam esse, non eo pertinet ut ne ipse fur, quive per vim possidet, usucapere possit (nam his alia ratione usucapio non competit, quia scilicet mala fide possident); sed ne ullus alius, quamvis ab eis bona fide emerit vel ex alia causa acceperit, usucapiendi jus habeat. Unde in rebus mobilibus non facile procedit ut bonæ fidei possessori usucapio competat: nam qui alienam rem vendit vel ex alia causa tradit, furtum ejus committit.

3. When it is said that the acquisition by use of things stolen or seized by violence is prohibited by these laws, it is not meant that the thief himself, or he who possesses himself of the thing by violence, is unable to acquire the property, for another reason prevents them, namely, that their possession is mala fide; but no one else, although he has in good faith purchased, or taken in any way from them, is able to acquire the property by use. Whence, as to moveables, it does not often happen that a bona fide possessor gains the property in them by use. For whenever anyone sells, or makes over for any other reason, a thing belonging to another, it is a theft.

Gai. ii. 49, 50.

In the case of moveables everything sold or delivered over by a person who knew himself not to be the owner was considered stolen, and therefore could not be acquired by use; and it could not often happen that a person who was not the real owner could sell or deliver a moveable, thinking himself to be the owner.

4. Sed tamen id aliquando aliter se habet. Nam si heres rem defuncto commodatam aut locatam vel apud eum depositam, existimans hereditariam esse, bona fide accipienti vendiderit aut donaverit aut dotis nomine dederit, quin is qui acceperit usucapere possit, dubium non est; quippe ea res in furti vitium non ceciderit, cum ntique heres qui bona fide tamquam suam alienaverit, furtum non committit.

4. Sometimes, however, it is otherwise; for, if an heir, supposing a thing lent or let to the deceased, or deposited with him to be a part of the inheritance, sells or gives it as a gift or dowry to a person who receives it bona fide, there is no doubt that the person receiving it may acquire the property in it by use; for the thing is not tainted with the vice of theft, as the heir who has bona fide alienated it as his own, has not been guilty of a theft.

Gai. ii. 50.

5. Item si is ad quem ancillæ ususfructus pertinet, partum suum esse credens vendiderit aut donaverit, furtum non committit; furtum enim sine affectu furandi non committitur.

5. So if the usufructuary of a female slave sells or gives away her child, believing it to be his property, he does not commit theft; for there is no theft, without the intention to commit theft.

Gai. ii. 50.

In such a case the usufructuary would make a legal mistake, but would not act with a criminal intention.

6. Aliis quoque modis accidere potest, ut quis sine vitio furti rem alienam ad aliquem transferat, et efficiat ut a possessore usucapiatur.

6. It may also happen in various other ways, that a man may transfer a thing belonging to another without committing a theft, so that the possessor acquires the property in it by use.

GAI. II. 50.

As, for instance, if a person who was not heir thought that he was (D. xli. 3. 36. 1), and sold a thing which was part of the inheritance; or if a person took possession of a thing which he believed the owner had intended to abandon. (D. xli. 7. 4.)

7. Quod autem ad eas res, quæ solo continentur, expeditius procedit: ut si quis loci vacantis possessionem, propter absentiam aut negligentiam domini, aut quia sine successore decesserit, sine vi nanciscatur. Qui, quamvis ipse mala fide possidet, quia intelligit se alienum fundum occupasse, tamen si alii bona fide accipienti, tradiderit, poteritei longa possessione res acquiri, quia neque furtivum neque vi possessum acceperit. Abolita est enim quorundam veterum sententia, existimantium etiam fundi locive furtum fieri; et eorum qui res soli possederint, principalibus constitutionibus prospicitur ne cui longa et indubitata possessio auferri debeat.

7. As to immoveables, it may more easily happen that a person may, without violence, take possession of a place vacant by the absence or negligence of the owner, or by his having died without a successor; and although his possession is mala fide since he knows that he has seized on land not belonging to him, yet if he transfers it to a person who receives it bona fide, this person will acquire the property in it by long possession, as the thing he receives has neither been stolen nor seized by violence. The opinion of the ancients, who thought that there could be a theft of a piece of land or a place, is now abandoned, and there are imperial constitutions which provide that no possessor of an immoveable shall be deprived of the benefit of a long and undoubted possession.

GAI. ii. 51; C. vii. 39. 1, 2.

If things immoveable could have been stolen, as was the opinion of Sabinus (AUL. GELL. xi. 18), the acquisition of immoveables by length of possession would have been as difficult as that of moveables; but as the *bona fides* of the actual possessor cured the *mala fides* of the first person who began the possession, it might very well happen that the property in immoveables should be gained in this way. By Novel 119 (cap. 7), A. D. 542, Justinian altered this, and only allowed the title by possession during ten or twenty years where the true owner was aware of his right, and of the transfer to the *bona fide* possessor; otherwise the right of ownership was not gained until after a possession of thirty years.

8. Aliquando etiam furtiva vel vi possessa res usucapi potest, veluti si in domini potestatem reversa fuerit; tunc enim, vitio rei purgato, procedit ejus usucapio.

8. Sometimes even a thing stolen or seised by violence may be acquired by use; for instance, if it has come back into the power of its owner, for then, the vice being purged, the acquisition by use may take place.

D. xli. 3. 4. 6.

In order that a thing once stolen should, after again falling under the power of its owner, be capable of being acquired by a *bona fide* possessor, it was necessary that the owner of the thing should recover it as a thing belonging to himself. If he purchased it, not knowing that it belonged to him, the vice or taint of theft was not purged. (D. xli. 3. 4. 6.)

9. Res fisci nostri usucapi non potest: sed Papinianus scripsit, bonis vacantibus fisco nondum nuntiatis, bona fide emptorem traditam sibi rem ex his bonis usucapere posse; et ita divus Pius, et divi Severus et Antoninus rescripserunt.

9. Things belonging to our *fiscus* cannot be acquired by use. But Papinian has given his opinion that if, before *bona vacantia* have been reported to the *fiscus*, a *bona fide* purchaser receives any of them, he can acquire the property by use. And the Emperor Antoninus Pius, and the Emperors Severus and Antoninus, have issued rescripts in accordance with this opinion.

D. xli. 3. 18. 2.

*Bona vacantia* was the term used to express the property of persons who died without successors. These goods belonged to the *fiscus* previously to being reported by the officers of the treasury (D. xlix. 14. 1. 1), but up to that time they could be acquired by usucapion.

10. Novissime sciendum est, rem talem esse debere ut in se non habeat vitium, ut a bonæ fidei emptore usucapi possit, vel qui ex alia justa causa possidet.

10. Lastly, it is to be observed that a thing must be tainted with no vice, that the *bona fide* purchaser or person who possesses it from any other just cause may acquire it by use.

D. xl. 1. 3. 24.

The word vice, as used here with reference to acquisition by use, includes every obstacle that prevented a thing being acquired by length of possession. First, the thing itself might be such as to be incapable of being acquired by use; to the instances of such things given above in paragraphs 1 and 9 may be added things belonging to pupils or to persons below the age of twenty-five years (C. vii. 35. 3), and things forming part of a dowry, unless the term of usucapion had begun to run before the marriage. (D. xxiii. 5. 16; C. v. 12. 30.) Secondly, it was necessary that the thing should be possessed *ex justa causa*, and if it was not, there would be *vitium* in the possession. By this it was meant that it must have come into the power of the possessor by a means, such as sale or gift, which was recognized by law as a good foundation for the transfer of ownership. It might have done so, and yet no title be acquired to the ownership, except by usucapion: the person who transferred it might not have been the real owner; the person who received it might not have had a right to do so; or, the thing itself might not have been capable of being acquired by mere possession.

The Digest (xli. 4, and seq.) gives a long series of Titles in which the several *justæ causæ* of possession are examined separately, and the different characters in which a person possessed are treated of. Thus, a person might possess *pro emptore* as having bought the thing; *pro donato*, as having received it as a gift; *pro dote*, as having received it in dowry; *pro soluto*, as the payment of a debt; *pro derelicto*, as having taken it when abandoned by its owner. In any of these cases the person who sold, gave, or abandoned the thing, might not have been the real owner, and then the possessor could only acquire the property in the thing by use; or again, he might possess *pro legato*, and then if he was not the person to whom the legacy had really been left, or if the legacy had been revoked, he might acquire by use the property in the thing. In this case it was not the testator not being the proprietor that made the possessor not the true owner, but it was his having no right to have the possession of the thing. Again, he might possess a thing *pro suo*, a general term specially employed to denote the possession of *fructus* gathered *bona fide*, or that of *res nullius*, such as wild animals. If he took possession of an animal, naturally wild, which had been tamed, and possessed it *pro suo*, he did not at once acquire the property in it, because it was not of a nature, since it had ceased to be wild, to be acquired by mere possession, but he became the owner by use. (D. xli. 10; D. xli. 2. 3. 21.)

Thirdly, it was necessary that there should be *bona fides*; the possessor must be quite ignorant of that which there was faulty in the manner he had gained possession. No ignorance of a leading principle of law, such as that a person below the age of puberty could not alienate his goods (D. xxii. 6. 4; D. xli. 3. 31), nor any wilful ignorance of facts, would be permitted as the commencement of usucapion. (D. xxii. 6. 6.) But if a person was only ignorant of a fact, of which it was excusable he should be ignorant, as that a vendor was under the age of puberty, his possession was *bona fide*. In the case

of sale, it was necessary that this *bona fides* should exist at
the moment of the contract being made, and also at that of its
being performed (D. xli. 3. 49), and in every case it was necessary it should exist at the commencement of possession.   But
after the possession was once commenced *bona fide*, a subsequent knowledge of the real facts did not vitiate the possession.

| | |
|---|---|
| 11. Error autem falsæ causæ usucapionem non parit : veluti si quis, cum non emerit, emisse se existimans possidet ; vel cum ei donatum non fuerit, quasi ex donatione possideat. | 11. But the mistake of thinking a false cause of possession is just, does not give rise to acquisition by use. As, for instance, if any one possesses in the belief that he has bought, when he has not bought, or that he has received a gift, when no gift has really been made to him. |

D. xli. 3. 27.

Supposing a person who thought that he had acquired *ex justa
causa* had not, supposing, for instance, he thought a person intended to give him a thing who did not, or if he had received a
thing in payment of a debt, while really no debt was due to him,
the question naturally suggested itself whether the imperfection
in the possession could be cured by *bona fides*, that is, an honest
belief that the *causa* was *justa*, that a gift had been made, or
that a debt was due.   The question had been much debated by
the jurists, and Justinian here decides it by declaring that the
imperfection could not be so cured, and that if the possessor
had been mistaken in this respect, length of possession would
not profit him.   We learn, however, from the Digest, that
where it was with respect to an act of some one through whom
the possessor believed his title to have been gained, as his procurator or slave, or the person whose heir he was, that the mistake was made, the possessor could acquire by use.   (D. xli. 4.
11.)   If, for instance, the possessor believed that his procurator
had bought a thing for him, although he might not have done
so, the possessor was not prevented by this mistake from
acquiring by use.

| | |
|---|---|
| 12. Diutina possessio quæ prodesse cœperat defuncto, et heredi et bonorum possessori continuatur, licet ipse sciat prædium alienum. Quod si ille initium justum non habuit, heredi et bonorum possessori, licet ignoranti, possessio non prodest.   Quod nostra constitutio similiter et in usucapionibus observari constituit, ut tempora continuentur. | 12. Long possession, which has begun to reckon in favour of the deceased, is continued in favour of the heir or *bonorum possessor*, although he may know that the immoveable belongs to another person ; but if the deceased commenced his possession *mala fide*, the possession does not profit the heir or *bonorum possessor*, although ignorant of this. And our constitution has enacted the same with respect to usucapions, in |

Q

which the benefit of possession is to
be in like manner continued.

D. xli. 4. 2, 19; D. xliv. 5. 11; C. vii. 31.

Persons who possessed *pro herede* or *pro possessore*, that is,
as *bonorum possessores*, did not themselves begin a new usucapion, but continued the *persona* of the deceased, and were
placed in the same position with reference to anything which
he had possessed, as if he had himself continued to possess it.
If the deceased had possessed the thing *pro emptore* or *pro
donato*, the *heres* or *bonorum possessor* continued to possess
it in the same way, and added to the time of his possession
the time during which the deceased had possessed it.

*Similiter in usucapionibus*, i. e. the continuation of possession by the heir shall apply to the usucapion of moveables by
three years' possession.

| | |
|---|---|
| 13. Inter venditorem quoque et emptorem conjungi tempora divi Severus et Antoninus rescripserunt. | 13. Between the buyer and the seller too, the Emperors Severus and Antoninus have decided by rescript that their several times of possession shall be reckoned together. |

D. xli. 4. 2. 20.

Persons who were merely successors of others in holding
particular things by sale, gift, legacy, &c., did not of course
continue the possession, for they did not continue the person,
of their predecessor. But if both the possession of their predecessor, and their own, was such as to give rise to usucapion, the
times of the two possessions were added together. If there was
something to prevent this in the possession of their predecessors, their own possession was the first commencement of the
usucapion.

The interruption of usucapion was termed *usurpatio*. (D.
xli. 3. 2.) It might take place in various ways. The thing
itself might be taken away from the possessor, or, if it was an
immoveable, be might be expelled from it (D. xli. 3. 5); or it
might become impossible, from physical causes, such as an in-
road of the sea, to occupy it (D. xli. 2. 3. 17); or, again, the
possessor might fall into the power of the enemy, and he would
not be reinstated in his possession by *postliminium*, for possession was a fact, and as he had ceased to possess, as a matter
of fact, he could only begin a new possession by again possessing the thing (D. xlix. 15. 12. 2); or the interruption might be
what was termed civil, that is, be produced by an action to
contest the right, and with respect to this Justinian (C. vii. 33.
10) made the time of the first raising of the controversy (*mota
controversia*) the period of interruption, instead of the *litis
contestatio*, which had no place in the civil process of his time.

There was also a prescription or possession, termed *longissimi temporis*. If there was a possession for thirty years, or, in the case of ecclesiastical property, for forty years, whatever *vitium* or obstacle there might be to the acquisition by use, for instance, theft, violence, absence of *justa causa*, or *mala fides*, the possessor could, before the time of Justinian, repel actions brought to claim the thing, and, after his legislation, became the legal owner.  (C. vii. 39.)

14. Edicto divi Marci cavetur, eum qui a fisco rem alienam emit, si post venditionem quinquennium praeterierit, posse dominum rei per exceptionem repellere. Constitutio autem divae memoriae Zenonis bene prospexit iis qui a fisco per venditionem aut donationem vel alium titulum aliquid accipiunt, ut ipsi quidem securi statim fiant, et victores existant, sive experiantur sive conveniantur; adversus autem sacratissimum aerarium usque ad quadriennium liceat intendere lis, qui pro dominio vel hypotheca earum rerum quae alienatae sunt, putaverint sibi quasdam competere actiones. Nostra autem divina constitutio quam nuper promulgavimus, etiam de iis qui a nostra vel venerabilis Augustae domo aliquid acceperint, haec statuit quae in fiscalibus alienationibus praefata Zenoniana constitutione continentur.

14. It is provided by an edict of the Emperor Marcus, that a person who has purchased from the *fiscus* a thing belonging to another person, may repel the owner of the thing by an exception, if five years have elapsed since the sale. But a constitution of Zeno of sacred memory has completely protected those who receive anything from the *fiscus* by sale, gift, or any other title, by providing that they themselves are to be at once secure, and made certain of success, whether they sue or are themselves sued, in an action. While they who think that they have a ground of action for the rights of ownership or mortgage over the things alienated, may bring an action against the sacred treasury within four years. An imperial constitution, which we ourselves have recently published, extends to those who have received as a gift anything from our palace, or that of the empress, the provision of the constitution of Zeno, relative to the alienations of the *fiscus*.

C. ii. 37. 3; C. vii. 37. 2. 2.

As Theophilus points out, the privilege really conceded by the constitution of Marcus Aurelius was, that no possession, if the thing had been received from the *fiscus*, should be attacked after five years had elapsed, however otherwise open to attack. If not otherwise open to attack, the time of usucapion, being so much shorter than five years, would give the property before the time fixed by the constitution had arrived.

## Tit. VII.  DE DONATIONIBUS.

Est et aliud genus acquisitionis donatio. Donationum autem duo sunt genera, mortis causa, et non mortis causa.

There is, again, another mode of acquiring property, donation, of which there are two kinds, donation *mortis causa* and donation not *mortis causa*.

· D. 1. 50. 10. 67.

The phrase *dono dare* was appropriated in Roman law to the mode of transferring property by gift; *dare* signifying that the whole property in the thing was passed, by delivery, and *dono* expressing the motive from which the delivery was made. (See *Vat. Fragm.* 275. 281. 283.) Viewed in its simple form, gift is not a peculiar mode of acquisition, but an acquisition by delivery with a particular motive for the transfer; but we shall see that in one species of *donatio mortis causa*, gift was really a peculiar mode of acquisition.

1. Mortis causa donatio est, quae propter mortis fit suspicionem: cum quis ita donat ut, si quid humanitus ei contigisset, haberet is qui accipit; sin autem superviximet is qui donavit, reciperet, vel si eum donationis poenituisset, aut prior decesserit is cui donatum sit. Hae mortis causa donationes ad exemplum legatorum redactae sunt per omnia. Nam cum prudentibus ambiguum fuerat, utrum donationis an legati instar eam obtinere oporteret, et utriusque causae quandam habebat insignia, et alii ad aliud genus eam retrahebant, a nobis constitutum est ut per omnia fere legatis connumeretur, et sic procedat quemadmodum nostra constitutio eam formavit. Et in summa mortis causa donatio est, cum magis se quis velit habere quam eum cui donat, magisque eum cui donat quam heredem suum. Sic et apud Homerum Telemachus donat Piraeo :—

Πειραῖ, οὐ γάρ τ' ἴδμεν ὅπως ἔσται τάδε ἔργα,
Εἰ κεν ἐμὶ μνηστῆρας ἀγήνορας ἐν μεγάροισι
Λάθρῃ κτείναντες, πατρώϊα πάντα δάσονται,
Αὐτὸν ἔχοντά σε βούλομ' ἐπαυρέμεν, ἤ τινα τῶνδε·
Εἰ δέ κ' ἐγὼ τούτοισι φόνον καὶ κῆρα φυτεύσω,
Δὴ τότε μοι χαίροντι φέρειν πρὸς δώματα χαίρων.

1. A donation *mortis causa* is that which is made to meet the case of death, as when anything is given upon condition, that, if any fatal accident befalls the donor, the person to whom it is given shall have it as his own; but if the donor should survive, or if he should repent of having made the gift, or if the person to whom it has been given should die before the donor, then the donor shall receive back the thing given. These donations *mortis causa* are now placed exactly on the footing of legacies. It was much doubted by the jurists whether they ought to be considered as a gift, or as a legacy, partaking as they did in some respects of the nature of both; and some were of opinion that they belonged to the one head, and others that they belonged to the other. We have decided by a constitution that they shall be in almost every respect reckoned amongst legacies, and shall be made in accordance with the forms our constitution provides. In short, it is a donation *mortis causa*, when the donor wishes that the thing given should belong to himself rather than to the person to whom he gives it, and to that person rather than to his own heir. It is thus that in Homer, Telemachus gives to Piraeus :—

'Piraeus, for we know not how these things shall be, whether the proud suitors shall secretly slay me in the palace, and shall divide the goods of my father, I would that thou thyself shouldst have and enjoy these things rather than that any of those men should: but if I shall plant slaughter and death amongst those men, then indeed bear these

> things to my home, and joying give
> them to me in my joy.'

D. xxxix. 6. 35. 4. 37. 1. 1; C. viii. 57. 4.

There are two essential conditions of a *donatio mortis causa*: it must be made with the view of meeting the case of death ; and it must be made to take effect only if death occurs, and so as to be revocable at any time previous.

It might be made conditional upon death in two ways. The donor might say, If I die in this enterprise I give you my horse; or he might say, I give you my horse, if I survive this enterprise you are to give it me back. In the latter method, the delivery of the thing is made at once, subject to a conditional redelivery : in the former the delivery is made conditional. (See D. xxxix. 6. 2. *et seq.*) The donation might be made conditional upon the death of a third person, as of a husband in a gift to a wife. (D. xxxix. 6. 11.) All who could make a testament could make a valid *donatio mortis causa* : and all who could receive under a testament could accept one. (D. xxxix. 6. 9. and 15.) Every kind of thing could be given in this way. (D. xxxix. 6. 18. 2.) Justinian, in the constitution alluded to in the text, required that a *donatio mortis causa* should be made in the presence of five witnesses. (C. viii. 57. 4.)

If the gift was made in the first of the two ways above mentioned, as there was no delivery, and the thing given was acquired *ipso jure* on the death of the donor, *donatio* was, in this case, a special mode of acquisition. If the gift was made in the second way, the whole property passed at once by the tradition to the recipient, and in the older and stricter law, as the *dominium* passed absolutely when it passed at all, the property in the thing could not revert to the donor merely by the condition having been accomplished. He would only have a personal action against the recipient to compel him to give the value of the thing if he did not choose to give back the thing itself. The later jurists seem, however, to consider that the *dominium* reverted *ipso jure*, and that the donor could bring a real action for the thing itself. (D. vi. 1. 41 ; D. xxxix. 6. 29.)

If the donor was insolvent at the time of his death this was considered as an implied revocation of the gift. (D. xxxix. 6. 17.)

*Ad exemplum legatorum redactæ sunt per omnia . . . per omnia fere legatis connumeretur*—the latter is the more correct expression ; gifts *mortis causa* were not exactly on the footing of legacies, especially because they had complete effect immediately on the death of the donor, whereas legacies, to take effect, required that the heir should first enter on the inheritance (D. xxxix. 6. 29): regard was had to the capacity to receive of the person to whom the gift was made, only at the time of the death, and not as in the case of legacies, also at the time of the disposition. (D. xxxiv. 9. 5. 17.) And a *filiusfamilias* who could not make a testament could, with his father's permission, make a *donatio mortis causa*. (D. xxxix. 6. 25. 1.) There was one remarkable mode in which they were placed on the footing of legacies. By a constitution of Severus the heir was permitted to retain as large a portion (one-fourth) of the gift as he could of a legacy by the *lex Falcidia*. (See C. viii. 57. 2.)

The lines quoted in the text are from Odyssey 17. 78.

2. Aliæ autem donationes sunt, quæ sine ulla mortis cogitatione fiunt, quas inter vivos appellamus, quæ non omnino comparantur legatis: quæ si fuerint perfectæ, temere revocari non possunt. Perficiuntur autem, cum donator suam voluntatem scriptis aut sine scriptis manifestaverit; et ad exemplum venditionis, nostra constitutio eas etiam in se habere necessitatem traditionis voluit, ut etiam si non tradantur, habeant plenissimum et perfectum robur, et traditionis necessitas incumbat donatori. Et cum retro principum dispositiones insinuari eas actis intervenientibus volebant, si majores fuerant ducentorum solidorum, constitutio nostra eam quantitatem usque ad quingentos solidos ampliavit, quam stare etiam sine insinuatione statuit; sed et quasdam donationes invenit, quæ penitus insinuationem fieri minime desiderant, sed in se plenissimam habent firmitatem. Alia insuper multa ad uberiorem exitum donationum invenimus: quæ omnia ex nostris constitutionibus quas super his exposuimus, colligenda sunt. Sciendum est tamen quod, et si plenissimæ sint donationes, si tamen ingrati existant homines in quos beneficium collatum est, donatoribus per nostram constitutionem licentiam præstavimus certis ex causis eas revocare; ne qui suas res in alios contulerunt, ab his quamdam patiantur injuriam

2. The other kind of donations are those which are made without any consideration of death, and are called donations *inter vivos*. They cannot, in any respect, be compared to legacies, and if completed cannot be revoked at pleasure. They are said to be completed when the donor has manifested his intention, whether by writing or not. Our constitution has declared that, after the example of sales, they shall involve the necessity of tradition; so, however, that even before tradition, they are completely effectual, and place the donor under the necessity of delivering them; previous Imperial constitutions have enacted that they should be registered by public deeds, if exceeding two hundred *solidi*, but our constitution has raised the limit to five hundred *solidi*, so that for a gift of this sum registration is not necessary. We have also marked out certain donations which need no registration at all, but are completely valid of themselves. We have, too, made many other new enactments, in order to extend and secure the effect of donations, all which may be collected from the constitutions we have promulgated on this subject. It must, however, be observed, that however absolutely a donation may be given, yet, if the object of the donor's bounty prove ungrateful, he is permitted by our constitution, in certain specified cases, to revoke the donation; for it is not right that they

vel jacturam, secundum enumeratos in constitutione nostra modos.

who have given their property to others should suffer from them injuries or losses of such a kind as those enumerated in our constitution.

D. xxxix. 6. 27; C. viii. 54. 35. 5; C. viii. 54. 34, pr. 3, 4; C. viii. 54. 30, pr. 2 and 3; C. viii. 54. 10.

A thing given was, if a *res mancipi*, given by mancipation, or *in jure cessio*, if a *res nec mancipi*, by tradition. But a mere agreement to give gratuitously (*pactum*) was not in the least binding on the person who agreed to give, and to make a promise to give binding, it was necessary that the agreement should assume the form of a stipulation. (See Introd. sec. 83.)

The *lex Cincia*, 560 A.U.C., introduced several new rules into the law respecting gifts, but did not make a mere agreement to give in any degree valid. The first step taken in this direction was by Constantine (Cod. Theod. viii. 12. 4. *et seq.*), who made the agreement binding if reduced to writing. And Justinian (C. viii. 54. 35. 5.) made the agreement binding, whether reduced to writing or not; but it is to be observed that he provided, not that the property should pass by the agreement, but that the donor should be bound thereby to make tradition of the thing. So that the property in the thing was acquired by tradition, and not by donation, as a distinct mode of acquisition.

Donations not registered were only void for the sum by which they exceeded the amount fixed by law. (C. viii. 54. 34.) Those valid without registration at all were such as donations made by, or to, the emperor, to redeem captives, or to rebuild edifices destroyed by fire. (C. viii. 54. 36.)

Gifts *inter vivos* were revocable in certain cases specified in the Code (viii. 56. 10), as, for instance, when the person benefited seriously injured, or attempted to injure, the person or property of the donor, or failed to fulfil the conditions of the gift. Revocation in such cases was personal to the donor and to the receiver, and could not be exacted by the heirs of the one, or against the heirs of the other.

3. Est et aliud genus inter vivos donationum, quod veteribus quidem prudentibus penitus erat incognitum, postea autem a junioribus divis principibus introductum est: quod ante nuptias vocabatur, et tacitam in se conditionem haberet ut tunc ratam esset, cum matrimonium fuerit insecutum, ideoque ante nuptias appellabatur, quod ante matrimonium efficiebatur, et

3. There is another kind of donation *inter vivos* entirely unknown to the ancient lawyers, and subsequently introduced by the more recent emperors. It was termed the *donatio ante nuptias*, and was made under a tacit condition that it should only take effect when the marriage had followed on it. Hence it was called *ante nuptias*, because it preceded the marriage, and never took place after their

nunquam post nuptias celebratas talis donatio procedebat. Sed primus quidem divus Justinus pater noster, cum augeri dotem et post nuptias fuerat permissum, si quid tale eveniret, etiam ante nuptias augeri donationem constante matrimonio sua constitutione permisit; sed tamen nomen inconveniens remanebat, cum ante nuptias quidem vocabatur, post nuptias autem tale accipiebat incrementum. Sed nos plenissimo fini tradere sanctiones cupientes, et consequentia nomina rebus esse studentes, constituimus ut tales donationes non augeantur tantum, sed et constante matrimonio initium accipiant, et non ante nuptias sed propter nuptias vocentur; et dotibus in hoc exaequentur, ut quemadmodum dotes constante matrimonio non solum augentur sed etiam fiunt, ita et istae donationes quae propter nuptias introductae sunt, non solum antecedant matrimonium, sed eo etiam contracto augeantur et constituantur.

celebration; but as it was permitted that dowries should be increased even after marriage, the Emperor Justin, our father, was the first to permit, by his constitution, that in case the dowry was increased, the donation *ante nuptias* might be increased also, even during the marriage; but the donation still retained what was thus an improper name, and was called *ante nuptias*, while this increase was made to it after marriage. Wishing, therefore, to perfect the law on the subject, and to make names appropriate to things, we have enacted that such donations may not only be increased, but may also be first made during marriage, and that they shall be termed, not *ante nuptias*, but *propter nuptias*, and that they shall be placed on the footing of dowries, so far that, as dowries may be not only increased, but first made during marriage, so donations *propter nuptias* may not only precede marriage, but also, after the tie of marriage has been formed, may be increased or made.

C. v. 3. 10, 20.

When the wife passed *in manum viri*, all that she had belonged to her husband; when she did not, all her property belonged exclusively to herself, and all gifts between husband and wife were strictly prohibited by law. But as a provision for the expenses of marriage, the wife contributed the *dos*, which, given before marriage, and sometimes increased after, belonged to the husband, subject, however, after the passing of a *lex Julia de adulteriis et de fundo dotali* in the time of Augustus, to the obligation of restoring all immoveables comprised in it at the end of the marriage; and, in the time of Justinian, subject also to the obligation of restoring the value of the moveables also. The power of the husband over the *dos* is treated of in the introductory paragraph of the next Title. The *donatio ante nuptias*, of which we first hear in a constitution of Theodosius and Valentinian (C. v. 17. 8. 4), which speaks of it as recognized by law, was a gift on the part of the husband as an equivalent to the *dos*. It was the property of the wife, but managed by the husband, and could not be alienated, even with her consent. Justinian provided (Nov. 97. 1) that the wife, if survivor, should receive an equal value from the *donatio propter nuptias* with that which the husband, if survivor, would have received from the *dos*, the actual amount reserved for the survivor being matter of agreement between the parties. By a constitution previous to Justinian (C. v. 14. 7), the wife had, if survivor, an equal portion of the *donatio* with that her husband had of the *dos*. Justinian substituted an equality of value for an equality of proportion.

4. Erat olim et alius modus civilis acquisitionis per jus accrescendi, quod est tale: si communem servum habeas aliquis cum Titio, solus libertatem ei imposuit vel vindicta, vel testamento, eo casu pars ejus amittebatur et socio accrescebat. Sed cum pessimum fuerat exemplo, et libertate servum defraudari et ex ea humanioribus quidem dominis damnum inferri, severioribus autem dominis lucrum accrescere, hoc quasi in ridia plenum pio remedio per nostram constitutionem mederi necessarium duximus; et invenimus viam per quam et manumissor, et socius ejus, et qui libertatem accepit, nostro beneficio fruantur: libertate cum effectu procedente (cujus favore et antiquos legislatores multa etiam contra communes regulas statuisse manifestum est), et eo qui eam imposuit suae liberalitatis stabilitate gaudente et socio indemni conservato, pretiumque servi secundum partem dominii quod nos definivimus, accipiente.

4. There was formerly another mode of acquiring property by the civil law, namely, that of accrual; as, if any one, having a slave in common with Titius, had himself alone enfranchised him, either by the *vindicta* or by testament, his share in that slave was lost, and accrued to the joint owner. But, as it was an example of very bad tendency, that both the slave should be defrauded of his freedom, and that the more humane master should suffer loss, while the more severe master profited, we have thought it advisable to apply by our constitution a pious remedy to what seemed so odious, and have devised means by which the manumittor, and the co-proprietor, and the freed slave, may be all benefited. Freedom, to favour which ancient legislators have often violated the ordinary rules of law, shall be really gained by the slave; he who has given this freedom, shall have the delight of seeing it maintained; and his co-proprietor shall be indemnified by receiving a price for the slave, proportioned to his interest in him, according to the rates fixed in our constitution.

C. vii. 7. 1. 5.

A man could not be partly free, partly a slave. If, then, a slave was enfranchised by one co-proprietor, was he a slave or free? The old law, as the text informs us, pronounced him the former. When under the old law the slave, if enfranchised, would have been a *Latinus-Junianus* (see Bk. i. Tit. 5. 3), he still remained the property of the same master as before. If he would have been a Roman citizen, the interest of the master who manumitted him accrued to the other proprietors. (PAUL. *Sent.* iv. 12. 1.)

The scale of prices alluded to in the concluding words of the text is given in the Code. (vii. 7. 1. 5.)

## Tit. VIII.   QUIBUS ALIENARE LICET, VEL NON.

Accidit aliquandout,quidominus sit, alienare non possit; et contra, qui dominus non sit, alienandæ rei potestatem habeat: nam dotale prædium maritus invita muliere per legem Juliam prohibetur alienare, quamvis ipsius sit dotis causa ei datum. Quod nos legem Juliam corrigentes, in meliorem statum deduximus: cum enim lex in soli tantummodo rebus locum habebat quæ italicæ fuerant, et alienationes inhibebat quæ invita muliere fiebant, hypothecas autem earum rerum etiam volente ea, utrique remedium imposuimus, ut et in eas res quæ in provinciali solo positæ sunt, interdicta sit alienatio vel obligatio, et neutrum eorum neque consentientibus mulieribus procedat, ne sexus muliebris fragilitas in perniciem substantiæ earum converteretur.

Sometimes it happens that he, who is owner of a thing cannot alienate it, while, on the contrary, he who is not owner has the power of alienation. Thus, the husband is prohibited by the *lex Julia* from alienating immoveables, which form part of the dowry, against the wish of the wife, although these immoveables, having been given him as a part of the dowry, belong to him. We have amended the *lex Julia*, and introduced a great improvement. This law only applied to things in Italy, and it prohibited alienations made against the wishes of the wife, and mortgages made even with her consent. Wishing to amend the law on each of these points, we have declared that the prohibition of alienation or mortgage shall extend to immoveables in the provinces, and that neither alienation nor mortgage shall be made even with the consent of the wife, lest the weakness of the female sex should be abused to the detriment of their fortunes.

GAI. ii. 62, 63; C. v. 13. 15.

The power of alienating belongs to the owner, and to him only; and every owner can alienate the thing belonging to him. There are, however, exceptions to the rule, and these exceptions form the subject of this Title.

The *dos* of the wife belonged to the husband, and his rights over it were in the ancient law unrestricted. Gradually a restraint was imposed on them, first, by the obligation to give up, after the dissolution of the marriage, those things of which the value had not been estimated; next by the *lex Julia de adulteriis* a *plebiscitum* of the time of Augustus, by which, as Paul, in his Sentences, ii. 21, informs us '*Cavetur ne dotale prædium maritus invita uxore alienet;*' that is, it rendered the consent of the wife necessary for the alienation of immoveables, and also prevented mortgage of immoveables even with the wife's consent, a distinction evidently arising from it being apprehended that a woman would be more easily persuaded to consent to mortgage than to sell her property. In the same way the *senatus consultum Velleianum* prevented a woman placing herself under an obligation for another person, but did not prevent her making a gift. (D. xvi. 1. 4. 1.) Any one can understand what they are doing when they sell or give a thing, but may easily not be aware how much is involved when they comply with the legal forms of mortgage or guarantee.

As a general rule *dotes* were given on the condition that, after the dissolution of the marriage, the things given should belong to the wife or her heirs; but a special agreement might decide that they should belong to the husband; and then, if alienated by him during the marriage, they could not be reclaimed on its dissolution. (D. xxiii. 5. 17.)

Under Justinian immoveables forming part of a *dos*, whereever situated, could no longer be either sold or subjected to a *hypotheca*, even with the wife's consent.

| 1. Contra autem creditor pignus ex pactione, quamvis ejus ea res non sit, alienare potest. Sed hoc sonitan ideo videtur fieri quod voluntate debitoris intelligitur pignus alienari, qui ab initio contractus pactus est ut liceret creditori pignus vendere, si pecunia non solvatur. Sed ne creditores jus suum persequi impedirentur, neque debitores temere suarum rerum dominium amittere videantur, nostra constitutione consultum est, et certus modus impositus est per quem pignorum distractio possit procedere: cujus tenore utrique parti creditorum et debitorum satis abundeque provisum est. | 1. On the other hand, a creditor may, according to agreement, alienate a pledge, although the thing is not his own property. But this alienation may perhaps be considered as taking place by the intention of the debtor, who in making the contract has agreed that the creditor might sell the thing pledged, if the debt were not paid. But that creditors might not be impeded in the pursuit of their rights, nor debtors seem too easily deprived of their property, a provision has been made by our constitution establishing a fixed method of procedure for the sale of pledges, by which the respective interests of the creditor and debtor have been fully secured. |

GAL ii. 64; C. viii. 34. 3, pr. *et seq.*

The power of a creditor to sell the thing pledged, forming an exception to the rule that none but the owner could alienate, was so necessary a part of his rights that it could not be taken from him even by express agreement; and an agreement *ne vendere liceat* had no other effect than to make it necessary for the creditor to give the debtor notice of his intention to sell. (D. xiii. 7. 4–6.) Justinian, by his constitution, permitted the parties to fix the time, and place, and manner of sale at their pleasure, and it was only if there was no special agreement that the regulations of his constitution were to take effect.

Tutors and curators might, in certain cases, alienate the goods of their pupils and of those committed to their care; but, at any rate in the later times of law, they had to obtain the permission of a magistrate for the alienation of rural immoveables. (See C. v. 37. 22.)

2. Nunc admonendi sumus neque pupillum neque pupillam, ullam rem sine tutoris auctoritate alienare posse. Ideoque si mutuam pecuniam sine tutoris auctoritate alicui dederit, non contrahit obligationem, quia pecuniam non facit accipientis; ideoque nummi vindicari possunt, sicubi extent. Sed si nummi quos mutuos dedit, ab eo qui accepit, bona fide consumpti sunt, condici possunt; si mala fide, ad exhibendum de his agi potest. At ex contrario, omnes res pupillo et pupillae sine tutoris auctoritate recte dari possunt. Ideoque si debitor pupillo solvat, necessaria est debitori tutoris auctoritas; alioquin non liberabitur. Sed hoc etiam evidentissima ratione statutum est in constitutione, quam ad Cæsarienses advocatos ex suggestione Triboniani viri eminentissimi, quæstoris sacri palatii nostri, promulgavimus: qua dispositum est, ita licere tutori vel curatori debitorem pupillarem solvere, ut prius judicialis sententia sine omni damno celebrata hoc permittat; quo subsecuto, si et judex pronuntiaverit et debitor solverit, sequatur hujusmodi solutionem plenissima securitas. Sin autem aliter quam depræmdimus solutio facta fuerit, pecuniam autem salvam habeat pupillus aut ex ea locupletior sit, et adhuc eamdem pecuniæ summam petat, per exceptionem doli mali poterit submoveri. Quod si aut male consumpserit aut furto amiserit, nihil proderit debitori doli mali exceptio, sed nihilominus damnabitur, quia temere sine tutoris auctoritate et non secundum nostram dispositionem solverit. Sed ex diverso pupilli vel pupillæ solvere sine tutoris auctoritate non possunt; quia id quod solvunt non fit accipientis, cum scilicet nullius rei alienatio eis sine tutoris auctoritate concessa est.

2. It must here be observed, that no pupil of either sex can alienate anything without the authority of a tutor. If, therefore, a pupil, without the tutor's authority, lend any one money, the pupil does not contract an obligation; for he does not make the money the property of the receiver, and the pieces of money may be claimed by vindication, if they still exist. But supposing these pieces which the pupil has lent are consumed by the borrower, then, if they are in bona fide, a personal action may be brought; if mala fide, an action ad exhibendum. On the contrary, the pupil of either sex may acquire anything whatsoever without the authority of the tutor; and therefore when a debtor pays a pupil, the debtor must have the authority of the tutor, or he does not free himself from the debt. And we have, for very obvious reasons, declared by a constitution, published to the advocates of Cæsarea on the suggestion of the very eminent Tribonian, quæstor of our sacred palace, that the debtor of a pupil may make payment to the tutor or curator, first receiving permission by the sentence of a judge, obtained free of all expenses, and if these forms are observed, a payment made according to the sentence of the judge will give the debtor the most complete security. If payment is made, not according to the mode we have sanctioned, the pupil who has the money still safe in his possession, or has been made richer by it, may, if he demand again the same sum, be repelled by an exception of dolus malus. But if he has spent the money uselessly, or lost it by theft, the debtor cannot profit by the exception of dolus malus, and he will be condemned to pay over again, because he has paid in a rash manner, without the authority of the tutor, and has not conformed to our rules. On the other hand, pupils of either sex cannot pay without the authority of the tutor, be-

cause that which they pay does not thereby become the property of the person who receives it, as they are incapable of alienating anything without the authority of the tutor.

GAI. ii. 60. 82–84; C. v. 37. 25 ; D. xlvi. 3. 14. 8.

The pupil might make his condition better, but not worse. (See Bk. i. Tit. 21.)  He could not transfer the property in anything belonging to him, but he could acquire the property in anything transferred to him.  If, therefore, he paid anything, he could not transfer the property in the money he paid to the creditor, and therefore his payment was of no effect.  Nor could he lend anything under the contract called *mutuum*, the essence of which was that the thing lent became the property of the borrower, who bound himself to give back a thing of equal value. (See Bk. iii. Tit. 14.) If the pupil attempted to lend a thing in this way, the thing lent could be recovered by vindication, if it were possible that the actual thing should be restored; if not, its value could be recovered by a personal action (*condictio*) against the borrower; or if the borrower had been guilty of *mala fides*, by an *actio ad exhibendum*, that is, the borrower was called upon to produce the thing borrowed; and on his being found unable to do so, he was condemned to pay not only the value of the thing, but damages to compensate for the injury inflicted.

If the debtor made a payment to the pupil, that which he paid became the property of the pupil; and as the pupil could not make his condition worse, he could not extinguish debts due to him; and thus the debt was still owing, although the pupil retained what was paid him.  If the tutor authorized the payment, the debt was extinguished; but the pupil had a right to receive from the tutor the money paid; and if he could not obtain it from him, the praetor would, under certain circumstances, grant a *restitutio in integrum* (see note on introductory paragraph of Bk. i. Tit. 23), and the creditor would then be obliged to pay over again, in order that the pupil might be kept free from all loss.  It was to guard against this that Justinian, in the constitution alluded to in the text, provided a means whereby the creditor should have *plenissima securitas*.

## TIT. IX.   PER QUAS PERSONAS NOBIS ACQUIRITUR.

Acquiritur nobis non solum per nosmetipsos, sed etiam per eos quos

We acquire not only by ourselves, but also by those whom we have in

in potestate habemus, item per servos in quibus usumfructum habemus, item per homines liberos et servos alienos quos bona fide possidemus: de quibus singulis diligentius dispiciamus.

our power; also by slaves, of whom we have the usufruct; and by those freemen and slaves belonging to others whom we possess bona fide. Let us examine separately these different cases.

GAI. ii. 80.

The rule of law was, that no one could acquire through another person; but if persons in the power of another acquired anything, that which they acquired became, by the mere force of their position, the property of the person in whose power they were; and thus the rule may be, perhaps, more accurately expressed by saying that nothing could be acquired *per extraneam personam*, i.e. through a person who was not in the *familia* of the acquirer.

1. Igitur liberi nostri utriusque sexus, quos in potestate habemus, olim quidem quidquid ad eos pervenerat (exceptis videlicet castrensibus peculiis), hoc parentibus suis acquirebant sine ulla distinctione. Et hoc ita parentium fiebat, ut esset eis licentia, quod per unum vel unam eorum acquisitum est, alii filio vel extraneo donare vel vendere vel, quocumque modo voluerant, adplicare. Quod nobis inhumanum visum est et, generali constitutione emissa, et liberis pepercimus et patribus debitum reservavimus. Sancitum etenim a nobis est, ut si quid ex re patris ei obveniat, hoc secundum antiquam observationem totum parenti acquirat; quae enim invidia est, quod ex patris occasione profectum est, hoc ad eum reverti? Quod autem ex alia causa sibi filiusfamilias acquisivit, hujus usumfructum patri quidem acquirat, dominium autem apud eum remaneat: ne quod ei suis laboribus vel prospera fortuna accessit, hoc ad alium pervениens luctuosum ei procedat.

1. Formerly, all that children under power of either sex acquired, excepting *castrensia peculia*, was without distinction acquired for the benefit of their parents; so much so, that the *paterfamilias* who had thus acquired anything through one of his children, could give or sell, or transfer it in any way he pleased to another child or to a stranger. This appeared to us very harsh, and by a general constitution we have relieved the children, and yet reserved for the parents all that was due to them. We have declared that all which the child obtains by means of the fortune of the father, shall, according to the old law, he acquired entirely for the father's benefit: for what hardship is there in that which comes from the father returning to him? But of everything that the *filiusfamilias* acquires in any other way, the father shall have the usufruct, but the son shall retain the ownership, so that another may not reap the profit of that which the son has gained by his labour or good fortune.

GAI. ii. 87; C. vi. 61. 6.

The *filiusfamilias* could not, in the strict law of Rome, have any property of his own. Sometimes, however, the father permitted the son to have what was called a *peculium*, that is, a certain amount of property placed under his exclusive control. This *peculium* remained in law the property of the father, but the son had the disposition and management of it by his father's permission, and as long as it remained in the son's possession it was, as far as I regarded third persons, exactly like property really belonging to the son only. (See Tit. 12. 1. of this Book.) In the early times of the Empire a *filiusfamilias* came to have, under the name of *castrense peculium*, property quite independent of his father. This *castrense peculium* consisted of all that was given to a son when setting out upon military service, or acquired while that service lasted. This belonged to the son as completely as if he had been *sui juris*, and he had full power of disposing of it either during his lifetime or by testament. *Filii familias in castrensi peculio vice patrum familiarum funguntur.* (D. xiv. 6. 2.) If, however, he did not choose to exercise his power of disposing of it by testament, his father took it at his death, not as succeeding to it *ab intestato*, but as the claimant of a *peculium*. (See Tit. 12. pr.) A further benefit was extended to the *filiusfamilias* by the institution of the *quasi-castrense peculium*, a privilege given to certain civil functionaries, corresponding to that given by the *castrense peculium* to soldiers. Constantine, by a constitution (C. xii. 31), placed on the footing of the *castrense peculium* things which a *filiusfamilias*, who was an officer of the palace, received from the emperor or gained by his own economy. The same advantage was subsequently extended to many other functionaries, as well as to advocates and certain ecclesiastical dignitaries. The *quasi-castrense peculium* must have existed in the time of Ulpian (D. xxxvi. 1. 1. 6; xxxvii. 13. 3. 5), unless the passages in the Digest in which he alludes to it are interpolated, but under what form it then existed we do not know. In one respect it slightly differed from the *castrense peculium*; for the power of disposing of it by testament did not always accompany it, but was only given to the more privileged classes of those who were allowed to have such a *peculium*. Justinian, however, altered this, and gave the power of disposing of it by testament to every one who had a *quasi-castrense peculium*. (See Tit. 11. 6.) Constantine also introduced another kind of *peculium*, termed the *peculium adventitium*. This consisted of everything received by a *filiusfamilias* in succeeding, whether by testament or not, to his mother. (C. vi. 60. 1.) Subsequent emperors included in it all received by succession or as a gift from maternal ascendants (C. vi. 60. 2), or by one of two married persons from the other (C. vi. 60. 1); and Justinian, as we learn from the text, included under the *peculium adventitium* all that came to the son from any other source than from the father himself. The father had the usufruct of the *peculium adventitium*, and it was only the ownership that was held by the son. The *peculium* which came to the son as part of the father's property, and which continued to belong to the father, has been termed by commentators *profectitium*, because it comes (*proficiscitur*) from the father.

The *peculium* in the time of Justinian, therefore, if *profectitium*, belonged to the father; in all other cases it belonged to the son; but the father had the usufruct of the *peculium adventitium*, while the son had as full power over the *castrense* or *quasi-castrense peculium* as if he had been *sui juris*.

2. Hæcquoque a nobis dispositum est et in ea specie ubi parens, emancipando liberum, ex rebus quæ acquisitionem effugiunt, si hi tertiam partem retinere si voluerat, licentiam ex anterioribus constitutionibus habebat, quasi pro pretio quodammodo emancipationis; et Inhumanum quiddam accidebat, ut filius rerum suarum, ex hac emancipatione, dominio pro parte tertia defraudetur, et quod honoris ei ex emancipatione additum est, quod sui juris effectus est, hoc per rerum diminutionem decrescat. Ideoque statuimus ut parens, pro tertia eorum bonorum parte dominii quam retinere poterat, dimidiam, non dominii rerum, sed ususfructus retineat: ita etenim res intactæ apud filium remanebunt, et pater ampliore summa fruetur, pro tertia dimidia potiturus.

2. We have also made some regulations with respect to the power which under former constitutions a father had, when emancipating his children, of deducting a third part from the things over which he had no right of acquisition, as if this were the price of the emancipation. It seemed very hard that the son should thus be deprived by emancipation of a third part of his property, and that what he gained in honour by being emancipated he should lose in fortune. We have therefore enacted that the father, instead of retaining a third as owner, shall retain half as usufructuary. Thus the ownership in the whole will remain with the son, unimpaired, while the father will enjoy the benefits of a larger portion, the half, namely, instead of the third.

### C. vi. 61. 6. 3.

The usufruct of the father over things, the ownership of which, as part of the *peculium adventitium*, belonged to the son, would be lost by emancipation. It was as an equivalent for this that the property in one-third of these things was given to the father on emancipation. Justinian substitutes the usufruct of one-half, for the ownership of one-third.

3. Item nobis acquiritur quod servi nostri ex traditione nanciscuntur, sive quid stipulentur, vel ex qualibet alia causa acquirant: hoc enim nobis et ignorantibus et invitis obvenit; ipse enim servus qui in potestate alterius est, nihil suum habere potest. Sed si heres institutus sit, non alias nisi nostro jussu hereditatem adire potest; et si nobis jubentibus adierit, nobis hereditas acquiritur, perinde ac si non ipsi

3. So, too, all that our slaves acquire by tradition, or stipulation, or in any other way, is acquired for us; and that even without our knowledge and against our wishes. For the slave who is in the power of any one cannot himself have anything as his own. And if he is instituted heir, he cannot enter on the inheritance except by our direction. And if he enters by our direction, we acquire the inheritance exactly as if we had ourselves

heredes instituti eramus; et convenienter scilicet nobis legatum per
eos acquiritur.  Non solum antem
proprietas per eos quos in potestate
habemus, nobis acquiritur, sed etiam
possessio; cujuscumque enim rei
possessionem adepti fuerint, id nos
possidere videmur: unde etiam per
eos usucapio vel longi temporis
possessio nobis accedit.

been instituted heirs. Legacies, again,
are equally acquired for us by our
slaves. And it is not only the ownership which is acquired for us by those
whom we have in our power, but
also the possession. Everything, of
which they have obtained possession,
we are considered to possess, and
consequently we have through them
the benefits of usucapion and possession longi temporis.

GAL. li. 67. 69.

All that the slave had belonged to his master; and this rule
was subject to no exceptions such as those which the indulgence of the emperors introduced for the benefit of the *filiusfamilias.*  His *peculium* was always at the disposition of his
master, and it made no difference what was the mode in which
he acquired: he acquired it for his master even though his
master had not consented or even known of the acquisition.
Therefore, if the slave received anything in pursuance of a
stipulation (*sive quid stipulentur*), he acquired it for his
master, although he could not bind his master by promising
anything to a person who stipulated for anything from him.
The slave could not make his master's condition worse; and as
an inheritance might be more onerous than lucrative, for the
debts of the deceased, which the heir was bound to pay, might
exceed the value of his property, a slave was not permitted to
accept an inheritance, except by his master's express command.
A legacy, on the other hand, could not be otherwise than advantageous, and therefore a legacy given to a slave immediately belonged to his master.  There was a minor difference
between the institution of a slave as heir, and a gift to him of
a legacy, which deserves mention.  The right to a legacy dated
from the death of the deceased; the right to an inheritance
dated from the time of entering on an inheritance.  The slave,
therefore, acquired a legacy for the benefit of the master to
whom he belonged at the time when the deceased died; but a
slave instituted heir, acquired for the master to whom he belonged at the time of entering on the inheritance.  If, therefore,
the slave changed masters or became free between these times,
he acquired a legacy for his former master, but took an inheritance for his new master, or, if free, for himself.

The physical fact of possession might be accomplished
through a slave, but not the intention, which was requisite
for legal possession.  It was necessary that the master should
have the intention of treating the thing possessed by the
slave as if he himself were the owner.  *Animo nostro,* says

R

Paul, *corpore etiam alieno, possidemus.* (D. xli. 2. 3. 12.) The master could not, therefore, acquire through the slave legal possession, as opposed to mere detention, without his knowledge and consent, as he could acquire ownership; except, indeed, when the slave possessed a thing as part of his *peculium*, for then the permission to have a *peculium* was considered as enabling the slave to exercise the intention of ownership. (D. xli. 2. 1. 5.)

4. De iis autem servis in quibus tantum usumfructum habemus, ita placuit, ut quidquid ex re nostra vel ex operibus suis acquirant, id nobis adjiciatur; quod vero extra eas causas persecuti sunt, id ad dominum proprietatis pertineat: Itaque si is servus heres institutus sit, legatumve quid ei aut donatum fuerit non usufructuario sed domino proprietatis acquiritur. Idem placet et de eo qui a nobis bona fide possidetur, sive is liber sit, sive alienus servus: quod enim placuit de usufructuario, idem placet et de bona fide possessore: itaque quod extra istas duas causas acquiritur, id vel ad ipsum pertinet, si liber est, vel ad dominum, si servus est. Sed bonae fidei possessor, cum usuceperit servum, quia eo modo dominus fit, ex omnibus causis per eum sibi acquirere potest; fructuarius vero usucapere non potest, primum quia non possidet, sed habet jus utendi fruendi, deinde quia scit servum alienum esse. Non solum autem proprietas per eos servos in quibus usumfructum habemus vel quos bona fide possidemus, aut per liberam personam quae bona fide nobis servit, nobis acquiritur, sed etiam possessio. Loquimur autem in utriusque persona secundum definitionem quam proxime exposuimus, id est, si quam possessionem ex re nostra vel ex suis operibus adepti fuerint.

4. As to slaves of whom we have only the usufruct, it has been decided that whatever they acquire by means of anything belonging to us, or by their own labour, shall belong to us; but that all they acquire from any other source shall belong to the owner. So if a slave is made heir, or anything is given him as a legacy or gift, it is the owner, not the usufructuary who receives the benefit of the acquisition. It is the same with regard to any one whom we possess bona fide, whether a freeman or the slave of another person (for the rule with regard to the usufructuary holds good with regard to the bona fide possessor), everything the person possessed acquires, except from one of the two sources above-mentioned, belongs to himself, if he is a freeman, and to his master, if he is a slave. When the bona fide possessor has gained the property in the slave by usucapion, be. of course, becomes the owner, and all that the slave acquires is acquired for him. But the usufructuary cannot acquire by use; first, because he has not the possession, but only the right of usufruct; and secondly, because he knows that the slave belongs to another. It is not only the ownership that is acquired for us by the slaves of whom we have the usufruct, or whom we possess bona fide, or by a free person whom we employ as our slave bona fide; we acquire also the possession. But in saying this we must be understood, with regard to both slaves and freemen, to adhere to the distinction laid down previously, and to refer only to the possession they have obtained by means of something belonging to us, or by their own labour.

The usufructuary was entitled to the fruits of the slave, that is, to his services, and to the profits derived from letting out his services to others; but what the slave acquired by stipulation, gift, legacy, or similar means, was no part of the fruits, and, therefore, did not belong to the usufructuary. If the means of acquisition were derived from the usufructuary, as, for instance, if the slave acquired by parting with any of the produce, then the case would be different.

What is true of the usufructuary, is true also of a *bona fide* possessor either of the slave of another, or of a person, in fact, free, but honestly believed to be a slave. And the *bona fide* possessor has the advantage over the usufructuary pointed out in the text, that as he has the possession, which no usufructuary can have, for no usufructuary intends to treat the thing as if he were the owner, this possession may, if continued long enough, give the rights of usucapion over a moveable, or of *possessio longi temporis* over an immoveable.

5. Ex his itaque apparet, per liberos homines quos neque nostro juri subjectos habemus, neque bona fide possidemus; item per alienos servos in quibus neque usumfructum habemus neque possessionem justam, nulla ex causa nobis acquiri posse. Et hoc est quod dicitur, per extraneam personam nihil acquiri posse: excepto eo quod per liberam personam, veluti per procuratorem, placet non solum scientibus sed et ignorantibus nobis acquiri possessionem, secundum divi Severi constitutionem, et per hanc possessionem etiam dominium, si dominus fuit qui tradidit, vel usucapionem aut longi temporis præscriptionem, si dominus non sit.

5. Hence it appears that we cannot acquire by means of free persons not in our power, or possessed by us *bona fide*; nor by the slave of another, of whom we have neither the usufruct, nor the possession. And this is meant, when it is said, that nothing can be acquired by means of a stranger; except, indeed, that according to the constitution of the Emperor Severus, possession may be acquired for us by a free person, as by a procurator, not only with, but even without our knowledge; and, by this possession we acquire the property, if it was the owner who delivered the thing, or the usucapion or prescription *longi temporis*, if it was not.

Gai. ii. 95; C. iv. 27. 1; D. xli. 1. 20. 2; C. vii. 32. 1.

The rule of the older law was that no person could be represented *per extraneam personam*, i. e. by a person who was not under his power, in any of those acts which were regulated by the civil law. Thus, no one could acquire the ownership of a thing for another; if he received anything, as, for instance, by mancipation or *in jure cessio*, although he received it expressly for another, still this other person did not thereby acquire the property in the thing. But a mere natural fact such as that of possession could take place for the benefit of one person through another person, if the person for whose benefit the thing was possessed bad but the intention of profiting by it, and then this possession might lead through usucapion to ownership. If, however, a person was charged with the management of the affairs of another, he could exercise an intention of possessing for the benefit of the person for whom he acted, which a mere stranger could not; and thus it was possible *non solum scientibus sed etiam ignorantibus*, i.e. for persons, who did not know even of the fact of possession, to acquire legal possession through an agent. But, though the text would be likely to mislead us, we learn from the constitution of Severus and Antoninus (vii. 32. 1), that usucapion did not commence until the person, for whose benefit the thing was possessed, knew of the possession. And a great change was made by the later law, which allowed that, when, in transferring the possession to the procurator, the owner also transferred the ownership, this ownership should be at once acquired for the person who employed the procurator.

6. Hactenus tantisperadmonuisse sufficit, quemadmodum singulæ res nobis acquirantur; nam legatorum jus, quo et ipso jure singulæ res nobis acquiruntur, item fidei commissorum ubi singulæ res nobis relinquuntur, opportunius inferiore loco referemus. Videamus itaque nunc quibus modis per universitatem res acquiruntur: si cui ergo heredes facti sumus, sive cujus bonorum possessionem petierimus, vel si quem arrogaverimus, vel si cujus bona libertatum conservandarum causa nobis addicta fuerint, ejus res omnes ad nos transeunt. Ac prius de hereditatibus dispiciamus, quarum duplex conditio est, nam vel ex testamento vel ab Intestato ad nos pertinent; et prius est, ut de his dispiciamus quæ ex testamento nobis obveniunt. Qua in re necessarium est initium de ordinandis testamentis exponere.

6. What we have said respecting the modes of the acquisition of particular things, may suffice for the present. For we shall speak more conveniently hereafter of the law of legacies, by which also we acquire property in particular things, and of *fideicommissa*, by which particular things are left us. Let us now speak of the modes of acquiring *per universitatem*. If we are made heir, or seek possession of the goods of any one, or arrogate any one, or goods are adjudged to us in order to preserve the liberty of slaves, in these cases all that belonged to the person to whom we succeed passes to us. First let us treat of inheritances, which may be divided into two kinds, according as they come to us by testament or *ab intestato*. We will begin with those which come to us by testament; and for this, it is necessary in the first place, to explain the formalities requisite in making testaments.

GAI. ii. 97-100.

We now pass to the acquisition of a *universitas rerum*, to the cases in which one man succeeded to the *persona* of another, and acquired in a mass all his goods and all his rights. (See Introd. sec. 74.)

## Tit. X. DE TESTAMENTIS ORDINANDIS.

| Testamentum ex eo appellatur, quod testatio mentis est. | The word testament is derived from testatio mentis; it testifies the determination of the mind. |
|---|---|

### D. xxviii. 1. 1.

With respect to this derivation it is scarcely necessary to say that *mentum* is merely a termination, and not derived from *mens*. Ulpian (*Reg.* 20.1) gives as a definition of a testament, *mentis nostræ justa contestatio, in id solemniter facta, ut post mortem nostram valeat*; and Modestinus (D. xxviii. 1.1) gives *voluntatis nostræ justa sententia, de eo quod quis post mortem suam fieri vult*; the word *justa* implying in each, that, in order to be valid, the testament must be made in compliance with the forms of law.

1. Sed ut nihil antiquitatis penitus ignoretur, sciendum est olim quidem duo genera testamentorum in usu fuisse: quorum altero in pace et in otio utebantur, quod calatis comitiis appellabant; altero, cum in prælium exituri essent, quod procinctum dicebatur. Accessit deinde tertium genus testamentorum, quod dicebatur per æs et libram, scilicet quia per emancipationem, id est, imaginariam quamdam venditionem, agebatur, quinque testibus et libripende civibus romanis puberibus præsentibus, et eo qui familiæ emptor dicebatur. Sed illa quidem priora duo genera testamentorum ex veteribus temporibus in desuetudinem abierunt; quod vero per æs et libram fiebat, licet diutius permansit, attamen partim, et hoc in usu esse desiit.

1. That nothing belonging to antiquity may be altogether unknown, it is necessary to observe, that formerly there were two kinds of testaments in use: the one was employed in times of peace, and was named *calatis comitiis*, the other was employed at the moment of setting out to battle, and was termed *procinctum*. A third species was afterwards added, called *per æs et libram*, being effected by mancipation, that is, an imaginary sale in the presence of five witnesses, and the *libripens*, all citizens of Rome, above the age of puberty, together with him who was called the *emptor familiæ*. The two former kinds of testaments fell into disuse even in ancient times: and that made *per æs et libram* also, although it continued longer in practice, has now in part ceased to be made use of.

### Gai. II. 101-104.

When the head of a family died, the law in ancient times determined on whom his *persona*, that is, the aggregate of his political and social rights, should devolve. But we cannot say that there was any definite period of Roman history when a man could not make a will. Originally, as we learn from the text which is borrowed from Gaius, testaments were made in the *comitia calata*, or in *procinctu*. By *calata comitia* is meant the *comitia curiata* summoned (*calata*) for the despatch of what we may term private business. This took place twice

a year.  We do not know how far it was open to any one at the
meeting to oppose a testament, or whether the *comitia* merely
registered the testaments declared in their presence.  Subsequently the mode of making testaments *per æs et libram*,
that is, by a fictitious sale, was introduced, and both this
mode and that of declaration before the *comitia curiata* were
used indifferently, nor is there any evidence to show that the
one form was considered more appropriate to the *patres* than
the other.   Only members of the patrician *gentes* sat in the
*comitia curiata*, but that is no reason why the plebeians
should not have come before these *comitia* to declare their
testaments.   The Twelve Tables declared *uti legassit super
pecunia tutelave suæ rei, ita jus esto*, that is, every one's
testamentary dispositions should be carried into effect, and
the necessity for the provision may have arisen from some
kind of tampering on the part of members of the *comitia*
with the testaments of plebeians.

*Procinctus* properly means an army in marching and fighting
order.   *Procinctus est expeditus et armatus exercitus* (GAI.
ii. 101).   The testament is said to be *procinctum*, but properly it ought to be *in procinctu factum*.   Cicero speaks (*de
Or.* i. 53) of the testament *in procinctu* as then in use, and
describes it as made *sine libra et tabulis*, that is, without the
forms usual in the *testamentum per æs et libram*.

In the *testamentum per æs et libram*, the *hereditas* was sold
by *mancipatio* to the purchaser.   Originally the testator sold
the inheritance to the person who was really to be the heir.  The
purchaser, as Gaius expresses it, *heredis locum obtinebat*, and
the testator instructed him how he wished his property to be
disposed of after his death.  But as the sale was irrevocable, a
testator might be very glad to escape from proclaiming an heir
whose position he could not afterwards affect.  The object was
attained by selling the inheritance to a third person; and the
*familiæ emptor* came to be thus a mere stranger, who was only
appointed *dicis gratia*, to go through the form of sale. (GAI. ii.
103.)   The process of selling to this fictitious stranger is given
at length in Gaius (ii. 104).   The testator summoned five witnesses, and a balanceholder (*libripens*), and then gave by mancipation his inheritance to the purchaser.   The purchaser, on
receiving it, instead of using the ordinary form, pronounced
these words, *Familiam pecuniamque tuam endo mandatam
tutela custodelaque mea recipio eaque quo tu jure testamentum facere possis secundum legem publicam hoc ære*
(or, as some added, *æneaque libra*) *esto mihi empta*: he
then, after striking the scale with it, gave the piece of copper

to the testator, as the price of the inheritance. The testator then stated aloud the terms of his will, if he wished to make his testament orally, or if he had written down the terms of his testament he produced the tablets on which his testament was written, and said, *Hæc ita, ut in his tabulis cerisque scripta sunt, ita do, ita lego, ita testor, itaque vos, Quirites, testimonium mihi perhibetote.* This announcement of his wishes was termed *nuncupatio. Nuncupare est palam nominare.* (GAI. ib.) The term is properly applicable to an oral statement; but the expression of the testator's wishes was really considered as always made orally, as the announcement that the written documents contained a declaration of the testator's wishes was taken as a compendious mode of stating what those wishes were. (GAI. ib.)

The concluding words of the paragraph, *partim et hoc in usu esse desiit,* allude to the change above-mentioned from a sale to the real heir to a sale to a stranger. The sale became a mere matter of form, and the testament was that which the testator wrote. When the mode of making testaments by the *calata comitia* fell into disuse we do not know, but probably at an early time of the Republic. The imperial constitutions (see next Title) gave all soldiers the power of making a testament without observing the usual forms, and the testaments of soldiers under the Empire were valid, not by being made *in procinctu,* that is, by virtue of the army being regarded as an assembly of citizens, but by the power which was given to each soldier of making an informal testament. In what way they gave greater liberty to the soldier than the old power of making the will *in procinctu* we cannot say; but probably the making of the testament *in procinctu* was connected with the taking of the auspices, and thus was more liable to be declared informal.

2. Sed prædicta quidem nomina testamentorum ad jus civile referebantur. Postea vero ex edicto prætoris forma alia faciendorum testamentorum introducta est: Jure enim honorario nulla emancipatio desiderabatur, sed septem testium signa sufficiebant, cum jure civili signa testium non erant necessaria.

2. These three kinds of testament belonged to the civil law, but afterwards another kind was introduced by the edict of the prætor. By the *jus honorarium* no sale was necessary, but the seals of seven witnesses were sufficient. The seals of witnesses were not required by the civil law.

There was no necessity, as the text tells us, that a written will made in the old form *per æs et libram* should be sealed. After the prætorian form of making wills became usual, a *senatus-consultum* provided (as we learn from Paulus, S. R. v. 25.6) that a written testament should be made on tablets of wax.

These tablets were held together at one margin with a wire, and in the opposite margin there was a perforation made through all the tablets, and through this was passed a triple linen thread, and then the tablets were covered with wax on the outside, and the witnesses placed their seal (that is, made a mark with their rings) on this external wax.   It was also customary for them to write their names, and to state whose will it was they had witnessed (D. xxviii. 1. 30), but this was not a necessary part of the form until made so by a constitution of Theodosius and Valentinian (C. vi. 23. 21).   This constitution also permitted a will to be made in a roll, which, if the testator wished to keep the terms secret, he might close and seal up, leaving the foot of the roll open, on which the witnesses were to put their seals and subscriptions.   The testator was under this constitution to subscribe his name or get an eighth witness to subscribe it for him.

The prætor, as the text informs us, permitted an heir instituted in a testament to have the inheritance, even though the form of mancipation was not gone through.   He could not, indeed, make this person heir, for it was necessary that an heir should derive his rights exclusively from the civil law: but he gave him the *bonorum possessio*, that is, permitted him to enjoy exactly what he would have enjoyed if he had been properly constituted heir, and then usucapion soon made him Quiritanian owner.   (See Bk. ii. Tit. 6.)   The prætor, however, required that the testament in which he was instituted should have been made in the presence and attested by the seals of seven witnesses.   This was really the number of witnesses which there would have been, had the form of mancipation been gone through, if the *libripens* and *familiæ emptor* were included.   Thus the prætor, while dispensing with the mere form of mancipation, retained exactly the same check against fraud, which that form would have afforded. (See ULP. *Reg.* 28. 6.)

3. Sed cum paulatim, tam ex usu hominum quam ex constitutionum emendationibus, cœpit in unam consonantiam jus civile et prætorium jungi, constitutum est ut uno eodemque tempore (quod jus civile quodammodo exigebat) septem testibus adhibitis, et subscriptione testium (quod ex constitutionibus inventum est) et ex edicto prætoris signacula testamentis imponerentur: ut hoc jus tripartitum esse videatur, ut testes quidem et eorum præsentia

3. But when the progress of society and the imperial constitutions had produced a fusion of the civil and the prætorian law, it was established that the testament should be made all at one time, in the presence of seven witnesses (two points required by the civil law), with the subscription of the witnesses (a formality introduced by the constitutions), and with their seals appended, according to the edict of the prætor.   Thus the law of testament seems to

uno contextu, testamenti celebrandi gratia, a jurecivili descendant; subscriptiones autem testatoris et testium ex sacrarum constitutionum observatione adhibeantur, signacula autem et testium numerus ex edicto praetoria.

have had a triple origin. The witnesses, and their presence at one continuous time for the purpose of giving the testament the requisite formality, are derived from the civil law; the subscriptions of the testator and witnesses, from the imperial constitutions; and the seals of the witnesses and their number, from the edict of the praetor.

C. vi. 23. 21.

The different formalities requisite were to be gone through one immediately following after another, so as to make the whole one transaction. *Est autem uno contextu nullum actum alienum testamento intermiscere* (D. xxviii. 1. 21. 3).

It was by the above-mentioned constitution, enacted in the reign of Valentinian the Third in the East, and of Theodosius the Second, his colleague, in the West, A.D. 439, that the new form of testament described in the text, and which received the name of *testamentum tripartitum*, was substituted for the ancient ones. But in the West the form *per æs et libram* was never quite superseded, and traces of it are to be found even in the middle ages.

4. Sed his omnibus a nostra constitutione. propter testamentorum sinceritatem, ut nulla fraus adhibeatur, hoc additum est: ut per manum testatoris vel testium nomen heredis exprimatur, et omnia secundum illius constitutionis tenorem procedant.

4. To all these formalities we have enacted by our constitution, as an additional security for the genuineness of testaments, and to prevent fraud, that the name of the heir shall be written in the handwriting either of the testator or of the witnesses; and that everything shall be done according to the tenor of that constitution.

C. vi. 25. 20.

This additional formality, imposed by Justinian, was afterwards abolished by him. (Nov. 119. 9.)

5. Possunt autem omnes testes et uno annulo signare testamentum. Quid enim si septem annuli una sculptura fuerint, secundum quod Pomponio visum est? Sed et alieno quoque annulo licet signare.

5. All the witnesses may seal the testament with the same seal; for, as Pomponius says, what if the engraving on all seven seals were the same? And a witness may use a seal belonging to another person.

D. xxviii. 1. 22. 2.

6. Testes autem adhibari possunt ii cum quibus testamenti factio est. Sed neque mulier, neque impubes, neque servus, neque furiosus, neque mutus, neque surdus, nec cui bonis

6. Those persons can be witnesses with whom there is *testamenti factio*. But women, persons under the age of puberty, slaves, madmen, dumb persons, deaf persons, prodigals re-

Interdictum est, nec is quem leges jubent improbum intestabilemque esse, possunt in numero testium adhiberi.

strained from having their property in their power, and persons declared by law to be worthless and incompetent to witness, cannot be witnesses.

D. xxviii. 1. 20. 4. 7; D. xxviii. 1. 20.

When testaments were made *per æs et libram*, as no one could take part in the ceremony of mancipation who did not share in the *jus Quiritium*, no *peregrinus*, no one who had not the *commercium*, could be a witness to a testament. It was equally necessary that the seller, i e. the testator, and the purchaser, that is (in the old form), the heir, should share in the *jus Quiritium*. And therefore no one who had not the *commercium* could take any part in the *testamenti factio*, the ceremony of making a testament, either as testator, heir, or witness; and this was expressed by saying that they were not persons with whom there was *testamenti factio*—not persons, that is, with whom any citizen could join in such a ceremony.

After the heir had ceased to take a part in the ceremony of mancipation, there was no longer any necessity for his having those qualifications which enabled him to join in the ancient ceremony. Accordingly, any one who could take under a testament, or acquire for another, although unable to make a testament, was then said to have the *testamenti factio*. An infant, for instance, a madman, or even a child born after the testator's death, had the *testamenti factio* in the sense of being able to be heir (see Tit. 19. 4), and a person might thus have the *testamenti factio* in one character without having it in another. He could be heir, and yet be unable to be a testator or a witness.

Women could take no part in such a solemn legal act as mancipation, and therefore could not be witnesses; nor could women make wills if in the power of their father, or in the *manus* of their husband. If they were not *in potestate*, nor *in manu*, they could make a will, provided that the will was confirmed by the *auctoritas* of their tutor. By a fictitious sale, however, *coemptio fiduciæ causa*, a woman could free herself from the power of her tutor, and then she could make a will independently of him. Infants and slaves could acquire by mancipation for those in whose power they were, but could not be witnesses. The *prodigus cui bonis interdictum est* was prevented from using his rights of *commercium*, and therefore could not take part in a mancipation. (D. xxviii. 1. 18.) The *mutus* had not the *testamenti factio*, because he could not utter the words of the *nuncupatio*, and the *surdus* also had not the *testamenti factio*, because he could not hear

the words of the *emptor familiæ*. (ULP. *Frag.* 20. 13.) By
the later law, however, provision was made for giving validity to the wills of the deaf and dumb. (See *infra*, Tit.
12. 3.)

A person who was made *intestabilis* for a crime could
neither make a testament nor take part in the making of one.
Among such persons were those condemned for libel, *ob carmen famosum* (D. xxviii. 1. 16. 1), for spoliation, *repetundarum* (D. xxii. 5. 15), or adultery (D. xxii. 5. 14); or who,
having acted as witnesses to a will, afterwards refused to acknowledge their signature and seal. (THEOPH. *Paraphr.*)

7. Sed cum aliquis ex testibus testamenti quidem faciendi tempore
liber existimabatur, postea vero servus apparuit, tam divus Hadrianus
Catonio Veroquam postea divi Seve-
ruset Antoninus rescripserunt, sub-
venire se ex sua liberalitate testamento, ut sic habeatur atque si ut
oportet factum esset; cum eo tempore quo testamentum signaretur,
omnium consensu hic testis liberorum loco fuerit, neque quisquam
esset qui status ei quæstionem mo-
veret.

7. A witness, who was thought to
be free at the time of making the testament, was afterwards discovered
to be a slave, and the Emperor Hadrian, in his rescript to Catonius
Verus, and afterwards the Emperors
Severus and Antoninus, by rescript
declared, that they would aid such a
defect in a testament, so that it
should be considered as valid as if
made quite regularly; since, at the
time when the testament was sealed,
this witness was commonly considered a free man, and there was no
one to contest his *status*.

C. vi. 23. 1.

Regard was had only to what was the condition of witnesses
at the time of signature, not at that of the death of the testator. (D. xxviii. 1. 22. 1.)

8. Pater nec non is qui in potestate ejus est, item duo fratres qui
in ejusdem patris potestate sunt,
utrique testes in uno testamento
fieri possunt; quia nihil nocet ex
una domo plures testes alieno negotio adhiberi.

8. A father, and a son under his
power, or two brothers, under the
power of the same father, may be
witnesses to the same testament;
for nothing prevents several persons
of the same family being witnesses
in a matter which only concerns a
stranger.

No one of the same family with the testator or heir could be
a witness to the testament, a family comprising, in this sense,
the head and those under his power; for they had so intimate
a connection with each other that they might be said to be
witnesses for themselves, if they were witnesses for each other.

9. In testibus autem non debet
esse, qui in potestate testatoris est.
Sed et si filiusfamilias de castrensi
peculio post missionem faciat testamentum, nec pater ejus recte adhi-

9. But no person under power of
the testator can be a witness. And
if a *filiusfamilias* makes a testament
giving his *castrense peculium* after
leaving the army, neither his father,

betur tertia, nec is qui in potestate ejusdem patris est; reprobatum est enim in ea re domesticum testimonium.

nor any one in power of his father can be a witness. For, in this case, the law does not allow of the testimony of a member of the same family.

GAI. E. 105, 106.

This had been a point on which the jurists were disagreed. Justinian here follows the opinion of Gaius (ii. 106), rejecting that of Ulpian and Marcellus. (D. xxviii. 1. 20. 2.) The question could only arise respecting a testament made *post missionem*, as, if it were made during service, it would be entitled to the exemptions accorded to military testaments.

10. Sed neque heres scriptus neque is qui in potestate ejus est, neque pater ejus qui eum habet in potestate, neque fratres qui in ejusdem patris potestate sunt, testes adhiberi possunt, quia totum hoc negotium quod agitur testamenti ordinandi gratia, creditur hodie inter testatorem et heredem agi: licet enim totum jus tale conturbatum fuerat, et veteres quidem familiae emptorem et eos qui per potestatem ei cognati fuerant, testimoniis repellebant, heredi et iis qui per potestatem ei conjuncti fuerant, concedebant testimonia in testamentis praestare. Licet ii qui id permittebant, hoc jure minime abuti eos debere suadebant. Tamen nos eamdem observationem corrigentes, et quod ab illis suasum est in legis necessitatem transferentes, ad imitationem pristini familiae emptoris, merito nec heredi qui imaginem vetustissimi familiae emptoris obtinet, nec aliis personis quae ei, ut dictum est, conjunctae sunt, licentiam concedimus sibi quodammodo testimonia praestare: ideoque nec ejusmodi veteres constitutiones nostro codici inseri permisimus.

10. No person instituted heir, nor any one in subjection to him, nor his father, in whose power he is, nor his brothers under power of the same father, can be witnesses; for the whole business of making a testament is in the present day considered a transaction between the testator and the heir. But formerly there was great confusion; for although the ancients would never admit the testimony of the *familiae emptor*, nor of any one connected with him by the ties of *patria potestas*, yet they admitted that of the heir, and of persons connected with him by the ties of *patria potestas*, only exhorting them not to abuse their privilege. We have corrected this, making illegal what they endeavoured to prevent by persuasion. For, in imitation of the old law respecting the *familiae emptor*, we refuse to permit the heir, who now represents the ancient *familiae emptor*, or any of those connected with the heir by the tie of *patria potestas*, to be, so to speak, witnesses in their own behalf; and accordingly we have not suffered the constitutions of preceding emperors on the subject to be inserted in our code.

GAI. ii. 108.

When the heir had ceased to be the *familiae emptor*, he was no party to the transaction, and therefore, it was considered, he could be a witness. Gaius (ii. 108) reprobates the custom, and Justinian here pronounces it illegal. Under his legislation, there being no longer any *familiae emptor*, the whole transaction, to use the language of the ancient mode, was between the testator and the heir.

| 11. Legatariis autem et fidelcom-missariis, quia non Juris succesores sunt, et aliis personis quae eis conjunctae sunt, testimonium non denegavimus. Imo in quadam nostra constitutione et hoc specialiter concessimus, et multo magis iis qui in eorum potestate sunt, vel qui eos habent in potestate, hujusmodi licentiam damus. | 11. But we do not refuse the testimony of legatees, or persons entrusted with fideicommissa, or of persons connected with them, because they do not succeed to the rights of the deceased. On the contrary, by one of our constitutions we have specially granted them this privilege; and we give it still more readily to persons in their power, and to those in whose power they are. |

GAI. iL 108.

It would appear that the objection of his being interested, which would make the heir an unfit witness, might also have been urged against the legatee; but the legatee was admitted as a witness on the technical ground of his not being the successor of the testator. The inheritance was not transmitted to him, and he was thus looked on as a stranger.

By the *Senatus-Consultum Libonianum*, passed in the reign of Tiberius, A.D. 16, it was provided that if a man wrote a testament for another, everything which he wrote in his own favour should be null. He could not, therefore, make himself a tutor (D. xxvi. 2. 29), an heir, or a legatee. (D. xxiv. 8.)

| 12. Nihil autem interest, testamentum in tabulis an in chartis membraneve, vel in alia materia fiat. | 12. It is immaterial, whether a testament be written upon a tablet, upon paper, parchment, or any other substance. |

D. xxxvii. 11. 1.

| 13. Sed et unum testamentum pluribus codicibus conficere quis potest, secundum obtinentem tamen observationem omnibus factis: quod interdum etiam necessarium est, veluti si quis navigaturus et secum ferre et domi relinquere judiciorum suorum contestationem velit, vel propter alias innumerabiles causas quae humanis necessitatibus imminent. | 13. Any person may execute any number of duplicates of the same testament, each, however, being made with prescribed forms. This may be sometimes necessary; as, for instance, when a man who is going a voyage, is desirous to carry with him, and also to leave at home, a memorial of his last wishes; or for any other of the numberless reasons, that may arise from the various necessities of mankind. |

D. xxviii. 1. 24.

Each *codex* was an original testament, valid only if itself made with all the solemnities which would have been requisite had it been the only one.

14. Sed hæc quidem de testamentis quæ in scriptis conficiuntur. Si quis autem sine scriptis voluerit ordinare jure civili testamentum, septem testibus adhibitis et sua voluntate coram eis nuncupata, sciat hoc perfectissimum testamentum jure civili firmumque constitutum.

14. Thus much may suffice concerning written testaments. But if any one wishes to make a testament, valid by the civil law, without writing, he may do so, if, in the presence of seven witnesses, he verbally declares his wishes, and this will be a testament perfectly valid according to the civil law, and confirmed by imperial constitutions.

Thus a testator under the legislation of Justinian might either make his testament according to the form described in paragraph 3, or orally before seven witnesses.

*Sua voluntate nuncupata.* The word *nuncupatio* was originally used to express the declaration of the testator's intentions whether the testament was written or not; but later usage appropriated the term *nuncupata* to testaments where there was no written will, and where the testator declared his wishes orally.

## Tit. XI. DE MILITARI TESTAMENTO.

Supradicta diligens observatio, in ordinandis testamentis, militibus propter nimiam imperitiam constitutionibus principalibus remissa est; nam quamvis ii neque legitimum numerum testium adhibuerint neque aliam testamentorum solemnitatem observaverint, recte nihilominus testantur: videlicet, cum in expeditionibus occupati sunt, quod meritonostra constitutio introduxit. Quoquo enim modo voluntas ejus suprema inveniatur, sive scripta sive sine scriptura, valet testamentum ex voluntate ejus. Illis autem temporibus, per quæ citra expeditionum necessitatem in aliis locis vel suis ædibus degunt, minime ad vindicandum tale privilegium adjurantur; sed testari quidem, etsi filiifamiliarum sunt, propter militiam concorduntur, jure tamen communi, eadem observatione et in eorum testamentis adhibenda, quam et in testamentis paganorum proxime exposuimus.

The necessity for the observance of these formalities in the construction of testaments, has been dispensed with by the imperial constitutions, in favour of military persons, on account of their excessive unskilfulness in such matters. For, although they neither employ the legal number of witnesses, nor observe any other requisite solemnity, yet their testament is valid, but only if made while they are on actual service, a proviso introduced by our constitution with good reason. Thus in whatever manner the wishes of a military person are expressed, whether in writing or not, the testament prevails by the mere force of his intention. But during the times when they are not on actual service, and live at their own homes, or elsewhere, they are not permitted to claim this privilege. A soldier, although a *filiusfamilias*, gains from military service the power of making a testament; but, in this case, the same formalities are required to be observed, as we above explained to be necessary for the testaments of civilians.

The privilege of making valid testaments, independent of any formality, was one given to soldiers, among many others of a similar kind, rather as a special favour to them than from any consideration for their *nimia imperitia*. It dates from the time of Julius Cæsar, who granted it as a temporary concession. It was made a general rule by Nerva, and confirmed by Trajan. If the testament of a soldier were written, no witness was necessary; but if not, it is doubtful whether one witness was sufficient to prove it; probably not, as the law required, as a general rule, that two witnesses at least should be produced in every case. (D. xxii. 5. 12; D. xlviii. 18. 17.) A soldier in the power of a father might make a testament disposing of his *castrense peculium*. If he made it while on service, he need observe no formality in making the testament; if he did not make it while on service, he was bound to observe the usual formalities. The concluding words of the section are meant to express this, and not to imply that a *filiusfamilias* could dispose by testament of anything besides his *castrense peculium*.

1. Plane de testamentis militum divus Trajanus Statilio Severo ita re-cripsit: 'Id privilegium quod militantibus datum est, ut quoquo modo facta ab iis testamenta rata sint, sic intelligi debet, ut utique prius constare debeat testamentum factum esse, quod et sine scriptura a non militantibus quoque fieri potest. Ia ergo miles de cujus bonis apud te quæritur, si convocatis ad hoc hominibus ut voluntatem suam testaretur, ita locutus est ut declararet quem vellet sibi heredem esse, et cui libertatem tribuere, potest videri sine scripto hoc modo esse te-tatus, et voluntas ejus rata habenda est. Ceterum, si (ut plerumque sermonibus fieri solet) dixit alicui, Ego te heredem facio, aut bona mea tibi relinquo, non oportet hoc pro testamento observari: nec ullorum magis interest quam ipsorum quibus id privilegium datum est, ejusmodi exemplum non admitti; alioquin non difficulter post mortem alicujus milites testes existerent, qui affirmarent se audisse dicentem aliquem relinquere se bona cui visum sit, et per hoc vera judicia subverterentur.'

1. The Emperor Trajan wrote as follows, in a rescript to Statilius Severus, with respect to military testaments: 'The privilege, given to military persons, that their testaments, in whatever manner made, shall be valid, must be understood as meaning that it must first be clear that a testament has been made (a testament may be made without writing even by persons not on military service). If, then, it appear, that the soldier, concerning whose goods the action before you is now brought, did, in the presence of witnesses, called expressly for the purpose, declare who he wished should be his heir, and to what state he wished to give freedom, he shall be considered to have made in this way a testament without writing, and effect shall be given to his wishes. But if, as is often the case, in the course of conversation, he said to some one, "I appoint you my heir," or, "I leave you all my estate," such words must not be regarded as a testament. No one is more interested than soldiers themselves, that such a precedent should not be admitted; otherwise it would not be difficult to procure witnesses who, after the death of a soldier, would

affirm, that they had heard him bequeath his estate to whomever they
pleased to name; and thus the real
intentions of soldiers might be defeated.'

D. xxix. 1. 24.

*Convocatis ad hoc hominibus*, there was no necessary
ceremony of calling witnesses. If there was but proof of
what the soldier's wishes were, and that he had declared them
while on service, that was enough.

2. Quinimo et mutus et surdus | 2. A soldier though dumb and
miles testamentum facere potest. | deaf may make a testament.

D. xxix. 1. 4.

It might happen, as Theophilus suggests, that a soldier, incapacitated for actual service by becoming deaf or dumb, might
yet not have received his *missio causaria* (discharge for an accidental reason). A testament made by him in the interval
between his loss of capacity and his discharge would be considered entitled to all the privileges of a military testament.

3. Sed hactenus hoc illis a prin- | 3. This privilege is only granted
cipalibus constitutionibus concedi- | by the imperial constitutions to mili-
tur, quatenus militant et in castris | tary men, as long as they are on ser-
degunt. Post missionem vero ve- | vice, and live in the camp. There-
terani, vel extra castra alii si faciant | fore, veterans after their discharge,
adhuc militantes testamentum, | or soldiers not in the camp, can only
communi omnium civium romano- | make their testaments by observing
rum jure facere debent; et quod in | the forms required of all Roman citi-
castris fecerint testamentum, non | zens. And if a testament be made
communi jure, sed quomodo volu- | in the camp, and the solemnities of
erint, post missionem intra annum | the law are not observed, it will con-
tantum valebit. Quid ergo si intra | tinue valid only for one year after
annum decreverit, conditio autem | discharge from the army. Suppose,
heredi adscripta post annum exti- | therefore, a soldier should die within
terit? An quasi militis testamen- | a year after his discharge, but the
tum valeat? Et placet valere | condition imposed on the heir should
quasi militis. | not be accomplished until after the
| year, would his testament be valid,
| on the analogy of the testament of
| a soldier? We answer, it would be
| so valid.

D. xxix. 1. 38, pr. and 1.

A soldier enjoyed the privilege of making a military testament while his name was inscribed on the list of the army
(*in numeris*), and also for a year after it had been taken off,
but this only provided he were not discharged *ignominiæ causâ*.
(D. xxix. 1. 38.)  The doubt as to the validity of a military

testament, containing a condition under the circumstances
mentioned in the text, arose from the doctrine of Roman law
that, when the institution of the heir was conditional, the
operation of the testament dated from the accomplishment of
the condition, not from the death of the testator.  If, therefore,
the soldier died within a year after he had quitted the service,
but the condition was not accomplished until the year was
expired, the testament did not, strictly speaking, take effect
within the year; and therefore Justinian removes a difficulty
which a rigorous adherence to the letter of the law suggested.

4. Sed et si quis ante militiam
non jure fecit testamentum, et miles
factum et in expeditione degens re-
signavit illud et quædam adjecit
sive detraxit, vel alias manifesta est
militia voluntas hoc valere volentis,
dicendum est valere hoc testamentum quasi ex nova militis voluntate.

4. If a man, before becoming a
soldier, has made his testament ir-
regularly, and afterwards, while on
service, opens it, and adds something
or strikes something out, or in any
other way makes his wish manifest,
that this testament should be valid,
it must be pronounced to be so, as
being, in fact, a new testament made
by a soldier.

D. xxix. 1. 20. 1.

If the soldier manifested his intention of adhering to the
dispositions of his old testament, this was as much a fresh
expression of his wishes as if he had made a new testament.
If he was altogether silent on the subject, an informal testament made before his becoming a soldier was not valid, as it
was necessary that there should be a positive declaration of
his wishes made while he was on service to make his testament valid as a military one.

5. Denique et si in adrogationem
datus fuerit miles, vel filiusfamilias
emancipatus est, testamentum ejus
quasi ex nova militis voluntate
valet, nec videtur capitis deminutione irritum fieri.

5. If a soldier is given in arrogation, or, being a filiusfamilias, is
emancipated, his testament is valid
as being a subsequent expression of
the wishes of a soldier; nor is it
considered as invalidated by the capitis deminutio he has undergone.

D. xxix. 1. 22, 23.

By the law of Rome every testament became void, irritum,
by the testator, after its execution, suffering any of the three
kinds of capitis deminutio.  With soldiers it was otherwise;
their testament was not invalidated by undergoing either of the
two greater kinds of deminutio, if it was for an infraction of
military law that they were condemned to a punishment involving either of these kinds of alteration of status.  (D. xxviii.
3. 6. 6.)  Nor was it ever invalidated by their undergoing the
third and least kind.  The will of the soldier was supposed to be

s

exercised so as to declare his wish that the old testament should
be valid (*quasi ex nova militiæ voluntate*); and in this case it
does not appear that any positive declaration of such a wish
was necessary. His testament, made previous to his change of
*status*, was effectual, to the fullest extent it could be in the new
position he occupied. The testament made by a *paterfamilias*
respecting his property became, after arrogation, an effectual
disposition of his *castrense peculium*; and one made by a
*filiusfamilias* respecting his *castrense peculium* became, after
emancipation, an effectual disposition of all his property.

| | |
|---|---|
| 6. Sciendum tamen est quod, ad exemplum castrensis peculii, tam anteriores leges quam principales constitutiones quibusdam quasi castrensia dederant peculia, et horum quibusdam permiserunt erat etiam in potestate degentibus testari. Quod nostra constitutio latius extendens permisit omnibus, in his tantummodo peculiis, testari quidem sed jure communi. Cujus constitutionis tenore perspecto, licentia est nihil eorum, quæ ad præfatum jus pertinent, ignorare. | 6. We may here observe, that, in imitation of the *castrense peculium*, both old laws and imperial constitutions have permitted certain persons to have a *quasi-castrense peculium*, and some of these persons have been permitted to dispose of this *peculium* by testament, although they were in the power of another. Our constitution has extended this permission to all those who have this kind of *peculium*, but their testaments must be made with the ordinary formalities. By reading this constitution a person may learn all that relates to the privilege we have mentioned. |

We must not suppose, from the expression *anteriores leges*,
that the *peculium quasi-castrense* belongs to a time of law
when *leges* were really made. It is even doubtful, as we have
said before, whether the passages in which it is mentioned by
Ulpian, the only writer before Constantine who is supposed to
refer to it, are genuine. (See note on Tit. 9. 1.)

*Horum quibusdam.* The right of disposing by testament
of the *quasi-castrense peculium* had, before Justinian, been
granted only to certain privileged classes, such as consuls and
presidents of provinces, among those who were permitted to
hold this kind of *peculium*. (C. iii. 28. 37.) Justinian
granted it to all. (C. vi. 22. 12.)

It is to be observed, that soldiers had other testamentary privileges besides those mentioned in the text. They could institute as heirs persons who were generally incapacitated, such as
those who had been *deportati*, or who were *peregrini*. (Gai. ii.
110.) They were not obliged formally to disinherit their
children, their testament was not set aside as inofficious (C. iii.
28. 9), they could give more than three-fourths of their property in legacies (C. vi. 21. 12), they could die partly testate
and partly intestate (D. xxii. 1. 6), and could dispose of the

inheritance by codicils (D. xxix. 1. 36). The succeeding
Title will show how much they thus differed from ordinary
citizens.

## Tit. XII. QUIBUS NON EST PERMISSUM FACERE TESTAMENTUM.

Non tamen omnibus licet facere
testamentum. Statim enim ii qui
alieno juri subjecti sunt, testamenti
faciendi jus non habent, adeo quidem ut quamvis parentes eis per-
miserint, nihilo magis jure testari
possint: exceptis iis quos antea
enumeravimus, et præcipue militibus qui in potestate parentium sunt,
quibus de eo quod in castris acqui-
sierunt, permissum est ex constitutionibus principum testamentum
facere. Quod quidem jus ab initio
tantum militantibus datum est, tam
ex auctoritate divi Augusti quam
Nervæ, nec non optimi imperatoris
Trajani; postea vero subscriptione
divi Hadriani etiam dimissis a militia, id est, veteranis concessum
est. Itaque si quod fecerint de castrensi peculio testamentum, pertinebit hoc ad eum quem heredem
reliquerint. Si vero intestati decesserint, nullis liberis vel fratribus
superstitibus ad parentes eorum jure
communi pertinebit. Ex hoc intelligere possumus, quod in castris acquisierit miles qui in potestate patris
est, neque ipsum patrem adimere
posse, neque patris creditores id
vendere vel aliter inquietare, neque
patre mortuo cum fratribus commune esse, sed scilicet proprium
ejus esse quid id in castris acquisierit; quamquam jure civili omnium qui in potestate parentium
sunt, peculia perinde in bonis parentium computantur ac si servorum
peculia in bonis dominorum numerantur; exceptis videlicet iis quæ ex
sacris constitutionibus et præcipue
nostris propter diversas causas non
acquiruntur. Præter hos igitur qui
castrense vel quasi castrense habent,
si quis alias filiusfamilias testamentum fecerit, inutile est, licet
suæ potestatis factus decesserit.

The power of making a testament
is not granted to every one. In the
first place, persons in the power of
others have not this right; so much
so, that, although parents give permission, still they cannot make a
valid testament. We must except
those whom we have already mentioned, and particularly *filiifamiliarum* who are soldiers, for the imperial
constitutions have given them the
power of bequeathing whatever they
have acquired while on actual service. This permission was at first
granted by the Emperors Augustus
and Nerva, and the illustrious Emperor Trajan to soldiers on service only;
but afterwards it was extended by the
Emperor Hadrian to veterans, that
is, to soldiers who had received their
discharge; and therefore, if a *filiusfamilias* disposes by testament of his
*castrense peculium*, this *peculium* will
belong to the person whom he makes
his heir; but, if he dies intestate,
without children or brothers, this
*peculium* will then belong, according
to the ordinary law of the *patria potestas*, to the person in whose power
he is. We may hence infer, that
whatever a soldier, although under
power, has acquired while on service,
cannot be taken from him even by
his father, nor can his father's creditors sell it, or otherwise disturb the
son in his possession, nor is he
bound to share it with brothers upon
the death of his father, but it remains his sole property, although, by
the civil law, the *peculia* of all those
who are in the power of parents, are
reckoned among the goods of their
parents, exactly as the *peculium* of a
slave is reckoned among the goods of
his master; those goods excepted,
which, by the constitutions of the
emperors, and especially by our own,

* 2

are prevented, for different reasons, from being so acquired. With the exception, therefore, of those who have a *castrense* or *quasi-castrense peculium*, if any other *filiusfamilias* make a testament, it is useless, although he become *sui juris* before his death.

D. xxviii. 1. 6; D. xxix. 1. 1; C. vi. 61. 3, 4; C. vi. 60. 11.; D. xliii. 17. 12; D. xxxvii. 6. 1. 16; D. xxviii. 1. 10.

The first thing, says Gaius (ii. 114), which we have to inquire, if we wish to know whether a testament is valid, is whether the person who made it had the *testamenti factio*, that is, in this instance, could take the part of testator in the making of a testament.   To be able to do this he must have the *commercium*; and further, he must be *sui juris*, or otherwise, as he could have no property, he could have nothing to dispose of by testament.   Every Roman citizen who was *sui juris* had the right of making a testament, and if he was capable of exercising his right, and made a formal testament, this testament was valid.

The text only gives one instance of persons who, as not being citizens *sui juris*, were unable to make a testament, viz., sons in the power of their father; but, of course, all who, like slaves, *peregrini*, and persons who had undergone the greater or middle *capitis deminutio*, were not in the possession of the rights of citizenship, were equally debarred from making testaments.

The *filiusfamilias* could have no property independently of his father, and he could not dispose of the property he might have if he became *sui juris* by outliving his father, because a future interest would not pass by mancipation.   This was a part of the public law (*testamenti factio non privati sed publici juris est*, D. xxviii. 1. 3), and could not be waived by the mere consent of a private individual.   It required express enactment to alter the law, and it was so far altered as to permit a *filiusfamilias* to dispose by testament of a *castrense* or *quasi-castrense peculium*. (See paragr. 6 of preceding Title.)   If, however, the possessor of the *peculium* did not dispose of it by testament, the head of the family took it, previously to the time of Justinian, not as heir *ab intestato*, but as lawful claimant of a *peculium*.   For the possessor, not having exercised the power the law gave him, was in the same position as if the law had never permitted such a disposition.   Justinian deferred this claim of the head of the family, when the possessor of the *peculium* had left children or brothers.   If he had not left any, the head of the family then took the *peculium*; whether in right of his headship, or as heir *ab intestato*, is a disputed point. We have, however, the authority of Theophilus in the paraphrase of this paragraph for supposing, that when Justinian in the text says he took it *jure communi*, it is meant that he took it by the right of *patria potestas*, and there seems no necessity for understanding the passage otherwise.

1. Praeterea testamentum facere non possunt impuberes, quia nullum eorum animi judicium est; item furiosi, quia mentis carent; nec ad rem pertinet, si impubes postea pubes, aut furiosus postea compos mentis factus fuerit et decesserit. Furiosi autem, si per id tempus fecerint testamentum quo furor eorum intermissus est, jure testati esse videntur: certe eo, quod ante furorem fecerint, testamento valente; nam neque testamenta recte facta, neque ullum aliud negotium recte gestum, postea furor interveniens peremit.

1. Persons, again, under the age of puberty cannot make a testament, because they have not the requisite judgment of mind, nor can madmen, for they are deprived of their senses. Nor does it make any difference that the former arrive at puberty, or the latter regain their senses before they die. But if a madman make a testament during a lucid interval, his testament is valid; and, of course, a testament which he has made before being seized with madness is valid, for subsequent madness can invalidate neither a previous testament validly made, nor any other previous act validly performed.

D. xxviii. 1. 20. 4.

In this and the succeeding paragraphs of this Title, instances are given of persons who have the right, but are not capable of exercising it. A testament made by a person incapable of exercising the right was not rendered valid by his subsequently becoming capable, nor one made by a person capable rendered invalid by his subsequently becoming incapable.

2. Item prodigus cui bonorum suorum administratio interdicta est, testamentum facere non potest; sed id quod ante fecerit quam interdictio suorum bonorum ei fiat, ratum est.

2. A prodigal, also, who is interdicted from the management of his own affairs, cannot make a testament; but a testament made before such interdiction is valid.

D. xxviii. 1. 18.

3. Item surdus et mutus non semper testamentum facere possunt. Utique autem de eo surdo loquimur qui omnino non exaudit, non qui tarde exaudit; nam et mutus is intelligitur qui loqui nihil potest, non qui tarde loquitur. Saepe etiam literati et eruditi homines variis causis et audiendi et loquendi facultatem amittunt. Unde nostra constitutio etiam his subvenit, ut certis casibus

3. Again, a deaf and dumb person is not always capable of making a testament: by deaf, we mean one who is so deaf as to be unable to hear at all, not one who hears with difficulty; and by dumb, we mean a person who cannot speak at all, not one who merely speaks with difficulty. For it often happens, that even men of good education lose by various accidents the faculty of hearing and

et modis secundum normam ejus
possint testari, aliaque facere quæ
eis permissa sunt. Sed si quis post
testamentum factum. adversa vale-
tudine aut quolibet alio casu mutus
aut surdus esse cœperit, ratum nihilominus ejus permanet testamentum.

speaking. Our constitution, therefore, comes to their aid, and permits
them, in certain cases, and with
certain forms, to make testaments,
and do many other acts according to
the rules therein laid down. But if
any one, after making his testament,
become deaf or dumb by reason of
ill health or any other accident, his
testament remains valid notwithstanding.

vi. 22. 10; D. xxviii. 1. 6. 1.

The constitution alluded to (C. vi. 22. 10) permits a testament to be made by any deaf or dumb person not physically
incapable of making one, i. e. by any one not deaf and dumb
from birth.

4. Cæcus autem non potest facere
testamentum. nisi per observationem quam lex divi Justini patris
nostri introduxit.

4. A blind man cannot make a
testament except by observing the
forms which the law of the Emperor
Justin, our father, has introduced.

C. vi. 22. 8.

Justin, besides the seven witnesses ordinarily necessary, required in the case of a testament made by a blind man, that
a notary (tabularius) should be present. or else an eighth
witness, who should either write at the dictation of the blind
man, or read aloud to him a testament previously prepared.
(C. vi. 22. 8.)

5. Ejus qui apud hostes est. testamentum quod ibi fecit non valet,
quamvis redierit. Sed quod, dum
in civitate fuerat, fecit, sive redierit,
valet jure postliminii, sive illic decesserit, valet ex lege Cornelia.

5. The testament of a captive in
the power of an enemy is not valid,
if made during his captivity, even
although he subsequently return.
But a testament made while he was
still in his own state is valid, either
by the jus postliminii, if he returns,
or by the lex Cornelia, if he die in
captivity.

D. xlix. 25. 18.

A captive was incapacitated from performing, during his
captivity, any act good in law; and thus, though his right to
make a testament was not lost, but only suspended, he was
incapable, while a captive, of exercising the right. But if he
had exercised it before his captivity, the testament was valid,
whether he returned to his country or not. If he did return,
the right not having been lost, and having been once duly
exercised, the testament was valid jure postliminii. If he

did not return, but died in captivity, it was still valid, as he
was supposed, by a fiction of law, to have died at the moment
when he was made captive, and so before his captivity had
begun. This fiction was introduced by a rather strained construction of the terms of the *lex Cornelia de falsis* (686
A.U.C.), which provided that the same penalty should attach
to the forgery of a testament of a person dying in captivity
as to that of a testament made by a person dying in his own
country. It was argued that the law could never have intended to attach a penalty to the forgery of a testament which
was invalid. If it was valid, it could only be so by treating it
as if made by a person who had not died in captivity, and
whose right was not suspended at the time of his death. For
it was necessary that a person should have the power of
making a testament, not only at the time when he made it,
but also at the moment of his death; but in this we must
distinguish between the right to make a testament and the
capacity of exercising that right; for the loss of capacity to
make a testament did not, as we have seen, affect a testament
made by one capable at the time of making it. This favourable interpretation of the *lex Cornelia (beneficium legis Corneliæ)* (PAUL. *Sent.* iii. 4. 8) was gradually extended, so as to
embrace every branch of law, such as tutorship, heirship, &c.,
to which it could be made applicable. *In omnibus partibus
juris is qui reversus non est ab hostibus quasi tunc decessisse videtur cum captus est.* (D. xlix. 15. 18.)

## Tit. XIII.   DE EXHEREDATIONE LIBERORUM.

Non tamen, ut omnimodo valeat
testamentum, sufficit hæc observatio
quam supra exposuimus; sed qui
filium in potestate habet, curare
debet ut eum heredem instituat, vel
exheredem eum nominatim faciat.
Alioquin si eum silentio præterierit,
inutiliter testabitur: adeo quidem
ut, etsi vivo patre filius mortuus sit,
nemo heres ex eo testamento existere possit, quia scilicet ab initio
non constiterit testamentum. Sed
non ita de filiabus, vel aliis per
virilem sexum descendentibus liberis utriusque sexus, antiquitati
fuerat observatum; sed si non
fuerant heredes scripti scriptæve
vel exheredati exheredatæve, testa-

The observation of the rules already laid down is not, however, all
that is required to make a testament
valid. A person who has a son in
his power must take care either to
institute him heir, or to disinherit
him by name, for if he pass him over
in silence, his testament will be of
no effect; so much so, that even if
the son die while the father is alive,
yet no one can be heir under the
testament, because it was void from
the beginning. But the ancients did
not observe this rule with regard
to daughters, or to grandchildren,
through the male line, of either sex;
for although these were neither instituted heirs nor disinherited, yet

mentum quidem non infirmabatur, jus autem accrescendi eis ad certam portionem præstabatur. Sed nec nominatim eas personas exheredare parentibus necesse erat, sed licebat inter ceteras hoc facere. Nominatim autem quis exheredari videtur, sive ita exberedetur, Titius filius meus exheres esto, sive ita, filius meus exheres esto, non adjecto proprio nomine, scilicet si alius filius non extet.

the testament was not invalidated, only they had a right of joining themselves with the instituted heirs so as to receive a portion of the inheritance. Parents, also, were not obliged to disinherit them by name, but might include them in the term *ceteri.* A child is disinherited by name, if the words used are 'let Titius my son be disinherited,' or thus, 'let my son be disinherited,' without the addition of a proper name, in case the testator has no other son.

GAI. li. 115. 123, 124. 127.

The power of making a testament was a derogation of the strict law regulating the devolution of the property of deceased persons. Of those whose claims a citizen *sui juris* was permitted thus to set aside, the first and most important class was that of what were called the *sui heredes,* that is, those persons in the power of the testator who became *sui juris* by the testator's death. They were necessarily either children of the testator, or his descendants in the male line, and their position in the testator's family, together with their claim to his property if he died intestate, was considered to entitle them to have an express declaration of his intention from a testator who wished to use his power of depriving them of the inheritance. We have already seen, in the case of the *castrense peculium* (see Introd. paragr. of preceding Title), that when the law permitted an exception to a general rule of law, unless advantage was taken of the exception, the general rule prevailed. So here, unless the testator expressly took advantage of his power of disinheriting the *sui heredes,* the general rule that they succeeded to him prevailed. The law would not permit his intention to disinherit them to be inferred from his silence, thus drawing a distinction in their favour as compared with the other classes of persons who might inherit *ab intestato.*

In order, therefore, as the text informs us, to disinherit a son, it was necessary that he should be referred to by name, or in a special and unmistakeable manner, as, *Titius filius meus exheres esto,* or, in case of an only son, *filius meus exheres esto.* But daughters and the descendants of sons (those of daughters would not, of course, be members of the family at all) might be disinherited by the general clause *ceteri exheredes sunto.* Whenever a person existed at the time the will was made, to disinherit whom it was necessary to refer to him by name, but who was passed over altogether, the whole testament was entirely bad, and the testator was considered to die intestate. Nor was the testament made valid by this person ceasing to exist before the death of the testator, although this was a point not established in the time of Gaius (ii. 123). If a person existed at the time of making the testament, to disinherit whom it was only necessary the general clause should be employed, the testament which did not contain this was good, but the person, if the heir named and instituted in the testament was among the *sui heredes*, took a *pars virilis* of the inheritance, that is, was joined so as to make one more heir and one more equal sharer in the inheritance (*jus accrescendi*); if the heirs instituted were strangers, the person took one-half the inheritance. *Scriptis heredibus accrescunt, suis quidem heredibus in partem virilem, extraneis autem in partem dimidiam.* (ULP. *Reg.* 22. 17.)

1. Postumi quoque liberi vel heredes instituti debent, vel exheredari; et in eo par omnium conditio est, quod et filio postumo et quolibet ex ceteris liberis, sive femini sexus sive masculini, praeterito, valet quidem testamentum, sed postea adquisitione postumi sive postumae rumpitur, et ea ratione totum infirmatur. Ideoque si mulier ex qua postumus aut postuma sperabatur, abortum ferent, nihil impedimento est scriptis heredibus ad hereditatem adeundam. Sed feminini quidem sexus postumae vel nominatim vel inter ceteros exheredari solebant: dum tamen, si inter ceteros exheredentur, aliquid eis legetur, ne videantur praeteritae esse per oblivionem. Masculos vero postumos, id est filium et deinceps, placuit non aliter recte exheredari, nisi nominatim exheredentur, hoc scilicet modo: Quicumque mihi filius genitus fuerit, exheres esto.

1. Posthumous children, too, must either be instituted heirs, or disinherited: and the condition of all such children is equal in this, that if a posthumous son, or any posthumous descendant of either sex, is passed over, the testament is still valid; but, by the subsequent agnation of a posthumous child of either sex, its force is broken, and it becomes entirely void. And therefore, if a woman from whom a posthumous child is expected, should miscarry, there is nothing to hinder the instituted heirs from entering upon the inheritance. Posthumous females may be either disinherited by name, or by using the general term *ceteri*. If, however, they are disinherited by using the general term, something must be left them as a legacy to show that they were not passed over through forgetfulness. But male posthumous children, i. e. sons, and other descendants, cannot be disinherited except by name, that is, in this form, 'whatever son is hereafter born to me, let him be disinherited.'

In the strictness of the old civil law, a child born after the death of the testator was incapable of taking, as heir or legatee, under a testament. He had not, at the time of the testator's death, any certain existence; and the law said, *Incerta persona heres institui non potest.* (ULP. *Reg.* 22. 4.) But still it might be that the child, when born, was a *suus heres* of the testator; and as his *agnatio* would be considered in law to date from the time of conception, not birth, the testator would pass over one of his *sui heredes* if he omitted to include him or exclude him in the will; although, if he had included him, the posthumous child could not have taken anything. In the course of time the law permitted the posthumous child, if a *suus heres*, to become an heir; but the civil law never permitted the posthumous child of a stranger, even after the testator's death, to be an heir or legatee. And thus the institution of a posthumous *suus heres* having once been permitted, the next step was to consider it imperative on the testator, if he wished to exclude the posthumous child from a share in the inheritance, to do so in the case of a son, by referring to him specially (*nominatim* does not, of course, here mean 'by name,' but by a phrase expressly referring to him, such as *postumus exheres esto*): and in the case of a daughter, or any descendant other than a son, by adopting the general clause of disinheritance, *ceteri exheredes sunto*, and also by giving the child some legacy, however trifling, in order to show that it was not by accident that the testator allowed this clause to embrace the case of a posthumous child.

2. Postumorum autem loco sunt et hi, qui in sui heredis locum succedendo, quasi adgnascendo fiunt parentibus sui heredes. Ut ecce: si quis filium et ex eo nepotem nepotemve in potestate habeat, quia filius gradu praecedit, is solus jura sui heredis habet, quamvis nepos quoque et neptis ex eo in eadem potestate sint; sed si filius ejus vivo eo moriatur, aut qualibet alia ratione exeat de potestate ejus, incipit nepos neptisve in ejus locum succedere, et eo modo jura suorum heredum quasi adgnatione nanciscuntur. Ne ergo eo modo rumpatur jus testamentum, sicut ipsum filium vel heredem instituere vel nominatim exheredare debet testator, ne non jure faciat testamentum, ita et nepotem neptemve ex filio necesse est el vel heredem instituere vel exheredare, ne forte eo vivo filio mortuo, succedendo in locum ejus nepos neptisve quasi adgnatione rumpat testamentum; idque lege Junia Velleia provisum est, in qua simul exheredationis modus ad similitudinem postumorum demonstratur.

2. Those ought also to be placed on the footing of posthumous children, who, succeeding in the place of a *suus heres*, become by a kind of agnation *sui heredes* of their parents. Thus, for instance, if any one has a son in his power, and by him a grandson or granddaughter, the son, being first in degree, has alone the rights of a *suus heres*, although the grandson or granddaughter by that son, is under the same parental power. But, if the son should die in his father's lifetime, or should by any other means cease to be under his father's power, the grandson or granddaughter would succeed in his place, and would thus, by this kind of agnation, obtain the rights of a *suus heres*. In order, then, that the force of his testament may not be broken, the testator, who is, as we have said, obliged, in order to make an effectual testament, to institute his son as heir or to disinherit him by name, is equally obliged to institute as heir, or to disinherit, a grandson or granddaughter by that son, lest, if, during his lifetime, his son should die, and the grandson or granddaughter succeed in his

place, the force of the testament may
be broken by this kind of agnation.
Provision has been made for this by
the *lex Junia Velleia*, in which is
given a mode of disinheriting in
such a case like that of disinheriting
posthumous children.

GAI. ii. 134.

A testament was made void, not only by the birth of a
posthumous *suus heres*, but by any one coming into the position of a *suus heres* after the time when the testament was
made. The testator might (under the ancient law) have subsequently married a wife *in manu*; an emancipated son might
be re-emancipated, and thus come again into his father's
power; a captive son might return home; or the testator
might adopt a person into his family. In all these cases, as
well as in that mentioned in the text, the testament would
be invalidated by a process which bore a close analogy to agnation, that is, by these persons becoming, otherwise than by
birth, the *sui heredes* of the testator, just as it would be by
direct agnation, if a son were born to the testator after the
date of the testament. The *lex Junia Velleia* (GAI. ii. 134),
passed in the time of Augustus (763 A.U.C.), provided (1st)
that a testator might institute or exclude any one who should,
after the date of the testament, be born his *suus heres*, and
(2ndly) that he might exclude a grandchild, or other descendant, stepping into the place of their father, as *suus heres*
during the testator's lifetime. It was not necessary to legal-
ize the institution of such a grandchild, as he was not, like
the person who might be born after the date of the will, a
*persona incerta*. (D. xxviii. 29. 12, 13.) If these latter
persons, who thus might be instituted, and who received the
name of *quasi postumi Velleiani*, were excluded, the *lex
Junia* required that, as in the case of posthumous *sui heredes*, the males should be excluded *nominatim*, and the females *inter ceteros*, but with a legacy; in the other cases of
quasi-agnation, no law helped the testator, and if he had a
new *suus heres* by any of the modes mentioned above, except
that of a descendant stepping into the place of a deceased *suus
heres*, he had to make a new testament in order to die testate.

3. Emancipatos liberos jurecivili
neque heredes instituere neque exheredare necesse est, quia non sunt
sui heredes. Sed praetor omnes tam
feminini sexus quam masculini, si
heredes non instituantur, exheredari jubet, virilis sexus nominatim,
feminini vero et inter ceteros; quod

3. The civil law does not make it
necessary either to institute emancipated children heirs, or to disinherit
them in a testament; because they
are not *sui heredes*. But the praetor
ordains, that all children, male or female, if they be not instituted heirs,
shall be disinherited; the males by

si neque heredes instituti fuerint, neque ita ut diximus exheredati, promittit eis prætor contra tabulas testamenti bonorum possessionem.

nam, the females under the general term cæteri: for, if they have neither been instituted heirs, nor disinherited in manner before mentioned, the prætor gives them possession of goods contra tabulas.

GAI. ii. 135.

An emancipated child, passing out of the testator's family, ceased to be his suus heres. But 'though he thus lost all legal claim upon the testator's inheritance, yet he had gained no provision by being emancipated, and the prætor, therefore, came to his relief, and set aside the testament, if he had not been expressly excluded. He did not do this nominally, for the testament was legally good, but he did what amounted to the same thing; he divided the property equally among all as if the testator had died intestate, giving the children what was termed 'possession of the goods;' a possession said, in this case, to be contra tabulas, as it overthrew the provisions contained in the tablets of the testament. An emancipated daughter might thus be in a better position than an unemancipated, if both were passed over. For if the emancipated daughter were passed over, the testament would be overthrown altogether, and she would, if an only child, take all the property; whereas, if the unemancipated daughter was passed over, she could only take half at most. Antoninus put them on an equality, by giving the emancipated only the share she would have had, had she not been emancipated. (GAI. ii. 125, 126.)

4. Adoptivi liberi quamdiu sunt in potestate patris adoptivi, ejusdem juris habentur cujus sunt justis nuptiis quæsiti: itaque heredes instituendi vel exheredandi sunt, secundum ea quæ de naturalibus exposuimus. Emancipati vero a patre adoptivo, neque jure civili, neque quod ad edictum prætoris attinet, inter liberos numerantur: qua ratione accidit ut ex diverso, quod ad naturalem parentem attinet, quamdiu quidem sint in adoptiva familia, extraneorum numero habeantur, ut eos neque heredes instituere neque exheredare necesse sit; cum vero emancipati fuerint ab adoptivo patre, tunc incipiant in ea causa esse in qua futuri essent, si ab ipso naturali patre emancipati fuissent.

4. Adoptive children, while under the power of their adoptive father, are in the same legal position as children sprung from a legal marriage; and therefore they must either be instituted heirs, or disinherited, according to the rules we have laid down respecting natural children. But neither by the civil nor the prætorian law, are children emancipated by an adoptive father reckoned among his natural children. Hence conversely, adoptive children, while in their adoptive family, are considered strangers to their natural parents, who need not institute them heirs, or disinherit them; but if they are emancipated by their adoptive father, they are in the same position in which they would have been, if emancipated by their natural father.

GAI. ii. 136, 137.

If an adopted son were emancipated by his adoptive father, he would, under the old law, have no legal claim on the inheritance of his adoptive or his natural father. But the prætor came to his aid, and gave him ' a possession of the goods' of his natural father, unless he was expressly excluded by his natural father's testament. On his adoptive father, he would, after emancipation, in no case have any claim whatever, until Justinian altered the law in the manner alluded to in the next paragraph.

5. Sed hæc quidem vetustas introducebat. Nostra vero constitutio inter masculos et feminas in hoc jure nihil interesse existimans, quia utraque persona in hominum procreatione similiter naturæ officio fungitur, et lege antiqua duodecim tabularum omnes similiter ad successionem ab intestato vocabantur, quod et prætores postea secuti esse videntur, ideo simplex ac simili jus et in filiis et in filiabus et in cæteris descendentibus per virilem sexum personis, non solum natis sed etiam postumis, introduxit: ut omnes, sive sui sive emancipati sunt, vel heredes instituan ur vel nominatim exheredentur, et eumdem habeant effectum circa testamenta parentium suorum infirmanda et hereditatem auferendam, quem filii sui vel emancipati habent, sive jam nati sint, sive adhuc in utero constituti postea nati sint. Circa adoptivos autem filios certam induximus divisionem, quæ nostra constitutione quam eu-per adoptivis tulimus, continetur.

5. Such was the ancient law. But thinking, that no distinction can reasonably be made between the two sexes, inasmuch as they equally contribute to the procreation of the species, and because, by the ancient law of the Twelve Tables, all children were equally called to the succession ab intestato, which law the prætors seem afterwards to have followed, we have by our constitution made the law the same both as to sons and daughters, and also as to all other descendants in the male line, whether already born or posthumous; so that all children, whether they are sui heredes or emancipated, must either be instituted heirs or be disinherited by name; and their omission has the same effect in making void the testaments of their parents, and taking away the inheritance from the instituted heirs, as would be produced by the omission of children who were sui heredes or emancipated, whether they have been already born, or having been already conceived are born afterwards. With respect to adoptive children, we have established a distinction between them, which is set forth in our constitution on adoptions.

C. i. 28. 4; O. viii. 47. 10, pr. and 1.

Under the legislation of Justinian a testament would be rendered invalid by the omission of any one male or female whom it was necessary either to institute or exclude, and every exclusion must be made nominatim. An adopted son, if adopted by a stranger, i. e. not an ascendant, lost none of his claims upon his natural father's property, but only had a claim upon that of his adoptive father, if his father died intestate; for if the adoptive father made a testament, it was not necessary he should notice the adoptive son. But an adopted son, if adopted by an ascendant, either a maternal grandfather or an emancipated father (see Bk. I. Tit. 11. 2), stood in the position of a *suus heres* to the ascendant, and a testament would be invalid in which he was passed over.

6. Sed si in expeditione occupatus miles testamentum faciat, et liberos suos jam natos vel postumos nominatim non exheredaverit, sed silentio preterierit non ignorans an habeat liberos, silentium ejus pro exheredatione nominatim facta valere constitutionibus principum cautum est.

6. If a soldier on actual service make his testament, and neither disinherit his children already born, or his posthumous children by name, but pass them over in silence although he is not ignorant that he has children, it is provided by the imperial constitutions of the emperors, that his silence shall be equivalent to disinheriting them by name.

D. xxix. 30. 2.

7. Mater vel avus maternus necesse non habent liberos suos aut heredes instituere aut exheredare, sed possunt eos omittere; nam silentium matris, aut avi materni et ceterorum per matrem ascendentium, tantum facit quantum exheredatio patria. Nec enim matri filium filiamve, neque avum materno nepotem neptemve ex filia, si eum eamve heredem non instituat, exheredare necesse est, sive de jure civili quærimus, sive de edicto prætoris quo præteritis liberis contra tabulas bonorum possessionem promittit: sed aliud eis adminiculum servatur, quod paulo post vobis manifestum fiet.

7. Neither a mother nor a maternal grandfather need either institute their children heirs, or disinherit them, but may pass them over in silence; for the silence of a mother or a maternal grandfather, or of any other ascendant on the mother's side, has the same effect as a father actually disinheriting them. For a mother is not obliged to disinherit her children, if she does not institute them her heirs; neither is a maternal grandfather under the necessity of instituting or of disinheriting his grandson or granddaughter by a daughter; whether we look to the civil law, or the edict of the prætor, which gives possession of goods contra tabulas to those children who have been passed over in silence. But children, in this case, have another remedy, which we will hereafter explain.

Gai. iii. 71.

The children could never be the *sui heredes* of their mother, for women never had any one in their power; nor could they be the *sui heredes* of a maternal ascendant, except by adoption, and the case of adoption is not spoken of here.

*Aliud adminiculum.* This refers to the action for setting aside the testament as inofficious, that is, made without proper regard for natural ties. (See Tit. 18. 2.)

## Tit. XIV. DE HEREDIBUS INSTITUENDIS.

Heredes instituere permissum est tam liberos homines quam servos, et tam proprios quam alienos. Proprios autem, olim quidem secundum plurium sententiam, non aliter quam cum libertate recto instituere licebat. Hodie vero etiam sine libertate ex nostra constitutione heredes eos instituere permissum est. Quod non per innovationem induximus, sed quoniam aequius erat, et Atilicino placuisse Paulus suis libris, quos tam ad Massurium Sabinum quam ad Plautium scripsit, refert. Proprius autem servus etiam is intelligitur in quo nudam proprietatem testator habet, alio usumfructum habente. Est tamen casus in quo nec cum libertate utiliter servus a domina heres instituitur, ut constitutione divorum Severi et Antonini cavetur, cujus verba haec sunt: 'Servum adulterio maculatum non jure testamento manomissum ante sententiam ab ea muliere videri, quae rea fuerat ejusdem criminis postulata, rationis est; quare sequitur, ut in eundem a domina collata institutio nullius momenti habeatur.' Alienus servus etiam is intelligitur, in quo usumfructum testator habet.

A man may institute as his heirs either freemen or slaves, and either his own slaves or those of another. Formerly, according to the more received opinion, no one could properly institute his own slaves, unless he also freed them; but now, by our constitution, a testator may institute his slave without expressly enfranchising him. And we have introduced this rule, not as an innovation, but because it seemed equitable; and Paulus in his writings on Massurius Sabinus and Plautius, informs us that this was the opinion of Atilicinus. Among a testator's own slaves is included one in whom the testator had only a bare ownership, another having the usufruct. But there is a case, in which the institution of a slave by his mistress is void, although his liberty is expressly given to him, according to the provisions of a constitution of the Emperors Severus and Antoninus, in these words: 'Reason demands that no slave, accused of adultery with his mistress, shall be allowed before his sentence is pronounced, to be made free by the mistress, who is alleged to be a partner in the crime. Hence, if a mistress institute such a slave as her heir, it is of no avail.' In the term, 'the slave of another,' is included a slave of whom the testator has the usufruct.

GAI. ii. 185-187; C. vi. 27. 5; C. vii. 15. 1; D. xxviii. 5. 48. 2; C. vii. 15. 1.

By institution is meant the declaration who is to be heir, that is, who is to carry on the legal existence, the *persona*, of the testator. And as, unless his existence were continued, there could be no thing or person from whom the testamentary dispositions could derive any force, or be of any efficacy, the institution was the all-important part of the testament. It was *veluti caput atque fundamentum totius testamenti*. All other dispositions were accessories to it, being only conditions or laws imposed upon the heir. In the older law a peculiar form of words was appropriated to the institution. '*Titius heres esto*' was the recognized form. Even in the days of Gaius and Ulpian (GAI. ii. 116, 117; ULP. *Reg.* 20), such expressions as '*Titius heres sit*,' '*Titium heredem esse jubeo*,'

terms of command, were considered right, and expressions
such as ' *Titium heredem esse volo*,' ' *heredem instituo*,' ' *heredem facio*,' were considered wrong.   And it was not till 389
A.D. that Constantine the Second permitted the institution to
be made in any terms by which the meaning of the testator
could be clearly ascertained.   (C. vi. 23. 15.)   Again, in the
older law, as everything else in the testament derived its force
from the institution, it was considered that the institution
ought to be put at the head or top of the testament, and any
legacy or other disposition placed before it was passed over,
and had no effect.   An exception was made in behalf of an
appointment of a tutor (see Bk. i. Tit. 14. 3); and the clause
in which the testator disinherited his *sui heredes* was naturally
placed before that in which he instituted testamentary heirs.
Justinian, as we shall see in the 20th Title, paragr. 34, enacted that, provided the institution appeared in some part of
the testament, it should be immaterial in what part it might
be placed.

Any one might be instituted, and consequently take as heir,
who had the rights of a citizen, or, as it was technically
termed, who had the *testamenti factio cum testatore*, i. e. the
power of joining with the testator in going through the ceremonies of the *jus Quiritium*.   This power was not enjoyed
by *peregrini, deportati, dedecitii*, nor by the *Latini Juniani*,
unless they became citizens before entering on the inheritance.   Women were prevented by the *lex Voconia* (585
A.U.C.) (GAI. ii. 274), unmarried persons by the *lex Julia*,
and *orbi* (childless persons) by the *lex Pupia Poppæa*, from
being instituted.   Neither could any uncertain person be instituted, nor any corporate body, or any of the gods, except
those in whose favour, as the Tarpeian Jupiter (ULP. *Reg.*
226), a special exception had been made by a *senatus consultum*.   All these distinctions had ceased in the time of Justinian, and none of those we have mentioned, except *peregrini* and persons who had lost their civil rights by *deportatio*,
were excluded.   There were still, however, some to whom the
capacity for institution was specially denied, such as the children of persons convicted of treason (C. ix. 8. 5. 1), apostates
and heretics (C. i. 7. 3), children of, and parties to, prohibited
marriages.   (C. v. 5. 6.)   A second husband or wife could not
be instituted, when there was issue of the first marriage (C.
v. 9. 6); nor natural, where there were legitimate children.
(C. v. 27. 2.)

If a person instituted his own slave, this was held to give the
slave his liberty by necessary implication.   If he instituted the

slave of another, the slave took the inheritance for his master's benefit, provided the master had the *testamenti factio* with the testator ; but if he had not, the institution of the slave was void.

In the law before Justinian, enfranchisement by a person who had only a bare property in a slave, was not held to confer freedom, *a proprietatis domino manumissus non liber fit, sed servus sine domino est.* (Ulp. *Reg.* l. 19.) Under Justinian the slave became free, and could acquire for himself, and could take as heir ; but he was obliged to serve as slave to the usufructuary, during such time as the usufruct continued.

The slave accused of adultery with his mistress might be subjected, as all slaves might, to the torture, to extract evidence of his guilt. If he had been enfranchised, he would have escaped this, and thus the mistress might have defeated justice, unless she had been restrained from using her power of enfranchising him.

1. Servus autem a domino suo heres institutus, si quidem in eadem causa manserit, fit ex testamento liber heresque necessarius ; si vero a vivo testatore manumissus fuerit, suo arbitrio adire hereditatem potest, quia non fit necessarius, cum utrumque ex domini testamento non consequitur. Quod si alienatus fuerit, jussu novi domini adire hereditatem debet, et ea ratione per eum dominus fit heres ; nam ipse alienatus neque liber neque heres esse potest, etiamsi cum libertate heres institutus fuerit ; destitisse enim a libertatis datione videtur dominus, qui eum alienavit. Alienus quoque servus heres institutus, si in eadem causa duraverit, jussu ejus domini adire hereditatem debet : si vero alienatus fuerit ab eo, aut vivo testatore, aut post mortem ejus antequam adeat, debet jussu novi domini adire ; at si manumissus est vivo testatore vel mortuo antequam adeat, suo arbitrio adire hereditatem potest.

1. A slave instituted heir by his master, if he remains in the same condition, becomes, by virtue of the testament, free and necessary heir. But, if his master has enfranchised him before dying, he may at his pleasure accept or refuse the inheritance, for he does not become a necessary heir, since he does not obtain both his liberty and the inheritance by the testament of his master. But, if he has been alienated, he must enter on the inheritance at the command of his new master, who thus through his slave becomes the heir of the testator. For a slave once alienated cannot gain his liberty, or himself take an inheritance by virtue of the testament of the master who alienated him, although his freedom was expressly given by the testament ; because a master who has alienated his slave, has shown that he has renounced the intention of enfranchising him. So, too, when the slave of another is appointed heir, if he remains in slavery he must take the inheritance at his master's bidding ; and if the slave be alienated in the lifetime of the testator, or after his death, but before he has actually taken the inheritance, it is at the command of his new master that he must accept it. But, if he be en-

franchised during the lifetime of the
testator, or after his death, and before he has accepted the inheritance,
he may enter upon the inheritance
or not, at his own option.

GAI. ii. 188, 189.

It was necessary that the heir, as being the person who carried on the legal existence of the testator, should be possessed
of civil rights. If, then, a slave of the testator was instituted,
as it was in the power of the testator to make him free, and he
had invested him with a character requiring freedom, this institution was considered to involve his freedom. The slave of
any one else, if instituted, was only a channel by which his
master, if possessed of civic rights, acquired the inheritance.
(See Bk. i. Tit. 6. 1.) If a slave of the testator were instituted his heir, and remained his slave at the time of the testator's death, the slave, immediately upon the testator dying,
became his *heres necessarius*, that is, became his heir without
any option of refusing or taking the inheritance. But if it
were given under any condition, and the condition failed, the
institution then became invalid.

If the slave instituted did not belong to the testator at the
time of the testator's death, his condition at the time of his
taking on him the inheritance (*aditio hereditatis*) determined
for whom the inheritance was acquired. If at that time he
was a slave, he acquired it for the person who was then his
master; if free, for himself.

Disposing of the slave to another revoked the gift of liberty,
because this was considered as a legacy, a mere accessory to
the inheritance, to revoke which anything was sufficient, which
showed a change of intention on the part of the testator; but
it did not revoke the institution, because this was the keystone
of the testament, and could only be revoked by a new testament, or destruction of the old one.

2. Servus autem alienus post domini mortem recte heres instituitur,
quia et cum hereditariis servis est
testamenti factio: nondum enim
adita hereditas personae vicem sustinet, non heredis futuri, sed defuncti: cum etiam ejus, qui in
utero est, servus recte heres instituitur.

2. The slave of another may be
instituted heir even after the death
of his master, as there is *testamenti
factio* with slaves belonging to an inheritance; for an inheritance not yet
entered on represents the person of
the deceased, and not that of the
future heir. So, too, the slave even
of a child in the womb may be instituted heir.

D. xxviii. 5. 31. 1; D. xxviii. 5. 64.

After the death of a testator, and before the inheritance was
entered on, the inheritance itself represented the person of the

deceased, as it did that of an unborn child until the birth. A slave, during this interval, was said to belong to theinheritance, and if a testament was made by any one instituting as heir a slave belonging to the inheritance, the slave took the inheritance thus given him for the benefit of that inheritance to which he belonged. And that he should do so, it was not necessary that the person by whose testament he was instituted heir should have *testamenti factio* with the future heir, but it was only necessary that he should have it with the testator to whose inheritance the slave belonged.

3. Servus plurinm cum quibus testamenti factio est, ab extraneo institutus heres unicuique dominorum cujus jussu adierit, pro portione dominii acquirit hereditatem.

3. If a slave belonging to several masters, all capable of taking by testament, is instituted heir by a stranger, he acquires a proportion of the inheritance for each master by whose command he took it, corresponding to the several interests they each have in him.

D. xxix. 2. 67, 68.

If the slave were instituted heir by one of his masters, then, if this master expressly gave him his freedom, he became the *heres necessarius* of the master instituting him, and free; a due proportion of the price at which he was valued being paid to each of his other masters. But if his liberty were not expressly given him, the share which the testator had in him accrued proportionately to all those of his masters by whose orders he entered on the inheritance. (See Tit. 7. 4 of this Book.)

4. Et unum hominem et plures in infinitum, quot quis velit, heredes facere licet.

5. Hereditasplerumque dividitur in duodecim uncias, quæ assis appellatione continentur. Habent autem et hæ partes propria nomina ab uncia usque ad assem, ut puta hæc: uncia, sextans, quadrans, triens, quincunx, semis, septunx, bes, dodrans, dextans, deunx, as. Non autem utique duodecim uncias esse oportet, nam tot unciæ assem efficiunt, quot testator voluerit; et si unum tantum quis ex semisse, verbi gratia, heredem scripserit, totus as in semisse erit: neque enim idem ex parte testatus et ex parte intestatus decedere potest, nisi sit miles cujus sola voluntas in testan-

4. A testator may appoint one heir or several, the number being quite unrestricted.

5. An inheritance is generally divided into twelve ounces, comprehended together under the term of an *as*, and each of these parts, from the ounce to the *as*, has its peculiar name, viz., *uncia, sextans, quadrans, triens, quincunx, semis, septunx, bes, dodrans, dextans, deunx, as.* But it is not necessary that there should be always twelve ounces, for an *as* may consist of as many ounces as the testator pleases. If, for example, a man names but one heir, and appoint him *ex semisse, i. e.* the heir of six parts, then these six parts will make up the whole *as*; for no one can die partly testate and partly intestate,

do spectatur. Et e contrario potest quis, in quantascumque voluerit plurimas uncias, suam hereditatem dividere.

except a soldier, whose intention in making his testament is alone regarded. Conversely, a testator may divide his estate into as many ounces more than twelve as he thinks proper.

D. xxviii. 5. 50. 2; D. xxviii 5. 13. 1, and seq.; D. xxix. 1. 6.

In making a testament, where the testator wished to give different shares to his heirs, the singular system, alluded to in the text, was often adopted. The testator did not give a fifth, a fourth, &c., to each heir, but gave so many parts, *e.g.* five or four parts to one heir, and so many more to another. The number of parts given to each was added up, and the total formed the number of which these parts were taken to be a fraction. For instance, if a testator gave to A five parts, to B six, and to C two, the whole number amounting to thirteen, A took five-thirteenths, B six-thirteenths, and C two-thirteenths.

So far all was simple, but a greater complication was introduced by adopting, conjointly with this calculation of parts, a mode of reckoning derived from the familiar measure of the *as*, or pound weight, and its division into twelve ounces. The *hereditas* was considered to be represented by the *as*, and the parts by the ounces. But the testator had the power of determining how many ounces there should be in this imaginary pound. In the instance above given, the *as* contains thirteen *unciæ*. But supposing the testator assigned a certain number of parts to some of his heirs, and not to others ; as, to A five parts, to B six parts, and then made C a co-heir, but without assigning him any number of parts; the law supposed the testator to have divided his pound into twelve ounces as the standard number, and gave the heir to whom no number of parts was assigned such a number as made up the *as*. In this instance, therefore, C would have one ounce or part. But if the whole number of parts expressly given exceeded twelve, then the testator was supposed to have been measuring out his inheritance by the double *as* (*dupondius*), and the heir to whom no express number was given took the number of parts wanting to make up 24. If the parts expressly given exceeded 24, then the *tripondius*, containing 36 ounces, was the measure, and so on. The testator never died only partly testate ; for whatever he gave was taken to make up the whole inheritance. If his testament only disposed of a portion of his property in the way mentioned in the text, viz. by his only giving six ounces (*semis*) to his heir, and his instituting only one heir, six was considered to be the number of ounces he wished to have in the *as*, and, therefore, he died testate as to all his property. If he did not use any expression referring to the parts of an *as*, but gave his heir specific things, having other property besides, what he did give was considered to represent what he did not give ; as, for instance, if a man possessed large estates, and made A his heir, giving him one farm, and named no other heir, A took all his property ; for this one farm was taken to be a description of the whole.

The *as* was thus divided : *uncia*, one ounce ; *sextans*, one-sixth of an *as*, or two ounces ; *quadrans*, one-fourth, or three ounces ; *triens*, one-third, or four ounces: *quincunx*, five ounces ; *semis*, one-half, or six ounces; *septunx*, seven ounces; *bes*, contracted from *bis triens*, eight ounces ; *dodrans*, contracted from *de quadrans*, the *as* minus a *quadrans*, nine ounces ; *dextans*, contracted from *de sextans*, ten ounces, and *deunx*, eleven ounces.

| | |
|---|---|
| 6. Si plures instituantur, ita demum partium distributio necessaria est, si nolit testator eos ex æquis partibus heredes esse ; satis enim constat, nullis partibus nominatis, ex æquis partibus eos heredes esse. Partibus autem in quorumdam personis expressis, si quis allus sine parte nominatus erit, si quidem aliqua pars æsl deerit, ex ea parte heres fiet ; et si plures sine parte scripti sunt, omnes in eandem partem concurrent. Si vero totus as completus sit, in dimidiam partem vocantur, et ille vel illi omnes in alteram dimidiam : nec interest primus an medius an novissimus sine parte heres scriptus sit ; ea enim pars data intelligitur, quæ vacat. | 6. If several heirs be appointed, it is not necessary that the testator should specify their several shares unless he intends that they should not take in equal portions. For if no division is made, the heirs clearly take equal portions. But if the shares of some should be specified, and another be named heir without having any portion assigned him, he will take the fraction that may be wanting to make up the as. And if several be instituted heirs without having any portion assigned them, they will all divide this fraction between them. But, if the whole as be given among those whose parts are specified, and there be then no fraction left, then they whose shares are not specified take one moiety, and he or they whose shares are specified the other moiety. It is immaterial whether the heir, whose share is not specified, hold the first, middle, or last place in the institution ; it is always the part not specifically given that is considered to belong to him. |

D. xxviii. 5. 9. 12; D. xxviii. 5. 17, pr. and 3, 4; D. xxviii. 5. 20.

From this paragraph we may add one more detail of the system pursued in calculating the parts of the inheritance. If the number of parts expressly given amounted exactly to twelve, and there was an heir instituted to whom no parts were given, as the parts given neither fell short of the *as*, nor broke into the *dupondius*, it was necessary to make some arbitrary regulation on the subject; and that adopted was, that the parts expressed should be taken to be equal to those not expressed; and these twelve expressed parts should cover one-half the inheritance.

7. Videamus, si pars aliqua vacet, nec tamen quisquam sine parte sit heres institutus, quid juris sit, veluti si tres ex quartis partibus heredes scripti sunt? Et constat vacantem partem singulis tacite pro hereditaria parte accedere, et perinde haberi ac si ex tertiis partibus heredes scripti essent; et ex diverso si plures in portionibus sint, tacite singulis decrescere, ut si verbi gratia quatuor ex tertiis partibus heredes scripti sint, perinde habeantur ac si unusquisque ex quarta parte scriptus fuisset.

7. Let us inquire how we ought to decide in case a part remains unbequeathed, and yet each heir has his portion assigned him: as, if three should be instituted, and a fourth part given to each. It is clear, in this case, that the undisposed part would be divided among them in proportion to the share bequeathed to each, and it would be exactly as if each had had a third part assigned him. And, on the contrary, if several heirs are instituted with such portions as in the whole to exceed the as, then each heir must suffer a proportionate diminution; for example, if four are instituted, and a third be given to each, this would be the same as if each of the written heirs had been instituted to a fourth only.

D. xxvii. 5. 13. 2, and seq.

In this section the division of the inheritance is into definite fractional parts, as one-third, one-fourth, one-fifth, a division the testator was always at liberty to adopt. If we were to use the terms derived from the as, and state the same case as that stated in the text, we should say, that if the testator gave a *quadrans* to three persons, he would thereby make his as to consist of nine ounces (which he was quite at liberty to do), and then a *quadrans* would give a third of the inheritance; if he gave a *triens* to four persons, he would make his as to consist of sixteen ounces, and then a *triens* would give a fourth of the inheritance.

8. Et si plures uncias quam duodecim distributae sint, is qui sine parte institutus est, quod dupondio deest habebit; idemque erit, si dupondius expletus sit. Quae omnes partes ad assem partes revocantur, quamvis sint plurium unciarum.

8. If more than twelve ounces are bequeathed, then he who is instituted without any prescribed share shall have the amount wanting to complete the second as; and so, if all the parts of the second as are already bequeathed, he shall have the amount necessary to make up the third as. But all these parts are afterwards reduced to one single as, however great may be the number of ounces.

D. xxviii. 5. 18.

The concluding sentence of the section means, that though,

for the sake of calculating the parts, we go beyond the *as* to the *dupondius* or *tripondius*, yet we must always consider the *as* as representing the inheritance. For example, to be quite correct, we must make 15-24ths into 7½—12ths, so that the portions of the inheritance may be expressed with reference to the twelve *unciæ* of the *as*.

| | |
|---|---|
| 0. Heres pure et sub conditione Institui potest, ex certo tempore aut ad certum tempus non potest, veluti post quinquennium quam moriar, vel ex calendis illis vel usque ad calendas illas heres esto. Itenique diem adjectum haberi pro supervacuo placet, et perinde esse ac si pure heres institutus esset. | 0. An heir may be instituted simply or conditionally, but not from or to any certain period: as, after five years from my death—or, from the calends of such a month, or until the calends of such a month. The term thus added is considered a superfluity, and the Institution is treated exactly as if unconditional. |

D. xxviii. 5.

If the institution is conditional, all those rights which otherwise would date from the death of the testator, date from the accomplishment of the condition. When the condition was accomplished, the heir entered on the inheritance, and then by this *aditio* (not by the accomplishment of the condition) his rights were carried back to the time when the testator died. *Heres quandoque adeundo hereditatem jam tunc a morte successisse defuncto intelligitur.* (D. xxix. 2. 54.)

It was a principle of Roman law that a person could not die partly testate and partly intestate; if his testament was valid at all, his *heredes ab intestato* were entirely excluded. It was also a rule of law, that a person who once became heir, could not cease to be heir. *Non potest (adjectus) efficere, ut qui semel heres exstitit desinat heres esse.* (D. xxviii. 5. 88.) But if a person were instituted heir from a certain time, there would be no one but the *heredes ab intestato* to take in the meantime, and they must cease to be heirs when the time arrived; if the Institution were to take effect only up to a certain time, the instituted heir would cease to be heir at the expiration of the time, and the *heredes ab intestato* would then take the inheritance. This would be making the testator die partly testate and partly intestate, and therefore the law did not permit such an institution. Such an institution would also have offended against the second rule we have just mentioned, viz. that a person who had once been heir could not cease to be heir (D. xxviii. 5. 88), whence the adage *semel heres semper heres*; for in the first case, the *heredes ab intestato*, in the second the instituted heir, would cease, at the end of a certain time, to be heir. But if the institution were conditional, the *heredes ab intestato* did not take until the condition was fulfilled, but were excluded by the possibility which existed at every moment of time that the testamentary heir would be able to enter on the inheritance by the condition being accomplished. (See D. xxix. 2. 39.)

The text speaks of *certum tempus*; if the time were uncertain, if, for instance, the testator said, let A be my heir from the date of B's death, this would operate to make the institution conditional. *Dies incertus conditionem in testamento facit.* (D. xxxv. 1. 75.) It would be uncertain whether A would outlive B; but if during A's lifetime, B died, which he might at any moment, the condition, viz. that A should outlive him, would be accomplished, and this possibility excluded the *heredes ab intestato.*

| | |
|---|---|
| 10. Impossibilis conditio in institutionibus et legatis, nec non fideicommissis et libertatibus, pro non scripta habetur. | 10. An impossible condition in the institution of heirs, gift of legacies, creation of *fideicommissa*, and gifts of freedom, is considered as not inserted at all. |

D. xxviii. 7. 1 ; D. xxviii. 7. 14.

That the institution was regarded as unconditional instead of void, when the condition was one not allowed by law, must be ascribed to the anxiety of Romans not to die intestate, and the consequent favour with which the law regarded any means of treating a will as valid. An obligation containing an impossible condition would be void. (Bk. iii. Tit. 9. 11.)

*Possibilis est quae per rerum naturam admitti potest: impossibilis quae non potest.* (PAUL. *Sent.* iii. 4. 2. 1.) But a thing contrary to law, or to *boni mores*, was considered as impossible as if it were impossible *per rerum naturam.* (PAUL. *Sent.* iii. 4. 2.)

| | |
|---|---|
| 11. Si plures conditiones institutioni adscriptae sunt, siquidem conjunctim, ut puta si illud et illud factum erit, omnibus parendum est; si separatim, veluti si illud aut illud factum erit, cuilibet obtemperare satis est. | 11. When several conditions are attached to the institution, if they are placed in the conjunctive, as, if this and that thing be done, all the conditions must be complied with. But, if the conditions are placed in the disjunctive, as, if this or that be done, it will be sufficient to comply with any one. |

D. xxviii. 7. 5.

| | |
|---|---|
| 12. Ii, quos nunquam testator vidit, heredes institui possunt, veluti si fratris filios peregri natos, ignorans qui essent, heredes instituerit; ignorantia enim testantis inutilem institutionem non facit. | 12. A testator may institute persons his heirs, whom he has never seen, as, his brother's sons, born in a foreign country, and unknown to him; for the want of this knowledge will not vitiate the institution. |

C. vi. 24. 11.

## TIT. XV.   DE VULGARI SUBSTITUTIONE.

Poteet antem quis in testamento uno plures gradus haeredum facere, ut puta si ille heres non erit ille heres esto, et deinceps in quantum velit testator substituere potest, et novissimo loco in subsidium vel servum necessarium heredem instituere.

A man by testament may appoint several degrees of heirs; as, for instance, if so and so will not be my heir, let so and so be my heir. And so on through as many substitutions as he shall think proper. He may even, in the last place, and as an ultimate resource, institute a slave his necessary heir.

D. xxviii. 6. 36.

Substitution was really a conditional institution. If A is not my heir, if, for instance, he die before me, I appoint B. The extent to which substitution was carried, was owing to the importance attached to dying testate; and partly also, in the time of the emperors, to the wish to guard against the operation of the *lex Julia et Papia*, which created numerous causes of incapacity to take under a testament, and gave the shares of those instituted, but incapable of taking, as *caduca*, to the public treasury.

This kind of substitution is termed *vulgaris*, as opposed to *substitutio pupillaris*, the subject of the next Title.

1. Et plures in unius locum possunt substitui, vel unus in plurium, vel singuli singulis, vel invicem ipsi qui heredes instituti sunt.

1. A testator may substitute several in the place of one, or one in the place of several, or one in the place of each one, or he may substitute the instituted heirs themselves reciprocally to one another.

D. xxviii. 6. 36. 1.

*Vel invicem ipsi qui heredes instituti sunt.* If any one instituted heir died before the testator, or refused to take his share of the inheritance, his share was, in fact, undisposed of. But as the testator was always supposed to have disposed of his whole estate if he disposed of any part, this share was divided among all those who entered on the inheritance in proportions corresponding to the share given them by the will. Their claim to this was called the *jus accrescendi*. But a testator sometimes produced nearly the same effect as the law would have produced for him, by substituting the heirs who entered on the inheritance in the place of those who did not, thus preventing any share from becoming vacant. The effect was nearly the same, but not quite so. It was open to the substituted heirs to refuse the inheritance of this new part, which required to be expressly entered on; whereas, if they once entered on the share given them by the testament, they could not decline accepting any further portion which devolved on them by the *jus accrescendi.* (D. xxix. 2. 35.) Again, the representatives of a deceased heir received his portion of the part given by the *jus accrescendi.* But only those living at the time when the choice of entering on the vacant share was offered them, took by substitution (D. xxviii. 6. 23; D. xxviii. 5. 59. 7), the benefit of substitution, like that of institution, being personal. The laws known under the joint name of the *lex Julia et Papia Poppæa*, had given a further reason for this mode of mutually substituting the heirs to each other. By these laws only the ascendants and descendants of the testator could take by the *jus accrescendi*, and the childless and the unmarried were entirely excluded. These laws, however, had been in a great measure abrogated by Constantine (C. viii. 58), and were completely so by Justinian in A.D. 434. (C. vi. 51). It is further to be observed, that, where there were more than two persons instituted, the devolution would not be the same by substitution and by the *jus accrescendi.* Supposing A, B, and C were all instituted heirs, and B substituted to A, and then D substituted to B; if A and B died, by B being substituted to A, the shares of A and B would both go to D; but by the *jus accrescendi* (*i. e.* supposing B had not been substituted to A), the share of A would have been vacant, and would have been divided between D and C.

2. Et si ex disparibus partibus heredes scriptos invicem substituerit, et nullam mentionem in substitutione partium habuerit, eas videtur in substitutione partes dedisse quas in institutione expressit; et ita divus Pius rescripsit.

2. If a testator, having instituted several heirs with unequal shares, substitute them reciprocally the one to the other, and make no mention of the shares they are to have in the substitution, he is considered to have given the same shares in the substitution, which he gave in the institution; thus the Emperor Antoninus decided by rescript.

C. vi. 26. 1.

If he chose, however, to specify the shares they were to take in that portion to which they were substituted, there was no necessity that they should be the same shares as those they were said to take by institution.

3. Sed si instituto heredi et coheredi suo substituto dato alius substitutus fuerit, divi Severus et Antoninus sine distinctione rescripserunt ad utramque partem substitutum admitti.

3. If a co-heir be substituted to any instituted heir, and a third person to that co-heir, the Emperors Severus and Antoninus have by rescript decided, that such substituted person shall be admitted to the portions of both without distinction.

D. xxviii. 6. 41.

A testator institutes two heirs, A and B.  He substitutes B
to A, but not A to B; to B he substitutes C.  Supposing
neither A nor B take the inheritance, C will take the part of
each, *utramque partem*, and will take it without any distinction (*sine distinctione*) as to what was the order in which the
testament was drawn up, or whether A or B first dies or refuses
or becomes incapable of taking the inheritance.  How he
would take the part of B is clear enough ; but if B died or
refused the inheritance before A, how would C take A's share,
by the *jus accrescendi* or by substitution ?  He did so by the
rule *substitutus substituto censetur substitutus instituto ;*
the person substituted to the substitute is considered substituted to the instituted heir ; C is substituted to B,
who is substituted to A, and therefore C is, by what was
termed a *tacita substitutio*, substituted to A, and takes his
part.

4. Si servum alienum quis patremfamilias arbitratus heredem scripserit, et si heres non esset, Mevium ei
substituerit, isque servus jussu domini adierit hereditatem, Mevius
in partem admittitur.  Illa enim
verba si heres non erit, in eo quidem
quem alieno juri subjectum esse
testator scit, sic accipiuntur, 'si
neque ipse heres erit, neque alium
heredem effecerit;' in eo vero quem
patremfamilias esse arbitratur, illud significant, 'si hereditatem
sibi, eive cujus juri postea subjectus
esse emperit, non acquisierit;' idque Tiberius Cæsar in persona
Parthenii servi sui constituit.

4. If a testator institute the slave
of another his heir, supposing him
to be *sui juris*, and if he does not become his heir, he substitutes Mævius
in his place; then, if that slave
should afterwards enter upon the
inheritance at the command of his
master, the substituted person, Mævius, would be admitted to a part.
For the words, 'if he do not become my heir,' in the case of a person, whom the testator knew to be
under the dominion of another, are
taken to mean, if he will neither become heir himself, nor cause another
to be heir; but in the case of a person whom the testator supposed to be
free, the words mean, if the heir will
neither acquire the inheritance for
himself, nor for him to whose dominion he may afterwards become subject.  This was decided by Tiberius
Cæsar, in the case of his own slave
Parthenius.

D. xxviii. 5. 40, 41.

The *pars* which each took was one-half.  (THEOPH. *Par.*)
That each should take half in such a case was a mere arbitrary
regulation, formed on no principle of law, but only meeting, as
was supposed, the equity of the case.  It seemed hard that
the master of the slave should lose all benefit from the institution, when the words of the testament gave him the whole
inheritance, and hard that the instituted heir should take

nothing when the master of the slave was profiting by a mistake of the testator. Accordingly Tiberius decided that each should have half.

## Tit. XVI.   DE PUPILLARI SUBSTITUTIONE.

Liberis suis impuberibus quos in potestate quis habet, non solum ita ut supra diximus substituere potest, id est ut, si heredes ei non extiterint, alius ei sit heres, sed eo amplius ut etsi heredes ei extiterint et adhuc impuberes mortui fuerint, sit eis aliquis heres, veluti si quis dicat hoc modo: Titius filius meus heres mihi esto: si filius meus heres mihi non erit, sive heres erit et prius moriatur quam in suam tutelam venerit, tunc Seius heres esto. Quo casu, si quidem non extiterit heres filius, tunc substitutus patri fit heres; si vero extiterit heres filius et ante pubertatem decesserit, ipsi filio fit heres substitutus; nam moribus institutum est ut, cum ejus aetatis filii sint, in qua ipsi sibi testamentum facere non possunt, parentes eis faciant.

A testator can substitute an heir in place of his children, under the age of puberty, and in his power, not only in the manner we have just mentioned, namely, by appointing some other person his heir in case his children did not become his heirs; but also, if they do become his heirs, but die under the age of puberty, he may substitute another heir; as for example, 'let Titius, my son, be my heir, and, if he should not become my heir, or, becoming my heir, should die before he comes to be his own master, i.e. before he arrives at puberty, let Seius be my heir.' In this case, if the son do not become the testator's heir, the substituted heir is heir to the father; but, if the son becomes heir, and then dies under the age of puberty, the substituted heir is then heir to the son. For custom has established, that parents may make testaments for their children, who are not of an age to make testaments for themselves.

Gai. ii. 179, 180.

A child under the age of puberty might be *sui juris*, and so have the legal capability of making a testament; his *status* might be such as to give him the *testamenti factio*, but he would not have the power of exercising his right to make a testament, according to the distinction between a right and the power of availing one's self of the right, so often met with in Roman law. If this child, then, died before attaining fourteen years, he would necessarily die intestate, which in Roman eyes was so great a misfortune for any one, that the father of the child was permitted to make the child's testament, but only as a part and as accessory to his own; except in the case of a soldier, who might make a child's testament without making one for himself. (D. xxviii. 6. 2.) The right to make a child's testament

depended on the possession of the *patria potestas*, and could
only be exercised with regard to those children who were in
the father's power.

In the words *si filius meus heres mihi non erit, sive heres erit
et prius moriatur*, we have an instance both of the vulgar and
the pupillary substitution. It was long a vexed question among
the jurisprudents (Cic. *de Orat.* 1. 39. 57), whether, if one only
was expressed, the other was implied; whether, for instance,
if the words *si filius meus heres mihi non erit* stood alone,
and the child became heir but died under the age of puberty,
the substituted heir would take as if he had been substituted by
pupillary substitution. Marcus Aurelius terminated the doubt
by deciding that each substitution implied the other (D. xxviii.
6. 4), so that, when the son was instituted heir, the person
substituted to him by pupillary substitution was considered as
substituted to him by vulgar substitution ; and conversely, the
person substituted by vulgar substitution was considered as
substituted by pupillary substitution, unless, in either case,
the testator had expressed a wish to the contrary.

1. Qua ratione excitati, etiam
constitutionem poenimus in nostro
codice, qua prospectum est, ut si
mente captos habeant filios vel nepotes vel pronepotes cujuscumque
sexus vel gradus, liceat eis, etsi puberes sint, ad exemplum pupillaris
substitutionis certas personas substituere; sin autem resipuerint,
eamdem substitutionem infirmari,
et hoc ad exemplum pupillaris substitutionis, quae postquam pupillus
adoleverit, infirmatur.

1. Guided by a similar principle,
we have also inserted a constitution
in our code, which provides that, if
a man have children, grandchildren,
or great-grandchildren, out of their
right minds, of whatever sex or degree, he may substitute certain persons as heirs in place of such children, on the analogy of pupillary
substitution, although they have attained the age of puberty. But if they
regain their reason, the substitution
is void, on the analogy of pupillary
substitution, which ceases to operate
when the minor attains to puberty.

C. vi. 26. 9; D. xxviii. 6. 14.

This kind of substitution is termed by the commentators
*quasi-pupillaris* or *exemplaris*, because made *ad exemplum
pupillaris substitutionis.* The power here given differs from
that of making a child's testament in two points : (1), it could
be made by any ascendant, whether paternal or maternal,
and not only by the *paterfamilias* ; and (2), the testator
could not substitute any one he pleased. He was obliged to
appoint one among *certas personas*, viz. one of the descendants of the insane, and, if there were none, then one of his
brothers. If he had no brother, the choice of the testator was
then unrestrained.  (C. vi. 26. 9.)

If for any other cause than insanity a descendant were incapable of making a testament, the emperor would, if he thought fit, give a licence to the head of the family to make a testament for him. (D. xxviii. 6. 43.)

2. Igitur in pupillari substitutione secundum præfatum modum ordinata duo quodammodo sunt testamenta, alterum patris, alterum filii, tanquam si ipse filius sibi heredem instituisset, aut certe unum est testamentum duarum causarum, id est, duarum hereditatum.

2. In a pupillary substitution, made in the way we have mentioned, there are in a manner two testaments, one of the father, the other of the son, as if the son had instituted an heir for himself; or at least there is one testament, operating on two objects, that is, two inheritances.

Gai. li. 160.

3. Sin autem quis ita formidolosus sit, ut timeret ne filius ejus pupillus adhuc, ex eo quod palam substitutum accepit, post obitum ejus periculo insidiarum subjiceretur, vulgarem quidem substitutionem palam facere et in primis testamenti partibus debet; illam autem substitutionem per quam, etsi heres extiterit pupillus et intra pubertatem decesserit, substitutus vocatur, separatim in inferioribus partibus scribere, eamque partem proprio lino propriaque cera consignare, et in priore parte testamenti cavere, ne inferiores tabulæ vivo filio et adhuc impubere aperiantur. Illud palam est, non ideo minus valere substitutionem impuberis filii, quod in iisdem tabulis scripta sit quibus sibi quisque heredem instituisset, quamvis pupillo hoc periculosum sit.

3. If a testator be so apprehensive as to fear lest, after his death, his son, being yet a pupil, should be exposed to the risk of having designs formed against him, from another person being openly substituted to him, he ought to make openly a vulgar substitution, and insert it in the first part of his testament; and to write the substitution, by which a substituted heir is called to the inheritance, if his son should become an heir and then die under the age of puberty, by itself, and in the lower part, which part ought to be separately tied up and sealed: and he ought also to insert a clause in the first part of his testament, forbidding the lower part to be opened, while his son is alive, and within the age of puberty. Of course a substitution to a son under the age of puberty is not less valid because written on the same tablet in which the testator has instituted him his heir, whatever danger it may involve to the pupil.

Gai. ii. 181.

4. Non solum autem heredibus institutis impuberibus liberis ita substituere parentes possunt, ut etsi heredes eis extiterint et ante pubertatem mortui fuerint, sit eis heres is quem ipsi voluerint; sed etiam exheredatis: Itaque eo casu, si quid pupillo ex hereditatibus legatisve aut donationibus propinquorum atque amicorum acquisitum fuerit, id omne ad substitutum pertinebit. Quæcunque diximus de substitu-

4. Parents may not only substitute to their children under the age of puberty, so that if such children become their heirs, and die under the age of puberty, any one whom the testator pleases shall be made their heir, but they may also substitute to their disinherited children; and therefore, in such a case, whatever a disinherited child, within the age of puberty, may have acquired by succession, by legacies, or by gift

tione impuberum liberorum vel
heredum institutorum vel exhere-
datorum, eadem etiam de postumis
intelligimus.

from relations and friends, will all
become the property of the substituted heir.  All we have said concerning the substitution of pupils,
instituted heirs, or disinherited children, is applicable also to posthumous children.

GAI. ii. 182, 183.

It was not because he instituted a child in his own testament that a *paterfamilias* could make the testament of that
child, but because the child was in his power, and hence he
could make the testaments even of children whom he disinherited.  Grandchildren and other descendants could also be
made subject to a pupillary substitution by their grandfather,
if they were immediately in his power, that is, if their own
father was dead or emancipated.

It was necessary that the child should be under the power
of the father at the time of making the testament, and also at
that of the father's death.  No testator could, therefore, substitute to an emancipated child.  (D. xxviii. 6. 2.)  If, after
the child became *sui juris*, he was arrogated, this vitiated the
substitution : but the person who arrogated him was obliged to
give security that if the child died under the age of puberty, he
would give up to the substituted heir, or to the *heredes legitimi*
if no one was substituted, all that would have to come to the
pupil if the substitution had remained valid.  It is, perhaps,
hardly necessary to observe, that in every case of pupillary
substitution, the substituted heir took not only what the pupil
received from the father, but all that the pupil would have had
to dispose of by testament, if he had been capable of making
a testament.

6. Liberis autem suis testamentum nemo facere potest, nisi et sibi
faciat ; nam pupillare testamentum
pars et sequela est paterni testamenti, adeo ut si patris testamentum non valeat, nec filii quidem
valebit.

6. No parent can make a testament
for his children, unless he also make
a testament for himself: for the pupillary testament is a part of, and
accessory to, the testament of the
parent, so much so, that if the testament of the father is not valid, neither is that of the son.

D. xxviii. 6. 2. 1.

The two testaments were generally contained in the same
instrument ; but a testator might, if he pleased, make his son's
testament by a different instrument, or might even make it by
verbal nuncupation, although his own testament was written.

0. Vel singulis autem liberis, vel ei qui eorum novissimus impubes morietur, substitui potest: singulis quidem si neminem eorum intestato decedere voluit, novissimo si jus legitimarum hereditatum integrum inter eos custodiri velit.

6. A parent may make a pupillary substitution to each of his children, or to him who shall die the last under the age of puberty; to each, if he be unwilling that any of them should die intestate; to the last who shall die within the age of puberty, if he wish that the order of legitimate succession should be rigidly preserved among them.

D. xxviii. 6. 37.

7. Substituitur autem impuberi aut nominatim, veluti Titius, aut generaliter, ut quisquis mihi heres erit: quibus verbis vocantur ex substitutione, impubere mortuo filio, qui et ei scripti sunt heredes et extiterunt, et pro qua parte heredes facti sunt.

7. A substitution may be made to a child under the age of puberty, by name, as, 'let Titius be heir;' or generally; for instance, 'whoever shall be my heir.' By these latter words, all are called to the inheritance by substitution, on the death of the son under the age of puberty, who have been instituted, and have become heirs to the father, and each in proportion to the share assigned to him as heir.

D. xxviii. 6. 8. 1.

*Quisquis mihi heres erit, heres filio meo impuberi esto,* would be the full expression.

8. Masculo igitur usque ad quatuordecim annos substitui potest, feminae usque ad duodecim annos; et si hoc tempus excesserint, substitutio evanescit.

8. A substitution may then be made to males, up to the age of fourteen: and to females, up to that of twelve years: this age once passed, the substitution is at an end.

D. xxviii. 6. 14.

The father could not extend the time beyond fourteen years, but he could make it less; as, for example, *si filius meus intra decimum annum decesserit.*

The *substitutio pupillaris* would be at an end not only by the pupil attaining the age of puberty, but by his undergoing a *capitis deminutio* before the age of puberty, or dying before his father, as, in either of these cases, it would be impossible he should make a testament. Or, again, if no one entered on the father's inheritance, or the father's testament was in any way made inoperative, the testament of the son was void, because it was on the validity of the testament of the father that the validity of the testament of the son depended.

9. Extraneo vero vel filio puberi heredi instituto ita substituere nemo potest, ut si heres extiterit et intra

9. After having instituted a stranger or son of full age, a testator cannot them go on to substitute another

aliquod tempus decesserit, aliusel sit heres; sed hoc solum permissum est, ut eum per fideicommissum testator obliget alii hereditatem ejus vel totam vel pro parte restituere: quod jus quale sit, suo loco trademus.

heir to him, if he dies within a certain time. All that is allowed is, to oblige, by a *fideicommissum*, the person instituted to give up all or a part to a third person. What the law is on this point we will explain in its proper place.

Gai. ii. 184.

It is to be observed that, in a *fideicommissum*, the testator does not attempt to deal with the inheritance of another; he only regulates the transmission of his own.

## Tit. XVII. QUIBUS MODIS TESTAMENTA INFIRMANTUR.

Testamentum jure factum usque adeo valet donec rumpatur irritumve fiat.

A testament, legally made, remains valid, until it be either revoked or rendered ineffectual.

If something were originally wanting to the validity of the testament, it was spoken of as being *injustum*, *non jure factum*; as *imperfectum*, if some formality were wanting; and as *nullius momenti*, if a child were not properly disinherited. But it might be quite valid when made, and subsequently lose its effect; in such a case it was either *ruptum*, i. e. its force was broken, it was revoked, either by agnation of a *suus heres*, or by a subsequent testament; or it was *irritum*, rendered useless by the testator undergoing a change of *status*, or by no one entering, under it, on the inheritance. In this last case it was specially said to be *destitutum*; but the general expression *irritum* was applied, as well as the more particular term *destitutum*, to a testament that had been abandoned.

We have no term nearer to *ruptum* than revoked; but it does not express it very accurately, as the rupture of the testament might be something quite independent of the testator's will, whereas revocation properly implies a voluntary act of the testator. We have hitherto, in order to keep up the metaphor, translated it, 'the force of the testament is broken;' but this paraphrase is too cumbrous to be retained when the expression occurs frequently.

1. Rumpitur autem testamentum cum in eodem statu manente testatore ipsius testamenti jus vitiatur. Si quis enim post factum testamentum adoptaverit sibi filium per

1. A testament is revoked when the testator still remaining in the same *status*, the effect of the testament is destroyed; for if, after making his testament, he arrogates a person *sui*

U

Imperatorem, eum, qui est sui juris, aut per prætorem secundum nostram constitutionem, eum qui in potestate parentis fuerit, testamentum ejus rumpitur quasi adgnatione sui heredis.

juris by licence from the emperor, or if, in the presence of the prætor, and by virtue of our constitution, he adopts a child under the power of his natural parent, then the testament would be revoked by this quasi-agnation of a suus heres.

GAI. ii. 138, and foll.

We have already seen how the rupture of the testament might be avoided by instituting or disinheriting posthumous children and *quasi-postumi*. But when a new *suus heres* came into the family by the civil agnation produced by adoption or arrogation, the stricter law of the time of Gaius pronounced that the testament was inevitably revoked. But in the times of the later jurists, if the new *suus heres* had been instituted by anticipation, the testament was considered as not revoked (D. xxviii. 2. 23), and it was only when he had been omitted or disinherited, that the rule making the testament of no effect was allowed to prevail. And Justinian seems here to countenance the opinion by omitting the word *omnimodo*, which Gaius adds to *rumpitur*.

2. Posteriore quoque testamento, quod jure perfectum est, superius rumpitur; nec interest, extiterit aliquis heres ex eo, an non; hoc enim solum spectatur, an aliquo casu existere potuerit. Ideoque si quis aut noluerit heres esse, aut vivo testatore aut post mortem ejus ante quam hereditatem adiret decesserit, aut conditione sub qua heres institutus est defectus sit, in his casibus paterfamilias intestatus moritur: nam et prius testamentum non valet ruptum a posteriore, et posterius æque nullas habet vires, cum ex eo nemo heres extiterit.

2. A former testament is equally revoked by a subsequent one made as the law requires, nor does it signify whether under the new testament any one becomes heir or not; the only question is, whether there could have been an heir under it: therefore, if an instituted heir renounces, or dies, either during the life of the testator, or after the testator's death, but before the heir can enter upon the inheritance, or if his interest terminates by the failure of the condition under which he was instituted—in any of these cases, the testator dies intestate: for the first testament is invalid, being revoked by the second, and the second is of as little force, as there is no heir under it.

GAI. ii. 144.

If the heir instituted in a second testament would have taken as *heres ab intestato*, the second testament, although it might be not formally made (*jure perfectum*), was still held valid, as an expression of the last will of the deceased, who died intestate indeed, but whose wishes were binding on the heir. (D. xxviii. 3. 2; C. vi. 23. 21. 3.)

The two modes mentioned in the text by which a testament could be revoked are the agnation of a *suus heres* and the making a subsequent testament.  But the testator could also revoke it by tearing or defacing it, or by signifying a wish to have it revoked before three witnesses, or by a formal deed, provided, in this last case, that ten years intervened between the making the testament and the testator's death.  Theodosius had enacted that a testament should be always invalid after ten years had expired from the time of its being made.  Justinian allowed testaments to remain valid for any length of time, but retained the effect of the lapse of time in the one case of the testator signifying his wish to have his testament revoked. (C. vi. 23. 27.)

When it is said that a subsequent testament to revoke a prior one must be regularly made, it must be understood that, in the case of soldiers, their privilege of making a testament in any way they pleased would permit them to revoke a prior testament by any testament that expressed their intentions.

3. Sed et si quis priore testamento jure perfecto, posterius æque jure fecerit, etiamsi ex certis rebus in eo heredem instituerit, superius testamentum sublatum esse divi Severus et Antoninus rescripserunt.  Cujus constitutionis verba inseri jussimus, cum aliud quoque præteres in ea constitutione expressum est.  'Imperatores Severus et Antoninus Cocceio Campano: Testamentum secundo loco factum, licet in eo certarum rerum heres scriptus sit, perinde jure valere ac si rerum mentio facta non esset; sed teneri heredem scriptum ut contentus rebus sibi datis, aut suppleta quarta ex lege Falcidia, hereditatem restituat his qui in priore testamento scripti fuerant, propter inserta verba secundo testamento, quibus ut valeret prius testamentum expressum est, dubitari non oportet.'  Et ruptum quidem testamentum hoc modo efficitur.

3. If any one, after having made a valid testament, makes another equally valid, although the heir is instituted therein for certain particular things only, yet as the Emperors Severus and Antoninus have decided by a rescript, the first testament is considered to be thereby destroyed.  We have ordered the words of this constitution to be here inserted, as it contains a further provision.  'The Emperors Severus and Antoninus to Cocceius Campanus : a second testament, although the heir named in it be instituted to particular things only, shall be as valid as if the things had not been specified, but unquestionably the heir instituted in the second testament must content himself either with the things given him, or with the fourth part, made up to him according to the *Falcidia lex*, and shall be bound to restore the rest of the inheritance to the heirs instituted in the first testament, on account of the words inserted in the second, by which it is declared, that effect shall be given to the first testament.'  This, therefore, is a mode in which a testament is revoked.

D. xxxvi. 1. 29.

It was not the *lex Falcidia*, but the *senatus-consultum*

*Peganianum,* by which this fourth was in such a case given to the heir. (See Tit. 23. 5.)

If the heir were instituted for a part only, *certæ res,* he would by law be instituted for the whole, as no one could die partly testate; but if in the second testament it were expressed that the first should be valid, this would be the same as imposing a *fideicommissum* on the heir under the second testament, the terms of the *fideicommissum* being contained in the first testament.

| | |
|---|---|
| 4. Alio quoque modo testamenta jure facta infirmantur, veluti cum is qui fecit testamentum, capite deminutus sit. Quod quibus modis accidat, primo libro retulimus. | 4. Testaments validly made are also invalidated in another way, viz. If the testator suffer a *capitis deminutio.* We have shown in the First Book under what circumstances this may happen. |

GAI. ii. 145.

As it was from his civil *status* that a testator's power of making a testament proceeded, any change in this was held to invalidate any exercise of the power made before the change.

| | |
|---|---|
| 5. Hoc autem casu irrita fieri testamenta dicuntur, cum alioquin et quæ rumpantur irrita fiant, et quæ statim ab initio non jure fiant irrita sunt, et ea quæ jure facta sunt et postea propter capitis deminutionem irrita fiunt, possumus nihilominus rupta dicere; sed quia sane commodius erat singulas causas singulis appellationibus distingui, ideo quædam non jure facta dicuntur, quædam jure facta rumpi vel irrita fieri. | 5. In such a case testaments are said to become ineffectual, although those which are revoked, or which, from the beginning, were not legally valid, may equally well be termed ineffectual. We may also term those testaments revoked, which, being at first legally made, are afterwards rendered ineffectual by a *capitis deminutio.* But, as it is more convenient to distinguish by different terms each cause that invalidates a testament, some are said to be irregularly made, and others, regularly made, to be revoked or rendered ineffectual. |

GAI. ii. 146.

Under *irrita testamenta,* we must include those which the jurisconsults termed *destituta, i. e.* abandoned, by no one entering on the inheritance.

| | |
|---|---|
| 6. Non tamen per omnia inutilia sunt ea testamenta, quæ ab initio jure facta propter capitis deminutionem irrita facta sunt. Nam si septem testibus signis signata sunt, potest scriptus heres secundum tabulas testamenti bonorum possessionem agnoscere, si modo defunctus et civis Romanus et suæ potestatis mortis tempore fuerit; nam si ideo irritum factum sit testamentum, | 6. But testaments at first validly made, and afterwards rendered ineffectual by a *capitis deminutio,* are not absolutely void; for if they have been attested by the seals of seven witnesses, the instituted heir can obtain possession of the goods according to the testament, provided that the testator was a Roman citizen, and was *sui juris* at the time of his death. For if a testament becomes void because |

quia civitatem vel etiam libertatem testator amisit, aut quia in adoptionem se dedit, et mortis tempore in adoptivi patris potestate sit, non potest scriptus heres secundum tabulas bonorum possessionem petere.

the testator has lost the right of a citizen, or his liberty, or because he has given himself in adoption, and at the time of his death was under the power of his adoptive father, then the instituted heir cannot demand possession of the goods according to the terms of the testament.

GAI. II. 147.

The meaning of the prætor giving the *bonorum possessio secundum tabulas* is, that he ordered that possession of the property should be given as the testator intended, though, by the rules of strict law, the testament in which he had expressed his intention was invalidated. The instance alluded to in the text is that of a testator, after making his testament, suffering a *capitis deminutio*, but returning to his old *status* before dying. In such a case the prætor gave the *bonorum possessio* as he did if a person, arrogated and then emancipated, expressly declared his wish to abide by his testament made before arrogation. (GAI. ii. 147.)

7. Ex eo autem solo non potest infirmari testamentum, quod postea testator id noluit valere: usque adeo ut, etsi quis post factum prius testamentum posterius facere cœperit, et aut mortalitate præventus, aut quia eum ejus rei pœnituit, non perfecerit, divi Pertinacis oratione cautum sit ne aliæ tabulæ priores jure factæ irritæ fiant, nisi sequentes jure ordinatæ et perfectæ fuerint; nam imperfectum testamentum sine dubio nullum est.

7. A testament cannot be invalidated solely because the testator is afterwards unwilling that it should take effect; so that, if any one, after making one testament, begins another, and then, being prevented by death, or from having changed his mind, does not complete it, it is decided in an address to the senate by the Emperor Pertinax, that the first testament shall not be revoked, unless the subsequent one is regularly made and complete, for an imperfect testament is undoubtedly null.

D. xxxiv. 4; C. vi. 23. 21. 3.

See note on paragraph 2.

8. Eadem oratione expressit, non admissurum se hereditatem ejus qui litis causa principem reliquerit heredem, neque tabulas non legitime factas in quibus ipse ob eam causam heres institutus erat probaturum neque ex nuda voce heredis nomen admissurum, neque ex ulla scriptura cui juris auctoritas desit aliquid adepturum. Secundum hæc divi quoque Severus et Antoninus sæpissime rescripserunt: licet enim

8. The emperor declared in the same address to the senate, that he would not accept the inheritance of any testator, who, on account of a suit, made the emperor his heir; that he would never make valid a testament legally deficient in form, if, in order to cover the deficiency, he himself was instituted heir; that he would not accept the title of heir, if he was instituted by word of mouth; and that he would never take anything by

(inquiunt) legibus soluti sumus, attamen legibus vivimus.

virtue of any writing wanting the authority of strict law. The Emperors Severus and Antoninus have also often issued rescripts to the same purpose: 'for although,' say they, 'we are above the laws, yet we live in obedience to them.'

D. xxxii. 23.

Testators occasionally made the emperor their heir, in order that their adversary in a lawsuit might have him to contend with.

An *oratio* was an address to the senate by the emperor, in which he explained to them what they were to enact; they then put his recommendations into the shape of a *senatus-consultum.*

## Tit. XVIII. DE INOFFICIOSO TESTAMENTO.

Quia plerumque parentes sine causa liberos suos exheredant vel omittunt, inductum est ut de inofficioso testamento agere possint liberi, qui queruntur aut inique se exheredatos aut inique praeteritos : hoc colore quasi non sanae mentis fuerint, cum testamentum ordinarent. Sed hoc dicitur non quasi vere furiosus sit, sed recte quidem fecerit testamentum, non autem ex officio pietatis; nam si vere furiosus sit, nullum testamentum est.

Since parents often disinherit their children, or omit them in their testaments, without any cause, children who complain that they have been unjustly disinherited or omitted, have been permitted to bring the action *de inofficioso testamento*, on the supposition that their parents were not of sane mind when they made their testament. This does not mean that the testator was really insane, but that the testament, though regularly made, is inconsistent with the duty of affection the parent owes. For, if a testator is really insane at the time, his testament is null.

D. v. 2. 2, 3. 5.

As we may gather from the text, a testament was termed *inofficiosum,* which was at variance with the dictates of natural affection, and those duties of near relationship which were expressed by the term *officium pietatis.* A presumption seemed to arise that the persons very closely connected with the testator, if passed over, must have done something to merit the testator's disapprobation. They might therefore naturally desire to have their character (*aestimatio*) protected against the imputations, and they therefore applied to the praetor to set the testament aside. A testament regularly and validly made, but liable to the objection that it was *inofficiosum,* was liable to be

set aside on the application of the children, or, if there were
no children, on that of the ascendants, or, if there were no
ascendants, on that of the brother or sister of the deceased,
the claim of these last, however, only prevailing where the
person instituted was *turpis.*

It is not known at what date the action *de inofficioso testamento* was first introduced. It is alluded to by Cicero (*In
Verr.* i. 42). It was brought before the *centumviri*, as were
all actions concerning inheritances, and if they pronounced
the testament '*inofficiosum,*' all its dispositions were set
aside, and the inheritance passed according to the succession
*ab intestato.* (See Introd. sec. 77.)

1. Non autem liberis tantum permissum est testamentum parentium
inofficiosum accusare, verum etiam
parentibus liberorum. Soror antem
et frater turpibus personis scriptis
heredibus ex sacris constitutionibus
praelati sunt; non ergo contra omnes
heredes agere possunt. Ultra fratres
igitur et sorores, cognati nullo modo
aut agere possunt, aut agentes vin-
cere.

1. It is not children only who are
allowed to attack the testaments of
their parents as inofficious. Parents
are also permitted to attack those of
their children. The brothers and
sisters of a testator, also, by the imperial constitutions, are preferred to
infamous persons, if any such have
been instituted heirs. Thus, then,
they cannot bring such an action
against any heir. Beyond brothers
and sisters no cognate can bring or
succeed in such an action at all.

C. iii. 28. 21. 27.

Before Justinian, brothers and sisters could only bring this
action while the tie of agnation was in existence. He permitted them to bring it *durante agnatione vel non* (C. iii.
28. 27), and thus made it sufficient that they should be merely
*consanguinei, i. e.* born of the same father. Subsequently, by
the 118th Novel, uterine brothers or sisters were placed on
the same footing as *consanguinei.*

2. Tam autem naturales liberi,
quam secundum nostrae constitutionis divisionem adoptati, ita
demum de inofficioso testamento
agere possunt, si nullo alio jure ad
defuncti bona venire possunt; nam
qui ad hereditatem totam vel
partem ejus alio jure veniunt, de
inofficioso agere non possunt. Postumi quoque qui nullo alio jure
venire possunt, de inofficioso agere
possunt.

2. But natural children, as well
as adopted (the distinction between
adopted children laid down in our
constitution being always observed),
can only attack the testament as inofficious, if they can obtain the effects
of the deceased in no other way : for
those who can obtain the whole or a
part of the inheritance by any other
means, cannot pursue this remedy.
Posthumous children, also, who are
unable to recover their inheritance
by any other method, are allowed
to bring this action.

D. v. 2. 6. 8. 15.

Those adopted by strangers could not impugn the testament of the adoptive father, if they were disinherited, or passed over, but those who were adopted by their ascendants could. This is the *divisio* here alluded to. (See Bk. i. Tit. 11. 2.)

The *actio de inofficioso testamento* was only a last resource open to those who had no other: a pupil, therefore, arrogated, and afterwards disinherited by the arrogator, could not bring this action, because he was entitled to the *quarta Antonina* (see Bk. i. Tit. 11. 2); nor, again, could an emancipated son, omitted in the testament of his father, because the praetor gave him possession of the goods *contra tabulas*. (See Tit. 13. 3.)

| | |
|---|---|
| 3. Sed hæc ita accipienda sunt, si nihil eis penitus a testatoribus testamento relictum est: quod nostra constitutio ad verecundiam naturæ introduxit. Sin vero quantacumque pars hereditatis vel res eis fuerit relicta, inofficiosi querela quiescente, id quod eis deest usque ad quartam legitimæ partis repleatur, licet non fuerit adjectum, boni viri arbitratu debere eam compleri. | 3. All this must be understood to take place only, when nothing has been left them by the testament of the deceased: a provision introduced by our constitution, out of respect for the rights of nature. For, if the least part of the inheritance, or any one single thing has been given them, they cannot bring an action *de inofficioso testamento*: but they must have made up to them one-fourth of what would have been their share, if the deceased had died intestate, supposing what is given does not amount to this fourth; and this, although the testator has not added to his gift any direction that this fourth is to be made up to them according to the estimate of a trustworthy person. |

C. iii. 28. 30, pr. and 1.

A *plebiscitum* was passed in the year 714 A.U.C., called the *lex Falcidia* (v. Tit. 22), which provided that one clear fourth of the inheritance must remain to the heir, and that legacies and trusts could only affect three-fourths. Either from the analogy of this law, or by some express enactment, it was decided that every one who was near enough in blood to the testator to bring the action *de inofficioso*, might bring it, though mentioned in the testament, unless one-fourth were thereby given him of what he would have received in a succession *ab intestato*. This fourth part was spoken of under different names. Sometimes it was itself termed the *Falcidia* (*Solam eis Falcidiam debitæ successionis relinquant*, Cod. Theod. xvi. 7. 28). Sometimes it is spoken of as the *portio legibus debita*, or *portio legitima* (C. iii. 28. 28), and commentators have called it simply the *legitima*.

Before the time of Justinian (Cod. Theod. ii. 19. 4), unless

a testator either expressly gave this fourth, or gave a direction
that such an additional share of the goods should be added
to that actually given, as some trustworthy person, who should
make an estimate of the value of all the goods of the deceased,
should consider would be necessary to make what was given
equal to the fourth, the testament could be attacked and set
aside as inofficious; but Justinian altered the law on this point,
and enacted that if the testator gave anything at all, the action
*de inofficioso* could not be brought, but only an action to
obtain what was wanting to make up the fourth, while the
testament itself remained valid. (C. iii. 28. 30.) There were
considerable differences between the action to make up what
was wanting to the fourth part (*actio in supplementum legitimæ*) and that *de inofficioso*: the former was a personal
action, there was no limit to the time in which it was to be
brought, it was transmissible to the heirs of the person who
could bring it, and it left the testament valid; the latter was a
real action, was obliged to be brought within a certain time
(see note to paragr. 6), could not be transmitted to the heirs,
unless the person entitled to bring it had manifested an intention to do so, and if it was successfully brought, the testament was set aside.

| | |
|---|---|
| 4. Si tutor nomine pupilli cujus tutelam gerebat, ex testamento patris sui legatum acceperit, cum nihil erat ipsi tutori relictum a patre suo, nihilominus poterit nomine suo de inofficioso patris testamento agere. | 4. If a tutor accepts in the name of the pupil under his charge a legacy given in the testament of the tutor's own father, while nothing has been left to the tutor himself by his father's testament, he may nevertheless in his own name attack the testament of his father as inofficious. |

D. v. 2. 10. 1.

To accept a legacy was to acquiesce in the validity of the
testament; but it was reasonable that a tutor, who had an
unavoidable duty to perform towards his pupil, should not be
personally bound by an act done in his capacity as tutor.

| | |
|---|---|
| 5. Sed et d e contrario pupilli nomine cui nihil relictum fuerit, de inofficioso egerit et superatus est, ipse tutor quod sibi in eodem testamento legatum relictum est, non amittit. | 5. Conversely, if a tutor, in the name of his pupil, to whom nothing has been left, attacks as inofficious the testament of his pupil's father, and attacks it unsuccessfully, he does not lose anything that may have been left himself in the same testament. |

D. v. 2. 30. 1.

Any heir who attacked a testament as inofficious, unsuccess-
fully, forfeited to the *fiscus* whatever was given him by the
testament.

6. Igitur quartam quis debet habere, ut de inofficioso testamento agere non possit, sive jure hereditario sive jure legati vel fideicommissi, vel si mortis causa ei donata quarta fuerit, vel inter vivos in iis tantummodo casibus quorum mentionem facit nostra constitutio, vel aliis modis qui constitutionibus continentur. Quod autem de quarta diximus, ita intelligendum est ut, sive unus fuerit sive plures quibus agere de inofficioso testamento permittitur, una quarta eis dari possit, ut pro rata eis distribuatur, id est, pro virili portione quarta.

6. That a person should be debarred from bringing the action de inofficioso testamento, it is necessary that be should have a fourth, either by hereditary right, or by a legacy, or a fideicommissum, or by a donatio mortis causa, or a donatio inter vivos in the cases mentioned in our constitution, or by any of the other means set forth in the constitutions. What we have said of the fourth must be understood as meaning that, whether there be one person only or several, who can bring an action de inofficioso testamento, only one-fourth is to be distributed among all proportionally, that is, each is to have the fourth of his proper share.

D. v. 2. 8. 6. 8; D. v. 2. 25; C. iii. 28–30. 2.

If the *donatio inter vivos* had been made on the express condition that it should be reckoned as part of the *quarta legitima* (D. v. 2. 25; C. iii. 28. 35), or had been advanced for the purchase of a military rank (C. iii. 28. 30), then it was taken into account in estimating how much the recipient was entitled to as his fourth; but, generally speaking, as it was the receipt of the fourth of that which a person would have received *ab intestato* that excluded him from bringing the action *de inofficioso*, the right to this action could not be taken away by the receipt of gifts, which, having been made *inter vivos*, could not have formed part of the inheritance *ab intestato*.

The words, *vel aliis modis*, &c., refer to *dotes*, and to *donationes propter nuptias* (C. iii. 28. 29 : C. vi. 20. 20, 1), which were taken into account in reckoning the amount due as the *portio legitima*.

The right to the action *de inofficioso* might be extinguished, (1) by the person entitled to the *quarta legitima* dying without having manifested an intention to dispute the testament: if he had done so, the right to the action passed to his heirs (D. v. 2. 6. 2); (2) if he had allowed a time fixed first at two and subsequently at five years (Cod. Theod. ii. 19. 5), to elapse without bringing the action; and (3) when he had acquiesced directly or indirectly in the testament; as, for instance, by making a contract with the persons instituted, in their capacity as heirs (D. v. 2. 20. 1), or by a demand against those persons for the payment of a legacy, or by desisting in the action when once brought. (D. v. 2. 8. 1.)

Justinian in his Novels introduced considerable changes in the law on these points. First, if those entitled to the *portio legitima* were more than four in number, they no longer took a fourth but a half; if less than four, then they took a third. (Nov. 18. 1.) Secondly, those who could claim a *portio legitima* were required to be made heirs, and it was no longer permitted to give them their portion by a legacy or trust. (Nov. 115. 3. 4.) Thirdly, if the testament were declared inofficious, it was only the institution of the heir or heirs that was to be set aside; the trusts, legacies, gifts of liberty, and appointments of tutors were to remain good. (Nov. 115. 4. 9.) And, fourthly, Justinian fixed and specified the reasons, limiting them to fourteen, for any one of which a testator might disinherit or omit his descendants, or ascendants; the one on which the testator had acted was to be expressly stated. (Nov. 115. 3.)

## Tit. XIX. DE HEREDUM QUALITATE ET DIFFERENTIA.

Heredes autem aut necessarii dicuntur, aut sui et necessarii, aut extranei.

Heirs are said to be *necessarii, sui et necessarii,* or *extranei.*

GAI. ii. 152.

1. Necessarius heres est servus heres institutus; ideo sic appellatus quia, sive velit sive nolit, omnimodo post mortem testatoris protinus liber et necessarius heres fit. Unde qui facultates suas suspectas habent, solent servum suum primo aut secundo aut etiam ulteriore gradu heredem instituere; ut si creditoribus satis non fiat, potius ejus heredis bona quam ipsius testatoris a creditoribus possideantur, vel distrahantur, vel inter eos dividantur. Pro hoc tamen incommodo illud ei commodum praestatur, ut ea quae post mortem patroni sui sibi acquisierit, ipsi reserventur; et quamvis bona defuncti non suffecerint creditoribus, iterum ex ea causa res ejus, quas sibi acquisierit, non veneunt.

1. A necessary heir is a slave instituted heir; and he is so called, because, whether he wish or not, at the death of the testator he becomes instantly free, and necessarily heir; he, therefore, who suspects that he is not in solvent circumstances, commonly institutes his slave to be his heir in the first, second, or some more remote place; so that, if he does not leave a sum equal to his debts, it may be the goods of this heir and not those of the testator himself, that are seized or sold by his creditors, or divided among them. But to compensate for this inconvenience, a slave enjoys the advantage of having reserved to him whatever he has acquired after the death of his patron; for although the goods of the deceased should be insufficient for the payment of his creditors, yet property so acquired by the slave is not on that account made the subject of a further sale.

GAI. II. 153-155; D. xlii. 0. 1. 17.

The sale of goods for the payment of debts, brought on the debtor an ignominy which was more than a matter of opinion, and had legal effects (GAI. ii. 154), and which a testator was, therefore, very anxious his memory should escape.

The *heres necessarius* was legally bound by all the debts of the deceased; but the prætor made a change in the strict law, and permitted the goods of the deceased to be distinctly separated from the possessions of the *heres necessarius*, if the *heres necessarius* demanded, before in any way interfering with the goods of the deceased, that this separation should take place. When it did take place, the creditors could only recover from him the amount of what actually came into his hands as heir, while he could deduct from the inheritance all that was due to him, himself, or that he had acquired after the demand was made. (D. xlii. 6. 1. 18.)

This *beneficium separationis*, the right to have the goods of the heir separated from those of the testator, was sometimes accorded in favour of the creditors of the testator. The heir might be insolvent, and then it was for their interest, that the testator's property should be kept distinct. (D. xlii. 6. 1. 17.)

If the reading, *iterum ex ea causa*, is to be retained, we must either construe *iterum* as 'further,' or with Du Caurroy make the passage mean, 'become the subject of a second sale, after the goods of the testator are disposed of.' There is another reading, *tamen ex alia causa*, instead of *iterum ex ea causa*.

2. Sui autem et necessarii heredes sunt, veluti filius, filia, nepos neptisve ex filio et deinceps ceteri liberi, qui modo in potestate morientis fuerint. Sed ut nepos neptisve sui heredes sint, non sufficit eum eamve in potestate avi mortis tempore fuisse; sed opus est ut pater ejus vivo patre suo desierit suus heres esse, aut morte interceptus aut qualibet alia ratione liberatus potestate; tunc enim nepos neptisve in locum patris sui succedit. Sed sui quidam heredes ideo appellantur, quia domestici heredes sunt, et vivo quoque patre quodammodo domini existimantur: unde etiam si quis intestatus mortuus sit, prima causa est in successione liberorum. Necessarii vero ideo dicuntur, quia omnimodo sive velint sive nolint, tam ab intestato quam ex testamento heredes fiunt;

2. Heirs are *sui et necessarii*, when they are, for instance, a son, a daughter, a grandson or granddaughter, by a son or other direct descendants, provided they are in the power of the deceased at the time of his death. That grandchildren should be *sui heredes*, it is not enough that they were in the power of their grandfather at the time of his decease, but it is also requisite, that their father should have ceased to be a *suus heres* in the life-time of his father, having been either cut off by death, or otherwise freed from paternal authority; for then the grandson or granddaughter succeeds in place of their father. *Sui heredes* are so called because they are family heirs, and, even in the life-time of their father, are considered owners of the inheritance in a certain degree. Hence, in case of

sed his pretor permittit volentibus abstinere se ab horeditate, ut potius parentis quam ipsorum bona similiter a creditoribus possideantur.

a person dying intestate, his children are first in succession. They are called necessary heirs, because, whether they wish or not, whether under a testament or in a succession *ab intestato*, they become heirs. But the pretor permits them to abstain from the inheritance if they wish, that if possession is taken of the goods of the deceased by his creditors, the goods may be not theirs, but those of their parent.

GAI. ii. 156-158.

There is no difficulty in understanding either who were *sui heredes*, or what was the position they occupied with reference to the inheritance. If the *paterfamilias* had had no power of making a testament, those persons in his power, who became *sui juris* at his death would necessarily have had the inheritance at his decease; they were in a manner, as the text says, owners during his lifetime of the inheritance, which must actually come into their possession at his death. And, although testaments were allowed to alter the legal succession, the rights of those who had this interest in the inheritance were so far guarded that it was necessary expressly to disinherit them in order to deprive them of their interest; while, on the other hand, if the testator appointed any one of them as his heir, he was considered thereby to exercise his *patria potestas*, so that the *suus heres* could not exercise any option as to accepting or refusing the inheritance, and was a *heres necessarius*, exactly as he was if he succeeded *ab intestato* until the prætor interfered to enable him to escape the burden. In every case the *suus heres* took the inheritance or his share in it, and without any act or exercise of his own will; if he were insane or beneath the age of puberty, no authority was needed to enable him to accept it, and he never had to enter formally on an inheritance that belonged to him immediately the *paterfamilias* died, unless he was instituted by the *paterfamilias* only conditionally, and then the inheritance belonged to him immediately on the condition being fulfilled. If the grandson, instituted while his father was disinherited, was in the power of the deceased at the time of his death, he became *suus heres et necessarius*, but becoming, on the testator's death, in the power of his own father, immediately placed his father in the position he himself occupied—*patrem suum sine aditione heredem fecit et quidem necessarium.*

Commentators are divided on the question whence the term *suus heres* arose. Why was such an heir termed *suus*? There are two modes of accounting for the term : one, which this passage, borrowed from Gaius, seems to countenance, and which Cujacius first brought forward in his notes to this passage, makes *sui heredes* mean persons who took an inheritance that was their own, who were heirs not of the *paterfamilias*, but of themselves, and being, as Cujacius expresses it by a Greek equivalent, αὐτοκληρονόμοι, took what thus belonged to them already, and only received possession of that over which they had always had a kind of ownership. As the *hereditas* might, with regard to them, have been termed especially and properly *sua*, so they themselves were termed *sui heredes*. The other opinion, which is sanctioned by the authority of Papinian (D. xxxviii. 6. 7), who says, if a grandson whose father was dead, *suus heres erit, cum et ipse fuerit in potestate*, refers the origin of the term to the common and well-known usage of *suus*, as a person in the power of the *paterfamilias*. The *sui heredes* were those who united the characters of *sui*, that is, were in the power of the *paterfamilias*, and were his *heredes*, which no one could have been who was not *sui juris* at the time of the death of the *paterfamilias*, as the *hereditas* would have immediately passed from them to the person in whose power they were. The latter origin of the term seems the more probable.

As the text informs us, the prætor interposed to prevent its being in every case obligatory on the *suus heres* to accept the inheritance ; he was only treated as an heir if he intermeddled with the inheritance ; and until he had in some way shown his intention of doing so, the prætor refused to permit any action to be brought against him as *suus heres* by the creditors of the deceased. The *beneficium abstinendi*, as this power of abstaining was termed, differed from the *beneficium separationis*, accorded to slaves, by no express demand being necessary, as it always existed in the absence of express intention to accept the inheritance, and also by its being a protection to the *suus heres* against all actions whatever brought against him in his capacity of heir, while the slave was liable to the amount of the property of the deceased.

The *suus heres* who had availed himself of this privilege, did not thereby cease to be heir. He could afterwards accept the inheritance if the goods were not sold by the creditors. (D. xxviii. 8. 8.)

| | |
|---|---|
| 3. Ceteri qui testatoris juri subjecti non sunt, extranei heredes appellantur: itaque liberi quoque nostri qui in potestate nostra non sunt, heredes a nobis instituti, extranei | 3. All those who are not subject to the power of the testator, are termed *extranei heredes*: thus, children, not within our power, whom we institute heirs, are *extranei heredes*. So, |

heredes videntur. Qua de causa et qui heredes a matre instituuntur, eodem numero sunt, quia feminae in potestate liberos non habent. Servus quoque heres a domino institutus et post testamentum factum ab eo manumissus, eodem numero habetur.

too, are children, instituted heirs by their mother, for a woman has not her children under her power. A slave also, whom his master has instituted by testament and afterwards manumitted, is considered a *heres extraneus*.

GAI. ii. 101.

4. In extraneis heredibus illud observatur, ut sit cum eis testamenti factio, sive ipsi heredes instituuntur, sive hi qui in potestate eorum sunt; et id duobus temporibus inspicitur, testamenti quidem facti ut constiterit institutio, mortis vero testatoris ut effectum habeat. Hoc amplius et cum adierit hereditatem, esse debet cum eo testamenti factio, sive pure sive sub conditione heres institutus sit; nam jus heredis eo vel maxime tempore inspiciendum est, quo acquirit hereditatem. Medio autem tempore inter factum testamentum et mortem testatoris vel conditionem institutionis existentem, mutatio juris non nocet heredi; quia, ut diximus, tria tempora inspicimus. Testamenti autem factionem non solum is habere videtur qui testamentum facere potest, sed etiam qui ex alieno testamento vel ipsi capere potest vel alii acquirere, licet non possit facere testamentum. Et ideo furiosus et mutus et posthumus et infans et filiusfamilias et servus alienus testamenti factionem habere dicuntur: licet enim testamentum facere non possint, attamen ex testamento vel sibi vel alii acquirere possunt.

4. As to *extranei heredes*, the rule is, that the testator must have *testamenti factio* with them, whether they are instituted heirs themselves, or whether those under their power are instituted. And this is required at two several times: at the making of the testament, that the institution may be valid, and at the testator's death, that it may take effect. Further, at the time of entering upon the inheritance, *testamenti factio* ought still to exist with the heir, whether he is instituted simply or conditionally; for his capacity as the heir is principally regarded at the time of acquiring the inheritance. But in the interval between the making of the testament and the death of the testator, or the accomplishment of the condition of the institution, the heir will not be prejudiced by change of status; because it is the three points of time which we have noted that are to be regarded. Not only is a man who can make a testament said to have *testamenti factio*, but also any person who under the testament of another can take for himself, or acquire for another, although he cannot himself make a testament; and therefore insane and dumb persons, posthumous children, infants, sons in power, and slaves belonging to others, are said to have *testamenti factio*. For although they cannot make a testament, yet they can acquire by testament either for themselves or others.

D. xxviii. 5, 49, 1; D. xxviii. 1, 16, 1.

The necessity for the heir having *testamenti factio* at the time of the making of the testament proceeded from the ancient mode of making testaments. When, in the *calata comitia*, the testator orally announced who it was on whom he wished his legal existence, his *persona*, to devolve after his

death, the person designated could not have accepted the
devolution unless he had been in the enjoyment of those rights
of citizenship implied in the *testamenti factio*; and when testaments were made *per æs et libram*, it was equally necessary
that the purchaser, that is, the heir, should have those rights
of citizenship which would enable him to go through a sale by
mancipation.

It will be observed that the text says that it was immaterial
whether the heir preserved his *testamenti factio* between the
two periods of the making the testament and the death of the
testator; if he lost it between the two later epochs, viz. the
death of the testator and the entrance on the inheritance, he
could not take, and it would not avail him that he had recovered
it at the time of entering on the inheritance. (D. xxviii. 2. 29. 5.)

The classes mentioned in the concluding portion of this
paragraph might have the rights of citizenship, and only be
accidentally prevented from exercising those rights.

| | |
|---|---|
| 5. Extraneis autem heredibus de-liberandi potestas est de adeunda hereditate val non adeunda. Sed sive is cui abstinendi potestas est, immiscuerit se bonis hereditatis, sive extraneus cui de adeunda hereditate deliberare licet, adierit, postea relinquendæ hereditatis facultatem non habet, nisi minor sit viginti quinque annis; nam hujus ætatis hominibus, sicut in ceteris omnibus causis, deceptis, ita et si temere damnosam hereditatem susceperint, prætor succurrit. | 5. *Extranei heredes* may deliberate whether they will enter upon the inheritance. But, if one, who has the liberty of abstaining, intermeddles with the property of the inheritance, or an *extraneus heres*, who is permitted to deliberate, enters on the inheritance, it will not afterwards be in his power to renounce the inheritance, unless he shall be under the age of twenty-five years; for the prætor, as in all other cases he relieves minors who have been deceived, so too he does when they have rashly taken upon themselves a burdensome inheritance. |

Gai. ii. 162, 163.

There was no fixed time within which it was necessary that
the heir should decide whether to accept or reject the inheritance, excepting when the testator fixed the time himself by
what was termed *cretio*. (See note to paragr. 7.) Those who
were interested in his making a decision could compel him by
action to do so, and the prætor then, if he wished, allowed him
time to deliberate, never less than one hundred days. Justinian
decides that the time given should not exceed nine months, or,
as a special favour from the emperor, a year. If he did not
decide within the appointed time, he was taken to have rejected
the inheritance, if the action to compel a decision was brought
by substituted heirs or a *heres ab intestato*; to have accepted
it, if the action was brought by legatees or creditors. If he

died before the expiration of the time, and within a year of the
first commencement of his right to enter on the inheritance, his
heir could, during the unexpired remainder of the time, decide
in his place.  (D. xxviii. 2. 28; Cod. vi. 30. 19.)

The mode by which the prætor interfered for the protection
of minors was called the *restitutio in integrum*.  (See Bk. i.
Tit. 23. 2.)

6. Sciendum tamen est divum Ha-
drianum etiam majori viginti quinque annis veniam dedisse, cum post
aditam hereditatem grande æs alienum, quod aditæ hereditatis tempore latebat, emersisset. Sed hoc
quidem divus Hadrianus cuidam
speciali beneficio præstitit; divus
autem Gordianus postea in militibus
tantummodo hoc extendit. Sed nostra benevolentia commune omnibus
subjectis Imperio nostro hoc beneficium præstitit, et constitutionem
tam æquissimam quam nobilem
scripsit, cujus tenorem si observaverint homines, licet eis et adire
hereditatem, et in tantum teneri
quantum valere bona hereditatis
contingit: ut ex hac causa neque
deliberationis auxilium eis fiat necessarium, nisi omissa observatione
nostræ constitutionis, et deliberan-
dum existimaverint, et sese veteri
gravamini aditionis supponere ma-
luerint.

6. The Emperor Hadrian, however,
once gave permission to a person of
full age, to relinquish an inheritance,
when it appeared to be encumbered
with a great debt, which had been
unknown at the time that he had
entered on the inheritance. But this
was granted as a special favour. The
Emperor Gordian afterwards extended this as a settled privilege, but
only to soldiers. But we in our goodness have rendered this benefit common to all our subjects, having dic-
tated a constitution as just as it is
illustrious, by which, if heirs will attend to its provisions, they may enter
upon their inheritance, and not be
liable beyond the value of the estate;
so that they need not have recourse
to deliberation, unless, neglecting to
conform to our constitution, they
prefer to deliberate, and submit
themselves to the liabilities attending the entering on the inheritance
under the old law.

Gal. ii. 163; C. vi. 30. 22.

Commentators have termed the privilege alluded to here the
*beneficium inventarii*.  Within thirty days after the heir became acquainted with his rights, an inventory of the property
might be begun, which was to be finished within ninety days
from the same time. This inventory was to be made in presence
of a *tabellio*, or public notary, and of any parties interested
who might wish to be present, or else of three witnesses.

If the heir chose to avail himself of this privilege, he entirely separated the estate of the testator from his own; he
could deduct anything that might be owing to him from it, and
had to pay to it anything he might owe.   He first paid the
expenses of the funeral and of the inventory, and then all the
creditors in the order they sent in their claims.  If there was
any surplus, he took it; if any deficiency, he was not liable.
(Cod. vi. 30. 22.)

x

7. Item extraneus heres testamento institutus, aut ab intestato ad legitimam hereditatem vocatus, potest aut pro herede gerendo aut etiam nuda voluntate suscipiendæ hereditatis heres fieri. Pro herede autem gerere quis videtur, si rebus hereditariis tamquam heres utatur vel vendendo res hereditarias vel prædia colendo locandove et quoquo modo, si voluntatem suam declaret vel re vel verbis de adeunda hereditate: dummodo sciat eum in cujus bonis pro herede gerit, testatum intestatumve obiisse et se ei heredem esse. Pro herede enim gerere est pro domino gerere; veteres enim heredes pro dominis appellabant. Sicut autem nuda voluntate extraneus heres fit, ita et contraria destinatione statim ab hereditate repellitur. Eum qui surdus vel mutus natus est, vel postea factus, nihil prohibet pro herede gerere et acquirere sibi hereditatem, si tamen intelligit quod agitur.

7. A stranger, instituted by testament, or called by law to a succession *ab intestato*, may become heir, either by doing some act as heir, or even by the mere wish to accept the inheritance. And a man acts as heir if he treat any of the goods of the Inheritance as his own, by selling any part, or by cultivating the ground, or letting it, or in any other way declare, either by act or word, his intention to enter on the inheritance, provided only that he knows that the person, with respect to whose estate he acts as heir, is dead, testate or intestate, and that he himself is the heir; for to act as heir is to act as proprietor; and the ancients frequently used the term heir to denote the proprietor. But as a stranger may become heir by a mere intention, so, on the contrary, by a contrary intention, he is at once barred from the inheritance. Nothing prevents a person, who was born deaf and dumb, or subsequently became so, from acting as heir, and acquiring the inheritance, if only he knows what he is doing.

GAI. II. 106, 107. 160; D. xxix. 2. 5.

Besides the two modes of entering on the inheritance here mentioned, namely, forming an intention to do so, and doing some act as heir, there was a mode, abolished by a constitution of Arcadius, Honorius, and Theodosius (A.D. 407), called *cretio*. *Cretio appellata est, quia cernere est quasi decernere et constituere.* (GAI. ii. 164.) The testator himself, in his will, fixed the time within which the heir was to decide whether he would accept the inheritance. Generally the time was made to run from the period when the heir became acquainted with his rights, and this was called the *cretio vulgaris*; sometimes from that when the rights accrued to him, and this was called the *cretio continua.* The heir could alter his decision at any time within the limited period. His decision was expressed, when made, by forms more solemn than when the *aditio* was made by a simple declaration of intention. (v. GAI. *in loc. cit.*) The heir was said *adire hereditatem* whenever he in any way entered on the inheritance, whether by doing some act as heir (*pro herede gerere*) or by the mere intention to be heir (*nuda voluntate*). Of course this intention would be manifested in some way or other; but it was the formation, not the expression, of the intention that constituted the entrance on the inheritance. Properly speaking, one person could not enter on an inheritance for another; but there were necessarily exceptions, such as that a tutor might accept an inheritance in behalf of his infant pupil. No one could enter on part of the inheritance, nor could he enter conditionally, or for a certain time. Directly he did enter, he was clothed with the *persona* of the deceased, whom he represented as if he had succeeded immediately on his death. (D. xlix. 2. 54.)

## Tit. XX. DE LEGATIS.

Post hæc videamus de legatis. Quæ pars juris extra propositam quidem materiam videtur, nam loquimur de iis juris figuris quibus per universitatem res nobis acquiruntur; sed cum omnino de testamentis deque hæredibus qui testamento instituantur, locuti sumus, non sine causa sequenti loco potest hæc juris materia tractari.

GAI. ii. 191.

We will now proceed to treat of legacies. This part of the law may not seem to fall within our present subject, namely, the discussion of those methods by which things are acquired *per universitatem*; but, as we have already spoken of testaments and testamentary heirs, we may not improperly pass to the subject of legacies.

A legacy, being a mode by which the property in one or more particular things is acquired, ought not, properly, to be discussed in the part of the Institutes devoted to the discussion of the modes of acquiring a *universitas rerum.*

In Roman law a legacy was an injunction given to the heir to pay or give over a part of the inheritance to a third person —*Legatum, quod legis modo id est imperativo, testamento relinquitur.* (ULP. *Reg.* 24. 1.) Without an heir there could be no legacy; and, therefore, if no instituted heir entered on the inheritance, the gift of the legacy was useless. The term was never applied, as in English law, to a direct bequest.

1. Legatum itaque est donatio quædam a defuncto relicta.

D. xxxi. 36.

1. A legacy is a kind of gift left by a deceased person.

2. Sed olim quidem erant legatorum genera quatuor, per vindicationem, per damnationem, sinendi modo, per præceptionem; et certa quædam verba cuique generi legatorum adsignata erant, per quæ singula genera legatorum significabantur. Sed ex constitutionibus divorum principum solemnitas hujusmodi

2. Formerly, there were four kinds of legacies, namely, *per vindicationem, per damnationem, sinendi modo,* and *per præceptionem.* There was a certain form of words proper to each of these, by which they were distinguished one from another. But these solemn forms have been wholly suppressed by imperial constitutions.

verborum penitus sublata est. Nostra autem constitutio, quam cum magna fecimus lucubratione, defunctorum voluntates validiores esse cupientes, et non verbis sed voluntatibus eorum faventes, disposuit ut omnibus legatis una sit natura, et quibuscumque verbis aliquid derelictum sit, liceat legatariis id persequi, non solum per actiones personales, sed etiam per in rem et per hypothecariam. Cujus constitutionis perpensum modum ex ipsius tenore perfectissime accipere possibile est.

We also, desirous of giving respect to the wishes of deceased persons, and regarding their intentions more than their words, have, by a constitution composed with great study, enacted that the nature of all legacies shall be the same; and that legatees, whatever may be the words employed in the testament, may sue for what is left them, not only by a personal, but by a real or an hypothecary action. The wisdom of this constitution may be easily seen by a perusal of its dispositions.

GAI. ii. 192, 193. 201. 209. 210; C. vi. 37. 21; C. vi. 43. 1.

*Per vindicationem.* The formula in this species of legacy ran thus: ' *Hominem Stichum do, lego,*' or ' *do*'; or ' *capito, sumito, sibi habeto.*' The legacy was said to be *per vindicationem*, because, immediately on the heir entering on the inheritance, the subject of the legacy became the property of the legatee *ex jure Quiritium*, who could accordingly claim it by *vindicatio.* The testator could only give, in this way, things of which he had the *dominium ex jure Quiritium*, both at the time of making the testament and of his death; excepting that such *dominium* at the time of death alone was sufficient when the subject of the legacy was anything appreciable by weight, number, or measure, as wine, oil, money, &c. (GAI. ii. 196.)

*Per damnationem.* The formula ran thus: ' *Heres meus damnas esto dare;*' or ' *Dato, facito, heredem meum dare jubeo.*' The legatee did not, by this legacy, become proprietor of the subject of the legacy; but he had a personal action against the heir to compel him to give (*dare*), to procure (*praestare*), or to do (*facere*), that which the terms of the legacy directed. Anything could be given by this legacy that could become the subject of an obligation, whether the property of the testator, the heir, or any one else. The rights it gave were, therefore, said to be the *optimum jus legati.* (ULP. *Reg.* 24. 11; GAI. ii. 204–208.)

*Sinendi modo.* The formula of this kind of legacy was: ' *Heres meus damnas esto sinere Lucium Titium sumere illam rem sibique habere.*' (GAI. ii. 209.) The heir is to allow the legatee to take the thing given. This form, then, was applicable to anything that belonged to the testator or to the heir, but not to anything belonging to a third person. The legatee did not become the owner of the thing given until he took possession. If the heir refused to allow the legatee to take possession, the legatee might compel him to do so by the personal action termed '*Quicquid heredem ex testamento dare facere oportet.*' (GAI. ii. 213. 214.)

*Per præceptionem.* The formula ran : '*Lucius Titius illam rem præcipito*' (i.e. take beforehand). The proper application of this form was to a gift made to one already instituted heir, of something which he was to take before receiving his share of the inheritance. The heir could enforce his claim to this something beyond his share by the action termed *judicium familiæ erciscundæ, i.e.* for having the inheritance portioned out by a judge, who assigned the thing given by the legacy to the heir as legatee. It was only by a mistake in language that this form was applied to a gift to a person not an heir; but a gift made in this form to a person not heir was not void; for the *senatus-consultum Neronianum*, about A.D. 60, made every such legacy valid as a legacy *per damnationem*. Gaius mentions that the Proculians attempted to get over the difficulty where the word *præcipito* was used to give a legacy to a person not heir, by reading '*præcipito*' as '*capito*;' and this construction was confirmed by a constitution of Adrian. (GAI. ii. 218–221.)

Under the imperial legislation the value attached to these *formulæ* was gradually lessened. By the *senatus-consultum Neronianum* it was enacted that any legacy given in a form of words not suited to the gift intended should be as valid as one given in the form most favourable to the legatee. '*Ut quod minus aptis verbis legatum est perinde sit ac si optimo jure legatum esset.*' (ULP. Reg. 24. 11 ; GAI. ii. 197. 218.) The *formulæ* remained, but a mistake in their use could no longer injure the legatee : and in every case the legacy, however expressed, had the effect of a legacy given *per damnationem*. In A.D. 342 a constitution of Constantine II., Constantius, and Constans, abolished the use of *formulæ* in all legal acts. (C. ii. 58. 1.) The division of legacies still theoretically remained, but the appropriate *formulæ* were no longer in use. Finally, Justinian, as we see in the text, enacted that all legacies should be of the same nature, and that the legatee might enforce the legacy by personal, real, or hypothecary actions, according to the nature of the gift.

3. Sed non usque ad eam constitutionem standum esse existimavimus : cum enim antiquitatem invenimus legata quidem stricte concludentem, fideicommissis autem quæ ex voluntate magis descendebant defunctorum, pinguiorem naturam indulgentem, necessarium esse duxi-

3. We have not, however, judged it expedient to confine ourselves within the limits of this constitution ; for, observing that the ancients confined legacies within strict rules, but accorded a greater latitude to *fideicommissa* as arising more immediately from the wishes of the deceased, we

mus omnia legata fideicommissis
exæquare, ut nulla sit inter ea differentia ; sed quod deest legatis, hoc
repleatur ex natura fideicommissorum, et si quid amplius est in legatis, per hoc crescat fideicommissorum natura. Sed ne in primis
legum cunabulis permixte de his
exponendo studiosis adolescentibus
quamdam introducamus difficultatem, operæ pretium esse duximus
interim separatim prius de legatis et
postea de fideicommissis tractare, ut
natura utriusque juris cognita facile
possint permixtionem eorum eruditi subtilioribus auribus accipere.

have thought it necessary to make
all legacies equal to gifts in trust, so
that no difference really remains between them. Whatever is wanting
to legacies they will borrow from
*fideicommissa*, and communicate to
them any superiority they themselves
may have. But, that we may not
raise difficulties, and perplex the
minds of young persons at their entrance upon the study of the law, by
explaining these two subjects jointly,
we have thought it worth while to
treat separately, first of legacies and
then of trusts, that, the nature of
each being known, the student thus
prepared, may more easily understand them when mixed up the one
with the other.

C. vi. 43. 2.

All that remained, after the changes noticed in the text, to
distinguish legacies from *fideicommissa*, was the general character of the expressions used. If they were imperative, the
gift was a legacy ; if they assumed the form of a request, and
were given *precative*, they were *fideicommissa*. If a gift was
in form imperative, but it was not valid as a legacy, it was valid
as a trust. If such a gift could be valid as a legacy, it was of
course regarded as a legacy, and not as a *fideicommissum*.

A difference still remained with respect to the gifts of liberty
to a slave. (Vid. Tit. 24. 2.) A direct legacy of liberty made
the slave the *libertus* of the testator ; a gift of liberty by a
*fideicommissum* made the slave the *libertus* of the *fideicommissarius*.

1. Non solum autem testatoris vel
heredis res, sed etiam aliena legari
potest, ita ut heres cogatur redimere
eam et præstare ; vel, si non potest
redimere, æstimationem ejus dare.
Sed si talis res sit cujus non est commercium, nec æstimatio ejus debetur, sicuti si Campum Martium vel
basilicas vel templa, vel quæ publico
usui destinata sunt, legaverit ; nam
nullius momenti legatum est. Quod
autem diximus alienam rem posse
legari, ita intelligendum est, si defunctus sciebat alienam rem esse,
non et si ignorabat ; forsitan enim
si scisset alienam, non legasset. Et
ita divus Pius rescripsit : et verius
esse, ipsum qui agit, id est legatarium, probare oportere scisse alienam
rem legare defunctum, non heredem

4. A testator may not only give as
a legacy his own property, or that of
his heir, but also the property of
others. The heir is then obliged
either to purchase and deliver it, or,
if it cannot be bought, to give its
value. But, if the thing given is not
in its nature a subject of commerce,
or purchasable, the heir is not bound
to pay the value to the legatee ; as if
a man should bequeath the Campus
Martius, the palaces, the temples, or
any of the things appropriated to
public purposes, for such a legacy is
of no effect. But when we say that
a testator may give the goods of
another as a legacy, we must be
understood to mean, that this can
only be done if the deceased knew
that what he bequeathed belonged to

probare oportere ignoraese alienam, quia semper necessitas probandi incumbit illi qui agit.

another, and not if he were ignorant of it ; since, if he had known it, he would not perhaps have left such a legacy. To this effect is a rescript of the Emperor Antoninus, which also decides that it is incumbent upon the plaintiff, that is, the legatee, to prove that the deceased knew that what he left belonged to another, not upon the heir to prove that the deceased did not know it, for the burden of proof always lies upon the person who brings the action.

GAI. ii. 202 ; D. xxx. 30. 7. 10 ; D. xxxi. 67. 8 ; C. vi. 37. 10 ; D. xxii. 3. 21.

5. Sed et si rem obligatam creditori aliquis legaverit, necesse habet heres luere. Et hoc quoque casu idem placet quod in re aliena, ut ita demum luere necesse habeat heres, si sciebat defunctus rem obligatam esse; et ita divi Severus et Antoninus rescripserunt. Si tamen defunctus voluit legatum luere et hoc expressit, non debet heres eam luere.

5. If a testator gives as a legacy anything in pledge to a creditor, the heir is bound to redeem it. But in this case, as in that of the property of another, the heir is not bound to redeem it, unless the deceased knew that the thing was pledged ; and this the Emperors Severus and Antoninus have decided by a rescript. But when it has been the wish of the deceased that the legatee should redeem the thing, and he has expressly said so, the heir is not bound to redeem it.

D. xxx. 5. 7.

6. Si res aliena legata fuerit, et ejus vivo testatore legatarius dominus factus fuerit, siquidem ex causa emptionis, ex testamento actione pretium consequi potest ; si vero ex causa lucrativa, veluti ex causa donationis vel ex alia simili causa, agere non potest: nam traditum est, duas lucrativas causas in eumdem hominem et in eamdem rem concurrere non posse. Hac ratione, si ex duobus testamentis eadem res eidem debeatur, interest utrum rem an aestimationem ex testamento consecutus sit : nam si rem, agere non potest, quia habet eam ex causa lucrativa ; si aestimationem, agere potest.

6. If a thing belonging to another be given as a legacy, and become the property of the legatee in the lifetime of the testator, then, if it become so by purchase, the legatee may recover the value, by an action founded on the testament ; but if the legatee obtained it by any way of clear gain to him, as by gift, or any similar mode, he cannot bring such an action, for it is a received rule, that two modes of acquiring, each being one of clear gain, can never meet in the same person with regard to the same thing. If, therefore, the same thing be given by two testaments to the same person, it makes a difference, whether the legatee has obtained the thing itself, or the value of it, under the first, for, if he has already received the thing itself, he cannot bring an action, for he has received it by a mode of clear gain to him ; but, if he has received the value only, he may bring an action.

D. xxx. 108 ; D. xliv. 7. 17 ; D. xxx. 34. 2.

It may be observed, that if a person acquired the subject of a legacy by a *causa lucrativa* during the lifetime of the testator, and the legacy was made, not in his own favour directly, but was given to his slave, or a descendant in his power, he could recover the value of the thing given from the heir.  In such a case the two *causæ lucrativæ* were not considered so to unite in one person as to violate the general rule, although, in fact, the result was the same as if the rule had been directly violated.  (D. xxx. 108.)

In the beginning of this paragraph it is said that if the legatee acquire the thing during the lifetime of the testator by a *causa lucrativa*, he could not regain it or its value by legacy.  The *vivo testatore* is merely an example ; it would be the same if the legatee acquired the thing by a *causa lucrativa* at any time before receiving it by way of legacy.

7. Ea quoque res quæ in rerum natura non est, si modo futura est, recte legatur : veluti fructus qui in illo fundo nati erunt, aut quod ex illa ancilla natum erit.

7. A thing not in existence, but which one day will be in existence, may be properly given as a legacy, as, for instance, the fruits which shall grow on such a farm, or the child which shall be born of such a slave.

Gai. ii. 203.

8. Si eadem res duobus legata sit sive conjunctim sive disjunctim, si ambo perveniant ad legatum, scinditur inter eos legatum ; si alter deficiat, quia aut spreverit legatum, aut vivo testatore decesserit, vel alio quolibet modo defecerit, totum ad collegatarium pertinet. Conjunctim autem legatur, veluti si quis dicat, Titio et Seio hominem Stichum do lego ; disjunctim ita, Titio hominem Stichum do lego, Seio Stichum do lego. Sed et si expresserit eumdem hominem Stichum, æque disjunctim legatum intelligitur.

8. If the same thing is given as a legacy to two persons, either conjointly or separately, and both take the legacy, it is divided between them. But should either of the legatees fail to take it, either from refusing it or from dying in the lifetime of the testator, or from any other reason, the whole goes to his co-legatee. A legacy is given conjointly, if a testator say, I give as a legacy my slave Stichus to Titius and Seius : but separately, if he say, I give as a legacy my slave Stichus to Titius ; I give as a legacy my slave Stichus to Seius.  And if the testator say, that he gives the same slave Stichus, yet the legacy is still taken to be given separately.

Gai. ii. 199.

A legacy might be void originally, when it was said to be taken *pro non scripto*, i.e. as if it had never been inserted ; or it might be valid originally, and yet before the rights of the legatee were fixed (i.e. to use the technical term (see note on paragr. 20), before the *dies cedit*) the legatee might die or refuse the legacy, or become incapable to take, when the legacy was called *irritum* or *destitutum* ; or the rights of the legatee

might be fixed, but before the legacy was actually delivered
over to him, it might be taken away from him on account of
something rendering him unworthy to receive it; the legacy
was then called *ereptitium* (*quæ ut indignis eripitur*).  If
there were no co-legatees, the legacy, if *ereptitium*, went to
the *fiscus*; in the two other cases the failure of the legacy was
for the benefit of the heir.   The legacies were burdens with
which he might have been, but was not, charged.

But if there was a co-legatee the case was different.  Co-legatees might be created, according to a division made by Paulus
(D. 1. 16, 142), *re, re et verbis*, or *verbis*; *re* being equivalent
to the *disjunctim* of the text, when the same gift was made
separately to two or more persons; *re et verbis*, equivalent to
the *conjunctim* of the text, when the same thing was given at
once to two or more; and *verbis*, in which the joint legacy was
only apparent, the gift being made at once to two or more, but
their respective shares being assigned them, as '*lego Titio et
Seio ex æquis partibus.*'

The rights of co-legatees were very different at different
periods of Roman law.  Originally the interest of the co-legatee
was determined by the formula under which the legacy was
given.  If it were *per vindicationem*, the right to the property
in the whole thing given passed to each legatee.  They might
divide it between them, but this was for their own convenience.
They each had, in the eye of the law, the whole.   If it were
given *per damnationem*, no right to the property passed, but
each legatee was a creditor of the heir in respect of the thing
given.  Accordingly each co-legatee could recover from the heir
the whole of the thing given, or its value in money. (*Singulis
solida res debebitur.*   Gai. ii. 205.)   Before the *lex Papia
Poppæa* there was no such thing as accrual of legacies between
co-legatees; each legatee was entitled to the property in the
whole thing, or was creditor for the whole.  When the legacy
was *per vindicationem*, it made a difference in fact, whether his
co-legatee took or not, but not in law, as in any case the law
considered him to have the whole legacy (*in solidum habuit*);
if it were given *per damnationem*, it made no difference in law
or fact, for each legatee was creditor for the whole.

The *lex Papia Poppæa* introduced a new system.  It took
away the legacies of the unmarried and the childless, and gave
them to those who were fathers and married.   No one could
take as heir or legatee who was unmarried (*cælebs*) or childless
(*orbus*).  At the same time the *dies cedit*, as it was called, that is,
the time when the rights were fixed (see note to paragr. 20) was
thrown forwards from the date of the testator's death to that

of the opening of the testament. Thus many legacies fell to
the ground ; they became *caduca*, and were diverted from the
course intended by the testator. *Quod quis sibi testamento
relictum, ita ut jure civili carpere possit, aliqua ex causa non
ceperit caducum appellatur, veluti ceciderit ab eo.* (ULP.
*Reg.* 17. 1.) The term *caduca* was strictly applied only to
these lapses of legacies caused by the provisions of the *lex
Papia Poppæa*, but was subsequently used for the failure of
any testamentary disposition. Failures in legacies, occasioned
by any of the rules of the civil law, and not by the *lex Papia
Poppæa*, were said to be *in causa caduci*, and were subjected
by that law to the same rules as governed the *caduca*. These
*caduca* were given, in the first place, to co-legatees having
children; but by a distinction, based apparently on no very good
reason, it was only those joined *re et verbis*, and those joined
*verbis*, who were considered co-legatees for this purpose;
those joined *re* were not. If there were no co-legatees with
children, the legacies went to the heir who had children.     If
there were none, then to legatees generally who had children.
If none had children, then to the *fiscus*. Any legacy given by
the *lex Papia Poppæa* might be refused : if accepted, it passed
with all the burdens attaching to it. *Caduca cum suo onere
fiunt.* (ULP. *Reg.* 17. 2.) The *lex Papia Poppæa* excepted
from its provisions the descendants and ascendants of the testator to the third degree, and left them *jus antiquum in caducis*
(ULP. *Reg.* 18) ; i. e. they were subject to the old rules of the
civil law. Legacies which were originally void did not come
within the scope of this law.

By a constitution of Caracalla (ULP. *Reg.* 17. 2), all *caduca*
were at once given to the *fiscus*, and no legatee or heir any
longer profited by the failure of legacies under the *lex Papia
Poppæa*.

Constantine abolished the law of incapacity arising from
celibacy. (Cod. viii. 58.) And Justinian did away with all
the law of *caduca* springing out of the *lex Papia Poppæa*.
The distinction between the kinds of legacies being no longer
in existence, new provisions on the subject were made. (C. vi.
51. 11.) The right to bring a real action was to attach to
every legacy ; and co-legatees were placed in the position they
would have occupied before the *lex Papia Poppæa* : but it was
enacted that in every case of a gift to a co-legatee falling, an
accrual should take place to the other, or others joined with
him. If they were joined *re*, the accrual was said to be
obligatory on those conjoined; but the burdens of the legacy
did not pass with it. Really there was no accrual at all ; the

co-legatees were in the same position as if the gift had only been made to one. If the co-legatees were joined *re et verbis*, the accrual was voluntary, but the burdens of the legacy passed with it. The co-legatees were looked upon as having really distinct interests, and, therefore, if the gift to one failed, the others had something to receive. But, at the same time, they took the share they gained, with all its burdens; it might, for instance, be encumbered with a *fideicommissum*. Legatees joined only *verbis* were not, properly speaking, co-legatees at all, and Justinian does not permit any accrual between them. There was thus a clear distinction made between legacies given jointly to legatees *re et verbis* and those given *verbis*. In both distinct interests were in effect given to all the legatees; but in the former case these interests were so united, that, through the failure of the legacy of one legatee, his interest accrued to those joined with him.

If the rights of a co-legatee were once fixed, then even if he died before he received his legacy, the accrual on any failure still took place for his benefit, or rather that of his representatives, and was said to be given to his *pars* or share. (D. vii. 1. 33. 1.)

| | |
|---|---|
| 9. Si cui fundus alienus legatus fuerit, et emerit proprietatem deducto usufructu, et usufructus ad eum pervenerit, et postea ex testamento agat, recte eum agere et fundum petere Julianus ait, quia usufructus in petitione servitutis locum obtinet; sed officio judicis continetur, ut deducto usufructu jubeat æstimationem præstari. | 9. If a testator give as a legacy land belonging to another, and the legatee purchase the bare ownership, and the usufruct comes to him, and he afterwards brings an action under the testament, Julian says that an action claiming the land is well brought, because, in this claim, the usufruct is regarded as a servitude only. It is the duty of a judge, in this case, to order the value of the property, deducting the usufruct, to be paid. |

D. xxx. 82. 2, 3; D. 1. 10. 25.

A *fundus*, or landed estate, is left by legacy; the legatee buys the naked ownership, but receives by a *causa lucrativa* (this is expressed by *pervenerit*) the usufruct. He is, of course, entitled to receive the value of what he has bought, but not of that which has already come to him by a *causa lucrativa*. Supposing he wishes to recover by action the value of the naked ownership from the heir, he can only demand exactly that which was given him by the testament. He, therefore, asks for the *fundus*; but the *fundus* includes both the naked ownership and the usufruct. Will he not, then, be asking too much, and thus fail in his action from what was termed *plus petitio*? (See Bk. iv. Tit. 6. 33.) Julian answers that he will not, because in every demand of a *fundus*, the plaintiff must necessarily ask for it, subject to all its servitudes. Usufruct was a servitude, and, therefore, in demanding the *fundus* from the heir, he does not demand the usufruct, if the *fundus* be subject to such a servitude.

10. Sed si rem legataril quis ei legaverit, inutile est legatum, quia quod proprium est ipsius amplius ejus fieri non potest; et licet alienaverit eam, non debetur nec ipsa nec æstimatio ejus.

10. If a testator give as a legacy anything that already belongs to the legatee, the legacy is useless; for what is already the property of a legatee cannot become more so. And, although the legatee has parted with the thing bequeathed, he would not be entitled to receive either the thing itself or its value.

D. xxx. 41. 2.

*Et licet alienaverit eam.* This is an application of what was called the rule of Cato, *regula Catoniana* (perhaps Cato Major), viz. *Quod, si testamenti facti tempore decessisset testator, inutile foret, id legatum quandocumque decesserit non valere* (D. xxxiv. 7. 1), i. e. a legacy invalid when the testament was made, could never become valid.

11. Si quis rem suam quasi alienam legaverit, valet legatum; nam plus valet quod in veritate est, quam quod in opinione. Sed et si legatarii putavit, valere constat, quia exitum voluntas defuncti potest habere.

11. If a testator give a thing belonging to himself, as if it were the property of another, the legacy is valid; for its validity is decided by what is the real state of the case, not by what he thinks. And if the testator imagine that what he gives belongs already to the legatee, yet, if it do not, the legacy is certainly valid, because the wish of the deceased can thus take effect.

D. xl. 2. 4. 1.

The words '*plus valet quod,*' &c., are not the statement of a general rule of law, but merely of what happens under the particular circumstances alluded to. Under other circumstances, exactly the opposite is laid down. Ulpian says, for instance, that a person thinking himself a *necessarius heres*, but really not being so, could not repudiate the inheritance, *Nam plus est in opinione quam in veritate*. (D. xxix. 2. 15.)

12. Si rem suam legaverit testator, postemque eam alienaverit, Celsus existimat, si non adimendi animo vendidit, nihilominus deberi; idemque divi Severus et Antoninus rescripserunt. Iidem rescripserunt eum qui, post testamentum factum, prædia quæ legata erant pignori

12. If a testator give his own property as a legacy, and afterwards alienate it, it is the opinion of Celsus that the legatee is entitled to the legacy, if the testator did not sell with an intention to revoke the legacy. The Emperors Severus and Antoninus have published a rescript

dedit, ademisse legatum non videri; et ideo legatarium cum berede agere posse, ut prædia a creditore luantur. Si vero quis partem rei legatæ alienaverit, pars quæ non est alienata ommimodo debetur; pars autem alienata ita debetur, si non adimendi animo alienata ait.

to this effect. And they have also decided by another rescript, that if any person, after making his testament, pledge immoveables which he has given as a legacy, be is not to be taken to have thereby revoked the legacy; and that the legatee may, by bringing an action against the heir, compel him to redeem the property. If, again, a part of the thing given as a legacy be alienated, the legatee is of course still entitled to the part which remains unalienated, but is entitled to that which is alienated only if it appear not to have been alienated by the testator with the intention of taking away the legacy.

GAI. ii. 108; D. xxxii. 11, 12; C. vi. 37. 3; D. xxx. 8.

Gaius informs us that the opinion confirmed by Severus and Antoninus was not that generally entertained when he wrote. When the legacy was given *per vindicationem*, it seemed impossible that if the thing were alienated the legatee could take anything ; and even if it were *per damnationem*, though there was nothing in the nature of the legacy to prevent the legatee making a valid claim (*licet ipso jure debeatur legatum*), it was considered that he might be repelled by an exception, because he would be acting against the wishes of the deceased. (GAI. ii. 198.)

13. Si quis debitori suo liberationem legaverit, legatum utile est, et neque ab ipso debitore neque ab herede, ejus potest berea, petere, nec ab alio qui heredis loco est; sed et potest a debitore conveniri, ut liberet eum. Potest autem quis vel ad tempus jubere ne heres petat.

13. If a testator gives as a legacy to his debtor a discharge from his debt, the legacy is valid, and the heir cannot recover the debt from the debtor, his heir, or any one in the place of his heir. The debtor may by action compel the heir to free him from his obligation. A man may also forbid his heir to demand payment of a debt during a certain time.

The debt was not extinguished by the legacy of *liberatio*. But if the heir sued the debtor, then the debtor could repel him by the plea of fraud (*exceptione doli mali*), and, if the debtor wished, he could, by suing under the testament, compel the heir to release the debt, by consent only, if the obligation had been made in that manner, by *acceptilatio*, i. e. by the heir acknowledging the receipt of the thing owed (See Bk. iii. Tit. 29. 1), if it had not.

A legacy of a discharge from debt might be made indirectly by giving as a legacy to the debtor the *chirographum*, or bond by which he was bound. (D. xxxiv. 3. 3. 1, 2.)

*Vel ad tempus.* The effect of such a legacy was, that if the heir sued the legatee before the time had expired, he could be repelled by an exception of *dolus malus.*

14. Ex contrario si debitor creditori suo, quod debet, legaverit, inutile est legatum, si nihil plus est in legato quam in debito, quia nihil amplius habet per legatum. Quod si in diem vel sub conditione debitum ei pure legaverit, utile est legatum propter repraesentationem. Quod si viro testatore dies venerit vel conditio extiterit, Papinianus scripsit utile esse nihilominus legatum, quia semel constitit: quod et verum est; non enim placuit sententia existimantium extinctum esse legatum, quia in eam causam pervenit a qua incipere non potest.

14. On the contrary, a legacy given by a debtor to his creditor of the money which he owes him, is ineffectual if it includes nothing more than the debt did, for the creditor thus receives no benefit from the legacy. But if a debtor give absolutely as a legacy to his creditor what was due only on the expiration of a term, or on the accomplishment of a condition, the legacy is effectual, because it thus becomes due before the debt. Papinian decides, that if the term expire, or the condition is accomplished, in the lifetime of the testator, the legacy is nevertheless effectual, because it was once good; which is true. For we may reject the opinion that a legacy once good, can afterwards become extinct, because circumstances have arisen which would have prevented its being originally valid.

D. xxxv. 2. 1. 10; D. xxxv. 2. 5; D. xxxi. 82.

The legacy would generally be more advantageous than the debt, on account of the actions that might be brought on it.

15. Sed si uxori maritus dotem legaverit, valet legatum, quia plenius est legatum quam de dote actio. Sed si quam non accepit dotem legaverit, divi Severus et Antoninus rescripserunt, si quidem simpliciter legaverit, inutile esse legatum; si vero certa pecunia vel certum corpus aut instrumentum dotis in praelegando demonstrata sunt, valere legatum.

15. If a man give as a legacy to his wife her marriage-portion, the legacy is valid, for the legacy is more beneficial than the action she might maintain for the recovery of her portion. But, if he bequeath to his wife her marriage-portion, which he has never actually received, the Emperors Severus and Antoninus have decided by a rescript, that if the portion be given without any specification, the legacy is void; but if in the terms of the gift a particular sum or thing, or a certain sum mentioned in the act of dowry, be specified as to be received as a legacy before it could be received as dowry, the legacy is valid.

D. xxxiii. 41. 2. 7, 8.

In the *de dote,* or, as it was otherwise called, the *rei uxoriae actio,* certain delays in the restitution of the dowry were permitted; and sums expended for the improvement of the property of the wife might be set off against the claim. The legacy had to be paid without delay, and no set-off was admissible. It was from the dowry being thus restored, when made the subject of a legacy, sooner than when the action was brought, that the expression *prælegare dotem* was used; the *dos* was given by legacy (*legare*) sooner (*præ*) than it could otherwise be obtained.

By the words '*certa pecunia*,' &c., is meant that if the testator said, 'I give to my wife the sum she brought me as dowry,' and she had not brought anything, the legacy would be useless; but if he said, 'I give her the 100 *aurei* she brought me,' then the words referring to her having brought them would be only a *falsa demonstratio*, that is, an unnecessary particularity of expression, which would be passed over as if not written.

*Instrumentum dotis.* So, if the testator said, 'I give the property mentioned in the act of dowry,' if there were no act of dowry, the gift would be useless; but if he said, 'I give such or such a particular thing mentioned in the act of dowry,' if there were no act of dowry, the wife would receive the thing specified, and the words, 'mentioned in the act of dowry,' would be treated as superfluous.

16. Si res legata sine facto heredis perierit, legatario decedit; et si servus alienus legatus sine facto heredis manumissus fuerit non tenetur heres. Si vero heredis servus legatus fuerit, et ipse eum manumiserit, teneri eum Julianus scripsit, nec interest utrum scierit an ignoraverit a se legatum esse; sed et si alli donaverit servum, et is cui donatus est eum manumiserit, tenetur heres, quamvis ignoraverit a se eum legatum esse.

16. If a thing given as a legacy perish without the act of the heir, the loss falls upon the legatee. And, if the slave of another, given as a legacy, should be manumitted without the act of the heir, the heir is not answerable. But if a testator give as a legacy the slave of his heir, who afterwards manumits that slave, Julian says that the heir is answerable, whether he knew or not that the slave was given away from him as a legacy. And it would be the same if the heir had made a present of the slave to any one who had enfranchised him: the heir, though ignorant of the legacy, would be answerable.

D. XXX. 35. 1; D. XXX. 112. 1.

The *factum* of the heir means anything by which, however innocently, he may have been the cause of the thing perishing, &c.

17. Si quis ancillas cum suis natis legaverit, etiamsi ancillæ mortuæ fuerint, partus legato cedunt. Idem

17. If a testator bequeath his female slaves and their offspring, although the mothers die, the issue

est, si ordinarii servi cum vicariis legati fuerint; et licet mortui sint ordinarii tamen vicarii legato cedunt. Sed si servus cum peculio fuerit legatus, mortuo servo vel manumisso vel alienato et peculii legatum extinguitur. Idem est, si fundus instructus vel cum instrumento legatus fuerit; nam fundo alienato et instrumenti legatum extinguitur.

goes to the legatee. And so, if ordinary slaves are bequeathed together with vicarial, although the ordinary slaves die, yet the vicarial slaves will pass by virtue of the gift. But, where a slave is bequeathed with his *peculium*, and afterwards dies, or is manumitted, or alienated, the legacy of the *peculium* becomes extinct. It is the same if the testator gives as a legacy, land ' provided with instruments,' or ' with its instruments of culture.' If the land is alienated, the legacy of the instruments of culture is extinguished.

D. xxxiii. 8. 1. 3; D. xxxiii. 7. 1, pr. and 1.

An *ordinarius servus* was a slave who had a special office in the establishment, as cook, barber, baker, &c. The *vicarii* were his attendants, and were generally reckoned as part of his *peculium*. But in the case of this legacy, the law considered them as having an independent existence (*propter dignitatem hominis*), and not merely as accessories to the *ordinarii*. So, the children of the female slaves are not treated as mere accessories to her. Had they been so, they could not have passed without the principal to which they were attached.

*Fundus instructus* is land, with everything on it, whether for use or ornament; *fundus cum instrumento*, land, with the instruments of its culture only.　(D. xxxiii. 7. 12. 27.)

18. Si grex legatus fuerit posteaque ad unam pervenerit, quod superfuerit vindicari potest. Grege autem legato, etiam eae oves quae post testamentum factum gregi adjiciuntur, legato cedere Julianus ait; est enim gregis unum corpus ex distantibus capitibus, sicut aedium unum corpus est ex cohaerentibus lapidibus.

18. If a flock is given as a legacy, and it be afterwards reduced to a single sheep, the legatee can claim what remains: and if a flock be given as a legacy, any sheep that may be added to the flock after the making of the testament, will, according to Julian, pass to the legatee. For a flock is one body, consisting of several different heads, as a house is one body, composed of several stones joined together.

D. xxx. 21, 22.

19. Aedibus denique legatis, columnas et marmora quae post testamentum factum adjecta sunt, legato dicimus cedere.

19. So, when a building is given as a legacy, any marble or pillars which may be added after the testament is made, will pass by the legacy.

D. xxxi. 30.

20. Si peculium legatum fuerit, sine dubio quicquid peculio accedit vel decedit vivo testatore, legatarii

20. When the *peculium* of a slave is given in a legacy, it is certain that if it is increased or diminished in

lucro vel damno est. Quod si post mortem testatoris ante aditam hereditatem servus acquisierit, Julianus ait, siquidem ipsi manumisso peculium legatum fuerit, omne quod ante aditam hereditatem acquisitum est, legatario cedere, quia hujus legati dies ab adita hereditate cedit; sed si extraneo peculium legatum fuerit, non cedere ea legato, nisi ex rebus peculiaribus auctum fuerit. Peculium autem, nisi legatum fuerit, manumisso non debetur; quamvis, si vivus manumiserit, sufficit si non adimatur, et ita dixi Severus et Antoninus rescripserunt. Iidem rescripserunt, peculio legato non videri id relictum, ut petitionem habeat pecuniæ quam in rationes dominicas impendit. Iidem rescripserunt peculium videri legatum cum rationibus redditis liber esse jussus est, et ex eo reliqua inferre.

the life of the testator, it is so much gained or lost to the legatee. And if the slave acquires anything between the death of the testator and the time of the heir entering on the inheritance, Julian makes this distinction: If it be to the slave himself that the *peculium*, together with his enfranchisement is given, then all that is acquired before the heir entering on the inheritance goes to the legatee, for the right to such a legacy is not fixed until the inheritance be entered on. But if it is to a stranger that the *peculium* is given, then anything acquired within the period above-mentioned will not pass by the legacy, unless the acquisition were made by means of something forming part of the *peculium*. This *peculium* does not go to a slave manumitted by testament, unless expressly given; although, if a master in his lifetime manumit his slave, it is enough if he do not expressly take it away from him; and to this effect is the rescript of the Emperors Severus and Antoninus, who have also decided, that when his *peculium* is given as a legacy to a slave, this does not entitle him to demand what he may have expended for the use of his master. The same emperors have further decided, that a slave is entitled to his *peculium* when the testator says he shall be free as soon as he has brought in his accounts, and made up any deficiency out of his *peculium*.

D. xxxii. 65; D. xxxiii. 8. 8. 8; D. xxxiii. 8. 0. 4; D. xxxiii. 8. 8. 7; D. xv. 1. 53.

*Dies cedit*, 'the day begins,' and *dies venit*, 'the day is come,' are the two expressions in Roman law which signify the vesting or fixing of an interest, and the interest becoming a present one. *Cedere diem* (says Ulpian, D. L. 16. 213), *significat incipere deberi pecuniam; venire diem, significat eum diem venisse, quo pecunia peti potest. Cedit dies* may, therefore, be translated, 'the right to the thing is fixed;' *venit dies*, 'the thing may be demanded.' For instance, if A buys a horse of B, without any terms being attached to the purchase, the right of B in the purchase-money is fixed at once, and also he may at once demand it, *et cessit et venit dies*. If A agrees

Y

that the purchase-money shall be paid by instalments, then, *dies cessit*, B has a fixed interest in the money ; but the *dies* can only be said *venisse*, as each instalment falls due, and with regard only to the portion becoming due.   If, again, A only buys it on condition that C will lend him the money, then until C has done so, *neque cessit neque venit dies*, B has no fixed interest in, or right to, the purchase money until the condition is accomplished.   With regard to legacies, the *dies cedit*, the time at which the eventual rights of the legatee were fixed, was the day of the testator's death, excepting when the vesting or fixing of these rights was suspended by a condition in the testament itself.   The *dies venit*, the time when the thing given could be demanded, was not till the heir entered on the inheritance, and there was thus some one of whom to make the demand ; if the legacy was given after a term, or on a condition, the demand, of course, could not be made (*dies non venit*) until the term had expired, or the condition was fulfilled.

An alteration was made by the *lex Papia Poppæa* in fixing the *dies cedit* at the day when the testament was opened, not at that when the testator died (see note to paragr. 8) ; but this had been done away with, and the old law was in force under Justinian.   (C. vi. 51. 1. 1.)

The legatee had the thing given exactly as it was at the time of the *dies cedit*.   He took it, with all the gains and losses that had accrued to it since the date of the testator's death, and directly his rights were fixed, they were transmissible to his heirs.

But if a testator gave his liberty to one of his slaves as a legacy, there was in this case an exception to the rule that the *dies cedit* dates from the death of the testator.   If the gift of liberty was given to a slave as a legacy, he could not begin to acquire for his own benefit until an heir had entered on the inheritance, as it was requisite there should be some one to free him.   The *peculium*, therefore, if given to him, would be such as it was when the heir entered on the inheritance ; while, if the *peculium* were given to a stranger, it would be such as it was at the death of the testator, excepting when the *peculium* was augmented by things derived from itself (*ex rebus peculiaribus*), as, for instance, if sheep or cattle, forming part of the *peculium*, had young.

There was another case, that of personal servitudes, in which the *dies cedit* dated from the entrance on the inheritance, not from the death of the testator.   These servitudes were exclusively attached to the person of the legatee,

and as they were not transmissible to his heirs, there could
be no interest in them until the actual enjoyment of them
was commenced.

The terms of the second rescript alluded to in the text are
given by Ulpian. (D. xxxiii. 8. 6. 4.) When the master enfranchised his slave himself, he was present to demand the
*peculium*, and if he did not, it was considered evident that he
intended the slave to keep it. Not so in a legacy of liberty, in
giving which the master might so easily forget the *peculium*
that some expressions were required to show that he remembered it, and wished to give it to the slave.

| | |
|---|---|
| 21. Tam antem corporales res legari possunt, quam incorporales; et ideo quod defuncto debetur, potest alicui legari, ut actiones suas heres legatario præstet, nisi exegerit vivus testator pecuniam; nam hoc casu legatum extinguitur. Sed et tale legatum valet: Damnas esto heres domum illius reficere vel illum ære alieno liberare. | 21. Things corporeal and incorporeal may be equally well given as a legacy. Thus, the testator may give a debt due to him, and the heir is then obliged to use his actions for the benefit of the legatee, unless the testator in his lifetime exacted payment, for in this case the legacy would become extinct. Such a legacy as this is also good: let my heir be bound to rebuild the house of such a one, or to free him from his debts. |

D. xxx. 41; D. xxx. 39. 3. 4.

The legacy of a debt due to the testator was usually called
*legatum nominis.* (See D. xxx. 44. 6.) Of course the legatee
could not sue for it, he could only compel the heir to sue for
his benefit.

| | |
|---|---|
| 22. Si generaliter servus vel res alia legetur, electio legatarii est, nisi aliud testator dixerit. | 22. If a testator give a slave or anything else as a legacy, without specifying a particular slave or thing, the choice belongs to the legatee, unless the testator has expressed the contrary. |

The jurists took care to lay down, with respect to what was
called a *legatum generis*, that the class of objects must not be
one too wide. *Legatum nisi certæ rei sit, et ad certam personam deferatur, nullius est momenti.* (Paul. Sent. iii. 6.
13.) For instance, the gift of 'an animal' would have seemed
rather intended to mock than to benefit the legatee, *magis
derisorium quam utile videtur.* (D. xxx. 7.)

Before Justinian, it depended on the formula with which the
legacy was given whether the choice of the particular thing to
be given to the legatee belonged to the heir or the legatee. In
a legacy *per vindicationem* it belonged to the latter; there was
a real action for a thing which must have formed part of the
testator's actual estate. In a legacy *per damnationem* it be

Y 2

longed to the heir; there was only a personal action against
the heir as debtor, and the debtor might discharge the obligation in the way most beneficial to himself. (ULP. *Reg.* 24. 14.)

23. Optionis legatum, id est, ubi
testator ex servis suis vel aliis rebus
optare legatarium jusserat, habebat
in se conditionem; et ideo, nisi ipse
legatarius vivus optaverit, ad heredem legatum non transmittebat. Sed
ex constitutione nostra et hoc ad
meliorem statum reformatum est, et
data est licentia heredi legatarii optare, licet vivus legatarius hoc non
fecit. Et diligentiore tractatu habito, et hoc in nostra constitutione additum est, ut sive plures legatarii
existant quibus optio relicta est, et
dissentiant in corpore eligendo, sive
unius legatarii plures heredes et inter se circa optandum dissentiant,
alio aliud corpus eligere cupiente, ne
pereat legatum (quod plerique prudentium contra benevolentiam in-
troducebant), fortunam esse hujus
optionis judicem, et sorte hoc even-
dirimendum, ut ad quem evenerint,
illius sententia in optione praecellat.

23. The legacy of election, that is,
when a testator directs his legatee
to choose any one from among his
slaves, or any other class of things,
was formerly held to imply a condition, so that if the legatee in his
lifetime did not make the election,
he did not transmit the legacy to his
heir. But, by our constitution, we
have altered this for the better, and
the heir of the legatee is now permitted to elect, although the legatee
in his lifetime has not done so. And,
pursuing the subject still further, we
have added, that if there be several
legatees to whom an option is left,
and they differ in their choice, or if
there be many heirs of one legatee,
and they cannot agree what to choose,
then to prevent the legacy becoming
ineffectual, which the generality of
ancient lawyers, contrary to all equity
decided would be the case, fortune
must be the arbitress of the choice,
and the dispute must be decided by
lot, so that his choice, to whom the
lot falls, shall prevail.

D. xl. 9. 3; D. xxxvi. 2. 12. 6; C. vi. 43. 3.

When once the *dies cedit* had fixed the rights of the legatee,
he could transmit to his heirs all the rights he had himself.
To this the Roman lawyers considered the *legatum optionis*
an exception, as intended to be personal to the legatee himself.
Justinian decides that the exception shall not exist. (C. vi.
43. 3.) We must distinguish the *legatum generis*, when an
object, though an uncertain one, was given, from the *legatum
optionis*, where only the right to select an object was given.
The former was never treated as an exception to the general
rule of the *dies cedit.*

24. Legari autem illis solis potest,
cum quibus testamenti factio est.

24. A legacy can be given to those
only, with whom the testator has
*testamenti factio.*

D. xli. 8. 7.

We have already said (Tit. 14. 2) that the necessity of having
the rights of citizenship in order to make, to witness, or to
profit by a testament, excluded all *peregrini.* But even among

those who were otherwise in a position to take as heirs or legatees, there were some who at different periods were specially precluded :

*First*, the *Latini Juniani* (see Bk. i. Tit. 5. 3.) could not be appointed tutors by testament, nor could they benefit at all by a testament, unless they had the full rights of citizenship at the time of the testator's death, or acquired them within a hundred days after his decease. (GAI. i. 23 ; ULP. *Reg.* 17. 1. and 22. 2.)

*Secondly*, by the *lex Voconia* (585 A.U.C.), the general object of which was to prevent the accumulation of large sums in the hands of women, no woman could be instituted by a person rated in the census as possessing a fortune of 100,000 asses. (GAI. ii. 274.)

*Thirdly*, by the *lex Julia de maritandis ordinibus*, unmarried persons could take nothing under a testament, unless they were married at the death of the testator, or within one hundred days after his decease ; and by the *lex Papia Poppaea* persons married, but childless, could only receive one-half of what was left them. (ULP. *Reg.* 17. 2. and 22. 3.)

*Lastly*, the disabilities of the *lex Julia* and the *lex Papia Poppaea* were removed by the Christian emperors ; but a new kind of disability was created, by enacting that no heretic should take anything whatever, even under a military testament. (C. i. 5. 4, 5. and 22.) In the time of Justinian it may be said that every one had the *testamenti factio*, excepting *barbari, deportati,* and heretics.

24. Incertis vero personis neque legata neque fideicommissa olim relinqui concessum erat ; nam nec miles quidem incertae personae poterat relinquere, ut divus Hadrianus rescripsit. Incerta autem persona videbatur, quam incerta opinione animo suo testator subjiciebat ; veluti si quis ita dicat : Quicumque filio filiam suam in matrimonium dederit, ei heres meus illum fundum dato. Illud quoque quod iis relinquebatur, qui post testamentum scriptum primi consules designati erunt, aeque incertae personae legari videbatur, et denique multo alia ejusmodi species sunt. Libertas quoque incertae personae non videbatur posse dari, quia placebat nominatim servos liberari. Sub certa vero demonstratione, id est, ex certis personis incertae personae recte

25. Formerly, it was not permitted that either legacies or *fideicommissa* should be given to uncertain persons, and even a soldier could not leave anything to an uncertain person, as the Emperor Hadrian has decided by a rescript. By an uncertain person was meant one who is not present to the mind of the testator in any definite manner, as if he should say : Whoever shall give his daughter in marriage to my son, to him let my heir give such a piece of land. So, if he had left anything to the persons first appointed consuls after his testament was written, this also would have been a gift to uncertain persons, and there are many other similar examples. Freedom likewise could not be conferred upon an uncertain person, for it was necessary that all slaves should be enfranchised by

legabatur; veluti, Ex cognatis meis qui nunc sunt, si quis filiam meam uxorem duxerit, ei heres meus illam rem dato. Incertis autem personis legata vel fideicommissa relicta, et per errorem soluta, repeti non possunt sacris constitutionibus cautum erat.

name; but a legacy given with a certain demonstration, that is, to an uncertain person, among a number of persons certain, was valid, as: Among my existing *cognati*, if any one shall marry my daughter, let my heir give him such a thing. But, if a legacy or *fideicommissum* to uncertain persons had been paid by mistake, it was provided by the constitutions, that such persons could not be called on to refund.

GAL. ii. 218, 230.

*Neque fideicommissa.* It was by a *senatus-consultum*, in the time of Hadrian, that the law was thus settled with respect to *fideicommissa.* (GAI. ii. 287.) Previously, a gift by way of *fideicommissum* to an uncertain person had been valid.

The *lex Furia Caninia* (GAI. ii. 239) required that slaves to whom freedom was given by testament should be expressly named, *jubet servos nominatim liberari.*

26. Postumo quoque alieno inutiliter legabatur. Est autem alienus postumus, qui natus inter suos heredes testatori futurus non est; ideoque ex emancipato filio conceptus nepos extraneus erat postumus aro.

26. Formerly, a legacy to a posthumous stranger was ineffectual; a posthumous stranger is any one who, if he had been born before the death of the testator, would not have been numbered among his *sui heredes*, and so a posthumous grandson, the issue of an emancipated son, was a posthumous stranger with regard to his grandfather.

GAI. ii. 241.

We have already seen (see Tit. 13. 1) how the rigour of this principle came to be modified with respect to a posthumous *suus heres.* It was as an *incerta persona* that the posthumous child was originally excluded from taking either as heir or legatee.

27. Sed hujusmodi species penitus est sine justa emendatione relicta; cum in nostro codice constitutio posita est, per quam et huic parti medemur, non solum in hereditatibus, sed etiam in legatis et fideicommissis: quod evidenter ex ipsius constitutionis lectione clarescit. Tutor autem nec per nostram constitutionem incertus dari debet, quia certo judicio debet quis pro tutela suae posteritati cavere.

27. These points have not, however, been left without proper alteration, for a constitution has been placed in our code by which the law has been altered, not only as regards inheritances, but also as regards legacies and *fideicommissa.* This alteration will appear from the constitution itself. But not even by our constitution is the nomination of an uncertain tutor permitted, for it is incumbent upon every parent to take care that his posterity have a tutor by a determinate appointment.

C. vi. 48.

There was, probably, a constitution treating of this subject inserted in the first code (see Introd. sec. 29), which was not given in the code we now have.

| | |
|---|---|
| 28. Postumus autem alienus heres Institui et antea poterat et nunc potest; nisi in utero ejus sit, quae jure nostro uxor esse non potest. | 28. A posthumous stranger could formerly, and may now, be appointed heir, unless it appear that he has been conceived by a woman, who by our law could not have been married to his father. |

GAI. II. 242. 287; D. xxviii. 2. 9. 1. 4.

Posthumous children, who, if born in the testator's lifetime, would not have been in his power (this is the meaning of *alienus*), could not be instituted heirs under the civil law; but the prætor gave them, if instituted, the *possessio bonorum*. Justinian permitted their institution.

*Nisi in utero ejus sit*, that is, unless the posthumous child be the child of the testator, and of a woman whom the testator could not have married. Such a child would be *extraneus* to the testator, as not being in his family, which no one could be who was not the offspring of a legal marriage. To take the expression as applicable to the child of any woman whom the testator could not marry, without limiting it to a child, also the offspring of the testator, would narrow the power of making a posthumous child heir, so much as to make it nugatory. For if either the testator or the woman were married, the child could not be made heir, nor could it, if it were the offspring of any very near relation of the testator. *Si ex ea quæ ulii nupta sit, postumum quis hæredem instituerit, ipso jure non valet quod turpis sit institutio.* (D. xxviii. 2. 9. 1.)

| | |
|---|---|
| 29. Si quis in nomine, cognomine, prænomine legatarii erraverit, si de persona constat, nihilominus valet legatum. Idemque in hæredibus servatur, et recte; nomina enim significandorum hominum gratia reperta sunt, qui si alio quolibet modo intelligantur, nihil interest. | 29. Although a testator may have mistaken the nomen, cognomen, or prænomen of a legatee, yet, if it be certain who is the person meant, the legacy is valid. The same holds good as to heirs, and with reason: for the use of names is but to point out persons; and, if they can be distinguished by any other method, it is the same thing. |

D. xix. 4.

| | |
|---|---|
| 30. Huic proxima est illa juris regula, falsa demonstratione legatum non perimi, veluti si quis ita legaverit, Stichum servum meum vernam do lego; licet enim non verna sed emptus sit, si de servo tamen con- | 30. Closely akin to this is the rule of law, that a legacy is not rendered void by a false description. For instance, if the testator were to say, I give as a legacy Stichus born my slave; in this case, although Stichus |

stat. utile est legatum. Et convenienter si ita demonstraverit, S ichum servum quem a Selo emi, sitque ab alio emptus, utile est legatum, si de servo constat.

was not born in the family, but bought, yet, if it be certain who is meant, the legacy is valid. And so if a testator marks out the particular slave in this way: I bequeath Stichus my slave, whom I bought of Seius; yet, although he was bought of another, the legacy is good, if no doubt exist as to the slave intended to be given.

D. xxxv. 1. 17, pr. and 1.

31. Longe magis legato falsa causa non nocet, veluti cum quis ita dixerit, Titio, quia me absente negotia mea curavit. Stichum do lego; vel Ita, Titio, quia patrocinio ejus capitali crimine liberatus sum, Stichum do lego. Licet enim neque negotia testat oris unquam gessit Titius, neque patrocinio ejus liberatus est, legatum tamen valet. Sed si conditionaliter enuntiata fuerit causa, aliud juris est, veluti hoc modo: Titio, si negotia mea curavit, fundum do lego.

31. Much less is a legacy rendered invalid by a false reason being assigned for giving it; as, if a testator says, I give my slave Stichus to Titius, because he took care of my affairs in my absence; or, because I was acquitted upon a cap'tal accusation, by his undertaking my defence. For, although Titius has never taken care of the affairs of the deceased, and although the testator was never acquitted by means of Titius defending him, the lega y will be valid. But it is quite different if the reason has been assigned under the form of a condition, as, I give to Titius such a piece of ground, if he has taken care of my affairs.

D. xxxv. 1. 17. 2, 3.

Ulpian shortly sums up the law of this and the two last paragraphs by the rule, ' *Neque ex falsa demonstratione, neque ex falsa causa legatum infirmatur.*' (ULP. Reg. 24. 19.)

Of course if the cause was so given as to constitute a condition, the legacy was only valid, if the condition had been accomplished.

32. An servo heredis recte legam s, queritur. Et constat pure inutiliter legari, nec quicquam profi ere si vivo testatore de potestate heredis exierit; quia quod inutile foret legatum, si statim post factum testamentum decessisset testator, non huc idem debet valere quia diutius testator vixerit. Subconditione vero recte legatur, ut requiramus an quo tempore dies leg ti cedit, in potestate heredis non sit.

32. The question has been raised, whether a testator can give a legacy to the slave of his heir; and it is evi'ent that such a legacy is quite ineffectual, nor is It at all helped by the slave having been freed from the power of the heir in the lifetime of the testator; for a legacy which would have been void if the testator had expired immediately after he had made the testament, ought not to become valid, merely because he happened to enjoy a longer life. But a testator may give the legacy to the slave under a condition, and then we

have to enquire whether at the time when the right to the legacy becomes fixed, the slave has ceased to be in the power of the heir.

GAI. ii. 244; D. xxxiv. 7. 1.

This paragraph is based on the *regula Catoniana* (see note on paragraph 10), though no express allusion to it is made. As to the doubts entertained on the subject, see GAI. ii. 244.

33. Ex diverso, herede Instituto servo, quin domino recte etiam sine conditione legetur, non dubitatur; nam etsi statim post factum testamentum decesserit testator, non tamen apud eum qui heres sit dies legati cedere intelligitur; cum hereditas a legato separata sit, et possit per eum servum alius heres effici, si priusquam jussu domini adeat, in alterius potestatem translatus sit, vel manumissus ipse heres efficitur: quibus casibus utile est legatum. Quod si in eadem causa permanserit, et jussu legatarii adierit, evanescit legatum.

33. On the contrary, it is not doubted, but that if a slave be appointed heir, a legacy may be given to his master unconditionally; for, although the testator should die instantly, yet the right to the legacy immediately after making the testament, does not immediately accrue to the heir; for the inheritance is here separated from the legacy, and another may become heir by means of the slave, if he should be transferred to the power of a new master, before he has entered upon the inheritance, at the command of the master, who is the legatee; or the slave himself, if enfranchised, may become heir; and, in these cases, the legacy would be good. But, if the slave should remain in the same state, and enter upon the inheritance by order of the legatee, the legacy is at end.

GAI. ii. 245.

34. Ante heredis institutionem inutiliter antea legabatur, scilicet quia testamenta vim ex institutione heredum accipiunt, et ob id veluti caput atque fundamentum intelligitur totius testamenti heredis institutio. Pari ratione nec libertas ante heredis institutionem dari poterat. Sed quia incivile esse putavimus, ordinem quidem scripturae sequi, quod et ipsi antiquitati vituperandum fuerit visum, sperni autem testatoris voluntatem, per nostram constitutionem et hoc vitium emendavimus: ut liceat et ante heredis institutionem et inter medias heredum institutiones legatum relinquere, et multo magis libertatem cujus usus favorabilior est.

34. Formerly, a legacy placed before the institution of the heir was ineffectual, because a testament receives its efficacy from the institution of the heir, and it is thus that the institution of the heir is looked on as the head and the foundation of the testament. So, too, freedom could not be given before the institution of the heir. But we have thought it unreasonable that the mere order of writing should be attended to, in contempt of the real intention of a testator—a thing of which the ancients themselves seem to have disapproved. We have, therefore, by our constitution, amended the law in this point; so that a legacy, and much more a grant of liberty, which is always favoured, may now be given before

the Institution of an heir, or among
the institution of heirs where more
than one.

Gai. ii. 229, 230; C. vi. 23, 24.

The nomination of a tutor, as not constituting any burden
on the inheritance, had already been made an exception to the
rule, that nothing in a testament could be valid that preceded
the institution of the heir. (Gai. ii. 231.)

35. Post mortem quoque heredis
aut legatarii simili modo inutiliter
legabatur, veluti si quis ita dicat:
Cum heres meus mortuus erit, do
lego. Item, pridie quam heres aut
legatarius morietur. Sed simili
modo et hoc correximus, firmitatem
hujusmodi legatis ad fideicommissorum similitudinem praestantes, ne
vel hoc casu deterior causa legatorum quam fideicommissorum inveniatur.

35. A legacy made to take effect
after the death of an heir or legatee,
was also ineffectual; as, If a testator
said, when my heir is dead, I give as
a legacy, or thus, I give as a legacy
on the day preceding the day of the
death of my heir, or of my legatee.
But we have corrected the ancient
rule in this respect, by giving all
such legacies the same validity as
fideicommissa; lest trusts should be
found in this respect to be more favoured than legacies.

Gai. ii. 232; C. iv. 38. 11; C. iv. 11.

Gaius remarks, that the second of these forms, *Pridie
quam*, though objected to because the time when the right was
fixed could not be known until the heir was dead, was not objected to on any very good ground. For all that the principles
of law forbad was, that the interest should not be fixed until
after the death of the heir, for then it would have been the
heir's heir, and not the heir that was charged; and that it
should not be fixed until after the death of the legatee, for if
he had no vested interest in his life, he could have nothing to
transmit. But a legacy made so as to give a fixed right the
day before either of their deaths, was not open to the same
objections.

36. Poenae quoque nomine inutiliter legabatur et adimebatur, vel
transferebatur. Poenae autem nomine legari videtur quod coercendi
heredis causa relinquitur, quo magis
aliquid faciat aut non faciat:
veluti si quis ita scripserit, Heres
meus, si filiam suam in matrimonium Titio collocaverit, vel ex diverso
si non collocaverit, dato decem
aureos Seio; aut si ita scripserit,
Heres meus, si servum Stichum

36. Also, formerly, if a testator
had given, revoked, or transferred a
legacy by way of penalty, he would
have done so ineffectually. A legacy
is considered as given by way of a
penalty, when it is intended to constrain an heir to do or not to do something; as. if a testator said, if my
heir give his daughter in marriage to
Titius, or. if he do not give her in
marriage to Titius, let him pay ten
aurei to Seius; or, thus, if my heir

alienaverit, vel ex diverso si non alienaverit, Titiodecemaureosdato. Et in tantum hæc regula observabatur, ut quam pluribus principalibus constitutionibus significatur, nec principem quidem agnoscere quod ei pœnæ nomine legatum sit. Nec ex militis quidem testamento talia legata valebant, quamvis alia militum voluntates in ordinandis testamentis valde observabantur. Quinetiam nec libertatem pœnæ nomine dari posse placebat. Eo amplius nec heredem pœnæ nomine adjici posse Sabinus existimabat, veluti si quis ita dicat, Titius heres esto, si Titius filiam suam Seio in matrimonium collocaverit, Seius quoque heres esto. Nihil enim intererat, qua ratione Titius coerceretur, utrum legati datione an coheredis adjectione. Sed hujusmodi scrupulosdias nobis non placuit, et generaliter ea quæ relinquuntur, licet pœnæ nomine fuerint relicta vel adempta vel in alios translata, nihil distare a ceteris legatis constituimus vel in dando vel in adimendo vel in transferendo: exceptis videlicet iis quæ impossibilia sunt, vel legibus interdicta, aut alias probrosa. Hujusmodi enim testamentorum dispositiones valere, secta meorum temporum non patitur.

shall alienate my slave Stichus, or, if my heir shall not alienate my slave Stichus, let him pay ten aurei to Titius. And this rule was so rigorously observed, that it was expressly ordained by many constitutions, that even the emperor would not receive a legacy, which was given by way of a penalty, nor could such a legacy be valid, even when given by the testament of a soldier; although, in every other respect, the intention of a testator in a military testament was scrupulously adhered to. And even freedom could not be given by way of a penalty; still less, in the opinion of Sabinus, could another heir be added; as if, for instance, a testator said, let Titius be my heir, but if he give his daughter in marriage to Seius, let Seius also be my heir. It made no difference how Titius was put under constraint, whether by the gift of a legacy, or the addition of a co-heir. But this scrupulous severity has not pleased us, and we have therefore ordained generally that things left, revoked, or transferred by way of penalty, shall be treated as other legacies, with the exception of anything that may be impossible, prohibited by law, or contrary to good manners, for the principles of our age will not permit testamentary dispositions of such a character.

GAI. ii. 235, 230, 243; C. vi. 41.

It is rather difficult to say how this rule sprang up in Roman law, or how the gift of a legacy *pœnæ nomine* differed from an ordinary condition. Theophilus, in his Paraphrase, gives us one reason that a legacy ought to spring from a feeling of kindness to the legatee, and not be used as a means to punish another. For want of a better reason, we may be content with this.

No principle of arrangement has been preserved in grouping the numerous paragraphs of this long title. If we are anxious to class the different paragraphs together under distinct heads, we could not, perhaps, adopt a better arrangement than that of Ducaurroy. He divides the title, or rather his explanation of it, into five paragraphs. The first gives the definition and general notions of a legacy (paragr. 1, 2, 3); the second treats of the objects given by a legacy (paragr. 4, 5, 6, 9, 10, 11, 13,

14, 15, 21, 22, and 23); the third treats of the persons to whom legacies can be given (paragr. 24, 25, 26, 27, 28, 32, and 33); the fourth of the different rules to be observed in the terms of the legacy (paragr. 29, 30, 31, 34, 35, and 36); and the fifth, of the effects of legacies (paragr. 8, 12, 16, 17, 18, 19, 20).

## Tit. XXI. DE ADEMPTIONE ET TRANSLATIONE LEGATORUM.

| | |
|---|---|
| Ademptio legatorum sive eodem testamento adimantur legata sive codicillis firma est, sive contrariis verbis illa ademptio, veluti si quod ita quis legaverit do lego, ita adimatur non do non lego; sive non contrariis, id est, aliis quibuscumque verbis. | The revocation of a legacy, whether made in the same testament or in a codicil, is valid, and may be made in terms contrary to those of the gift, as when a testator gives in three terms, I give as a legacy, and revokes it by saying, I do not give as a legacy; or in terms not contrary, that is, in any other form of expression. |

D. xxxiv. 4. 8. 11.

It was considered necessary, in the times when weight was attached to the formula under which the legacy was given, that the legacy should be revoked by words exactly opposite (*contrariis verbis*) to those by which it was given, as in a legacy *per vindicationem* the revocation ought to have been by the words ' *non do, non lego.*' (ULP. *Reg.* 24. 29.)

The text only speaks of direct revocation of legacies by an express declaration of the testator's wishes in some testamentary document; but it was also revoked by the mere wish of the testator (*nuda voluntate*, D. xxxiv. 4. 3. 11) that it should be revoked being in any way declared. In such a case the legacy was not, strictly speaking, taken away; but the legatee who brought an action for it might be repelled by an exception of *dolus malus*. We have seen, in the last Title (paragr 12), that a sale of the thing given as a legacy was held to be or not to be a revocation of the legacy, according as the testator intended or did not intend that such should be its effect.

A legacy was also considered to be revoked by implication if something occurred after it was given which made it impossible to believe that the testator could have continued to wish the legatee to profit by his bounty; as, for instance, if a notorious and deadly enmity sprang up between them. (D. xxxiv. 4. 3. 11.)

| | |
|---|---|
| 1. Transferri quoque legatum ab alio ad alium potest, veluti si quis | 1. A legacy may also be transferred from one person to another; as, I |

In dixerit hominem Stichum quem Titio legari Seio do lego, sive in eodem testamento sive in codicillis hoc fecerit. Quo casu simul Titio adimi videtur et Seio dari.

give as a legacy to Seius my slave Stichus, whom I have given as a legacy to Titius, whether this be done in the same testament or in codicils; and then at the same time a legacy is taken from Titius and given to Seius.

D. xxiv. 4, 5.

The translation had two effects: it took away a legacy from one person and gave it to another; but it might have either effect without the other. The original legatee might be dead, and thus the legacy useless, and yet the gift to the new legatee would be valid; or the new legatee might subsequently die, and yet the legacy would be lost to the original legatee. (D. xxxiv. 4. 20.)

## Tit. XXII.   DE LEGE FALCIDIA.

Supererat ut de lege Falcidia dispiciamus, qua modus novissime legatis impositus est. Cum enim olim lege Duodecim Tabularum libera erat legandi potestas, ut liceret vel totum patrimonium legatis erogare (quippe ea lege ita cautum esset, uti legassit suae rei, ita jus esto), visum est hanc legandi licentiam coarctare. Idque ipsorum testatorum gratia provisum est, ob id quod plerumque intestati moriebantur, recusantibus scriptis heredibus pro nullo aut minimo lucro hereditatis adire. Et cum super hoc tam lex Furia quam lex Voconia latae sunt, quarum neutra sufficiens ad rei consummationem videbatur, novissime lata est lex Falcidia, qua cavetur ne plus legare liceat quam dodrantem totorum bonorum, id est, ut sive unus heres institutus esset, sive plures, apud eum eosve pars quarta remaneret.

It remains to speak of the lex Falcidia, by which legacies have received their latest limitations. By the law of the Twelve Tables, a testator was permitted to dispose of his whole patrimony in legacies; for the law said, 'As a man has disposed of his property, so let the law be;' but it was thought proper to restrain this licence even for the benefit of testators themselves, because they frequently died intestate, the heirs they instituted refusing to enter upon an inheritance from which they could receive little or no profit. With this object the lex Furia and the lex Voconia were passed; and lastly, as neither of these was found adequate to the purpose, the lex Falcidia was enacted, which forbids a testator to give more in legacies, than three-fourths of all his property; so that, whether there be one or more heirs instituted, there must now remain to him, or them, at least one-fourth part of the whole.

GAI. ii. 224. 227.

The lex Furia testamentaria, which must not be confounded with the lex Furia, or Fusia Caninia, restraining the testamentary manumission of slaves (Bk. i, Tit. 7), was a plebiscitum, probably of the year 571 A.U.C. Gaius thus acquaints us with its provisions:—'*Quæ, exceptis personis quibusdam, cæteris plus mille assibus legatorum nomine mortisve causa capere permissum non est:*' more than 1000 asses could not be given as a legacy. The law failed to effect its object, as the testator was not restrained in the number of legacies he might give, but only in the amount of each legacy. (GAI. ii. 2. 25.)

The *lex Voconia*, also called *testamentaria*, was a *plebiscitum*, of which the year 585 A.U.C. is given as the date. Gaius says of it, '*Quæ cautum est, ne cui plus legatorum nomine mortisve causa capere liceret, quum heredes caperent:*' no legatee was to have more than each heir had. This law also failed in its object ; as, by multiplying the number of legatees and giving each a trifling amount, the sum received by the heirs, which would be equally small, might be too trifling to make it worth their while to enter on the inheritance. (GAI. ii. 226.)

The *lex Falcidia* was a *plebiscitum* passed in the year 714. A.U.C. Its principles were extended to *fideicommissa* by the *senatus-consultum Pegasianum* (see next Title); to *fideicommissa* imposed on *heredes ab intestato* by a rescript of Antoninus Pius (D. XXXV. 2. 18); to donations *mortis causa* by a rescript of Severus (C. vi. 50. 5); and lastly, to donations between husband and wife. (C. vi. 50. 12.) The mode in which the heir would avail himself of the *lex Falcidia* would be by repelling by an exception the legatee who demanded the whole of his legacy, when less than the whole was due by the *lex Falcidia*.

The part reserved to the heir is spoken of by the jurists as *quarta* or *Falcidia*. The commentators more usually employ the full term *quarta Falcidia*.

1. Et cum quæsitum esset duobus heredibus institutis, veluti Titio et Seio, si Titii pars aut tota exhausta sit legatis quæ nominatim ab eo data sunt aut supra modum onerata, a Seio vero aut nulla relicta sint legata aut quæ partem ejus duntaxat in partem dimidiam minuant, an quia in quartam partem totius hereditatis sit amplius habet, Titio nihil ex legatis quæ ab eo relicta sunt, retinere liceret. Placuit, ut quartam partem suæ partis salvam habeat, possæ retinere ; etenim in singulis heredibus ratio legis Falcidiæ ponenda est.

1. When two heirs are instituted, as Titius and Seius, a question has been raised : supposing the share of Titius in the inheritance is either entirely absorbed, or very heavily burdened with legacies specifically charged upon it, while the share of Seius is wholly free, or has legacies charged on it only up to half its amount, in such a case does the circumstance of Seius having a clear fourth or more of the inheritance, prevent Titius from retaining out of the legacies charged upon his share, enough to secure a fourth part of his own moiety to himself ? It has been decided that Titius may retain the fourth of his

own share, for the calculation of the
*lex Falcidia* is applicable to each heir
separately.

D. xxxv. 2. 77.

The case taken in the text is a simple one. If two heirs
are unequally burdened with legacies, each is to avail himself
separately of the *lex Falcidia*, and is secured in one-fourth of
that which was given him as a legacy; but supposing one co-
heir does not take under the testament, and his share accrues
to the other, are the fourth-parts to remain separate or to be
reckoned together? In answering this a distinction was made.
(1.) If the part burdened with legacies accrued to the part not
burdened, the latter remained unaffected, and the fourth was
deducted only from the former. (2.) If the two parts were each
burdened, the calculation was made for each of them. (3.) But
if the part not burdened accrued to the part burdened, as this
was a clear advantage to the latter, the two parts were reckoned
together, and the fourth of the whole which they made when
united was deducted. (D. xxxv. 2. 78.)

2. Quantitas autem patrimonii ad
quam ratio legis Falcidiae redigitur,
mortis tempore spectatur. Itaque si,
verbi gratia, is quicentum aureorum
patrimonium in bonis habebat, centum aureos legaverit, nihil legatariis
prodest, si ante additam hereditatem
per servos hereditarios aut ex partu
ancillarum hereditariarum aut ex
foetu pecorum tantum accesserit
hereditati, ut centum aureis legatorum nomine erogatis heres quartam
partem hereditatis habiturus sit; sed
necesse est ut nihilominus quarta
pars legatis detrahatur. Et diverso,
si septuaginta quinque legaverit, et
ante additam hereditatem in tantum
decreverint bona incendiis forte, aut
naufragiis aut morte servorum, ut
non amplius quam septuaginta quinque aureorum substantia vel etiam
minus relinquatur, solida legata
debentur. Nec ea res damnosa est
heredi, cui liberum est non adire
hereditatem: quae res efficit ut sit
necesse legatariis, ne destituto testamento nihil consequantur, cum
herede in portionem paciasci.

3. In order to apply the *lex Falcidia*, regard is had to the value of
the estate at the time of the testator's death. Thus, for instance, if
he, who is worth a hundred *aurei* at
his decease, bequeath the whole hundred in legacies, the legatees receive
no advantage, if the inheritance before
it is entered upon, should so increase
by the acquisition of slaves, the birth
of children to female slaves, or the
produce of cattle, that, after a full
payment of the one hundred *aurei* in
legacies, a clear fourth of the whole
estate would remain to the heir, for
the legacies notwithstanding would
still be liable to a deduction of one-
fourth. On the contrary, if the testator has given only seventy-five *aurei*
in legacies, then although, before the
entrance of the heir, the estate should
so decrease by fire, shipwreck, or the
loss of slaves, that its whole value
should not be more than seventy-five
*aurei* or less, yet the legacies would
still be due without deduction. Nor
is this prejudicial to the heir, who
is at liberty to refuse the inheritance,
but it obliges the legatees to come to
terms with the heir, so as to get a
part, lest if the testament were abandoned they should lose the whole.

D. xxxv. 2. 73.

The calculation under the *lex Falcidia* was made at the time of the testator's death, in accordance with the rule by which the *dies cedit* for most legacies was fixed at that time. It was, however, made then, even if the *dies cedit* was fixed at some other time. Between the death of the testator and the time of the heir entering on the inheritance, the estate might be so deteriorated as to make it disadvantageous to the heir to enter; and in order to persuade him to do so, the legatees would have to enter into a compromise with him.

3. Cum autem ratio legis Falcidiae ponitur, ante deducitur æs alienum, item funeris impensæ et pretia servorum manumissorum : tunc deinde in reliquo its ratio habetur, ut ex eo quarta pars apud heredes remaneat, tres vero partes inter legatarios distribuantur, pro rata scilicet portione ejus quod cuique eorum legatum fuerit. Itaque si fingamus quadringentos aureos legatos esse, et patrimonii quantitatem ex qua legata erogari oportet, quadringentorum esse, quarta pars legatariis singulis debet detrahi ; quod si trecentos quinquaginta legatos fingamus, octava debet detrahi. Quod si quingentos legaverit, initioque quintadeinde quarta detrahi debet ; ante enim detrahendum est, quod extra bonorum quantitatem est, deinde quod ex bonis apud heredem remanere oportet.

3. When the calculation of the *lex Falcidia* is made, the testator's debts, his funeral expenses, and the price of the manumission of slaves, are deducted, then what remains is divided, so that a fourth-part remains for the heir, and the other three parts are divided among the legatees in proportion to the amount of their respective legacies ; for example, let us suppose that four hundred *aurei* have been given in legacies, and the estate out of which the legacies are to be paid is worth no more, each legatee must have a fourth-part subtracted from his legacy ; but, if we suppose that the testator gave in legacies three hundred and fifty *aurei*, then an eighth ought to be deducted. And if he gave five hundred *aurei* in legacies, first, a fifth must be deducted, and then a fourth. For that which exceeds the real value of the goods of the deceased must first be deducted, and then that which is to remain to the heir.

D. xxxv. 2. 1. 10 ; D. xxxv. 2. 30 ; D. xxxv. 2. 73. 5.

*Octava debet detrahi,* i.e. one-eighth of the whole, or fifty *aurei*, must be deducted from the whole sum given to the different legatees, the sum to be deducted from each share being in proportion to the relative amount of that share. Each share would be diminished by one-seventh.

The *lex Falcidia* did not apply to military testaments. (D. xxxv. 2. 17.)

By a Novel (1. 2. 2) Justinian provided that the Falcidian fourth should never be retained by the heir if the testator expressly forbad its retention. If the heir renounced the inheritance, the legatees and other persons who were designed by the testator to take under the testament might, on giving security for carrying out all the dispositions of the testament, receive the inheritance. Even if the testator had not forbidden the retention of the fourth, it could not be retained unless the heir made an inventory of the property of the deceased. If he accepted the inheritance without making an inventory, he had to pay the legatees in full, even if he was obliged to draw upon his private funds to do so.

## Tit. XXIII. DE FIDEICOMMISSARIIS HEREDITATIBUS.

| | |
|---|---|
| Nunc transeamus ad fideicommissa. Et prius est ut de hereditatibus fideicommissariis videamus. | Let us now pass to *fideicommissa*; and first we will treat of fideicommissary inheritances. |

Gai. II. 246, 247.

*Fideicommissa*, that is, trusts, might be compared to the institution of heirs, if the trust embraced the whole inheritance, and to the gift of legacies, if it embraced only a part. In the former case they were termed by the jurists *fideicommissariæ hereditates*; in the latter, *fideicommissa singulæ rei*. The text proceeds to speak of the *fideicommissariæ hereditates*.

The word *fideicommissum* has been generally retained in the translation, instead of trusts, because, as *fideicommissa* include only trusts carrying out the last wishes of a deceased person, the word trusts, which is used much more widely in its application, might lead to confusion.

Ulpian gives (*Reg.* 25. 1) the following definition of a *fideicommissum*: ' *Quod non civilibus verbis, sed precatire relinquitur ; nec ex rigore juris civilis proficiscitur, sed ex voluntate datur relinquentis.*'

| | |
|---|---|
| 1. Sciendum Itaque et omnia fideicommissa primis temporibus infirma esse, quia nemo invitus cogebatur praestare id de quo rogatus erat. Quibus enim non poterant hereditatem vel legata relinquere, si relinquebant, fidei committebant eorum qui capere ex testamento poterant ; et ideo fideicommissa appellata sunt, quia nullo vinculo juris, sed tantum pudore eorum qui rogabantur, continebantur. Postea divus Augustus semel iterumque gratia personarum motus, vel quia per ipsius salutem rogatus quis diceretur, aut ob insignem quorumdam perfidiam, jussit consulibus | 1. At first *fideicommissa* were of little force ; for no one could be compelled against his will to perform what he was only requested to perform. When testators were desirous of giving an inheritance or legacy to persons, to whom they could not directly give either, they then entrusted them to the good faith of some person capable of taking by testament : and *fideicommissa* were so called, because their performance could not be enforced by law, but depended solely upon the good faith of the person to whom they were entrusted. Afterwards, the Emperor Augustus, having been frequently moved by |

z

auctoritatem suam interponere. Quod quia justum videbatur, et populare erat, paulatim conversum est in assiduam jurisdictionem; tantusque eorum favor factus est, ut paulatim etiam praetor proprius crearetur, qui de fideicommissis jus diceret, quem fideicommissarium appellabant.

consideration for certain persons, or because the request was said to have been made in the name of the emperor's safety, or on account of some striking instance of perfidy, commanded the consuls to interpose their authority. Their intervention being favoured as just by public opinion, gradually assumed the character of a regular jurisdiction, and trusts grew into such favour, that soon a special praetor was appointed to give judgment in these cases, and received the name of *fideicommissarius.*

GAI. ii. 274, 275. 278. 285; D. i. 2. 2. 32.

The limits within which the Roman law confined the power of a citizen over his property after his death were narrow; but the freedom given by the introduction of obligatory trusts was singularly wide. A testator, in order to give anything, was obliged to do so by a regular testament, to adopt prescribed formulæ, to use the Latin tongue. He could not give anything to a *peregrinus,* to a person proscribed, to a posthumous stranger, or to an uncertain person. The system of *fideicommissa* enabled him to give to almost any one he liked, and that in words the least formal, and even without a testament at all. The *heredes ab intestato,* if charged with a *fideicommissum* by the person to whose property they succeeded, were obliged to fulfil it. The licence given to *fideicommissa* was, indeed, diminished by different enactments, and they were gradually placed more and more on the footing of legacies. Thus by one *senatus-consultum,* passed in the time of Hadrian, the power of giving a *fideicommissum* to a *peregrinus* (GAI. ii. 285), by another, the power of giving one to a posthumous stranger or uncertain person, was taken away. (GAI. ii. 287.) Again, the *senatus-consultum Pegasianum* subjected *fideicommissa* to the rules of the *lex Papia Poppæa* (GAI. ii. 286); and a tutor could never be given by testament, except directly. (GAI. ii. 289.) *Fideicommissa* were, indeed, always something beside and foreign to the nature of Roman law. Augustus merely ordered that, in a case of great hardship, the consuls should interfere. Then a magistrate was created whose business it was to interfere in cases which warranted it; but there was nothing like an action at law to enforce *fideicommissa.* The *fideicommissarius* applied for aid as having equity on his side; and if the magistrate chose to interfere, the regular course of the law was stayed, and the trust enforced. (ULP. *Reg.* xxv. 12.) The proceeding was always *extra ordinem.* (GAI. ii. 258.)

The *fideicommissum* itself did not, like a legacy, directly transfer the property in an inheritance or in any particular thing, and of course did not give any right to a real action. The restitution or giving up of the inheritance was, however, effected by the mere consent of the heir, even before tradition.

2. In primis igitur sciendum est, opus esse ut aliquis recto jure testamento heres instituatur, ejusque fidei committatur ut eam hereditatem alii restituat; alioquin inutile est testamentum, in quo nemo heres instituitur. Cum igitur aliquis scripserit Lucius Titius heres esto, poterit adjicere, rogo te, Luci Titi, ut cum primum poteris hereditatem meam adire, eam Caio Seio reddas restituas. Potest autem quisque et de parte restituenda heredem rogare, et liberum est vel pure vel sub conditione relinquere fideicommissum, vel ex die certa.

2. We must first observe, that some one must be duly appointed heir in the testament: and then it must be entrusted to his good faith to restore the inheritance to some other person: for, the testament is ineffectual in which no one is instituted heir. And therefore, when a testator has said, Let Lucius Titius be my heir, he may add, and I request you, Lucius Titius, that, as soon as you can enter upon my inheritance, you will restore it and give it up to Caius Seius. A testator may also request his heir to restore a part of the inheritance only, and may leave the *fideicommissum* absolutely or conditionally, or on the expiration of a term.

GAI. ii. 248. 250.

Of course if there was no heir instituted, there could be no person to charge by testament with the trust (*nemo fiduciarius*); but the testator might charge the *heredes ab intestato*.

The person who made the *fideicommissum* was termed *fideicommittens*; the person requested to perform it, *fiduciarius*; and the person to be benefited by it, *fideicommissarius*.

3. Restituta autem hereditate, is quidem qui restituit, nihilominus heres permanet: is vero qui recipit hereditatem, aliquando heredis, aliquando legatarii loco, habebatur.

3. After an heir has restored the inheritance, he still continues heir. But he, who receives the inheritance, was sometimes considered in the light of an heir, and sometimes in that of a legatee.

GAI. ii. 251.

In order to protect himself, the heir who remained liable to all actions of creditors against the inheritance had recourse to a fiction of law. He sold the inheritance to the *fideicommissarius*, and they entered into mutual agreements called *emptæ et venditæ hereditatis stipulationes* (GAI. ii. 252), by which the *fiduciarius*, though remaining in the eye of the law responsible for the charges upon the inheritance, was protected from ultimate harm by having a remedy against the *fideicommissarius*. Thus Gaius says, 'Olim nec heredis loco erat, nec legatarii; sed potius emptoris.'

z 2

4. Et Neronis quidem temporibus, Trebellio Maximo et Annæo Seneca consulibus, senatus-consultum factum est: quo cautum est, ut si hereditas ex fideicommissi causa restituta sit, omnes actiones quæ jure civili heredi et in heredem competerent, ei et in eum darentur cui ex fideicommisso restituta est hereditas. Post quod senatus-consultum prætor utiles actiones ei et in eum qui recipit hereditatem, quasi heredi et in heredem dare cœpit.

4. During the reign of Nero, in the consulship of Trebellius Maximus and Annæus Senera, a senatus-consultum was passed, providing that, after an inheritance had been restored under a fideicommissum, all actions, which by the civil law might be brought by or against the heir, should be permitted for and against him, to whom the inheritance was restored. After this, the prætor began to give equitable actions for and against the person who received an inheritance, as if he were the heir.

GAI. ii. 251.

The *senatus-consultum Trebellianum* (A.D. 62) did away with the necessity of any such fiction as that of a sale. The *fideicommissarius* stepped at once into the place of the *heres institutus*. All the actions belonging to the inheritance were given him in the shape of *actiones utiles*. (See Introd. sec. 106.) If creditors sued the *heres institutus*, he had the *exceptio restitutæ hereditatis*; he might plead that he had parted with the inheritance as he had been directed.

5. Sed quia heredes scripti, cum aut totam hereditatem aut pene totam plerumque restituere rogabantur, adire hereditatem ob nullum vel minimum lucrum recusabant, atque ob id extinguebantur fideicommissa, prætra Vespasiani Augusti temporibus, Pegaso et Pusione consulibus, senatus censuit ut ei qui rogatus esset hereditatem restituere, perinde liceret quartam partem retinere, atque lege Falcidia ex legatis retinere conceditur. Ex singulis quoque rebus quæ per fideicommissum relinquuntur, eadem retentio permissa est. Post quod senatus-consultum ipse heres onera hereditaria sustinebat; ille autem qui ex fideicommisso recepit partem hereditatis, legatarii partiarii loco erat, id est, ejus legatarii cui pars bonorum legabatur: quæ species legati partitio vocabatur, quia cum herede legatarius partiebatur hereditatem. Unde quæ solebant stipulationes inter heredem et partiarium legatarium interponi, eædem interponebantur inter eum qui ex fideicommisso recepit hereditatem,

5. But, the instituted heirs being in most cases requested to restore the whole, or almost the whole of an inheritance, often refused to accept it, as they would receive little or no advantage, and thus *fideicommissa* were frequently extinguished. Afterwards, during the reign of the Emperor Vespasian, in the consulship of Pegasus and Pusio, the senate decreed, that an heir, who was requested to restore an inheritance, might retain a fourth, just as in the case of legacies he might by the Falcidian law. And the same deduction is allowed in particular things, which are left by a *fideicommissum*. For some time after this *senatus-consultum* the heir alone bore the charges of the inheritance; and he who had received a share or part of an inheritance, under a *fideicommissum*, was regarded as a part legatee, that is, a legatee having a legacy of a share of the property, a species of legacy which was called partitio, because the legatee took a part of the inheritance together with the heir. Thus the same stipulations

et heredem, id est, ut ei lucrum et damnum hereditarium pro rata parte inter eos commune esset.

which were formerly in use between the heir and partiary legatees, were likewise made between the person who received the inheritance under the *fideicommissum* and the heir, that is, they stipulated they would share the benefits and the charges of the inheritance between them, in proportion to their respective interests.

Gai. ii. 254.

The *senatus-consultum Trebellianum* protected the *fiduciarius* from any harm; but it gave him no incitement to enter on the inheritance. Why should he take an inheritance which he had instantly to transfer to another. The trust might thus perish; and, to remedy this, the *senatus-consultum Pegasianum* (A.D. 70) permitted the *heres institutus* to retain a fourth, just as the *lex Fulcidia* permitted in the case of legacies. Even the term *quarta Fulcidia* was applied to the fourth retained by the *fiduciarius heres*. (D. xxxvi. 1. 16. 9.) The *fideicommissarius* thus became exactly like a legatee; and, as having a definite part of the inheritance, he was considered in the light of a legatee of a part of the inheritance.

A testator sometimes gave a legatee not a particular thing, but a certain share in his whole property. The legatee (then termed *legatarius partiarius*) took, in this case, *per universitatem*; but he was not thereby made an heir, not having been formally instituted; and if there was no heir who entered on the inheritance, the legacy was extinguished. The claims of creditors against the inheritance were made exclusively against the heir, and the heir alone could recover sums due to the inheritance. Thus it was necessary that, if the heir paid a creditor, the legatee should account to him for a part of the payment proportionate to his share of the inheritance; while if the legatee wished that his share should be increased by the payment of a debt due to the inheritance, he could only effect this through the heir. Accordingly they made stipulations with each other, termed *stipulationes partis et pro parte*. By one of these stipulations the heir bound the legatee to pay a proportion of sums expended in satisfaction of claims against the inheritance; by the other the legatee bound the heir to account to him for his share of sums received in satisfaction of debts owing to the inheritance. Such legacies became obsolete from the time that *fideicommissa* and legacies were placed on the same footing.

α. Ergo si quidem non plus quam dodrantem hereditatis scriptus heres rogatus sit restituere, tunc ex

α. Therefore, if the instituted heir was not requested to restore more than three-fourths of the inheritance,

Trebelliano senatus-consulto restituebatur hereditas, et in utrumque
actiones hereditariæ pro rata parte
dabantur, in heredem quidem jure
civili, in eum vero qui recipiebat
hereditatem ex senatus-consulto
Trebelliano, tamquam in heredem.
At si plus quam dodrantem vel
etiam totam hereditatem restituere
rogatus sit, locus erat Pegasiano
senatus-consulto, et heres qui semel
adierit hereditatem, si modo sua
voluntate adierit, sive retinuerit
quartam partem sive retinere noluerit, ipse universa onera hereditaria
sustinebat: sed quarta quidem retenta, quasi partis et pro parte stipulationes interponebantur, tamquam inter partiarium legatarium
et heredem; si vero totam hereditatem restitueret, emptæ et venditæ
hereditatis stipulationes interponebantur. Sed si recuset scriptus heres
adire hereditatem, ob id quod dicat
eam sibi suspectam esse quasi damnosam, cavetur Pegasiano senatus-
consulto ut, desiderante eo cui restituere rogatus est, jussu prætoris
adeat et restituat hereditatem, pe-
rindeque ei et in eum qui recipit
hereditatem, actiones darentur ac
juris est ex Trebelliano senatus-
consulto. Quo casu nullis stipulationibus est opus; quia simul et
huic quia restituit, securitas datur,
et actiones hereditariæ ei et in eum
transferuntur qui recepit hereditatem, utroque senatus-consulto in
hac specie concurrentia.

he restored such part in accordance
with the provisions of the *senatus-
consultum Trebellianum*; and all actions which concern an inheritance,
might be brought against each according to their respective shares—
against the heir, by the civil law,
and against him who received the inheritance, by the *senatus-consultum
Trebellianum*, as against an heir.
But if the instituted heir was requested by the testator to restore the
whole inheritance, or more than
three-fourths, then the *senatus-consultum Pegasianum* became applicable: and the heir who had once
entered on the inheritance, provided
he did so voluntarily, was obliged to
sustain all the charges of the inheritance, whether he had retained, or
had declined to retain his fourth.
But, when the heir did retain a fourth
part, the stipulations termed *partis et
pro parte*, were entered into, as between a legatee of part and an heir;
and, when the heir did not retain a
fourth, then the stipulations termed
*emptæ et venditæ hereditatis*, were
made between them. But if the instituted heir refused to enter on the
inheritance, alleging that he feared
he should lose by doing so, it was
provided, by the *senatus-consultum
Pegasianum*, that, on the demand of
him to whom he had been requested
to restore the inheritance, he should,
under an order of the prætor, enter
on the inheritance, and restore it;
and that all actions might be brought
by or against him who received the
inheritance, as in a case falling under
the *senatus-consultum Trebellianum*.
And in this case stipulations are not
necessary, for the heir, who restores
the inheritance, is secured, and all
actions concerning an inheritance are
transferred to and against him, by
whom it is received, there being, in
this instance, a concurrent application of both *senatus-consulta*.

The *senatus-consultum Trebellianum* was not abrogated
by the *Pegasianum*. They applied to different cases. If the
fourth were expressly reserved to the *heres fiduciarius*, he took

the other three parts, and immediately restored or transferred them to the *fideicommissarius*, who had the position of *heres fideicommissarius*, and all the actions belonging to the inheritance, so far as his share extended. But if the fourth was not reserved, the *senatus-consultum Pegasianum* became applicable. The *fiduciarius heres* retained the fourth, and the *fideicommissarius* held the position of a legatee. The *heres institutus* might, however, not choose to retain the fourth. He might enter on the inheritance, and at once voluntarily transfer the whole to the *fideicommissarius*. Neither *senatus-consultum* then applied, and he had to protect himself by the old *stipulationes emptæ et venditæ hereditatis*. If he refused to enter on the inheritance, the prætor compelled him, by a power given in the *senatus-consultum Pegasianum*, and he was placed exactly in the same position as if he had entered under the *senatus-consultum Trebellianum*. He had no fourth reserved for him; and all action passed at once to the *fideicommissarius*.

7. Sed quia stipulationes ex senatus-consulto Pegasiano descendentes et ipsi antiquitati displicuerunt; et quibusdam casibus captiosas eas homo excelsi ingenii Papinianus appellat, et nobis in legibus magis simplicitas quam difficultas placet, ideo omnibus nobis suggestis tam similitudinibus quam differentiis utriusque senatus-consulti, placuit, exploso senatus-consulto Pegasiano quod punica supervenit, omnem auctoritatem Trebelliano senatus-consulto præstare, ut ex eo fideicommissariæ hereditates restituantur, sive habeat heres ex voluntate testatoris quartam, sive plus sive minus sive nihil penitus: ut tunc, quando vel nihil vel minus quarta apud eum remanet, liceat ei vel quartam vel quod deest ex nostra auctoritate retinere vel repetere solutum, quasi ex Trebelliano senatus-consulto pro rata portione actionibus tam in heredem quam in fideicommissarium competentibus. Si vero totam hereditatem sponte restituerit, omnes hereditariæ actiones fideicommissario et adversus eum competunt. Sed etiam id quod præcipuum Pegasiani senatus-consulti fuerat, ut quando recumbat heres scriptus sibi datam heredita-

7. But, as the stipulations, which arise from the *senatus-consultum Pegasianum*, were displeasing even to the ancients, and Papinian, a man of great genius, considers them in some cases as captious; and, as we prefer simplicity to complicity in matters of law, we have been pleased, upon comparing the points of agreement and disagreement in these two *senatus-consulta*, to abrogate the *senatus-consultum Pegasianum*, which was subsequent to the *senatus-consultum Trebellianum*, and to give an exclusive authority to the *senatus-consultum Trebellianum*, by which all fideicommissary inheritances shall be restored for the future, whether the testator has given by his will a fourth-part of his estate to the instituted heir, or more, or less, or even nothing, so that, when nothing is given to the heir, or less than a fourth-part, he may be permitted to retain a fourth, or as much as will make up the deficiency, by virtue of our authority, or to demand repayment of it if he has paid it over; and actions may be brought both against the heir and the *fideicommissarius* according to their respective shares, as if under the *senatus-consultum Trebellianum*. But, should the heir voluntarily re-

tem adire, necessitas ei imponeretur totam hereditatem volenti fidei-commissario restituerem, et omnes ad eum et contra eum transire actiones, et hoc transponimus ad senatus-consultum Trebellianum: ut ex hoc solo et necessitas heredi imponatur, si ipso nolente adire fidei-commissarius desiderat restitui sibi hereditatem, nullo nec damno nec commodo apud heredem remanente.

store the whole inheritance, all actions concerning an inheritance may be brought either by or against the *fideicommissarius*. And, as to the most important provision of the *senatus-consultum Pegasianum*, that, when an instituted heir refused to accept an inheritance, he might be constrained to restore it to the *fideicommissarius* if he demanded it, and to transfer all actions to and against him, we have transferred this provision to the *senatus-consultum Trebellianum*, by which alone this obligation is now laid upon the heir, when he himself refuses to enter on the inheritance, and the *fideicommissarius* is desirous that it should be restored, the heir in this case receiving neither gain nor loss.

Justinian unites the two *senatus-consulta* into one, giving them the name of the *senatus-consultum Trebellianum*. The heir is to retain the fourth, and the action will be, in all cases, transferred to the *fideicommissarius*, who will thus be always *in loco heredis*. Under the old system, either party was exposed to the risk of the other party to the stipulation becoming unable to fulfil his engagement.

Before the legislation of Justinian, the *heres* could not re-demand the fourth, if he had once paid it over. (Paul. Sent. iv. 3. 4.)

8. Nihil autem interest, utrum aliquis ex asse heres institutus aut totam hereditatem aut pro parte restituere, ao ex parte heres institutus aut totam eam partem aut partem partis restituere rogatus sit; nam et hoc casu eadem observari praecipimus, quae in totius hereditatis restitutione diximus.

8. But it makes no difference whether the heir is instituted to the whole inheritance, and is requested to restore the whole or a part, or whether being instituted to a part only, he is requested to restore that entire part, or a portion of it, for we enjoin that the same rules be observed in the latter case, as in case of restitution of the whole.

Gai. ii. 250.

9. Si quis una aliqua re deducta sive praecepta quae quartam continet, veluti fundo vel alia re, rogatus sit restituere hereditatem, simili modo ex Trebelliano senatus-consulto restitutio fiat, perinde ac si quarta parte retenta rogatus esset reliquam hereditatem restituere. Sed illud interest, quod altero casu, id est, cum deducta sive praecepta

9. If an heir be requested by a testator to give up an inheritance, after deducting or accepting some particular thing, equivalent to a fourth of the whole, as a piece of land, or anything else, he will give it up under the *senatus-consultum Trebellianum*, exactly as if he had been requested to restore the remainder of an inheritance, after reserving a fourth. But

aliqua re restituitur hereditas, in solidum ex eo senatus-consulto actiones transferuntur, et res quæ remanet apud heredem sine ullo onere hereditario apud eum remanet, quasi ex legato ei acquisita; altero vero casu, id est, cum quarta parte retenta rogatus est heres restituere hereditatem et restituit, scinduntur actiones, et pro dodrante quidem transferuntur ad fideicommissarium, pro quadrante remanent apud heredem. Quin etiam, licet una re aliqua deducta aut præcepta restituere aliquis hereditatem rogatus est, qua maxima pars hereditatis contineatur, æque in solidum transferuntur actiones, et secum deliberare debet is cui restituitur hereditas, an expediat sibi restitui. Eadem scilicet interveniunt, et si duabus pluribusve deductis præceptisve rebus restituere hereditatem rogatus sit; sed et si certa summa deducta præceptave, quæ quartam vel etiam maximam partem hereditatis continet, rogatus sit aliquis hereditatem restituere, idem juris est. Quæ autem diximus de eo qui ex asse heres institutus est, eadem transferemus et ad eum qui ex parte heres scriptus est.

there is this difference, that, in the first case, when an heir is requested to give up an inheritance, after deducting or excepting a particular thing, then, according to that *senatus-consultum*, all actions are transferred to and against the *fideicommissarius*, and what remains to the heir is free from all incumbrance, as if acquired by legacy. In the second case, when an heir is requested in general terms to give up an inheritance, after retaining a fourth to himself, all actions are proportionably divided; those which regard the three-fourths of the estate, being transferred to the *fideicommissarius*, and those which regard the one-fourth, to the heir. And, even if an heir be requested to give up an inheritance, after making a deduction or exception of some particular thing, which comprises the greatest part of the whole inheritance, all actions are still transferred to the *fideicommissarius*, who ought always, therefore, to consider whether it will be expedient or not, that the inheritance should be given up to him. All this applies equally, whether an heir be requested to give up an inheritance after a deduction or exception of two, or more, particular things, or of a certain sum of money, which may comprise a fourth or even the greatest part of the inheritance. What we have said of an heir, who is instituted to the whole of an inheritance, applies equally to one who is instituted only to a part.

D. xxxvi. 1. 1. 18. 21; D. xxxvi. 1. 30. 3.

If the testator give a particular object to the *heres institutus* which was equal in value to the fourth of the inheritance, the law considered this as a specific legacy given to the *heres*. The *fideicommissarius* took the whole inheritance except this part, and all the actions of the whole inheritance were transferred to him. Justinian retains this distinction between a particular object being given, and a general direction to retain a fourth. If a particular object were given not equal in value to a fourth, the heir would retain enough to complete his fourth; and all actions relating to the part so retained would pass to him, and all others to the *fideicommissarius*. (Cod. vi. 50. 11.)

10. Praeterea intestatus quoque moriturus potest rogare eum, ad quem bona sua vel legitimo jure vel honorario pertinere intelligit, ut hereditatem suam totam partemve ejus, aut rem aliquam, veluti fundum, hominem, pecuniam, alicui restituat; cum alioquin legata nisi ex testamento non valeant.

10. Moreover, a man about to die intestate, may request the person, to whom his estate will pass, either by the civil or prætorian law, to give up to a third person the whole inheritance, or a part of it, or any particular thing, as a piece of land, a slave, or a sum of money. Legacies, on the contrary, are only valid when given by testament.

Gai. ii. 270; D. xxxi. 36.

Antoninus Pius extended the provisions of the *senatus-consulta Trebellianum* and *Pegasianum*, to trusts imposed on *heredes ab intestato*. (D. xxxv. 2. 18.)

11. Eum quoque cui aliquid restituitur, potest rogare ut id rursum alii, aut totum aut pro parte, vel etiam aliquid aliud restituat.

11. A *fideicommissarius* may also himself be requested to give up to another, either the whole or a part of what he receives, or even anything else.

Gai. ii. 271.

The *fideicommissarius*, who was thus only a vehicle to pass on the inheritance to another *fideicommissarius*, could not retain a fourth for himself. The object of the *lex Falcidia* was merely to secure an heir, not in all cases to give a fourth to the person who virtually had the inheritance; but when the heir entered on the inheritance by order of the prætor, then the *fideicommissarius* stood in the place of the heir, so far as to be able to apply the *lex Falcidia*, as if representing the heir, against legatees, but not against a second *fideicommissarius*. (D. xxxvi. 1. 63. 4.)

12. Et quia prima fideicommissorum cunabula a fide heredum pendant, et tam nomen quam substantiam acceperunt, et ideo divus Augustus ad necessitatem juris ea detraxit, nuper et nos eumdem principem supremo contendentes, ex facto quod Tribonianus, vir excelsus, quæstor sacri palatii suggessit, constitutionem fecimus per quam disposuimus: si testator fidei heredis sui commisit ut vel hereditatem vel speciale fideicommissum restituat, et neque ex scriptura neque ex quinque testium numero qui in fideicommissis legitimus esse noscitur, possit res manifestari, sed vel pauciores quam quinque, vel nemo penitus testis intervenerit, tunc sive pater heredis sive alius

12. Originally all fiduciary gifts depended only upon the good faith of the heir; whence they took their name as well as their character. To remedy this the Emperor Augustus made them obligatory in law, and we have lately endeavoured to surpass that prince; and, on the occasion of a case brought to our notice by the most eminent Tribonian, the quæstor of our sacred palace, we have enacted by a constitution, that if a testator has entrusted to the faith of his heir the restoration of an inheritance, or any particular thing, and the fact cannot be proved either by any writing or by five witnesses (the legal number in such cases), there having been fewer, or perhaps no witnesses present, then,

quicumque sit qui fidem heredis elegerit, et ab eo restitui aliquid voluerit, si heres perfidia tentus adimplere fidem recusat negando rem ita esse subsecutam, si fideicommissarius jusjurandum ei detulerit, cum prius ipse de calumnia juraverit, necesse eum habere vel jusjurandum subire quod nihil tale a testatore audivit, vel recusantem ad fideicommissi vel universitatis vel specialis solutionem coarctari, ne pereat ultima voluntas testatoris fidei heredis commissa. Eadem observari censuimus, et si a legatario vel fideicommissario aliquid similiter relictum sit. Quod si is a quo relictum dicitur, confiteatur quidem a se aliquid relictum esse, sed ad legis subtilitatem decurrat, omnimodo solvere cogendus est.

whether it is his father who has thus trusted to the good faith of the heir, and begged him to restore the inheritance, or whether it is anyone else, if the heir perfidiously refuse to make the restitution, and deny the whole transaction, the *fideicommissarius* having previously himself sworn to his own good faith, may put the heir to his oath; and thus force him either to deny having received any such trust upon oath, or to fulfil it, whether it relate to the whole inheritance or to some particular thing; and this is allowed, lest the last wishes of a testator, committed to the faith of an heir, should be defeated. The same process may be adopted against a legatee, or a *fideicommissarius* charged with a restitution. And if any one so charged admits the trust, but endeavour to shelter himself in the subtleties of the law, he may be compelled to perform his duty.

C. vi. 42. 32.

*De calumnia juraverit*, that is, he must swear beforehand that he is acting *bona fide*, and not inventing a ground of litigation.

## TIT. XXIV. DE SINGULIS REBUS PER FIDEICOMMISSUM RELICTIS.

Potest autem quis etiam singulas res per fideicommissum relinquere, veluti fundum, hominem, vestem, aurum, argentum, pecuniam numeratam; et vel ipsum heredem rogare ut alicui restituat, vel legatarium, quamvis a legatario legari non possit.

A person may also leave particular things by a *fideicommissum*, as a piece of land, a slave, a garment, gold, silver, pieces of money; and he may request either his heir to restore them, or a legatee, although a legatee cannot be charged with a legacy.

GAL. li. 200. 271.

1. Potest autem non solum proprias res testator per fideicommissum relinquere, sed heredis aut legatarii aut fideicommissarii aut cujuslibet alterius. Itaque et legatarius et fideicommissarius non solum de ea re rogari potest, ut eam alicui restituat quae ei relicta sit, sed etiam de alia, sive ipsius sive aliena sit: hoc solum obser-

1. A testator may leave by *fideicommissum*, not only his own property, but also that of his heir, of a legatee, of a *fideicommissarius*, or of any other person; so that a legatee or *fideicommissarius* may not only be requested to give what hath been left to him, but what is his own, or even what is the property of another. The only rule to be observed is, that

vandum est, ne plus quisquam rogetur alicui restituere, quam ipse ex testamento ceperit; nam quod amplius est, inutiliter relinquitur. Cum autem aliena res per fideicommissum relinquitur, necesse est ei qui rogatus est, aut ipsam redimere et praestare aut aestimationem ejus solvere.

no one be requested to restore more than he has received under the testament: for as to the excess the disposition is ineffectual. And, when the property of another is left by a *fideicommissum*, the person requested to restore it is obliged either to obtain from the proprietor and deliver the thing itself, or to pay its estimated value.

GAI. II. 261, 262.

Ulpian (*Reg.* 25. 5) expresses the power of disposal by *fideicommissum*, by saying that everything could be disposed of in that way, that could be given by a legacy *per damnationem.*

*Quod amplius est, inutiliter relinquitur.* If, however, the thing which the *fideicommissarius* was to give belonged to him himself, he was obliged to give it, whatever might be its value, if he accepted what was given to him by the *fideicommissum*, as he was considered to have had an opportunity of exercising his judgment, and not to have valued his own thing more highly than that which he received. (D. xl. 5. 24. 12.)

2. Libertas quoque servo per fideicommissum dari potest, ut heres eum rogetur manumittere, vellegatarius vel fideicommissarius: nec interest utrum de suo proprio servo testator roget, an de eo qui ipsius heredis aut legatarii vel etiam extranei sit: itaque et alienus servus redimi et manumitti debet. Quod si dominus eum non vendat, si modo nihil ex judicio ejus qui reliquit libertatem, recepit, non statim extinguitur fideicommissaria libertas sed differtur; quia possit tempore providente, ubicunque occasio servi redimendi fuerit, praestari libertas. Qui autem ex fideicommissi causa manumittitur, non testatoris fit libertus, etiamsi testatoris servus sit, sed ejus qui manumittit; at is qui directo testamento liber esse jubetur, ipsius testatoris libertus fit, qui etiam Orcinus appellatur. Nec alius ullus directo ex testamento libertatem habere potest, quam qui utroque tempore testatoris fuerit, et quo faceret testamentum et quo moreretur: directo autem libertas tunc dari videtur; cum non ab alio

2. Freedom may also be conferred upon a slave by a *fideicommissum*: for an heir, legatee, or *fideicommissarius*, may be requested to enfranchise him; nor does it signify whether it be of his own slave that the testator requests the manumission, or of the slave of his heir, or of a legatee, or of a stranger; and therefore, when a slave is not the testator's own property, he must be bought, and enfranchised. But, if the proprietor of the slave refuse to sell him, as he may, if he has taken nothing under the testament, yet the freedom given by the *fideicommissum* is not extinguished, but deferred only until it may be possible in the course of time, on any occasion offering of purchasing the slave, to effect his enfranchisement. The slave who is enfranchised in pursuance of a *fideicommissum*, does not become the freedman of the testator, although he was the testator's own slave, but he becomes the freedman of that person who enfranchises him. But a slave who receives his liberty directly from the testament, becomes the freedman of the testator and is

servum manumitti rogat, sed velut
ex suo testamento libertatem si
competere vult.

said to be Orcinus; and no one can
obtain liberty directly by testament,
unless he were the slave of the
testator, both at the time of the
testator's making his testament, and
also at that of his death. Liberty
is given directly, when a testator
does not request that freedom be
given to his slave by another, but
gives it himself by virtue of his own
testament.

GAI. iL 203-207 ; C. vii. 4. 6.

This is an instance in which a difference is still allowed by
Justinian to subsist between legacies and *fideicommissa.* The
direct gift of liberty by a legacy differs from the indirect gift
by a *fideicommissum.* It was the opinion of Gaius, that if the
master of the slave refused to sell the slave for a reasonable
price, the *fideicommissum* perished. (GAI. ii. 265.) Justinian,
in accordance with a rescript of the Emperor Alexander
(C. vii. 4. 6.), decides that it is only delayed.

If a testator enfranchised directly a slave that could not be
so enfranchised, the gift of liberty would be as valid as a
*fideicommissum.*

*Orcinus,* from *Orcus* ; because he is the freedman of a
dead person.

3. Verba autem fideicommissorum hæc maxime in usu habetur : peto, rogo, volo, mando, fidei
tuæ committo. Quæ periode singula firma sunt, atque si omnia in
unum congesta essent.

3. The terms generally used in
making *fideicommissa* are the following : I request, I ask, I desire, I commit, I entrust to thy good faith ; and
each of them is of as much force
separately as all of them placed together.

GAI. li. 249.

The expressions by which a *fideicommissum* was created,
were quite immaterial, provided that the wishes of the testator
could be ascertained.

## Tit. XXV.   DE CODICILLIS.

Ante Augusti tempora constat
codicillorum jus non fuisse, sed
primus Luclus Lentulus, ex cujus
persona etiam fideicommissa coeperunt, codicillos introduxit. Nam
cum decederet in Africa, scripsit
codicillos testamento confirmatos,
quibus ab Augusto petiit per fideicommissum ut faceret aliquid ; et

Codicils were certainly not in use
before the reign of Augustus ; for
Luclus Lentulus, to whom the
origin of *fideicommissa* may be
traced, was the first who introduced
codicils. When dying in Africa, he
wrote several codicils, which were
confirmed by his testament ; and in
these he requested Augustus by a

cum divæ Augustæ voluntatem ejus implev, deinceps reliqui ejus auctoritatem secuti fideicommissa præstabant, et filia Lentuli legata quæ jure non debebat, solvit. Dicitur autem Augustus convocasse prudentes, inter quos Trebatium quoque cujus tunc auctoritas maxima erat, et quæsisse an posset hoc recipi, nec absonans a juris ratione codicillorum usus esset; et Trebatium suasisse Augusto, quod diceret utilissimum et necessarium hoc civibus esse propter magnas et longas peregrinationes quæ apud veteres fuissent, ubi si quis testamentum facere non posset, tamen codicillos posset. Post quæ tempora, cum et Labeo codicillos fecisset, jam nemini dubium erat quin codicilli jure optimo admitterentur.

fideicommissum to do something for him. The emperor complied with the request, and many other persons, following his example, discharged fideicommissa committed to them; and the daughter of Lentulus paid debts, which in strictness of law were not due from her. It is said, that Augustus, having called together upon this occasion persons learned in the law, and among others Trebatius, whose opinion was of the greatest authority, asked whether codicils could be admitted, and whether they were not repugnant to the principles of law? Trebatius advised the emperor to admit them, as they were most convenient and necessary to citizens, on account of the great and long journeys which they were frequently obliged to take, during which a man who could not make a testament, might be able to make codicils. And subsequently, Labeo himself having made codicils, no one afterwards doubted their perfect validity.

*Codicilli* were small tablets on which memorandums or letters were written. A testator might naturally address a short letter giving short directions to his heir. When *fideicommissa* came to be enforced, these letters or directions were enforced as creating *fideicommissa*. As under the Roman law a testator could make no alteration in his testament without making an entirely new testament, the use of codicils seemed so obvious as to make it a matter of wonder that the Romans were able so long to do without their legal recognition. Codicils might be made without there being any testament at all. They were then directions addressed to the *heredes ab intestato*. But if there was a testament, they were always considered as attached to it: if the testamentary dispositions failed they failed also, and all their provisions were taken with reference to the time when the testament was made. (D. xxix. 7. 2. 2. and 3. 2.)

A testator by inserting an express clause to that effect, termed by commentators *clausula codicillaris*, might provide that his testament, if invalid as a testament, should take effect as a codicil, or, to speak more accurately, as codicils, for the word was generally used in the plural.

1. Non tantum autem testamento facto potest quis codicillos facere,

1. Not only a person who has already made his testament, may

red intestato quis decedens fideicommittere codicillis potest. Sed
cum ante testamentum factum codicilli facti erant, l'apinianus ait non
aliter vires habere, quam si speciali
postea voluntate confirmentur; sed
divi Severus et Antoninus rescripserunt, ex iis codicillis qui testamentum precedunt, prose fideicommissum peti, si appareat eum
qui postea testamentum fecit, a
voluntate quam codicillis expresserat, non recessisse.

make codicils, but even a person
dying intestate may create fideicommissa by codicils. But when
codicils are made before a testament,
they cannot take effect, according to
l'apinian, unless confirmed by a
special disposition in the testament.
But the Emperors Severus and Antoninus have decided by rescript,
that a thing, left in trust by codicils, made before a testament, may
be demanded by the fideicommissarius, if it appear that the testator
has not abandoned the intention
which he at first expressed in the
codicils.

Gai. II. 270.

There was a distinction between codicils confirmed by testament, and those not so confirmed, for if codicils were confirmed
by testament, their provisions could operate as legacies, and
not only as *fideicommissa*. A testator could, by anticipation,
confirm in his testament any codicils he might thereafter make.
(D. xlix. 7. 8.)

2. Codicillis autem hereditas
neque dari neque adimi potest, ne
confundatur jus testamentorum et
codicillorum; et ideo nec exheredatio scribi. Directo autem hereditas codicillis neque dari neque
adimi potest; nam per fideicommissum hereditas codicillis jure relinquitur. Nec conditionem heredi
instituto codicillis adjicere neque
substituere directo potest.

2. An inheritance can neither be
given nor taken away by codicils, as
the different effect of testaments and
codicils would be thereby confounded, and of course, therefore, no
heir can be disinherited by codicils.
But it is only directly that an inheritance can neither be given nor
taken away by codicils, for it may
be legally disposed of in codicils by
means of a *fideicommissum*. Nor,
again, can a condition be imposed
on the institution of an heir, nor a
direct substitution be made, by
codicils.

Gai. ii. 273; D. xxix. 7. 0.

3. Codicillis autem etiam plures
quis facere potest, et nullam solemnitatem ordinationis desiderant.

3. A person may make several
codicils, and they require no solemnity in their form.

D. xxix. 7. 0. 1.

Codicils were not originally subjected to any rules determining the mode in which they were made. But by a constitution
of Theodosius, added to by Justinian, they were to be made
*uno contextu*, either verbally, or in writing, and in presence of
five witnesses casually or purposely gathered together; if the
codicils were in writing, the witnesses were to subscribe them.
(C. vi. 36. 8.)

# LIBER TERTIUS.

### Tit. I. DE HEREDITATIBUS QUÆ AB INTESTATO DEFERUNTUR.

Intestatus decedit, qui aut omnino testamentum non fecit, aut non jure fecit; aut id quod fecerat ruptum irritumve factum est, aut nemo ex eo heres extitit.

A person dies intestate, who either has made no testament at all, or has made one not legally valid; or if the testament he has made be revoked, or made useless; or if no one becomes heir under it.

D. xxxviii. 16. 1.

If a person died without a testament, the law regulated the succession to the inheritance. So also it did, if he left a testament that was fatally defective in form (*non jure factum*), or if his testament was revoked, or, in the language of Roman law, broken (*ruptum*), or if it was set aside as inofficious, or made useless by a change of *status* in the testator (*irritum*), or if no heir would accept the inheritance under it.

If there was no testament to determine the succession, the law of the Twelve Tables gave the inheritance first to the *sui heredes*, who were also *necessarii heredes*, that is, could not refuse to accept the inheritance; then to the *agnati*; and then, if the deceased was a member of a *gens*, to the *gentiles*. In default of *agnati*, the prætor called to the inheritance the *cognati*, or blood-relations. (See Introd. sec. 45.) Perhaps the succession of *gentiles* lasted to a time later than that of this Prætorian succession of the *cognati*; but, at any rate, it did not outlast the Republic, and, therefore, speaking of the times when we are most familiar with Roman law, we may say that the succession was given first to the *sui heredes*, then to the *agnati*, then to the *cognati*. But some complication was introduced into the rules of succession, by certain classes of persons being, by different changes in the law, raised from the rank of *agnati* to that of *sui heredes*, and from the rank of *cognati* to that of *agnati*. These changes are not, however,

very difficult to follow, if we divide them according as they
were effected, (1) by the Prætor, (2) by *senatus-consulta*, and
Imperial enactments previous to Justinian, (3) by Justinian
himself. This first Title treats of the succession of *sui heredes*,
and of those ranked among the *sui heredes*; the second and
two following Titles treat of the succession of *agnati*, and of
those ranked among *agnati*. At the end of this title will be
found a short summary of the changes in the law relative to
the succession of *sui heredes*: at the end of the fourth Title
one will be found of the changes relative to the succession of
*agnati*.

Justinian altered the whole mode of succession to intestates
by the 118th and 127th Novels. This change, being effected
several years after the publication of the Institutes, should not
be allowed to interfere with the consideration of the law of
succession existing when the Institutes were published. But,
as it is too remarkable and too well known a part of Justinian's
legislation to remain wholly unnoticed, a short account of it
will be given at the end of the ninth Title, which closes the
part of the Institutes treating of successions *ab intestato*.

1. Intestatorum autem hereditates ex lege Duodecim Tabularum
primum ad suos heredes pertinent.

1. The inheritances of intestates,
by the law of the Twelve Tables,
belong in the first place to the *sui
heredes*.

GAI. iii. 1.

2. Sui autem heredes existimantur, ut et supra diximus, qui in potestate morientis fuerint, veluti
filius filiave, nepos neptisve ex filio,
pronepos proneptisve ex nepote ex
filio nato pr gnatus pronatisve;
nec interest utrum naturales sint
liberi an adoptivi. Quibus connumerari necesse est etiam eos qui
ex legitimis quidem matrimoniis
non sunt progeniti, curiis tamen
civitatum dati, secundum divalium
constitutionum quæ super his positæ sunt tenorem, heredum suorum
jura nanciscuntur; necnon eos quos
nostræ amplexæ sunt constitutiones
per quas jusdimus, si quis mulierem
in suo contubernio copulaverit, non
ab initio affectione maritali, eam
tamen cum qua poterat habere conjugium, et ex ea liberos sustulerit,
postea vera affectione procedente
etiam nuptialia instrumenta cum
ea fecerit, et filios vel filias habuerit, non solum eos liberos qui post

2. And, as we have observed before, those are *sui heredes* who, at
the death of the deceased, were
under his power; as a son or a
daughter, a grandson or a granddaughter by a son, a great-grandson
or great-granddaughter by a grandson of a son; nor does it make any
difference, whether these children
are natural or adopted. We must
also reckon among them those, who,
though not born in lawful wedlock,
nevertheless, according to the tenor
of the imperial constitutions, acquire
the rights of *sui heredes*, by being
presented to the *curiæ* of their
cities; as also those to whom our
own constitutions refer, which enact
that, if any person has lived with a
woman not originally intending to
marry her, but whom he is not prohibited to marry, and shall have
children by her, and shall afterwards,
feeling towards her the affection of
a husband, enter into an act of mar-

A A

dotem editi sunt, justos et in potestate patris esse, sed etiam anteriores qui et iis, qui postea nati sunt, occasionem legitimi nominis praestiterunt. Quod obtinere censuimus, etiam si non progeniti fuerint post dotale instrumentum confectum liberi, vel etiam nati ab hac luce fuerint subtracti. Ita demum tamen nepos neptisve, pronepos proneptisve, suorum heredum numero sunt, si praecedens persona desierit in potestate parentis esse, sive morte id acciderit, sive alia ratione, veluti emancipatione: nam si per id tempus quo quis moreretur, filius in potestate ejus sit, nepos ex eo suus heres esse non potest; idque et in ceteris deinceps liberorum personis dictum intelligimus. Postumi quoque, qui si vivo parente nati essent, in potestate ejus futuri forent, sui heredes sunt.

riage with her, and have by her sons or daughters, not only those born after the settlement of the dowry shall be legitimate, and in the power of their father, but also those born before, who gave occasion to the legitimacy of the children born after. And this law shall obtain, although no children are born subsequent to the making of the act of dowry, or those born are all dead. But a grandson or granddaughter, a great-grandson or great-granddaughter, is not reckoned among the sui heredes, unless the person preceding them in degree has ceased to be under the power of the ascendant, either by death, or some other means, as by emancipation. For, if a son, when the grandfather died, was under the power of his father, the grandson cannot be suus heres of his grandfather; and so with regard to all other descendants. Posthumous children, also, who would have been under the power of their father, if they had been born in his lifetime, are sui heredes.

GAL. iii. 1, 2; C. v. 27. 3. 10, 11.

The *sui heredes* were the children, whether natural, adoptive, or made legitimate, in the power of the deceased at the time of his death. We must not confuse persons made *sui heredes* by the later legislation, as these legitimated children were, with those permitted to rank with *sui heredes*.

3. Sui autem etiam ignorantes fiunt heredes, et licet furiosi sint, heredes possunt existere, quia quibus ex causis ignorantibus nobis acquiritur, ex his causis et furiosis acquiri potest. Et statim morte parentis quasi continuatur dominium, et ideo nec tutoris auctoritate opus est pupillis, cum etiam ignorantibus acquiratur suis heredibus hereditas; nec curatoris consensu acquiritur furioso, sed ipso jure.

3. Sui heredes may become heirs without their knowledge, and even though insane; for in every case in which inheritances may be acquired without our knowledge, they may also be acquired by the insane. At the death of the father, ownership in an inheritance is at once continued; accordingly, the authority of a tutor is not necessary, as inheritances may be acquired by sui heredes without their knowledge: neither does an insane person acquire by assent of his curator, but by operation of law.

D. xxxviii. 10. 14.

Directly the succession *ab intestato* commenced, which it did when the deceased died if there was no testament, and as soon as it was ascertained that the testament was ineffectual if a testament had been made, the *suus heres* became at once heir without any act of his own.  We may, however, apply here what we have already said of the power to abstain altogether from the inheritance given him by the prætor.  (See Bk. ii. Tit. 19. 2.)

4. Interdum autem, licet in potestate parentis mortis tempore suus heres non fuerit, tamen suus heres parenti efficitur, veluti si ab hostibus reversus quis fuerit post mortem patris; jus enim postliminii hoc facit.

5. Per contrarium evenit ut, licet quis in familia defuncti sit mortis tempore, tamen suus heres non fiat, veluti si post mortem suam pater judicatus fuerit perduellionis reus, ac per hoc memoria ejus damnata fuerit: suum enim heredem habere non potest, cum fiscus ei succedit; sed potest dici ipso jure suum heredem esse, sed desinere.

4. But sometimes a child becomes a suus heres, although he was not under power at the death of his parent; as when a person returns from captivity after the death of his father. He is then made a suus heres by the jus postliminii.

5. On the contrary, it may happen that a child, who, at the death of his parent, was under his power, is not his suus heres: as when a parent, after his decease, is adjudged to have been guilty of treason, and his memory is thus made infamous. He can then have no suus heres, as it is the fiscus that succeeds to his estate. In this case it may be said that there has in law been a suus heres, but that he has ceased to be so.

D. xxxviii. 16. 1. 3.

As a general rule, if the accused died before conviction, the prosecution was at an end.  His succession went to his heirs by testament or in law.  But to this there was one exception.  If a person charged with perduellio (treason against the state or emperor) died before conviction, the prosecution was continued, and if he was found guilty, his memory was said to be condemned (memoria damnata fuit), and his sentence having a retrospective effect, his property was confiscated exactly as if he had been condemned in his lifetime.

6. Cum filius filiave et ex altero filio nepos neptisve existunt, pariter ad hereditatem avi vocantur, nec qui gradu proximior est, ulteriorem excludit: æquum enim esse videtur nepotes neptesque in patris sui locum succedere. Pari ratione, et si nepos neptisve sit ex filio, et ex nepote pronepos proneptisve, simul vocantur. Et quia placuit nepotes neptesque, item pronepotes et proneptes in parentis sui locum succedere, conveniens esse visum est non in capita sed in stirpes hereditatem dividi, ut filius partem dimidiam hereditatis habeat, et ex altero filio duo pluresve nepotes

6. A son, a daughter, and a grandson or granddaughter by another son, are all called equally to the inheritance; nor does the nearer in degree exclude the more remote: for it seems just, that grandsons and granddaughters should succeed in the place of their father. For the same reason, a grandson or granddaughter by a son, and a great-grandson or great-granddaughter by a grandson, are all called together. And since grandsons and granddaughters, great-grandsons and great-granddaughters, succeed in place of their parent, it appeared to follow that inheritances should not

alteram dimidiam. Item, si ex duobus filiis nepotes neptesve extant, ex altero unus forte aut duo, ex altero tres aut quatuor, ad unum aut duos dimidia pars pertineat, ad tres vel quatuor altera dimidia.

be divided per capita, but per stirpes; so that a son should possess one-half, and the grandchildren, whether two or more, of another son, the other half of an inheritance. So, where there are grandchildren by two sons, one or two perhaps by the one, and three or four by the other, the inheritance will belong, half to the grandchild, or the two grandchildren by the one son, and half to the three or four grandchildren by the other son.

GAI. LII. 7, 8.

The expressions ' dividing *per stirpes* and *per capita*' may be rendered, dividing by the ' stock' and ' by the head.' An inheritance is divided ' by the head' when each head or person of those who take has an equal share in it; it is divided ' by the stock' when one share is distributed among all who are descended from one stock, *i. e.* are descended from the person who would, if he had been living, have taken the whole share.

7. Cum autem quaeritur an quis suus heres existere possit, eo tempore quaerendum est quo certum est aliquem sine testamento decessisse, quod accidit et destituto testamento. Hac ratione, si filius exheredatus fuerit et extraneus heres institutus, et filio mortuo postea certum fuerit heredem institutum ex testamento non fieri heredem, aut quia noluit esse heres aut quia non potuit, nepos avo suus heres existet; quia quo tempore certum est intestatum decessisse patremfamilias, solus invenitur nepos: et hoc certum est.

7. When it is asked, whether such a person is a *suus heres*, we must look to the time at which it was certain, that the deceased died without a testament, including therein the case of the testament being abandoned. Thus, if a son be disinherited and a stranger be instituted heir, and after the death of the son it becomes certain that the instituted heir will not be heir, either because he is unwilling or unable to be so, in this case the grandson of the deceased becomes the *suus heres* of his grandfather; for, at the time, when it was certain that the deceased died intestate, there exists only the grandchild, and of this there can be no doubt.

D. xxxviii. 10. 1. 8 ; D. xxxviii. 6, 7.

8. Et licet post mortem avi natus sit, tamen avo vivo conceptus, mortuo patre ejus posteaque deserto avi testamento, suus heres efficitur. Plane, si et conceptus et natus fuerit post mortem avi, mortuo patre suo desertoque postea avi testamento, suus heres non existit, quia nullo jure cognationis patrem sui patris tetigit: sic nec ille est inter liberos avi, quem filius eman-

8. And although a child be born after the death of his grandfather, yet, if he were conceived in the lifetime of his grandfather, he will, if his father be dead, and his grandfather's testament be abandoned, become the *suus heres* of his grandfather. But a child both conceived and born after the death of his grandfather, could not become the *suus heres*, although his father should

cipatas adoptaverat. Ili autem, cum non sint quantum ad hereditatem liberi, neque bonorum possessionem petere possunt quasi proximi cognati. Haec de suis heredibus.

die and the testament of his grandfather be abandoned; because he was never allied to his grandfather by any tie of relationship. Neither is a person adopted by an emancipated son, to be reckoned among the children of the father of his adoptive father. And not only are these adoptive children of an emancipated son incapable of taking the inheritance as children of the deceased grandfather, but they cannot demand possession of the goods as the nearest *cognati*. Thus much concerning *sui heredes*.

D. xxxviii. 16. 6, 7.

9. Emancipati autem liberi jure civili nihil juris habent : neque enim sui heredes sunt, quia in potestate parentis esse desierunt, neque ullo alio jure per legem Duodecim Tabularum vocantur; sed praetor naturali aequitate motus dat eis bonorum possessionem unde liberi, perinde ac si in potestate parentis tempore mortis fuissent, sive soli sint, sive cum suis heredibus concurrant. Itaque duobus liberis extantibus, emancipato et qui tempore mortis in potestate fuerit, sane quidem is qui in potestate fuerit, solus jure civili heres est, id est, solus suus heres est; sed cum emancipatus beneficio pretoris in partem admittitur, evenit ut suus heres pro parte heres fiat.

9. Emancipated children by the civil law have no right to the inheritance of their father; being no longer under the power of their parent, they are not his *sui heredes*, nor are they called to inherit by any other right under the law of the Twelve Tables. But the praetor, obeying natural equity, grants them the possession of goods called *unde liberi*, as if they had been under the power of their father at the time of his death, and this, whether they stand alone, or whether there are also others, who are *sui heredes*. Thus, when there are two children, one emancipated, and the other under power at his father's death, the latter, by the civil law, is alone the heir, and alone the *suus heres*; but, as the emancipated son, by the indulgence of the praetor, is admitted to his share, the *suus heres* becomes heir only of a part.

Gai. iii. 19. 25, 20; D. xxxviii. 6. 1.

Not only emancipated children, but, if they themselves were dead, their children conceived after the emancipation, had the *possessio bonorum* given them by the praetor (D. xxxvii. 4. 6. 1); and a grandchild conceived before the emancipation, and who remained in the power of the grandfather, was allowed to succeed to the inheritance of the emancipated son. The praetor could not give these persons the title of 'heir,' as that only belonged to those who received it from the *jus civile*; but be gave them *possessio bonorum* for part of the inheritance (pro parte). Emancipated children were, however, obliged to bring into, and add to, the inheritance all the property they themselves possessed at the time of the father's death (*collatio bonorum*); because, if they had remained in the family, all that they had acquired, would have been acquired for the *paterfamilias*, and thus have formed part of the inheritance.  When a person, after a *capitis deminutio*, was *restitutus in integrum*, he also had the *possessio bonorum* given him, and received what he would have had if his disability had not prevented him succeeding as *suus heres*.  (D. xxxvii. 4. 1. 9.)

10. At hi qui emancipati a parente in adoptionem se dederunt, non admittuntur ad bona naturalis patris quasi liberi, si modo cum is moreretur in adoptiva familia sint; nam viro eo mancipati ab adoptivo patre, perinde admittuntur ad bona naturalis patris, ac si emancipati ab ipso essent, nec umquam in adoptiva familia fuissent; et convenienter, quod ad adoptivum patrem pertinet, extraneorum loco esse incipiunt. Post mortem vero naturalis patris emancipati ab adoptivo, et quantum ad hunc æque extraneorum loco fiunt, et quantum ad naturalis parentis bona pertinet, nihilo magis liberorum gradu nanciscuntur: quod ideo sic placuit, quia iniquum erat esse in potestate patris adoptivi, ad quos bona naturalis patris pertinerent, utrum ad liberos ejus an ad agnatos.

10. But those, who after emancipation have given themselves in adoption, are not admitted as children to the possession of the effects of their natural father, that is, if, at the time of his death, they are still in their adoptive family. But if, in the lifetime of their natural father, they have been emancipated by their adoptive father, they are then admitted to receive the goods of their natural father exactly as if they had been emancipated by him, and had never entered into the adoptive family. Accordingly, with regard to their adoptive father, they become from that moment strangers to him. But if they are emancipated by their adoptive father, after the death of their natural father, they are equally considered as strangers to their adoptive father; and yet do not gain the position of children with regard to the inheritance of their natural father. This has been so laid down, because it was unreasonable that it should be in the power of an adoptor to determine to whom the inheritance of a natural father should belong, whether to his children, or to the *agnati*.

D. xxxviii. 10. 4; D. xxxvii. 4. 6. 4.

Until the time of Justinian, an adopted son, during his continuance in his adoptive family, had no right of succession to his natural father, but was a *suus heres* of his adoptive father. If he left the adoptive family before the death of his natural father, he was called by the prætor to the succession of his natural father as a *suus heres*, but had, of course, no claim on the adoptive father. If he left the adoptive family after the death of his natural father, he had no claim to the succession of either natural or adoptive father, except as a *cognatus* of his natural father. Justinian, as we have seen in the First Book (Tit. 11. 2), altered this, and the adopted son, unless adopted by an ascendant, never lost his right to the succession of his natural father, although he gained a right to the succession *ab intestato* of his adoptive father. (See paragr. 14.)

11. Minus ergo juris habent adoptivi quam naturales: namque naturales emancipati beneficio prætoris gradum liberorum retinent, licet jure civili perdunt; adoptivi vero emancipati et jure civili perdunt gradum liberorum, et a prætore non adjuvantur, et recte: naturalia enim jura civilis ratio perimere non potest, nec quia desinunt sui heredes esse, desinere possunt filii filiæve aut nepotes neptesve esse. Adoptivi vero emancipati extraneorum loco incipiunt esse, quia jus nomenque filii filiæve quod per adoptionem consecuti sunt, alia civili ratione, id est emancipatione, perdunt.

11. The rights of adopted children are therefore less than those of natural children, who, even after emancipation, retain the rank of children by the indulgence of the prætor, although they lose it by the civil law. But adopted children, when emancipated, lose the rank of children by the civil law, and are not aided by the prætor. And the distinction between the two cases is very proper, for the civil law cannot destroy natural rights; and children cannot cease to be sons and daughters, grandsons or granddaughters, because they may cease to be *sui heredes*. But adopted children, when emancipated, become instantly strangers; for the rights and title of son or daughter, which they have only obtained by adoption, may be destroyed by another ceremony of the civil law, that, namely, of emancipation.

GAL. i. 158.

12. Eadem hæc observantur et in ea bonorum possessione, quam contra tabulas testamenti parentis liberis prætoritis, id est, neque heredibus institutis neque ut oportet exheredatis prætor pollicetur; nam eos quidem qui in potestate parentis mortis tempore fuerunt, et emancipatos vocat prætor ad eam bonorum possessionem; eos vero qui in adoptiva familia fuerint per hoc tempus quo naturalis parens moreretur, repellit. Item adoptivos liberos emancipatos ab adoptivo patre, sicut ab intestato, ita longe minus contra tabulas testamenti ad bona ejus non admittit; quia desinunt numero liberorum esse.

12. The same rules are observed in the possession of goods, which the prætor gives *contra tabulas* to children who have been passed over, that is, who have neither been instituted heirs, nor properly disinherited. For the prætor calls to this possession of goods those children under the power of their father at the time of his death, and those also who are emancipated; but he excludes those who were in an adoptive family at the decease of their natural father. So, too, adopted children emancipated by their adoptive father, as they are not admitted to succeed their adoptive father *ab intestato*, much less are they admitted to possess the goods of their adoptive father contrary to his testament, for they cease to be included in the number of his children.

D. xxxviii. 6. 1. 0; D. xxxvii. 4. 6. 4.

When a testament was made, but a person who was a *suus heres*, or who was raised to the rank of a *suus heres*, was not expressly disinherited in the testament, the prætor gave him the *possessio bonorum contra tabulas*, i. e. contrary to the testament.

13. Admonendi tamen sumus, eos qui in adoptiva familia sunt, quive post mortem naturalis parentis ab adoptivo patre emancipati fuerint, intestato parente naturali mortuo, licet ea parte edicti qua liberi ad bonorum possessionem vocantur, non admittantur, alia tamen parte vocari, id est, qua cognati defuncti vocantur. Ex qua parte ita admittuntur, si neque sui heredes liberi neque emancipati obstent, neque agnatus quidem ullus intervenial; sub enim prætor liberos vocat tam suos heredes quam emancipatos, deinde legitimos heredes, deinde proximos cognatos.

13. It is, however, to be observed, that children still remaining in an adoptive family, or who have been emancipated by their adoptive father, after the decease of their natural father, who dies intestate, although not admitted by the part of the edict, calling children to the possession of goods, are admitted by another part, by which the *cognati* of the deceased are called. They are, however, only thus admitted in default of *sui heredes*, emancipated children, and *agnati*. For the prætor first calls the children, both the *sui heredes* and those emancipated, then the *legitimi heredes*, and then the *cognati*.

GAI. iii. 31 ; D. xxxvii. 15. 1.

14. Sed ea omnia antiquitati quidem placuerunt, a iquam autem emendationem a nostra constitutione acceperunt, quam super his personis proximus quæ a patribus suis naturalibus in adoptionem aliis dantur: invenimus etenim nonnullos casus, in quibus filii et naturalium parentium successionem propter adoptionem amittebant, et adoptione facile per emancipationem soluta ad neutrius patris successionem vocabantur. Hoc solito more corrigentes constitutionem scripsimus per quam definivimus, quando parens naturalis filium suum adoptandum alii dederit, integra omnia jura ita servari atque si in patria naturalis potestate permansisset, nec penitus adoptio fuisset subsecuta, nisi in hoc tantummodo casu ut possit ab intestato ad patris adoptivi venire successionem. Testamento autem ab eo facto, neque jure civili neque prætorio aliquid ex hereditate ejus persequi potest, neque contra tabulas bonorum possessione agnita, neque inofficiosi querela instituta: cum nec necessitas patri adoptivo imponitur vel heredem eum instituere vel exheredatum facere,

14. Such were the rules that formerly obtained ; but they have received some emendation from our constitution, relating to persons given in adoption by their natural parents. For cases have occurred in which sons, who by adoption have lost their succession to their natural parents, and, the tie of adoption being easily dissolved by emancipation, have lost the right of succeeding to either parent. Correcting, therefore, as usual, what is wrong, we have promulgated a constitution, enacting that, when a natural father has given his son in adoption, the rights of the son shall be preserved exactly as if he had still remained in the power of his natural father, and no adoption had taken place; except only in this, that the person adopted may succeed to his adoptive father, if he die intestate. But, if the adoptive father make a testament, the adoptive son can neither by the civil law nor under the prætorian edict, obtain any part of the inheritance, whether he demand possession of the effects *contra tabulas*, or allege that the testament is inofficious; for an adoptive father is under no obligation to institute, or

utpote nullo vinculo naturali copulatum, neque ai ex Sabiniano senatus-consulto ex tribus maribus fuerit adoptatus; nam et in hujusmodi casu, neque quartae ei semiatur, nec ulla actio ad ejus persecutionem ei competit. Nostra autem constitutione exceptus est is quem parens naturalis adoptandum susceperit; utroque enim jure tam naturali quam legitimo in hanc personam concurrente, pristina jura illi adoptioni servavimus, quemadmodum si paterfamilias se dederit arrogandum: quae specialiter et sigillatim ex praefatae constitutionis tenore possunt colligi.

disinherit his adopted son, there being no natural tie between them; not even if the adopted son has been chosen among three brothers, according to the senatus-consultum Sabinianum, for even in this case the son does not obtain the fourth part of his adoptive father's effects, nor has he any action whereby to claim it. But persons adopted by an ascendant, are excepted in our constitution; for, as natural and civil rights both concur in their favour, we have thought proper to preserve to this adoption its effect under the old law, as also to the arrogation of a paterfamilias. But this, in all its details, may be collected from the tenor of the abovementioned constitution.

C. viii. 47. 10, pr. 1, 2, 3.

Theophilus, in his Paraphrase, tells us that when a person adopted one of three male children, he was obliged, by the senatus-consultum Sabinianum, to leave him a fourth part of his property, but gives no reason for the rule, and we have no means of ascertaining what the true reason was. Justinian did away with the provision of the senatus-consultum, because it was not, under his legislation, necessary to protect specially the person thus chosen, inasmuch as no adopted child lost his share of his inheritance of his natural father.

Children adopted by a stranger were, under Justinian's legislation, not, properly speaking, placed in the rank of sui heredes, but were sui heredes, for the adoption had no effect on their position in their natural family. The effect of adoption was destroyed, not its results specially provided against.

15. Item vetustas ex masculis progenitos plus diligens, solos nepotes qui ex virili sexu descendunt, ad eorum vocabat successionem, et juri agnatorum eos anteponebat; nepotes autem qui ex filiabus nati sunt, et pronepotes ex neptibus, cognationis loco numerans praeterquam line-ali eos vocabat, tam in avi vel proavi materni quam in avi vel proavi sive paterno sive materno successionem. Divi autem principes non passi sunt talem contra naturam injuriam sine competente emendatione relinquere : sed cum nepotis et pronepotis nomen commune est utriusque qui tam ex masculis quam

15. The ancient law, favouring descendants from males, called only grandchildren so descended, to the succession as sui heredes, in preference to the agnati, while grandchildren born of daughters, and great-grandchildren born of granddaughters, were reckoned among cognati, and succeeded only after the agnati to their maternal grandfather and great-grandfather, or to their grandmother, or great-grandmother, maternal or paternal. But the emperors would not suffer such a violence against nature to continue without an adequate alteration: and inasmuch as the name of grandchild and great-

ex feminis descendunt, idem eumdem gradum et ordinem successionis eis dumaverunt. Sed ut amplius aliquid sit eis qui non solum naturæ, sed etiam veteris juris suffragio muniuntur, portionem nepotum et neptum vel deinceps de quibus supra diximus, paulo minuendam esse existimaverunt: ut minus tertiam partem acciperent, quam mater eorum vel avia fuerat acceptura, vel pater eorum vel avus paternus sive maternus, quando femina mortua sit cujus de hereditate agitur; iisque, licet soli sint, adeuntibus agnatos minime vocabant. Et quemadmodum lex Duodecim Tabularum filio mortuo nepotes vel neptes, pronepotes vel proneptes in locum patris sui ad successionem avi vocat, ita et principalis dispositio in locum matris suæ vel aviæ eos cum jam designata partis tertiæ deminutione vocat.

grandchild is common, as well to descendants by females, as by males, they gave all the same right and order of succession. But, that persons whose privileges rest not only on nature, but also on the ancient law, might enjoy some peculiar advantage, they thought it right that the portions of grandchildren, great-grandchildren, and other lineal descendants of a female, should be somewhat diminished, so that they should not receive so much by a third part as their mother or grandmother would have received, or, when the succession is to the inheritance of a woman, as their father or grandfather, paternal or maternal, would have received; and, although there were no other descendants, if they entered on the inheritance, the emperors did not call the agnati to the succession. And, as upon the decease of a son, the law of the Twelve Tables calls the grandchildren and great-grandchildren, male and female, to represent their father in the succession to their grandfather, so the imperial legislation calls them to take in succession the place of their mother or grandmother, subject only to the above-mentioned deduction of a third part.

C. vi. 55. 9.

This section contains the substance of a constitution of the Emperors Theodosius, Valentinian, and Arcadius. (Cod. Theod. v. 5.) Justinian here says, that when there were descendants by a female who entered on the inheritance, the *agnati* were not called to the succession. We know, however, from the code itself, that the *agnati* had a fourth part of the inheritance, as a sort of *Falcidia*. (See next paragr.)

10. Sed nos, cum adhuc dubitatio manebat inter agnatos et memoratos nepotes, quartam partem substantiæ defuncti agnatis sibi vindicantibus ex cujusdam constitutionis auctoritate, memoratam quidem constitutionem a nostro codice segregavimus, neque inseri eam ex Theodosiano Codice in eo concessimus. Nostra autem constitutione promulgata, toti juri ejus derogatum est, et eximimus, talibus nepotibus ex filia vel pronepotibus ex nepte et deinceps

10. But, as there still remained matter of dispute between the *agnati* and the above-mentioned grandchildren, the *agnati* claiming the fourth part of the estate of the deceased by virtue of a constitution; we have rejected this constitution, and have not permitted it to be inserted into our code from that of Theodosius. And in the constitution we have ourselves promulgated, we have completely departed from the provisions of those former constitutions, and have enac-

superstitibus, agnatos nullam partem mortui successionis sibi vindicare: ne hi qui ex transversa linea veniunt, potiores iis habeantur qui recto jure descendunt. Quam constitutionem nostram obtinere secundum sui vigorem et temporis et nunc sancimus: ita tamen ut, quemadmodum inter filios et nepotes ex filio antiquitas statuit non in capita sed in stirpes dividi hereditatem, similiter hos inter filios et nepotes ex filia distributionem fieri jubemus, vel inter omnes nepotes et neptes et alias deinceps personas, ut utraque progenies matris suae vel patris avise vel avi portionem sine ulla deminutione consequatur; ut si forte unus vel duo ex una parte, ex altera tres aut quatuor extent, unus aut duo dimidiam, alteri tres aut quatuor alteram dimidiam hereditatis habeant.

ted that *agnati* shall take no part in the succession of the deceased, when there are grandchildren born of a daughter, or great-grandchildren born of a granddaughter, or any other descendants from a female in the direct line; as those in a collateral line ought not to be preferred to direct descendants. This constitution is to prevail, from the date of its promulgation in its full force, as we here again enact. And as the old law ordered, that between the sons of the deceased and his grandsons by a son, every inheritance should be divided *per stirpes*, and not *per capita*, so we also ordain, that a similar distribution shall be made between sons and grandsons by a daughter, and between grandsons and granddaughters, great-grandsons and great-granddaughters, and all other descendants in a direct line; so that the children of either branch may receive the share of their mother or father, their grandmother or grandfather, without any diminution; and, if of the one branch there should be one or two children, and of the other branch three or four, then the one or two shall have one-half, and the three or four the other half of the inheritance.

C. vi. 58. 12.

Those who, not being *sui heredes*, were admitted to rank as such, were not *necessarii*. They could accept the inheritance or not, which they only acquired when they entered on it, *iis adeuntibus*. (Paragr. 15.)

The changes in the succession of the *sui heredes* were these :—

1. Those at the time of his death in the power of the *de cujus* (i.e. the person of whose inheritance we are speaking), succeeded as *sui heredes* under the law of the Twelve Tables.

2. The prætor, by giving them the *possessio bonorum*, placed in the rank of *sui heredes* the following classes of persons: (1) emancipated children, and (2), if the emancipated father was dead, grandchildren conceived after his emancipation, or (3), if the *de cujus* were the emancipated son, grandchildren conceived before the emancipation of the father, and (4), *sui heredes* deprived of the power of inheriting by a *capitis deminutio*, but afterwards *restituti in integrum*.

3. A constitution of Theodosius permitted the children and

descendants of deceased daughters to succeed to the portion
their mother would have received as *suus heres*, giving up
one-third of it if there were other *sui heredes*, and one-fourth
if there were only *agnati*, who would share the inheritance
with the mother.

4. Under Justinian, adoption by a stranger ceased to have
any effect upon the position of the person adopted in his
natural family; and the persons referred to in the constitution
of Theodosius just mentioned succeeded to the whole share of
the deceased daughter without any deduction.

## Tit. II. DE LEGITIMA AGNATORUM SUCCESSIONE.

| | |
|---|---|
| Si nemo suus heres, vel eorum quam inter suos heredes prætor vel constitutiones vocant, extat qui successionem quoquo modo amplectatur, tunc ex leg. Duodecim Tabularum ad agnatum proximum pertinet hereditas. | When there is no *suus heres*, nor any of those persons called by the prætor or the constitutions, to inherit with *sui heredes*, to take the succession in any way, the inheritance, according to the law of the Twelve Tables, belongs to the nearest *agnatus*. |

Gai. iii. D.

All persons were *agnati* who, descended from a common
ancestor, would, if that ancestor had been living, have been in
his power. The *sui heredes* were thus *agnati*; but as they
had the title of *sui heredes* peculiar to themselves, only those
*agnati* received the name of *agnati* who were connected with
the *de cujus* by a collateral line.

| | |
|---|---|
| 1. Sunt autem agnati, ut p imo quoque libro tradidimus, cognati per virilis sexus personas cognationi juncti, quasi a patre cognati: itaque eodem patre nati fratres agnati sibi sunt, qui et consanguinei vocantur, nec requiritur an etiam eandem matrem habuerint. Item patruus fratris filio et invicem is illi agnatus est. Eodem numero sunt fratres patrueles, id est, qui ex duobus fratribus procreati sunt, qui etiam consobrini vocantur: qua ratione etiam ad plures gradus agnationis pervenire poterimus. Ii quoque qui post mortem patris nascuntur, jura consanguinitatis nanciscuntur. Non tamen omnibus simul agnatis dat lex hereditatem; sed iis qui tunc | 1. *Agnati*, as we have explained in the First Book, are those *cognati* who are related through males, that is, are *cognati* by the father; and therefore brothers, who are the sons of the same father, are *agnati* to each other (they are also called *consanguinei*), and it does not make any difference whether they have the same mother. An uncle is also *agnatus* to his brother's son, and vice versa, the brother's son to his paternal uncle. So also *fratres patrueles*, that is, the children of brothers (also called *consobrini*), are likewise *agnati*. We may thus reckon many degrees of agnation: children, too, who are born after the decease of their father, obtain the rights of consanguinity. The law |

proximiore gradu sunt, enm certum
esse ceperit aliquem intestatum de-
cessise.

does not, however, give the inheritance to all the *agnati*, but to those
only who are in the nearest degree,
at the time that it becomes certain
that the deceased has died Intestate.

GAI. l. 156 : iil. 10, 11.

2. Per adoptionem quoque agnationis jus consistit, veluti inter filios
naturales et eos quos pater eorum
adoptavit ; nec dubium est quin
proprie consanguinei appellentur.
Item, si quis ex ceteris agnatis,
veluti frater aut patruus, aut denique is qui longiore gradu est, adoptaverit aliquem, agnatos inter suos
esse non dubitatur.

2. The right of agnation arises also
through adoption ; thus the natural
and adopted sons of the same father
are *agnati*. And such persons are
without doubt properly included in
the term *consanguinei*.  Also, if one
of your *agnati*, as, for example, a
brother, a paternal uncle, or any
other *agnatus*, however remote, adopt
any one, then the person so adopted
is undoubtedly to be reckoned among
your *agnati*.

3. Ceterum inter masculos quidem agnationis jure hereditas, etiam
longi-simo gradu, ultro citroque ca-
pitur: quod ad feminas vero ita
placebat, ut ipsae consanguinitatis
jure tantum capiant hereditatem, si
sorores sint, ulterius non capiant;
masculi autem ad earum hereditates,
etiamsi longissimo gradu sint, admittantur. Qua de causa, fratris tui
aut patrui tui filiae vel sorori tuae
hereditas ad te pertinet, tua vero
ad illas non pertinebat: quod ideo
ita constitutum erat, quia commodius videbatur ita jura constitui, ut
plerumque hereditates ad masculos
confluerent. Sed quia sane iniquum
erat in universum eas quasi extra-
neas repelli, praetor eas ad bonorum
possessionem admittit ex parte qua
proximitatis nomine bonorum possessionem pollicetur: ex qua parte
ita scilicet admittuntur, si neque
agnatus ullus, neque proximior
cognatus intervenit. Et haec quidem lex Duodecim Tabularum nullo
malo introduxit ;sed simplicitate
legibus amicam amplexa, simili
modo omnes agnatos sive masculos,
sive feminas cujuscumque gradus,
ad similitudinem suorum, invicem
ad successionem vocabat. Media
autem jurisprudentia, quae erat post
Duodecim Tabularum junior imperiali autem dispositione anterior,
subtilitate quadam excogitata prae-
fatam differentiam inducebat, et

3. Agnation gives males, however
distant in degree, reciprocal rights to
the succession to inheritances. But it
has been thought right that females
should only inherit by title of consanguinity if they were sisters, and not,
if in a more remote degree ; while
their male *agnati*, in however remote
a degree, were admitted to succeed to
them. Thus, the inheritance of your
brother's daughter, or of the daughter
of your paternal uncle or aunt, will
belong to you; but not your inheritance to them. This distinction was
made, because it seemed expedient
that the law should be so ordered,
that inheritances should for the most
part fall into the possession of males.
But as it was contrary to equity that
females should be thus almost wholly
excluded as strangers, the praetor
admits them to the possession of
goods promised by his edict, on account of proximity; but they are only
admitted if there is no *agnatus*, nor
any nearer *cognatus*. The law of the
Twelve Tables did not introduce any
of these distinctions ; but with the
simplicity proper to all legislation,
called the a suti of either sex, or any
degree, to a reciprocal succession, in
the same manner as sui heredes. It was
an intermediate jurisprudence posterior to the law of the Twelve Tables,
but prior to the imperial constitutions, that in a spirit of subtle in-
genuity introduced this distinction,

penitus eas a successione agnatorum repellebat : omni alia successione incognita, donec prætores paulatim asperitatem juris civilis corrigentes, sive quod deerat implentes, humano proposito alium ordinem suis edictis addiderunt, et cognationis lines proximitatis nomine introducta per bonorum possessionem eas adjuvabunt, et pollicebantur his bonorum possessionem quæ unde cognati appellatur. Nos vero legem Duodecim Tabularum sequentes, et ejus vestigia in hac parte conservantes, laudamus quidem prætores suæ humanitatis, non tamen eos in plenum causæ mederi invenimus: quare etenim uno eodemque gradu naturali concurrente, et agnationis titulis tam in masculis quam in fœminis æqua lance constitutis, masculis quidem dabatur ad successionem venire omnium agnatorum, ex agnatis autem mulieribus nulli penitus, nisi soli sorori, ad agnatorum successionem patebat aditus? Ideo in plenum omnia reducentes et ad jus Duodecim Tabularum eamdem dispositionem exæquantes, nostra constitutione sanximus, omnes legitimas personas, id est, per virilem sexum descendentes, sive masculini generis sive feminini sint, simili modo ad jura successionis legitimæ ab intestato vocari secundum sui gradus prærogativam, nec ideo excludendas quia consanguinitatis jura, sicut germanæ, non habent.

and entirely excluded females from the succession of agnati, no other method of succession being then known, until the prætors, correcting by degrees the asperity of the civil law, or supplying what was deficient, were led by their feeling of equity to add in their edicts a new order of succession. The line of cognati was admitted according to the degrees of proximity, and relief was thus afforded to females by the prætor giving them the possession of goods called unde cognati. But we, turning to the law of the Twelve Tables, and following in its steps, in our legislation on this point, praise the kind feeling of the prætors, but cannot think they have provided a complete remedy for the evil. Why, indeed, when males and females are placed in the same degree of natural relationship, and have equally the title of agnation, should males be permitted to succeed to all their agnati, while females, with the single exception of sisters, are entirely excluded ? We therefore, making a complete change, and returning to the law of the Twelve Tables, have declared by our constitution, that all legitimæ personæ, that is, descendants from males, whether themselves male or female, shall be equally called to the rights of succession ab intestato, according to the proximity of their degree and that females shall not be excluded on the ground that none but sisters have the right of consanguinity.

GAI. lii. 14. 23. 29; C. vi. 58. 14.

The media jurisprudentia here spoken of consisted of the opinions of the jurisprudentes, who extended the principle of the lex Voconia, which limited the succession of females under a testament (see Bk. ii. Tit. 14. pr.) to their succession ab intestato. Fœminæ ad hereditates legitimas ultra consanguineas successiones non admittuntur. Idque jure civili Voconia ratione videtur effectum. (PAUL. Sent. 4. 8. 22.) Thus a distinction was made among the agnati themselves and the consanguinei, that is, agnati in the second degree ; or, in other words, brothers and sisters, natural or adoptive, of the de cujus, were made into a class apart and distinguished from the agnati properly so called. Consanguineus, when used to mark off a particular class of the *agnati*, merely means children of the same father, without any reference to the mother at all, and not, as it generally does, 'children of the same father, and not of the same mother.'

4. Hoc etiam addendum nostræ constitutioni existimavimus, ut transferatur unus tantummodo gradus a jure cognationis in legitimam successionem: ut non solum fratris filius et filia, secundum quod jam definivimus, ad successionem patrui sui vocentur, sed etiam germanæ consanguineæ vel sororis uterinæ filius et filia soli, et non deinceps personæ, una cum his ad jura avunculi sui perveniant; et mortuo eo qui patruus quidem est sui fratris filiis, avunculus autem sororis suæ soboli, simili modo ab utrinque latere incredant, tamquam si omnes ex masculis descendentes legitimo jure veniant, scilicet ubi frater et soror superstites non sunt. His etenim personis præcedentibus et successionem admittentibus, ceteri gradus remanent penitus semoti, videlicet hereditate non ad stirpes sed in capita dividenda.

4. We have also thought fit to add to our constitution, that one whole degree, but only one, shall be transferred from the line of *cognati* to the legal succession. Not only the son and daughter of a brother, as we have just explained, shall be called to the succession of their paternal uncle, but the son or daughter of a sister, though she is only by the same father or only by the same mother, but no one in a more distant degree than a son and daughter of such a sister, may also be admitted to the succession of their maternal uncle. Thus, when a person dies who is a paternal uncle to the children of his brother, and maternal uncle to the children of his sister, then the children of either branch succeed exactly as if they were all descendants from males, and had a right by law to the succession. But this is only if the deceased leaves no brother or sister, for if he leaves any, and they accept the inheritance, the more remote degrees are entirely excluded from the inheritance, as it is to be divided in this instance per *capita* and not *per stirpes*.

C. vi. 58. 14. 1.

The children of a sister, although only *consanguinea*, that is, having the same father, or *uterina*, having the same mother, were thus admitted to the succession as *agnati*. We might gather from this that uterine brothers and sisters themselves were admitted, although it is not expressed in the text. The Code contains a constitution of Justinian (C. vi. 56. 7) expressly admitting them. The changes in the law with respect to the admission of brothers and sisters and their children as *agnati* were as follows:—In A.D. 498 Anastasius gave the rights of agnation to emancipated brothers and sisters, except that they only received three-fourths of what they would have had if they had remained in the family. (See Tit. 5. 1.) The children of emancipated brothers and sisters still remained *cognati* only. Justinian gave the rights of agnation, in A.D. 528, to uterine brothers and sisters. (C. vi. 56. 7); and in

A.D. 532, to the children of uterine sisters (C. vi. 58. 14. 1); and though the children of uterine brothers are not mentioned in the constitution, they must undoubtedly have been placed in the same position. Finally, in a constitution dated October, A.D. 534 (C. vi. 58. 15), and therefore subsequent to the promulgation of the Institutes, Justinian admitted as *agnati* emancipated brothers and sisters without any deduction of a fourth, uterine brothers and sisters, and nephews and nieces being the children either of emancipated or uterine brothers and sisters. After that constitution there were not, therefore, any but *agnati* in the second degree, nor any in the third degree except the uncles and aunts of the *de cujus*.

*Agnatorum hereditates dividuntur in capita.* (ULP. *Reg.* 26. 4.) There was no division *per stirpes*, wh ch was originally only a consequence of the *patria potestas*, in the succession of *agnati*. If one of those in any degree of relationship was dead, his representatives did not take his share. He was entirely passed over, and the others in that degree of relationship were alone called to the succession.

*Agnati* were spoken of as *legitimi heredes*, because the inheritance was given to them by the law of the Twelve Tables, whereas the *cognati* only received it from the prætor.

5. Si plures sint gradus agnatorum, aperte lex Duodecim Tabularum proximum vocat. Itaque si (verbi gratia) sit defuncti frater et alterius fratris filius aut patruus, frater potior habetur. Et quamvis singulari numero usa lex proximum vocat, tamen dubium non est quin, si plures sint ejusdem gradus, omnes admittantur: nam et proprie proximus ex pluribus gradibus intelligitur, et tamen non dubium est quin, licet unus sit gradus agnatorum, pertineat ad eos hereditas.

5. When there are many degrees of *agnati*, the law of the Twelve Tables expressly calls the nearest; if, for example, there is a brother of the deceased, and a son of another brother, or a paternal uncle, the brother is preferred. And, although the law of the Twelve Tables calls the nearest *agnatus* (in the singular number), yet without doubt, if there be several in the same degree, they ought all to be admitted. And, although properly by the nearest degree must be understood the nearest of several, yet, if all the *agnati* are in the same degree, the inheritance undoubtedly belongs to them all.

GAI. iii. 15.

6. Proximus autem, si quidem nullo testamento facto quisquam decesserit, per hoc tempus requiritur, quo mortuus est is cujus de hereditate quæritur. Quod si facto testamento quisquam decesserit, per hoc tempus requiritur, quo certum esse coeperit nullum ex testamento heredem exstiturum; tunc enim proprie

6. When a man dies without a testament, the nearest *agnatus* is the *agnatus* who is nearest at the time of the death of the deceased. But, if he dies after having made a testament, then he is the nearest who is so when it becomes certain that there will be no testamentary heir; for it is only then, that a man who has made a

quisque intestato decessisse intelligitur. Quod quidem aliquando longo tempore declaratur; in quo spatio temporis sæpe accidit, ut proximiore mortuo proximus esse incipiat, qui moriente testatore non erat proximus.

testamento can be said to have died intestate, and this sometimes is uncertain for a long time. Meanwhile, the nearest agnatus may die, and some one become the nearest who was not so at the death of the testator.

GAI. iii. 18.

7. Placebat autem in eo genere percipiendarum hereditatum successionem non esse, id est, ut quamvis proximus qui, secundum ea quæ diximus, vocatur ad hereditatem, aut spreverit hereditatem, aut antequam adeat decesserit, nihilo magis legitimo jure sequentes admittantur. Quod iterum prætores imperfecto jure corrigentes, non in totum sine adminiculo relinquebant; sed ex cognatorum ordine eos vocabant, utpote agnationis jure eis recluso. Sed nos nihil decere perfectissimo juri cupientes, nostra constitutione quam de jure patronatus humanitate suggerente protulimus, sanximus successionem in agnatorum hereditatibus non esse denegandam; cum assis absurdum erat, quod cognatis a prætore apertum est, hoc agnatis esse reclusum, maxime cum in onere quidem tutelarum et proximo gradu deficiente sequens succedit, et quod in onere obtinebat, non erat in lucro permissum.

7. But it was settled, that in this order of succession there should be no devolution, so that if the nearest agnatus, called in the manner we have mentioned to the inheritance, either refused it, or died before he entered on it, his own legal heir was not thereby admitted to succeed him. Here, too, the prætors, though not introducing a complete reform, did not leave the agnati wholly without relief, but ordered that they should be called to the inheritance as cognati, since they were debarred from the rights of agnation. But we, desirous that our law should be as complete as possible, have decided by our constitution, which in our goodness we published concerning the right of patronage, that a devolution in the succession shall not be denied to agnati. It was indeed absurd, to refuse them a right which the prætor gave to cognati, especially as the burden of tutelage devolved on the second degree of agnati, if there was a failure of the first; and thus the principle of devolution was admitted to impose burdens, and was not admitted to confer advantages.

GAI. ii. 12. 22. 25. 28.

*In hereditate legitima successioni locus non est.* (PAUL. Sent. 4. 23.) The *suus heres* or *sui heredes* in the nearest degree became heirs by force of law. They could not help becoming so. But as to those who were only allowed to rank among the *sui heredes* without being strictly speaking *sui heredes*, if those in the nearest degree refused to accept the inheritance, or died before entering on it, the succession did not devolve upon any other *sui heredes*, but went at once to the *agnati*. If, in this case or any other, the nearest *agnatus* refused or died before entering on the inheritance, the succession passed to the *cognati* without first devolving on any of the more remote *agnati*. Justinian alters this; and under his system there was a devolution of the succession to the *agnati*, and therefore probably to those ranked among the *sui heredes*.

**8. Ad legitimam successionem** nihilominus vocatur etiam parens qui contracta fiducia filium vel filium, nepotem vel neptem ac deinceps emancipat. Quod ex nostra constitutione omnimodo indicitur, ut emancipationes liberorum semper videantur contracta fiducia fieri; cum apud antiquos non aliter hoc obtinebat, nisi specialiter contracta fiducia parens manumisisset.

**8.** An ascendant also is called to the legal succession who has emancipated a son, a daughter, a grandson, a granddaughter, or other descendant under a fiduciary agreement. And by our constitution, every emancipation is now considered to have been made under such an agreement, while among the ancients the ascendant was never called to the succession unless he had expressly made this agreement at the time of the emancipation.

D. xxxviii. 16. 10; C. viii. 48. 8.

Under the old law, the ascendant had nothing to do with the succession *ab intestato* of his descendant; for if the descendant were in the power of the ascendant, the latter took all the property of which the former could dispose, but did not, as belonging to him by right, of his *patria potestas*. If the descendant were emancipated, he was no longer in the family of the ascendant. The emancipated son, in short, had no *agnati*; and in default of *sui heredes* the inheritance went to his patron, that is, to the person who had emancipated him. This was the fictitious purchaser (see Introd. sec. 42), unless the ascendant who emancipated him made an agreement (*contracta fiducia*) with the purchaser, by which the purchaser made himself a trustee of the right of patronage for the ascendant. If this was done the ascendant succeeded in default of *sui heredes*.

By the later imperial constitutions three changes were made in the position of the ascendant. First, by a constitution of Theodosius and Valentinian (C. vi. 61. 3), and subsequently of Leo and Anthemius (C. vi. 61. 4), and lastly of Justinian (C. vi. 59. 11), in the case of goods coming to a son from his mother, the order of succession was thus fixed: 1st, his children and other descendants were admitted; 2ndly, his brothers and sisters, whether of the whole or the half blood; 3rdly, his nearest ascendant, i. e. his father, was preferred to his grandfather.

Secondly, Justinian, as we have seen in the 12th Title of the Second Book, arranged the order of succession to the *peculium* of a son, placing first the children, then the brothers and sisters, and lastly the father. But in this case the father was not preferred to the grandfather; for the ascendant did not really take in this instance *ab intestato*, but 'jure communi;' i. e. the

claims of the *patria potestas* had been deferred to let in the
children and brothers ; but if there were no children or
brothers, the ascendant, who is at the time the *paterfamilias*,
took the *peculium.*

Lastly, the succession of emancipated sons was altered by
the constitution of Justinian, which made a fiduciary contract
implied in every emancipation. The ancestor thus retained all
his rights of succession as patron to the emancipated son, and
would properly have succeeded immediately after the *sui
heredes* ; but Justinian admitted the brothers and sisters before
him, and the ascendant who emancipated the son had thus the
third place in the order of succession.   (C. vi. 56. 2.)

## Tit. III.   DE SENATUS-CONSULTO TERTULLIANO.

Lex Duodecim Tabularum ita
stricto jure utebatur, et preponebat
masculorum progeniem, et eos qui
per feminini sexus necessitudinem
sibi junguntur adeo expellebat, ut
ne quidem inter matrem et filium
filiamve ultro citroque her-ditatis
capiendæ jus daret : nisi quod prætores ex proximitate cognatorum
eas personas ad successionem, bonorum possessione unde cognati ac-
commodata, vocabant.

Such was the rigour of the law of
the Twelve Tables, so decided the
preference given to the issue of males,
and the exclusion of those related
by the female line, that the right of
reciprocal succession was not permitted between a mother and her
children. The prætors, however, admitted such persons, but only in
their rank as *cognati*, to the possession of goods called *unde cognati.*

GAL. iii. 24, 25. 30.

Until the *senatus-consultum Tertullianum* was made, a
mother and her children had no right of succession to each
other, except that which the prætor gave them as *cognati.* The
children were not in the power of the mother, and were, therefore, not her *sui heredes* ; they were not in her family, and
were, therefore, not her *agnati.* If, indeed, the mother at her
marriage passed *in manum viri,* she became, in the eye of the
law, the daughter of her husband, and as she was thus of the
same family with her children, she and they were *agnati* to
each other.   But even in the later days of the Republic, a
marriage *cum conventione in manum* had, probably, become
comparatively unusual.

1. Sed hæ juris angustiæ postea
emendatæ sunt, et primus quidem
divus Claudius matri, ad solatium
liberorum amissorum, legitimam
eorum detulit hæreditatem.

1. But this strictness of the law
was afterwards mitigated. The Emperor Claudius was the first who
gave the legal inheritance of deceased
children to a mother, to console her
grief for their loss.

2. Postea autem senatus-consulto Tertulliano, quod divi Hadriani temporibus factum est, plenissime detristi successione matri non etiam aviæ deferenda cautum est: ut mater ingenua trium liberorum jus habens, libertina quatuor, ad bona filiorum filiarumve admittatur intestato mortuorum, licet in potestate parentis est; ut scilicet, cum alieno juri subjecta est, jussu ejus adeat hereditatem cujus juri subjecta est.

2. Afterwards, the senatus-consultum Tertullianum, in the reign of the Emperor Hadrian, established the general rule that mothers, but not grandmothers, should have the melancholy privilege of succeeding to their children; so that a mother, born of free parents, having three children, or a freed woman having four, should be admitted, although in the power of a parent, to the goods of her intestate children. Except that a mother in the power of another can only enter upon the inheritance of her children at the command of him to whom she is subject.

This *senatus-consultum* was passed 158 A.D., in the time of Antoninus Pius, who is here called by his name of adoption. It was only an extension of the *lex Papia Poppæa.*

3. Præferuntur autem matri liberi defuncti qui sui sunt, quive suorum loco sunt, sive primi gradus sive alterioris. Sed et filiæ suæ mortuæ filius vel filia opponitur ex constitutionibus matri defunctæ, id est, aviæ suæ. Pater quoque utriusque, non etiam avus vel proavus, matri anteponitur, scilicet cum inter eos solos de hereditate agitur. Frater autem consanguineus tam filii quam filiæ excludebat matrem; soror autem consanguinea pariter cum matre admittebatur; sed si fuerat frater et soror consanguinei, et mater liberis honorata, frater quidem matrem excludebat, communis autem erat hereditas ex æquis partibus fratris et sororis.

3. The children of the deceased son being *sui hæredes*, or ranked as such, either in the first or another degree, are preferred to the mother. And if it is a daughter *sui juris* who is dead, her son, or daughter, is preferred by the constitutions to her mother, i. e. to their grandmother. The father of the deceased is preferred to the mother; not so the grandfather or great-grandfather, at least when they and the mother are the only claimants of the inheritance. The brother by the same father, either of a son or a daughter, excluded the mother; but the sister by the same father was admitted equally with the mother. If the deceased left a brother and a sister by the same father as himself, the brother excluded the mother, although rendered capable by the number of her children, and the inheritance was equally divided between the brothers and sisters.

D. xxxviii. 17. 2. 15. 18. 19; C. vi. 50. 5.

The mother was allowed to rank among the *agnati* by the *senatus-consultum Tertullianum*, but she had a relative position rather than a definitive position, as being in a certain degree of agnation.

First, she was, of course, as being only one of the *agnati*, excluded by the *sui heredes*; and, therefore, if her son died, she was excluded by his children.

Secondly, she was sometimes excluded by other *agnati*. If her daughter died, she was excluded by her daughter's children, although they were not *sui heredes*; for they were made *agnati* by the *senatus-consultum Orphitianum*, and a preference given them over the mother by imperial constitutions. (C. vi. 57. 4.) If there were no children of the deceased, the mother was excluded by the brothers of the deceased : if there were no brothers, but were sisters by the same father, the mother received half the inheritance, and these sisters received the other half.   All other *agnati* she excluded.

Thirdly, if the deceased child had been emancipated, which is the only case in which her claims could be compared with those of ascendants, the mother was excluded by the father, whether he took as being himself the emancipator, or as being the son of the deceased emancipator.   If the father's father was still living, the mother excluded him, if the father himself was dead, so that the question was between the mother and the grandfather.   But, if the father was living, the grandfather took the inheritance; for, if the mother had been preferred to the grandfather, she would herself have been excluded by the father, who would have been excluded by the grandfather, and, therefore, as the grandfather could not be excluded, it was simplest to say that the mother was not preferred to him. (D. xxxviii. 17. 5. 2.)

Fourthly, the rights of the mother were sometimes lessened in favour of certain *cognati*.   If there were children of the deceased in an adoptive family, who were thus only *cognati* of the deceased, the mother's rights depended on there being or not being any *agnati* of the deceased.   If there were *agnati*, the question was not whether the mother should exclude the children in the adoptive family, but whether she should take her place among the *agnati*.   She was allowed to do so, and, if there was no brother or sister of the deceased, she took the inheritance, or, if there were sisters, shared it with them.   But if there were no *agnati* of the deceased, the question was whether she should exclude the nearest *cognati* of the deceased, that is, the children in the adoptive family.   She did not : the *senatus-consultum Tertullianum* ceased to have any effect ; and she, as being equally with the children, in the first degree, received with them the *possessio bonorum*.   (D. xxxviii. 17. 2. 9.)   So, too, if the father of the deceased had been emancipated or given in adoption by the grandfather, he was no longer one of the *agnati* of the deceased.   If, then, the question lay between the mother and the *agnati*, more remote than a brother or sister, the mother succeeded ; but if there were no *agnati*, then the *cognati* came; and as the father still remained, she did not exclude *cognati*—the question lay between her and the father—but received with him, as *cognati* in the first degree, the *possessio bonorum.* His right was then the stronger, and she was excluded. (D. xxxviii. 17. 2. 17. 18.)

4. Sed nos constitutione quam in Codice nostro nomine decorato posuimus, matri subveniendum esse existimavimus, respicientes ad naturam et puerperium et periculum et sæpe mortem ex hoc casu matribus illatam ; ideoque impium esse credidimus casum fortuitum in ejus admitti detrimentum. Si enim ingenua ter vel libertina quater non peperit, Immerito defraudabatur successione suorum liberorum; quid enim peccavit, si non plures sed paucos peperit? Et dedimus jus legitimum plenum matribus, sive ingenuis sive libertinis, etsi non ter enixæ fuerint vel quater, sed cum tantum vel eam qui quæve morte intercepti sunt, ut et sic vocentur in liberorum suorum legitimam successionem.

4. But by a constitution, inserted in the Code, which bears our name, we have thought fit to come to the aid of the mother, from considering natural reason, as well as the pains of child-birth, the danger, and death itself, which they often suffer. We, therefore, have esteemed it highly unjust, that the law should turn to their detriment what is in its nature purely fortuitous ; for, if a married woman free-born, does not give birth to three children, or a freedwoman to four, they do not therefore deserve to be deprived of the succession to their children. For how can it be imputed to them as a crime, to have had few children? We, therefore, have given a full right to every mother, whether free-born or freed, to be called to the legal succession of her children, although she may not have given birth to three or four children, or may not have had any other than the child whose inheritance is in question.

C. viii. 50. 2.

5. Sed cum antea constitutiones jura legitimæ successionis promoventes, partim matrem adjuvabant, partim eam præravabant et non in solidum eam vocabant ; sed in quibusdam casibus tertiam ei partem abstrahentes certis legitimis dabant personis, in aliis autem contrarium faciebant, nobis visum est recta et simplici via matrem omnibus personis legitimis anteponi, et sine ulla diminutione filiorum suorum successionem accipere, excepta fratris et sororis persona, sive consanguinei sint, sive sola cognationis jure habentes; ut quemadmodum eam toti alii ordini legitimo præposuimus, ita omnes fratres et sorores, sive legitim sunt sive non, ad capiendas

5. The constitutions of former emperors, relative to the right of succession, were partly favourable to mothers, and partly unfavourable. They did not always give the mothers the entire Inheritance of their children, but in some cases deprived them of a third, which was given to certain *agnati* ; and in other cases, doing just the contrary, gave a third. But it seems right to us, that mothers should receive the succession of their children without any diminution, and that they should be decidedly and exclusively preferred before all legal heirs, except the brothers and sisters of the deceased, whether by the same father or having only the rights of cognation. And as we have preferred the

hæreditates simul vocamus; Ita
tamen ut, si quidem solæ sorores
agnatæ vel cognatæ et mater defuncti vel defunctæ supersint, dimidiam quidem mater, alteram vero
dimidiam partem omnes sorores habeant.  Si vero matre superstite et
fratre vel fratribus solis, vel etiam
cum sororibus sive legitima sive sola
cognationis jura habentibus, intestatus quis vel intestata moriatur, in
capita distribuatur ejus hæreditas.

mother to all other legal heirs, we call
all brothers and sisters, legal or not,
to the inheritance together with the
mother, the following rule being observed.   If there are living only
sisters agnate or cognate, and the
mother of the deceased, the mother
shall have one-half of the goods, and
the sisters the other half.   But if
there are living the mother, and also
a brother or brothers only, or brothers
and sisters, whether legal, or only
having the rights of cognati, then the
inheritance of the intestate son or
daughter shall be divided in capita.

C. vii. 50. 7.

In the code of Theodosius (v. 1. 1), we find two constitutions, one of Constantine, the other of Valentinian and Valens,
which were the first blow dealt to the *jus liberorum* introduced
by the *lex Papia Poppæa*.  By these constitutions it was
enacted that if there were persons in a certain degree of agnation with the deceased, namely, a paternal uncle, or a paternal
uncle's son or grandson, or an emancipated brother, then the
mother, instead of excluding them, as, if she had the *jus
liberorum*, she would have done, divided the inheritance with
them, taking two-thirds if she had the *jus trium liberorum*,
and one-third if she had not.  This enactment was, therefore,
a gain to those who had not the *jus liberorum*, and a loss
to those who had.  Justinian did away altogether with the *jus
liberorum* and the distinctions founded upon it.

6. Sed quemadmodum nos matribus prospeximus, ita eas oportet
suæ soboli consulere : scituris eis
quod, si tutores liberis non petierint,
vel in locum remoti vel excusati
intra annum petere neglexerint, ab
eorum impuberum morientium successione repellentur.

6. And as we have thus taken care
of the interests of the mothers, they
ought in return to consult the welfare
of their children.   Let them know,
then, that if they neglect, during the
space of a whole year, to demand a
tutor for their children, or to ask for
the appointment of a new tutor in the
place of one who has been removed
or excused, they will be deservedly
repelled from the succession of the
children, if they die before the age
of puberty.

D. xxxviii. 17. 2. 43.

7. Licet autem vulgo quæritus sit
filius filiave, non est tamen ad bona
ejus mater ex Tertulliano senatus-
consulto admitti.

7. Although a son or a daughter
is born of an uncertain father, yet
the mother may be admitted to succeed to their goods by the senatus-
consultum Tertullianum.

The natural tie is all that is regarded in this case; this is as strong between the mother and child, whoever may be the father.

## Tit. IV.  DE SENATUS-CONSULTO ORPHITIANO.

Per contrarium autem, ut liberi ad bona matrum intestatarum admittantur senatus-consulto Orphitiano, Orphito et Rufo consulibus, effectum est, quod latum est divi Marci temporibus; et data est tam filio quam filiæ legitima hereditas, etiamsi alieno juri subjecti sunt, et præferuntur consanguineis et agnatis defunctæ matris.

Reciprocally children are admitted to the goods of their intestate mothers, by the *senatus-consultum Orphitianum*, made in the consulship of Orphitius and Rufus, in the reign of the Emperor Marcus Antoninus. By the *senatus-consultum* the legal inheritance is given both to the sons and daughters, although in the power of another, and they are preferred to the *consanguinei*, and to the *agnati* of their deceased mother.

D. xxxviii. 17. 9; C. vi. 57. 1.

The *senatus-consultum Orphitianum* was made A.D. 178, in the time of Marcus Aurelius and Commodus. Previously, children could not succeed to their mother, except as *cognati*. But by this *senatus-consultum* they were preferred to the *consanguinei*, that is, the *agnati* of the second degree, or, in other words, brothers and sisters, natural or adoptive, as well as to all other *agnati*. They were not, however, preferred to the mother of the deceased, who derived her right of succession from the *senatus-consultum Tertullianum*, but they shared the inheritance with her. Her claim to share it with them was, however, subsequently taken away by a constitution (C. vi. 57. 4.) of Gratian, Valentinian, and Theodosius.

1. Sed cum ex hoc senatus-consulto nepotes ad aviæ successionem legitimo jure non vocabantur, postea hoc constitutionibus principalibus emendatum est, ut ad similitudinem filiorum filiarumque et nepotes et neptes vocentur.

1. But since grandsons and granddaughters were not called by this *senatus-consultum* to the legal succession of their grandmother, the omission was afterwards supplied by the imperial constitutions, and grandsons and granddaughters were called to inherit, just as sons and daughters had been.

C. vi. 55. 9.

The constitution enacting this given in the Code is one of Valentinian, Theodosius, and Arcadius.

2. Sciendum autem est, hujusmodi successione quae a Tertulliano et Orphitiano deferuntur, capitis deminutione non perimi, propter illam regulam qua novae hereditates legitimae capitis deminutione non perennt, sed illae solae quae ex lege Duodecim Tabularum deferuntur.

2. It must be observed, that these successions, derived from the *senatus-consulta Tertullianum* and *Orphitianum*, are not lost by a *capitis deminutio*. The rule is, that legitimate inheritances given by the late law are not destroyed by *capitis deminutio*, which affects those only that are given by the law of the Twelve Tables.

It is only the *minima capitis deminutio* which is here spoken of. Any one who sustained the *maxima* or *minor deminutio*, as he ceased to be a citizen, ceased to have any rights of succession.

3. Novissime sciendum est, etiam illos liberos qui vulgo quaesiti sunt, ad matris hereditatem in hoc senatus-consulto admitti.

3. Lastly, it must be observed, that even children born of an uncertain father are admitted by the *senatus-consultum Orphitianum* to the inheritance of their mother.

D. xxxviii. 17. 1, 2.

Justinian afterwards altered this, so as to exclude such children from the inheritance of their mother, if she was of high rank (*illustris*), or if she had other children born in lawful marriage. (C. vi. 57. 5.)

4. Si ex pluribus legitimis heredibus quidam omiserint hereditatem, vel morte vel alia causa impediti fuerint quominus adeant, reliquis qui adierint, accrescit illorum portio: et licet ante decesserint qui adierint, ad heredes tamen eorum pertinet.

4. When there are many legal heirs, and some renounce the inheritance, or are prevented by death, or any other cause, from accepting it, then the portions of such persons accrue to those who accept the inheritance: and if any of those who accept happen to die beforehand, the portions accruing to them will go to their heirs.

D. xxxviii. 10. 0.

This paragraph has nothing to do with the *S. C. Orphitianum*. It refers to the right of accrual enjoyed by all *heredes legitimi*. If any of those called to share an inheritance did not take his share, it was divided among all those who entered on the inheritance, and, if any of those who had entered died before receiving the share that accrued to him, this accruing share passed to his heirs, his interest in it having become fixed, and made transmissible to his heirs by his entering on the inheritance.

The following were the principal changes in the law of the succession of the *agnati*. By the law of the Twelve Tables, *agnati*, i. e. collaterals in the same civil family, succeeded

in default of *sui heredes.*  Subsequently, different classes of
persons were allowed to rank as *agnati* who were not so.
1.  Emancipated brothers and sisters were allowed to rank as
*agnati* by Anastasius, and their children were allowed to do so
by Justinian.   2.  Under Justinian, a peculiar order of succession was fixed on for persons emancipated ; first came their
children ; secondly, their brothers and sisters ; thirdly, the
ascendant emancipator.   3.  Justinian placed uterine brothers
and sisters, and their children, on the same footing as *consanguinei* and their children.    4.  The mother was allowed to succeed to her children by the *senatus-consultum Tertullianum,*
and children to their mother by the *senatus-consultum Orphitianum.*  The mother had not a definite place in the succession,
but one varying according as there were or were not certain
other persons to preclude or share her claim.  If the deceased
child were a daughter, and had left children, those children
shared the inheritance with the mother until the constitution of
Gratian (Tit. 4, pr.), and afterwards were preferred to her.   If
there were no children, it was necessary to consider whether the
deceased was emancipated ; if so, the father, or the grandfather,
if the grandfather and father were both living, was preferred ; if
not, or if the deceased had been emancipated, but the father
was dead, brothers *consanguinei,* and, under the legislation of
Justinian, brothers *uterini* (Tit. 2. 4), were preferred to the
mother ; sisters *consanguineæ,* and, under the legislation of
Justinian, *uterinæ,* shared with her.   She was preferred to all
more remote *agnati.*  But if a child, or the father of the
deceased, was in a different family from the deceased, and there
were *agnati,* the mother only received her share as one of the
*cognati.*  (Tit. 3. 3.)   5.  Grandchildren succeeded to their
grandmother by a constitution of Valentinian, Theodosius, and
Arcadius.   (Tit. 4. 1.)

There were also two other points, besides the admission of
these persons excluded by the strict definition of *agnati,* in
which the law underwent alterations.  First, the Twelve Tables
made no distinction of sex in the *agnati* ; the *prudentes*
limited the succession of females to the second degree.  Justinian restored the law of the Twelve Tables on this point, and
permitted no distinction of sex.   (Tit. 2. 3.)   Secondly, under
the law of the Twelve Tables, there was no devolution among
the *agnati* ; if the nearest refused, the more remote could not
come in their place ; Justinian permitted such a devolution to
take place.  (Tit. 2. 7.)

## Tit. V. DE SUCCESSIONE COGNATORUM.

Post suos heredes, eosque quos inter suos heredes prætor et constitutiones vocant, et post legitimos, quorum numero sunt agnati, et hi quos in locum agnatorum tam supra dicta senatus-consulta quam nostra erexit constitutio, proximos cognatos prætor vocat.

After the sui heredes and those whom the prætor and the constitutions call to inherit among the sui heredes, and after the legal heirs, that is, the agnati and those whom the above-mentioned senatus-consulta and our constitution have placed among the agnati, the prætor calls the nearest cognati.

D. xxxviii. 16. 1; D. xxxviii. 7. 2. 4.

The law of the Twelve Tables recognised only the succession of, (1) sui heredes; (2) agnati; (3) gentiles. If there were no gentiles, the inheritance lapsed to the state. In plebeian families, or rather in such plebeian families as were not parts of a plebeian gens, if there were no agnati, the inheritance would lapse at once.

The subject of gentilitas is too obscure, and repays investigation too little, to permit us to enter into it here. We know that the original notion of gentiles was that of members of some pure uncorrupted patrician stock, though not necessarily of the same descent, but bearing the same name, and having the same sacra. (See Introd. sec. 2.) We also know that freedmen and clients of gentiles were, in some degree, considered as themselves gentiles; probably if their property was not claimed by their patron, it went to the members of his gens, but they had not any claim on the property of any other gentilis. We know also that there were plebeian gentes, formed probably by the marriage of a patrician with a plebeian before the plebs received the connubium. Members of plebeian gentes would, we may suppose, have the rights of gentilitas towards other members of the same plebeian gens, but whether they had them towards the members of the patrician gens, from which they are an offset, is wholly uncertain. Of the mode in which the gentiles took the inheritance, we know nothing, nor at how late a period of history the gentes were still really in existence. Gaius (iii. 17) treats the subject as one of mere antiquarian interest. Probably at the time of the prætors' legislation there were few families that could boast a descent sufficiently pure and accurately known to satisfy the requisites of gentilitas. At any rate, the prætors felt themselves at liberty to favour, in every way, the tie of blood, and they accordingly called the cognati to the succession.

I. Qua parte naturalis cognatio spectatur : nam agnati capite deminuti, quique ex his progeniti sunt, ex lege Duodecim Tabularum inter legitimos non habentur, sed a praetore tertio ordine vocantur. Exceptis solis tantummodo fratre et sorore emancipatis, non etiam liberis eorum, quos lex Anastasiana cum fratribus integri juris constitutis vocat quidem ad legitimam fratris hereditatem sive sororis, non aequis tamen partibus, sed cum aliqua deminutione quam facile est ex ipsius constitutionis verbis colligere. Aliis vero agnatis inferioris gradus, licet capitis deminutionem passi non sunt, tamen eos anteponit, et procul dubio cognatis.

1. It is the natural relationship that is here looked to ; thus agnati who have undergone a *capitis deminutio* and their descendants, are not included among the legal heirs by the law of the Twelve Tables, but they are called by the praetor in the third order. We must except an emancipated brother or sister, but not their children. For the law of Anastasius, calling an emancipated brother or sister together with brothers whose rights still exist unaltered, to the legal succession of their brother or sister, not, indeed, giving them an equal share, but making a deduction set forth in the constitution, prefers them to all *agnati* of an inferior degree, even though these *agnati* have undergone no *capitis deminutio*, and, of course, prefers them to all *cognati*.

Gai. iii. 21. 27 ; C. v. 30. 4.

We have already spoken of this *lex Anastasiana* in the note to Tit. 2. 4, and noticed the constitution of 534, by which Justinian admitted as *agnati* the children of emancipated brothers and sisters, and did away with the deduction mentioned in the text, namely, that of one-fourth.

2. Hos etiam qui per feminini sexus personas ex transverso cognatione junguntur, tertio gradu proximitatis nomine praetor ad successionem vocat.

2. Collateral relations united only by the female line, are also called by the praetor in the third order of succession, according to their proximity.

Gai. iii. 30.

3. Liberi quoque qui in adoptiva familia sunt, ad naturalium parentum hereditatem hoc eodem gradu vocantur.

3. Children, who are in an adoptive family, are likewise called in the third order of succession to the inheritance of their natural parents.

Gai. iii. 31.

Justinian's change in the law of adoption left the adoptive child, unless adopted by an ascendant, in his natural family, and, therefore, he could come in as a *suus heres*, or *agnatus*, and not merely as a *cognatus*. But the text would still be applicable to persons *sui juris*, who arrogated themselves.

4. Vulgo quaesitos nullam habere agnatorum manifestum est, cum agnatio a patre, cognatio a matre sit: hi autem nullum patrem habere intelliguntur. Eadem ratione nec inter

4. It is manifest, that children born of an uncertain father, have no *agnati*, inasmuch as agnation proceeds from the father, cognation from the mother, and such children are

se quidem possunt videri consanguinei esse, quia consanguinitatis
jus species est agnationis; tantum
igitur cognati sunt sibi, sicut et
matris cognatia. Itaque omnibus
istis ea parte competit bonorum
possessio, qua proximitatis nomine
cognati vocantur.

looked upon as having no father.
And, for the same reason, consanguinity cannot be said to subsist
betv een the-e children, because consanguinity is a species of agnation.
They can, therefore, only be allied to
each other as *cognati*, by being related by their mother; and it is for
this reason that all such children are
admitted to the possession of goods,
which calls the *cognati* according to
their degree of proximity.

D. xxxviii. 8. 2. 4.

5. Hoc loco et illud necessario admonendi sumus, agnationis quidem
jure admitti aliquem adhereditatem,
etsi decimo gradu sit, sive de lege
Duodecim Tabularum quaeramus,
sive de edicto quo praetor legitimis
heredibus daturum bonorum possessionem pollicetur. Proximitatis
vero nomine iis solis praetor promittit bonorum possessionem, qui
usque ad sextum gradum cognationis sunt, et ex septimo a sobrino
sobrinaque nato natave.

5. Here we may observe, that by
right of agnation any one may be
admitted to inherit, although in the
tenth degree, both by the law of the
Twelve Tables, and by the edict in
which the praetor promises that he
will give the possession of goods to
the legal heirs. But the praetor promises the possession of goods to
*cognati* according to their proximity
only as far as the sixth degree of
cognation, and in the seventh degree
to those *cognati* who are the children
of a second cousin.

D. xxxviii. 16. 2. 2. 4; D. xxxviii. 8. 1. 3; D. xxxviii. 8. 9.

The *agnati* were not limited by the tenth degree. (See Tit.
6. 12.) This degree is only given as an instance of how far
the succession might go. But the sixth degree was the limit,
with the exception given in the text, of the succession of
*cognati.*

## Tit. VI.  DE GRADIBUS COGNATIONIS.

Hoc loco necessarium est exponere quemadmodum gradus cognationis numerentur: quare in primis
admonendi sumus cognationem
aliam supra numerari, aliam infra,
aliam ex transverso, quae etiam a
latere dicitur. Superior cognatio
est parentium, inferior liberorum,
ex transverso fratrum sororumve,
eorumque qui quove ex his progenerantur, et convenienter patrui,
amitae, avunculi, materterae. Et
superior quidem et inferior cognatio

It is necessary to explain here
how the degrees of cognation are
computed; and first we must observe, that one cognation is reckoned
by ascending, a second by descending
and a third by going transversely,
or, as it is also called, collaterally.
The cognation reckoned by ascending
is that of ascendants; that reckoned
by descending is that of descendants;
that reckoned transversely is that of
brothers and sisters, and their issue,
and consequently that of uncles and

a primo gradu incipit; at ea quæ ex transverso numerant, a secundo.

sunt, whether paternal or maternal. In the ascending and descending cognation the nearest cognatus is in the first degree; In the transverse, the nearest is in the second.

### D. xxxviii. 10. 1, pr. and 1.

1. Primo gradu est supra pater mater, infra filius filia.

1. In the first degree are, ascending, a father or a mother; descending, a son or a daughter.

### D. xxxviii. 10. 1. 3.

2. Secundo, supra avus avia, infra nepos neptis, ex transverso frater soror.

2. In the second degree are, ascending, a grandfather or a grandmother; descending, a grandson or granddaughter; on the collateral line, a brother or a sister.

### D. xxxviii. 10. 1. 4.

3. Tertio, supra proavus proavia, infra pronepos proneptis, ex transverso fratris sororisque filius filia, et convenienter patruus amita, avunculus matertera. Patruus est frater patris qui græce πάτρως vocatur; avunculus est frater matris, qui apud Græcos proprie μήτρως et promiscue θείος dicitur. Amita est patris soror, matertera vero matris soror: utraque θεία, vel apud quosdam τηθίς appellatur.

3. In the third degree are, ascending, a great-grandfather or a great-grandmother; descending, a great-grandson or great-granddaughter; on the collateral line, the son or daughter of a brother or sister; and so accordingly are an uncle or an aunt, whether paternal or maternal. Patruus is a father's brother, called in Greek πάτρως; avunculus is a mother's brother, in Greek μήτρως; θείος is applied indifferently to either; amita is a father's sister, matertera a mother's sister, and each is called in Greek, θεία, indifferently, and sometimes τηθίς.

### D. xxxviii. 10. 1. 5; D. xxxviii. 10. 10. 14.

Schræder substitutes in the text πάτρως and μήτρως, which are the forms used in classical Greek.

4. Quarto gradu, supra abavus abavia, infra abnepos abneptis, ex transverso fratris sororisque nepos neptis, et convenienter patruus magnus avita magna, id est, avi et soror: Item avunculus magnus et matertera magna, id est, aviæ frater et soror; consobrinus consobrina, id est, qui quæve ex fratribus aut sororibus progenerantur. Sed quidam recte consobrinos eos proprie dici putant, qui ex duabus sororibus progenerantur, quasi consororinos; eos vero qui ex duobus fratribus progenerantur, proprie fratres patrueles vocari: si autem ex duobus

4. In the fourth degree are, ascending, a great-great-grandfather, or a great-great-grandmother; descending, a great-great-grandson, or a great-great-granddaughter; in the collateral line, the grandson or the granddaughter of a brother or a sister; as also, a great-uncle or great-aunt, paternal, that is, the brother or sister of a grandfather; or maternal, that is, the brother or sister of a grandmother; and first cousins, that is, the children of brothers or sisters; but to speak strictly, according to some, it is the children of sisters that are properly called consobrini, as

fratribus filiæ nascuntur, sorores patruelee appellari; at eos qui ex fratre et sorore propagantur, amitinos proprie dici. Amitæ tuæ filii consobrinum te appellant, tu illos amitinos.

if *consororini*; the children of brothers are properly *fratres patrueles*, if males; *sorores patrueles*, if females; the children of a brother and of a sister are properly *amitini*; the children of your *amita* (aunt by the father's side) call you *consobrinus*, and you call them *amitini*.

D. xxxviii. 10. 1. 6.

We see from the concluding words of this paragraph, that *consobrinus* was used in another sense than its strict one of 'one of the children of two sisters.'

5. Quinto, supra atavus atavia, infra adnepten adneptis, ex transverso fratris sororisque pronepos pronepti, et convenienter propatruus proamita, id est, proavi frater et soror; proavunculus promaterlera, id est, proaviæ frater et soror. Item fratris patruelis sororis patruelis, consobrini consobrinæ, amitini amitinæ filius filia, propior sobrino propior sobrina. Ili sunt patrui magni amitæ magnæ, avunculi magni materteræ magnæ filius filia.

5. In the fifth degree, are, ascending a great-grandfather's grandfather, or a great-grandfather's grandmother; descending, a great-grandson, or a great-granddaughter, of a grandson or granddaughter; in the collateral line, a great-grandson or great-granddaughter of a brother or sister, as also a great-grandfather's brother or sister, or a great-grandmother's brother or sister; also, the son or daughter of a first cousin, that is, of a *frater* or *soror patruelis*, of a *consobrinus* or *consobrina*, or of an *amitinus* or *amitina*; also cousins who precede by a degree second cousins, that is, the son or daughter of a great-uncle or great-aunt, paternal or maternal.

D. xxxviii. 10. 1. 7.

*Propior sobrino* is, to use the exact equivalent, a first cousin once removed. He is one degree nearer (*propior*) than a *sobrinus* or second cousin.

6. Sexto gradu, supra tritavus tritavia, infra trinepos trineptis, ex transverso fratris sororisque abnepos abneptis, et convenienter abpatruus abamita, id est, abavi frater et soror, abavunculus abmatertera, id est, abaviæ frater at soror. Item sobrini sobrinæque, id est, qui quove ex fratribus vel sororibus patruelibus vel consobrinis vel amitinis progenerantur.

6. In the sixth degree, are, ascending, a great-grandfather's great-grandfather, or a great-grandfather's great-grandmother; descending, the great-grandson or great-granddaughter of a great-grandson or a great-granddaughter; in the collateral line, a great-great-grandson or a great-great-granddaughter of a brother or sister; as, also, a great-great-grandfather's brother or sister, and a great-great-grandmother's brother or sister; also, second cousins, that is, the sons and daughters of first cousins in general, whether the first cousins are sprung from two brothers or two sisters, or a brother and a sister.

D. xxxviii. 10. 3.

The nomenclature proper to the different degrees stops here, because the sixth degree was the limit of cognation.

7. Hactenus ostendimus sufficiet, quemadmodum gradus cognationis numerentur; namque ex his palam est intelligere quemadmodum ulteriores quoque gradus numerare debeamus, quippe semper generata quæque persona gradum adjiciat: ut longe facilius sit respondere quoto quisque gradu sit, quam propria cognationis appellatione quemquam denotare.

7. It is sufficient to have shown thus far, how degrees of cognation are reckoned; and, from the examples given, the more remote degrees may be computed; for each generation always adds one degree; so that it is much easier to determine in what degree any person is related to another, than to denote such person by his proper term of cognation.

D. xxxviii. 10. 10. 9.

8. Agnationis quoque gradus eodem modo numerantur.

8. The degrees of agnation are reckoned in the same manner.

9. Sed cum magis veritas oculata fide quam per aures animis botulinum infigitur, ideo necessarium duximus post narrationem graduum etiam eos præsenti libro inscribi, quatenus possint et auribus et oculorum inspectione adolescentes perfectissimam graduum doctrinam adipisci.

9. But as truth is fixed in the mind much better by the eye than by the ear, we have thought it necessary to subjoin, to the account given of the degrees, a table of them, that the young student, both by hearing and by seeing, may gain a perfect knowledge of them.

Justinian intended that a scheme of relationship should be here inserted; but as the degrees of relationship are sufficiently obvious, it is scarcely necessary to place a scheme before the eyes of the modern reader.

10. Illud certum est, ad serviles cognationes illam partem edicti, qua proximitatis nomine bonorum possessio promittitur, non pertinere; nam nec ulla antiqua lege talis cognatio computabatur. Sed nostra constitutione quam pro jure patronatus fecimus (quod jus usque ad nostra tempora satis obscurum atque nube plenum et undique confusum fuerat) et hæc humanitate suggerente concessimus, ut si quis in servili consortio constitutus liberum vel liberos habuerit sive ex libera sive ex servili conditionis muliere, vel contra serva mulier ex libero vel servo habuerit libere cujuscumque sexus, et ad libertatem his pervenientibus, et si qui ex servili ventre nati sunt libertatem meruerint, vel dum mulieres liberæ erant, ipsi in servitute eos habuerint, et postea ad libertatem pervenerint: ut hi

10. It is certain, that the part of the edict, in which the possession of goods is promised according to the degree of proximity, does not apply to servile cognation, which was not recognised by any ancient law. But, by our constitution concerning the right of patronage, a right hitherto so obscure, so cloudy and confused, we have enacted, from a feeling of humanity, that if a slave shall have a child or children, either by a free woman or a slave, and reciprocally if a female slave shall have a child or children of either sex, by a freeman or a slave, then if the father and mother are enfranchised, and the children, whose mother was a slave, become also free, or if the children of a free mother have a slave as father, and this slave afterwards attain his freedom, these children shall all succeed to their father or mother, the

omnes ad successionem patris vel
matris veniant, patronatus jure in
hac parte sopito. Hos enim liberos,
non solum in suorum parentum
successionem, sed etiam alterum in
alterius mutuam successionem vocavimus: ex illa lege specialiter eos
vocantes, sive soli inveniantur qui
in servitute nati et postea manumissi sunt, sive una cum aliis qui
post libertatem parentium concepti
sunt, sive ex eodem patre vel ex
eadem matre, sive ex aliis, ad similitudinem eorum qui ex justis nuptiis procreati sunt.

right of patronage in this case lying
dormant. And we have called these
children to succeed not only to their
parents, but also mutually to each
other, and that whether they have
all been born in servitude and afterwards enfranchised, or whether they
succeed with others who were conceived after the enfranchisement of
their parents; and also whether they
have all the same father and mother,
or have a different father or mother;
exactly as would be the case with the
issue of parents legally married.

D. xxxviii. 8. 1, 2.

Not even in the case of emancipated slaves did the law
recognize the claims of the kin of the slave to succeed to
him; all went to the patron if there were no *sui heredes.*

11. Repetitisitaqueomnibusquæ
jam tradidimus, apparet non semper
eos qui pares gradum cognationis
obtinent, pariter vocari; eoque amplius ne eum quidem qui proximior
sit cognatus, semper potiorem esse.
Cum enim prima causa sit suorum
heredum et eorum quos inter suos
heredes jam enumeravimus, apparet
pronepotem vel abnepotem defuncti
potiorem esse quam fratrem aut
patrem matremque defuncti: cum
alioquin pater quidem et mater (ut
supra quoque tradidimus) primum
gradum cognationis obtineant, frater vero secundum, pronepos autem
tertio gradu sit cognatus, et abnepos
quarto. Nec interest in potestate
morientis fuerit, an non, quod vel
emancipatus vel ex emancipato, aut
feminino sexu propagatus est.

11. To recapitulate what we have
said on this subject, it appears that
those who are in the same degree
of cognation are not always called
equally to the succession; and further, that even the nearest in degree
of cognation is not always preferred.
For, as the first place is given to *sui
heredes,* and to those who are numbered with them, it is evident that
the great-grandson or great-great-
grandson is preferred to the brother
or even the father or mother of the
deceased, although a father and
mother (as we have before observed)
are in the first degree of cognation,
a brother in the second, a great-
grandson in the third, and a great-
great-grandson in the fourth; neither
does it make any difference whether
the descendants were under the
power of the deceased at the time of
his death, or out of his power, either
by being themselves emancipated, or
by being the children of those who
were so, nor whether they were descended by the female line.

D. xxxviii. 10. 1, 2.

12. Amotis quoque suis heredibus, et quos inter suos heredes vocari
diximus, agnatus qui integrum jus
agnationis habet, etiam si longissimo
gradu sit, plerumque potior habetur
quam proximior cognatus; nam pa-

12. But, when there are no *sui
heredes,* nor any of those who are
called with them, then an *agnatus*
who has retained his full rights,
although he be in the most distant
degree, is generally preferred to a

trui nepos vel proneposavunculo vel materierae praefertur. Totiens igitur dicimus, aut potiorem haberi eum qui proximiorem gradum cognationis obtinet, aut pariter vocari eos qui cognati sunt, quotiens neque suorum heredum jure quique inter suos heredes sunt, neque agnationis jure aliquis praeferri debeat, secundum ea quae tradidimus. Exceptis fratre et sorore emancipatis, qui ad successionem fratrum vel sororum vocantur; qui et si capite deminuti sunt, tamen praeferuntur ceteris ulterioris gradus agnatis.

cognatus in a nearer degree; thus the grandson or great-grandson of a paternal uncle is preferred to a maternal uncle or aunt. Thus, when we say that the nearest in degree of cognation is called to the succession, or if there be many in the same degree, that they are all called equally, we only say so because there are no sui heredes, nor any of those who are called with them, nor any one who ought to be preferred by right of agnatio, according to the principles we have laid down. And we must notice the exception made in the case of an emancipated brother and sister who are called to the succession of their brothers and sisters: for, although they have suffered a capitis deminutio, they are nevertheless preferred to all agnati of a more remote degree.

Gai. iii. 27. 29; C. v. 30. 40.

## Tit. VII. DE SUCCESSIONE LIBERTORUM.

Nunc de libertorum bonis videamus. Olim itaque licebat liberto patronum suum impune testamento praeterire: nam ita demum lex Duodecim Tabularum ad hereditatem liberti vocabat patronum, si intestatus mortuus esset libertus nullo suo herede relicto: itaque intestato quoque mortuo liberto, si is suum heredem reliquisset, patrono nihil in bonis ejus juris erat. Et si quidem ex naturalibus liberis aliquem suum heredem reliquisset, nulla videbatur querela; si vero adoptivus filius fuisset, aperte iniquum erat nihil juris patrono superesse.

We will now speak of succession to freedmen. A freedman might formerly, with impunity, omit in his testament any mention of his patron, for the law of the Twelve Tables called the patron to the inheritance only when the freedman died intestate without leaving any suus heres. Therefore, though he had died intestate, yet if he had left a suus heres, the patron had no claim upon his estate. And when the suus heres was a natural child of the deceased, the patron had no cause of complaint: but when the suus heres was only an adopted son, it was manifestly unjust that the patron should have no claim.

Gal. iii. 39, 40.

The law of the Twelve Tables regulated the succession to enfranchised slaves as follows: an enfranchised slave had no agnati, for he belonged to no civil family; but he might marry and found a family of his own, and then his children would be his sui heredes, or he might gain sui heredes by adoption. If

be died intestate, his *sui heredes* succeeded to him; and in
default of *sui heredes*, the patron, or, if the patron were dead,
the children of the patron, took the place of *agnati* and received
the inheritance.   The enfranchised slave had, however, full
power to make a testament, and might pass over both his own
*sui heredes* and his patron.   A female slave, however, if emancipated, could not exclude the patron from her inheritance ; for
she could have no *sui heredes*, being a woman ; and as she
was always, on account of her sex, considered under the *tutela* of
her patron, she was incapable of making a testament unless with
the consent of her patron.  (ULP. *Reg.* 29. 2 ; GAI. iii. 43.)

1. Qua de causa, postea prætoris
edicto hæc juris iniquitas emendata
est.  Sive enim faciebat testamentum libertus, jubebatur ita testari ut
patrono partem dimidiam bonorum
suorum relinqueret, et si aut nihil
aut minus parte dimidia reliquerat,
dabatur patrono contra tabulas testamenti partis dimidiæ bonorum
possessio; sive intestatus moriebat-
ur suo herede relicto filio adoptivo,
dabatur æque patrono contra hunc
suum heredem partis dimidiæ bonorum possessio.  Prolixe autem
liberto solebant ad excludendum
patronum naturales liberi, non solum
quos in potestate mortis tempore
habebat, sed etiam emancipati et in
adoptionem dati, si modo ex aliqua
parte scripti heredes erant, aut
prætoriti contra tabulas bonorum
possessionem ex edicto petierant ;
nam exheredati nullo modo repellebant patronum.

1. This unfairness in the law was
therefore afterwards amended by the
edict of the prætor.  Every freedman
who made a testament was commanded to make such a disposition
of his property as to leave one-half
to his patron; and, if the testator
left him nothing, or less than a half,
then the possession of half was given
to the patron *contra tabulas*.  And if
a freedman died intestate, leaving an
adopted son as his *suus heres*, still the
possession of a half was given to the
patron.  But the patron was excluded
by the natural children of a freedman,
not only by those in his power at the
time of his death, but by those children also who had been emancipated,
or given in adoption, provided that
they were instituted heirs for any
part, or, in case they were omitted,
had demanded the possession *contra
tabulas*, under the prætorian edict.
For disinherited children did not
ever exclude the patron.

GAI. iii. 41.

The prætor considered it hard that a testament, or *sui heredes*
gained by adoption, or by the marriage of a wife *in manu*,
should exclude the patron.  This was to exclude him by purely
voluntary acts of the slave.   If the slave had children really
born to him, that constituted a good reason why the patron
should be excluded, and in this case the prætor did not interfere.  It is to be observed that the prætor left the law as it was
if it was a *patrona*, or a female child of the *patronus*, who was
excluded (GAI. iii. 49 ; ULP. *Reg.* 29. 4.) ; but by the *lex Papia
Poppæa* women with a certain number of children were placed
on a level with men in this respect.

2. Postea lege Papia adaucta sunt jura patronorum qui locupletiores libertos habebant: cautum est enim ut ex bonis ejus qui sestertium centum millium patrimonium reliquerat, et pauciores quam tres liberos habebat, sive in testamento facto sive intestato mortuus erat, virilis pars patrono deberetur. Itaque, cum unum quidem filium filiamve heredem reliquerat libertus, perinde pars dimidia debebatur patrono, ac si in sine ullo filio filiave testatus decessisset: cum vero duos duasve heredes reliquerat, tertia pars debebatur patrono, si tres reliquerat, repellebatur patronus.

2. But afterwards the rights of patrons, who had wealthy freedmen, were enlarged by the *lex Papia*, which provides that he shall have one equal share in the distribution of the effects of his freedman, whether dying testate or intestate, if the freedman has left a patrimony of a hundred thousand sesterces, and fewer than three children. Thus, if a freedman possessed of such a fortune has left only one son or daughter as heir, a half is due to the patron, exactly as if the deceased had died testate, without having any son or daughter. But, when there are two heirs, male or female, a third part only is due to the patron; and, when there are three, the patron is wholly excluded.

GAL. iii. 42.

3. Sed nostra constitutio quam pro omnium ratione graeca lingua compendiose tractatu habito composuimus, ita hujusmodi causas definivit, ut si quidem libertus vel liberta minores centenariis sint, id est, minus centum aureis habeant substantiam (sic enim legis l'apiae summam interpretati sumus, ut pro mille sestertiis unus aureus computetur) nullum locum habeat patronus In eorum successionem, si tamen testamentum fecerint: sin autem intestati decesserint nullo liberorum relicto, tunc patronatus Jus (quod erat ex lege Duodecim Tabularum) integrum reservavit. Cum vero majores centenariis sint, si heredes vel honorum possessores liberos habeant, sive unum sive plures cujuscumque sexus vel gradus, ad eos successionem parentium deduximus, patronis omnibus una cum sua progenie remotis: sin autem sine liberis decesserint, si quidem intestati, ad omnem hereditatem patronos patronasque vocavimus. Si vero testamentum quidem fecerint, patronos autem vel patronas praeterierint, cum nullos liberos haberent, vel habentes eos exheredaverint, vel mater sive avus maternus eos praeterierit, ita ut non possint argui inofficiosa eorum testamenta, tunc ex nostra constitutione per

3. But our constitution, published in a compendious form, and in the Greek language, for the benefit of all nations, established the following rules. If a freedman or freedwoman are less than *centenarii*, i.e. when their fortune does not reach a hundred *aurei*, (the amount at which we estimated the sum mentioned in the *lex Papia*, counting one *aureus* for a thousand sesterces,) the patron shall not be entitled to any share in the succession, provided the deceased has made a testament. But where a freed man or woman dies intestate, and without children, the right of patronage is maintained undiminished, and is as it formerly was, according to the law of the Twelve Tables. But if a freed person leave more than a hundred *aurei*, and has one child or several, whatever be their sex or degree, as his heirs or the possessors of his goods, such child or children shall succeed their parent to the exclusion of every patron and his issue: but if he die without children and intestate, we have called the patrons or patronesses to his whole inheritance. If he has made a testament, omitting his patron, and has left no children, or has disinherited them, or if a mother or maternal grandfather has omitted them, so however that such testa-

bonorum possessionem contra tabulas, non dimidiam (ut antea) sed tertiam partem bonorum liberti conquantur, vel quod deest eis ex constitutione nostra repleatur, si quando minus tertia parte bonorum suorum libertus vel liberta eis reliquerit: ita sine onere, ut nec liberis liberti libertaeve ex ea parte legata vel fideicommissa praestentur, sed ad cohaeredes hoc onus redundaret: multis aliis casibus a nobis in praefata constitutione congregatis quos necessarius esse ad hujusmodi juris dispositionem perpeximus, ut tam patroni patronaeque quam liberti eorum, nec non qui ex transverso latere veniunt usque ad quintum gradum, ad successionem libertorum vocentur, sicut ex ea constitutione intelligendum est, ut si ejusdem patroni vel patronae, vel duorum duarumve pluriumve liberi sint, qui proximior est ad liberti seu libertae vocetur successionem, et in capita non in stirpes dividatur successio, eodem modo et in iis qui ex transverso latere veniunt vorsando. Eno enim consonantia jura ingenuitatis et libertinitatis in successionibus ferimus.

ments cannot be attacked as inofficious, then, according to our constitution, the patron shall succeed by a possessio contra tabulas, not to a half as formerly, but to the third part of the estate of the deceased freedman, or shall have any deficiency made up to him in case the freed man or woman has left him a less share than a third of his or her estate. But this third part shall not be subject to any charge, so much so that it shall not furnish anything towards any legacies or fideicommissa, even though given for the benefit of the children of the deceased: but the whole burden shall fall exclusively on the co-heirs of the patron. In the same constitution we have collected many other decisions which we thought necessary to settle the law on the subject. Thus, patrons and patronesses, their children and collateral relations, as far as the fifth degree, are called to the succession of their freedmen and freedwomen; as may be seen in the constitution itself. And, if there be several children, whether of one, two, or more patrons or patronesses, the nearest in degree is called to the succession of the freedman or freedwoman; and the estate is divided per capita and not per stirpes. It is the same with collaterals; for we have made the laws of succession almost the same as regards persons free born and enfranchised slaves.

Doing away with all distinction of sex, and making the claim of the *patrona* the same as that of the *patronus*, and the position of the *liberta* the same as that of the *libertus*, Justinian thus regulates the succession *ab intestato*: first come the children of the freedman, whether in his power or not, or even if born before he was enfranchised; then, if he has no children, come the patron and his descendants; in default of these, the collaterals of the patron to the fifth degree. If the freedman has children, he can make any testament he pleases: if he has not, he can only make what testament he pleases provided his fortune is less than one hundred *aurei*; if it is more, he must leave the patron one unencumbered third, or the law will give this third *contra tabulas*.

4. Sed hæc de iis libertinis hodie dicenda sunt, qui in civitatem Ro-

4. What we have said relates in these days to freedmen who are citi-

manam pervenerunt, cum nec sint alii liberti, simul Dedititii et Latinis sublatis; cum Latinorum legitimae successiones nullae penitus erant, qui, licet ut liberi vitam suam peragebant, attamen ipso ultimo spiritu simul animam atque libertatem amittebant, et quam servorum ita bona eorum jure quodammodo peculii ex lege Junia manumissores detinebant. Postea vero senatus-consulto Largiano cautum fuerat, ut liberi manumissoris non nominatim exheredati facti extraneis heredibus eorum in bonis Latinorum praeponerentur. Quibus supervenit etiam divi Trajani edictum, quod eundem hominem, si invito vel ignorante patrono ad civitatem venire ex beneficio principis festinavit, faciebat vivum quidem civem Romanum, Latinum vero morientem. Sed nostra constitutione, propter hujusmodi conditionum vices et alias difficultates, cum ipsis Latinis etiam legem Juniam et senatus-consultum Largianum et edictum divi Trajani in perpetuum deleri censuimus, ut omnes liberti civitate Romana fruantur, et mirabili modo quibusdam adjectionibus ipsas vias quae in Latinitatem ducebant, ad civitatem Romanam capiendam transposuimus.

urbs of Rome; for there are now no others, there being no more *Dedititii* or *Latini*. And the *Latini* never enjoyed any legal right of succession; for although they lived as free, yet, with their last breath, they lost at once their life and liberty; and their goods, like those of slaves, were claimed by their manumittor, as a kind of *peculium*, by virtue of the *lex Junia Norbana*. It was afterwards provided by the *senatus-consultum Largianum*, that the children of a manumittor, not disinherited by name, should in the succession to the goods of a Latin, be preferred to any strangers whom a manumittor might institute his heirs. The edict of the Emperor Trajan followed, by which, if a slave, either against the will or without the knowledge of his patron, had obtained Roman citizenship by favour of the emperor, he was regarded as free during his life, but at his death was looked on as a Latin. But we, being dissatisfied with the difficulties attending these changes of condition, have thought proper, by our constitution, for ever to abolish the *Latini*, and with them the *lex Junia*, the *senatus-consultum Largianum*, and the edict of Trajan; so that all freedmen whatever become citizens of Rome. And we have happily contrived by some additional dispositions, that the manner of conferring the freedom of Latins has now become the manner of conferring Roman citizenship.

Gal. iii. 56–58. 63–65. 71–73; C. vii. 6.

*Latini Juniani.* See Bk. I. Tit. 5. 3.

*Senatus-consulto Largiano.* This *senatus-consultum* was passed in the time of Claudius, and in the consulate of Lupus and Largus. (Gai. iii. 63–67.) As we might infer from the text, the rights of the children of the patron to the succession of a *Latinus Junianus* remained if they were disinherited in any other way than by name.

By the edict of Trajan the rights of the patron were, in the case mentioned in the text, restored at the death of a *Latinus* exactly as if the *Latinus* had never become a citizen by imperial rescript. (Gai. iii. 72.) As to the modes in which a

*Latinus* could acquire the rights of full citizenship, see note on Bk. i. Tit. 5. 3.

## TIT. VIII.   DE ASSIGNATIONE LIBERTORUM.

In summa, quod ad bona libertorum, admonendi sumus consuisse senatum, ut quamvis ad omnes patroni liberos qui ejusdem gradus sunt, æqualiter bona libertorum pertineant, tamen licere parenti uni ex liberis assignare libertum: ut post mortem ejus solus is patronus habeatur cui assignatus est, et ceteri liberi qui ipsi quoque ad eadem bona, nulla assignatione interveniente, pariter admitterentur, nihil juris in iis bonis habeant; sed ita demum pristinum jus recipiunt, si is cui assignatus est decesserit nullis liberis relictis.

Finally, with regard to the goods of freedmen, we must remember that the senate has enacted, that although the goods of freedmen belong equally to all the children of the patron who are in the same degree, yet a parent may assign a freedman to any one of his children, so that, after the death of the parent, the child, to whom the freedman was assigned, is alone considered as his patron, and the other children, who would have been equally admitted had there been no assignation, are wholly excluded. But if the child to whom the assignation has been made, dies without issue, they regain their former right.

D. xxxviii. 4. 1.

The senate enacted this by the *consultum* mentioned in par. 3.

1. Nec tantum libertum, sed etiam libertam, et non tantum filio nepotive, sed etiam filiæ neptive assignare permittitur.

1. Not only a freedman, but a freedwoman may be assigned, and not only to a son or grandson, but to a daughter or granddaughter.

D. xxxviii. 4. 1, and 3. 1, 2.

But it was necessary that the child or grandchild should be in the power of the patron.

2. Datur autem hæc assignandi facultas ei qui duos pluresve liberos in potestate habebit, ut iis quos in potestate habet, assignare ei libertum libertamve liceat. Unde quærebatur, si eum cui assignaverit postea emancipaverit, num evanescat assignatio? Sed placuit evanescere, quod et Juliano et aliis plerisque visum est.

2. The power of assigning freed persons is given to him who has two or more children in his power, and it is to children in his power that a father may assign a freedman or freedwoman. Hence the question arose, supposing a father assigned a freedman to his son, and afterwards emancipated that son, whether the assignment would be destroyed. It has been determined that it is destroyed; such was the opinion of Julian and of most others.

D. xxxviii. 4. 1, and 13. 1.

The *senatus-consultum* did not allow the patron to give the freedman new heirs, but only to give a preference to particular heirs. If the children passed out of the power of the patron, they would cease to be heirs of the freedman.

| | |
|---|---|
| 3. Nec interest testamento quis assignet an sine testamento, sed etiam quibuscumque verbis patronis hoc permittitur facere ex ipso senatus-consulto, quod Claudianis temporibus factum est Suillo Rufo et Osterio Scapula consulibus. | 3. It makes no difference, whether the assignment of a freedman be made by testament, or without a testament. And patrons may make it in any terms whatever, by virtue of the *senatus-consultum* passed in the time of Claudian, in the consulship of Suillus Rufus and Osterius Scapula. |

D. xxxviii. 4. 1, pr. and 3.

The date of this *senatus-consultum* is given as A.D. 45.

Just as any expression of the wishes of the patron sufficed to make an assignation, so any expression of a contrary wish sufficed to revoke it. (D. xxxviii. 4. 1. 4.)

## Tit. IX.   DE BONORUM POSSESSIONIBUS.

| | |
|---|---|
| Jus bonorum possessionis introductum est a praetore, emendandi veteris juris gratia. Nec solum in intestatorum hereditatibus vetus jus eo modo praetor emendavit, sicut supra dictum est, sed in eorum quoque qui testamento facto decesserint; nam si alienus postumus heres fuerit institutus, quamvis hereditatem jure civili adire non poterat, cum institutio non valebat, bonorario tamen jure bonorum possessor efficiebatur, videlicet cum a praetore adjuvabatur: sed et is a nostra constitutione hodie recte heres instituitur, quasi et jure civili non incongruitus. | The system of *bonorum possessiones* was introduced by the praetors as an amendment of the ancient law, not only with regard to the inheritances of intestates, as we have said above, but of those also who die after making a testament. For if a posthumous stranger were instituted heir, although he could not enter upon the inheritance by the civil law, inasmuch as his institution would not be valid, yet by the praetorian law he might be made the possessor of the goods, because he received the assistance of the praetor. Such a person may now, by our constitution, be legally instituted heir as being no longer unrecognised by the civil law. |

GAI. ii. 242; D. i. 1. 71; D. xxxviii. 0. 1.

The *jus civile* knew of no other mode of succession than that of those who were strictly *heredes*. The praetor introduced a new mode, that by giving possession of the goods. This was, in its origin, merely the placing the heir under the civil law in possession of the *hereditas* in case this possession was withheld: and then the prætor being thus called on to admit to the possession, in process of time regulated this admission by the feeling of natural justice which it was part of his province to entertain, and admitted, in many cases, those whose blood gave a claim, in preference to those whom the course of the civil law marked out. He did not, indeed, admit any one whom the law expressly rejected; for the prætor could not openly violate the law; but when the law was silent, the prætor took advantage of this silence to admit persons whom the law passed over. (D. xxxvii. 1. 12. 1.) He never gave the *dominium Quiritarium* in any of the goods of the inheritance, but only the *dominium bonitarium* (see Introd. sec. 62), i.e. he made all that constituted the inheritance a part of the goods (' *in bonis* ') of the person to whom he gave the possession.

1. Aliquando tamen neque emendandi neque impugnandi veteris juris, sed magis confirmandi gratia pollicetur bonorum possessionem; nam illis quoque, qui recte facto testamento heredes instituti sunt, dat secundum tabulas bonorum possessionem. Item ab intestato suis heredes et agnatis ad bonorum possessionem vocat; sed et remota quoque bonorum possessione, ad eos pertinet hereditas jure civili.

1. But the prætor sometimes bestows the possession of goods with a wish not to amend or impugn the old law, but to confirm it, for he gives possession *secundum tabulas* to those who are appointed heirs by regular testament. He also calls *sui heredes* and *agnati* to the possession of the goods of intestates, and yet the inheritance would be their own by the civil law, although the prætor did not interpose his authority.

Gai. iii. 34; D. xxxvii. 1. 6. 1.

The person to whom the prætor gave the *bonorum possessio* could make use of the interdict (see Introd. sec. 107) beginning with the words ' *Quorum bonorum* ;' and as this was the readiest way of procuring the prætor's aid in being placed in possession, the heir might be glad to adopt it, though the *possessio bonorum* did not give him, as it did others, a title to succeed, which he would not otherwise have had.

2. Quos autem prætor solus vocat ad hereditatem, heredes quidem ipso jure non fiunt, nam prætor heredem facere non potest: per legem enim tantum vel similem juris constitutionem heredes fiunt, veluti per senatus-consulta et constitutiones principales; sed cum eis prætor dat bonorum possessionem, loco heredum constituuntur et vocantur bonorum possessores. Adhuc autem et aliæ complures gradus prætor fecit in bonorum possessionibus dandis, dum id agebat ne quis sine suc-

2. But those whom the prætor alone calls to an inheritance, do not in law become heirs, inasmuch as the prætor cannot make an heir, for heirs are made only by law, or by what has the effect of a law, as a *senatus-consultum*, or an imperial constitution. But when the prætor gives any persons the possession of goods, they stand in the place of heirs, and are called the possessors of the goods. The prætors have also devised many other orders of persons to whom the possession of goods may be granted,

remore moreretur; nam angustissimis finibus constitutum per legem Duodecim Tabularum jus percipiendarum hereditatum prætor ex bono et æquo dilatavit.

from a wish to ensure that no man should die without a successor. In short, the right of succeeding to inheritances, which was confined within very narrow limits by the laws of the Twelve Tables, has been extended by the prætors in conformity to the principles of justice and equity.

GAL. III. 18. 25. 32.

3. Sunt autem bonorum possessiones ex testamento quidem hæ: prima, quæ præteritis liberis datur, vocaturque contra tabulas; secunda, quam omnibus jure scriptis heredibus prætor pollicetur, ideoque vocatur secundum tabulas. Et cum de testamentis prius locutus est, ad intestatos transitum fecit; et primo loco suis heredibus, et iis qui ex edicto prætoris inter suos connumerantur, dat bonorum possessionem quæ vocatur unde liberi; secundo legitimis heredibus; tertio decem personis quas extraneo manumissori præferebat. Sunt autem decem personæ hæ: pater mater, avus avia tam paterni quam materni; item filius filia, nepos neptis tam ex filio quam ex filia; frater soror, sive consanguinei sunt sive uterini. Quarto cognatis proximis, quinto tum quem ex familia, sexto patrono et patronæ liberisque eorum et parentibus, septimo viro et uxori, octavo cognatis manumissoris.

3. The testamentary possessions of goods are these. First, that which is given to children passed over in the testament; this is called contra tabulas. Secondly, that which the prætor promises to all those legally instituted heirs, and is therefore called possessio secundum tabulas. After having spoken of these, he passes on to intestacies; and first he gives the possession of goods, called unde liberi, to the sui heredes, or to those who by the prætorian edict are numbered among the sui heredes; secondly, to the legal heirs; thirdly, to the ten persons who were preferred to a patron, if a stranger; and these ten persons were, a father; a mother; a grandfather or grandmother, paternal or maternal; a son; a daughter; a grandson or granddaughter, as well by a daughter as by a son; a brother or sister, either consanguine or uterine. Then, fourthly, he gave the possession of goods to the nearest cognati; fifthly, 'tum quem ex familia,' to the nearest member of the family of the patron; sixthly, to the patron or patroness, and to their children and parents; seventhly, to a husband and wife; eighthly, to the cognati of the manumittor.

GAL. III. 20, 27. 30; D. xxxviii. 0. 1.

The various kinds of possessions of goods may be divided according as they were testamentary (ex testamento) or ab intestato. Under the first head come the two kinds called contra tabulas and secundum tabulas.

1. The possessio contra tabulas was given, as it is said in the text, to children passed over in the testament. It was not given against the testament of women, as they had no sui heredes. (D. xxxvii. 4. 4. 2.)

2. The possessio secundum tabulas was given not only when

the testament was in due form and valid, but also when it would have had no effect according to the civil law. The prætor gave the possession though the testament was defective in form, as, for instance, if it contained no *familiæ mancipatio* or nuncupation.  (Ulp. Reg. 28. 6. See Bk. ii. Tit. 10.) The prætor, again, only required that the testator should have been capable of making a testament at the time he made it and at his death, without regard to the intermediate time. (See Bk. ii. Tit. 10 ; D. xxxvii. 11. 1. 8.) He permitted the institution of the posthumous child of a stranger (see Bk. ii. 13), and would, in cases where a gift was conditional, place the heir or legatee in possession of the goods while the condition was pending, and remove him if the condition was not fulfilled.  (D. xxxvii. 11. 5.)

The *possessio secundum tabulas* was not given until after that *contra tabulas*, that is, not until it was ascertained there were no children passed over, or that they had made no claim within the time fixed by law.  (D. xxxvii. 11. 2.)

If there was no testament, the prætor gave the possession under one of the following heads : *Unde liberi—Unde legitimi—Unde decem personæ—Unde cognati—Tum quem ex familia—Unde liberi patroni patronæque et parentes eorum—Unde vir et uxor—Unde cognati manumissoris.*

These are given in the text in the order in which they occurred in the edict ; and those beginning with *unde* are in that form, by a contraction for *ea pars edicti unde liberi vocantur: unde legitimi vocantur*, &c.

Four only have reference to the succession of persons of free birth : *Unde liberi, unde legitimi, unde cognati, unde vir et uxor.*  The other four are only applicable to freedmen.

1. The *possessio unde liberi* was given to the *sui heredes*, and those called with them.

2. That *unde legitimi* was given to all those who would be the heirs of the deceased by law, that is, to those summoned to the succession by the law of the Twelve Tables, and those placed in the same rank by subsequent legislation.  *Tum, quem ei heredem esse oporteret, si intestatus mortuus esset.* (D. xxxviii. 7. 1.)  It included the *sui heredes*, if they did not apply within the time prescribed to them as *sui heredes*, the *agnati*, those placed by the constitutions in the rank of *agnati*, the mother under the *senatus-consultum Tertullianum*, the children under the *senatus-consultum Orphitianum*, and the patron and his children as the *heredes legitimi* of their *libertus*.

3. That *unde decem personæ* was given to the ten persons mentioned in the text in preference to a stranger who might

have emancipated a free person, after having acquired him in
*mancipio* for the purpose of the fictitious sale necessary to
emancipation.   This emancipation made the emancipator the
patron, and gave him rights of succession, which the prætor
postponed by the edict.

4. The *possessio unde cognati* created a new class of persons
interested in the succession by ties of blood which gave no
claim except under the edict.  The *sui heredes* and *legitimi*, if
they had omitted to come in within the time prescribed to
them, might come in as *cognati*.

5. The *possessio tum quem ex familia* was given to the
nearest member of the family of the patron, in default of the
*sui heredes* taking under the *unde legitimi*.   The words are
an abridgement of part of the edict, '*tum quem ex familia
patroni proximum oportebit, vocabo.*' For the two first
words is read sometimes *tanquam*, sometimes *tum qua*; but
*tum quem* is much the most intelligible reading.

6. The *possessio unde liberi patroni patronaeque et parentes eorum* was given to the descendants of the patron,
whether they had been in the power of the patron or not, and
to the ascendants, whether the patron had been in their power
or not—thus going a step beyond the last-mentioned possession, which was only given to a person in the family of the
patron.   This is as probable an account as any of the use
of this and the last *possessio*: but so little is known respecting them, that we cannot be certain how they were applied.

7. The *possessio unde vir et uxor* gave husband and wife
reciprocal rights of succession.  The only mode in which one
married person succeeded by the *jus civile* to the goods of
another was when the wife passed into the power of her husband by *in manum conventio.*

8. The *possessio unde cognati manumissoris* was given to
all the blood relations of the patron.   In the possession given
exclusively with reference to the goods of freedmen, it was the
same as with those given alike of the goods of free persons and
of freedmen; any one who might have applied for an earlier
possession might, if he failed to do so within the prescribed
time, apply for a later possession, in the terms of which he was
included.    Thus the *quem proximum* might apply as for the
*possessio unde liberi patroni*, &c., and both he and one of the
*liberi patroni* might have applied for that *unde cognati
manumissoris.*

If there was no one to whom possession of goods could be
given, the right to the goods devolved to the people, i. e. in the
times of the emperors, to the *fiscus*. (*Si nemo sit, ad quem*

*bonorum possessio pertinere possit, aut sit quidem, sed jus suum amiserit, populo bona deferuntur ex lege Julia caducaria.*) (ULP. *Reg.* 28. 7.)

4. Sed eas quidem pretoria introduxit jurisdictio. A nobis tamen nihil incuriosum pretermissum est; sed nostris constitutionibus omnia corrigentes, contra tabulas quidem et secundum tabulas bonorum possessiones admisimus, utpote necessarias constitutas, nec non ab intestato unde liberi et unde legitimi bonorum possessiones. Quae autem in pretoris edicto quinto loco posita fuerat, id est unde decem personae, eam pio proposito et compendioso sermone supervacuam ostendimus. Cum enim prefata bonorum possessio decem personas praeponebat extraneo manumissori, nostra constitutio quam de enancipatione liberorum fecimus, omnibus parentibus eisdemque manumissoribus contracta fiducia manumissionem facere dedit, ut ipsa manumissio eorum hoc in se habeat privilegium, et supervacua fiat supradicta bonorum possessio. Sublata igitur prefata quinta bonorum possessione, in gradum ejus sextam bonorum possessionem induximus. et quintam fecimus quam pretor proximis cognatis pollicetur.

4. Such are the possessions of goods introduced by the praetor's authority. We ourselves, who have passed over nothing negligently, but have wished to amend everything, have admitted by our constitutions as indispensably necessary, the possession of goods *contra tabulas* and *secundum tabulas*, and also the possessions *ab intestato*, called *unde liberi* and *unde legitimi*; but with a kind intention, and in a few words, we have shown, that the possession called *unde decem personae*, which held the fifth place in the praetor's edict, was superfluous; for ten kinds of persons were therein preferred to a patron if a stranger; but by our constitution on the subject of the emancipation of children, parents themselves are the manumittors of their children, as if under a fiduciary contract, which has now become an understood part of the manumission, so that this privilege belongs necessarily to the manumission they go through, and the possession *unde decem personae* is now useless. We have suppressed it therefore, and, putting the sixth in its place, have now made that the fifth, by which the praetor gives the succession to the nearest *cognati*.

5. Cumque antea fuerat septimo loco bonorum possessiorum quem ex familia, et octavo unde liberi patroni patronaeque et parentes eorum, utrumque per constitutionem nostram quam de Jure patronatus fecimus, penitus vacuavimus. Cum enim ad similitudinem successionis ingenuorum, libertinorum successiones posuimus, quas usque ad quintum tantummodo gradum coarctavimus, ut sit aliqua inter ingenuos et libertinos differentia, sufficit eis tam contra tabulas bonorum possessio quam unde legitimi et unde cognati, ex quibus possunt sua jura vindicare, omni scrupolositate et

5. As to the possession *tam quem ex familia*, formerly in the seventh place, and the possession *unde liberi patroni patronaeque, et parentes eorum*, in the eighth, we have now annulled them both by our constitution concerning the right of patronage. And having made the successions of *libertini* like those of *ingenui*, except that we have limited the former to the fifth degree, so that there may still remain some difference between them, we think, that the possessions *contra tabulas*, *unde legitimi*, and *unde cognati* may suffice for the *ingenui* to vindicate their rights; all the subtle and intricate niceties of those two

inextricabili errore istarum duarum
bonorum possessionum resoluto.

6. Aliam vero bonorum possessionem quæ unde vir et uxor appellatur, et nono loco inter veteres bonorum possessiones posita fuerat, et
in suo vigore servavimus, et altiore
loco, id est sexto, eam posuimus:
decima veteri bonorum possessione,
quæ erat unde cognati manumissoris, propter causas enarratas merito sublata, ut sex tantummodo
bonorum possessiones ordinariæ
permaneant suo vigore pollentes.

7. Septima eas secuta, quam optima ratione prætores introduxerunt: novissime enim promittitur
edicto lis etiam bonorum possessio,
quibus ut detur, lege vel senatus-
consulto vel constitutione comprehensum est. Quam neque bonorum
possessionibus quæ ab intestato
veniunt, neque iis quæ ex testamento sunt, prætor stabili jure con-
numeravit: sed quasi ultimum et
extraordinarium auxilium, prout res
exigit, accommodavit, scilicet iis
qui ex legibus, senatus-consultis
constitutionibusve principum ex
novo jure, vel ex testamento vel ab
intestato, veniunt.

6. The other possession of goods,
called vir et uxor, which held the
ninth place among the ancient possessions, we have preserved in full
force, and have given it a higher place,
namely, the sixth. The tenth of the
ancient possessions, called unde cognati manumissoris, has been deservedly abolished for reasons already
given; and there now, therefore,
remain in force only six ordinary
possessions of goods.

7. To these a seventh possession
has been added, which the prætors
have most probably introduced. For
by the last disposition of the edict,
possession of goods is promised to
all those to whom it is given by any
law, senatus-consultum, or constitution. The prætor has not positively
numbered this possession of goods
either with the possessions of the
goods of intestates, or of persons who
have made a testament: but has given
it, according to the exigence of the
case, as the last and extraordinary resource of those who are called to the
succession of intestates, or under a
testament by any particular law,
senatus-consultum, or, in later times,
by an imperial constitution.

D. xxxviii. 14. 1, pr. and 2.

The difference between the *possessio quibus ut detur, lege
vel senatus-consulto vel constitutione comprehensum est*, or
as it was sometimes called, the *possessio tum quibus ex legibus*
(THEOPH. *Paraphr.*), and the *possessio unde legitimi*, was,
that the first was given when the law, &c., expressly declared
that the possession of goods was to be given; the latter when
the law, &c., gave the *hereditas*, and the prætor gave the *possessio*. It was, for instance, by means of the possession *uti ex
legibus*, that the patron took concurrently with the children
of the *libertus*, by virtue of the *lex Papia Poppæa*.

8. Cum igitur plures species successionum prætor introduxisset, eaque per ordinem disposuisset, et in
unaquaque specie successionis sæpe
plures extant dispari gradu personæ;

8. The prætor, having thus introduced and arranged in order many
kinds of successions, and as persons
in different degrees of relationship are
often found in the same place with

ne actiones creditorum differrentur, sed haberent quoscunvenirent, et ne facile in possessionem bonorum defuncti mitterentur, et eo modo sibi consulerent, ideo petendae bonorum possessionl certum tempus praefinivit. Liberis itaque et parentibus tam naturalibus quam adoptivis in petenda honorum possessione anni spatium, ceteris centum dierum dedit.

regard to the succession, thought fit to limit a certain time for demanding the possession of goods, that the actions of creditors might not be delayed, but there might be a proper person against whom to bring them, and that the creditors might not possess themselves of the effects of the deceased too easily, and consult solely their own advantage; the praetor therefore fixed a certain time within which the possession of the goods was to be demanded, if at all. To parents and children, whether natural or adopted, he allowed one year, within which they must either accept or refuse the possession. To all other persons, *agnati* or *cognati*, he allows only a hundred days.

D. xxxviii. 9. 1, pr. and 12.

The *species successionum* correspond to the different *possessiones*.

9. Et si intra hoc tempus aliquis bonorum possessionem non petierit, ejusdem gradus personis accrescit; vel si nemo sit deinceps, ceteris bonorum possessionem perinde ex successorio edicto pollicetur, ac si is qui praecedebat ex eo numero non esset. Si quis itaque delatam sibi bonorum possessionem repudiaverit, non quousque tempus bonorum possessioni praefinitum excesserit, expectatur; sed statim ceteri ex eodem edicto admittuntur. In petenda autem honorum possessione dies utiles singuli considerantur.

9. And if any person entitled do not claim possession within the time limited, his right of possession accrues first to those in the same degree with himself; and if there be none, the praetor, by the successory edict, gives the possession to the next degree, exactly as if he who preceded had no claim at all. If a man refuse the possession of goods when it is open to him, there is no necessity to wait until the time limited is expired, but the next in succession are instantly admitted under the same edict. In reckoning the time allowed for applications for the possession of goods, we only count those days which are *utiles*.

D. xxxvii. 1. 3. 9; D. xxxvii. 1. 4. 5; D. xxxviii. 9. 1. 9. 8. 10; D. xxxviii. 15. 2.

10. Sed bene anteriores principes et huic causae providerunt, ne quis pro petenda bonorum possessione curet; sed quocumque modo, si admittentis eam indicium iutra statuta tamen tempora ostenderit, plenum habeat earum beneficium.

10. Former emperors have wisely provided that no person need trouble himself to make an express demand of the possession of goods; for, if he has in any manner signified within the appointed time his wish to accept the succession, he shall enjoy the full benefit of it.

C. vi. 9. 8, 9.

Only those *dies* were considered *utiles* which were subse-

quent to the person entitled to the possession being aware of
his right, and which were not days on which magistrates did
not transact business (*dies nefasti*).  Demand of possession
was to be made before a magistrate, that is, before the prætor
in the city, and the *præses* in the province; for the possession
did not devolve, like the *hereditas*, by course of law, but
had to be expressly asked for within a prescribed time.  A
particular formality in the terms of the demand was held
necessary, the applicant having to say, '*da mihi hanc
bonorum possessionem*' (THEOPH. *Paraphr.*), until a constitution of the Emperor Constantius (C. vi. 0. 9) permitted
the application to be made in any terms, and before any
magistrate, and another constitution excused those whom
ignorance of what was the proper course, or whom absence
prevented from making an application.  (Cod. 6. 0. 8.)  In
the time of Justinian there was no application before a magistrate; any act that manifested the wish to have the possession
was enough.

Sometimes the possession of goods was said to be given *sine
re*.  (GAI. iii. 35; ULP. *Reg.* 28. 13.)  The possession might
be claimed, in many cases, by persons who were entitled to
enter on the inheritance as heirs under the civil law.  If these
persons entered on the inheritance without demanding possession of the goods, the right to this possession devolved, at the
expiration of the time in which they might have claimed it, to
the next class entitled to it.  But if the person standing next
in the order of prætorian succession demanded the possession
in such a case, he received it, but only *sine re*, i. e. he was
placed in the legal position of possessor of the goods, but did
not really have any share in those goods which formed the
inheritance of the heir under the civil law.

-----

As we have now finished the subject of successions *ab intestato*, as treated of in the Institutes, and seen the system prevailing when the Institutes were published, this is the most
natural place to notice briefly the complete change introduced
by the 118th and 127th Novels, which were issued respectively
in the years 543 and 547.  By this sweeping change, the difference between the *possessio bonorum* and the *hereditas*, and
that between *agnati* and *cognati* was entirely suppressed, and
three orders of succession were created ; the first, that of descendants ; the second, that of ascendants; the third, that of
collaterals.  (1.) The descendants succeeded, whether emancipated or not, and whether adoptive or natural, to the exclusion

of all other relations, and without distinction of sex or degree. When they were in the first degree, they shared the inheritance *per capita*; when in the second, they shared it *per stirpes*. (2.) If there were no descendants, the succession belonged to the ascendants, except that, when there were brothers or sisters of the whole blood, the ascendants shared the inheritance with them, each person who had a claim to succeed taking an equal share. When there were no such brothers or sisters, the nearest ascendant took, excluding the more remote; if two or more ascendants of the same degree were not in the same line, that is, were partly in the paternal, partly in the maternal line, then the ascendants of one line took one-half, and the ascendants of the other took the other half, although there might be more of the same degree in one line than in the other. (3.) If there were no ascendants, then came, first, brothers and sisters of the whole blood, then brothers and sisters of the half blood, no distinction being made between *consanguinei, æ,* and *uterini, æ.* The children of a deceased brother or sister were allowed to represent their deceased parent, and to receive the share that parents would have received; but the grandchildren of a brother or sister were not allowed to represent their grandfather or grandmother. If there were no brothers and sisters, or children of brothers and sisters, the nearest relation, in whatever degree, succeeded; if there were several in the same degree, they shared the inheritance *per capita.*

## TIT. X. DE ACQUISITIONE PER ARROGATIONEM.

Est et alterius generis per universitatem successio, quæ neque lege Duodecim Tabularum, neque prætoris edicto, sed eo jure quod consensu receptum est, introducta est.

There is also another kind of universal succession, introduced neither by the law of the Twelve Tables, nor by the edict of the prætor, but by the law which rests on general consent.

GAI. III. 82.

We now pass to other modes of acquiring *per universitatem.* And the first is that of arrogation.

1. Ecce enim, cum paterfamilias sese in arrogationem dat, omnes res ejus corporales et incorporales, quæque ei debitæ sunt, arrogatori antea quidem pleno jure acquirebantur, exceptis iis quæ per capitis deminutionem pereunt, quales sunt operarum obligationes et jus agnationis. Usus etamin et usufructus licet his

1. For if the father of a family gives himself in arrogation, his property corporeal or incorporeal, and the debts due to him, were formerly acquired in full ownership by the arrogator, with the exception only of those things which were extinguished by the *capitis deminutio,* as the obligation of services and the rights of

D D

antea connumerabantur, attamen capitis deminutione minima eas tolli nostra prohibuit constitutio.

agnatio. Formerly, ane and usufruct were numbered among these, but one of our constitutions prevents their extinction by the minima deminutio.

Gai. iii. 82, 83; C. iii. 33. 10, pr. and 1, 2.

Gaius remarks that the property of the wife who passed in *manum viri* was acquired by her husband exactly as fully as that of the *paterfamilias* was by the person who arrogated him. Everything belonging to them passed to the husband or arrogator, except only those things which were *ipso facto* destroyed by the change of *status*, as, for example, the services due from the freedman to the patron, *operarum obligationes*, were due to him personally, and were no longer due if the patron passed into the power of another. The ties of agnation were also lost by the change of *status*, as the person arrogated passed out of his civil family.

2. Nunc autem non eamdem acquisitionem quae per arrogationem debat, coarctavimus ad similitudinem naturalium parentium: nihil et enim aliud, nisi tantummodo usufructus, tam naturalibus patribus quam adoptivis per filiosfamilias acquiritur in iis rebus quae extrinsecus bliis obveniunt, dominio eis integro servato. Mortuo autem filio arrogato in adoptiva familia, etiam dominium ejus ad arrogatorem pertransit, nisi supersint aliae personae quae ex constitutione nostra patrem, in iis quae acquiri non possunt, antecedunt.

2. At the present day acquisitions by arrogation are restrained within the same limits as acquisitions by natural parents. Neither natural nor adoptive parents now acquire anything but the usufruct of those things which come to their children from any extraneous source, the children still retaining the dominium. But, if an arrogated son die in his adoptive family, then the property also will pass to the arrogator, provided there exist none of those persons who, by our constitution, are preferred to the father in the succession of those things, which cannot be acquired for him.

C. vi. 61. 6; C. vi. 59. 11.

See Bk. ii. Tit. 9. 1.

3. Sed ex diverso, pro eo quod is debuit qui se in adoptionem dedit, ipse quidem jure arrogator non tenetur, sed nomine filii convenietur; et si noluit eum defendere, permittitur creditoribus per competentes nostros magistratus bona quae ejus cum usufructu futura fuissent, si se alieno juri non subjecisset, providere et legitimo modo ea disponere.

3. On the other hand, an arrogator is not directly bound to satisfy the debts of his adopted son, but he may be sued in his son's name: and if he refuse to answer for his son, then the creditors may, by order of the proper magistrates, seize upon and sell in the manner prescribed by law those goods, of which the usufruct, as well as the property, would have been in the debtor, if he had not made himself subject to the power of another.

Gai. iii. 84.

The arrogator succeeded to all the rights of action for debt which the person arrogated had, but not to the debts. For the arrogator was in the position of a father, who was not bound by the obligations of a son. But the property of the arrogated son was held answerable for the debts, and the prætor gave the creditors a *utilis actio* against the son, in whose name the arrogator was thus sued.

## Tit. XI.  DE EO CUI LIBERTATIS CAUSA BONA ADDICUNTUR.

Accessit novus casus successionis ex constitutione divi Marci : nam si II, qui libertatem acceperunt a domino in testamento ex quo non aditur hereditas, velint bona sibi addici libertatum conservandarum causa, audiuntur.

A new species of succession has been added by the constitution of the Emperor Marcus Aurelius. For, if those slaves, to whom freedom has been given by the testament of their master, under which testament no one will accept the inheritance, wish that the property should be adjudged to them, in order that effect may be given to the disposition for their enfranchisement, their request is granted.

D. xl. 4. 50, pr. and 1.

If no *heres ex testamento* accepted the inheritance, it devolved to the *heredes ab intestato*, and if no *heres ab intestato* accepted it, it devolved to the *fiscus*; if the *fiscus* would not accept it, the creditors could have the goods of the deceased sold for their benefit. But if the deceased had by testament or codicil given freedom to any slaves, then, after the inheritance had been successively rejected by the *heredes ex testamento*, the *heredes ab intestato*, and the *fiscus*, application might be made to have the goods given up to the applicant instead of being sold by the creditors, the applicant undertaking to enfranchise the slaves, and to satisfy the creditors. If the inheritance was accepted by any heir, or if there were no slaves to whom the deceased had left their liberty, then this *addictio* could not take place.

Gaius makes no mention of this mode of acquisition *per universitatem*, a circumstance used to fix his date, as showing that he wrote before the time when Marcus Aurelius issued the rescript contained in the next paragraph.

1. Et ita divi Marci rescripto ad Popilium Rufum continetur. Verba rescripti ita se habent: 'Si Virginio

1. Such is the effect of a rescript addressed by the Emperor Marcus to Popilius Rufus, in the following

Valenti, qui testamento suo libertatem quibusdam adscripsit, nemine
successore ab intestato existente, in
ea causa bona ejus eam coeperunt ut
venumdarentur, is cujus de ea re notio
est, aditus rationem desiderii tui habebit: ut libertatum, tam earum
quae directo quam earum quae per
speciem fideicommissi relictae sunt,
tuendarum gratia addicantur tibi, si
idonee creditoribus caveris de solido
quod cuique debetur solvendo. Et
si quidem quibus directa libertas
data est, perinde liberi erunt ac si
hereditas adita esset; ii autem quos
heres manumittere rogatus est, a te
libertatem consequentur: ita ut, si
non alia conditione velis bona tibi
addici, quam ut etiam qui directo
libertatem acceperunt, tui liberti
fiant; nam huic etiam voluntati
tuae, si id quorum de statu agitur
consentiant, auctoritatem nostram
accommodamus. Et ne hujus re-
scriptionis nostrae emolumentum
alia ratione irritum fiat, si fiscus
bona agnoscere voluerit, et ii qui rebus nostris attendunt, scient commodo pecuniario praeferendam libertatis causam, et ita bona cogenda ut
libertas iis salva sit, qui eam adipisci potuerunt si hereditas ex testamento adita esset.'

terms: ' If the estate of Virginius
Valens, who by testament has given
their freedom to certain slaves, must
necessarily be sold, there being no
successor ab intestato, then the magistrate who has the cognisance of
the affair shall upon application attend to your request, that, for the
sake of preserving the liberty of those
to whom it was given, either directly
or by a fideicommissum, the estate of
the deceased may be adjudged to you,
on condition that you give good security to the creditors that their
claims shall be satisfied in full. And
all those, to whom freedom was
given directly, shall then become
free, exactly as if the inheritance had
been entered upon; but those whom
the heir was ordered to manumit
shall obtain their freedom from you
only. However, if you do not wish
that the goods of the deceased should
be adjudged to you on any other condition than that those slaves also
who received their liberty directly by
testament shall become your freedmen, and if those who are to receive
their freedom agree to this, we are
willing that your wishes in this respect shall be complied with. And,
lest you should lose the benefit of
this our rescript in another way,
namely, by the property being seized
on behalf of the imperial treasury,
be it known to the officers of our
revenue, that the gift of liberty is to
be attended to more than our pecuniary advantage; and seizure shall
be made of the property in such a
way as to preserve the freedom of
those who would have been in a situation to obtain it, had the inheritance been entered on under the
testament.'

D. xl. 5. 2, and 4. 8. 11, 12. 17.

By a constitution of Gordian, it was declared that the rescript
of Marcus Aurelius extended to cases in which a stranger, and
not one of the slaves of the deceased, applied for the addiction.
(Cod. vii. 2. 6.)

When the inheritance was not rejected, but accepted by the
heredes ab intestato or by the fiscus, the fiscus, so far as regards the enfranchisement of the slaves, was placed, by the

latter part of this rescript in a different position from that which was occupied by the *heredes ab intestato*; whichever accepted it, the *addictio* could not take place, but the *fiscus* was ordered to fulfil the wishes of the deceased, while the *heredes ab intestato* were at liberty to disregard them.

2. Hoc rescripto subventum est et libertatibus et defuncti, ne bona eorum a creditoribus possideantur et veneant. Certe si fuerint hac de causa bona addicta, cessat bonorum venditio: existit enim defuncti defensor, et quidem idoneus, qui de solido creditoribus cavet.

2. This rescript is meant to favour both the gift of liberty and also the deceased testator, whose effects it prevents being seized and sold by creditors: for, of course, when goods are thus adjudged, in order that liberty may be preserved, there cannot be a sale by creditors, for there is some one to answer for the deceased, who is solvent, and gives security to the creditors for the full satisfaction of their claims.

D. xlii. 4. 2, and 5. 3.

3. In primis hoc rescriptum toties locum habet, quoties testamento libertates datæ sunt. Quid ergo si quis intestatus decedens codicillis libertates dederit, neque adita sit ab intestato hereditas? favor constitutionis debebit locum habere. Certe si testatus decedat, et codicillis dederit libertatem, competere eam nemini dubium est.

3. This rescript is applicable whenever freedom is conferred by testament. But, what if a master die intestate, having bequeathed freedom to his slaves by codicils, and the inheritance *ab intestato* be not entered upon? The benefit of the constitution shall extend to this case; of course, if the deceased die testate, freedom given by codicils is effectual.

D. xl. 5. 2.

4. Tunc enim constitutioni locum esse verba ostendunt, cum nemo successor ab intestato existat; ergo quamdiu incertum erit utrum existat an non, cessabit constitutio. Si certum esse cœperit neminem extare, tunc erit constitutioni locus.

4. The words of the constitution show, that it is then in force, when there is no successor *ab intestato*. Therefore, as long as it remains doubtful, whether there be or be not a successor, the constitution is not applicable; but when it is certain that no one will enter upon the succession, it then takes effect.

D. xl. 5. 4.

5. Si is qui in integrum restitui potest, abstinuerit se ab hereditate, quamvis potest in integrum restitui, potest admitti constitutio et bonorum addictio fieri. Quid ergo si, post addictionem libertatum conservandarum causa factam, in integrum sit restitutus? Utique non erit dicendum revocari libertates, quæ semel competierunt.

5. If a person who has a right to be placed again in exactly the position he once held, should abstain from taking the inheritance, here too the constitution is applicable, and an adjudication of the goods may be made. Supposing then, after an adjudication has been made for the sake of preserving liberty, the heir is restored to his former position; still the freedom is not to be revoked, since it has been once gained.

D. xl. 5. 4. 1, 2.

The case most likely to have raised a doubt was that of a minor under 25 years, who was *heres ab intestato.* If he had accepted the inheritance at once, he would have taken it without any of the burdens, such as gifts of liberty, with which it was charged by the testament. But if he refused to accept it, and the slaves were enfranchised by addiction being granted, then when the minor attained the age of 25, and was entitled to the *restitutio in integrum,* was the freedom gained by the slaves to be revoked? Justinian says, undoubtedly not. The inheritance would be restored to the minor, but liberty once given could not be taken away again.

6. Hæc constitutio libertatum tuendarum causa introducta est; ergo si libertates nullæ sunt datæ, cessat constitutio. Quid ergo si vivus dederit libertatem, vel mortis causa, et ne de hoc quæratur utrum in fraudem creditorum an non factum sit, idcirco velint sibi addici bona, an audiendi sunt? Et magis est ut audiri debeant, etsi deficiant verba constitutionis.

6. This constitution was intended to make gifts of liberty effectual: and, therefore, when freedom is not given, the constitution is not applicable. Suppose, then, a master has given freedom to his slaves either *inter vivos* or *mortis causa,* and to prevent any question arising whether the creditors have been defrauded, the slaves intended to be enfranchised should petition, that the goods of the deceased may be adjudged to them: is this to be allowed? And we think that we ought, on the whole, to say that it is, although the constitution is silent on the point.

See Bk. i. Tit. 6.

7. Sed cum multas divisiones ejusmodi constitutionl deesse perspeximus, lata est a nobis plenissima constitutio, in qua multæ species collatæ sunt, quibus jus hujusmodi successionis plenissimum est effectum: quæ ex ipsa lectione constitutionis potest quis cognoscere.

7. Perceiving that the constitution was deficient in many respects, we have published a very complete constitution, containing many provisions, which complete the legislation on this kind of succession, and which may be easily learnt by reading the constitution itself.

C. vii. 2. 15, pr. 1, and foll.

## TIT. XII. DE SUCCESSIONIBUS SUBLATIS, QUÆ FIEBANT PER BONORUM VENDITIONEM, ET EX SENATUS-CONSULTO CLAUDIANO.

Erant ante prædictam successionem olim et aliæ per universitatem successiones: qualis fuerat bonorum

There were formerly many other kinds of universal succession prior to that of which we have just spoken;

emptio, quæ de bonis debitoris vendendis, per multas ambages fuerat introducta, et tunc locum habebat quando judicia ordinaria in usu fuerunt. Sed cum extraordinariis judiciis posteritas usa est, ideo cum ipsis ordinariis judiciis etiam bonorum venditiones expiraverunt. Et tantummodo creditoribus datur officio Judicis bona præsidere, et prout utile eis visum fuerit ea disponere: quod ex latioribus Digestorum libris perfectius apparebit.

such was the sale of goods which was employed to sell with numberless formalities the goods of debtors. It continued as long as the *judicia ordinaria* were in use; but afterwards, when the *judicia extraordinaria* were adopted, the sale of goods passed away with the *judicia ordinaria*. Creditors can now do no more than possess themselves of the goods of their debtors by order of a judge, and dispose of them as they think proper. This subject will be found treated of more at length in the larger work of the Digest.

GAI. III. 77-81; D. xlii. 5; C. vii. 72. 9.

This *bonorum emptio per universitatem* was a sale or transfer of the entire property of the debtor to the person who, in consideration of receiving it, would undertake to pay the largest proportion of the claims of the creditors. The creditors might apply for permission to have the goods sold in this way, not only when the debtor was dead, but (1) when he fraudulently hid himself, so that he could not be summoned before the magistrate, or (2) when he was absent, and no one appeared to defend his cause, or (3) if, after having been condemned, he did not satisfy the claims of the creditors within the time allowed by law, or (4) if he had made a *cessio bonorum*, i.e. had himself abandoned all his property to his creditors, as he was allowed to do by the *lex Julia*. (GAI. iii. 78.) The creditors were first placed in possession of the property, and this possession was continued during thirty days if the debtor were alive, and during fifteen if he were dead. They then announced the intended sale by *libelli*; and, by direction of the prætor, they chose one of their own body to conduct the business for them. He was called the *magister*, and received the proposals of those who wished to make an offer for the goods of the deceased. After a certain delay the creditors came again before the prætor, who directed them to fix the terms on which they finally consented to the transfer. The goods of the debtor, though not the Quiritarian ownership in them, were then transferred to the person whose offer they decided on accepting, and this person, termed the *bonorum emptor*, stepped into the place of the debtor, and might sue and be sued exactly as the debtor might have been. (THEOPH. *Par.*; GAI iii. 77. 80.)

*Judicia ordinaria, extraordinaria.* (See Introd. sec. 109.)

1. Erat et ex senatus-consulto Claudiano miserabilis per universi-

1. There was also, by virtue of the *senatus-consultum Claudianum*,

tatem acquisitio, cum libera mulier servili amore bacchata ipsam libertatem per senatus-consultam amittebat, et cum libertate substantiam. Quod indignum nostris temporibus esse existimantes, et a nostra civitate deleri, et non inseri nostris Digestis concessimus.

another most wretched method of universal acquisition per senatus-consultum: when a free woman indulged her passion for a slave, and lost her freedom under this senatus-consultum, and with her freedom her estate. This was, in our opinion, unworthy of our age, and we have therefore abolished it in our empire, and forbidden it to be inserted in the Digest.

GAL. i. 84. 91. 160; C. vii. 24.

There could be no marriage between a slave and a free person. If, therefore, a woman born free lived with a slave *in contubernio*, this was thought so disgraceful to her, that if the master of the slave complained, she was liable to the punishment mentioned in the text. The strong expression, '*servili amore bacchata*,' must not be taken as indicating anything more than cohabitation with a slave. If the woman was a freedwoman who thus lived with a slave, she became again the slave of her patron, if he had not known of, and assented to, her conduct, and the slave of the master of the slave with whom she lived, if the patron had been aware of how she was living. (PAUL. *Sent.* 2. 21; GAL. i. 84–91. 160; see also TACIT. *Annal.* xii. 53.)

## TIT. XIII.   DE OBLIGATIONIBUS.

Nunc transeamus ad obligationes. Obligatio est juris vinculum, quo necessitate astringimur alicujus solvendæ rei secundum nostræ civitatis jura.

Let us now pass to obligations. An obligation is a tie of law, which binds us, according to the rules of our civil law, to render something.

D. xliv. 7. 3.

We now pass to obligations. Having finished the subject of rights over things, and of the modes by which they are acquired, we now pass to rights against particular persons, expressed very inaccurately in later Latin by the term *jura ad rem*. (See Introd. sec. 61.) These rights are those which we have against some one or more particular persons, as opposed to the general rights, such as that of having the secure enjoyment of our property, which we have against all mankind. (See Introd. 61.) The indirect effect of rights against particular persons is, that we have a thing done for, or given to us, and hence, the *jus*, or right, was said to be *ad rem*; but the *res* was only the ultimate result, not the immediate object, of the right against the particular person.

Obligations are placed in the Institutes between the subject of things and the subject of actions; and as in Bk. i. 3, pr. it is said that the whole of private law relates to persons, things, and actions, it has been questioned whether obligations are meant to be included under things or actions. Theophilus understood them to be included under actions, as we see by his paraphrase on this Title, and on the 6th Title of the Fourth Book, but it is evident that Gaius, from whom Justinian borrows the arrangement, meant obligations to come under the discussion of *res*: otherwise, as Savigny remarks (*System des heut. röm. Rechts.* Bk. ii. ch. 1), we must consider the part specially relating to actions as a subsidiary part of the portion commencing with obligations, which is contradicted by the mode in which Gaius treats of the subject of actions. The subject of obligations does not properly fall under *res* or *actiones*, and it was from feeling this that Gaius placed it between the two, although his division of law obliged him to rank it under one or the other. He could not, consistently with this division, place obligations in his system according to their nature, and he preferred to consider them with reference to their ultimate result (*res*) rather than with reference to the mode by which the law secured this result (*actio*). The incorrectness of such a mode of treating obligations, and the inaccuracy of the expression *jus ad rem*, is evident when we consider that the *actio* did not really give the *res* which was the subject of the obligation, but only a pecuniary equivalent.

Unless an action could be brought to enforce an obligation, the obligation had no legal validity, and hence the text says, *astringimur secundum nostræ civitatis jura.* It is by having an action attached to it that an obligation, properly so called, a civil obligation, is distinguished from a natural obligation, which, however clearly it may be recognized as a part of man's duty, yet is not made compulsory by having an action to enforce it. Natural obligations were not, however, considered as entirely out of the pale of Roman law. For though no action could be brought to enforce them, yet they might furnish an exception, i. e. a ground of defence, and anything paid in fulfilment of them could not be recovered (D. xii. 6. 19); and at last a right of action was given in every case where the agreement was supported by a consideration. An action is so necessary a complement of a civil obligation, that in treating of an obligation, it is necessary to inquire what species of action is proper to it; and hence, in the Digest, obligations and actions are treated of in the same Title. (xliv. 7. *de obligationibus et actionibus.*)

The text says we are bound *necessitate alicujus solvendæ*

*rei; solvere* is used as a general expression for the fulfilment of an obligation. The three words, *dare, facere, præstare* (D. xliv. 7. 3), all here included in *solvere*, were used to embrace all the possible duties an obligation could create. Either the person bound by the obligation was obliged *dare*, i.e. to give the absolute ownership of a thing; or *facere*, i.e. to do, or not to do, some act; or *præstare*, i.e. to provide, or furnish, any advantage or thing, the yielding which could not be included in the limited sense of the word *dare*.

*Obligatio* is properly, as the text expresses it, a *vinculum*, a special tie between two or more particular persons; but it is also used to express the right thus gained (D. xii. 2. 9. 3), the duty thus owed (D. L. 16. 21), and also the mode by which the tie is created, being used as equivalent to *contractus*. (D. v. 1. 20.)

| | |
|---|---|
| 1. Omnium autem obligationum summa divisio in duo genera deducitur; namque aut civiles sunt aut prætoriæ. Civiles sunt, quæ aut legibus constitutæ aut certe jure civili comprobatæ sunt. Prætoriæ sunt, quas prætor ex sua jurisdictione constituit, quæ etiam honorariæ vocantur. | 1. The principal division of obligations is into two kinds, civil and prætorian. Civil obligations are those constituted by the laws, or, at least, recognized by the civil law. Prætorian obligations are those which the prætor has established by his own authority; they are also called honorary. |

D. xliv. 7. 52.

This division of obligations is based upon the difference of the sources, from which the actions given to enforce them were derived, the *obligatio civilis* being enforced by a civil action, the *prætoria obligatio* being enforced by prætorian action.

*Legibus constitutæ*, i. e. their force springing from the strict civil law of Rome, *jure civili comprobatæ*, i. e. originally belonging to the law of nations, but subsequently admitted into, and confirmed by, the civil law. The expression *secundum nostræ civitatis jura* in the last paragraph included both the civil and the prætorian law. If we use *civilis* not as opposed to *prætorius*, but as meaning 'municipal,' i. e. belonging to the particular state, all obligations derived their force from the *jus civile*, as they are only binding, because, under the system of Roman law, an action was attached to them.

| | |
|---|---|
| 2. Sequens divisio in quatuor species deducitur: aut enim ex contractu sunt, aut quasi ex contractu, aut ex maleficio, aut quasi ex maleficio. Prius est ut de iis quæ ex contractu sunt, dispiciamus: harum æquæ quatuor sunt species; aut enim re contrahuntur aut verbis aut li- | 2. A further division separates them into four kinds, for they arise *ex contractu* or *quasi ex contractu*, *ex maleficio* or *quasi ex maleficio*. Let us first treat of those which arise from a contract; which again are divided into four kinds, according as they are formed by the thing, by |

teris aut consensu, de quibus singulis dispiciamus.

word of mouth, by writing, or by consent. Let us examine each kind separately.

GAI. iii. 88, 89.

Gaius says (iii. 88), *omnis obligatio vel ex contractu nascitur, vel ex delicto*; and adds, in a passage given in the Digest (xliv. 7. 1), *aut proprio quodam jure ex variis causarum figuris*, which latter words include the various cases of obligations not properly belonging to either of the two heads of *ex contractu* or *ex delicto*, but which may be superficially assimilated to those belonging to one or the other. By *quasi ex contractu* is meant not that the obligation arises from a contract, but that there is an analogy between the mode in which the obligation arises and that in which an obligation, *ex contractu*, arises.

If we analyze the composition of a contract, we shall find that it includes three principal parts. First of all, there is what the Roman jurists termed *pollicitatio*, the offer made by one party for the acceptance of the other: then comes the *conventio*, or agreement on the terms terminating in the consent of the two parties. The third element of a contract is the obligation imposed by law on the parties to abide by what they have consented to. But the law only imposes this necessity, it only adds a *vinculum juris* to an agreement when the consent has been signified in certain prescribed ways. A mere agreement to which the law did not attach an obligation was termed a *pactum*; and the general notion of a pact is an agreement on which an action cannot be brought. Pacts might, however, be used by way of defence, and in the course of time many kinds of agreement, which had formerly been mere pacts, were clothed with an obligatory form by the prætor, or by constitutions of the Emperors, and could be enforced, thus losing the essential feature that distinguished pacts from contracts, although the name of pacts was still retained.

An agreement became a contract, that is, had a right of action attached to it, under the Roman law, when it was made in any of the four ways expressed by the words *re, verbis, literis* or *consensu*. If the subject-matter of an agreement was the transfer of a *res mancipi*, it could only be transferred by *mancipatio*, that is, by going through the form of the *nexum*. (See Introd. sec. 59.) But if the transfer of a *res mancipi* was not the subject-matter of the agreement, then the ancient law attached a *juris vinculum* whenever the agreement was made *re*, i. e. by a thing belonging to one person having been previously placed by him in the possession of another, or *verbis*, when a certain solemn form of words was used. Afterwards, contracts were permitted to be made *literis*, i.e. by entering the debt in the book of the creditor. Lastly, in four kinds of contracts, those of sale, letting, partnership, and mandate, there was nothing required more than the consent of the parties. Directly the consent was arrived at the *juris vinculum* attached.

The older actions of law (see Introd. sec. 94) afforded a very cumbrous machinery for the enforcement of rights against particular persons; and the *lex Silia* (510 A.U.C.) introduced a new kind of action, termed *condictio*, for the enforcement of obligations binding a person to give the absolute ownership (*dare*) of a certain sum of money (*pecunia certa*); and the *lex Calpurnia* (520 A.U.C.) extended its application to a similar demand of any certain thing, as a definite quantity of oil or wheat. (See Introd. sec. 95.) In process of time the *condictio* was made to embrace uncertain as well as certain things, and was applied to obligations binding a person *facere*, and hence Gaius says, *appellantur in personam actiones, quibus dare fierive intendimus, condictiones* (iv. 5). The *condictio certi*, i.e. the *condictio* in its older and stricter form, came thus to be opposed to the *condictio incerti*. We may therefore say that contracts *dare* or *facere* were enforced by a *condictio*, and that this *condictio* was *certi* or *incerti* according as a definite or indefinite thing was demanded. Whenever the contract was to do a thing, it was always uncertain, because the law could not compel the person bound by the contract to do the thing, but only to give a pecuniary equivalent; and what sum of money was a reasonable compensation for the loss sustained by the thing not being done was left to be settled by the judge. The formula of the *condictio certi* ran *si paret eum [decem aureos] dare oportere*. (See paragr. 1 of next Title.) That of the *condictio incerti* ran *Quicquid paret eum dare facere oportere*. The *condictio incerti*, besides its general name, received also a special name derived from the kind of contract it was brought to enforce, or from the subject-matter of the contract itself. For instance, the action brought to enforce a stipulation for an uncertain sum was termed an *actio ex stipulatu*. When the *condictio* was *certi*, it was generally spoken of simply as *condictio*. Sometimes, however, though rarely, it too received a special name, as the *condictio certi* brought to enforce a *mutuum*, sometimes termed the *actio mutui*. A *condictio* brought to enforce the demand of any certain thing, other than a certain sum of money, received the appellation of *condictio triticaria*, because wheat (*triticum*) was taken as a representative of those things of which a certain quantity could be claimed.

There were some actions in which a wide discretion was given to the judge, who was to take all the circumstances of the case into his consideration, and pronounce the sentence which equity demanded, thus acting as an *arbiter* rather than as a *judex*. Such actions were termed *bonæ fidei actiones*, and the obligations, to enforce which they were given, were termed *bonæ fidei obligationes*. The right to have this equitable consideration of the whole case was inherent in the nature of the obligation, i.e. the action brought to enforce any of the *bonæ fidei obligationes* was always *bonæ fidei*. All actions instituted by the prætorian law were of this description. There was thus an opposition made between *condictiones* which were derived from the civil law, and in which the judge was confined within the limits of the formula, and these *bonæ fidei actiones*. Among the *bonæ fidei actiones* we shall find several mentioned in the following Titles of this book, as, for instance, the action *ex empto, ex vendito, ex locato, ex conducto, mandati, depositi, pro socio*, &c. (See Bk. iv. Tit. 6. 38.)

There were agreements which, when executed on one side, were enforced, but which did not take the form of any of the four recognized kinds of contracts falling under the heads of contracts made *re, verbis, literis,* and *consensu*. We shall speak of these unnamed contracts, as they are termed, in the notes to Title 14. The action given by the prætor to enforce them was one specially adapted to meet the facts of the particular case, and it received the name of the *actio in factum præscriptis verbis*. The formula was drawn up to meet the facts of the particular case (*in factum*), and this was done by placing in the *demonstratio* a short statement of these facts (*præscriptis verbis*). (See Introd. sec. 106.) It may be proper to observe that such an action is to be distinguished from an *actio in factum concepta*, i.e. an action brought only to ascertain a fact, as opposed to an *actio in jus concepta*, i.e. an action in which the ordinary rules of law were applied to the facts ascertained. The *actio in factum præscriptis verbis* was *in jus concepta*. (See Introd. sec. 106.)

## Tit. XIV. QUIBUS MODIS RE CONTRAHITUR OBLIGATIO.

Re contrahitur obligatio, veluti mutui datione. Mutui autem datio in iis rebus consistit quæ pondere numero mensurave constant, veluti vino, oleo, frumento, pecunia numerata, ære, argento, auro: quas res

An obligation may be contracted by the thing, as, for example, by giving a *mutuum*. This always consists of things which may be weighed, numbered or measured, as wine, oil, corn, coin, brass, silver, or gold. In giving

aut numerando, aut metiendo, aut appendendo in hoc damus ut accipientium fiant, et quandoque nobis non eadem res, sed aliæ ejusdem naturæ et qualitatis redduntur: unde etiam mutuum appellatum est, quia ita a me tibi datur, ut ex meo tuum fiat. Et ex eo contractu nascitur actio quæ vocatur condictio.

these things by number, measure, or weight, we do so that they may become the property of those who receive them. The identical things lent are not returned, but only others of the same nature and quality; and hence the term *mutuum*, because, what I give from being mine becomes yours. From this contract arises the action termed *condictio*.

GAI. III. 90; D. xii. 1. 0, pr. and 3.

Obligations were said to be contracted *re* when the actual receipt of a thing under certain conditions imposed the necessity of fulfilling those conditions. Four kinds of contracts came under this head, all of which are noticed in this Title, viz. those named *mutuum, commodatum, depositum,* and *pignus*. The contract of *mutuum* was a contract of loan, where not the thing lent, but an equivalent, was to be returned. The obligation to return this equivalent arose on and by the delivery of the thing lent. It is scarcely necessary to say that the derivation from *ex meo tuum* is quite erroneous. Things which were of such a nature as that they could be replaced by equal quantities and qualities are termed, in barbarous Latin, *fungibiles*, because *mutua vice funguntur* (D. xii. 1. 6), they replace and represent each other : thus a bushel of wheat is said to be a *res fungibilis*, a particular picture is not. The distinction is much better expressed by saying that the classes of things which can represent each other are considered *in genere*, those which cannot are considered *in specie*. (See Introd. sec. 55.) If the person who lends the bushel of wheat receives in return a bushel of equally good wheat, consisting of grains totally different from those he lent, it is the same to him as if the identical grains were restored ; the wheat may be considered *in genere*; not so with the picture, which can only be considered *in specie*. But it is to be observed that it is the intention of the parties, not the nature of the thing, that makes the thing considered *in genere* rather than *in specie*. A person might lend a picture, and only require that a picture of some sort, whether the same picture or another, should be given in return to him, in which case the picture would be considered *in genere*; or a person might require the identical grains of wheat to be returned, and then the wheat would be considered *in specie*. A thing lent in a *mutuum* was always considered *in genere*, so that whenever it was the intention of the parties that the loan should be a *mutuum*, it was also their intention that the thing lent should be considered *in genere*.

The action for recovering the equivalent would be a *condictio certi*, as the equivalent was necessarily something fixed and determined on. In this case the *condictio* received the name of *condictio ex mutuo*, or sometimes *actio mutui*, but as it was always *certi*, it very seldom was termed anything but *condictio*, and perhaps the term *actio mutui* (C. vii. 35. 5) would not have been used in the time of strict legal language.

1. Is quoque qui non debitum accepit ab eo qui per errorem solvit, re obligatur, daturque agenti contra eum propter repetitionem condictitia actio : nam perinde ab eo condici potest, si paret eum dare oportere, ac si mutuum accepisset : unde pupillus, si ei sine tutoris auctoritate non debitum per errorem datum est, non tenebitur indebiti condictione, magis quam mutui datione. Sed hæc species obligationis non videtur ex contractu consistere, cum is qui solvendi animo dat, magis distrahere voluit negotium quam contrahere.

1. A person, also, who receives a payment which is not due to him, and which is made by mistake, is bound *re*, I. e. by the thing ; and the plaintiff may have against him an *actio condictitia* to recover what he has paid. For the *condictio* ' *Si paret eum dare oportere,*' may be brought against him, exactly as if he had received a *mutuum*. Thus a pupil, to whom a payment has been made by mistake without the authorisation of his tutor, is not subject to a *condictio indebiti*, any more than he would be by the gift of a *mutuum*. This species of obligation, however, does not seem to arise from a contract, since he, who gives in order to acquit himself of something due from him, intends rather to dissolve than to make a contract.

GAI. iii. 91.

In this case it is the law that imposes certain conditions, and not the intention of the parties, and, therefore, the obligation arises *quasi ex contractu*, and ought to have been placed under that head. A pupil could not be bound without the consent of his tutor. If, therefore, without the consent of his tutor, a loan was made him, he was not bound to repay it, or if money not due to him were paid him, he was not bound to refund it. (See Bk. i. Tit. 21, pr.)

2. Item is cui res aliqua utenda datur, id est commodatur, re obligatur et tenetur commodati actione. Sed is ab eo qui mutuum accepit, longe distat ; namque non ita res datur ut ejus fiat, et ob id de ea re ipsa restituenda tenetur. Et si quidem qui mutuum accepit, si quolibet fortuito casu amiserit quod accepit, veluti incendio, ruina, naufragio aut latronum hostiumve incursu, nihilo minus obligatus permanet : at is qui

2. A person, too, to whom a thing is given as a *commodatum*, i.e. is given that he may make use of it, is bound *re*, and is subject to the *actio commodati*. But there is a wide difference between him and a person who has received a *mutuum* ; for the thing is not given him that it may become his property, and he therefore is bound to restore the identical thing he received. And, again, he who has received a *mutuum*, if by any accident,

utendum accepit, mno quidem ex-actam diligentiam custodiendæ rei præstare jubetur, nec sufficit si tan-tam diligentiam adhibuiwe, quan-tam in suis rebus adhibere solitus est, si modo alius diligentior poterit eam rem custodire; sed propter majorem vim majoresve casus non tenetur, si modo non hujus ipsius culpa is casus intervenerit. Alioqui si id quod tibi commodatum est, peregre tecum ferre malueris, et vel incursu hostium prædonumve vel naufragio amiseris, dubium non est quin de restituenda ea re tenearis. Commodata autem res tunc proprie intelligitur, si nulla mercede ac-cepta vel constituta res tibi utenda data est: alioqui mercede interve-niente locatus tibi usus rei videtur; gratuitum enim debet esse commo-datum.

as fire, the fall of a building, ship-wreck, the attack of thieves or ene-mies, he loses what he received, still remains bound. But he who has received a thing lent for his use, is indeed bound to employ his utmost diligence in keeping and preserving it; nor will it suffice that he should take the same care of it, which he was accustomed to take of his own property, if it appear that a more careful person might have preserved it in safety; but he has not to answer for loss occasioned by superior force, or extraordinary accident, provided the accident is not due to any fault of his. If, however, you take with you on a journey the thing lent you to make use of, and you lose it by the attack of enemies or robbers, or by shipwreck, you are undoubtedly bound to restore it. A thing is properly said to be *commodatum*, when you are permitted to enjoy the use of it, without any recompense being given or agreed on; for, if there is any recompense, the contract is that of *locatio*, as a thing, to be a *commodatum*, must be lent gratuitously.

D. xliv. 7. 1. 3, 4.; D. xiii. 6, 6. 12.

As the advantage is, in almost every case, entirely on the side of the receiver of the *commodatum*, he was bound to take every care of it, or, as Gaius says, as great care as the most diligent *paterfamilias* takes of his own property. (D. xiii. 6. 18.)

To use the technical phrase, it was 'essential' to the *mutuum* that it should be gratuitous. Things incident to a contract may be *essential* to it, i. e. necessarily belonging, *natural*, i. e. belonging, in the absence of express agreement to the contrary, or *accidental*, i. e. belonging only by express agreement.

The *commodatum* gave rise to the *actio commodati*, which was either *directa* or *contraria*: by the *actio commodati directa*, the *commodans* made the receiver of the *commodatum* restore the thing lent, after the receiver had had it in his pos-session for the time agreed on (for he could not reclaim it before), or made him pay for any loss accruing through his fault. By the *actio commodati contraria*, the receiver of the *commodatum* obtained from the *commodans* compensation for any extraordinary expenses which the preservation of the thing had entailed, or for any losses occasioned by the fault of the *commodans*. The *actio* was, in the former case, termed *directa*, because it proceeded from what was a necessary part of the execution of the contract, viz. the thing lent being put in the possession of the receiver, while the *actio contraria* only arose from a thing which might happen or not, viz. there being some extraordinary expense, or some fault on the part of the *commodans*. (See D. xiii. 6. 17.)

| | |
|---|---|
| 3. Praeterea ct is apud quem res aliqua deponitur, re obligatur et actione depositi ; qui et ipse de ea re quam accepit restituenda tenetur. Sed is ex eo solo tenetur, si quid dolo commiserit ; culpae autem nomine, Id est, desidiae ac negligentiae non tenetur : Itaque securus est, qui parum diligenter custoditam rem furto amiserit, quia qui negligenti amico rem custodiendam tradidit, suae facilitati id imputare debet. | 3. A person with whom a thing is deposited, is bound *re*, and is subject to the *actio depositi*, because he must give back the identical thing which he received. But he is only answerable if he is guilty of fraud, and not for a mere fault, such as carelessness or negligence ; and he cannot, therefore, be called to account if the thing deposited, being carelessly kept, is stolen. For he who commits his property to the care of a negligent friend, should impute the loss to his own want of caution. |

D. xliv. 7. 1. 5.

Here the benefit is entirely on the side of the person who commits the thing to the care of him who receives it. The latter, therefore, unless he specially agrees to be answerable for the thing entrusted to him, or himself offers to take care of it (D. xiii. 65. 2), is not liable for its loss or deterioration, if he be not guilty of dishonesty, or of such gross neglect as amounts to dishonesty. He has, however, no right to make use of the thing (D. iv. 1. 6), and as it is deposited for the benefit of the person depositing it, that person can reclaim it when he pleases, and need not, like the *commodans*, wait for the expiration of the time agreed on.

The *depositum* gave rise to the *actio depositi*, which was *directa* or *contraria*, upon the same principle as the *actio commodati*. The depositary was entitled to be recompensed for every expense incurred, and to compensation for every loss incurred by the fault of the *deponens*, however light that fault might be. If the depositary had voluntarily offered to receive the deposit, he too would be answerable for loss occasioned by a *culpa levis*, i. e. a slight fault, as opposed to *culpa gravis*, gross negligence. (See Tit. 25. 9.) If a deposit was rendered necessary by circumstances of unforeseen and sudden misfortune, as a shipwreck or fire, and the thing deposited was lost by the negligence of the depositary, double the value of the thing could be recovered. (See Bk. iv. Tit. 6. 23.)

E E

4. Creditor quoque qui pignus accepit, re obligatur; qui et ipse de ea re quam accepit restituenda tenetur actione pigneratitia. Sed quia pignus utriusque gratia datur, et debitoris quo magis pecunia ei crederetur, et creditoris quo magis ei in tuto sit creditum, placuit sufficere quod ad eam rem custodiendam exactam diligentiam adhiberet: quam si prœstiterit, et aliquo fortuito casu eam rem amiserit, securum esse nec impediri creditum petere.

4. A creditor also, who has received a pledge, is bound re, for he is obliged to restore the thing he has received, by the actio pigneratitia. But, inasmuch as a pledge is given for the benefit of both parties, of the debtor that he may borrow more easily, and of the creditor that repayment may be better secured, it has been decided that it will suffice if the creditor employs his utmost diligence in keeping the thing pledged: if, notwithstanding this care, it is lost by some accident, the creditor is not accountable for it, and he is not prohibited from suing for his debt.

D. xliv. 7. 1. 6; D. xiii. 7. 13. 1.

The oldest form of the contract of pledge was that of *mancipatio*, or absolute sale of the thing subject to a contract of *fiducia* or agreement for redemption. There were so many things to which *mancipatio* was considered inapplicable, that the more simple contract of *pignus* quite superseded this *mancipatio contracta fiducia*. A further simplification of the contract or pledge was the *hypotheca* in which the thing pledged remained with the pledger. The *mancipatio*, it may be observed, transferred both the property and possession of the thing pledged; the *pignus* gave the possession to the creditor, but left the property in the thing with the debtor: the *hypotheca* left both the property and the possession with the debtor. (See note at end of Bk. ii. Tit. 5.)

The creditor was bound to take the same care of the pledge as he who received a *commodatum* was of the thing lent him. He could not, like the receiver of a *commodatum*, make use of the thing placed in his possession, and it was only by special agreement that the creditor could take the fruits of the thing pledged by way of interest.

Creditor and debtor are terms used more widely in Roman law than in our own. Every one who possessed a personal right against another was termed a *creditor*, and every one who owed the satisfaction of a claim, or was the subject of a personal right, was a *debitor*.

From the contract of *pignus* sprang the *actio pigneratitia*, which was *directa* when used by the debtor to constrain the creditor to give back the thing pledged if the debt had been paid, or to pay over the surplus if the thing pledged had been sold, and produced more than was due for the debt, or to obtain compensation from him for any injury to the thing pledged, arising through his fault. The *actio pigneratitia* was contra-

*riu* when used by the creditor to make the debtor reimburse him for all expenses incurred in keeping the thing safe, or compensate him for all injuries sustained by the thing pledged through the fault of the debtor (D. xiii. 7. 31); or, again, to compensate him if the thing pledged proved to be in reality not the property of the debtor, and was claimed by the real owner. Until it was claimed, the fact that it belonged to another did not prevent a thing being made the subject of a contract of *pignus*, and the creditor was as much bound to restore it to the debtor, if the sum due was paid, as if it had really been the debtor's property.

When an agreement did not take the shape of any of the ten forms of contract recognized in the civil law (it will be remembered that the heads *re* and *consensu* have each four subdivisions), it was, strictly speaking, not a contract at all, but if one party to it had executed it, the praetor would force the other party to execute it also. These contracts, as having no special name, have been termed *contractus innominati*, and as the contract sprang into existence by a thing having been done or given, by the fact, that is, of the contract being already executed by one party to it, these *contractus innominati* may be looked on as belonging more immediately to the head of contracts made *re*. Paulus (D. xix. 5. 5) thus sums up the heads of the cases in which such contracts might arise : '*Aut do tibi ut des, aut do ut facias, aut facio ut des, aut facio ut facias.*' I give something to you in such a way that by the fact of my gift (*re*) you are bound to give something to me, or I give so that you are bound to do something for me, or I do something for you so that you are bound to give me something, or I do something for you so that you are bound to do something for me. Contracts of this sort would, as we have said in the notes to the last Title, be enforced by an *actio in factum praescriptis verbis*, by one, that is, in which the formula would be arranged to meet the circumstances of this particular case (*in factum*), a short statement of these circumstances being placed in the *demonstratio* (*praescriptis verbis*).

## Tit. XV.  DE VERBORUM OBLIGATIONE.

Verbis obligatio contrahitur ex interrogatione et responsione, cum quid dari fierive nobis stipulamur; ex qua duae proficiscantur actiones, tam condictio si certa sit stipulatio, quam ex stipulata si incerta. Quae

An obligation by word of mouth is contracted by means of a question and an answer, when we stipulate that anything shall be given to, or done for us. It gives rise to two actions—the *condictio*, when the sti-

E E 1

hoc nomine inde utitur, quia stipulum apud veteres firmum appellabatur, forte a stipite descendens.

pulation is certain, and the *actio ex stipulatu*, when it is uncertain. The term stipulation is derived from *stipulum*, a word employed by the ancients to mean 'firm,' and coming perhaps from *stipes*, the trunk of a tree.

D. xliv. 7. 1. 7; D. xii. 1. 24.

The *stipulatio* was, properly speaking, not a contract, but a means of making a contract, a solemn form giving legal validity to an agreement. This form consisted of a question and answer, and it was the question only which was, properly speaking, the *stipulatio*, it being only by an extension of the term that the word was applied to the whole mode of contracting, and that the answerer as well as the questioner was said, as in paragr. 1, to be one of the *stipulantes*. Like all the old forms of obligation, this formula only bound one party, viz. the maker of the promise. The *promissor* had himself to become the *stipulator*, and to receive in his turn a promise, if he wished to secure reciprocal rights. Obligations may be divided according as they are *unilateral* and bind one party only, or *bilateral* and bind both parties. A stipulation gave rise to a unilateral obligation.

Festus derives *stipulatio* from *stips*, coined money; and Isodorus from *stipula*, a straw. ' *Veteres enim, quando sibi aliquid promittebant, stipulam tenentes frangebant, quam iterum jungentes, sponsiones suas agnoscebant.*' (Orig. iv. 24. Quoted by Ortolan.) *Stips* and *stipulum* are a more probable source of the derivation of the word.

When the stipulation was for something certain, it was enforced by the *condictio certi*; when for something uncertain, by the *condictio incerti*. The term *actio ex stipulatu* is sometimes used to denote the *condictio*, whether certi or incerti; but is more usually employed to denote the *condictio incerti*, as when the *condictio* was certi, that is, was employed in its proper form, it generally received no other name than *condictio*.

The stipulation was not the only contract made by going through a solemn form of words. By the *dictio dotis* the wife and her ascendants bound themselves to give the *dos* to the husband; and by a promise accompanied by an oath (*jurata promissio liberti*) the freedman bound himself to render his services to his patron.

1. In hac re olim talia verba tradita fuerunt: Spondes? Spondeo. Promittis? Promitto. Fidepromit-

1. Formerly the words used in making this kind of contract were as follows—*Spondes?* do you engage

tis? Fidepromittis? Fidejubes? Fidejubeo. Dabis? Dabo. Facies? Faciam. Utrum autem Latina an Graeca vel qua alia lingua stipulatio concipiatur, nihil interest, scilicet si uterque stipulantium intellectum ejus linguae habeat. Nec necesse est eadem lingua utrumque uti, sed sufficit congruenter ad interrogata respondere: quin etiam duo Graeci Latina lingua obligationem contrahere possunt. Sed haec solemnia verba olim quidem in usu fuerunt. Postea autem Leoniana constitutio lata est, quae solemnitate verborum sublata sensum et consonantem intellectum ab utraque parte solum desiderat, licet quibuscumque verbis expressus est.

yourself? Spondeo, I do engage myself. Promittis? do you promise? Promitto, I do promise. Fidepromittis? do you promise on your good faith? Fidepromitto, I do promise on my good faith. Fidejubes? do you make yourself fidejussor? Fidejubeo, I do make myself fidejussor. Dabis? will you give? Dabo, I will give. Facies? will you do? Faciam, I will do. And it is immaterial whether the stipulation is in Latin or in Greek, or in any other language, so that the parties understand it; nor is it necessary that the same language should be used by each person, but it is sufficient if the answer agrees with the question. So two Greeks may contract in Latin. Anciently indeed it was necessary to use the solemn words just mentioned, but the constitution of the Emperor Leo was afterwards enacted, which makes unnecessary this solemnity of the expressions, and only requires the apprehension and consent of each party, in whatever words it may be expressed.

Gai iii. 92, 93; D. xlv. I. l. 6; C. vii. 37. 10.

*Spondes? spondeo* was the form exclusively proper when both parties were Roman citizens; *adeo propria civium Romanorum est ut ne quidem in Graecum sermonem per interpretationem proprie transferri possit, quamvis dicatur a Graeca voce figurata esse.* (Gai. iii. 93.) This constitution of Leo was published A.D. 469. (C. viii. 37. 10.)

2. Omnis stipulatio aut pure aut in diem aut sub conditione fit: pure, veluti quinque aureos dare spondes? Idque confestim peti potest; indiem, cum adjecto die quo pecunia solvatur, stipulatio fit, veluti decem aureos primis calendis Martiis dare spondes? Id autem quod in diem stipulamur, statim quidem debetur; sed peti priusquam dies venerit, non potest. At ne eo quidem ipso die in quem stipulatio facta est, peti potest, quia totus is dies arbitrio solventis tribui debet; neque enim certum est hodie in quem promissum est, datum non esse, priusquam is praeterierit.

2. Every stipulation is made simply, or with the introduction of a particular time, or conditionally. Simply, as, 'Do you engage to give five aurei?' In this case the money may be instantly demanded. With the introduction of a particular time, as when a day is mentioned on which the money is to be paid, as, 'Do you engage to give me ten aurei on the first of the calends of March?' That which we stipulate to give at a particular time becomes immediately due, but cannot be demanded before the day arrives, nor can it even be demanded on that day, for the whole

of the day is allowed to the debtor
for payment, as it is never certain
that payment has not been made on
the day appointed until that day is
at an end.

D. xlv. 1. 46; D. 1. 10. 2. 13; D. xlv. 1. 18. 1.

In the technical language of the jurists, *Ubi pure quis
stipulatus fuerit, et cessit et venit dies; ubi in diem, cessit
dies, sed nondum venit.* (See note on Bk. ii. Tit. 20. 20.) If
the stipulation was made *pure*, the interest in the thing stipulated for passed at once to the stipulator (*cessit dies*), and he
could at once demand to have it (*venit dies*), giving, of course,
sufficient time for the debtor to fulfil his obligation. If the
stipulation was made *in diem*, the interest in the thing stipulated for passed at once to the stipulator, but he could not
demand it until the *dies* was passed.

There is a distinction in the respective effects of a stipulation *in diem* and of a conditional stipulation that deserves
notice. When stipulation was made *in diem* the promise was
binding at once, and the debt was already due, and therefore
if any part of the debt were paid before the day named, it
could not be recovered; whereas, when a stipulation was made
with a condition, if anything was paid before the condition
was accomplished, it could be recovered back, because, until
the condition was fulfilled, the stipulator had no interest in the
thing stipulated for (*nondum cessit dies*). (See paragr. 4.)

| | |
|---|---|
| 3. At si ita stipuleris, decem aureos annuos quoad vivam dare spondes? et pure facta obligatio intelligitur et perpetuatur, qula ad tempus deberi non potest; sed heres petendo pacti exceptione submovebitur. | 3. But, if you stipulate thus, 'Do you engage to give me ten aurei annually, as long as I live?' the obligation is understood to be made simply, and is perpetual; for a debt cannot be due for a time only: but the heir, if he demands payment, shall be repelled by the *exceptio pacti*. |

D. xlv. 1. 56. 4.

Lapse of time was not, in the Roman law, a mode by which
a debt could be extinguished. Consequently, if it was owed,
it was owed for ever; but this technicality was prevented from
working any injustice by the plea alluded to in the text,
namely, that there was an agreement to the contrary, or by
that of fraud. *Plane post tempus stipulator vel pacti conventi, vel doli mali exceptione submoveri poterit.* (D. xliv.
7. 44.)

| | |
|---|---|
| 4. Sub conditione stipulatio fit, cum in aliquem casum differtur obligatio, ut si aliquid factum fuerit aut non fuerit, stipulatio commit | 4. A stipulation is made conditionally, when the obligation is made subject to the happening of some uncertain event, so that it takes effect if |

tatur: veluti, si Titius consul fuerit factus, quinque aureos dare spondes? Si quis ita stipuletur, si in Capitolium non ascendero dare spondes? perinde erit ac si stipulatus esset, cum morietur sibi dari. Ex conditionali stipulatione tantum spes est debitum iri, eamque ipsam spem in heredem transmittimus, si prius quam conditio existat, mors nobis contigit.

such a thing happens, or does not happen, as, for instance, 'Do you engage to give five *aurei*, if Titius be made consul?' Such a stipulation as 'Do you engage to give five *aurei*, if I do not go up to the Capitol?' is In effect the same, as If the stipulation had been, that five *aurei* should be given to the stipulator at the time of his death. From a conditional stipulation, there arises only a hope, that the thing will become due; and this hope we transmit to our heirs, if we die before the condition is accomplished.

D. xlv. 1. 115. 1 ; D. I. 10. 54.

The heir or legatee, it may be remembered (see Bk. ii. Tit. 14. 9), who died before the condition was accomplished, did not transmit any interest in the inheritance or legacy to his heirs, whereas the stipulator did, as we learn from the text, transmit to his heirs the hope that the thing stipulated for would be one day due to him (*spes debitum iri*). The reason of this difference is, that the testamentary dispositions were considered to be made from a motive of kindness to the heir or legatee personally.

If the promissor attempted to defeat the condition by preventing its being fulfilled, he was treated as if he had promised *pure*, and the thing could be demanded from him at once.

It is here said that a promise to pay, if a person did not do a thing, was a promise to pay when he died. There was, however, this difference: the promissor was certain to die, and therefore, the stipulation, with the words *cum moriar*, was really made *in diem*; whereas it was not certain whether the promissor would or would not go up to the Capitol, and, therefore, the stipulation with the words *si in Capitolium non ascendero* was made *sub conditione*.

5. Loca etiam inseri stipulationi solent, veluti Carthagine dare spondes? Quae stipulatio, licet pure fieri videatur, tamen re ipsa habet tempus injectum, quo promissor ut illic ad pecuniam Carthagine dandam ; et ideo si quis Romae ita stipuletur, hodie Carthagine dare spondes? inutilis erit stipulatio, cum impossibilis sit repromissio.

5. It is customary to insert a particular place in a stipulation, as, for instance, ' Do you engage to give me at Carthage?' and this stipulation, although it appear to be made simply, yet necessarily implies a delay sufficient to enable the person who promises to pay the money at Carthage. And therefore, if any one at Rome stipulates thus, ' Do you engage to give to me this day at Carthage?' the stipulation is useless, because the thing promised is impossible.

D. xlv. 1. 73 ; D. xliii. 4. 2. 6.

6. Conditiones quæ ad præteritum vel præsens tempus referuntur, aut statim infirmant obligationem, aut omnino non differunt, veluti si Titius consul fuit, vel si Mævius vivit, dare spondes? nam si ea ita non sunt, nihil valet stipulatio; sin autem ita se habent, statim valet. Quæ enim per rerum naturam sunt certa, non morantur obligationem, licet apud nos incerta sint.

6. Conditions, which relate to time present or past, either instantly make the obligation void, or do not suspend it in any way; as, for instance, ' If Titius has been consul, or if Mævius is alive, do you engage to give me?' If the thing mentioned is not really the case, the stipulation is void; if it is the case, the stipulation is immediately valid. Things certain, if regarded in themselves, although uncertain as far as our knowledge is concerned, do not delay the formation of the obligation.

D. xlv. 1. 100; D. xil. 1. 37–30.

7. Non solum res in stipulatum deduci possunt, sed etiam facta, ut si stipulemur aliquid fieri vel non fieri. Et in hujusmodi stipulationibus optimum erit pœnam subjicere, ne quantitas stipulationis in incerto sit, ac necesse sit actori probare quid ejus intersit; itaque si quis ut fiat aliquid stipuletur, ita adjici pœna debet: si ita factum non erit, tunc pœnæ nomine decem aureos dare spondes. Sed si quædam fieri, quædam non fieri, una eademque conceptione stipuletur, clausula hujusmodi erit adjicienda: si adversus ea factum erit, sive quid ita factum non erit, tunc pœnæ nomine decem aureos dare spondes?

7. Not only things, but acts, may be the subject of a stipulation: as when we stipulate, that something shall, or shall not, be done. And, in these stipulations, it will be best to subjoin a penalty, lest the amount included in the stipulation should be uncertain, and the plaintiff should therefore be obliged to prove how great his interest is. Therefore, if any one stipulate, that something shall be done, a penalty ought to be added as thus: ' If the thing is not done, do you engage to give ten aurei by way of penalty?' But, if by one single question a stipulation is made, that some things shall be done, and that other things shall not be done, there ought to be added some such clause as this: ' If anything is done contrary to what is agreed on, or anything agreed on is not done, then do you engage to give ten aurei by way of penalty?'

D. xlv. 1. 137. 7; D. xlvi. 5. 11.

## Tit. XVI.   DE DUOBUS REIS STIPULANDI ET PROMITTENDI.

Et stipulandi et promittendi duo pluresve rei fieri possunt: stipulandi ita, si post omnium interrogationem promissor respondeat, spondeo, ut puta, cum duobus separatim stipu-

Two or more persons may be parties together in the stipulation or in the promise. In the stipulation, if after all have asked the question, the promisor answers ' Spondeo,' ' I

lantibus Ita promissor respondent, utrique reorum dare spondeo; nam si prius Titio spoponderit, deinde alio interrogante spondeat, alia atque alia erit obligatio, nec creduntur duo rei stipulandi esse. Duo pluresve rei promittendi Ita fiant: Mævi, quisque aureos dare spondes? Sei, eundem quinque aureos dare spondes? si respondent singuli separatim, spondeo.

engage;' for instance, when two stipulators, having each separately asked the question, the promisor answers, 'I engage to give to each of you.' For if he first answers Titius, and then, on another person putting the same question, he again answers him, there will be two distinct obligations, and not two co-stipulators. Two or more become co-promisors, thus: 'Mævius, do you engage to give five *aurei*?' 'Seius, do you engage to give five *aurei*?' each then separately answers, 'I do engage.'

D. xlv. 3. 28. 2; D. xlv. 2. 4.

The word *reus*, strictly speaking, signifies the person who is liable, or subject, to a demand, but is used more generally to signify a party to an obligation, whether active or passive: so here we have *rei stipulandi*, as well as *rei promittendi*.

It was immaterial whether the interrogation was put and answered in the plural, *spondetis? spondemus*; or in the singular, *spondes? spondeo*. (D. xlv. 2. 4.)

It was not only in contracts made *verbis* that there could be joint creditors and joint debtors. On a *commodatum* or *depositum*, for instance, the parties might agree that several persons should be subject to a common obligation, and each be bound for the whole. (D. xlv. 2. 9.)

1. Ex hujusmodi obligationibus, et stipulantibus solidum singulis debetur, et promittentes singuli in solidum tenentur; In utroque tamen obligatione una res vertitur, et vel alter debitum accipiendo, vel alter solvendo, omnium perimit obligationem et omnes liberat.

1. By virtue of such obligations, the whole thing stipulated for is due to each stipulator, and from each promisor. But, in each obligation, there is only one thing due, and if either of the joint parties receives the thing due, or gives the thing due, the obligation is at end for all, and all are freed from it.

D. xlv. 2. 2. 3. 1.

If we look to the thing which was the subject of the contract, we may say, however many were the joint parties, there was but one obligation, while, if we look to the persons by or to whom the promise was given, there were as many obligations as there were persons making or receiving the promise; if, therefore, the thing were given, that is, payment or performance made, the obligation was at an end, but the obligation binding on any one might be made to cease without those binding on the others ceasing also. If, indeed, the aid of the law had been called in to enforce the obligation, the position of the parties was different. If one co-stipulator sued the promissor, all the other parties to the stipulation were thereby prevented from suing him; and if one co-promissor were sued, none of the others could be sued, until it appeared that there was a deficiency in what had been obtained from the promissor that had been sued; the others might then be sued to make up this deficiency.　(C. viii. 41. 28.)

| | |
|---|---|
| 2. Ex duobus reis promittendi alius pure, alius in diem vel sub conditione obligari potest; nec impedimento erit dies aut conditio, quominus ab eo qui puro obligatus est, petatur. | 2. Of two co-promissors, one may engage simply, the other with the introduction of a particular time, or conditionally; and neither the time nor the condition will prevent payment being exacted from the one who binds himself simply. |

D. xlv. 2. 7.

## TIT. XVII.　DE STIPULATIONE SERVORUM.

| | |
|---|---|
| Servus ex persona domini jus stipulandi habet; sed hereditas in plerisque personæ defuncti vicem sustinet: ideoque quod servus hereditarius ante aditam hereditatem stipulatur, acquirit hereditati, ac per hoc etiam heredi postea facto acquiritur. | A slave derives from the persona of his master the power of making a stipulation. And as the inheritance in most respects represents the persona of the deceased, if a stipulation is made by a slave belonging to the inheritance before the inheritance is entered on, he acquires for the inheritance, and therefore for him who subsequently becomes heir. |

D. xli. 1. 34. 01.

A slave had no *persona*, that is, no capacity of acquiring civil or political rights.　But his master, who had such a capacity, could make his own *personæ* speak and act through the slave, who was thus only a channel by which the wishes of the master were expressed.　(See Bk. i. Tit. 3, pr.)　But although a slave could thus engage others for the benefit of his master, by a stipulation, he could not bind his master, and could not, therefore, be the promissor in a stipulation; hence, the text only speaks of the stipulations, and not of the promises, of slaves.

*In plerisque personæ defuncti vicem sustinet*; the inheritance represented the person of the deceased in most things, but there were some things which the slave could not acquire for the inheritance, which he could acquire for a living master; a usufruct, for instance, being always attached to a person, could not be stipulated for by a slave before the inheritance was entered on.　(D. xlv. 3. 29.)

1. Sive autem domino, sive sibi, sive conservo suo, sive impersonaliter servus stipuletur, domino acquirit. Idem juris est et in liberis qui in potestate patris sunt, ex quibus causis acquirere possunt.

1. Whether a slave stipulates for his master, or for himself, or for his fellow-slave, or without naming any person for whom he stipulates, he always acquires for his master. It is the same with children in the power of their father, in all cases in which they acquire for him.

D. xlv. 3. 15; D. xlv. 1. 45, pr. and 4.

What is said here of the children *in potestate* must be taken with all the limitations made necessary by the power they had to acquire a *peculium* for themselves. (See Bk. ii. Tit. 9.)

2. Sed cum factum in stipulatione continebitur, omnimodo persona stipulantis continetur, veluti si servus stipuletur ut sibi ire agere liceat; ipso enim tantum prohiberi non debet, non etiam dominus ejus.

2. If it is a licence to do something that is stipulated for, the benefit of the stipulation is personal to the stipulator; for instance, if a slave stipulate that he shall have a right of passage for himself or beasts and vehicles, it is he himself, not his master, who is not to be hindered from passing.

D. xlv. 1. 1:10.

Even in this case the slave really acquires for the master. It is the master, and not the slave, who could enforce the stipulation by action. Of course this personal licence to cross land is something quite different from a servitude. For a servitude *eundi* or *agendi*, stipulated for by the slave, could only be attached to the *prædium* of the master. (D. xlvi. 3. 17.)

3. Servus communis stipulando unicuique dominorum pro portione domini acquirit; nisi jussu unius eorum aut nominatim cui eorum stipulatus est; tunc enim ei soli acquiritur. Quod servus communis stipulatur, si alteri ex dominis acquiri non potest, solidum alteri acquiritur; veluti si res quam dari stipulatus est, unius domini sit.

3. If a slave held in common by several masters stipulates, he acquires a share for each master according to the proportion which each has in him, unless he stipulates at the command, or in the name of any one master, for then the thing stipulated for is acquired solely for that master. And, whatever a slave held in common stipulates for, is all acquired for one of his masters, if it is not capable of being acquired for the other; as for instance, if it belongs to one of his masters.

Gai. ii. 107; D. xlv. 3. 7. 1.

## Tit. XVIII.   DE DIVISIONE STIPULATIONUM.

Stipulationum aliæ sunt judiciales, aliæ prætoriæ, aliæ conventionales, aliæ communes tam prætoriæ quam judiciales.

Stipulations are either judicial, or
prætorian, or conventional, or common, that is, both prætorian and
judicial.

D. xlv. 5.

The division of stipulations here given is based on the
difference of the grounds on which they are entered into, the
ground being sometimes the will of the parties, sometimes the
direction of a person in authority.

1. Judiciales sunt dumtaxat, quæ
a mero judicis officio proficiscuntur:
veluti de dolo cautio, vel de perse-
quendo servo qui in fuga est, restituendove pretio.

1. Judicial stipulations are those
which proceed exclusively from the
office of the judge, such as the giving
security against fraud, or the engagement to pursue a fugitive slave, or to
pay his price.

D. xlv. 1. 5;  D. xxx. 69. 5.

Before the magistrate the parties were *in jure*, before the
*judex* they were *in judicio*. (See Introd. sec. 98.) The *judex*
sometimes ordered that the parties before him should enter
into stipulations.

Two instances are here given of stipulations directed by the
*judex*. The first is the *de dolo cautio*. This was a stipulation
directed for the benefit of a plaintiff, that the sentence given
in his favour might be executed, without any attempt at fraud
(*dolus malus*) on the part of the defendant. For instance, if
the defendant was ordered to make over the property in a
slave, the *judex* would direct that he should stipulate that he
had done nothing to lessen the value of the slave. Otherwise the
slave might be made over to the plaintiff, and the plaintiff's
claim be thus nominally satisfied, while it might really be
evaded by the defendant wilfully doing the slave some material harm.  (D. vi. 1. 20. and 45.)

The other instance given is that of the stipulation *de perse-
quendo servo qui in fuga est, restituendove pretio*. A slave
must be supposed to be demanded, and to run away before the
decision is given. As the defendant, being the actual possessor,
could only reclaim the slave against third parties, the *judex*
would compel him to engage by stipulation to follow and reclaim him, or to pay his price. If the slave escaped without any
fault whatsoever of the defendant, the judge merely directed
that the defendant should engage to give up the slave if he

came into his power, and to permit the plaintiff to bring an action in the defendant's name for the recovery of the slave from any one who might detain him. (D. iv. 2. 14. 11.)

2. Prætoriæ sunt, quæ a mero prætoris officio proficiscuntur, veluti damni infecti vel legatorum. Prætoriæ autem stipulationes nic exaudiri oportet, ut in his contineantur etiam Ædilitiæ; nam et hæ a jurisdictione veniunt.

2. Prætorian stipulations are those which proceed exclusively from the office of the prætor; as the giving security against *damnum infectum*, or for the payment of legacies. Under prætorian stipulations must be comprehended Ædilitian, for these, too, proceed from a magistrate pronouncing the law.

D. xl. 1. 5.

*Damnum infectum est damnum non factum quod futurum veremur.* (D. xxxix. 2. 2.) Supposing the *damnum futurum* which a man apprehended were an injury to his premises from the fall of the ill-repaired house of his neighbour, by the strict civil law, if he were to wait till the mischief were done, his neighbour might abandon his property in the fallen house, and the injured man could then obtain no reparation from him. To remedy this, the prætor would, if he saw fit, order the neighbour to give security (*cautio damni infecti*) to indemnify the person applying against any damage that might be done. If this order were not obeyed, the prætor authorized the complainant to enter upon and occupy the premises (*in possessionem mittebat*); and, finally, if security were still refused, the prætor gave the complainant full possession of the premises, but he was liable to be dispossessed, if within a certain time the original proprietor made compensation and complied with everything enjoined him. (See D. xxxix. 2. 4. 1.)

*Legatorum:* this was a stipulation binding the heir to pay legacies, when due, which were not yet payable; otherwise the heir might previously have spent and consumed all the inheritance.

*A jurisdictione veniunt,* that is, come from a magistrate *jus dicens,* as opposed to a *judex.*

3. Conventionales sunt, quæ ex conventione utriusque partis concipiuntur, hoc est, neque judicis, neque juris prætoris, sed ex conventione contrahentium. Quarum totidem genera sunt quot, pene dixerim, rerum contrahendarum.

3. Conventional stipulations are those which are made by the agreement of parties: that is, neither by the order of a judge nor by that of the prætor, but by the consent of the persons contracting. And of these stipulations there are as many kinds, so to speak, as there are of things to be contracted for.

D. xlv. 1. 5.

4. Communes stipulationes sunt, veluti rem salvam fore pupilli; nam et praetor jubet rem salvam fore pupillo caveri, et interdum judex sialiter expediri haec res non potest; vel de rato stipulatio.

4. Common stipulations are those, for example, providing for the security of the property of a pupil, for sometimes the praetor, and sometimes, too, when the matter cannot be managed in any other way, the judge orders it should be entered into: or, again, the stipulation that a thing shall be ratified.

D. xlv. 1. 5.

*Communes stipulationes* were those sometimes directed by the praetor, sometimes by the *judex*. They ought properly to have preceded the *conventionales*.

Mention has already been made of the security a tutor or curator was obliged to give. (Bk. i. Tit. 24, pr.) It was properly given before the tutor entered on his office, and it belonged to the praetor to see that it was given. But if, before it was given, the tutor sued a debtor of the pupil, and the debtor objected that security had not been given, the judge, in order that the proceedings might not be put an end to, would direct security to be then given before him.

The stipulation *de rato*, or *rem ratam haberi*, was one entered into by a procurator bringing an action in the name of his principal that what he did would be ratified by his principal. It properly belonged to the praetor to direct that this stipulation should be entered into before the *litis contestatio* (see Introd. sec. 105); but if he omitted to direct this, and there was ground for distrusting the authority of the procurator, the judge would direct that the procurator should bind himself by this stipulation. (See Bk. iv. Tit. 11. 1.)

## Tit. XIX. DE INUTILIBUS STIPULATIONIBUS.

Omnis res quae dominio nostro subjicitur, in stipulationem deduci potest, sive illa mobilia, sive soli sit.

Everything, of which we have the property, whether it be moveable or immoveable, may be the object of a stipulation.

A stipulation is *inutilis*, i.e. invalid, when it produces no tie binding on the parties to it. It would seem to have been proper to have examined here the causes which make contracts of any kind invalid, and not to limit the inquiry to stipulations. But the stipulation was so much the most important kind of contract that it is taken to represent all other kinds. Some few of the causes of invalidity noticed in this Title are peculiar to stipulations, but most are common to all contracts.

Lagrange thus classifies the reasons given in this Title for
the invalidity of stipulations: they might be invalid (1) on
account of their object (pr. paragr. 1, 2, 22, 24); (2) on account of the persons by whom (paragr. 7, 8, 9, 10, and 12),
for whom (paragr. 3, 4, 19, 20, 21), or between whom
(paragr. 6) they were made; (3) on account of the manner in
which they were made (paragr. 5, 18, 23); (4) on account of
the time (paragr. 13, 14, 15, 16, 26), or the condition (paragr.
11, 25) subject to which they were made.

1. At si quis rem quæ in rerum
natura non est aut esse non potest,
dari stipulatus fuerit, veluti Stichum qui mortuus sit, quem vivere
credebat, aut Hippocentaurum qui
esse non possit, inutilis erit stipulatio.

1. But, if any one stipulates for a
thing which does not, or cannot exist,
as for Stichus, who is dead, but whom
he thought to be living, or for a Hip-
pocentaur, which cannot exist, the
stipulation is void.

GAI. iii. 97.

In such a case no claim could be made for the supposed
value of the thing, nor even for a sum promised under a penal
clause in case of non-performance.   (D. xlv. 1. 69 and 103.)

2. Idem juris est, si rem sacram
aut religiosam quam humani juris
esse credebat, vel publicam quæ
usibus populi perpetuo exposita sit,
ut forum vel theatrum, vel liberum
hominem quem servum esse credebat, vel cujus commercium non
habuerit, vel rem suam dari quis
stipuletur : nec in pendenti erit stipulatio ob id quod publica res in
privatum deduci, et ex libero servus
fieri potest, et commercium adipisci
stipulator potest, et res stipulatoris
esse desinere potest ; sed prolinus
inutilis est. Item contra, licet
initio utiliter res in stipulatum deducta sit, si postea in earum qua
causa de quibus supra dictum est,
sine facto promissoris devenerit, extinguitur stipulatio. At nec statim
ab initio talis stipulatio valebit,
Lucium Titium, cum servus erit,
dare spondes ? et similia ; quia quæ
naturæ sui dominio nostro exempta
sunt, in obligationem deduci nullo
modo possunt.

2. It is the same if any one stipulates for a thing sacred or religious,
which he thought to be profane, or
for a public thing appropriated to the
perpetual use of the people, as a
forum, or theatre, or for a free man,
whom he thought to be a slave, or
for a thing of which he has not the
commercium, or for a thing belonging
to himself. Nor will the stipulation
remain in suspense, because the public thing may become private, the
freeman may become a slave, the
stipulator may acquire the commercium of the thing, or the thing which
now belongs to him may cease to be
his ; but the stipulation is at once
void. So, conversely, although a
thing may have been validly stipulated for originally, yet, if it afterwards fall under the class of any of the
things before-mentioned, without the
fault of the promisor, the stipulation
is extinguished. Such a stipulation,
too, as the following, is void ab initio,
' Do you promise to give me Lucius
Titius, when he shall become a
slave ?' for that which by its nature
belongs to no one, cannot in any way
be made the object of an obligation.

GAI. iii. 97 ; D. xlvi. 82, 83. 5.

*Cujus commercium non habuerit.* For instance, if, in the days of Gaius, a *peregrinus* had stipulated for a *fundus Italicus*; or if, in the times of the Lower Empire, a heathen had stipulated for a Christian slave (C. l. 10). Of course, if the promissor had not the *commercium* of the particular thing, while the stipulator had it, the promissor was answerable to the stipulator for a breach of contract if he did not fulfil his promise. (D. xlv. 1. 37.)

*Vel rem suam.* It cannot belong to him more than it does; but he might stipulate for its value, or for the thing itself if it ceased to belong to him. (D. xlv. 1. 31.)

*Extinguitur stipulatio.* And if it were once extinguished, no alteration of circumstances would renew it. *In perpetuum sublata obligatio restitui non potest.* (D. xlvi. 3. 98. 8.)

In a stipulation it made no difference that the stipulator was really ignorant that there was some character attaching to the object of the stipulation which made the stipulation invalid, as that it was sacred, or public. The fact that it was sacred or public invalidated the stipulation, and the stipulator had no further remedy against the promissor. We shall find (Tit. 24. 5) that if a person purchased in ignorance a thing of this nature, he would have a remedy against the seller to indemnify him for the loss he sustained by the purchase.

3. Si quis alium daturum facturumve quid spoponderit, non obligabitur, veluti si spondeat Titium quinque aureos daturum. Quod si effecturum se ut Titius daret, spoponderit, obligatur.

3. If a man promises that another shall give or do something, he is not bound, as if he promises, that Titius shall give five *aurei*. But, if he promise that he will manage that Titius shall give five *aurei*, he is bound.

D. xlv. 1. 83.

4. Si quis alii quam cujus juri subjectus sit, stipuletur, nihil agit. Plane solutio etiam in extranei personam conferri potest, veluti si quis ita stipuletur, mihi aut Seio dare spondes? ut obligatio quidem stipulatori acquiratur, solvi tamen Seio etiam invito eo recte possit; ut liberatio ipso jure contingat, sed ille adversus Seium habeat mandati actionem. Quod si quis sibi et alii cujus juri subjectus non sit, dari decem aureos stipulatus est, valebit quidem stipulatio; sed utrum totum debeatur quod in stipulationem deductum est, an vero pars dimidia, dubitatum est: sed placet non plus quam dimidiam partem ei acquiri. Ei qui juri tuo subjectus est, si stipulatus sis, tibi

4. If any one stipulates for the benefit of a third person, other than a person in whose power he is, the stipulation is void. But it may be arranged that payment shall be made to a third person, as if a person stipulates thus, 'Do you engage to pay to me or to Seius?' The stipulator alone, in this case, acquires the obligation; but payment may be made to Seius even against his will; the payer will then be at once freed from his obligation, while the stipulator will have against Seius an *actio mandati*. If any one stipulates that ten *aurei* shall be paid to him and to a third person, other than a person in whose power he is, the stipulation is valid; but it has been doubted, whether, in this case, the whole sum is due to

acquiris ; quia vox tua tamquam filii sit, sicul filiivox tamquam tua intelligitur in iis rebus quae tibi acquiri possunt.

the stipulator, or only half; and it has been decided that only half is due. But, if you stipulate for another, who is in your power, you acquire for yourself ; for your words are as the words of your son, and your son's words are as yours, with respect to all things which can be acquired for you.

GAL. lii. 103; D. xlv. 1. 141. 3 ; D. xlv. 1. 30. 130; D. xxxix. 2. 42.

No one who was not a party to a contract could gain or lose by it. *Res inter alios acta, aliis neque nocere, neque prodesse potest* (a maxim not to be found exactly in its present shape, but based on C. vii. 60. 1). And as this was true of all kinds of contracts, so was it specially of stipulations, in which a particular formula had to be spoken, and which could not properly be entered into by any one that was absent. The third person not being a party to the contract, could have no action to enforce it, and the stipulator could not enforce it because he had no interest in it. If, indeed, he had any interest in it, that is, any legal interest, which of course might happen, a stipulation for another was binding. *Si stipuler alii cum mea interessed ait Marcellus stipulationem valere.* (D. xlv. 1. 38. 20, and see paragr. 20 of this Title.) And when one person wished to stipulate for another, the object might generally be effected by adding a penalty for the non-performance of the promise. A stipulation binding the promissor to give something to Titius, or if it were not given, to pay a penalty to the stipulator, was binding. It was, indeed, nothing but a conditional contract. In the event of something not happening, which might have happened, a certain benefit was to accrue to the stipulator. (D. xlv. 1. 38. 17.) It is because the thing might have happened that such a penal clause differs in its effect from one made to enforce the performance of a thing physically impossible. (See note on paragr. 1.)

*Mihi aut Scio.* The third person, to whom payment might be thus made at the option of the payee, was said to be *solutionis causa adjectus.* (D. xlvi. 3. 95. 5.)

*Sibi et alii.* We learn from Gaius, that the Sabinians were of opinion that the whole sum specified was in this case due to the stipulator. Justinian adopts the contrary opinion. (GAL. iii. 103.)

Every one could stipulate and promise for his heir. Every *paterfamilias* could stipulate for those under his power and his slaves ; every person under power and every slave could stipulate for the *paterfamilias* or master, and could promise so as to bind the *paterfamilias* or master, if authorized, directly or indirectly, to do so. (See Bk. iv. Tit. 7.)

In the later law many kinds of stipulations could be made through another person, though this was contrary to the primary notion of a stipulation. For instance, the stipulation '*rem pupillo salvam fore*' (see Tit. 18. 4) could be made, for a pupil who was *infans*, or absent, by a public slave, by a person appointed by the prætor, or by a magistrate if the parties came before him. (D. xxvii. 8. 1. 15.)

5. Præterea Inutilis est stipulatio, si quis ad ea quæ interrogatus erit, non respondeat: veluti, si decem aureos a te dari stipuletur, tu quinque promittas, vel contra; aut si ille pure stipuletur, tu sub conditione promittas, vel contra, si modo scilicet id exprimas, id est, si cui sub conditione vel in diem stipulanti tu respondeas, præsenti die spondeo: nam si hoc solum respondeas, promitto, breviter videris in eamdem diem vel conditionem spopondisse; neque enim necesse est in respondendo eadem omnia repeti, quæ stipulator expresserit.

5. A stipulation, again, is void, if the answer do not agree with the demand: as when a person stipulates that ten aurei shall be given him, and you answer five, or vice versa. A stipulation is also void, if a person stipulates simply, and you promise conditionally, or vice versa; provided only, that the disagreement is expressly stated, as if, when a man stipulates conditionally, or for a particular time, you answer, 'I promise for to-day.' But, if you answer only, 'I promise,' you seem in a brief way to agree to the time or condition he proposes. For it is not necessary, that in the answer every word should be repeated which the stipulator expressed.

D. xlv. 1. 1. 3, 4; D. xlv. 1. 134. 1.

*Si decem aureos.* Ulpian, in the Digest, decides the question the other way. (D. xlv. 1. 1. 4.)

6. Item inutilis est stipulatio, si vel ab eo stipuleris qui tuo juri subjectus est, vel si is a te stipuletur. Sed servus quidem, non solum domino suo obligari non potest, sed ne alii quidem ulli; filii vero familiæ aliis obligari possunt.

6. A stipulation is also void if made with one who is in your power, or if such a person stipulate with you. A slave is incapable not only of entering into an obligation with his master, but of binding himself to any other person. But a *filiusfamilias* can enter into an obligation with others.

Gat. iii. 104. 30; D. xliv. 7. 14.

This paragraph must of course be taken as expressed without reference to the *peculia* of some persons in power and of slaves.

7. Mutum neque stipulari neque promittere posse palam est, quod et in surdo receptum est; quia et is qui stipulatur verba promittentis,

7. It is evident that a dumb man can neither stipulate nor promise. And this is considered to apply also to deaf persons, for he who stipu-

et is qui promittit verba stipulantis audire debet: unde apparet non de eo non loqui qui tardius exaudit, sed de eo qui omnino non audit.

later, ought to hear the words of the promissor, and he who promises, the words of the stipulator. Hence, it is clear that we are not speaking of a person who hears with difficulty, but of one who cannot hear at all.

Gai. lib. 105; D. xliv. 7. 1. 15.

8. Furiosus nullum negotium gerere potest, quia non intelligit quid agit.

8. A madman can go through no legal act, because he does not understand what he is doing.

Gai. iii. 106.

During lucid intervals a madman could make valid stipulations or promises.

9. Pupillus omne negotium recte gerit, ut tamen alicubi tutoris auctoritas necessaria sit, adhibeatur tutor, veluti si ipse obligetur: nam alium sibi obligare etiam sine tutoris auctoritate potest.

9. A pupil may go through any legal act, provided that the tutor takes a part in the proceeding in cases where his authorization is necessary; as for instance, when the pupil binds himself, for a pupil can bind others to him without the authorization of his tutor.

Gai. ii. 107.

10. Sed quod diximus de pupillis, utique de iis rerum est qui jam aliquem intellectum habent: nam infans et qui infanti proximus est, non multum a furioso distant, quia hujus ætatis pupilli nullum habent intellectum; sed in proximis infanti, propter utilitatem eorum, benignior juris interpretatio facta est, ut idem juris habeant quod pubertati proximi. Sed qui in potestate parentis est impubes, ne auctore quidem patre obligatur.

10. This must be understood only of pupils who already have some understanding: for an infant, or one still near to infancy, differs but little from a madman, for pupils of such an age have no understanding at all. But, in order to consult their interest, the law is construed more favourably to those who are near to infancy, and they are allowed the same rights as those near the age of puberty. A son in the power of his father, and under the age of puberty, cannot bind himself even if his father authorizes him.

Gai. iii. 109; D. xlv. 1. 141. 2.

An infant was properly one *qui fari non potest*, a child not yet old enough to speak. When a child could talk, and began to have some degree of understanding, he was termed *infanti proximus*. He could now pronounce the words of a stipulation, and the law permitted him to do so with the sanction of his tutor in certain cases, such as the acquisition of an inheritance, where his personal intervention was necessary. But the law did not allow him to stipulate except when the stipulation was clearly for his benefit. (D. xxix. 2. 9.)

Just as the child who was older than an infant was said to

be *infanti proximus*, so one a little younger than a *pubes* was
said to be *pubertati proximus*. Originally no fixed time was
assigned at which a child passed from one of these states to
another; but in later times the word *infans* had a new meaning; for, following a theory borrowed from the physicians, who
maintained that the human body underwent a marked change
every seven years, a constitution of Theodosius fixed the first
seven years as the period of infancy. (Cod. Theod. viii. 18. 8.)
The original meaning of the word was thus lost sight of, and
*infans* meant a person under seven years of age. Even in the
time of Justinian, however, the mode was not very accurately
fixed in which the different terms describing the age of a
child were employed. The terms *infans* and *infanti proximus*
are retained in the text as they stood in Gaius, although the
*infanti proximus* was now included in the *infans* (see Bk. i.
Tit. 21, pr.); and Theophilus, in his Paraphrase of this paragraph, says, *proximus infanti qualis fuerit qui septimum
aut octavum annum agit;* whereas the most accurate mode
of expression, after the constitution of Theodosius, would be
to consider *infanti proximus* as a term no longer needed, and
to say that, after a child commenced his eighth year, he was
*pubertati proximus*.

The *paterfamilias* could not, like a tutor, supply his
authority to make up what was deficient in the power of the
pupil. The concluding words of this paragraph are taken
from Gaius, who makes his statement more complete by adding
*pubes vero qui in potestate est, proinde ac si paterfamilias
obligari solet.* (D. xlv. 1. 141. 5.)

11. Si Impossibilis conditio obligationibus adjiciatur, nihil valet stipulatio. Impossibilis autem conditio habetur, cui natura impedimento est quominus existat, veluti si quis ita dixerit, si digito cœlum attigero dare spondes? At si ita stipuletur, si digito cœlum non attigero dare spondes? pure facta obligatio intelligitur, ideoque statim petere potest.

11. If an impossible condition is added to an obligation, the stipulation is void. A condition is considered impossible of which nature forbids the accomplishment; as, if a person says, ‘Do you promise if I touch the heavens with my finger?’ But if a stipulation is made thus, ‘Do you promise if I do not touch the sky with my finger?’ the obligation is considered as unconditional, and performance may be instantly demanded.

Gai. iii. 98 ; D. xlv. l. 7.

An impossible condition in a testamentary gift was treated
as if it had never been inserted. In a stipulation or any other
contract it made the contract void, a difference owing to the
favour with which testamentary gifts were regarded. (See
Bk. ii. Tit. 15. 10.)

In the stipulation, 'if I do not touch the heavens,' &c., there is really no condition; there is nothing left undecided in the mind of the speaker or hearer.

12. Item verborum obligatio inter absentes concepta inutilis est. Sed cum hoc materiam litium contentionis hominibus præstabat, forte post tempus tales allegationes opponentibus, et non præsentes esse vel se vel adversarios suos contendentibus, ideo nostra constitutio propter celeritatem dirimendarum litium introducta est, quam ad Cæsarienses advocatos scripsimus: per quam disposuimus tales scripturas quæ præsto esse partes Iudicant, omnimodo esse credendas, nisi ipse qui talibus utitur improbis allegationibus, manifestissimis probationibus vel per scripturam vel per testes idoneos approbaverit, in ipso toto die quo confiebatur instrumentum sese vel adversarium suum in aliis locis esse.

12. A verbal obligation, made between absent persons, is also void. But as this doctrine afforded matter of strife to contentious men, who alleged, after some time had elapsed, that either they or their adversaries were not present, we issued a constitution, addressed to the advocates of Cæsarea, in order to provide for the speedy determination of such suits. By this we have enacted, that written acts which declare that the contracting parties were present, shall be considered as indisputable evidence of the fact, unless the party who has recourse to such shameless allegations makes it evident, by the most manifest proofs, either by writing or by credible witnesses, that either he or his adversary was in some other place during the whole day in which the instrument was made.

GAL. iiL 138; C. viiL 38. 14.

No writing was necessary to make a verbal contract valid; but one was generally drawn up as a record of the transactions, and called *instrumentum* or *cautio*, as being a security for the stipulator.

13. Post mortem suam dari sibi nemo stipulari poterat, non magis quam post mortem ejus a quo stipulabatur; ac nec is qui in alicujus potestate est, post mortem ejus stipulari poterat, quia patris vel domini voce loqui videtur. Sed et si quis Ita stipuletur, pridie quam moriar vel pridie quam morieris dabis? inutilis erat stipulatio. Sed cum (ut ita dictum est) ex consensu contrahentium stipulationes valent, placuit nobis etiam In hunc juris articulum necessariam inducere emendationem: ut sive post mortem, sive pridie quam morietur stipulator sive promissor, stipulatio concepta est, valeat stipulatio.

13. A man could not formerly stipulate that a thing should be given him after his own death, any more than after the death of the promisor. Neither could any person in the power of another stipulate that anything should be given him after the death of the person in whose power he was, because it was his father or master who appeared to be speaking in him. And if any one stipulated thus, 'Do you promise to give the day before I die? or the day before you die?' the stipulation was invalid. But since all stipulations, as we have already said, derive their force from the consent of the contracting parties, we have thought it proper to introduce a necessary alteration in this respect, so that now, whether it be stipulated that a thing shall be given after, or immediately

before, the death either of the stipulator or the promisor, the stipulation is good.

Gai. iii. 100; C. viii. 38. 11; C. iv. 11.

A stipulation '*pridie quam moriar*' was held to be invalid,
because the date when the thing promised became due could
not be fixed until the death happened, and then the action
would only be acquired for or against the heirs, exactly as in
the case of a stipulation '*dabis post mortem.*' (Gai. iii. 100.)
Gaius says, *inelegans visum est ex heredis persona incipere
obligationem*: it was out of the due order of things that a
man should enter into an obligation in which no action could
be brought until after his death. Justinian does away with
all these subtleties.

| | |
|---|---|
| 14. Item si quis ita stipulatus erat, si navis ex Asia venerit, hodie dare spondes? inutilis erit stipulatio, quia praepostere concepta est. Sed cum Leo inclitae recordationis in dotibus eandem stipulationem quae praepostera nuncupatur, non esse reiiciendam existimavit, nobis placuit et huic perfectum robur accommodare, ut non solum in dotibus sed etiam in omnibus valeat hujusmodi conceptio stipulationis. | 14. Also, if any one stipulated thus, ' If a certain ship arrives to-morrow from Asia, do you engage to give to-day?' the stipulation would be void, as being praeposterous. But, since the Emperor Leo, of glorious memory, decided that such a stipulation, which is termed *praepostera*, ought not to be rejected with respect to marriage-portions, we have thought it right to give it complete validity, so that now, every stipulation made in this way is valid, not only with respect to marriage-portions, but whatever may be its object. |

C. vi. 23. 25.

Such a stipulation was said to be *praepostere concepta* (i. e.
the things which should come *post* are placed *prae*), because
the payment is to be made at once, and thus is placed before
(*prae*) instead of after (*post*) the fulfilment of the condition.
Under Justinian's enactment the contract was binding at
once, but payment could not be enforced until the condition
was fulfilled. (C. vi. 23. 25.)

| | |
|---|---|
| 15. Ita autem concepta stipulatio, veluti si Titius dicat, cum moriar dare spondes? vel cum morieris? et apud veteres utilis erat et nunc valet. | 15. A stipulation made thus, as if, for instance, Titius says, 'Do you promise to give when I die,' or 'when you die?' was considered valid by the ancients, and is so now. |

D. xlv. 1. 45. 3.

This stipulation was said to be valid because the thing was
to be given '*non post mortem, sed ultimo vitae tempore.*'

(GAL iL 232.) The same might be said of the stipulation *'dari pridie quam moriar.'*

16. Item post mortem alterius recte stipulamur.

16. We may also validly stipulate that a thing shall be given after the death of a third person.

D. xlv. 1. 45. 1.

The death of a third person was an uncertain term, which might be as legitimately affixed to a stipulation or any other uncertain time. The reason which prevented the stipulation *post mortem meam* or *tuam* did not apply.

17. Si scriptum in instrumento fuerit promissum aliquem, perinde habetur atque si interrogatione praecedente responsum sit.

17. If it be written in an instrument that a person has promised, the promise is considered to have been given in answer to a precedent interrogation.

See PAUL. *Sent.* v. 7. 2.　Ulpian says (D. il. 14. 7. 12) that if, at the end of the instrument of an agreement, the words usually added were found, viz. *rogavit Titius, spopondit Maevius,* the agreement was taken to be a stipulation unless it were expressly shown that it was in reality only a *pactum.*

18. Quoties plures res una stipulatione comprehenduntur, si quidem promissor simpliciter respondeat dare spondeo, propter omnes tenetur. Si vero unam ex his vel quasdam daturum se responderit, obligatio in iis pro quibus spoponderit, contrahitur: ex pluribus enim stipulationibus una vel quaedam videntur esse perfectae; singulas enim res stipulari, et ad singulas respondere debemus.

18. When many things are comprehended in one stipulation, a man binds himself to all, if he answer simply 'I promise to give.' But, if he promise to give one, or some of the things stipulated for, he is bound only with respect to the things comprised in his answer. For, of the different stipulations contained in the question, only some are considered to have been answered, as for each object a separate question and a separate answer is required.

D. xlv. 1. 83. 4 ; D. xlv. 1. 4, 5.

19. Alteri stipulari (ut supra dictum est) nemo potest: inventae sunt enim hujusmodi obligationes ad hoc ut unusquisque sibi acquirat quod sua interest; ceterum, ut alii detur, nihil interest stipulatoris. Plane si quis velit hoc facere, poenam stipulari conveniet, ut nisi ita factum sit ut comprehensum est, committatur poena stipulatio etiam ei cujus nihil interest; poenam enim quum stipulatur quis, non illud inspicitur quid intersit ejus, sed quae sit quantitas in conditione stipula-

19. No one, as we have already said, can stipulate for another, for this kind of obligations has been invented, that every person may acquire what it is for his own advantage to acquire ; and it cannot be for his interest that a thing should be given to another. But if any one wishes to stipulate for another, he should stipulate for a penalty payable to him, although he would otherwise receive no advantage from the obligation, so that if the promisor does not perform his promise,

tionis. Ergo si quis stipuletur
Titio dari, nihil agit ; sed si addi-
deritpœnam, nisi dederis tot aureos
dare spondes ? tunc committitur
stipulatio.

the stipulation for the penalty may
be valid even for a person who had
no interest in the performance of the
promise ; for when a penalty is stipulated for, it is not the interest of
the stipulator that is regarded, but
the amount of the penalty. If, therefore, any one stipulates that a certain
thing shall be given to Titius, this is
void ; but if he adds a penalty, ' Do
you promise to give me so many
aurei if you do not give the thing
to Titius?' this stipulation binds
the promisor.

D. xlv. 1. 38. 17.

20. Sed et si quis stipuletur alii,
cum ejus interesset, placuit stipulationem valere. Nam si is qui
pupilli tutelam administrare cœpe-
rat, cessit administratione contutori
suo, et stipulatus est rem pupilli
salvam fore ; quoniam interest stipulatoris fieri quod stipulatus est,
cum obligatus futurus esset pupillo
si male gesserit, tenet obligatio.
Ergo et si quis procuratori suo dari
stipulatus sit, stipulatio vires habebit ; et si creditori dari stipulatus
sit, quod sua interest, ne forte vel
pœna committatur, vel prædia distrahantur quæ pignori data erant,
valet stipulatio.

20. But, if any one stipulate for
another, having himself an interest in
the performance of the promise, the
stipulation is valid. Thus if he who
has begun to act as tutor afterwards
gives up the administration to his
co-tutor, and stipulates for the security of the estate of his pupil, since
it is for the interest of the stipulator
that the promise should be performed, as he is answerable to the
pupil for maladministration, the obligation is binding. So if a person
stipulates that a thing shall be given
to his procurator, the stipulation is
effectual. So, too, is a stipulation that
a thing shall be given to a creditor of
the stipulator, the stipulator having
an interest in the performance of the
promise ; as, for instance, that he
may avoid becoming liable to a penal
clause, or that his immoveables,
given in pledge, should not be sold.

D. xlv. 1. 38. 20. 23.

See note on paragr. 4.    The tutor was liable for all his co-
tutor did.    (See Bk. i. Tit. 24.)

21. Versa vice, qui alium facturum promisit, videtur in ea causa
ut non teneatur, nisi pœnam
ipse promiserit.

21. Conversely, he who undertakes
for the performance of another, is
not bound unless he promises under
a penalty.

D. xlv. 1. 38. 2.

22. Item nemo rem suam futu-
ram, in eum casum quo sua sit,
utiliter stipulatur.

22. No man can validly stipulate
that a thing which will hereafter
belong to him shall be given him
when it becomes his.

D. xlv. 1. 87.

When the time was come, the stipulation would have nothing on which to take effect.

23. Si de alia re stipulator senserit, de alia promissor, perinde nulla contrahitur obligatio, ac si ad interrogatum responsum non esset: veluti, si hominem Stichum a te quis stipulatus fuerit, tu de Pamphilo senseris quem Stichum vocari credideris.

23. If the stipulator intend one thing, and a promissor another, an obligation is no more contracted than if no answer had been made to the interrogation; for instance, if any one has stipulated that you should give Stichus, and you understood him to refer to Pamphilus, thinking that Pamphilus was called Stichus.

D. xlv. 1. 137. 1.

*Stipulatio ex utriusque consensu valet.* (D. xlv. 1. 83. 1.) And if the seeming consent implied in pronouncing the words of the stipulation was vitiated by a mistake under which one party spoke of one thing and the other of another, the stipulation was void; but if the mistake was only with reference to something in, or relating to, the thing they were speaking of, i. e. if they were really speaking of the same thing, but one party was under some misapprehension respecting it, the stipulation was valid. So it was valid if fraud or violence had been used to procure it; but though in such cases it was valid, the rights it gave were worthless under the jurisdiction of the praetor, who always allowed *exceptiones doli, metus*, &c., by which the action brought on the stipulation was repelled.

24. Quod turpi ex causa promissum est, veluti si quis homicidium vel sacrilegium se facturum promittat, non valet.

24. A promise made to effect a base purpose, as to commit homicide or sacrilege, is not binding.

D. xlv. 1. 26, 27.

A thing was said to be *promissum ex turpi causa*, when it was promised, being itself illegal or immoral, or was the reward, or depended on the happening, of anything illegal or immoral.

25. Cum quis sub aliqua conditione stipulatus fuerit, licet ante conditionem decesserit, postea existente conditione heres ejus agere potest. Idem est et ex promissoris parte.

25. If a stipulation be conditional, although the stipulator dies before the accomplishment of the condition, if, afterwards, the condition is accomplished, his heir can demand the execution of the promise; and so, too, the heir of the promissor may be sued.

D. xlv. 1. 57.

26. Qui hoc anno aut hoc mense dari stipulatus est, nisi omnibus partibus anni vel mensis praeteritis non recte petet.

26. A person who stipulates that a thing shall be given to him in such a year or month, cannot legally demand the thing promised, until the whole year or month has elapsed.

D. xlv. 1. 42.

27. Si fundum dari stipuleris vel hominem, non poteris continuo agere, nisi tantum spatium præterieris quo traditio fieri possit.

27. If you stipulate for a piece of ground, or a slave, you cannot instantly demand the thing, but must wait until enough time has passed for delivery to have been made.

D. xlv. 1. 73.

## Tit. XX.  DE FIDEJUSSORIBUS.

Pro eo qui promittit, solent alii obligari, qui fidejussores appellantur; quos homines accipere solent dum curant ut diligentius sibi cautum sit.

It is customary that other persons, termed *fidejussores*, should bind themselves for the promissor; creditors generally requiring that they should do so, in order that the security may be greater.

Gai. iii. 115. 117.

Besides the principal parties to a stipulation, the stipulator and the promissor, there might be accessory parties, called respectively *adstipulatores* and *adpromissores.* The *adstipulator* either received the same promise as his principal did, and could, therefore, have the same actions, and equally receive or exact payment; or he only stipulated for a part of that for which the principal stipulated, and then his rights were co-extensive with the amount of his own stipulation. In the early law, the chief use of an *adstipulator* was, probably, to supply the place of a procurator at a time when the law refused to allow stipulations to be made by procuration. A might make a stipulation, and know that at the time when payment would be due he would be abroad. He, therefore, joined B in the stipulation, who could receive payment, or bring an action in his place.

Before the time of Justinian no one could stipulate validly for a thing after his own death (see Tit. 19. 13), and, therefore, those who wished to make such a stipulation joined an *adstipulator* with them, and this *adstipulator* could bring an action, or receive payment, after the death of the stipulator. As in the days of Gaius, all contracts could be made by procuration, it appears from his account of the *adstipulator*, which is the only one we have, that the only use of the *adstipulator* was to make this stipulation *post mortem suam* valid. (Gai. iii. 117.)

The *adstipulator* could not transmit his right of action even to his heirs. His rights were purely personal, because he was selected by the stipulator, to whom he stood in the relation of

a mandatary, from motives of personal confidence. (GAI. iii.
114.)

The *adpromissores* were accessory to the promise, in order
to give the stipulator greater security. They were guarantees
for the fulfilment of the promise (GAI. iii. 116), and these
guarantees were termed *sponsores* when Roman citizens, as
they pledged themselves by the word *spondeo*, a word which
citizens alone could utter, and *fidepromissores* when *peregrini* (GAI. iii. 120), because, in binding themselves, they
used the expression *fide mea promitto.*

The *sponsores* and *fidepromissores* held a position, in many
respects, the exact converse of the *adstipulator.* They made
the same promise as their principal, or one not so extensive,
for they might only choose to become guarantees to a certain
extent; they could not bind themselves for more than their
principal was bound for. They were often employed to remove
any objections that might be made to the capacity of their
promisor, as, for instance, that he was *impubes* and contracting without the consent of his tutor. Their heirs were
not bound (GAI. iii. 120), and they might recover from their
principal by an *actio mandati* what they had advanced for
him. (GAI. iii. 127.)

By the *lex Furia* (circ. 95 B.C.) their obligation was only
binding for two years, and the amount of the liability of all
was divided equally among all living at the time when the
guarantee was enforced.

These restrictions, the limitation of the intervention of
*sponsores* and *fidepromissores* to verbal contracts, and their
obligation dying with them, made it necessary that there
should be a more unfettered mode of becoming surety for a
party to a contract. This was supplied by the introduction of
the *fidejussores*, who could bind themselves in every kind of
obligation, and who transmitted their obligation to their heirs.
In the time of Justinian, *sponsores* and *fidepromissores* had
been long obsolete, and as, under his legislation, stipulations
*post mortem suam* were allowed, there was no longer any
occasion for the intervention of *adstipulatores*, and, consequently, none of the additional parties to a verbal contract,
except *fidejussores*, are mentioned in the Institutes.

Gaius mentions other laws besides the *lex Furia*, bearing on
the subject of the additional parties to a contract, and as the
effect of some of their provisions is traceable in what we read
with respect to *fidejussores* in this Title, it may be as well to
notice them here. (1.) The *lex Apuleia* (102 B.C.) established
a kind of partnership (*quandam societatem*) between the dif-

ferent *sponsores* or *fidepromissores*; any one of them who had
paid the whole debt could recover from the others what he had
paid in excess of his own share by an action *pro socio*. (GAI.
iii. 122.) (2.) A law, the name of which is illegible in the
manuscript of Gaius, perhaps the *lex Apuleia*, required that
the creditor should give notice beforehand, for what amount he
was going to exact security, and how many *sponsores* or *fidepromissores* there were to be. (3.) The provisions of the *lex
Furia* (95 B.C.) have been noticed above. (4.) A *lex Cornelia*
(81 B.C.), referring not only to *sponsores* and *fidepromissores*,
but to all sureties, and therefore to *fidejussores* (which, perhaps,
shows the date of the first introduction of *fidejussores*), provided that no one should bind himself for the same debtor, to
the same creditor, in the same year (*idem pro eodem, apud
eundem, eodem anno*), for more than 20,000 sesterces. (GAI.
iii. 124, 125.) (5.) Lastly, *a lex Publilia* gave *sponsores* an
advantage over any other sureties, for they were allowed to
recover from their principal what they had paid, by a special
action (*actio depensi*), and, if he denied his liability, they
recovered double. (GAI. iii. 127.)

*Intercedere* was the proper term for becoming bound for the
debt of another; *satisdare* for the giving surety for the obligation of the principal; *satisaccipere* for the receiving it.

The *senatus-consultum Velleianum* (D. xvi. 1. 2. 1), 46
A.D., forbad women ever to bind themselves for another person.

| | |
|---|---|
| 1. In omnibus autem obligationibus assumi possunt, id est, sive re, sive verbis, sive literis, sive consensu contractae fuerint; at ne illud quidem interest utrum civilis an naturalis sit obligatio cui adjiciatur fidejussor, adeo quidem ut pro servo quoque obligetur, sive extraneus sit qui fidejussorem a servo accipiat, sive ipse dominus in id quod sibi naturaliter debetur. | 1. *Fidejussores* may be added in every kind of obligation, i.e. whether the obligation is contracted by the delivery of the thing, by words, by writing, or by the consent of the parties. Nor is it material, whether the obligation to which the *fidejussor* is made an additional party, is civil or natural; so much so, that a man may bind himself as a *fidejussor* for a slave, either to a stranger or to the master of the slave, when the thing due to him is due by a natural obligation. |

GAI. iii. 119; D. xlvi. 1. 8. 5.

*In omni obligatione.* This was the principal advantage
gained by the introduction of *fidejussores.*

| | |
|---|---|
| 2. Fidejussor non tantum ipse obligatur, sed etiam heredem obligatum relinquit. | 2. A *fidejussor* not only binds himself, but also his heir. |

D. xlvi. 1. 4. 1.

This was the second chief point of difference between *fidejussores* and *sponsores*, or *fidepromissores*.

| | |
|---|---|
| 3. Fidejussor et præcedere obligationem et æqui potest. | 3. A *fidejussor* may be added either before or after an obligation is entered into. |

D. xlvi. 1. 6, pr. and 2.

Probably the formality of verbal contracts exacted that the words of the principal should precede those of the accessory.

| | |
|---|---|
| 4. Si plures sint fidejussores, quotquot erunt numero, singuli in solidum tenentur: itaque liberum est creditori, a quo velit solidum petere. Sed ex epistola divi Hadriani compellitur creditor a singulis, qui modo solvendo sunt litis contestatæ tempore, partes petere: idemque, si quis ex fidejussoribus eo tempore solvendo non sit, hoc ceteros onerat. Sed si ab uno fidejussore creditor totum consecutus fuerit, hujus solius detrimentum erit, si is pro quo fidejussit solvendo non sit; et sibi imputare debet, cum potuerit adjuvari ex epistola divi Hadriani, et desiderare ut pro parte in se detur actio. | 4. Where there are several *fidejussores*, whatever is their number, each is bound for the whole debt; and the creditor may demand the whole from any of them he pleases. But, by a rescript of the Emperor Hadrian, the creditor is forced to divide his demand between all those *fidejussores* who are solvent at the time of the *litis contestatio*, so that, if any of the *fidejussores* is not solvent at that time, the rest have so much additional burden. But, if the creditor obtains his whole demand from one of the *fidejussores*, the whole loss falls upon him alone, if the principal debtor cannot pay; for he has no one but himself to blame, as he might have availed himself of the rescript of the Emperor Hadrian, and might have required that no action should be given against him for more than his share of the debt. |

Gai. III. 121; D. xlvi. 1. 26.

The provision of the *lex Furia* not applying to *fidejussores*, they were bound for all they had promised, and as each promised for himself alone, the one first sued had no remedy against the other *fidejussores*, until the rescript of Hadrian provided one, and gave him what was called the *beneficium divisionis*; but under the *lex Furia*, the liability was divided among the different sureties *ipso jure*, whereas the surety first sued was obliged expressly to claim the benefit given by the rescript of Hadrian.

There were two other privileges or *beneficia* of which the *fidejussor* might avail himself: one was, that *cedendarum actionum*, by which the surety could, before paying the creditor, compel him to make over to him the actions which belonged to the stipulator, and thus the *fidejussor* could sue those bound with him, or the principal debtor (D. xlvi. 1. 17), and this was often more advantageous than having recourse to actions which the *fidejussor* might himself have brought, because, if the creditor had taken pledges, they were transferred to the *fidejussor*. (D. xlvi. 1. 59.)

There was also a *beneficium ordinis*, or, as it was otherwise termed, *excussionis* or *discussionis*, introduced by Justinian (Nov. 4. 1) : by this a creditor was bound to sue the principal debtor first, and could only sue the sureties for that which he could not recover from the principal.

5. Fidejussores ita obligari non possunt, ut plus debeant quam debet is pro quo obligantur: nam eorum obligatio accessio est principalis obligationis, nec plus in accessione potest esse quam in principali re; at ex diverso, ut minus debeant, obligari possunt. Itaque si reus decem aureos promiserit, fidejussor in quinque recte obligatur; contra vero obligari non potest. Item si ille pure promiserit, fidejussor sub conditione promittere potest, contra vero non potest: non solum enim in quantitate, sed etiam in tempore minus et plus intelligitur; plus est enim statim aliquid dare, minus est post tempus dare.

5. *Fidejussores* cannot bind themselves for more than the debtor is bound for ; because their obligation is accessory to the principal obligation; and the accessory cannot contain more than the principal. They may, however, bind themselves for less. Therefore, if the principal debtor promises ten *aurei*, the *fidejussor* may be bound for five, but the *fidejussor* cannot be bound for ten, when the principal debtor is bound only for five. Again, when the principal promises unconditionally, the *fidejussor* may promise conditionally, but not *vice versa*. For the terms more and less are used not only with respect to quantity, but also with respect to time: it is more to give a thing instantly, it is less to give it after a time.

Gai. iii. 119. 120.

6. Si quid autem fidejussor pro reo solverit, ejus recuperandi causa habet cum eo mandati judicium.

6. If a *fidejussor* has made payment for the debtor, he may have an *actio mandati* against him to recover what he has paid.

Gai. iii. 127.

7. Graece fidejussor ita accipitur, τῇ ἐμῇ πίστει κελεύω, λίγω, ʼλω sive βούλομαι; sed et si φημι dixerit, pro eo erit ac si dixerit λίγω.

7. A *fidejussor* may bind himself in Greek, by using the expression τῇ ἐμῇ πίστει κελεύω (I order upon my faith), λίγω (I say), ʼλω or βούλομαι (I wish); if he uses the word φημι, it will be equivalent to λίγω.

D. xlvi. 1. 8.

The appropriate Latin formula was, ʻ*Idem fide mea esse jubeo*,ʼ but this formula was, probably, never insisted on, as the formulæ ʻ*spondeo*ʼ and ʻ*idem fide mea promitto*ʼ were.

8. In stipulationibus fidejussorum sciendum est generaliter hoc accipi, ut quodcumque scriptum sit

8. It is a general rule in all stipulations of *fidejussores*, that whatever is stated in writing to have been

quasi actum, videatur etiam actum; ideoque constat, si quis scripserit se fidejussisse, videri omnia solemniter acta.

done, is considered really to have been done. If, therefore, any one states in writing that he has bound himself as a *fidejussor*, it is presumed that all the necessary forms were observed.

D. xlvi. 1. 30.

## Tit. XXI. DE LITERARUM OBLIGATIONE.

Olim scriptura fiebat obligatio quæ nominibus fieri dicebatur, quæ nomina hodie non sunt in usu. Plane si quis debere se scripserit quod ei numeratum non est, de pecunia minime numerata post multum temporis exceptionem opponere non potest: hoc enim sæpissime constitutum est. Sic fit ut et hodie, dum queri non potest, scriptura obligetur, et ex ea nascitur condictio, cessante scilicet verborum obligatione. Multum autem tempus in hac exceptione antea quidem ex principalibus constitutionibus usque ad quinquennium procedebat. Sed ne creditores diutius præsint suis pecuniis forsitan defraudari, per constitutionem nostram tempus coarctatum est, ut ultra biennii metas hujusmodi exceptio minime extendatur.

Formerly there was made by writing a kind of obligation, which was said to be made *nominibus*. These *nomina* are now no longer in use. But if any one states in writing that he owes a sum which has never really been told out to him, he cannot, after a long time has elapsed, use the exception, *non numeratæ pecuniæ*, i.e. that the money has not been told out. This has been often decided by Imperial constitutions; and thus it may be said, even at the present day, as he cannot relieve himself from payment, he is bound by the writing, and that the writing gives rise to a condition. In the absence, that is, of any verbal obligation. The length of time fixed as barring this exception, was, under imperial constitutions antecedent to our time, not less than five years. But, that creditors might not be exposed too long to the risk of being defrauded of their money, we have shortened the time by our constitution, and this exception cannot now be used beyond the space of two years.

Gai. lib. 128–130. 133, 134 ; C. iv. 30. 14.

A contract was said to be formed *literis* when it originated in a certain entry or statement of it being made in the books of the creditor with the consent of the debtor. Regularity in keeping accounts, and in entering all matters of business in a private ledger, was considered one of the first duties of a Roman citizen. Cicero speaks of a failure in this duty as an almost insupposable act of negligence and dishonesty. (See *pro Roscio*, 3. 1 and 3.) Events, as they occurred, were jotted down in rough memorandums called *adversaria*, and these were transferred at least once a month to the ledger (*codex* or *tabulæ*). It was only this ledger which had any legal importance. If any one put down in his ledger that he had advanced such a sum of money to another (*expensum ferre*), this entry was an admissible proof of the fact. If the debtor also had made a corresponding entry in his ledger (*acceptum referre*), the tallying of the two together made what was called an *obligatio literis*. These two entries had, in fact, exactly the same effect as if the two parties had entered into a stipulation. But this was not all : the creditor was not to be placed entirely at the mercy of his debtor, whose wilful or accidental negligence preventing a proper entry, might make the obligation fail. The real source of the obligation was taken to be the consent of the debtor to the entry made by the creditor. If the debtor made a corresponding entry in his ledger, this was a conclusive proof that he had consented to the creditor's entry ; but if he did not, then the creditor might still prove, in any way that he could, that he had really made his entry with the debtor's consent. Of course, if he had really paid the money over, this, if proved, would show beyond a doubt that the debtor had consented.

The foundation of this contract *literis* being the payment of a sum certain by the creditor, the obligation was always for a sum or certain thing, and was therefore enforced by *condictio certi*, more usually termed simply *condictio*.

As the creditor put down the name of his debtor, the word '*nomen*' came to signify a debt ; and Gaius speaks of '*nomina transcriptia*,' referring to the *nomina* being transcribed from the *adversaria* to the *codex*. He says this *transcriptio* took place (1) *a re in personam*, as when something being already owed, as, for instance, under a contract of sale, or of letting to hire, the debtor assented to the creditor making an entry of the debt (GAI. iii. 129): this operated as a *novatio* (see Introd. sec. 89) of the old debt, and the creditor could now employ a *condictio* to enforce his claim ; (2) the *transcriptio* took place *a persona in personam*, viz. when one man took on himself the debt of another. (GAI. iii. 130.)

These contracts were peculiar to Roman citizens. *Peregrini* had, as a substitute, *syngraphæ*, signed by both parties, or *chirographa*, signed only by the debtor. These *syngraphæ* and *chirographa* were not mere proofs of a contract, but were instruments on which an action could be brought, and the making of which operated as a novation of an existing debt.

The word most usually employed for a mere memorandum intended to furnish a proof, and not to give a right of action, was *cautio*. In the time of Justinian there had ceased to be any real difference between *chirographa* and *cautiones*. Any writing stating that a sum was due sufficed as the ground of an action.

In every period of the law, if there was a formal verbal contract, the written contract was thought subsidiary, and was merged in the stipulation, as the text says, *nascitur condictio, cessante scilicet verborum obligatione.*

If the debtor had given a mere memorandum, a '*cautio*,' and then denied his liability, he had to prove that, in spite of the *cautio*, he was not bound. The burden of proof was against him ; but if a contract formed *literis* had been made, the civil law treated it exactly as it did a stipulation. The contract was conclusive evidence of the liability. Fairly or unfairly, the debtor must abide by this contract. The prætor, however, when the debtor had not really received the money, permitted him to repel the action of the creditor by an exception called the '*exceptio non numeratæ pecuniæ*,' by which the debtor insisted that the money which formed the consideration of the obligation had never been told or counted out to him ; and here the burden of proof was considered to fall on the creditor. It was for him to prove that he had paid the money ; not for the debtor to prove that he had not. The obligation was so often entered into before the money was really paid, that the law, to prevent fraud, insisted on the creditors proving the payment if it were denied ; but after a certain number of years, originally five, and reduced by Justinian to two, the *onus probandi* was shifted again, and the debtor had to prove that he had not received the payment. During this interval, however, if the debtor were really defrauded, he might protest in a public act against the writing which bound him, or bring an action against the creditor to compel him to give it up (C. iv. 30. 7); and a constitution in the Code (iv. 30. 14. 4) permitted him to make his exception perpetual by a formal announcement to the creditor of his intention to do so.

## Tit. XXII. DE CONSENSU OBLIGATIONE.

Consensu fiunt obligationes in emptionibus venditionibus, locationibus conductionibus, societatibus, mandatis. Ideo autem istis modis consensu dicitur obligatio contrahi, quia neque scriptura neque praesentia, omnimodo opus est, ac

Obligations are formed by the mere consent of the parties in the contracts of sale, of letting to hire, of partnership, and of mandate. An obligation is, in these cases, said to be made by the mere consent of the parties, because there is no necessity for any

ore dari quidquam necesse est ut substantiam capiat obligatio; sed sufficit eos qui negotia gerunt consentire: unde inter absentes quoque talia negotia contrahuntur, veluti per epistolam vel per nuntium. Item in his contractibus alter alteri obligatur in id quod alterum alteri ex bono et aequo praestare oportet, cum alloquin in verborum obligationibus alius stipuletur, alius promittat.

writing, nor even for the presence of the parties: nor is it requisite that anything should be given, to make the contract binding, but the mere consent of those between whom the transaction is carried on suffices. Thus these contracts may be entered into by those who are at a distance from each other, by means of letters, for instance, or of messengers. In these contracts, each party is bound to the other to render him all that equity demands, while in verbal obligations, one party stipulates and the other promises.

Gai. lii. 135. 137.

We now pass to contracts which belong to the *jus gentium*, which have nothing of the peculiar characteristics of the old civil law of Rome, and which are perfected by the simple consent of the parties. As is remarked in the concluding words of the text, these contracts by simple consent, unlike the contracts of which we have hitherto spoken, are bilateral; there is something which binds both parties; whereas the older and peculiarly Roman contracts were only unilateral. In a stipulation, for instance, it was only the *promissor* that was bound. These contracts ‘*consensu*’ were not enforced by actions *stricti juris*, such as were proper to the peculiarly Roman contracts of *mutuum*, stipulation, and contracts made *literis*, but by actions ‘*bonæ fidei*,’ i. e. prætorian actions, in which equitable principles were permitted to govern the decision. (See Introd. sec. 106.)


### Tit. XXIII. DE EMPTIONE ET VENDITIONE.

Emptio et venditio contrahitur simul atque de pretio convenerit, quamvis nondum pretium numeratum sit, ac ne arra quidem data fuerit: nam quod arrae nomine datur, argumentum est emptionis et venditionis contractae. Sed haec quidem de emptionibus et venditionibus quae sine scriptura consistunt, obtinere oportet; nam nihil a nobis in hujusmodi venditionibus innovatum est. In iis autem quae scriptura conficiuntur, non aliter perfectam esse venditionem et emptionem constituimus, nisi et instru-

The contract of sale is formed as soon as the price is agreed upon, although it has not yet been paid, nor even an earnest given; for what is given as an earnest only serves as proof that the contract has been made. This must be understood of sales made without writing; for with regard to these we have made no alteration in the law. But, where there is a written contract, we have enacted that a sale is not to be considered completed unless an instrument of sale has been drawn up, being either written by the contract-

menta emptionis fuerint conscripta, vel manu propria contrahentium, vel ab alio quidem scripta a contrahentibus autem subscripta, et si per tabelliones fiant, nisi et completiones acceperint, et fuerint partibus absoluta: donec enim aliquid deest ex his, et pœnitentiæ locus est, et potest emptor vel venditor sine pœna recedere ab emptione. Ita tamen impune eis recedere concedimus, nisi jam arrarum nomine aliquid fuerit datum: hoc etenim subsecuto, sive in scriptis sive sine scriptis venditio celebrata est, is qui recusat adimplere contractum, si quidem est emptor, perdit quod dedit; si vero venditor, duplum restituere compellitur, licet super arris nihil expressum est.

ing parties, or at least signed by them, if written by others; or if drawn up by a *tabellio*, it must be formally complete and finished throughout; for as long as anything is wanting, there is room to retract, and either the buyer or seller may retract without suffering loss: that is, if no earnest has been given. If earnest has been given, then, whether the contract was written or unwritten, the purchaser, if he refuse to fulfil it, loses what he has given as earnest, and the seller, if he refuse, has to restore double; although no agreement on the subject of the earnest was expressly made.

GAI. Iii. 139; C. Iv. 21. 17.

The contract of sale belonging to the *jus gentium* was attended with none of those material symbols which characterized the formation of contracts under the civil law. Directly one person agreed to sell a particular thing, and another to buy it, the contract was complete; no thing need be delivered, no money paid, in order that an obligation should arise. On the mutual consent being given, the seller was bound to deliver, the buyer to pay the price. The change which Justinian here introduced is that, when, in giving this mutual consent, they agree that the terms of the contract shall be reduced to writing, they shall be considered not to have consented to the contract until it is committed to writing.

The *arræ* were either signs of a bargain having been struck, as, for instance, when the buyer deposited his ring with the seller (D. xix. 1. 11. 6), or consisted of an advance of a portion of the purchase-money. They were also intended as a proof that the purchase had been made. Justinian gave these deposits a new character by making them the measures of a forfeit in case either party wished to recede from his bargain, it being open to either party to retract if he chose to incur this forfeit. This power of retracting by forfeiture of the deposit, or double its value, was a great change in the law; and when Justinian says *in hujusmodi venditionibus nihil innovatum est*, he must be understood only to he referring to unwritten contracts of sale, in which there was no deposit made as earnest. It will be seen from the text that this power of retraction was given whether the contract was made with writing or without.

Besides a buyer and a seller, there must, in a contract of
sale, be a fixed price and a particular thing sold. The jurists
are very minute in their distinctions of the nature of the thing
sold. There is a distinction with regard to things future and
uncertain forming the object of a sale, which is worth men-
tioning. Either a proportionate price may be agreed to be
paid on a greater or lesser number of things that may be
actually realized, as 'so much a-head for all the fish I catch
to-day,' which is termed *rei speratæ emptio*; or a definite sum
may be agreed on as the price of the possibility of any number
of things, more or less, being realized, as 'so much for the
chance of all the fish I catch to-day;' and this was termed
*spei emptio.* (D. xviii. 1. 8. 1.)

1. Pretium autem constitui oportet, nam nulla emptio sine pretio esse
potest; sed et certum esse debet.
Alioquin si inter aliquos ita convenerit, ut quanti Titius rem æstimaverit, tanti sit empta, inter veteres
satis abundeque hoc dubitabatur,
sive constat venditio sive non. Sed
nostra decisio ita hoc constituit, ut
quoties sic composita sit venditio
quanti ille æstimaverit, sub hac
conditione staret contractus ut, si
quidem ipse qui nominatus est pretium definierit, omnimodo secundum ejus æstimationem et pretium
persolvatur et res tradatur, ut venditio ad effectum perducatur emptore
quidem ex empto actione, venditore
ex vendito agente. Sin autem
ille qui nominatus est vel noluerit
vel non potuerit pretium definire,
tunc pro nihilo esse venditionem,
quasi nullo pretio statuto. Quod
jus, cum in venditionibus nobis placuit, non est absurdum et in locationibus et conductionibus trahere.

1. It is necessary that a price
should be agreed upon, for there can
be no sale without a price. And the
price must be fixed and certain. If
the parties agree that the thing shall
be sold at the sum at which Titius
shall value it, it was a question much
debated among the ancients, whether
in such a case there is a sale or not.
We have decided, that when a sale
is made for a price to be fixed by a
third person, the contract shall be
binding under this condition—that if
this third person does fix a price, the
price to be paid shall be determined
by that which he fixes, and that ac-
cord ng to his decision the thing shall
be delivered and the sale perfected.
But if he will not or cannot fix a
price, the sale is then void, as being
made without any price being fixed
on. This decision, which we have
adopted with respect to sales, may
reasonably be made to apply to contracts of letting to hire.

GAI. iii. 140; C. iv. 38. 15.

2. Item pretium in numerata
pecunia consistere debet; nam in
ceteris rebus an pretium esse possit,
veluti an homo aut fundus aut toga
alterius rei pretium esse possit, valde quærebatur. Sabinus et Cassius
etiam in alia re putant posse pretium
consistere: unde illud est quod
vulgo dicebatur, permutatione rerum emptionem et venditionem contrahi, eamque speciem emptionis et
venditionis vetustissimam esse; ar-

2. The price should consist in a
sum of money. It has been much
doubted whether it can consist in
anything else, as in a slave, a piece
of land, or a toga. Sabinus and Cassius thought that it could. And it is
thus that it is commonly said that
exchange is a sale, and that this form
of sale is the most ancient. The testimony of Homer was quoted, who
says that part of the army of the
Greeks procured wine by an ex-

gumentoque utebantur Græcopœta
Homero, qui aliqua parte exercitum
Achivorum vinum sibi comparasse
ait, permutatisquibusdam rebus, his
verbis :—

'Ἔνθεν ἄρ' οἰνίζοντο καρηκομόωντες
Ἀχαιοί,
'Ἄλλοι μὲν χαλκῷ, ἄλλοι δ' αἴθωνι
σιδήρῳ,
'Ἄλλοι δὲ ῥινοῖς, ἄλλοι δ' αὐτοῖσι
βόεσσιν,
'Ἄλλοι δ' ἀνδραπόδεσσι.

Diversæ scholæ auctores contra
sentiebant, aliudque esse existimabant permutationem rerum, aliud
emptionem et venditionem : alioquin non posse rem expediri permutatis rebus, quæ videatur res venisse etquæ pretii nomine data esse;
nam utramque videri et venisse et
pretii nomine datam esse, rationem
non pati. Sed Proculi sententia di-
centis, permutationem propriam esse
speciem contractus a venditione se-
paratam, merito prævaluit, cum et
ipsa aliis Homericis versibus adju-
vatur, et validioribus rationibus ar-
gumentatur.   Quod et anteriores
divi principes admiserunt, et in
nostris Digestis latius significatur.

change of certain things. The passage is this :—
'The long-haired Achæans procured wine, some by giving copper,
others by giving shining steel, others
by giving hides, others by giving
oxen, others by giving slaves.'
The authors of the opposite school
were of a contrary opinion: they
thought that exchange was one thing
and sale another, otherwise, in an
exchange, it would be impossible to
say which was the thing sold, and
which the thing given as the price;
for it was contrary to reason to consider each thing as at once sold, and
given as the price.   The opinion of
Proculus, who maintained that exchange is a particular kind of contract distinct from sale, has deservedly prevailed, as it is supported by
other lines from Homer, and by still
more weighty reasons adopted by
preceding emperors: it has been
fully treated of in our Digests.

Gai. iii. 141 ; D. xviii. L. I. 11 ; C. iv. 64. 7.

A sale and an exchange differ so little that it might seem
natural to treat the promise to exchange as raising an obligation equally with the promise to deliver a thing sold ; it was
indeed the opinion of the Sabinians that it did so ; but this
opinion did not prevail, and the law recognized no obligation
as existing under an agreement to exchange unless one party
had delivered to the other the thing he had promised.   *Ex
placito permutationis nulla re secuta, constat nemini actionem competere.*   (C. iv. 64. 3.)   If one party had delivered
the thing, he has a *condictio* to get it back, or an action
*præscriptis verbis* to recompense himself for all he lost by
delivering it.

In a contract of sale the seller was not bound to make the
buyer absolute master (*dominus*) of the thing sold, as he would
have been in a stipulation.   (D. xviii. 1. 25. 1.)   What he was
bound to do was this : 1st. He was bound to deliver the thing
itself ( *præstare, tradere*), (D. xix. 1. 11. 2), to give free and
undisturbed possession of it (*possessionem vacuam præstare*)
(D. xix. 1. 2. 1), and to give lawful possession of it (*præstare*

*licere habere*). (D. xix. 1. 30. 1.) 2ndly. He was bound, if the buyer was disturbed in his possession by the real owner (which was termed *evictio*), to recompense him for what he lost. (D. xix. 1. 11. 2.) And 3rdly. To secure the buyer against secret faults; if such faults were discovered, either compensation might be claimed to a greater or less amount according as the seller had or not knowledge of the defect (D. xix. 1. 13), or the contract might be rescinded, and the thing returned (which was termed *redhibitio—redhibere est facere ut rursus habeat venditor quod habuerit*). (D. xxi. 1. 21.) The buyer might also strengthen his position by exacting a stipulation from the seller, binding him to give possession, &c., and probably to do so was the only means of attaching the above-mentioned incidents to a contract of sale, until at a comparatively late time of Roman law these incidents were held to be attached to it by the nature of the contract. In the case of eviction it was customary, and under the provision of the Edict of the *Curule Ædiles* it was obligatory, when the thing sold was of some value, to stipulate for double the amount of the price. (D. xxi. 2. 37; xxi. 1. 31.)

The buyer was bound to make the seller the real owner of the money paid as the price (*emptor nummos venditoris facere cogitur*, D. xix. 1. 11. 2), and was also bound to pay interest on the purchase-money from the day when he had received the thing sold. (D. xix. 1. 13. 20.)

The lines cited in the text are from *Il.* 7 472; probably the *alii versus* alluded to are those describing the exchange between Glaucus and Diomede. (*Il.* 6. 235.)

3. Cum autem emptio et venditio contracta sit, quod effici diximus simul atque de pretio convenerit, cum sine scriptura res agitur, periculum rei venditae statim ad emptorem pertinet, tametsi adhuc ea res empta ri tradita non sit. Itaque si homo mortuus sit vel aliqua parte corporis laesus fuerit, aut aedes totae vel aliqua ex parte incendio consumptae fuerint, aut fundus vi fluminis totus vel aliqua ex parte ablatus sit, sive etiam inundatione aquae aut arboribus turbine dejectis longe minor aut deterior esse coeperit, emptoris damnum est, cui necesse est, licet rem non fuerit nactus, pretium solvere. Quicquid enim sine dolo et culpa venditoris accidit, in eo venditor securus est. Sed etsi post emptionem fundo

3. As soon as the sale is contracted, that is, in the case of a sale made without writing, when the parties have agreed on the price, all risk attaching to the thing sold falls upon the purchaser, although the thing has not yet been delivered to him. Therefore, if the slave dies or receives an injury in any part of his body, or a whole or a portion of the house is burnt; or a whole or a portion of the land is carried by the force of a flood, or is diminished or deteriorated by an inundation, or by a tempest making havock with the trees, the loss falls on the purchaser, and although he does not receive the thing, he is obliged to pay the price, for the seller does not suffer for anything which happens without any design or fault of his. On the other

aliquid per alluvionem accessit, ad emptoris commodum pertinet; nam et commodum ejus esse debet cujus periculum est. Quod si fugerit homo qui veniit, aut surreptus fuerit, ita ut neque dolus neque culpa venditoris interveniat, animadvertendum erit an custodiam ejus usque ad traditionem venditor susceperit: nam enim si susceperit, ad ipsius periculum is casus pertinet; si non susceperit, securus est. Idem et in ceteris animalibus ceterisque rebus intelligimus: utique tamen vindicationem rei et condictionem exhibere debebit emptori, quia rem qui nondum rem emptori tradidit, adhuc ipse dominus est. Idem et etiam de furti et de damni injuriae actione.

hand, if after the sale the land is increased by alluvion, it is the purchaser who receives the advantage, for he who bears the risk of harm, ought to receive the benefit of all that is advantageous. If a slave who has been sold, runs away or is stolen, without any fraud or fault on the part of the seller, we must inquire whether the seller undertook to keep him safely until he was delivered over; if he undertook this, what happens is at his risk; if he did not undertake it, he is not responsible. The same would hold in the case of any other animal or any other thing, but the seller is in any case bound to make over to the purchaser his right to a real or personal action, for the person who has not delivered the thing is still its owner; and it is the same with regard to the action of theft, and the action *damni injuriae*.

D. xviii. 6–8; D. xviii. 1. 35. 4.

If the seller were proprietor of the thing sold, he would retain this proprietorship (*dominium*) until he delivered it to the buyer, and the buyer received it, or until the property in it was passed by the buyer having paid the price, or given security for it, or in some way satisfied the seller (*ære soluto, vel fidejussore dato, vel alias satisfacto*, D. xiv. 4. 5. 18). Until this delivery, he retained the thing in his custody, and if it had, meanwhile, any accretion, or suffered any diminution, he was still the *dominus* of the thing which was increased or decreased, and so the rule *res domino perit* may be said to have been true of him. But his obligation bound him to deliver the thing exactly in the state in which it might happen to be at the time of delivery; and so it made no real difference to him whether there was an accretion or diminution. But whatever happened to the thing sold, the price fixed on remained due. For the obligation of the buyer being a distinct and independent obligation, the price could not alter, but remained fixed. The seller was, however, answerable for the care with which he preserved the thing while in his custody, *periculum rei ad emptorem pertinet dummodo custodiam venditor aut traditionem præstet*. (D. xlvii. 2. 14, pr.) And he was not only bound to guard against gross and ordinary negligence (*dolum et culpam præstare*, D. xiii. 6. 5. 2), but to preserve it more carefully even than his own property, *diligentiam præstet exactiorem, quam in suis rebus adhiberet.* (D. xviii. 6. 3.)

The *actio furti* and the *actio damni injuriæ* are noticed in Tit. 1 and 4 of the Fourth Book.

| | |
|---|---|
| 4. Emptio tam sub conditione quam pure contrahi potest: sub conditione, veluti si Stichus intra certum diem tibi placuerit, erit tibi emptus aureis tot. | 4. A sale may be made conditionally or unconditionally; conditionally, as for example, 'If Stichus suits you within a certain time, he shall be purchased by you at such a price.' |

GAI. iii. 146.

The exact opposite might be contracted for: if within a certain time you find *Stichus* does not suit you, let it be considered you have not bought him. The jurists then said that the sale was a *pura emptio, quæ sub conditione resolvitur.* (D. xli. 4. 2. 5.) *Stichus* is sold, but within a certain time the contract may be rescinded.

The generic name for the accessory agreements which modified the principal contract was *pacta.* Some of these *pacta* are treated of at considerable length in the Digest (D. xviii. 2 and 3), different names being appropriated to those most frequently in use; as, for instance, the *in diem addictio*, when the thing was sold, but if the seller had a better offer within a certain time, the contract might be rescinded (D. xviii. 2); and the *lex commissoria*, which was a general agreement for the rescission of the contract if either party violated its terms, and was especially used to enable the seller to demand back the thing sold, if the price was not paid by a certain day.

We may observe that the Code (iv. 44. 2 and 8) permits a seller, at all times, to rescind a contract if he had not received half its real value.

| | |
|---|---|
| 5. Loca sacra vel religiosa, item publica, veluti forum, basilicam frustra quis sciens emit. Quæ tamen si pro profanis vel privatis deceptus a venditore emerit, habebit actionem ex empto quod non habere ei liceat, ut consequatur quod sua interest deceptum non esse. Idem juris est, si hominem liberum pro servo emerit. | 5. A sale is void when a person knowingly purchases a sacred or religious place, or a public place, such as a Forum or Basilica. If, however, deceived by the vendor, he has supposed that what he was buying was profane or private, as he cannot have what he purchased, he may bring an action *ex empto* to recover whatever it would have been worth to him not to have been deceived. It is the same if he has purchased a free man, supposing him to be a slave. |

D. xviii. 1. 4. 6; D. xviii. 1. 62. 1.

This paragraph is probably inserted in order to contrast the effects of a contract of sale with those of a stipulation. In the strict civil law, ignorance that a thing was not a subject of commerce would not help the person who had stipulated for it.

But in a contract of sale, if the seller had, and the buyer had not, known the real character of the thing he was buying, the buyer could recover against the seller anything he lost by entering into the bargain; for instance, he would not only receive back the purchase-money, but also would be entitled to interest upon it from the date of its payment.

The contract of sale gave rise to two direct actions, the *actio ex vendito*, or *venditi*, belonging to the seller, and the *actio ex empto* or *empti*, mentioned in the text, belonging to the buyer.

### Tit. XXIV.   DE LOCATIONE ET CONDUCTIONE.

Locatio et conductio proxima est emptioni et venditioni, iisdemque juris regulis consistit: nam ut emptio et venditio ita contrahitur si de pretio convenerit, sic etiam locatio et conductio ita contrahi intelligitur si merces constituta sit; et competit locatori quidem locati actio, conductori vero conducti.

The contract of letting to hire approaches very nearly to that of sale, and is governed by the same rules of law. As the contract of sale is formed as soon as a price is fixed, so a contract of letting to hire is formed as soon as the amount to be paid for the hiring has been agreed on; and the latter has an action *locati*, and the hirer an action *conducti*.

D. xix. 2. 2, and 16, pr.

The contract of letting on hire (*locatio-conductio*), like that of sale, was complete by the mere consent of the parties, and, like it, produced only personal obligations, and not any real rights. The hirer was, however, not even entitled to the *possessio*; the latter still remained the possessor in the eye of the law, his duty not being *praestare rem licere habere*, but *praestare re frui, uti licere*.

There were three principal heads of this contract: 1, *locatio-conductio rerum*, when one person let a thing and another hired it; 2, *locatio-conductio operarum*, when one person let his services and another hired them; 3, *locatio-conductio operis*, where one person contracted that a particular piece of work should be done, and another contracted to do it. If in such a contract we look at the labour, &c. expended on the work, we should naturally call the person who did the work the *locutor*, as it was he who let out his services for its performance; but the Roman jurists generally looked at the work itself that was to be done, and spoke of the person who contracted for its performance, i.e. gave it out, as its *locutor*, and the person who engaged to perform or execute it, i.e. took it in, as the *conductor*. The price of, or consideration for, the letting, was generally called *merces*, sometimes *pretium*, and in the case of the letting of houses or land, *pensio* or *reditus*. In particular contracts, the *conductor* had special names, as the hirer of a house was called *inquilinus*, of a farm, *colonus*.

The duty of the letter was to guarantee the hirer against eviction, and to reimburse him for any useful or necessary expenses he had incurred; the duty of the hirer was to take care of the thing hired (see paragr. 4), to give up the thing hired at the end of the term for which it was let, and to pay the price agreed on.

The text gives us the names of the personal actions which belonged to the letter and the hirer respectively, the former having the *actio locati*, the latter the *actio conducti*. But actions of a very different kind were sometimes connected with this contract. In the case of land let to hire, certain instruments of farming and other property of the hirer were held as a security for the payment of the rent, and a real action, termed the *actio Serviana*, because first introduced by the prætor *Servius*, was given to the letter to enforce his right to these things in case of nonpayment of the rent; this action was gradually extended in its effects, and the extended action, under the name of *actio quasi-Serviana*, was used to enforce the rights of a creditor over anything given in pledge. (See Bk. iv. Tit. 6, 7.) The prætor, too, gave an interdict, termed the *interdictum Salvianum*, by which the letter enforced a claim to certain things, in case possession was refused by the hirer, after his hiring was at an end. (See Bk. iv. Tit. 15. 3.)

1. Et quæ supra diximus, si alieno arbitrio pretium promissum fuerit, eadem et de locatione et conductione dicta esse intelligamus, si alieno arbitrio mercea permissa fuerit. Qua de causa, si fulloni polienda curandave, aut sarcinatori sarcienda vestimenta quis dederit, nulla statim mercede constituta, sed postea tantum daturus quantum inter eos convenerit, non proprie locatio et conductio contrahi intelligitur, sed eo nomine actio præscriptis verbis datur.

1. What we have said above of a sale in which the price is to be fixed by the decision of a third person, may be applied to the contract of letting to hire, if the amount to be paid for the hire is left to the decision of a third person. Accordingly, if any one gives clothes to a fuller to be cleaned, or to a tailor to be mended, without fixing the sum to be paid for their work, a contract of letting to hire cannot properly be said to be made; but the circumstances furnish ground for an action *præscriptis verbis*.

Gai. iii. 143; D. xix. 2. 25, pr.

*Qua de causa*, i. e. ' the price ought to be determined, and therefore,' &c.; the passage is taken rather unconnectedly out of Gaius.

*Actio praescriptis verbis.*

2. Praeterea, sicut vulgo quaerebatur, an permutatis rebus emptio et venditio contrahitur, ita quaeri solebat de locatione et conductione, si forte rem aliquam tibi utendam sive fruendam quis dederit, et invicem a te aliam rem utendam sive fruendam acceperit. Et placuit non esse locationem et conductionem, sed proprium genus esse contractus: veluti si, cum unum bovem quis haberet et vicinus ejus unum, placuerit inter eos ut per denos dies invicem boves commodarent ut opus facerent, et apud alterum bos periit, neque locati vel conducti neque commodati competit actio, quia non fuit gratuitum commodatum; verum praescriptis verbis agendum est.

(See note on Tit. 13. 2.)

2. Moreover, just as the question was often asked, whether a contract of sale was formed by exchange, a similar question arose with respect to the contract of letting to hire, in case any one gave you a thing to use or take the fruits of, and in return received from you something else of which he was to have the fruits or use. It has been decided that this is not a contract of letting to hire, but a distinct kind of contract. For example, if two neighbours have each an ox, and agree each to lend the other his ox, for ten days to make use of, and one of the oxen dies while in the care of the person to whom it does not belong, there will not be an action *locati*, or *conducti*, or *commodati*, since the loan was not gratuitous, but an action *praescriptis verbis*.

GAL. iii. 144; D. xix. 5. 17. 3.

3. Adeo autem familiaritatem aliquam inter se habere videntur emptio et venditio, item locatio et conductio, ut in quibusdam causis quaeri soleat, utrum emptio et venditio contrahatur, an locatio et conductio: ut ecce de praediis quae perpetuo quibusdam fruenda traduntur, id est, ut quamdiu pensio sive reditus pro his domino praestetur, neque ipsi conductori neque heredi ejus, cuive conductor heresve ejus id praedium vendiderit aut donaverit aut dotis nomine dederit, aliove quoquo modo alienaverit, auferre liceat. Sed talis contractus quia inter veteres dubitabatur, et a quibusdam locatio, a quibusdam venditio existimabatur, lex Zenoniana lata est, quae emphyteuseos contractus propriam statuit naturam, neque ad locationem neque ad venditionem inclinantem, sed suis pactionibus fulciendam. Et si quidem aliquid pactum fuerit, hoc ita obtinere ac si natura talis esset contractus: sin autem nihil de periculo rei fuerit pactum, tunc si quidem totius rei interitus acciderit, ad dominum super hoc redundare peri-

3. Contracts of sale and of letting to hire are so nearly connected, that in some cases it is questioned whether the contract is one or the other. For instance, when lands are delivered over to be enjoyed for ever, that is, that as long as the rent is paid for the land to the owner, he cannot take away the land from the hirer or his heir, or any one to whom the hirer or his heir has sold, or given, or made a dowry of the land. As the ancients were in doubt as to this contract, some regarding it as a letting to hire, and some as a sale, the constitution of Zeno was made, which declared that the contract of *emphyteusis* was of a special nature, and was not to be confounded either with letting to hire, or with sale, but rested upon its own peculiar agreements; and that if any special agreement was made, it was to be observed as if to have such an agreement was part of the nature of the contract; but if no agreement was made as to the risks the thing might undergo, the risk of a total loss should fall upon the owner, and the detriment of a partial loss upon the occupier; and

culum: sin particularia, ad emphy- this we still wish to be considered
teuticarium hujusmodi damnum the law.
venire. Quo jure utimur.

GAI. lii. 145; O. iv. 66. 1.

We have already given an account of *emphyteusis* in the
note to Blk. ii. Tit. 5, 6.

The law would naturally contemplate the contract under
which the possessor entered as a *locatio-conductio*; but the
*dominus* seemed to have parted with so much of his interest,
that it appeared doubtful whether it ought not rather to be
considered as a sale.

4. Item quæritur, si cum aurifice Titius convenerit ut is ex auro suo certi ponderis certæque formæ anulos ei faceret, et acciperet verbi gratia aureos decem, utrum emptio et venditio contrahi videatur, an locatio et conductio? Cassius ait, materia quidem emptionem et venditionem contrahi, opera autem locationem et conductionem; sed placuit tantum emptionem et venditionem contrahi. Quod si suum aurum Titius dederit mercede pro opera constituta, dubium non est quin locatio et conductio sit.

4. It is also questioned whether, when Titius has agreed with a goldsmith to make him rings of a certain weight and pattern, out of gold belonging to the goldsmith himself, the goldsmith to receive, for example, ten aurei, whether the contract is one of sale or letting to hire. Cassius says that there is a sale of the material, and a letting to hire of the goldsmith's work; but it has been decided that there is only a contract of sale. If Titius gives the gold, and a sum is agreed on to be paid for the work, there is no doubt that the contract is then one of letting to hire.

GAI. iii. 147.

5. Conductor omnia secundum legem conductionis facere debet: et si quid in lege prætermissum fuerit, id ex bono et æquo debet præstare. Qui pro usu aut vestimentorum aut argenti aut jumenti mercedem aut dedit aut promisit, ab eo custodia talis desideratur, qualem diligentissimus paterfamilias suis rebus adhibet: quam si præstiterit, et aliquo casu rem amiserit, de restituenda ea non tenebitur.

5. The hirer ought to do everything according to the terms of his hiring, and if anything has been omitted in these terms, he ought to supply it according to the rules of equity. He who has given or promised a sum for the hire of clothes or silver, or a beast of burden, is required to bestow as great care on the safe custody of the thing he hires, as the most careful father of a family bestows on the custody of his own property. If he bestows such care, but loses the thing through some accident, he is not bound to restore it.

D. xix. 1. 25. 3. 7.

The subject of the distinctions, in the amount of care
required in different cases, will be treated of in the notes to
paragr. 9 of the next Title.

6. Mortuo conductore intra tempora conductionis, heres ejus eodem jure in conductione succedit.

6. If the hirer dies during the time of his hiring, his heir succeeds to all the rights given him by the contract.

C. iv. 65. 10.

Of course in a *locatio-conductio operarum* or *operis*, the death of the person who gave his services terminated the contract.

The contract, in the case of a *locatio-conductio rei*, was also terminated by the sale of the thing hired. The buyer was not considered bound by the contract. *Emptori fundi non necesse est stare colonum cui prior dominus locavit*; *nisi ea lege emit* (C. iv. 65. 9); but the *conductor* could demand compensation from the *locator*. The contract ceasing if the thing was sold serves clearly to distinguish the interest of the *conductor*, from a usufruct. The *conductor* had no real interest in the thing, but only a personal right against the *locator*, while the usufructuary had a servitude, i.e. a real right, in the thing. The whole of the thing over which the usufruct extended could not be sold, because part of it, namely the usufruct, had already been parted with.

The contract was also terminated if the rent was two years in arrear (D. xix. 2. 54. 1); if the *conductor* grossly misused the thing hired (C. iv. 65. 3); if the *locator* had indispensable need of it (C. ib.); or if the *conductor* was prevented from getting benefit from it. (D. xix. 2. 13. 7.)

## Tit. XXV. DE SOCIETATE.

Societatem coire solemus aut totorum bonorum, quam Graeci specialiter κοινοπραξίαν appellant, aut unius alicujus negotiationis, veluti mancipiorum emendorum vendendorumque, aut olei, vini, frumenti emendi vendendique.

A partnership is formed either of the whole goods of the contracting parties, to which the Greeks give the special name of κοινοπραξία, or for some particular business, as the sale or purchase of slaves, wine, oil, or wheat.

Gai. iii. 148.

The text, borrowed from Gaius (iii. 148), gives the general division of partnerships into two classes according as they are universal or particular. In the Digest we have a further division by distinguishing five kinds of partnership. (D. xvii. 2. 5.)

1. *Societas universorum bonorum*, in which everything belonging or accruing in any way to each partner is held in common. (D. xvii. 2. 1. 1.)

2. *Societas universorum quae ex quaestu veniunt*, i.e. of all things which are gained or acquired by each partner through

such transactions as were contemplated in the formation of the contract; but not of things belonging or accruing in other ways, such as inheritances or legacies.

3. *Societas negotiationis alicujus*, formed to carry on a particular business.

4. *Societas vectigalis*, formed to carry on the farming of public lands—a mere branch of the last, but subject to special rules. (D. xvii. 2. 5.)

5. *Societas rei unius*, when one or more particular things are held in common.

| | |
|---|---|
| 1. Et quidem si nihil de partibus lucri et damni nominatim convenerit, aequales scilicet partes et in lucro et in damno spectantur. Quod si expressae fuerint partes, hae servari debent; nec enim unquam dubium fuit quin valeat conventio, si duo inter se pacti sunt ut ad unum quidem duae partes et lucri et damni pertineant, ad alium tertia. | 1. Unless the proportions of gain and loss have been specially agreed on, the shares of gain and loss are equal. If they have been agreed on, effect ought to be given to the agreement, for, indeed, the validity of the agreement has never been questioned, if two partners have agreed that two-thirds of the gain and loss should belong to the one, and one-third to the other. |

Gai. iii. 150.

*Æquales partes*, i. e. one equal share of the whole, not proportional to what each contributes.

| | |
|---|---|
| 2. De illa sane conventione quaesitum est, si Titium et Seium inter se pacti sunt ut ad Titium lucri duae partes pertineant, damni tertia, ad Seium duae partes damni, lucri tertia, an rata deberi haberi conventio? Quintus Mutius contra naturam societatis talem pactionem esse existimavit, et ob id non esse ratam habendam. Servius Sulpitius cujus sententia praevaluit, contra sensit, quia saepe quorundam ita pretiosa est opera in societate, ut eos justum sit conditione meliore in societatem admitti: nam et ita coiri posse societatem non dubitatur, ut alter pecuniam conferat, alter non conferat, et tamen lucrum inter eos commune sit, quia saepe opera alicujus pro pecunia valet. Et adeo contra Quinti Mutii sententiam obtinuit, ut illud quoque constiterit posse convenire, ut quis lucri partem ferat, damno non teneatur; quod et ipsum Servius convenienter sibi existimavit. Quod tamen ita intelligi oportet, ut si in | 2. But doubts have been raised as to the following agreement; supposing Titius and Seius have agreed that two-thirds of the profit and one-third of the loss shall belong to Titius, and two-thirds of the loss and one-third of the profit shall belong to Seius, ought such an agreement to be valid? Quintus Mutius considered it as contrary to the nature of partnership, and as therefore not to be held valid. Servius Sulpitius, on the contrary, whose opinion has prevailed, thought it valid, as frequently the services of particular partners are so valuable that it is just to give them advantages in the terms of the partnership. There can be no doubt that a partnership may be formed on the terms of one partner contributing money, and of the other not contributing, while yet the profit is common to both, as often a man's labour is equivalent to money. The opinion, therefore, contrary to that of Quintus Mutius, has prevailed, and it is admitted that by special agreement a partner may share the |

aliqua re lucrum, in aliqua damnum allatum sit, compensatione facta solum quod superest intelligatur lucri esse.

profit, and yet not be responsible for the loss, as Servius consistently held. This must be understood as meaning, that, if there is profit on one transaction and loss on another, the accounts must be balanced, and only the net profit be reckoned as profit.

Gai. Iii. 149; D. xvii. 2. 30.

A partnership in which one partner was totally excluded from gain was void. The jurists called it a *leonina societas*, as the other partner would have the lion's share. (D. xvii. 2. 29. 1.)

With respect to the power of one partner to bind another, a point not touched on by Justinian, we may observe that as between the partners themselves, any one who acted in behalf of the rest was their mandatary, and, beyond acts of pure administration of their affairs, could only be empowered to act by their express desire (*mandatum*). If he were so empowered he had an action against them for all expenses and losses he incurred, and was bound to account to them for the profits. With regard to third persons, as the Roman law, strictly speaking, took no notice of any one who was not a party to the particular contract, they could not sue, or be sued by, the remaining partners, who were not parties. The prætor, however, allowed the remaining partners to sue if they had no other means of protecting their interests (D. xiv. 3. 1, 2); and the stranger to sue, if the partners had benefited by the contract. (D. xvii. 2. 82.)

3. Illud expeditum est, si in una causa pars fuerit expressa, veluti in solo lucro vel in solo damno, in altera vero omissa, in eo quoque quod prætermissum est, eandem partem servari.

3. Of course if the share on one side only is expressly agreed on, as on the side of profit only, or on that of loss only, the same share is to be considered as held on the side of which no mention is made.

Gai. iii. 150.

4. Manet autem societas eousque donec in eodem consensu perseveraverint: at cum aliquis renuntiaverit societati, solvitur societas. Sed plane si quis callide in hoc renuntiaverit societati, ut obveniens aliquod lucrum solus habeat: veluti si totorum bonorum socius, cum ab aliquo heres esset relictus, in hoc renuntiaverit societati ut hereditatem solus lucrifaceret, cogetur hoc lucrum communicare; si quid vero lucrifaciat quod non captaverit, ad ipsum solum pertinet. Ei vero cui renuntiatum est, quidquid omnino

4. A partnership continues as long as the partners continue to agree that it shall do so; but if any one partner renounces the partnership, then the partnership is dissolved. If, however, he makes this renunciation with a secret motive, such as that he may alone enjoy a gain which he knows awaits him; for instance, if when a member of a partnership embracing all the property of each of the partners, he renounces the partnership to enjoy alone the advantage of an inheritance left him, he is compelled to share this source of gain with his partners.

post renuntiatam societatem acquiritur, soli conconditur.

But if he gains anything without
such previous design, he alone profits
by it: while the partner who has received his renunciation acquires alone
all that falls to him subsequently.

Gal. iii. 151.

The contract of partnership may have different modifications. It may be made during or from a certain time, or
conditionally. (D. xvii. 2. 1.)   But there can be no partnership to last for ever, as no one can be forced to remain
a partner against his will. (D. xvii. 2. 70.)   Any partner may
renhounce, i.e. withdraw, when he pleases.

The remaining paragraphs of this Title treat of the modes
in which the partnership may be dissolved.   Ulpian, enume-
rating the causes of the dissolution of partnerships, says,
' *Societas solvitur ex personis, ex rebus, ex voluntate, ex
actione.*' (D. xvii. 2. 63. 10.)   *Ex personis,* when one of the
parties is dead or incapacitated; *ex rebus,* when the purpose
of the partnership is effected, or its subject-matter has ceased
to exist (this will include the cases of confiscation and cession
of goods given in paragraphs 7 and 8); *ex voluntate,* when
one partner wishes to withdraw; and *ex actione,* when one
partner compels a dissolution of partnership by action.   We
may add *ex tempore,* if the partnership was only temporary.

5. Solvitur adhuc societas etiam
morte socii, quia qui societatem
contrahit, certam personam sibi
eligit. Sed et si consensu plurium
societas contracta sit, morte unius
socii solvitur, etsi plures supersint,
nisi in coeunda societate aliter convenerit.

5. A partnership is also dissolved
by the death of a partner, as he who
enters into a partnership chooses a
particular person to whom he binds
himself. And even if there are more
than two partners, the death of any
one dissolves the partnership although more than one survive, unless
on the formation of the partnership
it has been otherwise agreed.

Gal. iii. 152;  D. xvii. 2. 65. 0.

Although, in forming the partnership, the parties might agree
that, if any one ceased to be a partner, the rest should still
continue partners, or, to speak more accurately, should immediately and without fresh agreement form a new partnership,
yet no one could validly make it part of the contract that his
heirs should, on his death, be admitted partners (D. xvii. 2. 59),
the contract being personal. There was an exception made to
this rule in the case of *societates vectigales.* (D. xvii. 2. 59.)

6. Item si alicujus rei contracta
societatis sit, et unius negotio impositus est, finitur societas.

6. If the partnership has been
formed for a single transaction, when
the transaction is completed, the
partnership is ended.

D. xvii. 2. 65. 10.

7. Publicatione quoque distrahi societatem manifestum est, scilicet si universa bona socii publicentur; nam cum in ejus locum alius succedat, pro mortuo habetur.

7. It is evident, also, that a partnership is dissolved by the confiscation of all the property of a partner; for this partner, as he is replaced by a successor, is considered dead.

D. xvii. 2. 65. 12.

8. Item si quis ex sociis mole debiti praegravatus bonis suis cesserit, et ideo propter publica aut privata debita subdentia ejus veneat, solvitur societas; sed hoc casu, si adhuc consentiant in societatem, nova videtur incipere societas.

8. So, too, if one of the partners, borne down by the weight of his debts, makes a cession of his goods, and his property is therefore sold to satisfy his debts, public or private, the partnership is dissolved. But in this case, if the parties agree still to continue partners, a new partnership would seem to be begun.

Gai. iii. 153, 154.

The *persona* of an individual might, we know, be destroyed even in his lifetime, as, for instance, by the *maxima* and *minor capitis deminutio*, by the sale of his property in the mass, either for the profit of the treasury in the case of criminals (*sectio bonorum*), or of private individuals in certain cases of insolvency (*emptio bonorum*), or when he had made a *cessio bonorum* under the *lex Julia*. (See Tit. 12 of this Book.) In the time of Justinian sales in one mass of a whole patrimony were obsolete, and therefore confiscation (*publicatio*) and *cessio bonorum* are alone mentioned here, and these as taking away the fortune of the partner, and not as destroying his *persona*.

Of course the partnership might be immediately renewed with the partner whose goods had been confiscated or ceded to creditors, if the other partners were willing to enter into what was really a new partnership, as it might if the partner had suffered the *minor deminutio*; for partnership, being a contract of the *jus gentium*, could be formed with a stranger. (Gai. iii. 154.)

0. Socius socio utrum eo nomine tantum teneatur praescio actione, si quid dolo commiserit, sicut is qui deponi apud se passus est, an etiam culpae, id est desidiae atque negligentiae nomine, quaesitum est: praevaluit tamen etiam culpae nomine teneri eum. Culpa autem non ad exactissimam diligentiam dirigenda est: sufficit enim talem diligentiam in communibus rebus adhibere socium, qualem suis rebus adhibere solet; nam qui parum diligentem socium sibi assumit, de se queri debet.

9. It has been questioned whether one partner can be made answerable to another by the action *pro socio*, if he has been guilty of malicious wrong, as a depositary is, or whether also for a fault, that is, for carelessness and negligence. The opinion has prevailed that he is also answerable for a fault, but the fault is not to be measured by a standard of the most perfect carefulness possible. It is sufficient that he should be as careful of things belonging to the partnership as he is of his own property.

H H

For he who accepts as partner a
person of careless habits, has only
himself to blame.

D. xvii. 2. 72.

*Societas jus quodammodo fraternitatis in se habet.* (D.
17. 2. 63.) Hence each partner had something of a brotherly
allowance (termed the *beneficium competentiæ*) made for him,
and was only held responsible to the extent of his means and
power of action; while, if he were condemned in an action
*pro socio*, he was marked with infamy.

The action *pro socio* was the remedy in almost every case
that could arise between partners. It was employed, for instance, to enforce accounts, to get compensation for losses, and
to dissolve the partnership. If any partner was guilty of a de-
linquency, such as theft, he would be made amenable by such
actions as the *actio furti, vi bonorum raptorum legis Aquiliæ*,
of which we read in the Fourth Book. There was also another
action peculiar to partnerships, called the *actio communi
dividundo*, which was brought to procure a partition, by the
*judex*, of the common property. (See Introd. sec. 103.)

The mention of *culpa* in the text gives occasion to notice
a subject of importance not only as regards the particular
contract of partnership, but as regards all other contracts.

If one person who was bound to another by a contract,
designedly subjected him to harm or loss (*damnum*) with
respect to anything included in the contract, the wrongdoer,
in inflicting this wilful injury, was said to be guilty of *dolus*;
if he was the means of an injury not designed being inflicted,
that unless the *damnum* was the result of unavoidable accident, he was said to be guilty of *culpa*. This *culpa* would
naturally admit of degrees. The fault might be one which
any man in his senses would have scrupled to commit, and it
was then termed *lata culpa* (*lata culpa est nimia negligentia,
id est, non intelligere quod omnes intelligunt*; D. L. 16. 213.
2); or it might consist in falling short of the highest standard
of carefulness to avoid injury that could be found; such, for
instance, as the carefulness employed in the management of
affairs by a person who would deserve to be called *bonus paterfamilias*, and the *culpa* was then termed *levis* or *levissima*.
Or, again, it might consist in falling short of the care which
the person guilty of the *culpa* was accustomed to bestow on
his own affairs. In this last case we no longer measure by an
absolute standard, but a relative one; what is *culpa* in one
man is not in another, and modern writers have therefore
spoken of it as being *culpa levis in concreto*, i.e. as seen in

and measured by the particular individual, opposed to the *culpa levis in abstracto*, i. e. estimated by an absolute standard. The *lata culpa* was treated very much on the same footing with *dolus*, as there always seems something wilful in the extreme negligence, the *crassa negligentia*, which characterized the *lata culpa*. The text affords us an example of the difference between the *culpa levis in abstracto* and the *culpa levis in concreto*. The *socius* is not bound to render *exactissima diligentia*, he is not to be answerable for the perfect care of a *bonus paterfamilias*, but he is to be judged by the amount of care which he bestows on his own property. This may happen to be as great as that of a *bonus paterfamilias*, but it may also happen to be much less; so that, practically, though not necessarily, the *culpa levis in concreto* implies a lower degree of responsibility than the *culpa levis in abstracto*; and hence many commentators arrange the *culpa*, when thus considered *in concreto*, as belonging to the *culpa lata*, and not to the *culpa levis*. We cannot properly consider it as belonging to the one more than the other, because it would depend on the character of the individual to which it most nearly approached. The technical term for to be responsible for malicious injury or a fault was *dolum, culpam præstare*. Every contract bound all parties *dolum præstare*, and a special agreement that the parties should not be so bound was void. (D. ii. 14. 27. 3.) The person for whose benefit or sake, or to whose profit, the contract was made, was answerable for *culpa levis*; and if both parties were benefited, both were answerable. The person who only had the burden, without the advantage of the contract or whom the matter in hand did not concern, was only answerable for *lata culpa*, unless he had, either directly or tacitly, promised to use greater diligence than the nature of the contract would make incumbent on him. A person, for instance, who meddled, unbidden, in the affairs of another, was bound to use *exactissima diligentia*. Lastly, those who, like partners, had their own property intermixed with the property of others, or those, as tutors and curators, who were obliged by law to administer the property of others, were bound to exert the diligence which they employed in the management of their own affairs.

We may add, that when a person bound by a contract delayed to execute it, and this delay (*mora*) was of such a kind that *culpa* could be imputed to him, he was subjected to something more than the necessity of fulfilling the contractd, and especially he was in most cases liable to pay interest (*usuræ*). (D. xxii. 1.)

## Tit. XXVI.  DE MANDATO.

Mandatum contrahitur quinque modis: sive sua tantum gratis aliquis tibi mandet, sive sua et tua, sive aliena tantum, sive sua et aliena, sive tua et aliena: at si tua tantum gratia mandatum sit, supervacuum est, et ob id nulla obligatio nec mandati inter vos actio nascitur.

The contract of mandate is formed in five modes; according as a mandator gives you anything for his benefit only, or for his benefit and for yours; or for the benefit of a third person only, or for his benefit and that of a third person, or for your benefit and that of a third person. A mandate made for your benefit only is useless, and does not produce between you any obligation or action *mandati.*

D. xvii. 1. 2.

In the theory of Roman law one person could not represent another. The person who actually made the contract, who uttered the binding words, or went through the binding formalities, was the only legal contractor; he alone could sue and be sued. The law would not take notice that it was really in behalf of another that he made the contract.

But a friend on whom reliance could be placed might be persuaded to make the contract in his own name. Honour and friendship would then effect what the law would not compel. This friend would give up all that he gained by the contract to the person at whose request he entered into it. The promise to perform this act of friendship was given, in the old times of Roman manners, with an appropriate formality. The person really interested took the friend by the right hand, and told him that he placed in his hand the trust he was anxious to have discharged. The trust, or commission itself, was hence called mandatum (*manu datum*). Plautus thus describes the ceremony. (*Captiv.* ii. 3.)

Tynd.—*Hœc per dexteram tuam, te dextera retinens manu,*
*Obsecro, infidelior mihi ne fuas, quam ego sum tibi.*
*Tu hoc age, tu mihi herus nunc es, tu patronus, tu pater,*
*Tibi commendo spes opesque meas.*

Ph.—*Mandavisti satis.*

The execution of a *mandatum* was thus a discharge of an office of friendship. *Originem ex officio atque amicitia trahit.* (D. xvii. 1, l. 4.) And it never lost the traces of its origin. It was always necessarily gratuitous; the *mandatarius,* i.e. the person charged with the *mandatum,* was obliged to bestow on it the care of the most diligent *pater-*

*familias*, i. e. the greatest possible (C. iv. 35. 13), and if he failed to discharge the trust, and was condemned in an *actio mandati*, he was stamped with infamy. (D. iii. 2. 1.)

When the introduction of the praetorian system furnished a method by which every equitable claim could be enforced, friends who entered into such an agreement were obliged to discharge their reciprocal duties. The praetor, by the *actio mandati directa* given to the mandator, compelled the *mandatarius* to account for all he received, and to pay over the profits, and by the *actio mandati contraria* given to the *mandatarius*, compelled the *mandator* (i. e. the person who requested the favour) to reimburse, with interest, the *mandatarius* for all expenses incurred, to indemnify him for all losses, and to free him from all obligation contracted in the execution of the mandate.

The praetorian law went a great step further, by allowing the mandator to bring equitable actions against, and to be sued by, the third party, with whom the *mandatarius* contracted. Whatever direct actions the *mandatarius* would properly have brought or was liable to, the *mandator* was allowed to bring or was liable to, in their equitable form. As, for instance, where the *mandatarius* would have brought a *condictio*, or an *actio empti* or *venditi*, the *mandator* was allowed to bring a *condictio utilis*, or an *actio utilis empti*, or *venditi*. (D. iii. 5. 31.) In the case of a special mandate, these actions were allowed, as of course; in the case of a general mandate, only when the *mandator* had no other way of protecting his interests, a mandate being termed special when one man charged another with the execution of one or more particular things, and general when he asked him to represent him in all his affairs. (D. xvii. 1. 10. 5.)

There were some acts, of a solemn character, in which one citizen could, at no time of Roman law, act for another, such as bringing any of the *legis actiones*, mancipation, making testaments, or the *cretio* or *aditio* of an inheritance. But it must be remarked that, apart from the praetorian enforcement of claims arising out of a *mandatum*, there were some exceptions to the rule that one man could not represent another. The civil law, indeed, never permitted it, but the praetorian system, in some instances, expressly recognized the intervention of an agent. Thus, a *cognitor* was allowed to conduct a suit on behalf of another (see Bk. iv. Tit. 10), and an agent was permitted by the edict to be appointed in carrying on trading operations before the *mandatum* received its full legal force. (See Bk. iv. Tit. 7.)

1. Mandantis tantum gratia intervenit mandatum, veluti si quis tibi mandet ut negotia ejus gereres, vel ut fundum si emeres, vel ut pro eo sponderes.

1. A mandate is made for the benefit of the mandator only; if, for instance, any one gives you a mandate to transact his business, to buy an estate for him, or to become surety for him.

D. xvii. 1. 2. 1.

This is the usual case of a *mandatum*. Justinian employs here, it may be remarked, the word *sponderes*, although *sponsores* no longer existed. (See Tit. 20.)

2. Tua et mandantis, veluti si mandet tibi, ut pecuniam sub usuris crederes el qui in rem ipsius mutuaretur; aut si, volente te agere cum eo ex fidejussoria causa, tibi mandet ut cum reo agas periculo mandantis, vel ut ipsius periculo stipuleris ab eo quem tibi deleget in id quod tibi debuerat.

2. A mandate is made for your benefit and that of the mandator; if, for instance, he gives a mandate to you to lend money at interest to a person who borrows it for the purpose of the mandator; or if, when you are about to sue him as a *fidejussor*, he gives you a mandate to sue the principal at his risk, or to stipulate at his risk for something owed by him to you, from a person whom he appoints as his substitute.

D. xvii. 1. 2. 4; D. xvii. 1. 45. 7, 8.

*Volente te agere cum eo ex fidejussoria causa.* Under the law anterior to Justinian, the creditor could sue either the debtor or the *fidejussor*, but not both. If he proposed to sue the latter, the *fidejussor* might give him a *mandatum* to sue the debtor, and then, if the creditor did so, the *fidejussor* would be freed from any obligation as *fidejussor*, but would be bound as mandator; and thus the mandate would be for the benefit of the *fidejussor*, because he would be sued after the principal, and for the benefit of the creditor, because he could sue the principal first and then the surety in his quality of mandator, whereas he could not ordinarily sue both the principal and the surety, but was obliged to make his choice between them. This could not be of any use after Justinian had decided that the principal debtor should be sued first, and then, if there was any deficiency, the *fidejussor*. (See Tit. 20. 4.)

*Ab eo quem tibi delegat.* The debtor points out to the creditor a third person who owes the debtor a sum equal to his debt to the creditor; and asks the creditor to stipulate with this third person for payment of the amount due from the debtor. If the third person does not pay, the debtor is held responsible as *mandator*. The creditor thus benefits, as he has two persons to sue, and the debtor benefits, because he employs his creditor to collect a debt due to him.

3. Aliena autem causa intervenit mandatum, veluti si tibi mandet ut Titii negotia gerere, vel ut Titio fundum emeres, vel ut pro Titio spondere.

3. A mandate is made for the benefit of a third person; if, for example, the mandator bids you manage the affairs of Titius, or buy an estate for Titius, or become surety for Titius.

D. xvii. 1. 2. 2.

Here, as the *mandator* has no interest in the affair, no ground for action can arise against him until the execution of the mandate. The *mandatarius* has an action to indemnify himself, and the *mandator* one to make the *mandatarius* account.

4. Sua et aliena, veluti si de communibus suis et Titii negotiis gerendis tibi mandet, vel ut sibi et Titio fundum emeres, vel ut pro eo et Titio sponderes.

4. A mandate is made for the benefit of the mandator and of a third person, if, for example, the mandator gives you a mandate to manage affairs common to himself and Titius, or to buy an estate for himself and Titius, or to become surety for himself and Titius.

D. xvii. 1. 2, 3.

5. Tua et aliena, veluti si tibi mandet ut Titio sub usuris crederes; quod si ut sine usuris crederes, aliena tantum gratia intercedit mandatum.

5. A mandate is made for your benefit and for that of a third person, if, for instance, the mandator bids you to lend money at interest to Titius. Were the money lent without interest, the mandate would be only for the benefit of a third person.

D. xvii. 1. 2. 5.

6. Tua gratia intervenit mandatum, veluti si tibi mandet ut pecuniam tuam in emptiones potius praediorum collocares, quam foeneres; vel ex diverso, ut foeneres potius quam in emptiones praediorum collocares. Cujus generis mandatum, magis consilium est quam mandatum, et ob id non est obligatorium; quia nemo ex consilio obligatur, etiamsi non expediat ei cui dabitur, cum liberum cuique sit apud se explorare an expediat consilium. Itaque si otiosam pecuniam domi te habentem hortatus fuerit aliquis ut rem aliquam emeres, vel eam crederes, quamvis non expediat tibi eam emisse vel credidisse, non tamen tibi mandati teneatur. Et adeo haec ita sunt, ut quaesitum sit an mandati teneatur, qui mandavit tibi ut pecuniam Titio foenerares? sed obtinuit Sabini sententia, obligatorium esse

6. A mandate is made for your benefit only, if, for example, the mandator bids you invest your money in the purchase of land rather than put it out to interest, or, vice versa. Such a mandate is rather a piece of advice than a mandate, and consequently is not obligatory, as no one is bound by giving advice, although it be not judicious, as each may judge for himself what the worth of the advice is. If, therefore, you have a sum of money lying idle in your house, and any one advises you to make a purchase with it, or put it out to interest, although it may not be advantageous to you to have made this purchase, or to have lent your money, yet your adviser is not bound by an action *mandati*. So much so, that it has been questioned whether a person is bound by this action who has given you a mandate to lend your money at

| | |
|---|---|
| In hoc casu mandatum, quia non aliter Titio credidisses, quam si tibi mandatum esset. | interest to Titius. But the opinion of Sabinius has prevailed, that such a mandate is obligatory, as you would not have lent your money to Titius unless the mandate had been given. |

GAT. iii. 156; D. xvii. 1. 2. 4.

It was a very narrow line which divided the expression of a mere opinion advising another person to do a thing, and such a request to him to do it as involved the responsibilities of a *mandatum*. Everything depended on the intention of the parties. The question was, did the person who expressed the opinion, or made the request, mean to say that, if the opinion would not be adopted, or the request granted, unless he made himself responsible for the consequences, he was willing to become responsible? If he did mean this, he was treated as a *mandator*.

A *mandator* stood in this and similar cases almost exactly in the place of a *fidejussor*. Accordingly, in the Digest, and the Code, the two are treated of under the same head, *de fidejussoribus et mandatoribus*. For the mandate was an *intercessio*, i.e. a mode in which a third party steps in between two others as a surety for one of them, and was subject to the general rules common to accessory contracts, such as the prohibition of the *senatus-consultum Velleianum*, with respect to women. the benefits of discussion, of division, if there were more than one *mandator*, and of cession of actions. (See Tit. 20. 4.)

But the *mandatum* being a distinct, and not an accessory contract, it was, in some parts, distinguished from a *fidejussio*. The action brought by the *mandatarius* against the *mandator* did not free the debtor. Justinian, however, by a constitution (C. viii. 41, 28), placed *fidejussores* on the same footing in this respect. Secondly, the payment by the *mandator* of the sum due did not free the debtor. (D. xvii. 1. 28.) Lastly, if the *mandator* paid the sum, he could compel the *mandatarius* to transfer to him, after the payment, all his actions against the debtor. (D. xliv. 3. 76.)

| | |
|---|---|
| 7. Illud quoque mandatum non est obligatorium, quod contra bonos mores est, veluti si Titius de furto aut de damno faciendo, aut de injuria facienda tibi mandet; licet enim pœnam istius facti nomine præstiteris, non tamen ullam habes adversus Titium actionem. | 7. A mandate, again, is not obligatory which is contrary to *boni mores*; as, for instance, if Titius gives you a mandate to commit a theft, or do a harm or injury; although you pay the penalty of what you may do, you have not in such a case an action against Titius. |

GAI. iii. 157; D. xvii. 1. 22. 6.

8. Is qui exequitur mandatum, non debet excedere finem mandati: ut ecce, si quis usque ad centum aureos mandaverit tibi ut fundum emeres, vel ut pro Titio spunderes, neque pluris emere debes, neque in ampliorem pecuniam fidejubere; alioquin non habebis cum eo mandati actionem, adeo quidem ut Sabino et Cassio placuerit, etiamsi usque ad centum aureos cum eo agere velis, inutiliter te acturum. Diversae scholae auctores recte usque ad centum aureos te acturum existimant, quae sententia sane benignior est. Quod si minoris emeris, habebis scilicet cum eo actionem; quoniam qui mandat ut sibi centum aureorum fundus emeretur, is utique mandasse intelligitur ut minoris, si possit, emeretur.

8. A mandatary must not exceed the limits of the mandate; for instance, if a mandator bids you buy land or become surety for Titius up to the amount of a hundred aurei, you must not exceed this sum in making the purchase or becoming surety, otherwise you will not have an action mandati; so much so, that Sabinus and Cassius thought that even if you limited your action to a hundred aurei, you would bring it in vain. The authors of the opposite school think that you may rightly bring an action limited to a hundred aurei, and this opinion is doubtless the more favourable. If you lay out less on the purchase, you can certainly bring an action against the mandator; for a person who gives a mandate that an estate shall be bought for him at the price of a hundred aurei, is understood to mean that it should be bought for less if possible.

Gai. iii. 161; D. xvii. 1. 3. 2; D. xvii. 1. 4, 5.

*Qui excessit, aliud quid facere videtur.* (D. xvii. 1. 5.) Sabinus, in giving the opinion mentioned in the text, insisted very rigorously on the effect of the thing done being *aliud quid.*

9. Recte quoque mandatum contractum, si dum adhuc integra res sit, revocatum fuerit, evanescit.

9. The mandate, although validly formed, is extinguished, if before it has been executed it is revoked.

Gai. iii. 159.

10. Item si adhuc integro mandato mors alterius interveniat, id est, vel ejus qui mandaverit, vel illius qui mandatum susceperit, solvitur mandatum; sed utilitatis causa receptum est, si eo mortuo qui tibi mandaverat, tu ignorans eum decessisse executus fueris mandatum, posse te agere mandati actione; alioquin justa et probabilis ignorantia tibi damnum afferet. Et huic simile est quod placuit, si debitores manumisso dispensatore Titii per ignorantiam liberto solverint, liberari eos; cum alioquin stricta juris ratione non possent liberari, quia alii solvissent quam cui solvere debuerint.

10. A mandate is also extinguished, if, before it is executed, the mandator or mandatary dies. But motives of convenience have given rise to the decision, that if, after the death of the mandatary, you, in ignorance of his decease, execute the mandate, you may bring an action mandati: otherwise you would be prejudiced by what was allowable and natural ignorance. Similarly it has been decided that, if debtors make a payment to the steward of Titus, after he has been enfranchised, in ignorance of his enfranchisement, they are freed from their obligation, although, in strict law, they could not be freed, as they have made the payment to a person other than him to whom they ought to have made it.

Gai. iii. 160.

*Manumisso.*  It would be the same if the slave had not
been enfranchised, but had been sold, or had his office of
*dispensator* taken from him, without the knowledge of the
debtors.  (D. xlvi. 3. 51.)

11. Mandatum non suscipere cuilibet liberum est, susceptum autem
consummandum est, aut quampri-
mum renuntiandum, ut per semetipsum aut per alium eundem rem
mandator exequatur; nam nisi ita
renuntiatur ut integra causa man-
datori reservetur eandem rem ex-
plicandi, nihilominus mandati actio
locum habet, nisi justa causa intercessit aut non renuntiandi aut in-
tempestive renuntiandi.

11. Every one is free to refuse accepting a mandate, but if it is once
accepted, it must be executed, or else
renounced soon enough to permit the
mandator executing it himself or
through another.  For, unless the
renunciation is made so that the
mandator is still in a position to do
this, an action *mandati* may be
brought in spite of the renunciation
of the mandatary, unless some good
reason has prevented him making the
renunciation, or making it within a
proper time.

D. xvii. 1. 22. 11.

*Nisi justa causa.*  For example, a sudden and serious illness, a deadly enmity springing up between the *mandator*
and the *mandatarius*, or the insolvency of the former.  (D.
xvii. 1. 23.)

12. Mandatum et in diem dif-
ferri, et sub conditione fieri potest.

12. A mandate may be made to
take effect from a particular time, or
may be made conditionally.

D. xvii. 1. 1. 3.

13. In summa, sciendum est mandatum, nisi gratuitum sit, in aliam
formam negotii cadere, nam mercede constituta incipit locatio et
conductio esse.  Et, ut generaliter
dixerimus, quibus casibus sine mercede suscepto officio mandati aut
depositi contrahitur negotium, iis
casibus interveniente mercede locatio et conductio contrahi intelligitur; et ideo si fulloni polienda
curandave vestimenta dederis, aut
sarcinatori sarcienda, nulla mercede
constituta neque promissa, mandati
competit actio.

13. Lastly, it may be observed,
that unless a mandate is gratuitous,
it will take the form of some other
contract, for, if a price is fixed on, it
is a contract letting to hire.  And
generally we may say, that in every
case in which, whenever the duty
being undertaken without pay, there
is a contract of mandate or deposit,
in every such case, if pay is received,
the contract is one of letting to hire.
If, therefore, a person gives his
clothes to a fuller to be cleaned, or
to a tailor to be mended, without any
pay being agreed on or promised, an
action *mandati* may be brought.

Gai. ii. 162; D. xvii. 1. 1. 4.

Although the execution of the *mandatum* was necessarily
gratuitous, yet, without making the contract a *locatio conductio*, a mandator might offer a reward to the *mandatarius*,

not exactly in payment of, but in gratitude for, his services.
Such a recompense was called a *honorarium*, a term that was
especially applied to the recompense offered to those who
exercised the liberal professions, such as philosophers, rhetoricians, physicians, advocates, &c. These *honoraria* could
not be made the subject of an action; but the magistrate,
prætor, or præses of the province pronounced *extra ordinem*
(see Introd. sec. 108) whether they were due and what was
the proper amount. (D. L. 13. 1.)

## Tit. XXVII. DE OBLIGATIONIBUS QUASI EX CONTRACTU.

Post genera contractum enume-
rata, dispiciamus etiam de iis obligationibus quæ non proprie quidem
ex contracto nasci intelliguntur;
sed tamen, quia non ex maleficio
substantiam capiunt, quasi ex contractu nasci videntur.

Having enumerated the different
kinds of contracts, let us treat of
those obligations which do not spring,
properly speaking, from a contract,
but yet, as they do not take their
origin from a delict, seem to arise, as
it were, from a contract.

If obligations were to be considered as always arising either
*ex contractu*, or *ex delicto*, one man could only be bound to
another in one of two ways; either by a mutual exercise of
will he had entered into an agreement with him, or he had
done him some injury which he ought to repair. But there
were many instances in which justice required that he should
be considered bound, where no contract had been made, and
where nothing to which the law gave the technical term of
*delictum* had been committed. Such cases, however, if separately examined, would approach more nearly either to an
*obligatio e contractu* or to one *e delicto*. If it more nearly
resembled the former, the binding tie was called an *obligatio
quasi e contractu*; if the latter, it was called an *obligatio
quasi e delicto*. (See Introd. sec. 87.)
The leading distinction between obligations *e contractu* and
those *quasi e contractu* is, that in the former one person
chooses to bind himself to another, in the latter he is placed
in such circumstances that he is thereby bound to another.
To take, for instance, the examples given in the Title: if I
take upon me the management of my neighbour's affairs,
become tutor, have things in common with others who are yet
not my partners, accept an inheritance, or receive money not
due to me, the mere fact of my so conducting myself imposes
on me certain duties which the law will force me to fulfil. Of

course, if I make an express agreement in any of these cases, I am then bound by the agreement, and not by the circumstances of my position. It is only in the absence of any agreement that I am bound by an *obligatio quasi e contractu.* An *obligatio quasi e contractu* does not rest on any contract at all; it rests on a fact or event, but there is an analogy between a contract and the kind of fact or events which give rise to an *obligatio quasi e contractu,* for they both create rights *in personam.* (See Austin, *Province of Jurisprudence Determined,* Appendix xL.)

1. Igitur cum quis absentis negotia gesserit, ultro citroque inter eos nascuntur actiones quae appellantur negotiorum gestorum; sed domino quidem rei gestae adversus eum qui gessit, directa competit actio, negotiorum autem gestori contraria. Quae ex nullo contractu proprie nasci manifestum est; quippe ita nascuntur istae actiones, si sine mandato quisque alienis negotiis gerendis se obtulerit, ex qua causa ii quorum negotiis gesta fuerint, etiam ignorantes obligantur. Idque utilitatis causa receptum est, ne absentium qui subita festinatione coacti, nulli demandata negotiorum suorum administratione, peregre profecti essent, desererentur negotia: quae sane nemo curaturus esset, si de eo quod quis impendisset, nullam habiturus esset actionem. Sicut autem is qui utiliter gesserit negotia, habet obligatum dominum negotiorum, ita et e contra iste quoque tenetur ut administrationis rationem reddat: quo casu ad exactissimam quisque diligentiam compellitur reddere rationem, nec sufficit talem diligentiam adhibuisse qualem suis rebus adhibere soleret, si modo alius diligentior commodius administraturus esset negotia.

1. Thus, if a person has managed the affairs of another in his absence, they have reciprocally actions *negotiorum gestorum,* the action belonging to the owner against him who has managed his affairs, being an *actio directa,* and the action given to this person against the owner being an *actio contraria.* It is evident that these actions cannot properly be said to arise from a contract, for they arise only when one person has, without receiving a mandate, taken upon himself the management of the affairs of another, and consequently those whose affairs are thus managed, are bound by an obligation, even without their knowing it. It is from motives of convenience that this has been admitted, to prevent the entire neglect of the affairs of absent persons, who may be forced to depart in haste, without having entrusted the management to any one; and certainly no one would pay any attention to them, unless he could recover by action any expenses he might be put to. On the other hand, just as he who has advantageously managed the affairs of another, makes this person liable to him by an obligation, so he himself is bound to render an account of his management. And the standard which he is bound to observe in rendering an account, is that of the most exact diligence, nor is it sufficient that he should use such diligence as he employs in the management of his own affairs, that is, if it is possible a person of greater diligence could manage the affairs of the absent person better.

D. iii. 5. 2; D. xliv. 7. 5; C. ii. 18. 20.

*Etiam ignorantes.*   If the owners had known of the part taken in the management of their affairs, there would have been a *mandatum lucitum.*

2. Tutores quoque qui tutelæ judicio tenentur, non proprie ex contractu obligati intelliguntur(nullum enim negotium inter tutorem et pupillum contrahitur) ; sed quia sane non ex maleficio tenentur, quasi ex contractu teneri videntur.  Et hæc autem casu mutuæ sunt actiones: non tantum enim pupillus cum tutore habet tutelæ actionem, sed ex contrario tutor cum pupillo habet contrariam tutelæ, si vel impenderit aliquid in rem pupilli, vel pro eo fuerit obligatus, aut rem suam creditoribus ejus obligaverit.

2. Tutors, again, who are liable to the action *tutelæ*, are not, properly speaking, bound by a contract, for there is no contract made between the tutor and the pupil, but as they are certainly not bound by a delict, they seem to be bound *quasi ex contractu.*  In this case, too, there are reciprocal actions, for not only has the pupil an action *tutelæ* against the tutor, but, in his turn, the tutor has an *actio contraria tutelæ* against the pupil, if he has incurred any expenses in managing the pupil's property, or has entered into an obligation for him, or given his own property as security to the pupil's creditors.

D. xliv. 7. 5. 1.

We should add here the corresponding case of the curator.

His *negotiorum gestio* did not give rise to a special action, but to the action *negotiorum gestorum contrarius,* which he could avail himself of to reimburse himself for all reasonable expenses.  (D. iii. 5. 3. 5.)

*Quasi ex contractu teneri videntur.*  The exact translation would be, 'seem to be bound by a tie analogous to that by which persons are bound under contracts;' but as this is too long a phrase to repeat every time the words *quasi ex contractu* occur, the Latin has been retained in the translation.

3. Item si inter aliquos communis sit res sine societate, veluti quod pariter eis legata donatave esset, et alter eorum alteri ideo teneatur communi dividundo judicio, quod solus fructus ex ea re perceperit, aut quod in eam rem solus necessarias impensas fecerit, non intelligitur proprie ex contractu obligatus, quippe nihil inter se contraxerunt; sed quia non ex maleficio tenetur, quasi ex contractu teneri videtur.

3. So, again, if a thing is common to two or more persons, without there being any partnership between them, as, for instance, if they have received a joint legacy or gift, and one of them is liable to the other by an action *communi dividundo,* because he alone has enjoyed the fruits of the thing, or because the other has incurred expenses necessary for the thing, he cannot be said to be bound by a contract, for no contract has been made ; but as he is not bound by a delict, he is said to be bound by something analogous to a contract.

D. xvii. 2. 31. 34.

*Necessarias impensas.*  Useful expenses, and not merely necessary ones, could be recovered.  (D. x. 3. 6. 3.)

4. Idem juris est de eo qui coheredi suo familiæ erciscundæ judicio ex his causis obligatus est.

4. It is the same with regard to a person who is bound to his heir by an action *familiæ erciscundæ*.

D. xviL 2. 34.

The *actio familiæ erciscundæ* was that by which any one *heres* applied to the judge to make a fair division of the inheritance.

5. Heres quoque legatorum nomine non proprie ex contractu obligatus intelligitur (neque enim cum herede, neque cum defuncto ullum negotium legatarius gessisse proprie dici potest); et tamen quia ex maleficio non est obligatus heres, quasi ex contractu debere intelligitur.

5. The heir, too, is not bound to the legatee by a contract, for the legatee cannot be said to have made a contract with the heir or with the deceased; and yet, as the heir is not bound by a delict, he seems to be bound *quasi ex contractu*.

D. xliv. 7. 5. 2.

The circumstance of accepting the inheritance imposed on the heir the obligation of carrying out the testator's wishes, and this he was compelled to do by the *actio ex testamento.* If a particular thing were given as a legacy, the legatee would also be able to bring a *vindicatio*, and might exercise his choice between the personal and the real action.

6. Item is cui quis per errorem non debitum solvit, quasi ex contractu debere videtur. Ideo enim non intelligitur proprie ex contractu obligatus, ut si certiorem rationem requiramur, magis (ut supra diximus) ex distractu quam ex contractu possit dici obligatus esse: nam qui solvendi animo pecuniam dat, in hoc dare videtur ut distrahat potius negotium, quam contrahat; sed tamen perinde is qui accepit obligatur, ac si mutuum illi daretur, et ideo condictione tenetur.

6. A person to whom money not due has been paid by mistake, is bound *quasi ex contractu.* For so far is he from being bound by a contract, that, to reason strictly, we may say, as we have said before, that he is bound rather by the dissolution than by the formation of a contract; for a payment is generally made to dissolve, not to form, a contract; and yet he who receives it in the case we have mentioned is bound exactly as if it had been given him as a *mutuum,* and is therefore liable to a *condictio.*

D. xliv. 7. 8. 3.

If the person who paid what was not due was one who, like a pupil or madman, had not legally the power of passing the property in what he gave, no property in the thing paid passed by the transfer, and the tutor or curator recovered it by a *vindicatio,* unless the thing ceased to exist, and then recourse was had to a *condictio indebiti* ; but if he had this power, the property was transferred by the delivery, and he could not recover the thing itself but could only bring a *condictio,* in which he claimed that the defendant should re-transfer the thing, given in payment (*dare oportere.*)

If a person knowingly made a payment not due, he could not recover what he paid, as the payment was treated as a gift; nor could he, if he paid what was naturally, though not legally, due.

The word 'pay,' 'solvo,' must be taken in a much more extended sense than the payment of money. It must be considered as including anything given to or done for another.

7. Ex quibusdam tamen causis repeti non potest quod per errorem non debitum solutum sit; namque definierunt veteres, ex quibus causis infidiando lis crescit, ex iis causis non debitum solutum repeti non posse, veluti ex lege Aquilia, item ex legata. Quod veteres quidem in iis legatis locum habere voluerunt, quæ certa constituta per damnationem cuicumque legata fuerant. Nostra autem constitutio, cum unam naturam omnibus legatis et fideicommissis indulsit, hujusmodi augmentum in omnibus legatis et fideicommissis extendi voluit; sed non omnibus legatariis præbuit, sed tantummodo in iis legatis et fideicommissis quæ sacrosanctis ecclesiis et cæteris venerabilibus locis, quæ religionis vel pietatis intuitu honorificantur, derelicta sunt. Quæ, si indebita solvantur, non repetuntur.

7. In some cases, however, money paid by mistake cannot be recovered; the ancients have decided that this is so, in cases in which the amount recovered is doubled if the liability is denied; as, for instance, in actions brought under the lex Aquilia, or with respect to a legacy. The rule was only applied by the ancients, in the case of legacies, where a fixed sum was given per damnationem. But our constitution, which has placed all legacies and fideicommissa on the same footing, has extended to all the effect of denial in doubling the amount required. It has not, however, given it in behalf of all legatees, but only in the case of legacies and fideicommissa left to churches and other holy places; such legacies, although paid when not due, cannot be recovered.

GAI. ii. 283; iv. 9. 171; C. iv. 5. 4; C. 1. 2. 23.

In all cases where by denying his liability the person liable might have an increased amount ultimately recovered against him, it was considered that paying the thing for which he was, or for which he thought himself, liable, was but a mode of escaping from paying a penalty, and that it was paid in order to attain security. If, therefore, it was discovered that the thing need not have been paid, yet, as the person who paid it had paid it to purchase security, he could not recover it back.

*Nostra constitutio.* This constitution is not to be found in the Code, but we have provisions in the Code bearing on the subject. (See C. vi. 43. 2. 1–3.)

*Ceteris venerabilibus locis.* Such, for instance, as monasteries, asylums for strangers, orphans, the aged, &c. (C. i. 2. 23.)

## Tit. XXVIII.  PER QUAS PERSONAS NOBIS OBLIGATIO ACQUIRITUR.

Expositis generibus obligationum quae ex contractu vel quasi ex contractu nascuntur, admonendi sumus acquiri nobis, non solum per nosmetipsos, sed etiam per eas personas quae in nostra potestate sunt, veluti per servos et filios nostros; ut tamen quod per servos quidem nobis acquiritur, totum nostrum fiat; quod autem per liberos quos in potestate habemus, ex obligatione fuerit acquisitum, hoc dividatur secundum imaginem rerum proprietatis et ususfructus quam nostra discrevit constitutio: ut quod ab actione commodum perveniat, hujus ususfructum quidem habeat pater, proprietas autem filio servetur, scilicet patre actionem movente secundum novellae nostrae constitutionis divisionem.

After having gone through the different kinds of obligations which arise from a contract, or arise quasi ex contractu, we may observe that we may acquire an obligation, not only by ourselves, but also by those who are in our power, as our slaves or children. But there is this distinction in acquiring by slaves or by children, that what is acquired for us by our slaves is entirely ours, while the benefit of the obligation acquired by our children is divided in the same way as our constitution has laid down with respect to the ownership and usufruct of things. Thus, of all that is gained by an action, the father will have the usufruct, and the ownership will be reserved for the son, that is to say, when the action is brought by the father in conformity with what is laid down by our new constitution.

Gai. iii. 103; C. vi. 61. 6. 3.

By acquiring an obligation is meant that we become creditors, and have a right to the action necessary to enforce the obligation.

As to the division of the usufruct and ownership, see Bk. ii. Tit. 9. 1. It is the object of the obligation, it may be observed, not the obligation itself, that is thus divided between the father and the son. Only the father could bring the action to enforce the obligation. (C. vi. 61. 1. 3.)

1. Item per liberos homines et alienos servos quos bona fide possidemus, acquiritur nobis; sed tantum ex duabus causis, id est, si quid ex operibus suis vel ex re nostra acquirant.

1. An obligation is also acquired for us by freemen, and by slaves belonging to others, whom we possess bona fide, but only in two cases, namely, when it arises from their labours, or from something belonging to us.

Gai. iii. 104.

See Bk. ii. Tit. 9. 4.

2. Per eum quoque servum in quo usumfructum vel usum habemus, similiter ex duabus istis causis nobis acquiritur.

2. It is equally acquired for us in the same two cases by a slave of whom we have the usufruct or use.

Gai. iii. 105; D. vii. 8. 14.

See Bk. ii. Tit. 9, 4.

In the case of a slave of whom we have only the use, we can only acquire when the two cases unite, i.e. when his labour is expended on something that is our property, for we cannot derive any benefit from his labour expended elsewhere.

3. Communem servum pro domini parte dominis acquirere certum est, excepto eo quo l uni nominatim stipulando ant per traditionem accipiendo, illi soli acquirit: veluti cum ita stipulatur, Titio domino meo dare spondes? Sed si unius domini jussu servus fuerit stipulatus, licet antea dubitabatur, tamen post nostram decisionem res expedita est, ut illi tantum acquirat qui hoc ei facere jussit, ut supra dictum est.

3. A slave held in common, undoubtedly acquires for his different masters in proportion to their interests in him, excepting that, in stipulating or receiving by tradition for one only, whom he mentions by name, he acquires only for this one; for instance, if he stipulates thus, 'Do you engage to give to Titius my master?' But if the slave has stipulated by order of one master only, in spite of former doubts, there is no question since our constitution, but that he acquires, as we have already said, for him alone who has given him the order.

Gai. iii. 107; C. iv. 27, 3.

## Tit. XXIX. QUIBUS MODIS OBLIGATIO TOLLITUR.

Tollitur autem omnis obligatio solutione ejus quod debetur, vel si quis consentiente creditore aliud pro alio solverit. Nec tamen interest quis solvat, utrum ipse qui debet, an alius pro eo: liberatur enim et alio solvente, sive sciente debitore sive ignorante vel invito solutio fiat. Item si reus solverit, etiam si qui pro eo intervenerunt, liberantur. Idem ex contrario contingit, si fidejussor solverit: non enim solus ipse liberatur, sed etiam reus.

Every obligation is dissolved by the payment of the thing due, or of something else given in its place with the consent of the creditor. And it makes no difference whether it is the creditor himself who pays, or some one else for him; for the debtor is freed from the obligation, if payment is made by a third person, and that either with or without the knowledge of the debtor, or even against his will. If the debtor pays, all those who have become surety for him are thereby freed, just as if a surety pays, not only he himself is freed, but the principal is freed also.

Gai. iii. 168; D. xlvi. 3. 53; D. xlvi. 3. 38. 2; D. xlvi. 3. 43; D. xlvi. 1. 60.

We now pass to considering how an obligation once formed may be dissolved. Solvere, to unloose, dissolve the tie, is the appropriate term for the process, in whatever way it may be accomplished—Solutionis verbum pertinet ad omnem liberationem quoquo modo factam (D. xlvii. 3. 54)—although most

II

generally applied to the payment of money, as the mode by which contracts are usually terminated. It is by a slight extension of the strict use of the word that a person was said not *solvere obligationem*, but *solvere rem* or *pecuniam*.

The civil law, which imposed forms on the formation of a contract, imposed corresponding forms on its dissolution. And when these were fulfilled, the debtor was said to be freed from his obligation '*ipso jure*.' In later times, in cases where these forms had not been gone through, but yet equity demanded that the debtor should he considered free, the prætor allowed him to repel, by an exception, the creditor who sued him; and it has thence been said, '*obligatio aut ipso jure, aut per exceptionem tollitur*.'

Of course, in every stage of the law, payment put an end to the contract. The claims of the contracting parties were satisfied, and nothing more remained to he done. But, supposing payment were not made, but one of the parties was willing to release the other, or one party could claim, for some reason, to be released, certain forms had been entered into, which could not he made of no effect by the mere consent of the parties. Such forms were too solemn in the eyes of the law to lose their power unless other forms equally solemn were gone through. Accordingly, in every case where no real payment was made, there was what Gaius calls an *imaginaria solutio*, varying in the method in which it was made according to the forms with which the contract had been formed.

If, for instance, the contract had been formed *per œs et libram*, not less than five witnesses and a *libripens* were called together. The debtor struck the scale with a piece of money and gave it to the creditor in the name of the whole sum owing. (GAI. iii. 174.) This form was also adopted in cases where payment of a legacy given *per damnationem* was remitted, probably because the testament was itself supposed to he made *per œs et libram*; and also in cases where payment of money due by a judicial sentence was remitted, probably because the most formal mode of imaginary payment was adopted when the money was due in a way which the law considered as specially solemn. (GAI. iii. 175.) This form of imaginary payment was also applicable wherever anything certain of those things which '*pondere, numero, mensurave constant*' was due.

If the contract had been made '*verbis*,' the debtor asked the creditor if he held what wa due, as received, '*Quod ego tibi promisi, habesne acceptum?*' The creditor answered that he did, '*Habeo*.' The creditor was said, '*acceptum ferre*,' and the process was called '*acce tilatio*.' (See next paragr.)

If the contract had been made '*literis*,' the debtor probably entered on his *tabulæ* the expenditure (*expensilatio*) of the sum due, with the consent of the creditor, but we cannot learn anything from Gaius on the subject.

If the contract had been made *re*, the mere return of the thing was a sufficient sign that the contract was at an end. There was a visible act, and the whole object of the forms by which contracts were made and dissolved, was to substitute visible acts for mere expressions of consent. Where the contract as belonging to the *jus gentium*, could be made merely by consent, it could also be dissolved by consent. (See paragr. 4.)

1. Item per acceptilationem tollitur obligatio. Est autem acceptilatio imaginaria solutio: quod enim ex verborum obligatione Titio debetur, id si velit Titius remittere, poterit sic fieri ut patiatur hæc verba debitorem dicere, Quod ego tibi promisi habesne acceptum? et Titius respondeat, Habeo. Sed et Græce potest acceptum fieri, dummodo sic fiat, ut Latinis verbis solet: ἔχεις λαβὼν δηνάρια τόσα; ἔχω λαβών. Quo genere, ut diximus, tantum eæ solvuntur obligationes quæ ex verbis consistant, non etiam cæteræ: consentaneum enim visum est, verbis factam obligationem aliis possе verbis dissolvi. Sed et id quod alia ex causa debetur, potest in stipulationem deduci et per acceptilationem dissolvi. Sicut autem quod debetur, pro parte recte solvitur, ita in partem debiti acceptilatio fieri potest.

1. An obligation is also put an end to by acceptilation. This is an imaginary payment, for if Titius wishes to remit payment of that which is due to him by a verbal contract, he can do so by permitting the debtor to put to him the following question, 'Do you acknowledge to have received that which I promised you?' Titius then answering, 'I do.' The acknowledgment may also be made in corresponding Greek words, ἔχεις λαβὼν δηνάρια τόσα; ἔχω λαβών. In this way verbal contracts are dissolved, but not contracts made in other ways: it seemed natural that an obligation formed by words should be dissolved by words; but anything due by any other kind of contract may be made the subject of a stipulation, and the debtor be freed by acceptilation. And as part of a debt may be paid, so acceptilation may be made of a part only.

GAL. iii. 100, 170. 172; D. xlvi. 4. 8. 4; D. xlvi. 4. 9.

Properly the *acceptilatio* only operated as a release when the contract had been made *verbis*, but it was held, in all cases, to contain by implication a pact or agreement not to sue, and, therefore, an *exceptio* could be grounded on it to repel the creditor who had entered into it. *Si acceptilatio inutilis fuit, tacita pactione id acturus videtur, ne peteretur.* (D. ii. 14. 27. 9.) The jurists, however, found a means of making the *acceptilatio* extend to every kind of contract. It was looked on as a stipulation which operated as a novation of the old contract, that is, which did away with the former contract, and substituted a new one in its place.

2. Est prodita stipulatio quæ vulgo Aquiliana appellatur, per quam stipulationem contingit ut omnium rerum obligatio in stipulatum deducatur, et ea per acceptilationem tollatur; stipulatio enim Aquiliana novat omnes obligationes, et a Gallo Aquilio ita composita est: 'Quicquid te mihi ex quacumque causa dare facere oportet oportebit, præsens in diemve, quarumque rerum mihi tecum actio, quæque adversus te petitio vel adversus te persecutio est eritve, quodve tu meum habes, tenes possidesve, dolove malo fecisti quominus possideas: quanti quæque earum, rerum res erit,' tantam pecuniam dari stipulatus est Aulus Agerius; spopondit Numerius Negidius. Item ex diverso Numerius Negidius interrogavit Aulum Agerium: 'Quicquid tibi hodierno die per Aquilianam stipulationem spopondi, id omne habesne acceptum?' respondit Aulus Agerius: 'Habeo, acceptumque tuli.'

2. A stipulation has been invented, commonly called the Aquilian, by which every obligation, whatever may be the thing it concerns, is put into the form of a stipulation, and afterwards dissolved by acceptilation. This Aquilian stipulation effects a novation of all obligations, and was framed in the following terms by Gallus Aquilius:—'Whatever for any cause you are or shall be bound to give or do for me, either now or at a future day, everything for which I have or shall have against you, actions, personal or real, or right to have recourse to the extraordinaria judicia of the magistrate; everything of mine which you have, hold, or possess, or which you only do not possess through some wilful fault of your own, whatever shall be the value of all these things,' so much Aulus Agerius stipulated should be given him in money, and Numerius Negidius engaged to give it: on the other hand, Numerius Negidius put to Aulus Agerius the question, 'All that I have promised you to-day by the Aquilian stipulation, do you acknowledge it as received?' and Aulus Agerius answered that he did acknowledge it.

D. ii. 15. 4; D. xlvi. 4. 18. 1.

This Aquilius Gallus was the friend of Cicero, whose colleague he was in the prætorship. (B.C. 65.) He was the pupil of Mucius, and the teacher of Sulpicius, and is mentioned in the Digest (I. 2. 2. 42) as of great authority with the people. He is said to have devised a means by which *posthumi sui* might be instituted (D. xxviii. 2. 29); and Cicero informs us that he was also the author of certain formulæ in the actions of theft. (*De Off.* iii. 14.)

We may remark with what care and forethought Aquilius Gallus has made his formula applicable to all possible cases. '*Causa*' is the general expression. '*Oportet, oportebit*' embrace the present and the future. '*Præsens in diemve*' (most texts add, '*aut sub conditione*') refer to what are termed the 'modalities' to which contracts are liable. '*Actio*' is the '*actio in personam*;' '*petitio*' is the '*actio in rem*;' '*persecutio*' is the extraordinary proceeding before a magistrate; '*habes*' refers to '*vindicatio*;' '*tenes*' to physical detention; '*possides*' to civil possession. The expression,

' *dolove malo fecisti quominus possideas*' was added to express the obligation which bound a person who had fraudulently
destroyed a thing in his possession to prevent the owner
reclaiming it. The *stipulatio Aquiliana* was equally applicable if the object was to effect a novation intended to operate
as the foundation of a new contract to be really fulfilled by
the parties. (D. ii. 15. 2. and 9. 2.)

3. Praeterea novatione tollitur
obligatio, veluti si id quod tu Seio
debeas, a Titio dari stipulatus sit;
nam interveniu nova persona nova
nascitur obligatio et prima tollitur
translata in posteriorem; adeo ut
interdum, licet posterior stipulatio
inutilis sit, tamen prima novationis
jure tollatur, veluti si id quod tu
Titio debebas, a pupillo sine tutoris
auctoritate stipulatus fueris. Quo
casu nec amittitur, nam et prior
debitor liberatur, et posterior obligatio nulla est. Non idem Juris
est, si a servo quis fuerit stipulatus;
nam tunc prior perinde obligatus
manet, ac si postea nulli stipulatus
fuisset. Sed si eadem persona sit
a qua postea stipularis, ita demum
novatio fit, si quid in posteriore
stipulatione novi sit, forte si conditio aut dies aut fid-jussor adjiciatur aut detrahatur. Quod autem
diximus, si conditio adjiciatur novationem fieri, sic intelligi oportet ut
ita dicam factam novationem si
conditio extiterit; alioquin si defecerit, durat prior obligatio. Sed
cum hoc quidem inter veteres con-
stabat, tunc fieri novationem cum
novandi animo in secundam obligationem itum fuerat; per hoc
autem dubium erat, quando novandi animo videretur hoc fieri,
et quasdam de hoc praesump-
tiones alii in aliis casibus intro-
ducebant. Ideo nostra processit
constitutio quae apertissimo definivit, tunc solum novationem fieri
quoties hoc ipsum inter con-
trahentes expressum fuerit, quod
propter novationem prioris obligationis convenerunt; alioquin manere
et pristinam obligationem, et secundam ei accedere, ut maneat ex
utraque causa obligatio secundum

3. An obligation is also dissolved
by novation, as for instance, if Seius
stipulates from Titius for that which
is due to Seius from you. For by
the intervention of a new debtor a
new obligation arises, and the former
obligation is extinguished by being
transferred into the latter; so much
so, that it may happen, that although
the latter stipulation is void, yet the
former, by the effect of the novation,
ceases to exist; as for instance, if
Titius stipulates from a pupil not
authorized by his tutor, for a debt
due to Titius from you. In this case
Titius loses his whole claim, for the
first debtor is freed, and the second
obligation is void. But the case is
different, if it is a slave from whom
he stipulates, for then the original
debtor remains bound as if the subsequent stipulation had never been
made. But if it is the original debtor
himself from whom you make the
second stipulation, there will be no
novation, unless the subsequent stipulation contains something new, as
for instance, the addition or suppression of a condition, a term, or a
surety. In saying that if a condition
is added there is a novation, we must
be understood to mean that the novation will take place if the condition
be accomplished, but that if it be not
accomplished, the former obligation
remains binding. The ancients were
of opinion that the novation only
took place when the second obligation was entered into for the purpose
of making the novation, and doubts
consequently arose as to the existence of this intention, and different
presumptions were laid down by
those who treated the subject according to the different cases they
had to settle. In consequence, our

nostræ constitutionis definitionem, quam licet ex ipsius lectione apertius cognoscere.

constitution was published, in which it was clearly decided that novation shall only take place when the contracting parties have expressly declared that their object in making the new contract is to extinguish the old one; otherwise the former obligation will remain binding, while the second is added to it, so that each contract will give rise to an obligation still in force, according to the provisions of our constitution, which may be more fully learnt by reading the constitution itself.

Gai. lii. 176, 177. 170; D. xlvi. 2. 0. 8. 1, and foll.; C. viii. 41. 8.

Novation is the dissolution of one obligation by the formation of another. Ulpian says, ' *Novatio est prioris debiti in aliam obligationem transfusio atque translatio: hoc est, cum ex præcedente causa ita nova constituatur, ut prior perimatur. Novatio enim a novo nomen accepit, et a nova obligatione.* (D. xlvi. 2. 1.)

Although every kind of contract could be superseded by a novation, it was not every kind of contract that could supersede a contract already existing. We may, in fact, say that it was necessary that the new contract should be a stipulation. No other mode of contracting was solemn enough, in the eyes of the law, to blot out an existing contract.

It was necessary that the obligation superseded should be existing at the time; but whether it were civil, prætorian, or natural, was immaterial. (D. xlvi. 2. 1, 2.) And it was also necessary that the stipulation which superseded it should be binding, either civilly or naturally. In the text we have two instances of contracts which are not binding, owing to the incapacity of the parties, one made with a pupil, and one with a slave, and a distinction is drawn between them. The stipulation made with the pupil is a stipulation, though only one binding naturally: the pupil is a Roman citizen, and can pronounce the word *spondeo*; but a stipulation made with a slave, except when the slave speaks merely as the mouthpiece of his master, is no stipulation at all. The slave cannot use the words of the formulary. There is no contract *verbis* to supersede the existing obligation.

By a novation a new debtor might be substituted, even without the consent of the original debtor. If it were done with the consent of the original debtor, the new debtor was termed *delegatus*, and the process *delegatio*. If it were done without his consent, the new debtor was termed the *expromissor*, and the process, *ex promissio*; but these terms, *expromissor* and *expromissio*, were also used in a wider sense, as implying the new debtor and the mode of contracting generally, without implying that the consent of the old debtor had not been given to the substitution.   (D. xiii. 7. 10.)

Of course, if both parties to the original contract were willing, a new creditor could he substituted as well as a new debtor, by a novation.

In the passage of Gaius (iii. 177) on which the text is based, it is said that if a sponsor were added, there was a new contract.   This was because a sponsor was obliged to be a party to the same contract as his principal ; and so after the principal had made his contract, no sponsor could he added as a party to it ; but a new contract was necessary.   *Sponsores* being obsolete, Justinian substitutes *fidejussor*, although *fidejussores* could be added at any time.

If the original contract were made in any other way than a stipulation, it could be superseded by a stipulation containing the same terms.   But if it were made by a stipulation, then, unless some alteration were made in it, the new stipulation would be, in fact, the old one, and there could he no *novatio*, unless some new term were added.   But suppose a new stipulation were made with a condition introduced into it, was the old stipulation extinguished at once by novation ?   The text lays down the general principle that it was not extinguished, as it is said in the Digest ( xlvi. 2. 14) *non statim fit novatio, sed tunc demum cum conditio extiterit*, the old contract endured until the condition was accomplished, and if the condition failed the old contract remained binding.   But some of the jurists said that this might be the intention of the parties in making the second contract, or it might not.   The question of novation was therefore a question of the intention of the parties in each particular case.   Justinian decides against this, and lays down in the text that, unless the parties expressly declare it to be their wish that the first contract shall be extinguished by the second, the first contract shall be considered as subsisting.

In personal actions something like novation took place at two points of the suit (GAI. iii. 180)—at the *litis contestatio* (see Introd. paragr. 105), and when judgment had been given.   After the *litis contestatio*, the plaintiff could sue in a fresh action on what was, at this period of the suit, ascertained to be his legal position, but not on the contract itself.   After judgment was given, he could sue on the judgment.   But all the beneficial accessories of the original contract were continued on to the new—such, for instance, as pledges given in security,

and so this juridical novation did not, like novation proper,
quite supersede the original contract. (D. xlvi. 2. 29.)

4. Hoc amplius, eae obligationes
quae consensu contrahuntur, contraria voluntate dissolvuntur; nam
si Titius et Seius inter se consen-
serint, ut fundum Tusculanum
emptum Seius haberet centum aureorum, deinde re nondum secuta,
id est, neque pretio soluto neque
fundo tradito, placuerit inter eos ut
discederetur ab ea emptione et venditione, invicem liberantur. Idem
est in conductione et locatione, et
in omnibus contractibus qui ex
consensu descendunt.

4. Those obligations which are
formed by consent alone, are dissolved
by the expression of a contrary wish.
If Titius and Seius have agreed that
Seius shall purchase an estate at
Tusculum for a hundred aurei, and
then, before the contract has been
executed, that is, before the price
has been paid, or delivery made of
the estate, they agree to abandon
the agreement for the sale, they are
mutually freed from their obligation.
It is the same in the contract of letting to hire, and in all other contracts
formed by consent alone.

D. xlvi. 3. 80; D. xviii. 5. 5. 1.

This paragraph must be understood with the limitation that
the contract could only be rescinded *integris omnibus*, i.e. if
each party could possibly be placed in the position he held before. The text rather loosely expresses this, by '*re nondum
secuta*.' If all things were not *integra*, but the parties agreed
to restore them, this would be a new contract extinguishing
the old contract by novation, not an extinction of the contract
by mere consent.

There were other modes by which a contract was dissolved,
as, if the subject of the contract being a thing certain perished
without the fault of any party, or if the qualities of debtor
and creditor were united in the same person, as, for instance, if
the debtor became heir of the creditor, which is termed *confusio*, or if one debt was set off against another (*compensatio*),
which, however, if the actions proper to the contract were
actions *stricti juris*, would only give rise to an exception, and
not to an extinction of the contract: in actions *bonae fidei*,
where equitable grounds of defence need not be stated in the
formula, the *compensatio* would be necessarily taken notice of,
and in such cases the contract may be said to have been really
put an end to by the *compensatio*. And there were also many
other things which, although they left the contract still subsisting, prevented an action being brought on it. These will be
treated of in the next Book under the head of Exceptions.

# LIBER QUARTUS.

## Tit. I. DE OBLIGATIONIBUS QUÆ EX DELICTO NASCUNTUR.

Cum expositum sit superiore libro de obligationibus ex contractu et quasi ex contractu, sequitur ut de obligationibus ex maleficio dispiciamus. Sed illæ quidem, ut suo loco tradidimus, in quatuor genera dividuntur: hæ vero unius generis sunt; nam omnes ex re nascuntur, id est, ex ipso maleficio, veluti ex furto aut rapina aut damno aut injuria.

As we have treated in the preceding Book of obligations arising *ex contractu* and *quasi ex contractu*, we have now to inquire into obligations arising *ex maleficio*. Of the obligations treated of in the last Book, there were, as we have said, four kinds; of those we are now to treat of, there is but one kind, for they all arise from the thing, that is, from the delict, as, for example, from theft, from robbery, or damage, or injury.

GAL. iii. 182; D. xliv. 7. 4.

This part of the Institutes only treats of *delicta* so far as they produce obligations and are the grounds of private actions. It is not the evil intent which makes an act a delict. Many acts done with evil intent are excluded, many done without are included in the number. Those acts only were delicts which had been characterized and provided against as such by the ancient civil legislation, and to which a particular action was attached. (See Introd. paragr. 88.) In this and the three following Titles we have the four principal kinds of delicts treated of, viz. *furtum, vi bona rapta, damni injuria,* and *injuriæ.*

All the obligations attached to delicts are said in the text *nasci ex re,* i.e. from the evil act or thing done *ex ipso maleficio,* to contrast them with the various modes in which obligations *e contractu* are formed.

*Ut de obligationibus ex maleficio dispiciamus.* Many texts read, *ut de obligationibus ex maleficio, et quasi ex*

| | |
|---|---|
| 1. Furtum est contrectatio rei fraudulosa, vel ipsius rei, vel etiam usus ejus possessionisve: quod lege naturali prohibitum est admittere. | 1. Theft is the fraudulent dealing with a thing itself, with its use, or its possession; an act which is prohibited by natural law. |

D. xlvii. 2. 1. 3.

The definition of theft includes the term *contrectatio rei*, to show that evil intent is not sufficient; there must be an actual touching or seizing of the thing: *fraudulosa*, to show that the thing must be seized with evil intent, and *rei, usus, possessionis*, to show the different interests in a thing that might be the subject of theft. It might seem that it would have made the definition more complete to have said *contrectatio rei alienæ*. Perhaps the word *alienæ* was left out because it was quite possible that the *dominus* or real owner of a thing should commit a theft in taking it from the possessor, as, for instance, in the case of a debtor stealing a thing given in pledge; and yet the *res* was scarcely *aliena* to the *dominus*.

Many texts, after the words *contrectatio fraudulosa*, add *lucri faciendi gratiâ*, i.e. with a design to profit by the act, whether the profit be that of gaining a benefit for one's self, or that of inflicting an injury on another. These words are found in the passage of the Digest (xlvii. 2. 1. 3), from which this definition of theft is taken, but the authority of the manuscripts seems against admitting them here.

Only things moveable could be the subject of theft. (D. xlvii. 2. 25.)

| | |
|---|---|
| 2. Furtum autem vel a furvo, id est nigro, dictum est, quod clam et obscure fit, et plerumque nocte; vel a fraude, vel a ferendo, id est auferendo, vel a Græco sermone, qui φῶρας appellant fures. Imo et Græci ἀπὸ τοῦ φέρειν φῶρας dixerunt. | 2. The word *furtum* comes either from *furvum*, which means 'black,' because it is committed secretly, and often in the night; or from *fraus*; or from *ferre*, that is, 'taking away,' or from the Greek word φῶρ, meaning a thief, which again comes from φέρειν, to carry away. |

D. xlvii. 2. 1.

| | |
|---|---|
| 3. Furtorum autem genera duo sunt, manifestum et nec manifestum: nam conceptum et oblatum species potius actionis sunt furto cohærentes, quam genera furtorum, sicut inferius apparebit. Manifestus fur est, quem Græci ἐπ' αὐτοφώρῳ appellant, nec solum is qui in furto deprehenditur, sed etiam is qui eo loco deprehenditur quo fit: veluti qui in domo furtum fecit, et nondum egressus januam deprehensus fuerit; et qui in oliveto olivarum aut in | 3. Of theft there are two kinds, theft manifest and theft not manifest; for the thefts termed *conceptum* and *oblatum* are rather kinds of actions attaching to theft than kinds of theft, as will appear below. A manifest thief is one whom the Greeks term ἐπ' αὐτοφώρῳ, being not only one taken in the fact, but also one taken in the place where the theft is committed; as, for example, before he has passed through the door of the house where he has com- |

vincto uvarum furtum fecit, quamdiu in oliveto aut vineto fur deprehensus sit. Imo ulterius furtum manifestum extendendum est, quamdiu eam rem fur tenens visus vel deprehensus fuerit, sive in publico sive in privato, vel a domino vel ab alio, antequam eo pervenerit quo perferre ac deponere rem destinasset; sed si pertulit quo destinavit, tametsi deprehendatur cum re furtiva, non est manifestus fur. Nec manifestum furtum quid sit, ex iis quae diximus intelligitur; nam quod manifestum non est, id scilicet nec manifestum est.

mitted a theft, or in a plantation of olives, or a vineyard where he has been stealing. We must also extend manifest theft to the case of a thief seen or seized by the owner or any one else in a public or private place, while still holding the thing he has stolen, before he has reached the place where he meant to take and deposit it. But if he once reaches his destination, although he is afterwards taken with the thing stolen on him, he is not a manifest thief. What we mean by a not manifest thief may be gathered from what we have said, for a theft, which is not a manifest theft, is a not manifest theft.

(Gai. iii. 183-185; D. xlvii. 2, 3; D. xlvii. 2. 5, pr. and 1.

The distinction between *furtum manifestum* and *nec manifestum* is found in the law of the Twelve Tables, which affixed to a *furtum manifestum* the penalty of death if committed by a slave, and the penalty of being given over as a slave to the person injured if the thefts were committed by a freeman; and attached to a *furtum nec manifestum* the penalty of double the value of the thing stolen, whether committed by a freeman or a slave. The praetor retained the penalty fixed in the latter case, but in the former altered the penalty to the payment of four times the value of the thing stolen, whether the theft was committed by a slave or a freeman. (Gai. iii. 189.)

Gaius tells us that the jurists were divided on the point of what it was that constituted a *furtum manifestum*; some thinking the thief must be taken in the act, some that he need only be taken on the spot, some that he need only be taken with the thing stolen on him before he had transported it to its destination (this is the opinion received in the text), and some that time and place were immaterial so that he were taken with the thing stolen on him. (Gai. iii. 184.)

4. Conceptum furtum dicitur, cum apud aliquem testibus praesentibus furtiva res quaesita et inventa sit; nam in eum propria actio constituta est, quamvis fur non sit, quae appellatur concepti. Oblatum furtum dicitur, cum res furtiva ab aliquo tibi oblata sit, eaque apud te concepta sit, utique si ea mente tibi data fuerit, ut apud te potius quam apud eum qui dedit, conciperetur; nam tibi apud quem conceptasit, propria

4. There is what is termed *conceptum furtum*, when a thing stolen has been sought and found in the presence of witnesses in any one's house, for although this person may not be the actual thief, he is liable to a special action termed *concepti*. There is what is termed *furtum oblatum*, if a thing stolen has been placed in your hands and then seized in your house; that is, if the person who placed it in your hands did so,

adversus enm qui obtulit, quamvis
fur non sit, constituta est actio quæ
appellatur oblati. Est etiam prohibiti furti actio adversus eum, qui
furtum quærere tertibus præsentibus volentem prohibuerit. Præterea
pœna constituitur edicto prætoris
per actionem furti non exhibiti, adversus eum qui furtivam rem apud
se quæsitam et inventam non exhi-
buit. Sed hæ actiones, id est, concepti et oblati et furti prohibiti, nec
non furti non exhibiti, in desuetudinem abierunt: cum enim requi-
sitio rei furtivæ hodie secundum
veterem observationem non fit, merito ex consequentia etiam præfatæ
actiones ab usu communi recesse-
runt, cum manifestissimum est,
quod omnes qui scientes rem furtivam susceperint et celaverint, furti
nec manifesti obnoxii sunt.

that it might be found rather in your
house than in his. For you, in
whose house it had been seized,
would have against him who placed
it in your hands, although he were
not the actual thief, a special action
termed *oblati*. There is also the
action *prohibiti furti* against a person
who prevents another who wishes to
seek for a thing stolen in the presence of witnesses; there is, too, by
means of the action *furti non exhibiti*,
a penalty provided by the edict of the
prætor against a person who has not
produced a thing stolen which has
been searched for and found in his
possession. But these actions, con-
*cepti, oblati, furti prohibiti,* and *furti
non exhibiti,* have fallen into disuse;
for search for things stolen is not
now made according to the ancient
practice, and therefore these actions
have naturally ceased to be in use, as
all who knowingly have received and
concealed a thing stolen are liable
to the action *furti nec manifesti*.

GAI. iii. 186–188.

To the *furtum conceptum* and the *furtum oblatum* a
penalty of triple the value of the thing stolen was affixed by
the Twelve Tables. To the *furtum prohibitum*, not noticed
in the Twelve Tables, a penalty of quadruple the value was
affixed by the prætor. (GAI. iii. 192.) The Twelve Tables
noticed a kind of *furtum conceptum* of which no mention is
made here; it was called *furtum lance licioque conceptum*.
The searcher entered the house of the supposed receiver,
having nothing on his person but a cincture (*licium*) round
his waist, and a plate (*lanx*) which he held with both his
hands, so that there could be no suspicion that he had brought
in with him the thing supposed to be stolen. If he then
found the thing in the house, the receiver was punished as if
he had committed a *furtum manifestum*. (GAI. iii. 192.)
This mode of search and the action founded on it were suppressed by the *lex Æbutia*. (AUL. GELL. *Noct. Att.* xvi. 10.)
The actions *furti concepti, oblati,* and *prohibiti,* were still
in use in the time of Gaius.

Ulpian (D. L., 16. 13) explains the meaning of the word
*pœna*. *Pœna* is the punishment of an offence, *noxæ vindicta*.
It is contrasted with *multa*. *Pœna* is a punishment imposed
by some general law, affecting possibly the *caput* and *existimatio* of the person punished. *Multa* is a fine, a money

fine in later law, a fine of cattle and sheep in earlier times (*pecuaria*).

5. Prona manifesti furti, quadrupli est, tam ex servi quam ex liberi persona; nec manifesti, dupli.

5. The penalty for manifest theft is quadruple the value of the thing stolen, whether the thief be a slave or a freeman; that for theft not manifest is double.

GAI. iii. 180, 190.

6. Furtum autem fit non solum cum quis intercipiendi causa rem alienam amovet, sed generaliter cum quis alienam rem invito domino contrectat. Itaque, sive creditor pignore, sive is apud quem res depasita est, ea re utatur, sive is qui rem utendam accepit, in alium usum eam transferat quam cujus gratia ei datu est, furtum committit: veluti, si quis argentum utendum acceperit quasi amicos ad coenam invitaturus, et id peregre secum tulerit, aut si quis equum gestandi causa commodatum sibi longius aliquo duxerit. Quod veteres scripserunt de eo qui in aciem equum perduxisset.

6. It is theft, not only when any one takes away a thing belonging to another, in order to appropriate it, but generally when any one deals with the property of another contrary to the wishes of its owner. Thus, if the creditor uses the thing pledged, or the depositary the thing deposited, or the usuary even lays the thing for another purpose than that for which it is given, it is a theft; for example, if any one borrows plate on the pretence of intending to invite friends to supper, and then carries it away with him to a distance, or if any one borrows a horse, as for a ride, and takes it much farther than suits such a purpose, or, as we find supposed in the writings of the ancients, takes it into battle.

GAI. iii. 195, 196; D. xlvii. 2. 54.

7. Placuit tamen eos qui rebus commodatis aliter uterentur quam utendas acceperint, ita furtum committere si se intelligant id invito domino facere, eumque si intellexisset non permissurum, at si permissurum credant, extra crimen videri: optima sane distinctione, quia furtum sine affectu furandi non committatur.

7. A person, however, who borrows a thing, and applies it to a purpose other than that for which it was lent, only commits theft, if he knows that he is acting against the wishes of the owner, and that the owner, if he were informed, would not permit it; for if he really thinks the owner would permit it, he does not commit a crime; and this is a very proper distinction, for there is no theft without the intention to commit theft.

GAI. iii. 197; D. xli. 3. 37.

8. Sed et si credat aliquis invito domino se rem commodatam sibi contrectare, domino autem volente id fiat, dicitur furtum non fieri. Unde illud quaesitum est, cum Titius servum Maevii sollicitaverit ut quasdam res domino subriperet et ad eum perferret, et servus id ad Maevium pertulerit;

8. And even if the borrower thinks he is applying the thing borrowed contrary to the wishes of the owner, yet if the owner as a matter of fact approves of the application, there is, it is said, no theft. Whence the following question arises; Titius has urged the slave of Maevius to steal from his master certain things, and

Maevius dum vult Titium in ipso delicto deprehendere, permiserit servo quaedam res ad eum perferre, utrum furti an servi corrupti judicio teneatur Titius, an neutro. Et cum nobis super hac dubitatione suggestum est, et antiquorum prudentium super hoc altercationes perspeximus, quibusdam neque furti neque servi corrupti actionem praestantibus, quibusdam furti tantummodo. Nos hujusmodi calliditati obviam euntes per nostram decisionem sanximus, non solum furti actionem, sed et servi corrupti contra eum dari. Licet enim in servus deterior a sollicitatore minime factus est, et ideo non concurrant regulae quae servi corrupti actionem introducerent, tamen consilium corruptoris ad perniciem probitatis servi introductum est: ut sit poenalis actio imposita, tamquam si re ipsa fuisset servus corruptus, ne ex hujusmodi impunitate et in alium servum qui facile possit corrumpi, tale facinus a quibusdam perpetretur.

to bring them to him; the slave informs his master, who, wishing to seize Titius in the act, permits his slave to take certain things to Titius; is Titius liable to an action *furti*, or to one *servi corrupti*, or to neither? This doubtful question was submitted to us, and we examined the conflicting opinions of the ancient jurists on this subject, some of whom thought Titius was liable to both these actions, while others thought he was only liable to the action of theft; and to prevent subtleties, we have decided that in this case both these actions may be brought. For, although the slave has not been corrupted, and the case does not seem therefore within the rules of the action *servi corrupti*, yet the intention to corrupt the slave is indisputable, and he is therefore to be punished exactly as if the slave had been really corrupted, lest his impunity should incite others to act in the same criminal way towards a slave more easy to corrupt.

GAI. iii. 198; C. vI. 2. 20.

Was the slave corrupted? No, he had given a signal proof of his fidelity. Was the thing stolen? No, the owner had consented to its being taken. Thus had reasoned those who refused either action. Justinian avoids these subtleties, and decides that crime shall at any rate be punished, and reparation be made for a wrongful act.

9. Interdum etiam liberorum hominum furtum fit, veluti si quis liberorum nostrorum qui in potestate nostra sit, subreptus fuerit.

9. Sometimes there may be a theft of free persons, as, if one of our children in our power is carried away.

GAI. iii. 199.

Gaius adds, as an example, the case of a wife *in manu* being stolen. It was not the value of the person stolen which in such cases formed the measure of the penalty, for the value of a free person was inappreciable; but it was the loss occasioned by the theft to the person in whose power the subject of the theft was.

10. Aliquando etiam suae rei furtum quisque committit, veluti si debitor rem quam creditori pignoris causa dedit, subtraxerit.

10. A man may even commit a theft of his own property, as, if a debtor takes from a creditor a thing he has pledged to him.

GAI. iii. 200.

11. Interdum furti tenetur qui ipse furtum non fecit, qualis est cujus ope consilio furtum factum est. In quo numero est, qui tibi nummos excussit ut alius eos raperet, aut tibi obstitit ut alius rem tuam exciperet, aut oves tuas vel boves fugavit ut alius eas caperet; et hoc veteres scripserunt de eo qui panno rubro fugavit armentum. Sed si quid eorum per lasciviam, et non data opera ut furtum admitteretur, factum est, in factum actio dari debet. At ubi ope Mævii Titius furtum fecerit, ambo furti tenentur. Ope consilio ejus quoque furtum admitti videtur, qui scalas forte fenestris supposuit, aut ipsas fenestras vel ostium effregit ut alius furtum faceret; quive ferramenta ad effringendum, aut scalas ut fenestris supponerentur, commodaverit, sciens cujus gratia commodaverit. Certe qui nullam opem ad furtum faciendum adhibuit, sed tantum consilium dedit atque hortatus est ad furtum faciendum, non tenetur furti.

11. A person may be liable to an action of theft, although he has not himself committed a theft, as, for instance, a person who has lent his aid and planned the crime. Among such is one who makes your money fall from your hand that another may seize upon it; or has placed himself in your way that another may carry off something belonging to you; or has driven your sheep or oxen that another may make away with them, or, to take an instance given by the old lawyers, frightens a herd with a piece of scarlet cloth. But if such acts are only the fruit of reckless folly, with no design of assisting in the commission of a theft, the proper action is one in factum. But if Mævius assists Titius to commit a robbery, both are liable to an action of theft. A person, again, assists in a theft who places ladders under a window, or breaks a window or a door, that another may commit a theft; or who lends tools to break a door, or ladders to place under a window, knowing the purpose to which they are to be applied. But a person who does not actually assist, but only advises and urges the commission of a theft, is not liable to an action of theft.

GAI. iii. 202; D. xlvii. 2. 54. 4; D. xlvii. 2. 30.

12. Hi qui in parentium vel dominorum potestate sunt, si rem eis subripiant, furtum quidem illis faciunt, et res in furtivam causam cadit, nec ob id ab ullo usurapi potest antequam in domini potestatem revertatur: sed furti actio non nascitur, quia nec ex alia ulla causa potest inter eos actio nasci. Si vero ope consilio alterius furtum factum fuerit, quia utique furtum committitur, convenienter ille furti tenetur, quia verum est ope consilio ejus furtum factum esse.

12. Those who are in the power of a parent or master, if they steal anything belonging to the person in whose power they are, commit a theft. The thing stolen, in such a case, is considered to be furtiva, and therefore no right in it can be acquired by usucapion before it has returned into the hands of the owner; but no action of theft can be brought, because the relation of the parties is such, that no action whatever can arise between them. But if the theft has been committed by the assistance and advice of another, as a theft is actually committed, this person will be subject to the action of theft, as a theft is undoubtedly committed through his means.

D. xlvii. 2. 17; D. xlvii. 2. 36. 1.

13. Furti autem actio ei competit cujus interest rem salvam esse, licet

13. An action of theft may be brought by any one who is interested

dominus non sit. Itaque nec domino aliter competit, quam si ejus intersit rem non perire.

in the safety of the thing, although he is not the owner; and the proprietor, consequently, cannot bring this action unless he is interested in the thing not perishing.

GAI. iii. 203.

The right to bring the *actio furti* may belong to several persons at the same time. For instance, both the owner and the usufructuary had sufficient interest in the thing to support an action. But mere interest in a thing was not sufficient unless the thing had been delivered to, and was or had been in the possession of the plaintiff. A person, for instance, to whom a thing was due by stipulation could not bring an '*actio furti*' if the thing were stolen; he could only compel the actual owner to allow him to bring an *actio furti* in the owner's name. (D. xlvii. 2. 13.)

14. Unde constat creditorem de pignore subrepto furti actione agere posse, etiamsi idoneum debitorem habeat, quia expedit ei pignori potius incumbere quam in personam agere: adeo quidem ut, quamvis ipse debitor eam rem subripuerit, nihilominus creditori competit actio furti.

14. Hence, a creditor may bring this action if a thing pledged to him is stolen, although his debtor is solvent, because it may be more advantageous to him to rely upon his pledge than to bring an action against his debtor personally; so much so, that although it is the debtor himself that has stolen the thing pledged, yet the creditor can bring an action of theft.

GAI. iii. 204.

15. Item si fullo polienda curanda, aut sarcinator sarcienda vestimenta mercede certa acceperit, eaque furto amiserit, ipse furti habet actionem, non dominus; quia domini nihil interest eam rem non perire, cum judicio locati a fullone aut sarcinatore rem suam persequi potest. Sed et bonae fidei emptori subrepta re quam emerit, quamvis dominus non sit, omnimodo competit furti actio, quemadmodum et creditori. Fulloni vero et sarcinatori non aliter furti competere placuit, quam si solvendo sint, hoc est, si domino rei aestimationem solvere possint; nam si solvendo non sunt, tunc quia ab eis suum dominus consequi non possit, ipsi domino furti competit actio, quia hoc casu ipsius interest rem salvam esse. Idem est, et si in partem solvendo sint fullo aut sarcinator.

15. So, too, if a fuller receives clothes to clean, or a tailor receives them to mend, for a certain fixed sum, and has them stolen from him, it is he and not the owner who is able to bring an action of theft, for the owner is not considered as interested in their safety, having an action *locati*, by which he may recover the thing stolen, against the fuller or tailor. But, if a thing be stolen from a *bona fide* purchaser, he is entitled, like a creditor, to an action of theft, although he is not the proprietor. But an action of theft is not maintainable by the fuller or tailor, unless he be solvent, that is, unless he is able to pay the owner the value of the thing lost; for if the fuller or tailor is insolvent, then the owner, as he cannot recover anything from them, is allowed to bring an action of theft, as he has in this case an

interest in the safety of the thing. And it is the same although the fuller or tailor is partially solvent.

GAI. liL 205; D. xlvii. 2. 20. 1.

The owner has no interest in recovering the penalty if he can get compensation from the person whose services he has hired to the full amount of any loss he sustains by the theft; but he would still be able to bring an action, i. e. a *vindicatio*, an *actio ad exhibendum*, or a *condictio*, to get the thing itself, or its value, from the thief.

16. Quæ de fullone et sarcinatore diximus, eadem et ad eum cui commodata res est, transferenda retorse existimabant; nam, ut ille fullo mercedem accipiendo custodiam præstat, ita is quoque qui commodum utendi percipit, similiter necesse habet custodiam præstare. Sed nostra providentia etiam hoc in nostris decisionibus emendavit ut in domini voluntate sit, sive commodati actionem adversus eum qui rem commodatam accepit, movere desiderat, sive furti adversus eum qui rem subripuit, et alterutra earum electa dominum non posse ex pœnitentia ad alteram venire actionem. Sed si quidem furem elegerit, illum qui rem utendam accepit, penitus liberari; sin autem commodator veniat adversus eum qui rem utendam accepit, ipsi quidem nullo modo competere posse adversus furem furti actionem, eum autem qui pro re commodata convenitur, posse adversus furem furti habere actionem: ita tamen, si dominus sciens rem esse subreptam, adversus eum cui res commodati fuit, pervenit. Sin autem nescius, et dubitans rem non esse apud eum, commodati actionem instituit, postea autem re comperta voluit remittere quidem commodati actionem, ad furti autem pervenire, tunc licentia ei concedatur et adversus furem venire, nullo obstaculo ei opponendo, quoniam incertus constitutus movit adversus eum qui rem utendam accepit, commodati actionem, nisi domino ab eo satisfactum est. Tunc etenim omnimodo furem a domino quidem furti actione liberari, suppositum

16. What we have said of the fuller and tailor was applied by the ancients to the borrower. For as the fuller by accepting a sum for his labour makes himself answerable for the safe keeping of the thing, so does a borrower by accepting the use of the thing he borrows. But our wisdom has introduced in our decisions an improvement on this point, and the owner may now bring an action *commodati* against the borrower, or of theft against the thief; but when once his choice is made, he cannot change his mind and have recourse to the other action. If he elects to sue the thief, the borrower is quite freed; if he elects to sue the borrower, he cannot bring an action of theft against the thief, but the borrower may, that is, provided that the owner elects to sue the borrower, knowing that the thing has been stolen. If he is ignorant or uncertain of this, and therefore sues the borrower, and then subsequently learns the true state of the case, and wishes to have recourse to an action of theft, he will be permitted to sue the thief without any difficulty being thrown in his way, for it was in ignorance of the real fact that he sued the borrower; unless, indeed, his claim has been satisfied by the borrower, for then the thief is quite free from any action of theft on the part of the owner, but the borrower takes the place of the owner in the power of bringing this action. On the other hand, it is very evident that if the owner originally brings an action *commodati*, in ignorance that the thing has been stolen, and subsequently learning this, prefers to

autem esse ei qui pro re sibi commodata domino satisfecit; cum manifestissimum est, etiamsi ab initio dominus actionem commodati instituit ignarus rem esse subreptam, postea autem hoc ei cognito adversus furem transivit, omnimodo liberari eum qui rem commodatam accepit, quemcumque causae exitum dominus adversus furem habuerit: eadem definitione obtinente, sive in partem sive in solidum solvendo sit is qui rem commodatam accepit.

proceed against the thief, the borrower is thereby entirely freed, whatever may be the issue of the suit against the thief; as, in the previous case, the thief would be freed, whether the borrower was wholly or only partially able to satisfy the claim against him.

GAI. ili. 206; C. vi. 2. 23. 1, 2.

17. Sed is apud quem res deposita est, custodiam non praestat; sed tantum in eo obnoxius est, si quid ipse dolo malo fecerit. Qua de causa, si res ei subrepta fuerit, quia restituendae ejus rei nomine depositi non tenetur, nec ob id ejus interest rem salvam esse, furti agere non potest; sed furti actio domino competit.

17. A depositary is not answerable for the safe keeping of the thing deposited, but is only answerable for wilful wrong; therefore, if the thing is stolen from him, as he is not bound by the contract of deposit to restore it, and has no interest in its safety, he cannot bring an action of theft, but it is the owner alone who can bring this action.

GAI. ill. 207.

We must, in all cases of theft, bear in mind that an *actio furti* might also be brought against any one who had 'ope consilio' participated in the theft, and the whole amount of the penalty could be recovered separately against each thief and each person taking an indirect part in the theft. (D. xlvii. 2. 21. 9.)

18. In summa sciendum est quaesitum esse an impubes, rem alienam amovendo, furtum faciat? Et placet, quia furtum ex affectu consistit, ita demum obligari eo crimine impuberem si proximus pubertati sit, et ob id intelligat se delinquere.

18. It should be observed, that the question has been asked whether, if a person under the age of puberty takes away the property of another, he commits a theft. The answer is, that as it is the intention that makes the theft, such a person is only bound by the obligation springing from the delict if he is near the age of puberty, and consequently understands that he commits a crime.

GAI. lli. 208.

19. Furti actio, sive dupli sive quadrupli, tantum ad poenae persecutionem pertinet; nam ipsius rei persecutionem extrinsecus habet dominus, quam aut vindicando aut condicendo potest auferre. Sed vindicando quidem adversus possessorem est, sive fur ipse possidet,

19. The action of theft, whether brought to recover double or quadruple, has no other object than the recovery of the penalty. For the owner has also a means of recovering the thing itself, either by a *vindicatio* or a *condictio*. The former may be brought against the possessor, whe-

sive alius, quilibet; condictio autem adversus furem ipsum heredemve ejus, licet non possideat, competit.

ther the thief or any one else; the latter may be brought against the thief or the heir of the thief, although not in possession of the thing stolen.

GAI. Iv. 8; D. xlviI. 2. 54. 3.

The thief and those who assisted him had to pay a penalty as a punishment for their wrong-doing; but something more remained for the thief himself to do; he had to restore the thing stolen. The owner of the thing, therefore, who alone could insist on having the thing back, could compel its restoration by bringing against the thief, if he still had the thing in his possession, the action of *vindicatio* or that of *ad exhibendum*, the actions by which particular things were generally recovered by their owners. But if the thief had not the thing any longer in his possession, it was useless to bring an action which could do no more than make him restore it. The owner was therefore allowed to bring a *condictio* (having in this case the especial name of ' *condictio furtiva* '), by which he recovered from the thief the value of the things stolen, with interest for the time of its detention; and though it was a general rule (see Tit. 6. 14) that, where a person could bring a *vindicatio*, he should not be allowed to bring a *condictio*, i.e. where he could recover the thing itself, he should not be allowed, at his option, to recover its value instead; yet, ' *in odium furum* ' this was allowed against a thief, and the plaintiff might select which action he pleased. (See Tit. 6. 14.)

This action might be brought against the heirs of the thief, whereas the *actio furti*, which inflicted a punishment for a personal wrongful act, could only be brought against the thief himself. Every action against a thief or those who assisted him might be brought by the heirs of any one entitled to bring it. (See Tit. 12.)

## Tit. II.   DE BONIS VI RAPTIS.

Qui res alienas rapit, tenetur quidem etiam furti: quis enim magis alienam rem invito domino contrectat, quam qui vi rapit? Ideoque recte dictum est, eum improbum furem esse; sed tamen propriam actionem ejus delicti nomine praetor introduxit, quae appellatur vi bonorum raptorum, et est intra annum quadrupli, post annum simpli. Quae actio utilis est, etiam si quis unam rem licet minimam rapuerit. Quad-

A person who takes a thing belonging to another by force is liable to an action of theft, for who can be said to take the property of another more against his will than he who takes it by force? And he is therefore rightly said to be an *improbus fur*. The praetor, however, has introduced a peculiar action in this case, called *vi bonorum raptorum*; by which, if brought within a year after the robbery, quadruple the value of

ruplum autem non totum pœna est, et extra pœnam rei persecutio, sicut in actione furti manifesti diximus; sed in quadruplo inest et rei persecutio, ut pœna tripli sit, sive comprehendatur raptor in ipso delicto, sive non: ridiculum est enim levioris conditionis esse eum qui vi rapit, quam qui clam amovet.

the thing taken may be recovered; but if brought after the expiration of a year, then the single value only can be recovered. This action may be brought even against a person who has only taken by force a single thing, and one of the most trifling value. But this quadruple of the value is not altogether a penalty, as in the action of *furtum manifestum*; for the thing itself is included, so that, strictly, the penalty is only of three times the value. And it is the same, whether the robber was, or was not taken in the actual commission of the crime. For it would be ridiculous that a person who uses force should be in a better condition than he who secretly commits a theft.

GAI. iv. 8.

The edict of the prætor, introducing this action, ran as follows: *Si cui dolo malo, hominibus coactis, damni quid factum esse dicetur, sive cujus bona rapta esse dicentur: in eum, qui id fecisse dicitur judicium dabo.* (D. xlvii. 8. 2.)

It was necessary that the act of violence should be committed with evil intent (*dolo malo*). If, for instance, a *publicanus* carried off a flock of sheep, thinking that some offence had been committed against the *lex vectigalis*, although he was mistaken, this action could not be brought against him. (D. xlvii. 8. 2. 20.) Even if the thief was alone, or one thing, however small, were carried off, yet the action might be brought although the words *hominibus coactis* and *bona rapta* occur in the edict. It, like the action of theft, could only be brought if the thing or things taken were moveables. (C. ix. 33. 1.)

The text explains how the amount recovered under it differed from that recovered under an *actio furti*. Under the *actio vi bonorum raptorum* the thing itself was recovered, or its value if the thief no longer had it in his possession, and also three times the estimated value of the thing itself; while the *actio furti* was only penal. (See paragr. 19 of last Title.)

The plaintiff might, if he pleased, bring the *actio furti* instead; and he might also bring this action after the expiration of a year prevented his bringing that '*vi bonorum raptorum.*'

This action united in its effects the *vindicatio* or *condictio*, and also the recovery of a penalty. As it was partly penal, it could not be brought against the heirs of the thief. (D. xlvii. 8. 2. 27.)

1. Quia tamen ita competit haec actio, si dolo malo quisque rapuerit, qui aliquo errore inductus suam rem esse existimans et imprudens juris eo animo rapuit, quasi domino liceat etiam per vim rem suam auferre a possessoribus, absolvi debet: cui scilicet conveniens est, nec furti teneri eum qui eodem hoc animo rapuit. Sed ne, dum talia excogitentur, inveniatur via per quam raptores impune suam exercerent avaritiam, melius divalibus constitutionibus pro hac parte prospectum est, ut nemini liceat vi rapere rem mobilem vel se moventem, licet suam eamdem rem existimet: sed si quis contra statuta fecerit, rei quidem suae dominio carere; sin autem aliena sit, post restitutionem ejus etiam aestimationem ejusdem rei praestare. Quod non solum in mobilibus rebus quae rapi possunt, constitutiones obtinere censuerunt, sed etiam in invasionibus quae circa res soli fiunt, ut ex hac causa omni rapina homines abstineant.

1. As, however, this action can only be brought against a person who robs with the intent of committing a wilful wrong, if any one takes by force a thing, thinking himself, by a mistake, to be the owner, and, in ignorance of the law, believing it permitted to an owner to take away, even by force, a thing belonging to himself from persons in whose possession it is, he ought to be held discharged of this action, nor in such a case would he be liable to an action of theft. But lest robbers, under the cover of such an excuse, should find means of gratifying their avarice with impunity, the imperial constitutions have made a wise alteration, by providing that no one may carry off by force a thing that is moveable, or moves itself, although he thinks himself the owner. If any one acts contrary to these constitutions, he is, if the thing is his, to cease to be owner of it; if it is not, he is not only to restore the thing taken, but also to pay its value. The constitutions have declared these rules applicable, not only in the case of moveables of a nature to be carried off by force, but also to the forcible entries made upon immoveables, in order that every kind of violent robbery may be prevented.

D. xlvii. 8. 2. 18; C. viii. 4. 7.

2. Sane in hac actione non utique expectatur rem in bonis actoris esse; nam sive in bonis sit sive non sit, si tamen ex bonis sit, locum haec actio habebit: quare sive locata, sive commodata, sive pignorata, sive etiam deposita sit apud Titium sic ut intersit ejus eam rem non auferri, veluti si in re deposita culpam quoque promisit, sive bona fide possideat, sive usumfructum in ea quis habeat, vel quod aliud jus ut intersit ejus non rapi, dicendum est competere ei hanc actionem, ut non dominium accipiat, sed illud solum quod ex bonis ejus qui rapinam passus est, id est, quod ex substantia ejus ablatum esse proponatur. Et generaliter dicendum est, ex quibus causis furti actio competit in re clam facta, ex iis-

2. In this action it is not necessary that the thing should have been part of the goods of the plaintiff; for whether it has been part of his goods or not, yet if it has been taken from among his goods, the action may be brought. Consequently, if anything has been let, lent, or given in pledge to Titius, or deposited with him, so that he has an interest in its not being taken away by force, as, for instance, he has engaged to be answerable for even any fault committed respecting it; or if he possesses it bona fide, or has the usufruct of it, or has any other legal interest in its not being taken away by force, this action may be brought, not to give him the ownership in the thing, but merely to restore him what he has lost by the thing being taken away from out of

dem casmis omnes habere hanc actionem.

his goods, that is, from out of his
property. And generally, we may
say, that the same causes which
would give rise to an action of theft,
if the theft is committed secretly,
will give rise to this action, if it is
committed with force.

D. xlvii. 8. 2. 92-94.

In order to make the punishment of an open and flagrant
violation of law more severe than that of a secret theft, the
very slightest interest in the thing taken was sufficient to enable
a plaintiff to bring the action *vi bonorum raptorum*. For
instance, a mere depositary could bring it, although his interest
was not great enough to permit of his bringing an *actio furti*.

## Tit. III.   DE LEGE AQUILIA.

Damni injuriæ actio constituitur
per legem Aquiliam: cujus primo
capite cautum est ut si quis alienum
hominem, alienamve quadrupedem
quæ pecudum numero sit, injuria
occiderit, quanti ea res in eo anno
plurimi fuerit, tantum domino dare
damnetur.

The action *damni injuriæ* is established by the *lex Aquilia*, of which
the first head provides, that if any
one shall have wrongfully killed a
slave, or a four-footed beast, being
one of those reckoned among cattle,
belonging to another, he shall be
condemned to pay the owner the
greatest value which the thing has
possessed at any time within a year
previously.

Gai. iii. 210.

The *lex Aquilia* was, as Ulpian informs us (D. ix. 2. 1), a
*plebiscitum* made on the proposition of the tribune Aquilius.
It made an alteration in all the previous laws, including those
of the Twelve Tables, which had treated of damage wrongfully done (*de damno injuria*). Theophilus says it was
passed at the time of the secession of the plebs, meaning,
probably, that to the *Janiculum*, in the year 468 A.U.C.
(Paraphrase on paragr. 15.)

A fragment of Gaius in the Digest (D. ix. 2. 2) contains
the terms of this first head of the *lex Aquilia*: ' *Qui servum
servumve alienum alienamve quadrupedem vel pecudem injuria occiderit, quanti id in eo anno plurimi fuerit, tantum
æs dare domino damnatus esto.*'

1. Quod autem non precise de
quadrupede, sed de ea tantum quæ
pecudum numero est, cavetur, eo
pertinet ut neque de feris bestiis

1. As the law does not speak generally of four-footed beasts, but only
of those which are reckoned among
cattle, we may consider its provisions

neque de canibus cautum esse intelligimus, sed de iis tantum quæ proprie pecci dicuntur, quales sunt equi, muli, asini, oves, boves, capræ. De suibus quoque, idem placuit; nam et suem pecudum appellatione continentur, quia et bi gregatim pascuntur. Sic denique et Homerus in Odyssea ait, sicut Ælius Marcianus in suis Institutionibus refert:—
Δήεις τόνγε σύεσσι παρήμενον· αἱ δὲ νέμονται
Πὰρ Κόρακος πέτρῃ, ἐπί τῇ κρήνῃ Ἀρεθούσῃ.

as not applying to dogs or wild animals, but only to animals which may be properly said to feed in herds, as horses, mules, asses, sheep, oxen, goats, and also swine, for they are included in the term cattle, for they feed in herds. Thus Homer says, as Ælius Marcianus quotes in his Institutes,—
'You will find him seated by his swine, and they are feeding by the rock of Corax, near the spring Arethusa.'

D. xi. 2. 2. 2; D. xxxii. 65. 4.

The passage is from Od. 13. 407.

2. Injuria autem occidere intelligitur, qui nullo jure occidit. Itaque latronem qui occidit, non tenetur, utique si aliter periculum effugere non potest.

2. To kill wrongfully is to kill without any right; consequently, a person who kills a thief is not liable to this action, that is, if he could not otherwise avoid the danger with which he was threatened.

D. ix. 2. 5, pr. and 1.

It was not necessary to consider the intent with which the damage was done. Was it done 'nullo jure?' if so, the lex Aquilia applied.

3. Ac ne is quidem hac lege tenetur, qui casu occidit, si modo culpa ejus nulla inveniatur; nam alioquin non minus quam ex dolo ex culpa quisque hac lege tenetur.

3. Nor is a person made liable by this law, who has killed by accident, provided there is no fault on his part, for this law punishes fault as well as wilful wrong-doing.

Gat. iii. 202. 211.

4. Itaque si quis dum jaculis ludit vel exercitatur, transeuntem servum tuum trajecerit, distinguitur: nam si id a milite in campo eove ubi solitum est exercitari, admissum est, nulla culpa ejus intelligitur; si alius tale quid admisit, culpæ reus est. Idem juris est de milite, si in alio loco quam qui exercitandis militibus destinatus est, id admisit.

4. Consequently, if any one playing or practising with a javelin, pierces with it your slave as he goes by, there is a distinction made; if the accident befalls a soldier while in the camp, or other place appropriated to military exercises, there is no fault in the soldier, but there would be in any one else besides a soldier, and the soldier himself would be in fault. If he inflicted such an injury in any other place than one appropriated to military exercises.

D. ix. 2. 9. 4.

5. Item si putator, ex arbore dejecto ramo, servum tuum transcun-

5. If, again, any one, in pruning a tree, by letting a bough fall, kills your

tem occiderit: si prope viam publicam aut vicinalem id factum est, neque proclamavit ut casus evitari possit, culpæ reus est: si proclamavit, nec ille curavit cavere, extra culpam esse putatur. Æque extra culpam esse intelligitur, si seorsum a via forte vel in medio fundo cædebat, licet non proclamavit; quia in eo loco nulli extraneo jus fuerat veniendi.

slave who is passing, and this takes place near a public way, or a way belonging to a neighbour, and he has not cried out to make persons take care, he is in fault; but if he called out, and the passer-by would not take care, he is not to blame. He is also equally free from blame if he was cutting far from any public way, or in the middle of a field, even though he has not called out, for by such a place no stranger has a right to pass.

D. ix. 2. 31.

6. Præterea si medicus qui servum tuum secuit, dereliquerit curationem, atque ob id mortuus fuerit servus, culpæ reus est.

6. So, again, a physician who has performed an operation on your slave, and then neglected to attend to his cure, so that the slave dies, is guilty of a fault.

D. ix. 2. 8.

7. Imperitia quoque culpæ adnumeratur: veluti si medicus ideo servum tuum occiderit, quod eum male secuerit, aut perperam ei medicamentum dederit.

7. Unskilfulness is also a fault, as, if a physician kills your slave by unskilfully performing an operation on him, or by giving him wrong medicines.

D. ix. 2. 7. 8; D. ix. 2. 8; D. 1. 17. 132.

8. Impetu quoque mularum, quas mulio propter imperitiam retinere non potuerit, si servus tuus oppressus fuerit, culpæ reus est mulio; sed et si propter infirmitatem eas retinere non potuerit, cum alius firmior retinere potuisset, æque culpæ tenetur. Eadem placuerunt de eo quoque qui, cum equo veheretur, impetum ejus aut propter infirmitatem aut propter imperitiam suam retinere non potuerit.

8. So, too, if a muleteer, through his want of skill, cannot manage his mules, and runs over your slave, he is guilty of a fault. As, also, he would be if he could not hold them in on account of his weakness, provided that a stronger man could have held them in. The same decisions apply to an unskilful or infirm horseman, unable to manage his horse.

D. ix. 2. 8. 1.

9. Illis autem verbis legis, quanti in eo anno plurimi fuerit, illa sententia exprimitur, ut si quis hominem tuum qui hodie claudus aut mancus aut luscus erit, occiderit, qui in eo anno integer et pretiosus fuerit non tanti teneatur quanti hodie erit, sed quanti in eo anno plurimi fuerit. Qua ratione creditum est pœnalem esse hujus legis actionem, quia non solum tanti quisque obligatur quantum damni dederit, sed aliquando longe pluris: ideoque constat in heredem eam

9. The words above quoted, 'the greatest value the thing has possessed at any time within a year previously,' mean that if your slave is killed, being at the time of his death lame, maimed, or one-eyed, but having been within a year quite sound and of considerable value, the person who kills him is bound to pay, not his actual value, but the greatest value he ever possessed within the year. Hence, this action may be said to be penal, as a person is bound under it not only for the damage he has done,

actionem non transire, quæ transituræ fuisset, si ultra damnum numquam lis æstimaretur.

but for much more; and, therefore, the action does not pass against his heir, as it would have done if the condemnation had not exceeded the amount of the actual damage.

GAI. iii. 214; D. ix. 2, 23, 3, 8.

10. Illud non ex verbis legis, sed ex interpretatione placuit, non solum perempti corporis æstimationem habendam esse, secundum ea quæ diximus, sed eo amplius quidquid præterea perempto eo corpore damni nobis allatum fuerit: veluti si servum tuum heredem ab aliquo institutum antea quis occiderit, quam jussu tuo adiret, nam hereditatis quoque amissæ rationem esse habendam constat. Item si ex pari mularum unam, vel ex quadriga equorum unum occiderit, vel ex comœdis unus servus occisus fuerit, non solum occisi fit æstimatio; sed eo amplius id quoque computatur, quanti depretiati sunt qui supersunt.

10. It has been decided, not by virtue of the actual wording of the law, but by interpretation, that not only is the value of the thing perishing to be estimated as we have said, but also the loss which in any way we incur by its perishing; as, for instance, if your slave having been instituted heir by some one is killed before he enters at your command on the inheritance, the loss of the inheritance should be taken account of. So, too, if one of a pair of mules, or of a set of four horses, or one slave of a band of comedians, is killed, account is to be taken not only of the value of the thing killed, but also of the diminished value of what remains.

GAI. iii. 212; D. ix. 2, 22, 1.

11. Liberum autem est ei cujus servus occisus fuerit, et judicio privato legis Aquiliæ damnum persequi, et capitalis criminis eum reum facere.

11. The master of a slave who is killed may bring a private action for the damages given by the lex Aquilia, and also bring a capital action against the murderer.

GAI. iii. 213.

A crimen capitale was one which affected the caput of the condemned. The lex Cornelia (D. ix. 2. 23. 9; see also Title 18. 5, of this Book) gave the master the power to bring a criminal accusation against the murderer. The Code (iii. 35. 3) contains a rescript of the Emperor Gordian, stating it as undoubted law that a criminal accusation did not prevent a master also bringing a private action under the lex Aquilia.

12. Caput secundum legis Aquiliæ in usu non est.

12. The second head of the lex Aquilia is not now in use.

GAI. iii. 215; D. ix. 2. 27. 4.

We learn from Gaius (GAI. iii. 215) that the second head of the lex Aquilia gave an action for the full value of the injury sustained to a stipulator, whose claim was extinguished by an adstipulator releasing the debtor by acceptilation. (See Bk. iii. Tit. 29.) The stipulator might also bring an actio mandati against the adstipulator, if he preferred doing so; but, as we see from Title 16 of this Book (paragr. 1), proceeding under the *lex Aquilia* gave the plaintiff the advantage of having the amount he recovered increased if the defendant denied his liability.

13. Capite tertio de omni cetero damno cavetur. Itaque si quis servum, vel eam quadrupedem quae pecudum numero est, vulneraverit, sive eam quadrupedem quae pecudum numero non est, veluti canem aut feram bestiam vulneraverit aut occiderit, hoc capite actio constituitur. In ceteris quoque omnibus animalibus, item in omnibus rebus quae anima carent, damnum injuria datum hac parte vindicatur: si quid enim ustum aut ruptum aut fractum fuerit, actio ex hoc capite constituitur, quamquam poterit sola rupti appellatio in omnes istas causas sufficere; ruptum enim intelligitur, quod quoquo modo corruptum est. Unde non solum fracta aut usta, sed etiam scissa et collisa et effusa, et quoquo modo perempta atque deteriora facta, hoc verbo continentur: denique responsum est, si quis in alienum vinum aut oleum id immiserit quo naturalis bonitas vini aut olei corrumperetur, ex hac parte legis eum teneri.

13. The third head provides for every kind of damage; and, therefore, if a slave is wounded or killed, or a four-footed beast, whether of those reckoned among cattle or not, as a dog or wild beast, an action may be brought under the third head. Compensation may also be obtained under it for all wrongful injury to animals or inanimate things, and, in fact, for anything burnt, broken, or fractured although the word broken (*ruptum*) would have sufficed for all these cases; for a thing is *ruptum* which is in any way spoilt (*corruptum*), so that not only things fractured or burnt, but also things cut, bruised, spilt, or in any way destroyed or deteriorated, may be said to be *rupta*. It has also been decided, that any one who mixes anything with the oil or wine of another, so as to spoil the goodness of the wine or oil, is liable under this head of the *lex Aquilia*.

GAI. iii. 217; D. ix. 2. 27. 15.

The terms of this third head of the Aquilian law are given by Ulpian (D. ix. 2. 27. 5): '*Ceterarum rerum, praeter hominem et pecudem occisos, si quis alteri damnum facit, quod usserit, fregerit, ruperit injuria quanti ea res erit in diebus triginta proximis, tantum aes domino dare damnas esto.*'

14. Illud palam est, sicut ex primo capite ita demum quisque tenetur si dolo aut culpa ejus homo aut quadrupes occisus occisave fuerit, ita ex hoc capite de dolo aut culpa de cetero damno quemquam teneri. Hoc tamen capite, non quanti in eo anno, sed quanti in diebus triginta proximis res fuerit, obligatur is qui damnum dederit.

14. It is evident that, as a person is liable under the first head, if by wilful injury or by his fault he kills a slave or a four-footed beast, so by this head, a person is liable for every other damage, if there is wrongful injury or fault in what he does. But in this case, the offender is bound to pay the greatest value the thing has possessed, not within the year next preceding, but the thirty days next preceding.

GAI. iii. 218; D. ix. 2. 30. 3.

15. Ac ne plurimi quidem verbum adjicitur; sed Sabino recte placuit, perinde habendam æstimationem ac si etiam hac parte plurimi verbum adjectum fuisset: nam plebem Romanam quæ Aquilio tribuno rogante hanc legem tulit, contentam fuisse quod prima parte eo verbo usa est.

15. Even the word *plurimi*, i.e. of the greatest value, is not expressed in this case. But Sabinus was rightly of opinion, that the estimation ought to be made as if this word were in the law, since it must have been that the plebeians, who were the authors of this law on the motion of the tribune Aquilius, thought it sufficient to have used the word in the first head of the law.

GAI. iii. 216; D. ix. 2, 1. 1.

16. Ceterum placuit ita demum directam ex hac lege actionem esse, si quis præcipue corpore suo damnum dederit. Ideoque in eum qui alio modo damnum dederit, utiles actiones dari solent, veluti si quis hominem alienum aut pecus ita incluserit ut fame necaretur, aut jumentum tam vehementer egerit ut rumperetur, aut pecus in tantum exagitaverit ut præcipitaretur, aut si quis alieno servo persuaserit ut in arborem ascenderet vel in puteum descenderet, et is ascendendo vel descendendo aut mortuus ant aliqua corporis parte læsus fuerit, utilis actio in eum datur. Sed si quis alienum servum aut de ponte aut de ripa in flumen dejecerit, et is suffocatus fuerit, eo quod projecit corpore suo damnum dedisse non difficulter intelligi poterit, ideoque ipsa lege Aquilia tenetur. Sed si non corpore damnum datum, neque corpus læsum fuerit, sed alio modo damnum alicui contigerit, cum non sufficit neque directa neque utilis Aquilia, placuit, eum qui obnoxius fuerit, in factum actione teneri: veluti si quis misericordia ductus alienum servum compeditum solverit, ut fugeret.

16. But the direct action under this law can only be brought if any one has, with his own body, done damage, and consequently *utiles actiones* are given against the person who does damage in any other way, as, for instance, against one who shuts up a slave or a beast, so as to produce death by hunger: who drives a horse so fast as to knock him to pieces, or drives cattle over a precipice, or persuades another man's slave to climb a tree, or go down into a well, and the slave in climbing or descending is killed or maimed, then a *utilis actio* is given against him. But if any one has flung the slave of another from a bridge or a bank into a river, and the slave is drowned, then, as he has actually flung him down, there can be no difficulty in deciding that he has caused the damage with his own body, and consequently he is directly liable under the *lex Aquilia*. But if no damage has been done by the body, nor to the body, but damage has been done in some other way, the *actio directa* and the *actio utilis* are both inapplicable, and an *actio in factum* is given against the wrong-doer; for instance, if any one through compassion has loosed the fetters of a slave, to enable him to escape.

GAI. iii. 219; D. ix. 2. 33. 1; D. iv. 3. 7. 7.

If the injury were done, to use the language of the jurists, *corpore corpori*, that is, with direct bodily force, to the body of a slave or beast, the *actio (legis) Aquiliæ* had place. If it were done *corpori*, but indirectly and not *corpore*, the *actio utilis Aquiliæ* had place. If it were done neither to the body, nor yet with direct bodily force, the *actio* must be brought *in factum*, that is, on the particular circumstances of the case.

The *directa actio Aquiliæ* could only be brought by the owner; the *utilis* might be brought by the possessor, usufructuary, and others having an interest less than that of ownership.

As the action under the *lex Aquilia* was penal, the whole sum recoverable against one could be recovered separately against each or more than one offender.

If the defendant denied his liability, the *lex Aquilia* inflicted a double penalty, *adversus inficiantem in duplum actio est.* (D. ix. 2. 2. 1.)

It might very often happen that the person injured could also bring an action arising from a contract against the doer of the injury, as, for instance, an *actio pro socio, mandati, depositi,* if the person who did the injury were a partner, a mandatary, or depositary of the person to whom the injury was done. In such a case he could either bring the action on the contract, or proceed under the *lex Aquilia.* He could not do both, but if he brought the action on the contract, and then found that if he had proceeded under the *lex Aquilia* he would have recovered a larger sum, he was allowed to bring an action under the *lex Aquilia* to recover the surplus. (D. ix. 2. 7. 8; D. xliv. 7. 34. 2.)

The subject of *damnum* is hardly noticed in the Institutes except in connection with the *lex Aquilia.* (See Bk. iii. Tit. 18. 2.) By *damnum* is meant the diminution of a man's property, and it is treated of in the Digest according as it is *factum,* that is already done, or *infectum,* that is apprehended. (D. xxxix. 2.) *Damnum factum,* more usually termed simply *damnum,* might arise from a mere accident, or from the free will of another. If it arose in the latter way, it might have arisen in the exercise of a right enjoyed by the person causing it, and then no reparation had to be made for causing it, *non videtur vim facere qui jure suo utitur* (D. L. 17. 155); or it might have been done wrongfully, *damnum injuria datum,* and then the person injured was entitled to compensation according to the rates provided by the *lex Aquilia,* if the damage came within the scope of the law; if it did not, then an *actio in factum* was given (D. ix. 2. 33. 1), and compensation was made at rates differing according to the degree of wrong. If there had been *dolus* or *culpa lata,* the compensation was regulated by the value peculiar to the person injured : if the degree of *culpa* had been less, the common value was the measure of the compensation. In cases of *damnum infectum*, the owner of the property threatened could call on the owner of the property from which danger was apprehended to give security against any loss which might thus arise. (D. xxx. 12. 2. 5. 1.)

## Tit. IV. DE INJURIIS.

Generaliter injuria dicitur omne quod non jure fit: specialiter, alias contumelia quæ a contemnendo dicta est, quam Græci ὕβριν appellant; alias culpa, quam Græci ἀδίκημα dicunt, sicut in lege Aquilia damnum injuriæ accipitur; alias iniquitas et injustitia, quam Græci ἄδικον vocant. Cum enim prætor vel judex non jure contra quem pronuntiat, injuriam accepisse dicitur.

Injuria, in its general sense, signifies every action contrary to law; in a special sense, it means, sometimes, the same as *contumelia* (outrage), which is derived from *contemnere*, the Greek ὕβρις; sometimes the same as *culpa* (fault), in Greek ἀδίκημα, as in the *lex Aquilia*, which speaks of damage done *injuria*; sometimes it has the sense of iniquity, injustice, or in Greek ἄδικον; for a person against whom the prætor or judge pronounces an unjust sentence, is said to have received an *injuria*.

D. xlvii. 10, 1.

*Injuria*, then, is used in three senses—1, a wrongful act, an act done *nullo jure*; 2, the fault committed by a judge who gives judgment not according to *jus*; 3, an outrage or affront.

1. Injuria autem committitur, non solum cum quis pugno, puta, aut fustibus cæsus vel etiam verberatus erit, sed et si cui convicium factum fuerit; sive cujus bona quasi debitoris, qui nihil deberet, possessa fuerint ab eo qui intelligebat nihil eum sibi debere; vel si quis ad infamiam alicujus libellum aut carmen scripserit, composuerit, ediderit, dolove malo fecerit quo quid eorum fieret; sive quis matremfamilias aut prætextatum prætextamve adsectatus fuerit, sive cujus pudicitia attentata esse dicetur, et denique aliis pluribus modis admitti injuriam manifestum est.

1. An injury is committed not only by striking with the fists, or striking with clubs or the lash, but also by shouting till a crowd gathers round any one; by taking possession of any one's goods, pretending that he is debtor to the inflicter of the injury, who knows he has no claim on him; by writing, composing, publishing a libel or defamatory verses against any one, or by maliciously contriving that another does any of these things; by following after an honest woman, or a young boy or girl; by attempting the chastity of any one; and, in short, by numberless other acts.

Gai. iii. 220.

*Convicium.* Ulpian gives (D. xlvii. 10. 15. 4) the following derivation of the word:—' *Convicium autem dicitur vel a conciliatione vel a conventu, hoc est, a collatione vocum, quum enim in unum complures voces conferuntur, convicium appellatur, quasi convocium,*' any proceeding which publicly insults or annoys another, as gathering a crowd round a man's house, or shouting out scandal respecting another to a mob.

*Matremfamilias*, i.e. every married woman of honest character.

*Praetextatum, am*, i.e. still wearing the *praetexta*, which was put off at the age of puberty.

*Adsectatus fuerit.* Ulpian says (D. xlvii. 10. 15. 22), '*Adsectatur qui tacitus frequenter sequitur, assidua enim frequentia quasi praebet nonnullam infamiam.*'

*Pudicitia attentata.* Paul says (D. xlvii. 10. 10), '*Attentari pudicitia dicitur cum id agitur, ut ex pudico impudicus fiat.*'

2. Patitur autem quis injuriam non solum per semetipsum, sed etiam per liberos suos quos in potestate habet; item per uxorem suam, id enim magis praevaluit. Itaque si filiae alicujus quae Titio nupta est, injuriam feceris, non solum filiae nomine tecum injuriarum agi potest, sed etiam patris quoque et mariti nomine. Contra autem si viro injuria facta sit, uxor injuriarum agere non potest; defendi enim uxores a viris, non viros ab uxoribus aequum est. Sed et socer nurus nomine cujus vir in potestate est, injuriarum agere potest.

2. A man may receive an injury, not only in his own person, but in that of his children in his power, and even in that of his wife, according to the opinion that has prevailed. If, therefore, you injure a daughter in the power of her father, and married to Titius, the action for the injury may be brought, not only in the name of the daughter herself, but also in that of the father or the husband. But, if a husband has sustained an injury, the wife cannot bring the *actio injuriarum*, for the husband is the protector of the wife, not the wife of the husband. The father-in-law may also bring this action in the name of his daughter-in-law, if her husband is in his power.

Gai. iii. 221; D. xlvii. 10. 2; D. xlvii. 10. 1. 3.

Each person injured could bring an action. Take, for instance, the case of a married woman. She, her husband, her own father, and her husband's, have each an action, supposing both she and her husband are *in potestate*. But a person *in potestate*, though he had an action, could not bring it himself, except in certain cases, as in the absence of the *paterfamilias*. The *paterfamilias* would bring the action, and could sue either in his son's name, or his own. The amount recovered in the respective actions differed according to the dignity of the person bringing it. It might happen, for instance, that the son was of higher rank than the father. *Cum utrique tam filio quam patri, adquisita actio sit, non eadem utique facienda aestimatio est: cum possit propter filii dignitatem major ipsi quam patri injuria facta esse.* (D. xlvii. 10. 30. 31.) Although the wife was in power of the father, yet her husband could always bring an action for injury done to her, grounded on his natural duty to protect her.

3. Servis autem ipsis quidem nulla injuria fieri intelligitur, sed domino per eos fieri videtur, non tamen iisdem modis quibus etiam per liberos et uxores, sed ita cum quid atrocius commissum fuerit, et quod aperte ad contumeliam domini respicit: veluti si quis alienum servum verberaverit, et in hunc casum actio proponitur. At si quis servo convicium fecerit, vel pugno eum percusserit, nulla in eum actio domino competit.

3. An injury cannot, properly speaking, be done to a slave, but it is the master who, through the slave, is considered to be injured; not, however, in the same way as through a child or wife, but only when the act is of a character grave enough to make it a manifest insult to the master, as if a person has flogged severely the slave of another, in which case this action is given against him. But a master cannot bring an action against a person who has collected a crowd round his slave, or struck him with his fist.

GAI. iii. 222.

Under the civil law the master could not bring an action for injury done to his slave, unless the injury were done with intent to hurt or annoy the master. But the prætor gave an action *pleno jure*, i. e. which could be brought as a matter of right, if the slave were beaten or tortured without the master's orders, and an action *cognita causa*, i. e. allowed if the circumstances of the case seemed, on inquiry, to furnish good ground for it, if the injury had been slighter. Regard was had, in making this inquiry, and in estimating the amount of damage, to the class of slaves to which the slave belonged. (See paragr. 7.) The slave himself could in no case bring an action for injury sustained by him. (D. xlvii. 10. 15. 34.)

4. Si communi servo injuria facta sit, æquum est, non pro ea parte qua dominus quisque est, æstimationem injuriæ fieri, sed ex dominorum persona, quia ipsis fit injuria.

4. If an injury has been done to a slave held in common, equity demands that it shall be estimated not according to their respective shares in him, but according to their respective position, for it is the masters who are injured.

If the co-proprietors brought the action for injury done, or intended to be done to them through their slave, then, as it is said in the text, it made no difference what was the amount of their interest in the slave. Each had equally had an insult offered him. But the co-proprietors might bring a prætorian action for harm done to the slave, when no insult or hurt was intended to them, but the only question was, how much was the slave damaged, and made unfit for work, and then the amount recovered was divided between them, proportionately to their respective interests in the slave. (See note on last paragr.)

5. Quod si ususfructus in servo      5. If Titius has the usufruct, and
Titii est, proprietas Mævii, magis    Mævius the property in a slave, the
Mævio injuria fieri intelligitur.      injury is considered to be done rather
                             to Mævius than to Titius.

D. xlvii. 10. 15. 47.

It might, however, happen that it could be shown that the
intention was to injure and insult the usufructuary more than
the proprietor. (D. xlvii. 10. 15. 48.) No one but the proprietor could bring the prætorian action for the injury done
to the slave.

6. Sed si libero qui tibi bona fide    6. If the injury has been done to a
servit, injuria facta sit, nulla tibi    freeman, who serves you *bona fide*,
actio dabitur: sed suo nomine is    you have no action, but he can bring
experiri poterit, nisi in contumeliam   an action in his own name, unless he
tuam pulsatus sit: tunc enim com-   has been injured merely to insult
petit et tibi Injuriarum actio. Idem   you, for, in that case, you may bring
ergo est et in servo alieno bona fide   the *actio injuriarum*. So, too, with
tibi serviente, ut toties admittatur   regard to a slave of another who
injuriarum actio, quoties in tuam   serves you *bona fide*, you may bring
contumeliam injuria ei facta sit.    this action whenever the slave is in-
                            jured for the purpose of insulting
                            you.

D. xlvii. 10. 15. 48.

7. Pœna autem injuriarum ex    7. The penalty for injuries under
lege Duodecim Tabularum, propter   the law of the Twelve Tables, was a
membrum quidem ruptum talio   limb for a limb, but if only a bone
erat; propter os vero fractum sum-   was fractured, pecuniary compensa-
mariæ pœnæ erant constitutæ, quasi   tion was exacted proportionate to the
in magna veterum paupertate: sed   great poverty of the times. After-
prætor, prætores permittebant ipsis   wards, the prætor permitted the in-
qui injuriam passi sunt, eam æsti-   jured parties themselves to estimate
mare, ut judex vel tanti reum con-   the injury, so that the judge should
demnet, quanti injuriam passus   condemn the defendant to pay the
æstimaverit, vel minoris, prout ei   sum estimated, or less, as he may
visum fuerit. Sed pœna quidem   think proper. The penalty appointed
injuriarum quæ ex lege Duodecim   by the Twelve Tables has fallen into
Tabularum introducta est, in de-   desuetude, but that introduced by
suetudinem abiit; quam autem præ-   the prætors, and termed honorary,
tores introduxerunt, quæ etiam   is adopted in the administration of
honoraria appellatur, in judiciis   justice. For, according to the rank
frequentatur, nam secundum gra-   and character of the person injured,
dum dignitatis vitæque honestatem   the estimate is greater or less; and a
crescit aut minuitur æstimatio in-   similar gradation is observed, not im-
juriæ: qui gradus condemnationis   properly, even with regard to a slave,
et in servili persona non immerito   one amount being paid in the case of
servatur, ut aliud in servo actore,   a slave who is a steward, a second in
aliud in medii actus homine, aliud   that of a slave holding an office of an
in vilissimo vel compedito consti-   intermediate class, and a third in
tuatur.                          that of one of the lowest rank, or
                            one condemned to wear fetters.

Gai. iii. 223, 224; D. xlvii. 10. 15. 44.

The greater part of the edict of the prætor on this subject is given by Ulpian in different parts of the extracts from his writings (see Digest, xlvii. 10. 15).

8. Sed et lex Cornelia de injuriis loquitur, et injuriarum actionem introduxit, quæ competit ob eam rem quod se pulsatum quis verberatumve, domumve suam vi introitam esse dicat. Domum autem accipimus, sive in propria domo quis habitat, sive in conducta vel gratis sive hospitio receptus sit.

8. The *lex Cornelia* also speaks of injuries, and introduced an *actio injuriarum*, which may be brought when any one alleges that he has been struck or beaten, or that his house has been broken into. And the term ' his house ' includes one which belongs to him and in which he lives, or one he hires, or one in which he is received gratuitously or as a guest.

D. xlvii. 10. 5, pr. and 2.

The *lex Cornelia de Sicariis* (see Tit. 18. 5), though chiefly directed against murderers, also contained provisions against other deeds of violence. *Lex itaque Cornelia ex tribus causis dedit actionem : quod quis pulsatus verberatusve domusve ejus vi introitu sit.* (D. xlvii. 10. 5.)

0. Atrox injuria æstimatur vel ex facto, veluti si quis ab aliquo vulneratus fuerit vel fustibus cæsus; vel ex loco, veluti si cui in theatro vel in foro vel in conspectu prætoris injuria facta sit; vel ex persona, veluti si magistratus injuriam passus fuerit, vel si senatori ab humili injuria facta sit, aut parenti patronove fiat a liberis vel libertis : aliter enim senatoris et parentis patronique, aliter extranei et humilis personæ injuria æstimatur. Nonnunquam et locus vulneris atrocem injuriam facit, veluti si in oculo quis percusserit. Parvi autem refert, utrum patrifamilias an filiofamilias talis injuria facta sit : nam et hæc atrox æstimabitur.

0. An injury is said to be of a grave character, either from the nature of the act, as if any one is wounded or beaten with clubs by another, or from the nature of the place, as when an injury is done in a theatre, a forum, or in the presence of the prætor: sometimes from the quality of the person, as when it is a magistrate that has received the injury, or a senator has sustained it at the hands of a person of low condition, or a parent or patron at the hands of a child or freedman. For the injury done to a senator, a parent, or a patron is estimated differently from an injury done to a person of low condition or to a stranger. Sometimes, it is the part of the body injured that gives the character to the injury, as if any one has been struck in the eye. Nor does it make any difference whether such an injury has been done to a *paterfamilias* or a *filiusfamilias*, it being in either case considered of a grave character.

Gai. iii. 225; D. xlvii. 10. 7, 8; D. xlvii. 8, 0. 1, 2.

If the injury was *atrox*, a freedman might bring an action against his patron, and the emancipated son against his father, but not otherwise. (D. xlvii. 10. 7. 3.) And the prætor himself, in cases of *atrox injuria*, when he gave the formula to

L L

the judge, fixed the maximum of the condemnation, and the judge would not condemn the defendant in a less sum. (GAI. iii. 224.)

10. In summa sciendum est, de omni injuria eum qui passus est, posse vel criminaliter agere vel civiliter. Et si quidem civiliter agatur, æstimatione facta secundum quod dictum est, pœna imponitur; sin autem criminaliter, officio judicis extraordinaria pœna reo irrogatur. Hoc videlicet observando quod Zenoniana constitutio introduxit, ut viri illustres quique super eos sunt, et per procuratorem possint actionem injuriarum criminaliter vel persequi vel suscipere, secundum ejus tenorem qui ex ipsa manifestius apparet.

10. Lastly, it must be observed, that in every case of injury he who has received it may bring either a criminal or a civil action. In the latter, it is a sum estimated as we have said that constitutes the penalty; in the former, the judge, in the exercise of his duty, inflicts on the offender an extraordinary punishment. We must, however, remark, that a constitution of Zeno permits men of the rank of *illustres*, or of any higher rank, to bring or defend the *actio injuriarum* if brought criminally by a procurator, as may be seen more clearly by reading the constitution itself.

D. xlvii. 10. 6; C. ix. 35. 11.

It was only as a very peculiar exception that criminal actions could, like private actions, be brought or defended through a procurator.

11. Non solum autem is injuriarum tenetur, qui fecit injuriam, id est, qui percussit; verum ille quoque continebitur, qui dolo fecit vel curavit ut cui mala pugno percuteretur.

11. Not only is he liable to the *actio injuriarum* who has inflicted the injury, as, for instance, the person who has struck the blow; but he also who has maliciously caused or contrived that any one should be struck.

D. xlvii. 10, 11. 1.

12. Hæc actio dissimulatione aboletur; et ideo si quis injuriam dereliquerit, hoc est, statim passus ad animum suum non revocaverit, postea ex pœnitentia remissam injuriam non poterit recolere.

12. This action is extinguished by a person dissembling to have received the injury; and, therefore, a person who has taken no account of the injury, that is, who immediately on receiving it has shown no resentment at it, cannot afterwards change his mind and resuscitate the injury he has allowed to rest.

D. xlvii. 10, 11. 1.

If the person injured, though expressing indignation at the time, did not take any steps towards enforcing reparation within a year, the action was extinct. (D. xlvii. 10. 17. 6; C. ix. 35. 5.) The action was personal to the person injured, and could not be transmitted to his heirs, unless before his death the action had already proceeded as far as the *litis contestatio*.

## Tit. V.   DE OBLIGATIONIBUS QUÆ QUASI EX DELICTO NASCUNTUR.

Si judex litem suam fecerit, non proprie ex maleficio obligatus videtur: sed quia neque ex contractu obligatus est, et utique peccasse aliquid intelligitur, licet per imprudentiam, ideo videtur quasi ex maleficio teneri; et in quantum de ea re æquum religioni judicantis videbitur, pœnam sustinebit.

If a judge makes a cause his own, he does not, properly speaking, seem to be bound *ex maleficio*: but as he is neither bound *ex maleficio*, nor *ex contractu*, and as he has, nevertheless, done a wrong, although perhaps only from ignorance, he seems to be bound as it were *ex maleficio*, and will be condemned to the amount which seems equitable to the conscience of the judge.

D. 1. 13. 6.

The Roman law characterized rather arbitrarily certain wrongful acts as delicts, and then, as there were many other wrongful acts which bound the wrong-doer to make reparation, and as it could not be said that the wrong-doer was bound *ex delicto*, he was said to be bound *quasi ex delicto*, i. e. there was an evident analogy between the mode in which the obligation arose from other kinds of wrong-doing and that in which it arose from the kinds of wrong-doing technically called delicts. The principle was exactly the same, but the particular act did not happen to be among those technically termed delicts. The first instance given is that of a judge *qui litem suam fecerit*, that is, who, through favour, corruption, or fear (D. v. 1. 15. 1), or even ignorance of law (*licet per imprudentiam*), gives a manifestly wrong sentence, and who thus makes the *lis* or suit to be *sua*, that is, affect himself by rendering him responsible for the sentence. Gaius gives an example, in the case of a judge condemning a defendant in a sum different from that fixed in the *formula*. (GAI. iv. 52.)

The defendant might, if be pleased, instead of bringing an action against the judge, appeal from his decision; and in some cases, as when the judge had violated public law, or been corrupted, he might treat the decision as null, and commence the action afresh (D. xlix. 1. 5. 19); but his adversary might be insolvent, or his indignation, or many other reasons, might make him prefer suing the judge.

Ducaurroy points out that the distinction made between the seemingly parallel cases of an ignorant physician and an ignorant judge, the fault of the former being punished under the *lex Aquilia*, the latter being bound *quasi ex delicto*, arises from the injury of the physician being done to the body. The severity of the penalty against a judge who was merely ignorant of the law, is owing probably to the great checks against ignorance which the judge possessed if he pleased to avail himself of them in the advice of the '*prudentes*,' whose business it was to assist him, and in the possibility of having recourse to the magistrate who had given the action to him.

1. Item is ex cujus cœnaculo, vel proprio ipsius vel in quo gratis habitabat, dejectum effusumve aliquid est, ita ut alicui noceretur, quasi ex maleficio obligatus intelligitur. Ideo autem non proprie ex maleficio obligatus intelligitur quia plerumque ob alterius culpam tenetur, aut servi aut liberi. Cui similis est is qui, ea parte qua vulgo iter fieri solet, id positum aut suspensum habet quod potest, si ceciderit, alicui nocere: quo casu pœna decem aureorum constituta est. De eo vero quod dejectum effusumve est, dupli quanti damnum datum sit, constituta est actio: ob hominem vero liberum occisum, quinquaginta aureorum pœna constituitur; si vero vivat nocitumque ei esse dicatur, quantum ob eam rem æquum judici videtur, actio datur. Judex enim computare debet mercedem medicis præstitas, ceteraque impendia quæ in curatione facta sunt, præterea operarum quibus caruit aut cariturus est, ob id quod inutilis factus est.

1. So, too, be who occupies, whether as proprietor or gratuitously, an apartment, from which anything has been thrown or poured down, which has done damage to another, is said to be bound *quasi ex maleficio*, for be is not exactly bound *ex maleficio*, as it is generally by the fault of another, a slave, for instance, or a freedman, that be is bound. It is the same with regard to a person who, on a public way, keeps something placed or suspended, which may, if it fall, hurt any one; in this case, a penalty has been fixed of ten *aurei*. With respect to things thrown or poured down, an action is given for double the amount of the damage done; and if a freeman has been killed, there is a penalty of fifty *aurei*. If be is not killed, but only hurt, the action is given for the amount which the judge considers equitable under the circumstances; the judge ought to take into account the fees paid to the physician, and all the other expenses of the man's illness, as well as the employment which he has lost, or will lose, by being incapacitated.

D. xliv. 7. 5. 6; D. ix. 3. 5, 6; D. ix. 3. 1; D. ix. 3. 7.

The edict of the prætor, in both cases alluded to in the text, is given, D. ix. 3. 1; and D. ix. 3. 5, 6.

The action given in each case was *popularis*, that is, any one might bring it, but in the case of a freeman being killed, his heirs or relations, if they brought an action, were preferred to strangers.

2. Si filiusfamilias seorsum a patre habitaverit, et quid ex cœnaculo ejus dejectum, effusumve sit, sive quid positum suspensumve habuerit, cujus casus periculosus est, Juliano placuit in patrem nullam esse actionem, sed cum ipso filio agen-

2. If a *filiusfamilias* lives apart from his father, and from a room in his house anything is thrown or poured down, or is placed or suspended, the fall of which would be dangerous, Julian thinks that no action could be brought against the

dum. Quod et in filiosfamilias judice observandum est, qui litem suam fecerit.

father, but only against the son. The same holds good with respect to a filiusfamilias, who, being a judge, has made a cause his own.

D. xliv. 7. 5. 5; D. v. 1. 15.

In the case of a *filiusfamilias*, the father was not obliged even to repair the injury done to the extent of the son's *peculium* (see Tit. 5. 10); but if a slave had done the injury, the master was always bound to repair the damage, or to abandon the slave. (See Tit. 8.)

3. Item exercitor navis aut cauponae aut stabuli de damno aut furto quod in navi aut caupona aut stabulo factum erit, quasi ex maleficio teneri videtur, si malo ipsius nullum est maleficium, sed alicujus eorum quorum opera navem aut cauponam aut stabulum exerceret; cum enim ne que ex contractu sit adversus eum constituta haec actio, et aliqua tenus culpae reus est, quod opera malorum hominum uteretur, ideo quasi ex maleficio teneri videtur. In his autem casibus in factum actio competit, quae heredi quidem datur, adversus heredem autem non competit.

3. The master of a ship, of an inn, or a stable, is liable *quasi ex maleficio*, for any damage or loss through theft occurring in the ship, inn, or stable, that is, if it is not he who has committed the wrongful deed, but some one employed in the service of the ship, inn, or stable. For as the action given against him does not arise *ex maleficio* or *ex contractu*, and yet he is in fault in employing dishonest persons as his servants, he seems to be bound *quasi ex maleficio*. In these cases it is an action *factum* that is given, and it may be brought by the heir, but not against the heir.

D. xliv. 7. 5, 6; D. ix. 3. 5. 13.

The person injured might also, at his option, have an *actio furti*, or *Aquiliae*, as the case might be, against the actual wrong-doer. (D. xlvii. 5.)

## Tit. VI.  DE ACTIONIBUS.

Superest ut de actionibus loquamur. Actio autem nihil aliud est, quam jus persequendi judicio quod sibi debetur.

It now remains that we speak of actions. An action is nothing else than the right of suing before a judge for that which is due to us.

D. xliv. 7. 51.

A sketch has been given in the Introduction (secs. 90–111) of the Roman System of Civil Process. In the time of Justinian the system of *extraordinaria judicia* (Introd. sec. 108) had long been established, and the praetorian system of *formulae* abolished. But it was under the system of *formulae* that Roman law received its characteristic shape, and the great jurists wrote. In this Title of the Institutes Justinian, bor-

rowing from writers who treated all actions with reference to
the system of *formulæ*, uses the language of the prætorian
system.　A knowledge, therefore, of the outlines of that system
is indispensable for the comprehension of this Title.　For an
account of its main features the reader is referred to sections
98 to 106 of the Introduction.

| | |
|---|---|
| 1. Omnium actionum quibus inter aliquos apud judices arbitrosve de quacomque re quæritur, summa divisio in duo genera deducitur: aut enim in rem sunt, aut in personam. Namque agit unusquisque aut cum eo qui ei obligatus est vel ex contractu vel ex maleficio, quo casu proditæ sunt actiones in personam, per quas intendit adversarium ei dare facere oportere, et aliis quibusdam modis; aut cum eo agit qui nullo jure ei obligatus est, movet tamen alicui de aliqua re controversiam, quo casu proditæ actiones in rem sunt: veluti si rem corporalem possidet quis, quam Titius suam esse affirmet et possessor dominium se esse dicat; nam si Titius suam esse intendat, in rem actio est. | 1. All actions whatever, by which any matter whatever is submitted to the decision of judges or of arbitrators may be divided into two classes; for actions are either real or personal. Either the plaintiff sues the defendant, because he is made answerable to him by contract, or by a delict, in which case the plaintiff brings a personal action, alleging that his adversary is bound to give to, or to do something for him, or making some other similar allegation. Or else the plaintiff brings an action against a person not made answerable to him by any obligation, but with whom he disputes the right to some corporeal thing, and for such cases real actions are given: as, for example, if a man is in possession of land, which Titius maintains to be his property, while the possessor says that he himself is the proprietor, the action is real. |

Gai. iv. 1. 3; D. xliv. 7. 25.

The first and most important division of actions is that into
actions *in rem* and actions *in personam*, by the first of which
we assert a right over a thing against all the world, by the
second we assert a right against a particular person.　(See
Introd. sec. 61.)　And, accordingly, speaking technically, an
action was called real when the formula in which it was conceived embodied a claim to a thing without saying from whom
it was claimed, and personal, when the formula stated upon
whom a claim was made.　If Titius said that a piece of land
belonged to him, there was no necessity that the name of the
wrongful occupier should appear in the formula; at any rate
not in the *intentio*, the part of the formula always considered
characteristic of the *actio*.　'*Si paret Titii esse rem.*'　This
was all; the question to be decided was, does the thing belong
to Titius?　It was only as a consequence of Titius' proprietorship being established that the wrongful occupier, whose name
might appear in the *condemnatio*, was condemned to lose the
possession.　But in an action arising on a contract, the name
of a person was necessarily introduced into the *intentio*.　Titius

could not merely say a thing was owed to him; he must add
that it was owed by a particular person.  There are, indeed,
some cases, as, for instance, a deposit, in which the action may
be equally well shaped with or without the insertion of the
name of a particular person.  There may either be a real action
in which the plaintiff claims the thing, or a personal one in
which he says that the depositary ought to give it him.
Whenever the action is made to rest on an obligation, it is
personal, when on a right of proprietorship it is real.

The words *aliis quibusdam modis* in the text refer to the
*intentio* of the formula, which did not, in a personal action,
always run either *dare oportere*, or *facere oportere*, but in
other ways, especially that of *præstare oportere*.

A real action was termed *vindicatio* or *petitio*.  A personal
action, when brought *dare* or *facere*, received the name of
*condictio*.  Ulpian gives *condictio* as a generic name for all
actions *in personam*.  (D. xliv. 7. 25.)  For an account of
the different kinds of *condictio*, in a limited sense, see note
on Bk. iii. Tit. 13. 2; and see also paragr. 15 of this Title.

As preliminary to the divisions of actions given in this Title,
it may be useful to repeat that actions *in personam*, if based
on a contract, and raising a question of law as well as of fact,
may be divided into (1) condictions, given to enforce unilateral
contracts, and being *certi* when the claim was certain, *incerti*
when it was not; (2) prætorian actions, having special names,
given principally to enforce bilateral contracts; and (3) actions
*in factum præscriptis verbis*, given to enforce contracts not
falling under the four heads of contracts, and not having special
names.  (See Bk. iii. Tit. 13. 2.)  All conditions were *stricti
juris*, that is, the judge was bound by the strict rules of law,
unless there was an exception appealing to equity introduced
into the formulæ.  All the prætorian actions given to enforce
bilateral contracts, as well as certainly most, and probably all,
other actions of exclusively prætorian origin, were *bonæ fidei*,
i.e. the judge needed no exception to enable him to consider
the equitable circumstances of the case.  The *intentio* of every
personal action, except a *condictio certi*, was *incerta*, i.e. it
ran '*quicquid paret*,' not *si paret*.  Personal actions brought
on a delict were either in the form of the particular action
given by the law which made the offence a delict, or were *in
factum præscriptis verbis*.

We have said, ' based on a contract, and raising a question
of law, as well as of fact,' because there was an important kind
of personal actions, those *in factum conceptæ* (to be carefully
distinguished from those *in factum præscriptis verbis*), in

which the magistrate merely directed the judge to ascertain whether a particular statement was true, and if it was, to condemn the defendant. There was, in such an action, no application of the rules of law to be made by the judge, as there was in those which ran *si paret oportere*, and were *in jus conceptæ*. (See Introd. sec. 106, and note on paragr. 28.)

2. Æque si agat jus sibi esse fundo forte vel ædibus utendi fruendi, vel per fundum vicini eundi agendi, vel ex fundo vicini aquam ducendi, in rem actio est. Ejusdem generis est actio de jure prædiorum urbanorum : veluti, si agat jus sibi esse altius ædes suas tollendi, prospiciendive, vel projiciendi aliquid, vel immittendi in vicini ædes. Contra quoque de usufructu et de servitutibus prædiorum rusticorum, item prædiorum urbanorum, invicem quoque proditæ sunt actiones, ut si quis intendat jus non esse adversario utendi fruendi. eundi agendi, aquamve ducendi, item altius tollendi, prospiciendi, projiciendi, immittendi. Istæ quoque actiones in rem sunt, sed negativæ. Quod genus actionis in controversiis rerum corporalium proditum non est, nam in his is agit qui non possidet; ei vero qui possidet, non est actio prodita per quam neget rem actoris esse. Sane uno casu, qui possidet uihilominus actoris partes obtinet, sicut in latioribus Digestorum libris opportunius apparebit.

2. So, too, if any one alleges that he has a right to the usufruct of land, or of a house, or that he has a right of going or driving his cattle, or of conducting water, over the land of his neighbour, the action is real: as also are actions relating to prædial servitudes, as when a man alleges a right to raise his house, a right to an uninterrupted view, a right to make part of his house project, or of inserting the beams of his building into his neighbour's walls. There are also actions relating to usufructs, and the servitudes of country and city estates, which are the reverse of these; as when the complainant alleges that his adversary is not entitled to the usufruct, or has not the right to go, to drive, to conduct water, to raise his house, to have an uninterrupted view, to throw out projections, or to insert his beams. These actions are equally real, but are negative, and cannot therefore be used in disputes respecting things corporeal, for in these disputes it is the person out of possession who brings the action: for a possessor cannot bring an action to deny that the thing is the property of the plaintiff. There is, however, one case, in which a possessor may act the part of plaintiff; which will be more fully seen if reference is made to the books of the Digest.

Gai. iv. 3; D. viii. 5. 2; D. xxxix. 1. 15.

Usufructs, uses, rural and urban servitudes, might be the objects of real actions. These actions were either *confessoriæ*, or *negativæ*; in the former the plaintiff claimed to exercise a servitude over the immoveables of another, in the latter he maintained that a servitude which another attempted to exercise over an immoveable belonging to the plaintiff was not due.

Both the *actio confessoria* and the *actio negativa* might be brought, whether the claimant was or was not in the *quasi possessio* of the servitude in question. If the *actio confessoria* was brought by a person not in quasi-possession, the action falls very obviously under actions *in rem*. A claims a servitude over the land of B; the servitude is a *res*, and the action is as much one *in rem* as if the claim was for the land itself. But A might really be in quasi-possession of this servitude, and yet bring an *actio confessoria* to secure his possession, supposing it were threatened or made insecure, and such an action is a wide departure from an ordinary action *in rem*. If a claim of a servitude was resisted by an *actio negativa* brought by the owner of the immoveable over which it was claimed, then, supposing the owner was not in quasi-possession of the servitude, but the person was in quasi-possession of it who claimed the servitude, the *actio negativa* amounted, in fact, to an affirmative action *in rem*. It has a *res*, viz. the servitude, which A says is part of his *dominium*, and has never been separated from it, and belongs to him, and A might very well bring an ordinary action *in rem* to recover it; but in the case of a servitude the action took a form which it could not take in the case of a claim to a *res corporalis*. The claimant of a *res corporalis* would gain nothing by having it declared that B was not the owner of the thing, for that would not show that he himself was; but if the owner of an immoveable had it declared that a servitude claimed did not exist, he had, as the result of the action, the immoveable freed from the servitude. If the person who brought the *actio negativa* was in quasi-possession of the servitude, or, rather, if he was in possession of the immoveable, so that the servitude did not exist, but was only claimed by another, then this action was, like the *actio confessoria*, brought by the quasi-possessor only as a means of securing himself in the possession. And the reason why such actions were brought in the case of servitudes, and not of *res corporales*, was, that possession of the latter was sufficiently protected by the interdicts *uti possidetis* and *utrubi*, of which more will be said in the 15th Title. These interdicts were not granted to quasi-possessors, and though interdicts were, in process of time, given by the prætors to protect quasi-possession, yet these actions remained as a concurrent means of security.

*Sane uno casu.* It is a subject of much dispute what is the one case in which the possessor could be plaintiff. Probably the words are but a summary of what has gone before. ' There is, indeed, but one case of a person in possession being plaintiff, that, namely, of the possessor of an incorporeal thing.'

3. Sed istæ quidem actiones quarum mentionem habuimus, et si quæ sunt similes, ex legitimis et civilibus causis descendunt. Aliæ autem sunt quas prætor ex sua jurisdictione comparatas habet tam in rem quam in personam, quas et ipsas necessarium est exemplis ostendere: ecce plerumque ita permittitur in rem agere, ut vel actor diceret se quasi usucepisse quod non usuceperit, vel ex diverso possessor diceret adversarium suum non usucepisse quod usuceperit.

3. The actions just mentioned, and those of a similar nature, are derived from particular laws and from the jus civile; but there are others, both real and personal, which the prætor, by virtue of his jurisdiction, has introduced, and of which it is necessary to give some examples: thus the prætor often permits a real action to be brought, by which the plaintiff is allowed to allege, that he has acquired something by prescription, which he has not acquired; or by which, on the contrary, the possessor alleges that his adversary has not acquired something by prescription, which, in reality, he has acquired.

D. xliv. 7. 25. 2.

The second division of actions, given in this Title, is that of civil and prætorian. The two methods principally adopted by the prætor to give an action in cases not provided for by the civil law, were either to construct a formula on a fictitious hypothesis, or make the action one *in factum concepta*. (See Introd. paragr. 106.) The three following paragraphs give examples of fictitious actions *in rem*.

Justinian notices five prætorian actions *in rem*, viz. the *actio Publiciana*, the *actio quasi Publiciana*, the *actio Pauliana*, the *actio Serviana*, and the *actio quasi Serviana*, and gives as instances of the numerous prætorian actions *in personam*, the actions *de pecunia constituta*, *de peculio*, &c. (See paragr. 8, and foll.)

4. Namque si cui ex justa causa res aliqua tradita fuerit, veluti ex causa emptionis aut donationis aut dotis aut legatorum, necdum ejus rei dominus effectus est; si ejus rei possessionem casu amiserit, nullam habet directam in rem actionem ad eam persequendam, quippe ita proditæ sunt jure civili actiones ut quis dominium suum vindicet: sed quia sane durum erat eo casu deficere actionem, inventa est a prætore actio in qua dicit is qui possessionem amisit, eam rem se usucepisse, et ita vindicat suum rem. Quæ actio Publiciana appellatur, quoniam primum a Publicio prætore in edicto proposita est.

4. For instance, if anything is delivered for a just cause, as a purchase, gift, dowry, or legacy, to a person who has not yet become proprietor of the thing delivered, if he chances to lose the possession, he has no direct action for its recovery; inasmuch as the civil law only permits such actions to be brought by the proprietor. But, as it was very hard that there should be no action given in such a case, the prætor has introduced one, in which the person who has lost the possession, alleges he has acquired the thing in question by prescription, although he has not really so acquired it, and he thus claims it as his own. This action is called the *actio Publiciana*, because it was first placed in the edict by the prætor Publicius.

GAI. iv. 30.

When any one except the real owner of a thing (*dominus*) delivered over a thing on a ground and in a mode which would have sufficed to have passed the property, if he had had it to pass, or if an owner of a thing transferred a thing by a mode insufficient to pass the *dominium*, as if a *res mancipi* was delivered without mancipation, the person, in either of these cases, to whom the thing was delivered, being a *bona fide* possessor, could perfect his title to it by usucapion; but if he lost the thing out of his possession after it was delivered to him, but before the time necessary to complete the usucapion had expired, the civil law gave him no remedy, for he was not the *dominus*, and none but a *dominus* could claim a thing by ' *vindicatio.*' The *actio Publiciana* was therefore given for his relief by the prætor Publicius, perhaps the Publicius mentioned as prætor by Cicero. (*Pro Cluent.* 45.) In this action the plaintiff was allowed to state what was in fact not true, that the usucapion was complete, and thus to claim as if his ownership was absolute. If the thing had fallen into the hands of a person who himself claimed to be really the *dominus*, and to have a *bona fide* ground of repelling the *actio Publiciana*, it could be repelled by an exception termed the *exceptio justi dominii.* (D. vi. 2. 16.)

If it had fallen into the hands of a person who did not claim to be the owner, but who had so acquired it as to be in a situation to perfect his title by usucapion, i. e. who was also a *bona fide* possessor, and the plaintiff brought an *actio Publiciana* for it before the time of the usucapion had expired, the title of the actual holder of the thing was considered the better; for *in pari causa melior est conditio possidentis.* The formula of the action ran thus: '*Judex esto. Si quem hominem Aulus Agerius emit, quique ei traditus esset, anno possedisset, tum si eum hominem, de quo agitur, ejus ex jure Quiritium esse oporteret.*' (GAI. iv. 36.)

The *actio Publiciana* might also be useful to a person who was really the owner; for while the distinction between *res mancipi* and *nec mancipi* was retained, the owner of a thing requiring to be passed by mancipation might have himself received it by mancipation, but be unable to show that the person who transferred it to him was really the *dominus*, and had in his turn received it by mancipation. If he lost the thing before he had perfected the title by usucapion, he could not bring a *vindicatio*, but was obliged to have recourse to the *actio Publiciana*; and before the legislation of Justinian this action was especially useful to persons who had received a transfer of things which, like the provincial lands, could not be made the subject of a perfect *dominium*, and the title to which could not be perfected by usucapion (see Bk. ii. Tit. 6); for they were allowed to bring this fictitious action if they were deprived of the possession, at any rate after the time entitling them to use the *præscriptio longi temporis* had elapsed. (C. vii. 39. 8.)

5. Rursus ex diverso si quis, cum reipublicæ causa abesset vel in hostium potestate esset, rem ejus qui in civitate esset usuceperit, permittitur domino, si possessor reipublicæ causa abesse desierit, tunc intra annum rescissa usucapione eam rem petere, id est, ita petere ut dicat possessorem usu non cepisse, et ob id suam rem esse. Quod genus actionis quibusdam et aliis simili æquitate motus prætor accommodat, sicut ex latiore Digestorum seu Pandectarum volumine intelligere licet.

5. On the contrary, if any one, while abroad in the service of his country, or a prisoner in the hands of the enemy, has acquired by usucapion a thing which belongs to another person resident at home, then the proprietor is permitted within a year after the return of the possessor, to bring an action by rescinding the usucapion; that is, he may allege that the possessor has not acquired by prescription, and that the thing therefore is his. Similar feelings of equity have led the prætor to grant this species of action in certain other cases, as may be learnt from the larger treatises of the Digest or Pandects.

D. iv. 6. 21; D. iv. 1. 1, 2; D. iv. 0. 1.1.

This paragraph gives the converse case. Before, the usucapion was not complete, and the action supplied what was wanting to it. Here the usucapion is complete, and the action takes away its effect.

Such an action might be wanted in either of two cases. Either the proprietor of the thing might be absent, or deprived, on the legitimate ground, of the power of attending to his affairs; and during this time the usucapion might have been completed against him; or the possessor, the person in whose favour the time of usucapion was running, might have been absent, and the proprietor, not being able to sue him, might have been unable to stop the usucapion. In either of these cases this kind of *actio Publiciana*, called *rescissoria*, because the usucapion was rescinded, came to the aid of the proprietor. It is to be remarked that Justinian notices only the latter of the two cases, and yet he had provided a much more simple remedy in behalf of proprietors, who were allowed to interrupt the usucapion of an absent possessor by a protestation made before a magistrate. (C. vii. 40. 2.)

The *actio Publiciana rescissoria* had to be brought within a year, commencing from the time when it first became possible to bring the action. *Intra annum, quo primum de ea re experiundi potestas erit.* (D. iv. 6 1. 1.) The year was a *utilis annus*, and its length, therefore, varied in different cases, for which Justinian substituted the uniform term of four years.

*Quibusdam et aliis.* Such as the *restitutio in integrum,* by which the prætor protected a person under the age of twenty-five years. (See Bk. i. Tit. 23, pr.)

6. Item, si quis in fraudem creditorum rem suam alicui tradiderit, bonis ejus a creditoribus ex sententia præsidis possessis, permittitur ipsis creditoribus rescissa traditione eam rem petere, id est, dicere eam rem traditam non esse, et ob id in bonis debitoris mansisse.

6. Again, if a debtor deliver to a third person anything that is his property, in order to defraud his creditors, who have seized on his goods by order of the prætor, the creditors are permitted to rescind the delivery, and bring an action for the thing delivered; that is, they may allege that the thing was not delivered, and that it therefore continues to be a part of the debtor's goods.

D. xlii. 8. 1, pr. 1, 2.

Theophilus tells us that this action was called the *actio Pauliana.* The *lex Ælia Sentia* (see Bk. i. Tit. 7) had made enfranchisements in fraud of creditors void; but the law did not extend to alienations; and the prætor, therefore, when the creditors had taken possession of the effects of the debtor, permitted them to reclaim anything which had been alienated after insolvency and with intent to defraud.

The *actio Pauliana in rem* (says Ortolan) is not spoken of elsewhere in the works of Roman law which have come down to us. It must not be confounded with the *actio Pauliana in personam* treated of in the Digest (xxii. 1. 38, pr. and 4), which was given, not only in case of alienation, but of every act whereby the debtor had diminished his assets, and the *intentio* of which was directed against the particular person who had profited by such an act, and not as that of the *actio in rem,* which forms the subject of this paragraph, against any one who happened to be the person detaining the thing claimed.

7. Item Serviana, et quasi Serviana, quæ etiam hypothecaria vocatur, ex ipsius prætoris jurisdictione substantiam capiunt. Serviana autem experitur quis de rebus coloni, quæ pignoris jure pro mercedibus fundi ei tenentur; quasi Serviana autem, qua creditores pignora hypothecasve persequuntur. Inter pignus autem et hypothecam, quantum ad actionem hypothecariam attinet, nihil interest: nam de qua re inter creditorem et debitorem convenerit ut sit pro debito obligata, utraque hac appellatione continetur, sed in aliis differentia est: nam pignoris appellatione eam proprie rem contineri dicimus, quæ simul etiam traditur

7. The *actio Serviana,* and the *actio quasi-Serviana* also called *hypothecaria,* equally take their rise from the prætor's jurisdiction. The *actio Serviana* is brought to get possession of the effects of a farmer which are held as a pledge to secure the rent of the land. The *actio quasi-Serviana* is that, by which creditors sue for things pledged or mortgaged to them; and, as regards this action, there is no difference between a pledge and a *hypothecha;* for the two terms are indifferently applied to anything which the debtor and creditor agree shall be bound as security for the debt; but in other points there is a distinction between them. The term pledge

creditori, maxime si mobilis sit; at eam quæ sine traditione nuda conventione tenetur, proprie hypothecæ appellatione contineri dicimus.

is properly applied to a thing which has actually been delivered to a creditor, especially if the thing be a moveable; the term *hypotheca* means anything bound by simple agreement without delivery.

D. xt. 2. 4; D. xx. 1. 17. 5. 1; D. xiiL 7. 9. 2.

We have already given a slight sketch of the *jus pignoris*, and the relative position of the creditor and debtor, at the end of the fifth Title of the Second Book. The interest of the creditor was not thought sufficient to support a *vindicatio* if he lost the thing pledged out of his possession, or wished to get the thing subjected to a *hypotheca* into his possession; but a prætorian action enabled him to effect this. The *actio Serviana* mentioned in this paragraph was given to enforce the claim of the landlord to the farming instruments, which, without any special agreement, were considered, in law, to be held as a pledge for the rent of the farm, and the *actio quasi-Serviana* was an extension of this, giving a means to every creditor of enforcing his right to anything pledged or mortgaged.

*Maxime si mobilis sit.* An immoveable might of course be given in pledge; but it would generally happen that things given in pledge were moveables.

A thing subjected to successive *hypothecæ* belonged, as we have said in treating of the real right given by the *jus pignoris* (Bk. ii. Tit. 5), to the person in whose favour the first *hypotheca* was constituted. If, therefore, a creditor, whose *hypotheca* was subsequent, brought the *actio quasi-Serviana* against a creditor whose *hypotheca* was prior, he would be repelled by an exception. (C. viii. 18. 6.)

8. In personam quoque actiones ex sua jurisdictione propositas habet prætor, veluti de pecunia constituta, cui similis videbatur receptitia. Sed ex nostra constitutione, cum et si quid plenius habebat, hoc in actionem pecuniæ constitutæ transfusum est, ea quasi supervacua jussa est cum sua auctoritate a nostris legibus recedere. Item prætor proposuit de peculio servorum filiorumque familias, et ex qua quæritur an actor juraverit, et alias complures.

8. There are also personal actions which the prætor has introduced in the exercise of his jurisdiction, as, for instance, the action *de pecunia constituta*, which that called *receptitia* much resembled. But the *actio receptitia* has been rendered superfluous by all its advantages being transferred to the *actio pecuniæ constitutæ*, and has, therefore, by one of our constitutions, lost its authority, and disappeared from our legislation. The prætor has likewise introduced an action concerning the *peculium* of slaves, and of *filiifamiliarum*, an action in which the question is tried, whether the plaintiff has made oath, and many others.

C. iv. 18. 2, pr. and 1.

See notes to succeeding paragraphs.

9. De constituta autem pecunia cum omnibus agitur quicumque pro se vel pro alio soluturos se constituerint, nulla scilicet stipulatione interposita; nam alioquin, si stipulanti promiserint, jure civili tenentur.

9. The *actio de constituta pecunia* may be brought against any person who has engaged to pay money, either for himself or another, without having made a stipulation; for, if he has promised a stipulator, he is bound by the civil law.

D. xiii. 5. 14. 3.

The *actio de constituta pecunia* was an action by which the prætor enforced a mere pact or agreement (not a stipulation, for then the action would have been *ex stipulatu*) by which a person promised again what he already owed, or promised what another owed, fixing the time for payment. This agreement (*constitutum*) did not operate as a novation, and was enforced as subsidiary to the main contract. The *actio de constituta pecunia* could only be brought within a year, and only applied to things which could form the subject of a *mutuum*, i.e. things *quæ numero, pondere, mensurive constant*. The *pecunia* was said to be *constituta* because it was agreed to be paid on a particular day. The *actio receptitia* was an action given against bankers (*argentarii*) who promised to satisfy the demands of a creditor of one of their customers. This creditor was said *recipere diem*, to have a day fixed by the banker for payment of his claim, and hence the action was called *receptitia*. The mere promise of the banker was considered enough to ground an action on, an exception to the ordinary rules of the civil law which must have grown out of the peculiar character of a banker's business. What the civil law confined to bankers only the prætor extended to every one alike; and whenever any one, who owed a debt to another or had funds of another in his hand, promised to pay the money owed by or deposited with him on a particular day, the prætor gave the action *de constituta pecunia* to enforce the fulfilment of the promise. Justinian abolished the *actio receptitia*, and invested the *actio de constituta pecunia* with privileges which had before belonged exclusively to the *actio receptitia*; for he made it perpetual, and he allowed it to be brought whatever was the nature of the thing promised. (C. iv. 18. 2.)

10. Actiones autem de peculio ideo adversus patrem dominumve comparavit prætor, quia licet ex contractu filiorum servorumve ipso jure non teneantur, æquum tamen est peculio tenus, quod veluti patri-

10. The prætor has introduced actions *de peculio* against fathers and masters, because, although they are not, according to the civil law, bound by the contracts of their children and slaves, yet they ought in equity to be

monium est filiorum filiarumque, item servorum, condemnari eos.

bound to the extent of the *peculium*, which is a kind of patrimony of sons and daughters, and of slaves.

D. xv. 1. 47. 6.

The actions *de peculio*, of which there were several, are treated of in paragr. 4 of next Title.

11. Item si quis, postulante adversario, juraverit deberi sibi pecuniam quam peteret, neque ei solvatur, justissime accommodat ei talem actionem, per quam non illud queritur an ei pecunia debeatur, sed an juraverit.

11. Also, if any one, when called upon by his adversary, makes oath, that the debt which he sues for is due and unpaid, the prætor most justly grants him an action, in which the inquiry is not whether the debt is due, but whether the oath has been made.

D. xii. 2. 3. 5. 2.

Either party might challenge the other to swear to the truth of his statement. This was done out of court, and if the party challenged took the oath, his statement could no longer be impugned by the person who had challenged him. For instance, if the creditor, being challenged, swore that the debt was due, the debtor was obliged to pay. The only question, therefore, which could be subsequently referred to a court of justice was whether the oath had or had not been taken, inquiry into which circumstance was made under an *actio in factum* given by the prætor.

12. Pœnales quoque actiones bene multas ex sua jurisdictione introduxit; veluti adversus eum qui quid ex albo ejus corrupisset, et in eum qui patronum vel parentem in jus vocasset, cum id non impetrasset; item adversus eum qui vi exemerit eum qui in jus vocaretur, cujusve dolo alius exemerit, et alias innumerabiles.

12. The prætor has also introduced many penal actions by virtue of his jurisdiction. As, for instance, against a person who has damaged any part of the prætor's *album*; against those who summon before the prætor their patron or father without previous permission from the proper magistrate; against those who carry away by force any one summoned to appear before the prætor, or fraudulently induce a third person to carry him off; and very many other actions.

Gai. iv. 46.

The *album* was the tablet suspended in the forum, containing the ordinances of the prætor. Any attempt to injure or deface it was punished by an action *de albo corrupto*.

The descendant or freedman who summoned before a magistrate (*in jus*) his ascendant or patron without the permission of the prætor, was liable to an action termed *de parente aut patrono in jus vocato*.

The *actio de in jus vocato vi exempto* was given against a

person who rescued with violence any one who, after disobeying a notice to appear *in jure*, was being forcibly conveyed before the magistrate. The penalty was a sum equivalent to that which the plaintiff would have received from the action he had commenced against the person rescued, while this person rescued remained still liable to the action he had been summoned to answer.

13. Præjudiciales actiones in rem esse videntur; quales sunt per quas quæritur an aliquis liber, an libertus sit, vel de partu agnoscendo. Ex quibus fere una illa legitimam causam habet, per quam quæritur an aliquis liberssit: ceteræ ex ipsius prætoris jurisdictione substantiam capiunt.

13. Prejudicial actions seem to be real actions; such are those by which it is inquired whether a man is born free, or has been made free; whether he be a slave, or whether he is the offspring of his reputed father. But of these, that alone by which it is inquired whether a man is free, belongs to the civil law. The others spring from the prætor's jurisdiction.

GAI. iv. 44; C. viii. 47. 9.

The object of a *prejudicialis actio* was to ascertain a fact, the establishing of which was a necessary preliminary to further judicial proceedings. (See Introd. paragr. 104.) Such actions differ from actions *in rem*, because in an *actio prejudicialis* no one is condemned, only the fact is ascertained; but they are said in the text to resemble actions *in rem* because they were not brought on any obligation, and because in the *intentio*, which indeed composed the whole formula in this case, no mention was made of any particular person.

Questions of *status*, such as those of paternity, filiation, patronage, and the like, were most commonly the subjects of *actiones prejudiciales*, but were by no means the only ones. We hear of others, such as *quanta dos sit* (GAI. iv. 44); an *res de qua agitur major sit centum sestertiis; an bona jure venierint.* (D. xlii. 5. 30.)

The *liberalis causa*, the suit in which the *status* of a supposed slave was ascertained, was originally nothing else but a *vindicatio*. The person called the *assertor libertatis* claimed him, and the master of the slave defended his possession. If the decision was in favour of the *assertor*, it was still open to another person to attempt to prove that the subject of the suit was really a slave; if the decision was in favour of the master, another *assertor* could bring a fresh suit; but there could only be three *assertores* in all. If the supposed slave was thrice adjudged a slave, his *status* could be no further questioned. Justinian entirely altered the action, by allowing the slave himself to claim his liberty, and making the first decision final. (C. vii. 16.)

M M

It was Appius Claudius who inserted the law respecting the *liberalis causa*, which had existed previously, in the Twelve Tables. (D. i. 2. 2. 24.)

14. Sic itaque discretis actionibus, certum est non posse actorem suam rem ita ab aliquo petere, si paret eum dare oportere; nec enim quod actoris est, id ei dari oportet, quia scilicet dari cuiquam id intelligitur, quod ita datur ut ejus fiat, nec res quae jam actoris est magis ejus fieri potest. Plane odio furum, quo magis pluribus actionibus teneantur, effectum est ut, extra poenam dupli aut quadrupli, rei recipiendae nomine fures etiam hac actione teneantur si paret eos dare oportere, quamvis sit adversus eos etiam haec in rem actio per quam rem suam quis esse petit.

14. Actions being thus divided, it is certain that a plaintiff cannot sue for his own property by such a formula as this, ' If it appear that the defendant ought to give.' For it is not a duty to give the plaintiff that which is his own. To give a thing is to transfer the property in it, and that which is already the property of the plaintiff cannot belong to him more than it does already. However, to show detestation for thieves, and to make them liable to a greater number of actions, it has been determined, that besides the penalty of double or quadruple the amount taken, they may, for the recovery of the thing taken, be subjected to the action, ' If it appear that they ought to give.' Although the party injured may also bring the real action against them, by which the plaintiff demands the thing as proprietor.

Gai. iv. 4.

15. Appellamus autem in rem quidem actiones, vindicationes; in personam vero actiones quibus dare facere oportere intenditur, condictiones. Condicere enim est denuntiare, prisca lingua: nunc vero abusive dicimus, condictionem actionem in personam esse qua actor intendit dari sibi oportere; nulla enim hoc tempore eo nomine denuntiatio fit.

15. Real actions are called vindications; and personal actions, in which it is maintained that something ought to be done or given, are called condictions; for *condicere*, in old language, meant the same as *denuntiare*; and it is improperly that condiction is now used as the name of the personal action, by which the plaintiff contends that something ought to be given to him, for there is no *denuntiatio* now actually in use.

Gai. iv. 5. 18.

Gaius says, ' *actor adversario denuntiabat, ut ad judicem capiendum die xxx. adesset* ' (iv. 18). Thus the proper meaning of *condictio* is the appointing of a day.

16. Sequens illa divisio est, quod quaedam actiones rei persequendae gratia comparatae sunt, quaedam poenae persequendae, quaedam mixtae sunt.

16. Actions may be next divided into actions given to recover the thing, actions given to recover a penalty, and mixed actions.

Gai. iv. 6.

We now come to the third division of actions, that, namely,

according to the object for which they were brought; they were thus divided into three classes—those in which it was sought to get a thing, those in which it was sought to enforce a penalty, and those in which both these objects were united.

17. Rei persequendæ causa comparatæ sunt omnes in rem actiones. Earum vero actionum quæ in personam sunt, eæ quidem quæ ex contractu nascuntur fere omnes rei persequendæ causa comparatæ videntur: veluti, quibus mutuam pecuniam vel in stipulatum deductam petit actor, item commodati, depositi, mandati, pro socio, ex empto vendito, locato conducto. Plane si deponi agatur eo nomine quod tumultus, incendii, ruinæ, naufragii causa depositum sit, in duplum actionem prætor reddit si modo cum ipso apud quem depositum sit, aut cum herede ejus ex dolo ipsius agetur: quo casu mixta est actio.

17. For the recovery of the thing are given all real actions; and of personal actions almost all those which arise from contract, as the action for a sum lent or stipulated for, a commodatum, a deposit, a mandate, a partnership, a sale, or a letting to hire. But when the action on a deposit is brought for a thing deposited by reason of a riot, a fire, the fall of a building, or a shipwreck, the prætor always gives the action for the double of the value of the thing deposited, provided the suit be brought against the depositary himself, or against his heir, by reason of personal fraud, in which case the action is mixed.

GAI. iv. 7; D. xvi. 3. 1. 1–4; D. xvi. 3. 18.

The action against a depositary for fraud only was not in *duplum*, unless the depositor had been forced, by fire, shipwreck, the fall of a building, or other sudden calamity, to make the deposit. If, without being so forced, he had selected the depositary, then the action was only for the single value. It was his own fault not to have chosen an honester man. (See Bk. iii. Tit. 13. 3.)

18. Ex maleficiis vero proditæ actiones aliæ tantum pœnæ persequendæ causa comparatæ sunt, aliæ tam pœnæ quam rei persequendæ, et ob id mixtæ sunt. Pœnam tantum persequitur quis actione furti: sive enim manifesti agitur quadrupli, sive nec manifesti dupli, de sola pœna agitur, nam ipsam rem propria actione persequitur quis, id est, suam esse petens, sive fur ipse eam rem possideat sive alius quilibet. Eo amplius, adversus furem etiam condictio est rei.

19. Actions arising from a delict are either for the penalty only, or both for the thing and the penalty, which makes them mixed. But in no action of theft, nothing more is sued for than the penalty; whether, as in manifest theft, the quadruple, or, in theft not manifest, the double, is sued for, the owner recovers the thing itself by a separate action, by claiming it as proprietor, whether it be in the possession of a thief or of any one else. He may also bring against the thief a condiction for the thing.

GAI. iv. 8, 9; D. xiii. 1. 7. 1.

Persons who suffered from crimes had a private action against the wrong-doer for compensation, quite apart from, and independent of, the prosecution of the offender for his outrage on the laws of society. There was, indeed, something more than an exact compensation enforced by the private actions: for, by way of penalty, the defendant had often to pay two, three, or four times the amount of loss actually sustained; but still this penalty was given as a punishment for the injury to the individual, and not as a punishment for the infraction of public law.

10. Vi autem bonorum raptorum actio mixta est, quia in quadruplum rei persecutio continetur; pœnæ autem tripli est. Sed et legis Aquiliæ actio de damno injuriæ mixta est, non solum si adversus inficiantem in duplum agatur, sed interdum et si in simplum quisque agit: veluti si quis hominem claudum aut luscum occiderit, qui in eo anno integer et magni pretii fuerit; tanti enim damnatur, quanti is homo in eo anno plurimi fuerit, secundum jam traditam divisionem. Item mixta est actio contra eos qui relicta sacrosanctis ecclesiis vel aliis venerabilibus locis legati vel fidei-commissi nomine dare distulerint, usque adeo ut etiam in judicium vocarentur: tunc enim et ipsam rem vel pecuniam quæ relicta est, dare compelluntur, et aliud tantum pro pœna, et ideo in duplum ejus fit condemnatio.

10. An action for goods taken by force, is a mixed action; because the thing taken is included under the quadruple value to be recovered by the action; and thus the penalty is but triple. The action introduced by the lex Aquilia, for wrongful damage, is also a mixed action: not only when brought for double value against a man denying the fact, but sometimes, when the action is only for the single value; for instance, according to the distinction previously laid down, when a man has killed a slave, who at the time of his death was lame, or wanted an eye, but within the year, previous to his decease, was free from any defect, and of great value. The action is also mixed which is brought against those who have delayed the payment of a legacy, or fideicommissum, left to our holy churches, or any other sacred place, until at last they have been summoned before a magistrate; for then they are compelled to give the thing, or to pay the money left by the deceased, and in addition an equivalent thing or an equal sum besides, by way of penalty; and thus they are condemned in a double amount.

C. ix. 33. 1; D. ix. 2. 23. 3–8; C. i. 3. 40, pr. and 7.

*Interdum si in simplum.* An action could be brought *in simplum* under the *lex Aquilia*, if the object of the action was not to determine whether the defendant had done the injury, but to fix the sum which would be the proper compensation for it. It could not be brought *in simplum* to determine the fact of the defendant having done the injury: for if he denied it, the action was *in duplum*; if he confessed it, there was no need of an action to prove what he confessed.

*Sacrosanctis ecclesiis.* The punishment had formerly been enforced in the case of all legacies in which a certain sum had been given *per damnationem.* (See Bk. iii. Tit. 27. 7.)

*Dare distulerint.* Formerly the punishment had only

been inflicted in case of an absolute refusal of the legacy. (C. i. 3. 46. 7.)

20. Quædam actiones mixtam causam obtinere videntur, tam in rem quam in personam: qualis est familiæ erciscundæ actio, quæ competit coheredibus de dividenda hereditate; itemcommuni dividundo, quæ inter eos redditur inter quos aliquid commune est, ut id dividatur; item finium regundorum, quæ inter eos agitur qui continuas agros habent. In quibus tribus judiciis permittitur judici, rem alicui ex litigatoribus ex bono et æquo adjudicare, et si unius pars prægravare videbitur, eum locuples certa pecunia alteri condemnare.

20. Some actions are also mixed, as being both real and personal; as, for instance, the action *familiæ erciscundæ*, brought between co-heirs for the partition of the inheritance; the action *de communi dividundo*, between partners for the division of things held in common; also, the action *finium regundorum*, between owners of contiguous estates. And, in these three actions, the judge, following the rules of equity, may give any particular thing to any of the parties to the suit, and then condemn him, if he seems to have an undue advantage, to pay the other a certain sum of money.

D. x. 1. 2. 1; D. x. 1. 3; D. x. 2. 55.

These actions, though entirely personal, as being founded on obligations and brought against particular persons, are here said to seem in one aspect like real actions, because they involved not only a *condemnatio*, but an *adjudicatio*. A particular thing was adjudged and given over to the plaintiff. Even here, however, the analogy to real actions was not very complete, as real actions were always brought for some definite thing, ascertainable before the action was brought; but in the actions mentioned in the text, the thing to be adjudged was only ascertained by the action.

As to the formula in these actions, see Introd. sec. 103. In these actions no distinction can properly be made of plaintiff and defendant. Ulpian says, ' *Mixtæ sunt actiones, in quibus uterque actor est.*' (D. xliv. 7. 37. 1.) The judge discharged the function assigned him equally for the benefit of all persons interested in the subject-matter of the action.

21. Omnes autem actiones vel in simplum conceptæ sunt, vel in duplum, vel in triplum, vel in quadruplum; alterius autem nulla actio extenditur.

21. All actions are for the single, double, triple, or quadruple value; beyond that no action extends.

D. ii. 8. 3.

We have now the fourth division of actions, that, namely, according to the amount of the condemnation.

In actions which were *in duplum, in triplum,* or *in quadruplum conceptæ,* the *intentio* only contained an estimate of the single value the amount of actual loss, and then in the *condemnatio* this was doubled, tripled, or quadrupled, as the case might be ; the word *conceptæ*, therefore, which properly refers to the *intentio*, is not very strictly used.

| | |
|---|---|
| 22. In simplum agitur: veluti ex stipulatione, ex mutui datione, ex empto vendito, locato conducto, mandato, et denique ex aliis compluribus causis. | 22. The single thing itself, or its simple value, is sued for: as, for example, in case of a stipulation, a loan, a mandate, a sale, a letting to hire, and in numberless other cases. |

If a person stipulated that in a certain case his debtor should give him double or triple of the value of the sum owed, the action brought to enforce the stipulation would still be *in simplum conceptæ*. It would be the agreement, and not the action, which would double or triple the sum to be paid.

| | |
|---|---|
| 23. In duplum agimus: veluti furti nec manifesti, damni injuriæ ex lege Aquilia, depositi ex quibusdam casibus: item æris corrupti, quæ competit in eum cujus hortatu consilioque servus alienus fugerit, aut contumax adversus dominum factus est, aut luxuriose vivere cœperit, aut denique quolibet modo deterior factus sit. In qua actione etiam earum rerum quas fugiendo servus abstulit, æstimatio deducitur. Item ex legato quod venerabilibus locis relictum est, secundum ea quæ supra diximus. | 23. The double value is sued for: as, for example, in an action of theft not manifest, of wrongful injury by the *lex Aquilia*, and, in certain cases, in an action of deposit. Also in an action on account of the corruption of a slave brought against him by whose advice or instigation the slave has fled from his master, has grown disobedient towards him, become dissolute in his habits, or been made in any manner worse; and, in this action, an estimate is also to be made of whatever things the slave has stolen from his master before his flight. An action also for the detention of a legacy, left to a sacred place, is brought for double value, as we have before remarked. |

GAL. iii. 180; GAI. iv. D. 171; D. xvi. 3. I. 1; D. xi. 9. 1; C. i. 3. 40. 7.

*Depositi ex quibusdam casibus*, i.e. when made under the pressure of a sudden calamity.  See note on paragr. 17.

| | |
|---|---|
| 24. Tripli vero, cum quidam majorem veræ æstimationis quantitatem in libello conventionis inseruit ut ex hac causa viatores, id est executores litium, ampliorem summam sportularum nomine exegerint: tunc enim id quod propter eorum causam damnum passus fuerit reus, in triplum ab actore consequetur, ut in hoc triplo et simplum in quo damnum passus est, connumeretur. Quod contra constitutio induxit, quæ in nostro Codice fulget, ex qua dubio procul est ex lege condicticiam emanare. | 24. The triple value is sued for when any person inserts a greater sum than is due to him, in his statement of demand, so that the *viatores*, that is, the officers of suits, exact a larger sum as their fee. In this case the defendant may obtain the triple value of the loss he has sustained by giving the fee from the plaintiff, but the amount actually expended in the fee is included in the triple value. Thus, a constitution inserted in our code has established, on which constitution, without doubt, a legal condiction may be grounded. |

C. iii. 10. 2. 2.

In the old law there had been other actions *in triplum*, as those *furti concepti* and *furti oblati*. (GAI. iii. 191; see Tit. 1. 4, of this Book.) The action, of which Justinian speaks in this paragraph, had been substituted by him for the penalty of entirely losing all right of action, to which a plaintiff who sued for more than was due to him had been liable.

The *libellus conventionis* in the system of civil process obtaining in the Lower Empire, was the notification of an action and its grounds delivered by a bailiff of the court (*executor*) to a defendant, who, on the receipt of it, had to give security for his appearance before the *judex*. It thus, in the extra-*ordinaria judicia*, replaced the old *vocatio in jus*.

25. Quadrupli, veluti furti manifesti: item de eo quod metus causa factum sit, deque ea pecunia quae in hoc data sit, ut is cui datur calumniae causa negotium alicui servret, vel non sacret. Item ex lege condictitia a nostra constitutione oritur, in quadruplum condemnationem imponens iis executoribus litium, qui contra constitutionis normam a reis quidquam exegerint.

25. The quadruple value is sued for; as, for example, in an action for manifest theft, in an action *quod metus causa*, and an action relating to money given to any one to set on foot or to desist from a vexatious suit. The legal condiction is also for the quadruple value, which is established in our constitution against those officers of suits, who demand anything from the defendant, contrary to the regulations of the constitution.

GAI. iii. 189; D. iv. 2. 14. 1; D. iii. 0. 1; C. iii. 2. 4.

26. Sed furti quidem nec manifesti actio, et servi corrupti, a ceteris de quibus simul locuti sumus eo differunt, quod hae actiones omnimodo dupli sunt; at illae, id est, damni injuriae ex lege Aquilia et interdum depositi indicatione duplicantur, in confitentem autem in simplum dantur. Sed illae quae de iis competit quae relicta venerabilibus locis sunt, non solum inficiatione duplicatur, sed etiam si distulerit relicti solutionem usquequo jussu magistratuum nostrorum conveniatur; in confitentem vero, et antequam jussu magistratuum conveniatur solventem, simplum redditur.

26. But an action of theft not manifest, and an action on account of a slave corrupted, differ from the others, which we have placed under the same head, in that they are always brought for double the value; but the others, that is, the action given by the *lex Aquilia* for a wrongful injury, and sometimes the action of deposit, are brought for the double value in case of denial; but if the defendant confesses, the single value only can be recovered. In actions brought for things given to sacred places, double is recovered, not only on the denial of the defendant, but also on payment being delayed until a magistrate orders an action to be brought; but it is the single value only that can be recovered, if the debt be acknowledged and paid before such an order is given.

GAI. iv. 9. 171. 173; C. i. 3 40. 7.

27. Item actio de eo quod metus causa factum sit, a ceteris de qui-

27. The action *quod metus causa* differs also from the other actions

bus simul locuti sumus eo differt, quod ejus natura tacite continetur, ut qui Judicis jussu ipsam rem actori restituat, absolvatur. Quod in ceteris casibus non ita est sed omnimodo quisque in quadruplum condemnatur; quod est et in furti manifesti actione.

included under the same head, because it is tacitly implied in the nature of this action, that a defendant, who, in obedience to the command of the judge, restores the things taken, ought to be acquitted; in all the other actions, on the contrary, the defendant must always be condemned to pay the fourfold value, as, for instance, in the action of manifest theft.

D. iv. 2. 14. 1. 4.

The *actio quod metus causa* was given to a person who had, while under constraint from the fear of actual or threatened violence, alienated anything, created real rights, or entered into an obligation. The action was, as the text informs us, *arbitraria.* (See Introd. sec. 106.)

28. Actionum autem quædam bonæ fidei sunt, quædam stricti juris. Bonæ fidei sunt hæ: ex empto vendito, locato, conducto, negotiorum gestorum, mandati, depositi, pro socio, tutelæ, commodati, pigneratitia, familiæ erciscundæ, communi dividundo, præscriptis verbis quæ de æstimato proponitur, et ea quæ ex permutatione competit, et hereditatis petitio. Quamvis enim usque ad huc incertum erat, sive inter bonæ fidei judicia connumeranda sit hereditatis petitio, sive non, nostra tamen constitutio aperte eam esse bonæ fidei disposuit.

28. Again, some actions are *bonæ fidei*, some are *stricti juris*. Of those *bonæ fidei* there are the following:— the actions *empti* and *venditi*, *locati* and *conducti*, *negotiorum gestorum*; those brought on a mandate, deposit, partnership, tutelage, loan, or pledge; the action *familiæ erciscundæ*; that *communi dividundo*; the action *præscriptis verbis*, arising from a commission to sell at a fixed price, or an exchange; and the demand of an inheritance. For, although it was, till recently, doubtful whether this last action should be included, among those *bonæ fidei*, our constitution has clearly decided that it is to be included among them.

Gai. iv. 62; C. iii. 31. 12. 3.

We here enter on the fifth division of actions, that, namely, according to the powers given to the judge, and according to which they are divided into *actiones bonæ fidei, actiones stricti juris*, and *actiones arbitrariæ.*

In actions *bonæ fidei*, the words *ex bona fide* were permitted to be added to the formula, so that the *intentio* ran, *quicquid dare*, or *facere*, or *præstare oportet ex bona fide.* The actions in which this was permitted were all prætorian. Justinian here gives a list of them; and probably, though not quite certainly, the list is meant to be a complete one. The principal effects of this addition to the formula were:— (1.) That all circumstances tending to show *dolus malus* were taken into consideration, without an exception *doli mali* being inserted. (D. xxx. 84. 5.)

(2.) Every assistance which the consideration of customs and common use could give to the determination of the particular question was permitted to affect the decision of the judge. (D. xvi. 1. 31. 20.) (3.) The judge would notice any counter claims which the defendant might have arising out of the same set of circumstances which gave rise to the action of the plaintiff (GAI. iv. 63.) (4.) And, lastly, interest was due on the thing withheld from the time it ought to have been given. (D. xxii. 1. 32. 2.)

In the actions *stricti juris*, the judge was obliged to adhere strictly to the principles of the civil law. *Dolus malus*, or counter claims, could not be taken into consideration unless exceptions were inserted bringing them before the notice of the judge. And interest could not generally be claimed from before the time of the *litis contestatio*, except by special stipulation. (D. xii. 1. 31.) It was the actions derived from the *jus civile* that were *stricti juris*. That a real action should, as in the case of the *petitio hereditatis*, be *bonæ fidei*, was quite an exception.

The nature of *actiones arbitrariæ* will appear from paragr. 31.

An action *præscriptis verbis*, otherwise *in factum præscriptis verbis*, or *in factum*, was, as we have elsewhere said, an action in which at the head of the formula were placed words stating the facts giving rise to a contract which did not come under any of the heads of contracts bearing a particular name. In the contract *permutatio*, each party made a contract re, i.e. by depositing the thing bartered with the other, but the thing given was not given as a *mutuum*, a *commodatum*, a *depositum*, or a *pignus*, and, therefore, the circumstances had to be stated specially. The action *de æstimato* was given when a thing was entrusted to another to sell for a certain sum; the agent being permitted to retain all he received above that given, and to give back the thing if he could not obtain the price fixed. This was not precisely a *locatio*, a *societas*, or a *mandatum*, and, therefore, the action was given in the form of one *præscriptis verbis*. (See Bk. iii. Tit. 13. 2.)

It may be useful to take this opportunity of again referring to a division of actions alluded to in the note to Bk. iii. Tit. 13. 2, but not treated of in this Title because belonging entirely to the system of *formulæ*, viz. that according as they were *in jus conceptæ* or *in factum conceptæ*. In some actions the prætor did not raise a question of law as he did when he adopted the usual form *si paret oportere*, but he merely directed the judge to ascertain a definite fact, and then instructed him if he found the fact to be in a particular way to condemn the

defendant.  Such an action was said to be *in factum conceptu*, while one in which the judge was guided in his decision
by the rules of law was *in jus conceptu*.

29.  Fuerat antea et rei uxoriæ
actio una ex bonæ fidei judicii.
Sed cum pleniorem esse ex stipulatu actionem Invenientes, omne
jus quod res uxoria ante habebat,
cum multis divisionibus in actionem ex stipulatu quæ de dotibus
exigendis proponitur, transtulimus:
merito rei uxoriæ actione sublata,
ex stipulatu quæ pro ea introducta
est, naturam bonæ fidei judicii
tantum in exactione dotis meruit,
ut bonæ fidei sit ; sed et tacitam
ei dedimus hypothecam.  Præferri
autem aliis creditoribus in hypo-
thecis tunc censuimus, cum ipsa
mulier de dote sua experiatur,
cujus solius providentia hoc induximus.

29.  Formerly, the action *rei uxoriæ*
was included among the actions *bonæ
fidei*; but finding the action *ex stipulatu* to be more advantageous, we
have, while establishing many distinctions, transferred to the action
*ex stipulatu*, when given for the recovery of marriage portions, all the
effects before attaching to the action
*rei uxoriæ* ; the *actio rei uxoriæ* being then reasonably done away with,
the action *ex stipulatu*, by which it
is replaced, naturally assumed the
character of an action *bonæ fidei*, but
assumed it only when brought for
the recovery of a marriage portion.
We have also given the wife an implied mortgage, but when we prefer her to mortgagees, we do so only
whenever she herself sues for her
marriage portion.  For it is to her
personally that we grant the privilege.

D. iv. 5. 8; C. v. 13; C. viii. 18. 12. 1.

In order to enforce the restitution of a marriage portion,
the *actio rei uxoriæ* was given ; but sometimes the wife or
other person entitled, not content with the remedy, stipulated
with the husband for the restitution, and thus secured the
power of bringing an action *ex stipulatu.*

In the *actio rei uxoriæ*, which was an action *bonæ fidei*, the
husband could, for different reasons, make certain deductions
in his restitution of the *dos*.  He had three years in which to
make restitution of all things, *quæ numero, pondere, mensurave constant*, and he could oppose to the action the *beneficium competentiæ*, that is, he was only condemned to pay
*quantum facere potest.*  The wife could not transmit the
action to her heirs, and if her husband were deceased, and she
had benefited by his testament, she could not both accept the
gift under the testament, and also ask for the restitution of her
portion, but was obliged to abandon either the one advantage
or the other.  (ULP. *Reg.* 6.)

None of these drawbacks attended the action *ex stipulatu.*
There could be no deductions, no delay in payment, no regard
to the husband's power to pay.  The action passed to the
heirs of the wife, and she could take, in addition, anything
given her by her husband's testament.

Justinian united the two actions into one. However the *dos* might have been given, and whether there had really been any stipulation to restore it, a *tacita stipulatio*, was, in every case, to be supposed. The *actio rei uxoriæ* was to be abolished, and all actions for the restitution of a marriage portion to be brought *ex stipulatu*. But then, this action was treated as one *bonæ fidei*, and produced most of the advantages which the husband had enjoyed under the *actio rei uxoriæ*. He had a year in which to restore all moveables, and he could claim the *beneficium competentiæ*. (See paragr. 37.) Lastly, in order to make the position of the wife more secure, Justinian gave her an implied mortgage on the effects of her husband, taking priority over all other incumbrances—a privilege, however, personal to herself. (C. iv. 13.)

30. In bonæ fidei autem judiciis libera potestas permitti videtur judici ex bono et æquo æstimandi, quantum actori restitui debeat : in quo et illud continetur, ut si quid invicem præstare actorem oporteat, eo compensato in reliquum is cum quo actum est, debeat condemnari. Sed et in strictis judiciis ex rescripto divi Marci, opposita doli mali exceptione compensatio inducebatur. Sed nostra constitutio eas compensationes quæ jure aperto nituntur, latius introduxit, ut actiones ipso jure minuant, sive in rem sive in personam, sive alias quascumque : excepta sola depositi actione, cui aliquid compensationis opponi satis impium esse credidimus, ne sub prætextu compensationis depositarum rerum quis exactione defraudetur.

30. In all actions *bonæ fidei* full power is given to the judge to determine, according to the rules of equity, how much ought to be restored to the plaintiff; whence it follows that when the plaintiff also is found to be indebted to the defendant, the debtor ought to be allowed to set off the sum due to him, and to be condemned only to pay the difference. Even in actions *stricti juris*, a rescript of the Emperor Marcus permitted a set-off to be claimed, by opposing the exception of fraud ; but our constitution, when the debt due to the defendant is evident, has given a greater latitude to claims of set-off; for now actions, real or personal, or of whatever kind, are *ipso jure* reduced by the claim, with the exception only of the action of deposit, against which we have not judged it proper to permit any claim of set-off to be made, lest under this pretence any one should be fraudulently prevented from recovering the thing deposited.

Gai. Iv. 61 ; C. iv. 31. 14, pr. and 1 ; C. iv. 34. 11.

The subject of *compensatio* will be treated of more fully under paragr. 39.

31. Præterea quasdam actiones arbitrarias, id est, ex arbitrio judicis pendentes, appellamus : in quibus, nisi arbitrio judicis is cum quo agitur actori satisfaciat, veluti rem restituat, vel exhibeat, vel solvat, vel ex noxali causa servum

31. Some actions, again, are called arbitrary, as depending upon the arbitrium of the judge. In these, if the defendant do not, on the order of the judge, give the satisfaction awarded by the judge, and either restore, exhibit, or pay the thing, or give up a

dedat, condemnari debeat. Sed
istæ actiones tam in rem quam in
personam inveniuntur: in rem, veluti Publiciana, Serriana de rebus
coloni, quasi Serriana quæ etiam
hypothecaria vocatur; in personam,
veluti quibus de eo agitur quod aut
metus causa aut dolo malo factum
est, item cum id quod certo loco
promissum est petitur; ad exhibendum quoque actio ex arbitrio
judicis pendet. In his enim actionibus et ceteris similibus permittitur judici ex bono et æquo,
secundum cujusque rei de qua actum est naturam, æstimare quemadmodum actori satisfieri oporteat.

slave that has committed an injury,
he ought to be condemned. Of
these arbitrary actions some are real
and some personal: real, as the actions *Publiciana, Serriana*, and *quasi
Serviana*, also called *hypothecaria*;
personal, as those, by which a suit is
commenced on account of something
done through fear or fraud, and that
for which something was promised
to be paid at a particular place; the
action *ad exhibendum* also depends
on the *arbitrium* of the judge: in
these actions, and others of a like
nature, the judge may determine,
according to the principles of equity
and the circumstances of the particular case, the satisfaction which the
plaintiff ought to receive.

D. vi. 1. 68; D. iv. 2. 14. 4; D. xiii. 4. 4. 1; D. x. 4. 3. 9; D. xx. 1. 16.
3; D. iv. 3. 18.

In the *actiones arbitrariæ* the judge was instructed only to
condemn the defendant in a sum of money, if he did not satisfy
the demands of the plaintiff, supposing that demand was well-
founded. When, therefore, the judge had ascertained the
validity of the plaintiff's claim, he issued an order (*arbitrium*)
to the defendant, and at the same time, condemned him to pay,
in case of his refusal, a sum proportionate to the value of what
was claimed, *quanti ea res erit*. But though the option
seemed thus to be given the defendant of complying with
the *arbitrium*, or paying the amount of the *condemnatio*, it
appears that the prætor used the *manus militaris*, the strong
arm of the law, to enforce compliance with the *arbitrium*.
But this, perhaps, was not always the case, and it might happen
that, instead, the amount of the *condemnatio* was exacted.
This had, therefore, to be reduced from the vague term *quanti
ea res erit*, to a particular sum, fixed, if there was any appearance of fraud on the part of the defendant, by the plaintiff
himself, who stated on his oath (D. xii. 3. 5) the amount he
considered fairly due to him as compensation; otherwise the
*judex* fixed the amount according to the circumstances of the
case.

Actions *in rem* were enforced by being made *arbitrariæ*, and
all actions *in rem* were so enforced. (See Tit. 17. 2.) In real
actions the satisfaction ordered by the judge was to restore the
thing, except that in the *actio Serviana* and *quasi-Serviana*
the defendant was permitted either to give up the thing pledged,
or to pay the debt. (D. xx. 1. 16. 3.) When the thing claimed
was restored, the *condemnatio* might still be made available for
the *fructus*. Among personal actions, those *quod metus causa*,

*de dolo malo,* and *ad exhibendum* were *arbitrariæ,* because
they were brought virtually to have something restored or
exhibited. The action *de eo quod certo loco promissum est*
was made *arbitraria,* for the peculiar reason mentioned below.
With respect to the *actio quod metus causa,* see paragr. 25
and 27. The *actio de dolo malo* was given to avoid the consequences of a *dolus malus,* but only when there was no other
means of avoiding them (D. iv. 3. 1. 2); it was *in simplum;*
it subjected the defendant, if condemned, to infamy, and had
to be brought within a year. (D. iv. 3. 29.)

*Cum id quod certo loco promissum est petitur.* When a
contract was made in which it was agreed that payment should
be made at a particular place, the creditor could not demand
payment anywhere else. If he did, he asked for more than was
his due, and was subject to the consequences of a *pluris-petitio.*
(See paragr. 33.) Supposing, indeed, the action brought on
the obligation was one *bonæ fidei,* or had an *intentio incerta,*
as being for an undetermined object, then, as the judge would
take into account all the circumstances of the case, and allow
the defendant the benefit of whatever difference being sued in
a wrong place could be supposed to make to him, the consequence of this *pluris-petitio* would be immaterial. But if the
action was one *stricti juris,* the plaintiff would fail altogether
in his action. But it might happen that the debtor absented
himself from the place where payment was to be made, and
then the creditor would not be able to sue him there. And,
again, it might be, in some cases, to the mutual advantage of
both parties that, if all just allowance were made for any inconvenience either might sustain, the demand should be made
at a different place from that agreed on. The prætor provided
for these two cases by altering the *condictio certa* which would
be brought on the obligation in two points : first, he made the
action arbitrary, so that before sentence was given there was an
opening for the defendant to pay a sum in satisfaction of the
plaintiff's claim ; and secondly, though the *intentio* was left
certain, the *condemnatio* was made to be for *quanti ea res erit,*
so that the real amount which the defendant would have to pay,
would be that which the judge, on an equitable consideration
of the whole circumstances, fixed on as reasonable.

32. Curare autem debet judex
ut omnimodo, quantum possibile
ei sit, certæ pecuniæ vel rei sententiam ferat, etiam si de incerta
quantitate apud eum actum est.

32. A judge ought, as much as
possible, to take care that his sentence awards a thing or sum certain,
even though the demand on which
he pronounces may have been for an
uncertain quantity.

[Gai. iv. 48. 52 ; C. vii. 4. 17.

*Certæ pecuniæ vel rei.* It was only under the system of *judicia extraordinaria* that the *condemnatio* might be not only for a certain sum of money, but also for any other definite thing, that thus the object of the demand might be directly obtained.

The *condemnatio* was always certain, even if the action was brought for a sum or thing uncertain; the nature of the action might, indeed, be such as to give the defendant the choice of two alternatives, and then the *condemnatio* would, of course, correspond; but even then the condemnation cannot properly be said to have been uncertain, as it compelled the defendant to choose between two definite things.

32. Si quis agens in intentione sua plus complexus fuerit quam ad eum pertineret, causa cadebat, id est, rem amittebat; nec facile in integrum a prætore restituebatur, nisi minor erat viginti quinque annis: huic enim, sicut in aliis causis causa cognita succurrebatur, si lapsus juventute fuerat, ita et in hac causa succurri solitum erat. Sane, si tam magna causa justi erroris interveniebat, ut etiam constantissimus quisque labi posset, etiam majori viginti quinque annis succurrebatur: veluti, si quis totum legatum petierit, post deinde prolati fuerint codicilli quibus aut pars legati adempta sit, aut quibusdam aliis legata data sint, quæ efficiebant ut plus petiisse videretur petitor quam dodrantem, atque ideo lege Falcidia legata minuebantur. Plus autem quatuor modis petitur, re, tempore, loco, causa; re, veluti si quis pro decem aureis qui ei debebantur, viginti petierit; aut si is cujus ex parte res est, totam eam vel majore ex parte suam esse intenderit; tempore, veluti si quis ante diem vel ante conditionem petierit: qua ratione enim qui tantius solvit quam solvere deberet, minus solvere intelligitur, eadem ratione qui præmature petit, plus petere videtur. Loco plus petitur, veluti cum quis id quod certo loco sibi stipulatus est, alio loco petit sine commemoratione illius loci in quo sibi dari stipulatus fuerit: verbi gratia, si is qui ita stipulatus fuerit, Ephesi dare spondes?

39. Formerly, if a plaintiff claimed in his *intentio* more than his due, he failed in his action, that is, he lost the thing owing to him, nor was it easy for him to get reinstated by the prætor unless he was under the age of twenty-five years, for in this, as well as in other cases, it was usual to aid the plaintiff if it appeared that he had made an error owing to his youth. If, however, the reasons which betrayed him into the mistake were such as might have misled the most careful man relief was given even to persons of full age. For example, if a legatee had demanded his whole legacy, and codicils were afterwards produced by which a part of it was taken away, or new legacies given to other persons, so that, the legacies being reduced by the *lex Falcidia*, the plaintiff appeared to have demanded more than three-fourths. A man may demand more than what is due to him in four ways—in respect to the thing, to the time, to the place, and to the cause. In respect to the thing, as when the plaintiff, instead of ten *mori*, which are due to him, demands twenty; or if, although owner of but part of some particular thing, he claims the whole, or a greater share than he is entitled to. In respect to time, as when the plaintiff makes his demand before the day of payment, or before the time of the performance of a condition; for just as he who does not pay so soon as he ought is held to pay less than he ought, so

Romae pure intendat sibi dare oportere. Ideo autem plus petere intelligitur, quia utilitatem quam habuit promissor si Ephesi solveret, adimit ei pura intentione. Propter quam causam alio loco petenti arbitraria actio proponitur, in qua scilicet ratio habetur utilitatis quae promissori competitura fuisset, si illo loco solveret: quae utilitas plerumque in mercibus maxima invenitur, veluti vino, oleo, frumento, quae per singulas regiones diversa habent pretia; sed et pecuniae numeratae non in omnibus regionibus sub iisdem usuris foenerantur. Si quis tamen Ephesi petat, id est, eo loco petat quo ut sibi detur stipulatus est, pura actione recte agit; idque etiam praetor monstrat, scilicet quia utilitas solvendi salva est promissori. Huic autem qui loco plus petere intelligitur, proximus est is qui causa plus petit: ut ecce, si quis ita a te stipulatur, hominem Stichum aut decem aureos dare spondes? deinde alterutrum petat, veluti hominem tantum aut decem aureos tantum. Ideo autem plus petere intelligitur, quia in eo genere stipulationis promissoris est electio, utrum pecuniam an hominem solvere malit; qui igitur pecuniam tantum vel hominem tantum sibi dari oportere intendit, eripit electionem adversario, et eo modo suam quidem conditionem meliorem facit, adversarii vero sui deteriorem: qua de causa talis in ea re prodita est actio, ut quis intendat hominem Stichum aut aureos decem sibi dari oportere, id est, ut eodem modo peteret quo stipulatus est. Praeterea, si quis generaliter hominem stipulatus sit, et specialiter Stichum petat, aut generaliter vinum stipulatus specialiter campanum petat, aut generaliter purpuram stipulatus sit, deinde specialiter tyriam petat, plus petere intelligitur; quia electionem adversario tollit, cui stipulationis jure liberum fuit aliud solvere quam quod peteretur. Quin etiam, licet vilissimum sit quod quis petat, nihilominus plus petere intelligitur; quia saepe accidit ut promissori facilius sit illud sol-

whoever makes his demand prematurely, demands more than his due. In respect to place, as when any person demands that something stipulated to be delivered at a particular place, should be delivered at some other place, without noticing the place fixed by the stipulation; for example, if, after stipulating in these words, 'Do you promise to give at Ephesus?' any one should afterwards bring an action at Rome, merely stating that the defendant ought to give. In this case the plaintiff would demand more than his due, as he would, by his *intentio* thus conceived simply, deprive the promisor of the advantage he might have in paying at Ephesus. And it is thus, that an arbitrary action is given to a plaintiff demanding payment in a place different from that agreed on, in which action allowance is made for the advantage which the debtor might have reaped from paying his debt in the place agreed on. This advantage is generally found to be most considerable in the different kinds of merchandise, as in wine, oil, corn, of which the price differs in different places. Money itself, again, is not lent everywhere at the same interest. But if a man bring his action at Ephesus, that is, at the place fixed by the stipulation, he may validly bring an action conceived simply; and this the pretor, too, points out, because all the advantage the debtor will have in paying at the particular place is secured to him. To him who demands more than his due in regard to place, he approaches very nearly who demands more than his due in regard to the cause; as, for instance, if any one stipulate thus with you, 'Do you promise to give either your slave Stichus or ten aurei?' and then demand either the slave only, or the money only. He would in this case be held to have demanded more than his due, because in such a stipulation the promisor has the right to choose whether he will give the slave or the money. He, therefore, who claims either the money only, or the slave only, takes away his

vere, quod majoris pretii est. Sed hæc quidem antea in usu fuerant. Postea autem lex Zenoniana et nostra rem coercuit; et si quidem tempore plus fuerit petitum, quid statui oportet, Zenonis divæ memoriæ loquitur constitutio. Sin autem quantitate vel alio modo plus fuerit petitum, omne si quod forte damnum ex hac causa acciderit, ei contra quem plus petitum fuerit, commissa tripli condemnatione, sicut supra diximus, puniatur.

adversary's power of choice, and thus makes his own condition better, and that of his adversary worse. An action, therefore, has been given by which in such a case the plaintiff maintains that either the slave Stichus ought to be given him, or the money, and thus makes a demand in conformity with the stipulation. So, too, if a man stipulates generally that wine, or purple, or a slave be given him, and afterwards sues for the wine of Campania, the purple of Tyre, or the slave Stichus in particular, he is held to demand more than his due, for he thus takes the power of election from his adversary, to whom it was open by the terms of the stipulation to pay something different from what is demanded. Nay, even if the thing actually sued for be of little or no value, yet the plaintiff is held to claim more than his due, because it is often easier for the debtor to pay a thing of greater value. Such was the law formerly in use. But the severity of the law on this point has been greatly restrained by the constitution of the Emperor Zeno, and by our own. If more than is due be demanded in respect of time, the constitution of Zeno must be applied; if in respect of quantity, or in any other way, then, as we have said above, the plaintiff is to be condemned in a sum triple the amount of any loss sustained by the defendant.

Gai. iv. 53; D. iv. 4. 1. 1; D. iv. 4. 7. 4; D. iv. 0. 1. 1; D. xiii. 4 and foll.; C. iii. 10. 1, 2.

Under the system of *formulæ*, a *plus-petitio* or *pluris-petitio* had the effect of making the plaintiff fail entirely in his action in one case only; namely, when the error was in the *intentio*, and the *intentio* was for a thing certain. Supposing this were the case, as the formula would run *si paret decem nummos, &c., condemna si non absolve*, then, if the defendant owed only nine *nummi*, he did not owe ten, and so the *judex* could not condemn him. The plaintiff failed, and having once come in *judicio*, the *litis contestatio* operated as a novation of the cause of action (see Bk. iii. Tit. 29), and his original claim being thus cut away, he was left entirely without remedy, and could take no further proceedings to enforce his demand.

Of course, if the demand was for a thing uncertain, there could be no *plus-petitio*. If there were an error in the *demonstratio*, the plaintiff was not at all prejudiced. If there were a mistake in the *condemnatio*, making it more unfavourable to the defendant than it ought to have been, it was the defendant who would be prejudiced, excepting that, if the prætor would grant a *restitutio in integrum*, he could regain his right position. (See GAI iv. 53–60.)

Under the system of the *judicia extraordinaria* a *plus-petitio* would mean any claim in excess contained in the *libellus conventionis*. The text informs us of the mode in which such a mistake or misstatement was punished when the *plus-petitio* was not one *tempore*. If the *plus-petitio* was *tempore*, i.e. if the plaintiff sued before the proper time, he was condemned by the constitution of Zeno (C. iii. 10. 1) to wait double the time he ought originally to have waited, and to reimburse the defendant all expenses he might have been put to by the action improperly brought.

34. Si minus in intentione complexus fuerit actor quam ad eum pertineret, veluti si, cum si decem deberentur, quinque sibi dari oportere intenderit; aut si, cum totus fundus ejus esset, partem dimidiam suam esse petierit, sine periculo agit. In reliquum enim nihilominus judex adversarium in eodem judicio condemnat, ex constitutione divæ memoriæ Zenonis.

34. If a plaintiff include less in his *intentio* than he has a claim to, demanding, for instance, only five *aurei* when ten are due, or the half of an estate, when the whole belongs to him, he runs no risk, for the judge may, by the constitution of Zeno, of glorious memory, condemn in the same action the adverse party to pay the remainder of what is due to the plaintiff.

GAI. iv. 50; C. iii. 10. 1. 3.

Under the prætorian system, a plaintiff who claimed a less amount than was really due to him, could bring another action for the surplus if he waited until another prætor came into office. (GAI. iv. 56.) Justinian allowed the *judex* to add the surplus in condemning the defendant.

35. Si quis aliud pro alio intenderit, nihil eum periclitari placet; sed in eodem judicio, cognita veritate, errorem suum corrigere ei permittimus: veluti, si is qui hominem Stichum petere deberet, Erotem petierit; aut si quis ex testamento sibi dari oportere intenderit, quod ex stipulatu debetur.

35. When a plaintiff demands one thing instead of another, he incurs no risk. For if he discover the truth, he is allowed to correct his mistake in the same action: as if he should demand the slave Eros instead of Stichus, or should claim as due by virtue of a testament, what is really due upon a stipulation.

GAI. iii. 55.

Under the older law, a plaintiff who demanded one thing

N N

instead of another, lost the action, but could recover the thing really due in a subsequent action.

30. Sunt praeterea quaedam actiones quibus non solidum quod nobis debetur, persequimur, sed modo solidum consequimur, modo minus, ut ecce, si in peculium filii servive agamus: nam si non minus in peculio sit quam persequimur, in solidum dominus paterve condemnatur: si vero minus inveniatur, eatenus condemnat judex, quatenus in peculio sit. Quemadmodum autem peculium intelligi debeat, suo ordine proponemus.

30. There are, again, certain actions by which we do not always sue for the whole of what is due to us, but sometimes for the whole, sometimes for less. For example, when a suit is brought so as to form a claim against the peculium of a son or a slave, then if the peculium be sufficient to answer the demand, the father or master is condemned to pay the whole debt; but if the peculium be not sufficient, he is condemned to pay only to the extent of the peculium. We will hereafter explain, in its proper place, how the peculium is to be estimated.

C. iv. 20. 12.

We here enter on another division of actions, according to which actions, by which the whole of what was due was obtained, are distinguished from those by which sometimes the whole, sometimes less than the whole, of what was due was obtained.

37. Item, si de dote judicio mulier agat, placet eatenus maritum condemnari debere quatenus facere possit, id est, quatenus facultates ejus patiuntur: itaque, si dotis quantitati concurrant facultates ejus, in solidum damnatur; si minus, in tantum quantum facere potest. Propter retentionem quoque dotis repetitio minuitur; nam ob impensas in res dotales factas marito retentio concessa est, quia ipso jure necessariis sumptibus dos minuitur, sicut ex latioribus Digestorum libris cognoscere licet.

37. Thus, too, if a wife bring an action for the restitution of her marriage portion, the husband must be condemned to pay only as far as he is able, i.e. as far as his means permit. Therefore, if his means admit of his paying the whole amount of the portion, he must do so; if not, he must pay as much as it is in his power to pay. The claim of a wife for the restitution of her marriage portion may also be lessened by the husband having a right to retain something, for the husband is permitted to retain a sum equivalent to the expenses he has incurred about the things given, since the marriage portion is by law diminished by the amount of all necessary expenses, as may be seen in fuller detail in the Digest.

D. xxiv. 3. 12. 14; D. xxv. 1. 5.

The privilege of being condemned only in an amount which he could pay without being reduced to a state of destitution (D. L. 17. 173), a privilege called by the commentators the *beneficium competentiæ*, was accorded to the defendant in several other cases besides those mentioned in the text and in the next paragraph and in paragr. 40. We may instance the cases of one brother sued by another, and every case arising between man and wife, except claims grounded on delicts. This privilege was always personal, and did not avail either heirs or sureties.

*Propter retentionem dotis.* The husband might deduct the amount of all necessary expenses incurred in the management of the property constituting the marriage portion. If the expenses had been only profitably and not necessarily incurred, that is, were *utiles*, and not *necessariæ*, Justinian only allowed the husband to bring an *actio mandati*, or an *actio negotiorum gestorum*, to reimburse himself; whereas, previously, he had been able to deduct such expenses as well as those that were *necessariæ*. (D. I. 16. 79. 1; C. v. 13. 1.) As to expenses merely incurred for pleasure and ornament, *voluptariæ* (D. L. 16. 79. 2), the husband had nothing more than the *jus tollendi*, that is, he might remove anything which he had contributed, and which he could take away without doing damage to the property. (See ULP. *Reg.* 6. 14.)

| | |
|---|---|
| 38. Sed et si quis cum parente suo patronove agat, item si socius cum socio judicio societatis agat, non plus actor consequitur quam adversarius ejus facere potest. Idem est, si quis ex donatione sua conveniatur. | 38. If any person sue his parent or patron, or one partner sue another in an action of partnership, he cannot obtain a greater sum than his adversary is able to pay. It is the same when a donor is sued for his gift. |

D. xlii. 1. 18. 19, pr. and 1.

| | |
|---|---|
| 39. Compensationes quoque oppositæ plerumque efficiunt, ut minus quisque consequatur quam ei debebatur; namque ex bono et æquo habita ratione ejus, quod invicem actorem ex eadem causa præstare oportet, in reliquum eum cum quo actum est condemnare, sicut jam dictum est. | 39. When a set-off is opposed by the defendant to the demand of the plaintiff, it generally happens that the plaintiff recovers less than what he demands, for the judge, proceeding on equitable principles, may deduct from the demand of the plaintiff whatever he owes under the same head to the defendant, and may condemn the defendant to pay the remainder only, as has been already observed. |

GAI. iv. 61.

If the defendant was not only a debtor but a creditor of the plaintiff, if he had something owing to him from the plaintiff as well as owed something to him, it was evidently the most convenient way that he should be allowed to balance one debt against the other (*compensatio pensare cum*), and only account for the surplus, supposing a surplus were still due from him.

Under the prætorian system, in all actions *bonæ fidei*, the judge, who could take all the circumstances of the case into his consideration, set off as a matter of course any debt due to the defendant from the plaintiff in consequence of the same set of circumstances (*ex eadem causa*) by which the debt on which the action was brought, became due. (GAI. iv. 61.) In one case, however, viz. that of a banker (*argentarius*), a much stricter system prevailed. The *argentarius* could only sue a customer for the sum due to him after deducting what he owed to the customer. If he sued for more, it was a *plus-petitio.* (GAI. iv. 64.) In the actions *stricti juris*, which arose from unilateral, not bilateral contracts, there could be no reciprocal rights, as in a bilateral contract, giving the defendant a claim *ex eadem causa.* But the rule grew up and was confirmed by a rescript of Marcus Aurelius (see paragr. 31), *dolo facit qui petit quod redditurus est.* (D. xliv. 4. 8.) If the plaintiff claimed a sum which directly he had obtained he would have to repay back to the defendant, he was guilty of a *dolus*; he had acted as if he had a right to the money, whereas he had not. Accordingly the defendant could avail himself of the exception of *dolus*; and the effect of this exception was that if the plaintiff was found to owe the defendant anything of a similar kind, although *ex dispari causa*, which he had not allowed for in stating the amount of his claim, he entirely failed in his action. He did not recover any surplus which might be really due to him. The exception stopped the action altogether. The formula ran : *Si in ea re nihil dolo malo Auli Agerii factum sit neque fiat . . . con-demna, si non paret, absolve. Dolus malus* did appear, and all the *judex* could do was to absolve the defendant. (PAUL. *Sent.* ii. 5. 3.)

But we must not suppose that *compensatio* was looked on as a means of extinguishing an obligation. In theory of law, each debt subsisted separately. Certainly in the case of the *argentarius* it is hard to draw any line between an extinction of obligation and the way in which debts due to customers were necessarily deducted ; but it was necessary that the debts due to and from the *argentarius* should be *in eadem re*, that is, should both consist, for instance, of money or wine. This was an exceptional case, and, generally speaking, the two debts clearly subsisted together, although, when, by submitting the facts to the knowledge of the *judex* in the case of actions *bonæ fidei,* and by the *exceptio doli* in the action of law, the set-off was claimed, its effects were retroactive, and may be said to have commenced from the moment when the two debts first began to exist together. (C. iv. 31. 4.)

Under Justinian the debts were held to operate as mutually
extinguishing each other *ipso jure.* When the parties came
before the *judex,* he ascertained their respective claims on
each other, and if there was, on the whole, a balance in favour
of the plaintiff, awarded the amount to him. All the old distinctions were done away, and it no longer made any difference whether the two debts arose from the same transaction,
or whether things of the same kind were payable (the words,
*ex eadem causa,* in the text are, therefore, under Justinian's
legislation, inaccurate). But Justinian made it requisite that
the defendant's claim should be clearly well founded, and that
the amount should be at once ascertainable, and not need further
inquiry to determine it (*causa liquida*). (See C. iv. 31. 14. 1.)

40. Eum quoque qui creditoribus
suis bonis cessit, si postea aliquid
acquisierit quod idoneum emolumentum habeat, ex integro in id
quod facere potest, creditores cum
eo experiuntur: inhumanum enim
erat spoliatum fortunis suis in solidum damnari.

40. So, when a debtor who has
made a cession of his goods to his
creditors acquires a fortune which
makes it worth their while, the creditors may compel him by action to
pay as much as he is able, but not
more, for it would be inhuman to
condemn a man to pay the whole
debt who has already been deprived
of all his property.

D. xlii. 3, 4. 6.

## Tit. VII. QUOD CUM EO CONTRACTUM EST, QUI IN ALIENA POTESTATE EST.

Quia tamen superius mentionem
habuimus de actione, quæ in peculium filiorumfamiliæ servorumve
agitur, opus est ut de hac actione et
de ceteris quæ eorumdem nomine in
parentes dominosve dari solent, diligentius admoneamus. Et quia,
sive cum servis negotium gestum
sit, sive cum his qui in potestate
parentis sunt, his fere eadem jura
servantur, ne verbosa fiat disputatio,
dirigamus sermonem in personam
servi dominique, idem intellecturi
de liberis quoque et parentibus
quorum in potestate sunt; nam si
quid in his proprie observatur, separatim ostendemus.

We have already spoken of the
action which may be brought relative to the *peculium* of *filiifamiliarum*
or of slaves. And we must now
speak of it more fully, and also of
all other actions which may be
brought against parents and masters
as representing children and slaves.
But, as the law is almost the same,
whether the dealing be with a slave,
or with one under the power of a
parent, to avoid prolixity, we will
treat only of slaves and their masters, leaving what we say of them
to be understood as applicable also
to children and the parents, under
whose power they are. For anything
which is peculiar to children and parents we will point out separately.

Gai. iv. 69.

By the strict rule of the civil law, the parent or master could not be bound or prejudiced by any act of a child or slave. But a sense of equity gradually broke in upon this rule, and, in certain cases, the contracts and delicts of persons *alieni juris*, came to affect those in whose power these persons were.

This Title treats of the contracts of persons *alieni juris*, which were considered to concern the master or parent (1) whenever they were made by his order; and (2) whenever he had profited by them.

1. Si igitur jussu domini cum servo negotium gestum erit, in solidum prætor adversus dominum actionem pollicetur; scilicet quia qui ita contrahit, fidem domini sequi videtur.

1. Thus, then, if any one deal with a slave acting under the command of his master, the prætor will give an action against the master for the whole of what is due under the contract; for with a slave, in this case, the person who contracts does so as relying on the faith of the master.

GAI. iv. 70.

The *jussus domini* extended to cases where the master subsequently ratified the contract, the ratification being equivalent to a mandate. (D. xv. 4. 1. 6.)

If the slave had been merely the instrument of his master, if, for instance, the master arranged that money borrowed for himself should be told out to his slave, the prætor would give a *condictio*, not an action *quod jussu*. (D. xv. 4. 5, pr.)

2. Eadem ratione prætor duas alias in solidum actiones pollicetur, quarum altera exercitoria, altera institoria appellatur. Exercitoria tunc habet locum, cum quis servum suum magistrum navi præposuerit, et quid cum eo ejus rei gratia cui præpositus erit contractum fuerit: ideo autem exercitoria vocatur, quia exercitor appellatur is ad quem quotidianus navis quæstus pertinet. Institoria tunc locum habet, cum quis tabernæ forte aut cuilibet negotiationi præposuerit, et quid cum eo ejus rei causa cui præpositus erit contractum fuerit: ideo autem institoria appellatur, quia qui negotiationibus præponuntur, institores vocantur. Istas tamen duas actiones prætor reddit, et si liberum quis hominem aut alienum servum navi aut tabernæ aut cuilibet negotiationi præposuerit, scilicet quia eadem æquitatis ratio etiam eo casu intervenisset.

2. For the same reason the prætor also gives two other actions for the whole sum due, the one called the *actio exercitoria*, the other the *actio institoria*. The action *exercitoria* may be brought when a master has made his slave commander of a vessel, and a contract has been entered into with the slave relating to the business he has been appointed to manage. This action is named *exercitoria*, because he, to whom the daily profits of a ship belong, is said to be an *exercitor*. The action *institoria* may be brought when a master has intrusted his slave with the management of a shop or any particular business, and a contract has been made with the slave relating to the business he has been appointed to manage. This action is called *institoria*, because persons to whom the management of a business is intrusted are called *institores*. The prætor likewise permits these two actions to be brought if any one

commits to a free person, or to the
slave of another, the management of
a ship, a warehouse, or any particular affair, as the principle of equity
is the same.

GAL. iv. 7l.

*Liberum hominem.* We have seen at how late a period of
Roman law it was that one freeman could act for another. (See
Bk. iii. Tit. 26.) It was, in fact, by extending these actions
*institoria* and *exercitoria*, so as to embrace the case of a mandatary, that the prætor made the principal directly responsible,
and thus enabled him to be really represented by the agent.

3. Introduxit et aliam actionem
prætor, quæ tributoria vocatur:
namque si servus in peculiari merce
sciente domino negotietur, et quid
cum eo ejus rei causa contractum
erit, ita prætor jus dicit, ut quidquid in his mercibus erit, quodque
inde receptum erit, id inter dominum si quid ei debetur, et ceteros
creditores pro rata portione distribuatur. Et quia ipsi domino distributionem permittit, si quis ex
creditoribus queratur quasi minus
ei tributum sit quam oportuerit,
hanc ei actionem accommodat, quæ
tributoria appellatur.

3. The prætor has also introduced
another action called *tributoria*; for,
if a slave with the knowledge of his
master trade with his *peculium*, and
contracts are made with him in the
course of business, the prætor ordains
that all the merchandise or money
arising from his traffic shall be distributed between the master, if anything be due to him, and the rest of
the creditors of the slave in proportion to their claims. And as the
master himself is permitted to make
the distribution, if any creditor complain that he has received too small
a share, the prætor will permit him
to bring the *actio tributoria.*

GAI. iv. 72; D. xiv. 4. 1; D. xiv. 4, 5. 11; D. xiv. 4. 7. 1, 2.

The *actio tributoria* was only given against the master when
there was fraud (*dolus*) in the distribution; but there would
be *dolus* directly the master had notice that a creditor had
received nothing, or less than his share. (D. xiv. 4. 7. 2, 3.)

4. Præterea introducta est actio
de peculio deque eo quod in rem
domini versum erit: ut quamvis
sine voluntate domino negotium
gestum erit, tamen sive quid in rem
ejus versum fuerit, id totum præstare debeat, sive quid non sit in
rem ejus versum, id eatenus præstare debeat, quatenus peculium patitur. In rem autem domini versum intelligitur, quidquid necessario in rem ejus impenderit servus:
veluti, si mutuatus pecuniam creditoribus ejus solverit, aut ædificia
ruentia fulserit, aut familiæ fru-

4. The prætor has also introduced
an action relating at once to a *peculium*, and to things by which the
master has profited: for although
the slave contracts without the consent of his master, yet the master
ought, if he has profited by anything,
to pay all up to the amount of his
profit; if he has not received any
profit, he ought to pay the amount
of the slave's *peculium*. Everything
is understood as profiting the master
which is laid out in his necessary expenses by the slave; as, for instance,
if the slave borrows money with

mentum emerit, vel etiam fundum
aut quamlibet aliam rem necessariam mercatus erit. Itaque, si ex
decem ut puta aureis quos servus
tuus a Titio mutuos accepit, creditori tuo quinque solverit,
reliquos vero quinque quolibet modo
consumpserit, pro quinque quidem
in solidum damnari debes; pro ceteris vero quinque, eatenus quatenus
in peculio sit. Ea quo scilicet apparet, si toti decem aurei in rem
tuam versi fuerint, totos decem
aureos Titium consequi posse; licet
enim una est actio qua de peculio
deque eo qnod in rem domini versum sit agitur, tamen duas habet
condemnationes. Itaque judex apud
quem de ea actione agitur, ante dispicere solet an in rem domini versum sit; nec aliter ad peculii aestimationem transit, quam si aut nihil
in rem domini versum esse intelligatur, aut non totum. Cum autem
queritur quantum in peculio sit,
ante deducitur quidquid servus domino, eive qui in potestate ejus sit
debet, et quod superest id solum
peculium intelligitur. Aliquando
tamen id quod ei debet servus qui
in potestate domini sit, non deducitur ex peculio, veluti si is in hujus ipsius peculio sit: quod eo pertinet, ut si quid vicario suo servus
debeat, id ex peculio ejus non deducatur.

which he pays the debts of his master, repairs his buildings in danger of
falling, purchases wheat for the establishment, or land for his master, or
any other necessary thing. Thus if
your slave borrow ten *aurei* of Titius,
pay five to one of your creditors,
and spend five, you would be condemned to pay the whole of the first
five, and so much of the other five
as the slave's *peculium* would cover;
whence it will appear, that if all the
ten *aurei* had been spent to your
profit, Titius might have recovered
the whole from you; for although
it is the same action in which the
plaintiff seeks to obtain the *peculium*,
and the amount by which the master
has profited, yet this action contains
two condemnations. The judge before whom the action is brought,
first inquires whether the master
has received any profit; and then,
when he has ascertained that so
part or not the whole of the sum due
from the slave has been expended to
the profit of the master, he proceeds
to estimate the value of the *peculium*, in estimating which, a deduction is first made of what the slave
owes his master, or any one under
the power of his master, and the remainder only is considered as the
*peculium*. But it sometimes happens that what a slave owes to a
person in the power of his master is
not deducted, as when he owes something to a slave who forms part of
his own *peculium*. For if a slave
is indebted to his *vicarius*, the sum
due cannot be deducted from the
*peculium*.

GAI. Iv. 73, 74 ; D. xlv. 5. 1 ; D. xv. 3. 3. 1 ; D. xv. 1. 17.

This action is generally called *de peculio et in rem verso*,
because, in most cases, the judge had to take notice of both
the profit derived by the master and of the amount of the
slave's *peculium*. But in some cases, as, for instance, where
the slave had no *peculium*, the action could be brought *de in
rem verso* only, and so it would naturally be, if it could be
shown that the master had reaped all the benefit of the contract. (See end of next paragraph.)

*Si quid vicario*. The *vicarii* formed part of the *peculium* of the ordinary slave ; anything, therefore, deducted from the *peculium*, as owed to the *vicarii*, would, if paid, again enter into the *peculium* as the property of the ordinary slave. It was, therefore, useless to pay it.

5. Ceterum dubium non est quin is quoque qui jussu domini contraxerit, cuique institoria vel exercitoria actio competit, de peculio deque eo quod in rem domini versum est, agere possit; sed erit stultissimus, si omissa actione qua facillime solidum ex contractu consequi possit, se ad difficultatem perducat probandi in rem domini versum esse, vel habere servum peculium, et tantum habere ut solidum sibi solvi possit. Is quoque cui tributoria actio competit, æque de peculio et in rem verso agere potest; sed sane huic modo tributoria expedit agere, modo de peculio et in rem verso. Tributoria ideo expedit agere, quia in ea domini conditio præcipua non est, id est, quod domino debetur non deducitur, sed ejusdem juris est dominus cujus et ceteri creditores; at in actione de peculio ante deducitur quod domino debetur, et in id quod reliquum est creditori dominus condemnatur. Ita rursus de peculio ideo expedit agere, quod in hac actione totius peculii ratio habetur; at in tributoria, ejus tantum quo negotiatur, et potest quisque tertia forte parte peculii aut quarta vel etiam minima negotiari, majorem autem partem in prædiis et mancipiis aut fœnebri pecunia habere. Prout ergo expedit, ita quisque vel hanc actionem vel illam eligere debet: certe, qui potest probare in rem domini versum esse, de in rem verso agere debet.

6. It need hardly be said that a person who has contracted with a slave acting by his master's command, and who may bring either the action *institoria* or *exercitoria*, may also bring the action *de peculio*, or that *de in rem verso*. But it would be the height of folly in any one to give up an action by which he might easily recover his whole demand, and have recourse to another by which he would be reduced to the difficulty of proving that the money he lent to the slave was employed to the profit of the master, or that the slave is possessed of a *peculium*, and that sufficient to answer the whole debt. Any one, again, in whose power it is to bring the *actio tributoria*, may equally bring the action *de peculio*, or that *de in rem verso*; and it is expedient, in some cases, to employ the former, and in some cases one of the two latter. On the one hand, the *actio tributoria* is preferable, because in this no privilege is accorded to the master, i.e. there is no previous deduction made in his favour of what is due to him, but he stands in the same position as the rest of the creditors; whereas in the action *de peculio*, there is first deducted the debt due to the master, who is only condemned to distribute the remainder among the creditors. On the other hand, in some cases, it may be more convenient to bring the action *de peculio*, because it affects the whole *peculium*, whereas the action *tributoria* affects only so much of it as has been employed in trade; and it is possible that a slave may have traded only with a third, a fourth, or some very small part of it, and that the rest may consist in lands, slaves, or money lent at interest. Every one ought, therefore, to select this or that action as may promise to be most advantageous to him. If, however, a creditor can prove that anything has

been employed to the profit of the master, he ought to bring the action *de in rem verso*.

GAL. iv. 74; D. xiv. 4. 11.

Any one who could bring an *actio quod jussu, exercitoria,* or *institoria,* could also, at option, bring an *actio de peculio et de in rem verso,* but not at all necessarily *vice versa.*

| | |
|---|---|
| 6. Quæ diximus de servo et domino, eadem intelligimus et de filio et filia aut nepote et nepte, et patre avove in cujus potestate sunt. | 6. What we have said in relation to a slave and his master, is equally applicable to children and grandchildren, and to their ascendants, in whose power they are. |

D. xiv. 4. 1. 4.

It may be observed that the master was never bound, if the slave engaged himself by mandate, or fidejussion, for a third person, but the father was bound by an engagement contracted for another by a son in his power. (D. xv. 1. 3. 9.)

| | |
|---|---|
| 7. Illud proprie servatur in eorum persona, quod senatus-consultum Macedonianum prohibuit mutuas pecunias dari eis qui in parentis erunt potestate, et ei qui crediderit, denegator actio tam adversus ipsum filium filiamve, nepotem neptemve, sive adhuc in potestate sunt, sive morte parentis vel emancipatione sua potestatis eam coeperint, quam adversus patrem avumve, sive eos habeat adhuc in potestate, sive emancipaverit. Quæ ideo senatus prospexit, quia sæpe onerati ære alieno creditarum pecuniarum quas in luxuriam consumebant, vitæ parentium insidiabantur. | 7. A peculiar provision has, however, been made in their favour by the *senatus-consultum Macedonianum,* which prohibits money to be lent to children under power of their parents; and refuses any action to the creditor, either against the descendants, whether still under power, or become *sui juris* by the death of the parent or by emancipation, or against the parent, whether he still retain them under his power, or has emancipated them. This provision was adopted by the senate, because they thought that persons under power, when loaded with debts contracted by borrowing sums to be wasted in debauchery, often attempted the lives of their parents. |

D. xiv. 6. 1; D. xiv. 6. 3. 3; D. xiv. 6. 7. 10.

The *senatus-consultum Macedonianum* was made, according to Tacitus, in the reign of Claudius (ANN. xi. 31); according to Suetonius, in that of Vespasian (VESP. 11). Perhaps it was only renewed in the latter reign. Theophilus informs us that it was made to meet the case of a young prodigal named Macedo, who attempted the life of his father. The terms of the *senatus-consultum* (D. xiv. 6. 1) would rather lead us to suppose Macedo was the name of a usurer.

8. Illud in summa admonendi animus, id quod jussu patris dominive contractum fuerit, quodque in rem ejus versum erit, directo quoque posse a patre dominove condici, tamquam si principaliter cum ipso negotium gestum esset. Ei quoque qui vel exercitoria vel institoria actione tenetur directo posse condici placet, quia hujus quoque jussu contractum intelligitur.

8. Lastly, we may observe, that whenever any contract has been made by command of a parent or master, or anything employed to their profit, a *condictio* may be brought directly against the father or master exactly as if the contract had been originally made with them. So when any one is liable to the action *institoria* or *exhibitoria*, a *condictio* may also be brought directly against him, as in this case also it is by his order that the contract has been made.

D. xvii. 2. 84 ; D. xiv. 3. 17. 5 ; D. xii. 1. 20.

*Posse condici.* If a condiction could be brought, of what use were the peculiar prætorian actions of which, as the text informs us, the plaintiff could avail himself? Probably the institution of these actions was long antecedent to the time when the condiction was admitted as an appropriate form of action in cases where a *paterfamilias* was to be made responsible for the acts of his son or slave. It was only by a great extension of the scope of the condiction that it was given, first, when one man profited in any way by the property of another (D. xii. 1. 23. 32); and, secondly, against a person by whose order another person had contracted, or whose manager (*institor*) the person contracting was. (D. xii. 1. 9. 2.) After it had received this extension, the *condictio* would be a concurrent remedy with the prætorian actions. But there would still be cases, namely, bilateral contracts, giving rise to prætorian actions, such as those *empti*, or *venditi*, *pro socio*, *locati* or *conducti*, or contracts giving rise to actions *in factum*, in which the condiction would not be given against the *paterfamilias*, and in which recourse must be had to the prætorian actions proper to the kind of contract. These prætorian actions would, in the particular case of the *paterfamilias*, receive a slight modification of form, and a new name, and be termed *quod jussu*, *de in rem verso*, *de peculio*, &c., though remaining substantially *empti*, *locati*, *pro socio*, &c., according to the character of the transaction.

It will be observed that the text says *directo posse condici.* The action could be brought as if we had treated directly with the *paterfamilias.* An *actio* was said to be *directa*, in this sense, when brought against a person bound by some act of his own, *indirecta* when brought against a person bound by some act of a person or thing belonging to him. And thus this Title and the two following may, if we please, be considered as treating of a seventh division of actions into *directæ* and *indirectæ*. *Directa*, when applied to an action, was also opposed to *contraria*, i.e. protecting the rights principally contemplated in the kind of contract as opposed to one protecting rights only incidentally attaching to it (see Bk. iii. Tit. 26); and it was also opposed to *utilis*, i.e. given directly by the law, as opposed to one given by an extension of the law. (See Introd. sec. 106.)

## TIT. VIII. DE NOXALIBUS ACTIONIBUS.

Ex maleficiis servorum, veluti si furtum fecerint, aut bona rapuerint, aut damnum dederint, aut iujuriam commiserint, noxales actiones proditæ sunt, quibus domino damnato permittitur, aut litis æstimationem sufferre, aut hominem noxæ dedere.

The wrongful acts of a slave, whether he commits a theft or robbery, or does any damage or injury, give rise to noxal actions, in which the master of the slave, if condemned, may either pay the estimated amount of damage done, or deliver up his slave in satisfaction of the injury.

GAI. iv. 75.

We now pass to actions given to enforce obligations arising from the delicts of persons *alieni juris*. These actions, which were given against the master of the slave, and, in ancient times, against the parent of the *filiusfamilias*, were termed *noxales*, because the master or parent could rid himself of all liability, by abandoning the slave or child committing the delict to the person injured. There was, however, no distinct *actio noxalis*. The action brought on the delict was one *furti*, *vi bonorum raptorum*, &c., as the case might be, the difference being that the *condemnatio* was alternative, either to pay so much or to abandon the slave, instead of simply to pay so much.

If at any time, either before or after the *litis contestatio*, the master abandoned the slave, all right of action for damages against him became immediately extinct. The *actio noxalis* had thus a kind of resemblance to the *actiones arbitrariæ*, in which the *judex* first ordered the defendant to make satisfaction, and then if he did not comply, proceeded to condemn him.

1. Noxa autem est corpus quod nocuit, id est, servus: noxia, ipsum maleficium, veluti furtum, damnum, rapina, injuria.

1. *Noxa* is the doer of the wrongful act, i.e. the slave. *Noxia* is the act itself, that is, the theft, the damage, the robbery with violence, or injury.

D. ix. 1. 1. 1.

2. Summa autem ratione permissum est noxæ deditione defungi; namque erat iniquum nequitiam eorum ultra ipsorum corpora dominis damnosam esse.

2. It is with great reason that the master is permitted to deliver up the offending slave: for it would be very unjust, when a slave does a wrongful act, to make the master liable to lose anything more than the slave himself.

GAL. iv. 75.

3. Dominos noxali judicio servi sui nomine conventus, servum actori noxæ dedendo liberatur: nec minus perpetuum ejus dominium a domino transfertur; sin autem damnum ei cui deditus est servus resarcierit quæsita pecunia, auxilio prætoris invito domino manumittetur.

3. A master sued in a noxal action on account of his slave, clears himself if he gives up his slave to the plaintiff, and then the property in the slave is thus transferred for ever; but, if the slave can procure money, and satisfy the master to whom he has been given up for all damage he has sustained, he may be manumitted by the intervention of the prætor, though against the wish of his new master.

D. ix. 4. 20.

4. Sunt autem constitutæ noxales actiones, aut legibus, aut edicto prætoris: legibus, veluti furti lege Duodecim Tabularum, damni injuriæ lege Aquilia; edicto prætoris, veluti injuriarum et vi bonorum raptorum.

4. Noxal actions are established either by the laws, or by the edict of the prætor. By the laws, as for theft, by the law of the Twelve Tables; for wrongful damage, by the lex Aquilia; by the prætor's edict, as for injuries and robbery with violence.

GAL. iv. 76.

These are but examples; any delict whatsoever committed by a slave would furnish ground for an *actio noxalis*.

5. Omnis autem noxalis actio caput sequitur: nam si servus tuus noxiam commiserit, quamdiu in tua potestate sit, tecum est actio; si in alterius potestatem pervenerit, cum illo incipit actio esse; at si manumissus fuerit, directo ipse tenetur, et extinguitur noxæ deditio. Ex diverso quoque directa actio noxalis esse incipit: nam si liber homo noxiam commiserit, et is servus tuus esse cœperit (quod quibusdam casibus effici primo libro tradidimus), incipit tecum esse noxalis actio quæ antea directa fuisset.

5. Every noxal action follows the delinquent. The delicts committed by your slave are a ground of action against you, while the slave belongs to you; if the slave becomes subject to another, the action must be brought against the new master: but if the slave is manumitted, the action is brought directly against him, and there cannot then be any giving up of the slave in satisfaction. Conversely, an action, which was at first direct, may afterwards become noxal; for if a freeman commit a wrongful act, and then become your slave, which may happen in some cases, of which we have spoken in our First Book, then the direct action against the slave is changed into a noxal action against you.

If the slave were not in the possession of his owner (*dominus*), of course the owner would not be liable for his delicta.

6. Si servus domino noxiam commiserit, actio nulla nascitur: namque inter dominum et eum qui in potestate ejus est, nulla obligatio nasci potest: Ideoque et si in alienam potestatem servus pervenerit ant manumissus fuerit, neque cum ipso, neque cum eo cujus nunc in potestate sit, agi potest. Unde, si alienus servus noxiam tibi commiserit, et is postea in potestate tua esse coeperit, intercidit actio, quia in eum casum deducta sit, in quo consistere non potuit; ideoque licet exierit de tua potestate, agere non potes: quemadmodum si dominus in servum suum aliquid commiserit, nec si manumissus aut alienatus fuerit servus, ullam actionem contra dominum habere potest.

6. If a slave commit a wrongful act against his master, no action can be brought; for no obligation can arise between a master and his slave: and if the slave pass under the power of another master, or is manumitted, no action can be brought either against him or his new master; whence it follows, that, if the slave of another should commit a wrongful act against you, and become your slave, the action is extinguished; as it has become impossible, in the actual position of the parties. And although he subsequently passes out of your power, yet you cannot bring an action. Neither, if a master injures his slave in any way, can the slave after having been alienated or manumitted, bring any action against his master.

GAI. iv. 78.

The Proculians had thought that a master could, after a slave had passed out of his power, bring an action against the slave, for anything done by him whilst his slave. (GAI. iv. 78.)

7. Sed veteres quidem haec et in filiisfamilias masculis et feminis admisere. Nova autem hominum conversatio hujusmodi asperitatem recte respuendam esse existimavit, et ab usu communi hoc penitus recessit. Quis enim patiatur filium suum et maxime filiam in noxam alii dare, ut pene per corpus pater magis quam filius periclitetur, cum in filiabus etiam pudicitiae favor hoc bene excludit? Et ideo placuit in servos tantummodo noxales actiones esse proponendas, cum apud veteres legum commentatores invenimus saepius dictum, ipsos filiosfamilias pro suis delictis posse conveniri.

7. The ancients, indeed, applied the same rules to children of both sexes in the power of ascendants; but the feeling of later times has rightly rejected such extreme rigour, and it has therefore passed wholly into disuse. For who could bear to deliver up as a forfeiture a son, and still more a daughter? for, in the person of his son, the father would suffer more than the son himself, and mere regard to decency forbids such treatment of a daughter. Noxal actions have, therefore, been allowed to apply to slaves only; and we find it often laid down in th older jurists, that an action may be brought directly against sons in power, for their wrongful acts.

GAI. iv. 75, 77–79; D. ix. 4. 33–35.

It is true that the sons of a family could be sued, but then the plaintiff could only recover up to the amount of the *peculium*; and, therefore, the old *actio noxalis* may have been a much more efficient remedy, though one which the more lenient idea of parental power, current in the later days of Roman law, would not sanction.

## Tit. IX. SI QUADRUPES PAUPERIEM FECISSE DICATUR.

Animalium nomine quae ratione carent, si qua lascivia aut fervore aut feritate pauperiem fecerint, noxalis actio lege Duodecim Tabularum prodita est. Quae animalia, si noxae dedantur, proficiunt reo ad liberationem, quia ita lex Duodecim Tabularum scripta est, ut puta, si equus calcitrosus calce percusserit, aut bos cornu petere solitus petierit. Haec autem actio in iis quae contra naturam moventur locum habet: ceterum, si genitalis sit feritas, cessat. Denique si ursus fugit a domino et sic nocuit, non potest quondam dominus conveniri, quia desiit dominus esse ubi fera evasit. Pauperies autem est damnum sine injuria facientis datum: nec enim potest animal injuriam fecisse dici, quod sensu caret. Haec quod ad noxalem pertinet actionem.

A noxal action is given by the law of the Twelve Tables, when irrational animals, through wantonness, rage, or ferocity, have done any damage; but if the animals are delivered up in satisfaction for the damage done, the owner is secured against any action; such is the law of the Twelve Tables; as, for example, if a kicking horse should kick, or an ox, apt to gore, should inflict an injury with his horns. But this action can only be brought in the case of animals acting contrary to their nature, for, when the ferocity of a beast is innate, no action can be brought, so that, if a bear break loose from his master, and mischief be done, the master cannot be sued; for he ceased to be the master as soon as the wild beast escaped. The word *pauperies* denotes a damage done without any wrong intent; for an animal, void of reason, cannot be said to have had a wrong intent. Thus much as to noxal actions.

D. ix. 1. 1, pr. 3, 4. 7. 10.

Although in the Twelve Tables the word *quadrupes* was used, all animals were held to be included under it.

The distinction noticed in the text is that between an animal with an inborn fierceness (*genitalis feritas*) and one with a confirmed vicious habit (*calcitrosus, petere solitus*). The owner of the latter only was liable to the *actio noxalis* given by the Twelve Tables.

If an animal fierce by nature did any damage while in the keeping of any one, his keeper would be liable to an *actio utilis*, though not to the direct *actio noxalis* given by the law of the Twelve Tables. (See next paragraph.)

L. Ceterum sciendum est aedilitio edicto prohiberi nos canem, verrem, aprum, ursum, leonem, ibi habere qua vulgo iter fit; et si adversus ea factum erit, et nocitum libero homini esse dicetur, quod bonum et aequum judici videtur, tanti dominus condemnetur; ceterarum rerum, quanti damnum datum sit dupli. Praeter has autem aedilitias actiones, et de pauperie locum habebit; numquam enim actiones, praesertim poenales, de eadem re concurrentes alia aliam consumit.

L. It must be observed, that the edict of the aedile forbids any man to keep a dog, a boar, a bear, or a lion, where there is a public road: and, if this prohibition be disobeyed, and any freeman receive hurt, the master of the beast may be condemned at the discretion of the judge; and, in case of damage to anything else, the condemnation must be in double the amount of damage done. Besides the aedilitian action, the action de pauperie may also be brought against the same person; for when different actions, especially penal actions, may be each brought on account of the same thing, the employment of one does not prevent the employment of another.

D. ix. 4. 2. 1; D. xxi. 1. 40. 1; D. xxi. 1. 41, 42; D. xliv. 7. 60.

## Tit. X. DE IIS PER QUOS AGERE POSSUMUS.

Nunc admonendi sumus agere posse quemlibet hominem aut suo nomine, aut alieno: alieno velut procuratorio, tutorio, curatorio; cum olim in usu fuisset alterius nomine agere non posse, nisi pro populo, pro libertate, pro tutela. Praeterea lege Hostilia permissum est furti agere eorum nomine qui apud hostes essent, aut reipublicae causa abessent, quive in eorum cujus tutela essent. Et quia hoc non minimam incommoditatem habebat, quod alieno nomine neque agere neque excipere actionem licebat, coeperunt homines per procuratores litigare; nam et morbus et aetas et necessaria peregrinatio, itemque aliae multae causae saepe impedimento sunt quominus rem suam exequi possint.

We must now remark, that a person may conduct an action either in his own name, or in that of another, as, for instance, if he is a procurator, a tutor, or a curator; but anciently, custom forbad one person conducting an action in the name of another, unless for the people, for freedom, or for a pupil. The lex Hostilia afterwards permitted an actio furti to be brought in the names of those who were prisoners in the hands of an enemy, of persons absent in the service of the state, or under the care of tutors. But, as it was found to be exceedingly inconvenient, that one man should be prohibited from bringing or defending an action in the name of another, it by degrees became a practice to sue by procurators. For ill-health, old age, unavoidable journeys, and many other causes, continually prevent mankind from being able to attend personally to their own affairs.

GAI. iv. 82; D. l. 17. 123; D. lii. 3. 1. 2.

The old principle of Roman law was, that no one could

represent another, and with the exceptions noticed in the text this principle was rigorously observed during the period of the actions of law.

By *agere pro populo* was meant bringing an *actio popularis* (*eum popularem actionem dicimus quae suum jus populi tuetur*, D. xlvii. 23. 1); by *agere pro libertate*, was meant becoming *assertor libertatis* for a slave; and by *agere pro tutela*, bringing an action on behalf of a pupil.

Under the system of *formulae*, the first step towards breaking through the old rule was the permitting a *cognitor* to be appointed. A *cognitor* was a person who was appointed by one of the parties to a suit to conduct it for him. The *cognitor* himself was not necessarily present when he was appointed, but it was necessary that the appointment should be made before the magistrate, in presence of the adversary, and by a certain form of words. For instance, a plaintiff speaking generally of his action would say, '*Quod ego tecum agere volo, in eam rem Lucium Titium cognitorem do.*' Other forms, adapted to other cases, are given in Gaius (iv. 83).

The next step was to permit a procurator appointed by a mandate to conduct a suit, but he did so in his own name, for it was not till a late period of Roman law that a procurator could expressly represent his principal. He had accordingly to give security *ratam rem dominam habiturum*, that his principal would ratify what he did. When a *cognitor* or procurator appeared instead of the real party to the suit, the *intentio* of the formula was left as it would have been if the party himself had appeared, as, for instance, *Si paret Numerium Negidium Publio Marvio sestertium X. millia dare oportere*, and then in the *condemnatio* the name of the *cognitor* was substituted, *judex Numerium Negidium Lucio Titio sestertium X. millia condemna*. (GAI. iv. 86, 87.)

In the time of Justinian a procurator, however appointed, and even the *negotiorum gestor*, if he procured a subsequent ratification from his principal, could in every way represent the principal. The procurator need not give any security, provided that, if his principal were absent, he could satisfactorily show that he had authority to act for him. The *negotiorum gestor*, generally in such a case called *defensor*, because he would seldom take the responsibility on himself, except when the person for whom he appeared was the attacked party, had to give security *ratam rem dominum habiturum*, or *judicatum solvi*.

1. Procurator neque certis verbis, neque praesente adversario, immo plerumque ignorante eo constitui-

1. A procurator is appointed without any particular form of words, nor is the presence of the adverse

O O

tur; cuicunque enim permiseris rem tuam agere aut defendere, is procurator intelligitur.

party required: Indeed, it is generally done without his knowledge. For any one is considered to be your procurator who is employed to bring or to defend an action for you.

GAI. iv. 84; D. iii. 3. 1. 1, 3.

2. Tutores et curatores quemadmodum constituuntur, primo libro expositum est.

2. How tutors and curators are appointed has been already explained in the First Book.

GAI. iv. 85.

If the tutor, in appearing for the pupil, had merely discharged a duty forced upon him, the *actio judicati* (i. e. the action brought to enforce the sentence) was given to or against the pupil. If the tutor chose to appear for the pupil when he need have done nothing more than authorize the pupil to appear himself, the *actio judicati* was given to or against the tutor. The case was the same as regards the curators of persons under the age of 25.

## TIT. XI. DE SATISDATIONIBUS.

Satisdationum modus alius antiquitati placuit, alium novitas per usum amplexa est. Olim enim, si in rem agebatur, satisdare possessor compellebatur, ut si victus esset, nec rem ipsam restitueret nec litis aestimationem ejus, potestas esset petitori aut cum eo agendi, aut cum fidejussoribus ejus: quae satisdatio appellatur judicatum solvi. Unde autem sic appellatur, facile est intelligere; namque stipulatur quis ut solvatur sibi quod fuerit judicatum. Multo magis is qui in rem actione conreniebatur, satisdare cogebatur, si alieno nomine Judicium accipiebat. Ipse autem qui in rem agebat, si suo nomine petebat, satisdare non cogebatur, procurator vero, si in rem agebat, satisdare jubebatur ratam rem dominum habiturum: periculum enim erat ne iterum dominus de eadem re experiretur. Tutores et curatores, eodem modo quo et procuratores, satisdare debere verba edicti faciebant: sed aliquando his agentibus satisdatio remittebatur. Haec ita erant, si in rem agebatur.

One system of taking securities prevailed in ancient times; custom has introduced another in modern times. Formerly, in a real action, the possessor was compelled to give security, so that if he lost his cause, and did not either restore the thing itself, or pay the estimated value of it, the plaintiff might either sue him or his fidejussors; this species of security is termed *judicatum solvi*, nor is it difficult to understand why it is so called. For the plaintiff used to stipulate that what was adjudged to him should be paid, and with still greater reason was a person sued in a real action obliged to give security if he was defendant in the name of another. A plaintiff in a real action suing in his own name, was not obliged to give security; but a procurator had to give security that his acts would be ratified by the person for whom he acted; for there was a danger lest the person should bring a fresh action for the same thing. By the words of the edict, tutors and curators were bound to give security, as well as procurators, but it was sometimes dispensed with when they were the plaintiffs. Such was the practice with regard to real actions.

GAI. Iv. 60. 01, 90. 98–100; D. xlvi, 7. 0.

*Judicatum solvi stipulatio tres clausulas in unum collatas habet; de re judicata, de re defendenda, de dolo malo.* (D. xlvi. 7. 6.) There were three objects secured by the *cautio judicatum solvi*; the surety promised (1), that the *litis æstimatio*, the amount of what was adjudged by the sentence, should be paid if the defendant should be condemned and should not give back the thing: (2), that the defendant should appear to receive the sentence of the judge; (3), that the defendant should use no *dolus malus*, should not, for instance, give back the thing, but give it in a state deteriorated by his fault. The object of the defendant, as well as the sureties, binding himself for the *litis æstimatio* (*aut cum eo agendi*, says the text, *aut cum fidejussoribus*), was to give the plaintiff his choice between an action *ex stipulatu*, which was often preferred, or one *ex judicato*, i. e. upon, or to enforce, the sentence. The object of making the defendant directly liable, by a stipulation, if he did not appear to defend the action, was to avoid having recourse to the less direct mode in which the disobedience of the defendant to obey the magistrate's summons was made to benefit the plaintiff.

*Satisdare possessor compellebatur.* If the possessor would not give the *cautio judicatum solvi*, the possession, by means of an interdict (see Tit. 15. 3), was transferred to the plaintiff, if he were willing to give the security which his adversary refused to give.

*Litis æstimatio. Lis* here signifies the subject of the suit.

*Multo magis si alieno nomine.* This applied to the procurator in the days when he did not really represent the principal. The *cognitor* never gave security. The person really interested in the action was called *dominus litis*; when the procurator did not represent him, but came forward as if he were the *dominus litis*, it was necessary to guard against the real *dominus litis* bringing another action.

Tutors had probably to give security in all cases where they were the party defendant.

| | |
|---|---|
| 1. Si vero in personam, ab actoris quidem parte eadem obtinebant, quæ diximus in actione qua in rem agitur. Ab ejus vero parte cum quo agitur, si quidem alieno nomine aliquis interveniret, omnimodo satisdaret, quia nemo defensor in | 1. In personal actions, on the part of the plaintiff, the same rules as to giving security were observed as in real actions. As to the defendant, if he appeared in the name of another, he was obliged to give security, for no one was considered a competent |

o o 2

aliena re sine satisdatione idoneus esse creditur. Quod si proprio nomine aliquis judicium accipiebat in personam, judicatum solvi satisdare non cogebatur.

defendant in behalf of another unless he gave security: but any one who defended a personal action in his own name was not compelled to give the security *judicatum solvi.*

Gai. iv. 100-102.

*If the defendant was a cognitor, the dominus litis gave security for him. (Vat. Fragm. 317.)*

2. Sed haec hodie aliter observantur: sive enim quis in rem actione convenitur sive in personam suo nomine, nullam satisdationem pro litis aestimatione dare compellitur, sed pro sua tantum persona, quod in judicio permaneat usque ad terminum litis; vel committitur suo promissioni cum jurejurando, quam juratoriam cautionem vocant; vel nudam promissionem vel satisdationem pro qualitate personae suae dare compellitur.

2. At present a different practice prevails. A defendant who is sued in his own name, either in a real or personal action, is not forced to give security for the payment of the estimated value of the thing sued for, but only for his own person, that is, that he will remain and abide the judgment until the end of the suit. For this security recourse may be had to the promise on oath of the party, when the security is called a *cautio juratoria,* or to his simple promise without oath, or to a *satisdatio,* according to the quality of the person.

C. xii. 1. 17.

*In judicio permaneat.* An earlier writer would have said *in jure,* as the *cautio* was given when the parties were before the praetor that the defendant would go before the *judex.* But in Justinian's time the distinction of *in jure* and *in judicio* was done away.

We gather from the text, that whereas under the old law the defendant would have had to give security both for the payment of the amount at which the subject-matter of the action was valued, and that he would appear to defend himself (*pro re defendenda,* or, as here, *in judicio permaneat*), under Justinian's legislation he did not engage at all for the former, and for the latter he did not necessarily give the security of a fidejussor, but if a *vir illustris,* only pledged himself by oath, or even by a simple promise. (C. xii. 1. 17.)

3. Sin autem per procuratorem lis vel infertur vel suscipitur, in actoris quidem persona, si non mandatum actio insinuatum est, vel praesens dominus litis in judicio procuratoris sui personam confirmaverit, ratam rem dominum habiturum satisdationem procurator dare compellitur: eodem observan-

3. But, where a suit is commenced or defended by a procurator. If the procurator of the plaintiff does not either register a mandate of appointment, or if the person who really brings the action does not himself appear before the judge to confirm the appointment of the procurator, then the procurator himself is obliged

do, et si tutor vel curator vel aliæ tales personæ quæ alienarum rerum gubernationem receperunt, litem quibusdam per alium inferunt.

to give security, that the person for whom he acts will ratify his proceedings. The same rule applies also if a tutor, curator, or any other person, who has undertaken to manage the affairs of another, brings an action through a third party.

4. Si vero aliquis convenitur, si quidem præsens procuratorem dare paratus est, potest vel ipse in judicium venire, et sui procuratoris personam per judicatum solvi satisdationis solemnes stipulationes firmare, vel extra judicium satisdationem exponere, per quam ipse sui procuratoris fidejussor existat pro omnibus judicatum solvi satisdationis clausulis: ubi et de hypotheca rnarum rerum convenire compellitur, sive in judicio promiserit, sive extra judicium cavarit, ut tam ipse quam heredes ejus obligentur; alia insuper cautela vel satisdatione propter personam Ipsius exponenda, quod tempore sententiæ recitandæ in judicio invenietur, vel si non venerit omnia dabit fidejussor quæ condemnatione contineatur, nisi fuerit provocatum.

4. As to the defendant, if he appears and wishes to appoint a procurator, he may either himself come before the judge, and there confirm the appearance of the procurator, by giving with a solemn stipulation the caution called *judicatum solvi*, or he may give such a security elsewhere, and become himself the fidejussor of his own procurator, as to each clause of the caution *judicatum solvi*, and he is then compelled to subject all his property to a *hypotheca*, whether he promises before the judge or not, and this obligation binds not only himself but his heirs. He must also give a further caution that he will himself appear at the time when judgment is given, or if he fails to do so, his *fidejussor* will be obliged to pay all that is fixed to be paid by the sentence, unless the decision be appealed against.

For the *clausulæ* of the *cautio judicatum solvi*, see note on the introductory paragraph of this Title.

*Alia insuper cautela.* This was to insure that the *actio judicati* should be given against the real *dominus litis.*

5. Si vero reus præsto ex quacumque causa non fuerit, et alius velit defensionem ejus subire, nulla differentia inter actiones in rem vel in personam introducenda, potest hoc facere, ita tamen ut satisdationem judicatum solvi pro litis æstimatione præstet; nemo enim secundum veterem regulam (ut jam dictum est) alienæ rei sine satisdatione defensor idoneus intelligitur.

5. But if, from any cause, a defendant does not appear, and another person is willing to defend the action for him, he may do so (nor does it make any difference whether the action is real or personal), but he must give security *judicatum solvi* to the amount of what is at stake; for, according to the old rule of law we have just mentioned, no one can be defendant for another without giving security.

6. Quæ omnia apertius et perfectissime a quotidiano judiciorum usu in ipsis rerum documentis apparent.

6. All this will be learnt more easily and fully by attending the sittings of Judges, and by the teaching of actual practice.

7. Quam formam non solum in hac regia urbe, sed etiam in omni-

7. We order that those rules shall be observed not only in this our

bus nostris provinciis, et si propter imperitiam forte aliter celebrantur, obtinere censemus; cum necesse sit omnes provincias caput omnium nostrarum civitatum, id est, hanc regiam urbem ejusque observantiam sequi.

royal city, but also in all our provinces, although other usages may be now adopted there through ignorance; for it is necessary that all the provinces should conform to the practice of our royal city, the capital of our whole empire.

## Tit. XII.　DE PERPETUIS ET TEMPORALIBUS ACTIONIBUS, ET QUÆ AD HEREDES ET IN HEREDES TRANSEUNT.

Hoc loco admonendi sumus, eas quidem actiones quæ ex lege senatusve consulto sive ex sacris constitutionibus proficiscuntur, perpetuo solere antiquitus competere, donec sacræ constitutiones tam in rem quam in personam actionibus certos fines dederunt; eas veroque ex propria prætoris jurisdictione pendent, plerumque intra annum vivere : nam et ipsius prætoris intra annum erat imperium. Aliquando tamen et in perpetuum extenduntur, id est, usque ad finem ex constitutionibus introductum: quales sunt eæ quæ bonorum possessori, ceterisque qui heredis loco sunt, accommodat. Furti quoque manifesti actio, quamvis ex ipsius prætoris jurisdictione proficiscatur, tamen perpetuo datur; absurdum enim esse existimavit anno eam terminari.

We ought here to observe that the actions derived from the law, from a senatus-consultum, or from imperial constitutions, could formerly be exercised at any length of time, however great; until imperial constitutions assigned fixed limits both to real and to personal actions. Of the actions derived from the jurisdiction of the prætor, the greater part only last during one year, for this was the limit of the prætor's authority. Sometimes, however, these actions are perpetual, that is, last until the time fixed by the constitutions; such are those given to the bonorum possessor and to others standing in the place of the heir. The action furti manifesti, also, though proceeding from the jurisdiction of the prætor, is yet perpetual, for it seemed absurd to limit its duration to a year.

Gai. iv. 110, 111.

This Title gives us two more divisions of actions, making an eighth and a ninth, viz. actions perpetual and temporary, and actions transmissible and not transmissible to and against heirs.

Although the duration of the prætor's authority may have suggested the particular length of time during which actiones temporales could be brought, we must not suppose that they had to be either brought or concluded while the same person was prætor during whose tenure of office the right to bring them first accrued. As an exception to the rule that prætorian actions lasted only for a year, we have mentioned in the Text the actio furti manifesti, which was perpetual because it was really derived from the Twelve Tables, the prætor having only substituted a pecuniary for a capital penalty. (GAI. iv. 111.) Also, almost all prætorian actions, the object of which was to establish a right to a particular thing (*actiones rei persecutoriæ*), were perpetual. (D. xliv. 7. 35.) In A.D. 424, Theodosius II. enacted that, as a general rule, actions, real or personal, should not be brought after a lapse of thirty years. (C. vii. 39. 3.) Subsequently the time was, in the case of some actions, as in that of an *actio hypothecaria*, when the thing hypothecated remained in the hands of the debtor, extended to forty years. (C. vii. 39. 71.) The term *perpetua*, however, still continued to be applied to these actions, though, properly speaking, in the time of Justinian it meant nothing more than an action which could be brought within thirty or forty years, as opposed to those which could only be brought within a shorter period. The effect of the lapse of time, in cases where actions could only be brought within thirty or forty years, was, it may be observed, to bar the action, not, as in the case of prescription by the lapse of ten or twenty years under the legislation of Justinian (see Bk. ii. Tit. 6), to transfer the property.

1. Non omnes autem actiones quæ in aliquem aut ipso jure competunt aut a prætore dantur, et in heredem æque competunt aut dari solent: est enim certissima juris regula, ex maleficiis pœnales actiones in heredem rei non competere, veluti furti, vi bonorum raptorum, injuriarum, damni injuriæ; sed heredibus hujusmodi actiones competunt, nec denegantur, excepta injuriarum actione, et si qua alia similis inveniatur. Aliquando tamen etiam ex contractu actio contra heredem non competit, cum testator dolose versatus sit, et ad heredem ejus nihil ex eo dolo pervenerit. Pœnales autem actiones quas supra diximus, si ab ipsis principalibus personis fuerint contestatæ, et heredibus dantur, et contra heredes transeunt.

1. It is not all the actions allowed against any one by the law, or given by the prætor, that will equally be allowed or given against his heir. For it is a fixed rule of law, that actions arising from delicts are not allowed against the heir of the delinquent, as, for instance, the actions furti, vi bonorum raptorum, injuriarum, damni injuriæ. These actions are, however, given to heirs, with the exception of the action injuriarum, and others that may resemble it. Sometimes an action, arising from a contract, is not allowed against an heir; for instance, the action given against any one for wilful wrong committed by him, is not allowed against the heir under his testament. But penal actions, such as those of which we have just spoken from the moment of the *litis contestatio*, pass both to and against the heirs to the parties.

GAI. iv. 112, 113; D. iv. 3. 17. 1; D. xliv. 7. 20. 59.

*Aliquando ex contractu actio contra heredem non competit.* This is taken from Gaius, who means it to apply to the heirs of *adstipulatores, sponsores,* and *fidepromissores*; for their heirs

were not bound; but it is difficult to say to what it could apply
in the time of Justinian. It would also be supposed, from the
text, that an action making a testator responsible for *dolus
malus* did not ordinarily pass against his heirs, if his heirs
were not benefited by the wrong he had committed; but there
was only one case in which the action did not pass against his
heirs whether they had benefited by the *dolus malus* or not,
namely, the action *in duplum* against a person who had been
guilty of *dolus malus* with regard to a deposit placed in his
custody under the pressure of an accidental misfortune (see
Tit. 6. 23); and even in this case an *actio in simplum* passed
against the heirs. (D. xvi. 3. 18.) The whole of the passage
in the text seems inaccurate.

2. Superest ut admoneamus,
quod, si ante rem judicatam is cum
quo actum est satisfaciat actori,
officio judicis convenit eum absol-
vere, licet judicii accipiendi tempore in ea causa fuisset, ut damnari deberet: et hoc est quod ante
vulgo dicebatur, omnia judicia ab-
solutoria esse.

2. It remains that we should remark, that if, before the sentence,
the defendant satisfies the plaintiff,
the judge ought to absolve the defendant, although, from the time of
the action being commenced before
the magistrate, it was evident the
defendant would be condemned. It
is in this sense that in former times
it was commonly said that in all
actions the defendant might be ab-
solved.

GAI. iv. 114.

The Proculians, we may suppose from what Gaius tells us
(iv. 114), had maintained that, as the question on which the
condemnation depended was whether a certain fact did or did
not exist at the time when the action was given, the judge
could not avoid condemning the defendant, if the defendant
was at that time in a position to be condemned. The contrary
opinion of the Sabinians is here confirmed by Justinian.

## TIT. XIII.　DE EXCEPTIONIBUS.

Sequitur ut de exceptionibus dispiciamus. Comparatae autem sunt
exceptiones defendendorum eorum
gratia cum quibus agitur: saepe
enim accidit, ut licet ipsa persecutio qua actor experitur justa sit,
tamen iniqua sit adversus eum cum
quo agitur.

It now follows that we should
speak of exceptions. They have been
introduced as a means of defence for
those against whom the action is
brought. For it often happens that
the action of the plaintiff, although
in itself justly brought, is yet unjust with respect to the person
against whom it is brought.

GAI. iv. 115, 116.

Exceptions belonged properly to the system of formulae
only. Under that system the praetor or other magistrate who

pronounced on the right, *qui jus dicebat*, decided whether, on the statement of facts, the plaintiff had a right to an action. If he had, the parties were sent to the judge. But though the plaintiff might have a right to an action, the defendant might have some ground to urge why, in the particular instance, the action should be defeated. He stated these grounds to the prætor, and the statement was incorporated in the formula sent to the judge, and was called the *exceptio*; it excepted, or took away from the power of the action. (See Introd. sec. 104.) The judge was bound by the instructions he received in the *intentio*. He could take notice of no reason urged by the defendant why the action should fail, if the only question submitted to him by the prætor was whether the plaintiff had a good ground of action. It was necessary that the prætor should also expressly instruct him to inquire whether the action, however well grounded, ought not to be defeated.

For instance, supposing an action was brought on a stipulation, the formula would run *Si paret Numerium Negidium Aulo Agerio sestertium X. millia dare oportere*. The only question which the *judex* could have to decide would be, was the stipulation made or not? If it was, the right of the plaintiff to have a sentence in his favour was indisputable. But supposing the prætor went on to add an exception, and say *Si in ea re nihil dolo malo Auli Agerii factum sit neque fiat*, then a further inquiry would have to be made; was there any fraud on the part of the creditor which made it unjust that he should recover in the action?

The defendant, in making an exception, was not supposed to admit the truth of the plaintiff's statement. (D. xliv. 1. 9.) The plaintiff had first to prove his *intentio*, and unless he did so the action failed. Supposing he proved it to the satisfaction of the *judex*, it was then for the defendant to prove his exception. He affirmed the facts on which the exception rested, and he must prove them; he was in his turn the attacking party; *Reus in exceptione actor est.* (D. xliv. 1. 1.)

There was, however, a class of actions, viz. those *bonæ fidei*, in which, as we have already said (see Tit. 6. 31), exceptions were never used; for here the judge was bound by the character of the action to examine into all the circumstances, and only to condemn the defendant if justice demanded he should do so. The action itself was said to imply any exception that could be set up. (D. xxxv. 1. 84. 5.)

In the time of Justinian there were, properly speaking, no such things as exceptions. The word came to mean any defence other than a denial of the subsistence of the right of action, which was urged before the magistrate by the defendant.

1. Verbi gratia, si metu coactus, aut dolo inductus, aut errore lapsus, stipulanti Titio promisisti quod non debueras, palam est jure civili te obligatum esse, et actio qua intenditur dare te oportere, efficax est. Sed iniquum est te condemnari; Ideoque datur tibi exceptio metus causa, aut doli mali, aut in factum composita ad impugnandam actionem.

1. For instance, if forced by fear, inveigled by fraud, or fallen into a mistake, you promise Titius in a stipulation that which you did not owe him, it is evident that, according to the civil law, you are bound, and the action, in which it is maintained that you ought to give, is validly brought. Yet it is unjust that you should be condemned; and, therefore, to repel the action, you have given you the exception *metus causa*, or *doli mali*, or one made to raise the question of a particular fact.

D. xliv. 4. 4. 16. 33; D. xliv. 7. 30.

*Errore lapsus*, i. e. not a mistake as to the thing forming the subject of the stipulation, for such a mistake would make the stipulation void; but a mistake in the apprehension of some fact which, if the defendant had known rightly, he would not have entered into the stipulation. (See Bk. iii. Tit. 19. 23.)

The *exceptio metus causa* ran thus: *Si in ea re nihil metus causa factum est.* The *exceptio doli mali* thus: *Si in ea re nihil dolo malo Auli Agerii factum sit neque fiat.* (D. xliv. 4. 4. 2 and 4.) We may remark that the former is general, (fear inspired by any one whomsoever,) the latter personal, (the fraud of *Aulus Agerius*,) and that the *exceptio doli mali* relates not only to the character of the action at the particular time when the obligation was formed, but also to its subsequent character, *neque factum sit neque fiat.* A claim might be perfectly fair in the first instance, and afterwards become only partially so, or even wholly unfair. For instance, the real owner of an estate might claim it, and then find that the possessor, having improved it during the time he held it, is entitled to compensation. If the owner refuses the compensation, his claim, in itself fair, becomes, in the way he urges it, unfair.

*In factum composita*, i. e. shaped so as to raise the question whether a statement of a particular fact was or was not true. Some particular fact is submitted by the prætor to the *judex*, instead of such a general inquiry as whether the plaintiff has been guilty of fraud. For instance, to use the example given in the Digest (xlv. 1. 22), the inquiry directed to be made might be whether the plaintiff has not made the defendant believe that the subject of stipulation, which is made of brass, was made of gold

The *exceptio in factum composita* was thus, like the *actio in factum composita*, opposed to one *in jus concepta.* For instance, the *exceptio doli mali*, which was in *jus concepta,*

not only raised a question of fact, but made it requisite that
the *judex* should affix a certain character to the acts of the
parties.   It may be observed that this general exception *doli
mali* would always answer every purpose which could be gained
by using an exception *in factum composita*; for any particular fact which, if stated as an exception and proved, would
furnish a bar to the action, would be taken notice of under
the exception *doli mali*.   But the magistrate would not
always allow an exception *doli mali* to be inserted when he
would give permission to employ one *in factum composita*;
for infamy was attached to a plaintiff against whom an exception *doli mali* was proved; and when the plaintiff stood to
the defendant in any such near relation as that of patron or
ascendant, the magistrate would not allow an exception to be
used which would have any further consequence than to protect the defendant.

2. Idem juris est. si quis quasi
credendi causa pecuniam stipulatus
fuerit. neque numeraverit; nam
eam pecuniam a te petere posse
eum certum est, dare enim te
oportet, cum ex stipulatione tenearis; sed quia iniquum est eo nomine te condemnari, placet per
exceptionem pecunio non numeratæ te defendi debere, cujus tempora nos (secundum quod jam
superioribus libris scriptum est)
constitutione nostra coarctavimus.

2. It is the same, if any one should
stipulate from you for the repayment of money he is to lend you, and
then does not pay to you the sum
borrowed; in such a case, he could
certainly demand from you the
amount you have engaged to repay
him, and you are bound to give it, for
you are tied by the stipulation.   But
as it would be unjust that you should
be condemned in such an action.   It
has been thought right you should
have the defence of the exception
*pecuniæ non numeratæ*.   The time
within which this exception can be
used, has, as we have said in a former
Book, been shortened by our constitution.

GAL. Iv. 116; C. iv. 30. 14.

*Quasi credendi causa*, i.e. had made the defendant promise
to pay a sum, as if he, the plaintiff, were going to lend the
sum to the defendant.

It will be remembered that, in this exception, the burden
of proof was on the plaintiff, instead of, as in other exceptions,
on the defendant.   (See Bk. iii. Tit. 21.)

3. Præterea debitor, si pactus
fuerit cum creditore ne a se peteretur, nihilominus obligatus manet,
quia pacto convento obligationes
non omnimodo dissolvuntur.   Qua
de causa efficax est adversus eum
actio qua actor intendit, si paret
eum dare oportere; sed quia iniquum est contra pactionem eum
damnari, defenditur per excep-

3. Again, the debtor who has
agreed with his creditor that payment shall not be demanded from
him, still remains bound.   For an
agreement is not a mode by which
obligations are always dissolved.
The action, therefore, in which the
*intentio* runs, 'If it appears that he
ought to give,' may be validly
brought against him; but as it would

tionem pacti conventi.

be unjust that he should be condemned in contravention of the agreement. he may use in his defence the exception *pacti conventi.*

GAI. iv. 110.

Obligations formed *re* or *verbis* could not be dissolved by a simple pact. As the contract was a subsisting one, an exception was necessary. The exception *pacti conventi* ran thus: *Si inter Aulum Agerium et Numerium Negidium non convenit, ne ea pecunia peteretur.* (GAI. iv. 119.)

4. Æque si debitor creditore deferente juraverit nihil se dare oportere, adhuc obligatus permanet; sed quia iniquum est de perjurio queri, defenditur per exceptionem jurisjurandi. In iis quoque actionibus quibus in rem agitur, æque necessariæ sunt exceptiones, veluti si petitore deferente possessor juraverit eam rem suam esse, et nihilominus petitor eandem rem vindicet; licet enim verum sit quod intendit, id est, rem ejus esse, iniquum tamen est possessorem condemnari.

4. So, too, if the debtor, when the creditor challenges him to swear, affirms on oath that he ought not to give, he still remains bound. But as it would be unjust to examine whether he has perjured himself, he is allowed to defend himself with the exception *jurisjurandi*. In actions *in rem*, these exceptions are equally necessary; for instance, if the possessor, on being challenged by the defendant, swears that the property is his, and yet the plaintiff still persists in his real action. For the claim of the plaintiff might be well founded, and yet it would be unjust to condemn the possessor.

D. xli. 2. 0, pr. and 1; D. xii. 2, 3. 1; D. xii. 2. 11. 1.

The *exceptio jurisjurandi* was only necessary when the fact whether the defendant had accepted the oath when offered him was disputed. If it was acknowledged, the prætor would not give an action at all. (D. xii. 2. 3.) The oath terminated the right of the plaintiff to an action; *jusjurandum speciem transactionis continet, majoremque habet auctoritatem quam res judicata.* (D. xii. 2. 2.)

5. Item si judicio tecum actum fuerit, sive in rem sive in personam, nihilominus obligatio durat, et ideo ipso jure de eadem re postea adversus te agi potest; sed debes per exceptionem rei judicatæ adjuvari.

5. Again, if an action real or personal has been brought against you, the obligation still subsists, and, in strict law, an action might still be brought against you for the same object, but you are protected by the exception *rei judicatæ.*

GAI. iv. 106, 107.

Under the system of the actions of law, if a cause had once been decided, no further action could again be brought on the same grounds (GAI. iv. 108); but this was not the case under the prætorian system. To understand the effect of a previous action having been brought under the prætorian system, we must notice the distinction drawn by Gaius in the part of his Fourth Book which treats of exceptions between *judicia legitima* and *judicia imperio continentia.* A *judicium legitimum,* i. e. founded on the old *jus civile,* was an action given in the city of Rome, or within the first milestone round the city, between Roman citizens, and tried by a single judge. A *judicium imperio continens,* i. e. founded on the authority of the praetor, was an action given out of Rome or by *recuperatores,* or when one or both parties was a *peregrinus.* The latter, the *imperio continentia,* never extinguished the right of action, and therefore the plaintiff who brought an action for the second time had to be met with an exception. With respect to *judicia legitima,* a further distinction is to be made. If they were *in rem* or *in factum,* the nature of these actions prevented the *litis contestatio* in their case operating as a novation ; and therefore, if a fresh action was brought, the defendant had to repel it by the exception *rei judicatae,* or *in judicium deductae,* as the case might be. Accordingly we may say, in brief, that under the praetorian system none but *judicia legitima in personam* extinguished the right of action, and therefore in all other cases an exception was necessary.

In the time of Justinian these distinctions had disappeared, and therefore he says generally that the *res judicata* produces an exception. It was to have the same force as it had formerly had in the case of *judicia imperio continentia,* and not that it had received in *judicia legitima.* Whether the action was real or personal, as the text informs us, the principal obligation still subsisted, and, no novation having taken place, a second action could only be repelled by an exception. But, practically speaking, under the system of *judicia extraordinaria,* as the judge did not receive instructions from a magistrate, and was not bound within the limits of a formula, the distinction between the *res judicata* operating as a bar or as an exception was a very immaterial one.

In order that a *res judicata* should be available either as a bar or an exception, it was necessary that there should have been, in the former action, the same thing as the subject-matter of the litigation, the same quantity, the same right, the same ground of action, the same persons suing in the same character: *Cum quaeritur haec exceptio noceat necne, inspiciendum est an idem corpus sit: Quantitas eadem, idem jus: an eadem causa petendi, eadem conditio personarum—quae nisi omnia concurrant alia res est.* (D. xliv. 2. 12. lib. 14.)

0. Haec exempli causa retulisse sufficiet. Alioquin, quasi ex multis variisque causis exceptiones neces-

0. The above examples of exceptions may suffice. It may be seen in the larger work of the Digest or

moriæ sint, ex latioribus Digestorum
seu Pandectarum libris intelligi potest.

7. Quarum quædam e legibus
vel ex iis quæ legis vicem obtinent,
vel ex ipsius prætoris jurisdictione
substantiam capiunt.

Pandects how numerous and how
different are the causes which make
exceptions necessary.

7. Some of these exceptions are
derived from the laws, and from
other enactments having the force
of law, or from the jurisdiction of
the prætor.

GAL. iv. 118.

*E legibus;* such as the exception *nisi bonis cesserit,* relative to the cession of the debtor's goods, under the *lex Julia.*
*Ex iis quæ legis vicem obtinent,* i. e. *senatus-consulta* and
*constitutiona.* The exception under the rescript of Hadrian,
permitting the employment of an exception *doli mali* when a
plaintiff neglected to notice a counter-claim (see Tit. 6. 39),
may serve as an example.

8. Appellantur autem exceptiones, aliæ perpetuæ et peremptoriæ,
aliæ temporales et dilatoriæ.

8. Exceptions are either perpetual
and peremptory, or temporary and
dilatory.

D. xliv. 1. 3.

The duration according to which exceptions are said to be
*perpetuæ* or *temporales,* is the length of time in which they
can be used by the defendant if he has occasion, not the
length of time during which their effect continues if they are
employed.

All *exceptiones perpetuæ* were necessarily *peremptoriæ;* if
found to be justified by the facts, they set the matter in litigation at rest for ever. All *exceptiones temporales* were necessarily *dilatoriæ;* they did but defer the decision of the matter
in question till the expiration of a certain time.

9. Perpetuæ et peremptoriæ sunt,
quæ semper agentibus obstant, et
semper rem de qua agitur perimunt:
qualis est exceptio doli mali, et
quod metus causa factum est, et
pacti conventi, cum ita convenerit
ne omnino pecunia peteretur.

9. Those are perpetual and peremptory which always present an
obstacle to the demand, for we cut
away the ground on which it is
brought; as, for instance, the exception *doli mali,* that *metus causa,* and
that *pacti conventi,* when it has been
agreed that no demand for the money shall ever be made.

D. xliv. 1. 3.

An act might be used for ever as an exception; and yet if
an action were brought grounded on it, that action might possibly have to be brought within a certain time. For instance,
if fraud or violence had been used in the making of a contract,
the exception would be good whenever an action was brought
on the contract; but the person injured could only bring an
*actio doli* or *metus causa* within a limited time. Hence it

came to be said that such things were *temporalia ad agendum, perpetua ad excipiendum.* (See D. xliv. 4, 5, 6.)

10. Temporales atque dilatoriæ sunt, quæ ad tempus norent, et temporis dilationem tribuunt: qualis est pacti conventi, cum ita convenerit ne intra certum tempus ageretur, veluti intra quinquennium; nam finito eo tempore non impeditur actor rem exequi. Ergo si quibus intra certum tempus agere volentibus objicitur exceptio aut pacti conventi aut alia similis, differre debent actionem et post tempus agere; Ideo enim et dilatoriæ intæ exceptiones appellantur. Alioquin, si intra tempus egerint, objectaque sit exceptio, neque eo judicio quidquam consequerentur propter exceptionem, neque post tempus olim agere poterant, cum temere rem in judicium deducebant et consumebant, qua ratione rem amittebant. Hodie autem non ita stricte hæc procedere volumus: sed eum qui ante tempus pactionis vel obligationis litem inferre ausus est, Zenonianæ constitutioni subjacere censemus, quam sacratissimus legislator de iis qui tempore plus petierint, protulit: ut si inducias quas ipse actor sponte indulserit vel natura actionis continet, contempsit, erit, in duplum habeant ii qui talem injuriam passi sunt; et post eas finitas non aliter litem suscipiant, nisi omnes expensas litis antea acceperint, ut actores tali pœna perterriti tempora litium doceantur observare.

10. Those are temporary and dilatory which present an obstacle for a certain time and procure delay. Such is the exception *pacti conventi* when it has been agreed that no action shall be brought for a certain time, as, for instance, for five years; when once this period has elapsed, the plaintiff is not prevented from bringing his action. Those, therefore, who seek to bring the action before the expiration of the time, and are repelled by the exception *pacti conventi*, or any similar one, ought to put it off and to bring it after the time has elapsed; hence these exceptions are termed dilatory. If plaintiffs have brought the action before the expiration of the time, and been repelled by the exception, they will not gain anything by the action they bring, because of the exception: and, formerly, they would not have been able again to bring an action on the expiration of the time, because they had rashly brought their claim before a judge, and so used up their right to bring an action, and lost all they could claim. But at the present day we do not wish to proceed so rigorously; any one who shall venture to bring an action before the time fixed by the agreement or obligation, shall be subject to the dispositions of the constitution of Zeno, published by that emperor with respect to those who, in regard to time, ask more than is due to them. Consequently, if the plaintiff shall disregard the delay which he himself has voluntarily accorded, or which results from the nature of the action, the delay shall be doubled for the benefit of those who have sustained such a wrong; and even after the expiration of the time, these persons shall not be obliged to defend the action unless they have been first reimbursed for all the expenses of the former action, that a penalty so heavy may teach plaintiffs to have due regard to the delays that are to elapse before actions are brought.

*Alia similis.* Gaius gives, as an instance, the *exceptio litis dividuæ*, given to repel a plaintiff who broke up into two actions his remedy for a single thing, and sued within the same prætorship for the part he did not include in his first action. Gaius defines dilatory exceptions as those *quæ non semper locum habent, sed evitari possunt.* (iv. 122.)

*Zenonianæ constitutioni.* See Tit. 6. 33.

11. Præterea etiam ex persona dilatoriæ sunt exceptiones, quales sunt procuratoriæ, veluti si per militem aut mulierem agere quis velit: nam militibus, nec pro patre vel matre vel uxore, nec ex sacro rescripto, procuratorio nomine experiri conceditur; suis vero negotiis superesse sine offensa disciplinæ possunt. Eas vero exceptiones quæ olim procuratoribus propter infamiam vel dantis vel ipsius procuratoris opponebantur, cum in judiciis frequentari nullo modo perspeximus, conquiescere sancimus; ne dum de his altercatur, ipsius negotii disceptatio proteletur.

11. There are also dilatory exceptions by reason of the person: such are those objecting to a procurator; as, for instance, if a plaintiff wishes to have his cause conducted by a soldier or woman, for soldiers cannot be procurators even for their father, or mother, or wife, not even by virtue of an imperial rescript: but they may conduct their own affairs without any breach of discipline. As to the exceptions formerly opposed to procurators on account of the infamy, either of the person appointing the procurator, or of the procurator himself, since we found that they were no longer used in practice, we have enacted that they shall be abolished, that no discussion as to their effect may prolong the course of the action itself.

D. xliv. 1. 3; C. ii. 13. 7. 0.

The exception to the procurator as an improper person only produced a delay; directly the plaintiff appointed a proper person as procurator, the action proceeded.

The *infamia* alluded to was that produced by being condemned in certain actions as in the *actio tutelæ, depositi, pro socio,* &c.

## Tit. XIV.    DE REPLICATIONIBUS.

Interdum evenit ut exceptio, quæ prima facie justa videatur, inique noceat. Quod cum accidit, alia allegatione opus est adjuvandi actori gratia, quæ replicatio vocatur, quia per eam replicatur atque resolvitur jus exceptionis: veluti, compactus est aliquis cum debitore suo ne ab eo pecuniam petat, deinde postea in contrarium pacti sunt, id

Sometimes an exception which at first sight seems just, is really unjust. In this case, to place the plaintiff in a right position, it is necessary there should be another allegation termed a replication, because it unfolds and resolves the right given by the exception. For example, supposing a creditor has agreed with a debtor not to demand payment, and then

est, ut creditori petere liceat. Si agat creditor, et excipiat debitor, ut ita demum condemnetur, si non convenerit ne eam pecuniam creditor petat, nocet ei exceptio. Convenit enim ita: namque nihilominus hoc verum manet, licet postea in contrarium pacti sint; sed quia iniquum est creditorem excludi, replicatio ei dabitur ex posteriore pacto contento.

GAI. IV. 126.

makes an agreement to the contrary; that is, that he may demand payment; if, when the creditor brings his action, the debtor uses the exception, alleging that he ought only to be condemned if his creditor so not under an agreement not to demand payment, this exception presents an obstacle to the creditor. For it remains true that this agreement was made, although a contrary agreement was afterwards made. But as it would be unjust to deprive the creditor of his remedy, he will be permitted to use a replication founded on the latter agreement.

All that has been said on the use and nature of exceptions is applicable to replications, which are but exceptions of an exception. (D. xliv. 1. 22.)

It is to be remarked that there could not be an *exceptio doli mali* to an *exceptio doli mali*. If the plaintiff had been guilty of fraud, it could not strengthen his right of action that the defendant had also been guilty. (D. xliv. 4. 4. 13.)

1. Rursus interdum evenit ut replicatio, quae prima facie justa est, inique noceat. Quod cum accidit, alia allegatione opus est, adjuvandi rei gratia, quae duplicatio vocatur.

GAI. IV. 127.

1. The replication, in its turn, may, at first sight, seem just, and yet be really unjust. In this case, to aid the defendant, it is necessary there should be a further allegation, termed a *duplicatio*.

2. Et si rursus ea prima facie justa videatur, sed propter aliquam causam actori inique noceat, rursus alia allegatione opus est, qua actor adjuvetur, quae dicitur triplicatio.

GAI. IV. 128.

2. And if, again, the *duplicatio* may seem just, but is really unjust, there is wanted to aid the plaintiff a still further allegation, termed a *triplicatio*.

3. Quarum omnium exceptionum usum, interdum ulterius quam diximus, varietas negotiorum introducit: quae omnes apertius ex Digestorum latiore volumine facile est cognoscere.

GAI. IV. 129.

3. The great diversity of affairs has made it requisite to carry still farther the use of these exceptions. A clearer knowledge of them all may be obtained by reading the fuller work of the Digest.

4. Exceptiones autem quibus debitor defenditur, plerumque accommodari solent etiam fidejussoribus ejus et recte; quia quod ab iis petitur, id ab ipso debitore peti videtur, quia mandati judicio redditurus

4. The exceptions given for the protection of the debtor are also for the most part given in behalf of his *fidejussores*, and rightly so; for what is demanded from them is really demanded from the debtor, because by

P P

est eis quod ii pro eo solverint. Qua ratione, et si de non petenda pecunia pactus quis cum reo fuerit, placuit perinde succurrendum esse per exceptionem pacti conventi illis quoque qui pro eo obligati essent, ne si cum ipsis pactus esset ne ab eis ea pecunia peteretur. Sane quædam exceptiones non solent his accommodari; ecce enim debitor, si bonis suis cesserit, et cum eo creditor experiatur, defenditur per exceptionem nisi bonis cesserit; sed hæc exceptio fidejussoribus non datur, ideo scilicet quia qui alios pro debitore obligat, hoc maxime prospicit, ut cum facultatibus lapsus fuerit debitor, possit ab iis quos pro eo obligavit, suum consequi.

the actio mandati he will be forced to repay them what they have paid for him. Hence, if a creditor agrees with his debtor not to demand payment, the exception pacti conventi may be employed by those who are bound for him, exactly as if the agreement not to demand payment had been made with them personally. There are, however, some exceptions not allowed them; for instance, if the debtor has made a cession of his property, and the creditor sues him, he may protect himself by the exception nisi bonis cesserit; but this exception is not allowed to fidejussores. For, in taking security for the payment of a debt, what the creditor principally looks to is, recovering what is owed him from the sureties, in case of the insolvency of the principal.

D. xliv. 1. 10; D. ii. 14. 32.

Exceptions were divided into rei cohærentes, which affected the right to claim, and personæ cohærentes, which only protected the debtor himself. Fidejussors could avail themselves of the former, but not of the latter.

As an instance of an exceptio cohærens rei may be given an exceptio doli mali, or a general pact not to sue. As an instance of an exceptio cohærens personæ may be given that mentioned in the text, where the debtor was protected by having given up all his property, or a particular pact not to sue the debtor personally. In such a case as the last, however, the fidejussors would have an actio mandati against the debtor for what they paid for him, and, therefore, he would get no good by the pact, except, perhaps, that of delay.

## Tit. XV.   DE INTERDICTIS.

Sequitur ut dispiciamus de interdictis, seu actionibus quæ pro his exercentur. Erant autem interdicta formæ atque conceptiones verborum quibus prætor aut jubebat aliquid fieri, aut fieri prohibebat: quod tunc maxime faciebat, cum de possessione aut quasi possessione inter aliquos contendebatur.

We have now to treat of interdicts and the actions which supply their place. Interdicts were certain formulæ by which the prætor ordered or forbad something to be done: they were chiefly employed in disputes as to possession or quasi possession.

Gai. iv. 138, 139.

An interdict was a decree or edict of the prætor made in a

special case. The prætor published a general edict stating the leading principles on which he would act. But in certain cases he would make an edict applicable only to particular persons and particular things. Instead, for instance, of referring the party applying to him for relief to the general rule of law that one man should not be allowed to interfere with the watercourses of another, he made an edict that A should not interfere with the watercourses of B. According to the circumstances of the case such a command might be either positive or negative; and though, as is remarked in paragr. 1, the word *interdictum* was considered to apply more properly to a negative command only, it was, as a matter of usage, applied to all such special edicts indifferently.

If the person to whom the special edict was addressed obeyed its directions, no further proceedings were necessary; if he disobeyed, the prætor allowed an action to be brought grounded on the interdict. A sketch of the mode in which the proceedings grounded on an interdict were conducted will be found in the notes to paragr. 8.

There was always something of a public character in the reasons which induced the prætor to grant an interdict. He adopted it as a speedy and sure remedy in cases when danger was threatened to objects which public policy is especially interested to preserve uninjured, such as public roads and waters, burial-grounds, or sacred places; and though interdicts were granted where the quarrel was entirely between private parties, it was only when the subject of dispute was such as to render a breach of the public peace the probable result, unless the matter was set at rest by the summary interposition of legal authority. If, for instance, it was a possession or quasi-possession that was disputed, it was feared that the claimant would adopt force to eject the actual occupier, that force would be met by force, and the public peace be broken. This public character attaching to interdicts would make us naturally conclude that they were originally given to protect public, not private interests. Niebuhr (*Hist. Rom.* vol. ii. 149) and Savigny (*Possess.* Bk. iv. 44) think that in the private occupancy of the *ager publicus* may be seen an interest so little protected otherwise, and calling so precisely for some such aid as the interdict, that it can hardly be doubted that the early use of interdicts was directed to meet the exigencies of this particular case. When the prætorian system was fully established, the prætors still continued to give interdicts in cases where it had been usual, yet a character of settled law was imposed upon the mode of giving them by the prætor announcing in his edict that he would grant a particular interdict under particular circumstances. Even before the introduction of the system of *extraordinaria judicia*, the interdicts had become, probably, less frequently used, there being a tendency to go direct to the action grounded on them, and to do away with the interdict as a preliminary step.

Interdicts were wholly based on the prætorian authority. In the time of Justinian persons who under the prætorian system would have applied for an interdict, brought an action. In conducting this action, the magistrate would be greatly guided by the old law relating to interdicts; but otherwise, the subject of interdicts was one with which the law of the Lower Empire had very little to do.

1. Summa autem divisio interdictorum hæc est, quod aut prohibitoria sunt, aut restitutoria, aut exhibitoria. Prohibitoria sunt, quibus velat aliquid fieri, veluti vim sine vitio possidenti, vel mortuum inferenti quo ei jus erat inferendi, vel in loco sacro ædificari, vel in flumine publico ripave ejus aliquid fieri quo prius navigetur. Restitutoria sunt, quibus restitui aliquid jubet, veluti bonorum possessori possessionem eorum quæ quis pro herede aut pro possessore possidet ex ea hereditate, aut cum jubet ei qui vi possessione fundi dejectus sit, restitui possessionem. Exhibitoria sunt per quæ jubet exhiberi, veluti eum cujus de libertate agitur, aut libertum cui patronus operas indicere velit, aut parenti liberos qui in potestate ejus sunt. Sunt tamen qui putant proprie interdicta ea vocari quæ prohibitoria sunt quia interdicere est denuntiare et prohibere: restitutoria autem et exhibitoria proprie decreta vocari: sed tamen obtinuit omnia Interdicta appellari, quia inter duos dicuntur.

1. The principal division of interdicts is, that they are prohibitory, restitutory, or exhibitory. Prohibitory interdicts are those by which the prætor forbids something to be done, as, for example, to use force against a person in lawful possession, or against one who carries a dead body to a spot where he has a right to carry it, or to build on a sacred place, or to do anything in a public river, or on its bank, which may impede the navigation. Restitutory interdicts are those by which the prætor orders something to be restored, as, for instance, when he orders to be restored to the possessor the possession of the goods of an inheritance possessed by another as heir or as possessor, or when he orders the possession of land to be restored to the person who has been violently expelled from it. Exhibitory interdicts are those by which the prætor orders to exhibit; for instance, to exhibit the person whose freedom is being questioned, or the freedman whose services are claimed by the patron, or to exhibit to the father the children in his power. Some, however, think that the term interdict ought, strictly speaking, to be applied to those which are prohibitory, because *interdicere* means 'to denounce, to prohibit,' while those that are restitutory, or exhibitory, ought to be called *decreta*. But usage has applied the word interdict to all alike, as they are all given between two parties.

The formula of many of the interdicts most ordinarily in use is preserved to us in the Digest. It would take up too much space to give many of these at length. One or two examples of each kind must suffice.

The formula of the prohibitory interdict generally ended with the words *veto* or *vim fieri veto.* That forbidding nuisances in public ways ran thus :—

*In via publica itinerere publico facere, immittere quid, quo ea via idve iter deterius fiat, veto.* (D. xliii. 8. 2. 20.)

That forbidding interruption in the use of a burial-ground ran thus :—

*Quo quave illi* (the person protected), *inferre invito te* (the person against whom the interdict was granted), *jus est, quominus illi eo eave mortuum inferre et ibi sepelire liceat, vim fieri veto.* (D. xi. 8. 1.) Other prohibitory interdicts may be found relating to sacred places (D. xi. 8. 1), tombs (D. xi. 8. 1), public places (D. xliii. 8. 2. 20), navigation (D. xliii. 12. 1).

Restitutory interdicts ran, for example, thus :—

*Quod in flumine publico ripave ejus factum, sive quid in flumen ripamve ejus immissum habes, si ob id aliter aqua fluit, atque uti priore æstate fluxit, restituas.* (D. xliii. 13. 11.)

Of exhibitory interdicts we may take as a specimen that *de libero homine exhibendo*, granted to make any one who had a freeman in his custody produce him ; and thus render it impossible that he should be illegally retained in his custody, It ran thus :—

*Quem liberum dolo malo retineas, exhibeas.* (D. xliii. 29. 1.)

2. Sequens divisio interdictorum hæc est, quod quædam adipiscendæ possessionis causa comparata sunt, quædam retinendæ, quædam recuperandæ.

2. The second division of Interdicts is, that they are given to some to acquire, some to retain, and others to recover possession.

GAI. iv. 143.

3. Adipiscendæ possessionis causa interdictum accommodatur bonorum possessori, quod appellatur quorum bonorum. Ejusque vis et potestas hæc est, ut quod ex iis bonis quisque quorum possessio alicui data est, pro herede aut pro possessore possideat, id ei cui bonorum possessio data est restituere debeat. Pro herede antem possidere videtur, qui putat se heredem esse : pro possessore is possidet.

3. To acquire possession an Interdict is given to the *bonorum possessor*, termed *Quorum bonorum*, of which the effect is to compel the person possessing, as heir or possessor, any of the goods of which the possession is given, to make restitution to the *bonorum possessor*. A person is said to possess as heir, who thinks himself to be heir, and as possessor, who, without any right, and knowing that it does not belong to him, possesses a

qui nullo jure rem hereditariam vel etiam totam hereditatem, sciens ad se non pertinere, possidet. Ideo autem adipiscendæ possessionis vocntur interdictum, quia ei tantum utile est qui nunc primum conatur adipisci rei possessionem : itaque si quis adeptus possessionem amiserit eam, hoc interdictum ei inutile est. Interdictum quoque quod appellatur Salvianum, adipiscendæ possessionis causa comparatum est, eoque utitur dominus fundi de rebus coloni, quas is pro mercedibus fundi pignori futuras pepigisset.

part or the whole of an inheritance. It is said of this interdict, that it is given to acquire possession, because it is only available for a person who wishes to gain, for the first time, possession of a thing. If, then, a person who has gained possession loses it, he cannot avail himself of this interdict. There is, too, another interdict given to acquire possession, viz. the *interdictum Salvianum*, to which an owner of land has recourse to enforce his right over the things belonging to the farmer, which the farmer has pledged as a security for his rent.

GAI. iv. 144. 147.

The interdict *Quorum bonorum* ran thus :—

*Quorum bonorum ex edicto meo illi possessio data est, quod de his bonis pro herede aut pro possessore possides, possiderave si nihil usucaptum esset, quod quidem dolo fecisti ut desineres possidere, id illi restituas.* (D. xliii. 2.)

Although the interdict was only given when the *bonorum possessor* had never before had possession, yet it was said to be a restitutory one, and the word *restituas* appears in its terms. *Restituas*, therefore, must be used in a wide sense, as meaning 'to give up,' not 'to give back.'

The use of this interdict was to give the possession to those whom the prætor treated as having a right to the inheritance, but who had not a right recognised by the civil law. Not being heirs, properly so called, they could not bring a real action for the inheritance. (See Bk. iii. Tit. 9.)

We must not confound the *interdictum Salvianum* with the *actio Serviana* (see Tit. 6. 7), but it was probably only a step to that action, and may have fallen into disuse when the *actio Serviana* was established as a means of redress for the creditor. The *interdictum Salvianum* was not given to every mortgage creditor, but only to the owner of a rural estate, as a means of getting possession of the goods of the occupier of the estate which had been pledged for the rent. Probably the interdict was granted even if the goods had passed into the hands of a third party. (D. xliii. 33. 1. but see C. viii. 9. 1.)

4. Retinendæ possessionis causa comparata sunt interdicta uti possidetis et utrubi, cum ab utraque parte de proprietate alicujus rei controversia sit, et ante quæritur uter ex litigatoribus possidere, et

4. To retain possession there are given the interdicts *uti possidetis* and *utrubi*, when, in a dispute as to the ownership of a thing, a dispute first rises which of the parties ought to be possessor and which plaintiff.

uter petere debeat: namque, nisi ante exploratum fuerit utrius eorum possessio sit, non potest petitoria actio institui, quia et civilis et naturalis ratio facit ut alius possideat, alius a possidente petat. Et quia longe commodius est possidere potius quam petere, ideo plerumque et fere semper ingens existit contentio de ipsa possessione. Commodum autem possidendi in eo est, quod etiamsi ejus res non sit qui possidet, si modo actor non potuerit suam esse probare, remanet suo loco possessio: propter quam causam, cum obscura sunt utriusque jura, contra petitorem judicari solet. Sed interdicto quidem uti possidetis de fundi vel ædium possessione contenditur, utrobi, vero interdicto de rerum mobilium possessione. Quorum vis ac potestas plurimam inter se differentiam apud veteres habebat: nam uti possidetis interdicto is vincebat, qui interdicti tempore possidebat si modo nec vi nec clam nec precario nactus fuerat ab adversario possessionem, etiamsi alium vi expulerat, aut clam arripuerat alienam possessionem, aut precario rogaverat aliquem ut sibi possidere liceret; utrubi vero interdicto is vincebat, qui majore parte ejus anni nec vi nec clam nec precario ab adversario possidebat. Hodie tamen aliter observatur; nam utriusque interdicti potestas (quantum ad possessionem pertinet) exæquata est: ut ille vincat et in re soli et in re mobili, qui possessionem nec vi nec clam nec precario ab adversario litis contestatæ tempore detinet.

For, unless it is first determined to which the possession belongs, it is impossible to shape the real action, as law and reason both require that one party should possess, and the other bring his claim against him. And as it is much more advantageous to possess than to claim the thing, there is generally a keen dispute as to the right to possess. The advantage of possession consists in this, that even if the thing does not really belong to the possessor, yet, if the plaintiff does not prove himself to be the owner, the possessor still remains in possession, and, therefore, when the rights of the parties are doubtful, it is customary to decide against the claimant. The interdict uti possidetis applies to the possession of land and buildings, the interdict utrubi to that of moveables. There were among the ancients great differences in their effects; for, in the interdict uti possidetis, he prevailed who was in possession at the time of the interdict, provided that he had not acquired possession from his adversary by force, or clandestinely, or as a concession; but it made no difference if he had acquired it from anyone else, by forcibly expelling him, secretly depriving him of possession, or obtaining from him possession as a concession. In the interdict utrubi, on the contrary, he prevailed, who during the greater part of the preceding year had had the possession without having obtained it as against his adversary by force, clandestinely, or as a concession. At the present day it is different, for the two interdicts have the same effect as regards possession, so that whether the thing claimed is an immoveable or a moveable, he prevails, who, at the time of the litis contestatio, is in possession, without having obtained it as against his adversary by force, clandestinely, or as a concession.

GAI. iv. 148–160; D. vi. 1. 24; D. xliii. 17. 1: D. xliii. 31; C. iv. 19. 2.

The interdict *uti possidetis* ran thus :—

*Uti eas ædes, quibus de agitur, nec vi, nec clam, nec pre-*

*curio alter ab altero possidetis, quominus ita possidentis vim fieri veto.* (D. xliii. 17. 1.)

It was granted to defend the possession of all immoveables, except *cloacæ*, which were expressly excepted by the prætor's edict. The word *ædes* in the text of the interdict is only an example.

By possessing *precario* is meant possessing by having extorted possession by prayer and entreaties. When the person from whom the possession had been extorted wished to do so, he could always resume it; and hence the word *precarius* came to mean uncertain. Perhaps the origin of *precuria possessio* was the interest that clients had in a portion of the *ager publicus*, which their patron might permit them to use, and which they were bound to restore immediately if their patron demanded it back.

The words *alter ab altero* are inserted, because it would be no ground for disturbing the possession that it had been obtained *vi*, *clam*, or *precario*, unless it had been so obtained from the other litigant party.

It was necessary that application should be made for this interdict within a year after the security of the possession had been threatened. (D. xliii. 17. 1.) It did not signify how it had been threatened. The text only refers to the case of an action being brought to dispute it, but the interdict would be granted in whatever way the possession had been attacked.

The interdict *utrubi* ran thus:—

*Utrubi hic honno quo de agitur majore parte hujusce anni fuit, quominus is eum ducat, vim fieri veto.* (D. xliii. 31.)

The example is taken from the case of the disputed possession of a slave, but the interdict applied to the case of all moveables. In the older law, this interdict was considered one *retinendæ possessionis*, although, as it was granted to the person who had possessed during the greater part of the preceding year, it might happen that it was granted to a person who had not the possession at the exact time it was granted. He was, however, considered the possessor by a legal fiction, although not actually so.

6. Possidere autem videtur quisque, non solum si ipse possideat, sed et si ejus nomine aliquis in possessione sit, licet is ejus juri subjectus non sit, qualis est colonus et inquilinus. Per eos quoque apud quos deposuerit quis, aut quibus commodaverit, ipse possidere videtur; et hoc est quod dicitur,

6. A person is considered to possess not only when he is himself in possession, but also if any one is in possession in his name, although not a person in his power, as the tenant of a farm or building. He may also possess through a depositary or a borrower, and this it is that is meant by saying, that a person may retain

retinere possessionem posse aliquem
per quemlibet qui ejus nomine sit
in possessione. Quinetiam animo
quoque retineri possessionem placet,
id est, ut quamvis neque ipse sit
in possessione, neque ejus nomine
alius, tamen si non derelinquendæ
possessionis animo, sed postea re-
versurus inde discesserit, retinere
possessionem videatur. Adipisci
vero possessionem per quos aliquis
potest, secundo libro exposuimus;
nec ulla dubitatio est quin animo
solo adipisci possessionem nemo
potest.

possession by any other who possesses in his name. Moreover, it is
held that possession may be retain-d
by mere intention only, that is, that
although he is not in possession himself, nor is any one else in his name,
yet, if it is not with any intention of
abandoning the thing, but of returning again to it, that he has placed
himself at a distance from it, he is
considered still to retain the possession. Through whom possession
may be acquired, we have already
explained in the Second Book. But
it most certainly can never be acquired by mere intention only.

GAI. iv. 153.

The person actually in possession, in the case mentioned in
the text, viz. the *colonus* or *inquilinus*, would have no right
to any interdicts to protect the possession, because he did not
possess *animo domini*. (See Bk. ii. Tit. 1.)

6. Recuperandæ possessionis causa
solet interdici, si quis ex possessione fundi vel ædium vi dejectus
fuerit; nam ei proponitur interdictum unde vi, per quod is qui
dejecit, cogitur ei restituere possessionem, licet is ab eo qui dejecit
vi vel clam vel precario possidebat.
Sed ex constitutionibus sacris, ut
supra diximus, si quis rem per vim
occupaverit, si quidem in bonis
ejus est, dominio ejus privatur; si
aliena, post ejus restitutionem
etiam æstimationem rei dare vim
passo compellitur. Qui autem aliquem de possessione per vim dejecerit, tenetur lege Julia de vi
privata, aut de vi publica: sed de
vi privata, si sine armis vim fecerit;
sin autem cum armis eum de possessione expulerit, de vi publica.
Armorum autem appellatione non
solum scuta et gladios et galeas sig-
nificari intelligimus, sed et fustes
et lapides.

6. To recover possession an interdict is given in case any one has
been expelled by violence from the
possession of land or a building. He
has then given him the interdict
unde vi, by which he who has expelled him is forced to restore to him
the possession, although the person
to whom the interdict is given has
himself taken by force, clandestinely,
or as a concession, the possession
from the person who has expelled
him. But, as we have said above,
the Imperial constitutions provide
that if any one seizes on a thing by
violence, be shall lose the ownership of it, if it is a part of his own
goods, and if it belongs to another,
he shall not only restore it, but, in
addition, pay to the person who has
sustained the injury, the amount at
which the thing is estimated. Moreover, a person who has expelled by
violence another from his possession,
is liable under the *lex Julia* for private or for public violence; for private violence, if his violence was
exercised without the use of arms;
for public violence, if the expulsion
from possession was made by armed
force. Under the term arms are in-

cluded not only shields, swords, and
helmets, but sticks and stones.

GAI. iv. 154, 155; D. xlviii. 7; D. l. 16. 41; C. viii. 4. 7.

The interdict *unde vi* ran thus :—
*Unde tu illum vi dejecisti, aut familia tua dejecit, de eo,
quæque ille tunc ibi habuit, tantummodo intra annum, post
annum de eo quod ad eum qui vi dejecit pervenerit, judicium
dabo.* (D. xliii. 16. 1.)

Formerly a distinction was made in granting this interdict,
according to the degree of violence used. If it had been ordinary violence (*vis quotidiana*), the interdict was only granted
if the possession had not been obtained *vi, clam,* or *precario,*
with respect to the adversary (GAI. iv. 144); but if *vis armata*
had been employed, the interdict was granted in all cases.
This difference had ceased long before the time of Justinian,
and apparently before the time when the interdict assumed
the shape in which we now find it in the Digest.

The interdict *unde vi* only applied to immoveables until
the constitution of Valentinian, Theodosius, and Arcadian,
alluded to in the text, which applied to moveables as well as
to immoveables. (C. viii. 4. 7.)

The *lex Julia de vi* is treated of in Tit. 18. 8.

7. Tertia divisio interdictorum
hæc est, quod aut simplicia sunt,
aut duplicia. Simplicia sunt, veluti
in quibus alter actor, alter reus
est, qualia sunt omnia restitutoria
aut exhibitoria: namque actor est,
qui desiderat aut exhiberi aut restitui, reus est is a quo desideratur
ut restituat aut exhibeat. Prohibitoriorum autem interdictorum
alia simplicia sunt, veluti cum
prohibet prætor in loco sacro vel in
flumine publico ripave ejus aliquid
fieri ; nam actor est qui desiderat
ne quid fiat, reus est qui aliquid facere conatur. Duplicia sunt, veluti uti possidetis interdictum et
utrubi; ideo autem duplicia vocantur, quia par utriusque litigatoris in his conditio est, nec
quisquam præcipue reus vel actor
intelligitur, sed unusquisque tam
rei quam actoris partes sustinet.

7. The third division of interdicts
is, that they are either simple or
double. Those are simple in which
one person is plaintiff and the other
defendant, as is the case in all that
are restitutory or exhibitory. For
he is the plaintiff who wishes that a
thing shall be exhibited or restored,
and he is defendant against whom
the claim is made. But of prohibitory interdicts some are simple,
some double: simple, as for instance,
when the prætor forbids anything to
be done in a sacred place, or in a
public river, or on its banks; for he
is plaintiff who wishes that the thing
should not be done, and he is defendant who wishes to do it: double,
as in the case of the interdicts *uti
possidetis,* and *utrubi*; and these interdicts are called double, because in
them the position of each party is
equal, for neither can be said to be
properly plaintiff or defendant, but
each is at once plaintiff and defendant.

*Duplicia sunt, veluti uti possidetis interdictum et utrubi.*
These interdicts here and in Gaius(GAI.iv. 160)are, seemingly,
only adduced as examples, but we know of no others having
the same character.

8. De ordine et vetere exitu interdictorum supervacuum est hodie
dicere; nam quoties extra ordinem
jus dicitur(qualia sunt hodie omnia
judicia), non est necesse reddi interdictum; sed perinde judicatur
sine interdictis, ac si utilis actio ex
causa interdicti reddita fuisset.

8. Of the process and effect of
Interdicts in former times it would
be now superfluous to speak. For
whenever the jurisdiction is extraordinary, as is the case now in all
actions, there is no necessity for an
interdict; for judgment is given
without interdicts, exactly as if a
*utilis actio* had been given in pursuance of an interdict.

C. viii. 1. 3.

From the Institutes of Gaius we gather a general notion
of the manner in which the proceedings on an interdict were
conducted. But the text of Gaius is, in this part, very imperfect and difficult to understand, and as the whole process
was obsolete in the time of Justinian, a very short sketch of
the proceedings must suffice here.

The parties were made to appear *in jure* exactly in the same
way when an interdict was to be applied for as when an action
was to be brought. The praetor heard the statement of the
party who made the application, and if the adversary confessed
the truth of the statement, or the facts were manifest, the praetor
announced his decree at once, and had it executed, if necessary,
by the strong arm of the law (*manu militari*). If the merits
of the case were doubtful, or the defendant refused to obey,
the praetor gave an action based upon the interdict, that is,
the *intentio* of the formula was the language of the interdict
put as a hypothetical case. The interdict would run,—*Hoc
vel illud te facere velo*; the *intentio, Si hoc vel illud A. A.
fecerit* (*condemna*, &c.). The parties bound themselves by a
*sponsio* and *restipulatio* in a penal sum, which the defendant
was to pay if he had violated the terms of the interdict, and
to receive if he had not. But this practice, which was always
adopted when the interdict was prohibitory, was probably
gradually abandoned when the interdict was restitutory or
exhibitory; and in these cases, in order to compel the actual
performance of the act ordered by the praetor, an action was
given with a *formula arbitraria*, so that the *judex* might
issue a preparatory order to the defendant, and if it was not
complied with, might make him pay the amount of all damage
sustained (*quanti ea res erit*). (GAI. iv. 161, and foll.)

## Tit. XVI. DE PŒNA TEMERE LITIGANTIUM.

Nunc admonendi sumus, magnam curam egisse eos qui Jura sustinebant, ne facile homines ad litigandum procederent, quod et nobis studio est; idque eo maxime fieri potest, quod temeritas tam agentium quam eorum cum quibus agyretur, modo pecuniaria pœna, modo jurisjurandi religione, modo infamiæ metu corrcetur.

We may here observe, that the authors and preservers of our law have always sought most anxiously to hinder men from engaging too recklessly in law-suits, and it is what we ourselves desire also. And the best method of succeeding in it is, to repress the rashness alike of plaintiffs and of defendants, sometimes by a pecuniary penalty, sometimes by the sacred tie of an oath, sometimes by the fear of infamy.

Gai. iv. 174, and foll.

In the days of Gaius, the means of punishing persons who recklessly brought or defended a suit were more numerous. First, there was the action of calumny, the word *calumnia* meaning in Roman law the offence committed by a man who, in the language of Gaius, *intelligit non recte se agere sed vexandi adversarii gratia actionem instituit.* (Gai. iv. 174.) This action might also be brought against the defendant for improperly defending an action. Secondly, by a *sponsio* and *restipulatio,* each party could make the other liable to forfeit a fixed sum in case the sentence was against him. Thirdly, there was also the oath, which was retained by Justinian, with this difference—previously to the time of Justinian, either party might, but neither need necessarily, challenge his adversary to swear that he had good grounds for bringing or defending the action; but if he adopted this course, and his adversary accepted the challenge, he thereby abandoned the power of bringing an action to punish his adversary for reckless litigation. (Gai. iv. 179.) Justinian made the oath a necessary preliminary to bringing or defending the action. (C. ii. 5. 9. 2.) Further, as in the time of Justinian, rashly defending certain actions subjected the defendant to a pecuniary loss, and rashly defending certain others, to infamy. And, lastly, the defendant could, in particular cases, bring against the plaintiff a contrary action, *contrarium judicium*; and the plaintiff, in these cases, was liable to pay a tenth part of the sum demanded, even though he had not actually brought the action from any bad motive.

1. Ecce enim jusjurandum omnibus qui conveniuntur, ex constitutione nostra defertur; nam reus non aliter suis allegationibus utitur,

1. And first, under our constitution, an oath is administered to all defendants. And the defendant is not admitted to state his defence

nisi prius juraverit quod putans sese bona instantia uti ad contradicendum pervenit. At adversus inficiantes ex quibusdam causis dupli vel tripli actio constituitur, veluti si damni injuriæ aut legatorum locis venerabilibus relictorum nomine agatur. Statim autem ab Initio pluris quam simpli est actio, velut furti manifesti quadrupli, nec manifesti dupli; nam ex his causis et aliis quibusdam, sive quis neget sive fateatur, pluris quam simpli est actio. Item actoris quoque calumnia coercetur, nam etiam actor pro calumnia jurare cogitur ex nostra constitutione; utriusque etiam partis advocati jusjurandum subeunt, quod alia nostra constitutione comprehensum est. Hæc autem omnia pro veteris calumniæ actione introducta sunt, quæ in desuetudinem abiit, quia in partem decimam litis actores mulctabat, quod numquam factum esse invenimus: sed pro his introductum est et præfatum jusjurandum, et ut improbus litigator et damnum et impensas litis inferre adversario suo cogatur.

until he has sworn that it is from a persuasion of the goodness of his own cause that he resists the demand of the plaintiff. In many cases the action is raised so as to be for the double or treble value against those who deny: for instance, in the case of wrongful damage, or of legacies left to holy places. There are other cases, in which, from the beginning, the action is more than for the single value, as, for instance, the action *furti manifesti* for the quadruple, and *furti nec manifesti* for the double. In these cases and in some others, whether the defendant denies or confesses, the action is for more than the single value. The litigiousness of the plaintiff is also restrained, for he is obliged by our constitution to take the oath *de calumnia*. The advocates also of each party take an oath prescribed by another of our constitutions. All these formalities have been introduced to replace the old action *calumniæ*, which is fallen into disuse, for it subjected the plaintiff to a fine of the tenth of the value of the thing in dispute; but we have never known this penalty enforced. In its stead, there has, in the first place, been introduced the oath we have just mentioned: and, in the next place, a person who brings a groundless action is made to reimburse his adversary for all losses and expenses he has been put to.

GAL. iv. 173; C. ii. 59. 2; C. iii. 1. 13. 0; C. lii. 1. 14. L.

For the terms of these oaths see C. ii. 59. 2; C. iii. 1. 14. 1. *Vel tripli.* We know of no actions in which there was a penalty of treble against a defendant who denied the claim. Perhaps the word *tripli* has slipped in from the text of Gaius, in which it refers to actions *furti oblati*, &c. (GAL. iv. 171. 173.)

2. Ex quibusdam judiciis damnati ignominiosi fiunt: veluti furti, vi bonorum raptorum, injuriarum, de dolo; item tutelæ, mandati, depositi directis non contrariis actionibus; item pro socio, quæ ab utraque parte directa est, et ob id quilibet ex sociis eo judicio dam-

2. In certain actions the person condemned becomes infamous, as in the actions *furti, vi bonorum raptorum, injuriarum, de dolo:* as also in the actions *tutelæ, mandati, depositi*, if direct, but not if contrary: and also in the action *pro socio*, which is direct, by whichever of the contract-

natus ignominia notatur. Sed furti
quidem aut vi bonorum raptorum,
aut injuriarum, aut de dolo, non
solum damnati notantur ignominia,
sed etiam pacti, et recte: plurimum
enim interest, utrum ex delicto aliquis an ex contractu debitor sit.

ing parties it may be brought, and
in which infamy is attached to
whichever of these parties may be
condemned. But in the actions furti, vi bonorum raptorum, injuriarum,
and de dolo, it is not only to have
been condemned that makes a person infamous, but also to have agreed
for the commission of the offence;
and rightly, for there is a great difference in being debtor by a delict,
or by a contract.

GAI. iv. 182; D. iii. 2, 7.

*Directis non contrariis.*  Contrariæ actiones were such as
those brought against the pupil, the mandator, or depositor,
by the tutor, mandatary, or depositary. There could be no
reason why infamy should attach to a pupil who did not
know the amount of the claims of the tutor, or to a depositor
who did not know the amount of the expenses to which the
depositary had been put.

The consequences of infamy were to prevent the guilty
person from being a witness, receiving any public honours, or
bringing a public prosecution. We have also seen (Tit. 13. 11)
that, previous to the legislation of Justinian, a person declared
infamous could not appear as procurator in the cause of another.

3. Omnium autem actionum in-
stituendarum principium ab ea
parte edicti proficiscitur, qua prætor
edicit de in jus vocando; utique
enim in primis adversarius in jus
vocandus est, ad eum qui jus dic-
turus sit. Qua parte prætor parentibus et patronis, item parentibus
liberisque patronorum et patrona-
rum hunc præstat honorem, ut non
aliter liceat liberis libertisque eos
in jus vocare, quam si id ab ipso
prætore postulaverint et impetra-
verint; et si quis aliter vocaverit,
in eum pœnam solidorum quinquaginta constituit.

3. In bringing any action, the first
thing is, to comply with that part of
the edict in which the prætor treats
of the vocatio in jus. For the defendant must always be summoned
in jus, i.e. before the magistrate who
has the jurisdiction. In this part of
the edict the prætor wishes that such
respect should be shown towards ascendants, patrons, and even towards
the ascendants and children of patrons, that children and freedmen
cannot summon them in jus, unless
they have first obtained permission
from the prætor; and he subjects
persons who summon them without
having obtained the prætor's permission, to a penalty of fifty solidi.

GAI. iv. 46; D. ii. 4. 1; D. ii. 4. 4. 1; D. II. 4. 24.

The earliest method of *vocatio in jus* was to seize on the
defendant, and drag him before a magistrate. Afterwards
the seizing became symbolical, and the plaintiff called some
one to witness that the defendant had been seized, but would
not come.

## Tit. XVII. DE OFFICIO JUDICIS.

Superest ut de officio judicis dispiciamus. Et quidem imprimis illud observare debet judex, ne aliter
judicet quam legibus aut constitutionibus aut moribus proditum est.
D. v. 1. 40. 1; D. xlviii. 10. 1. 3.

It remains to treat of the office of
the judge. His first care ought to
be, never to judge otherwise than
according to the laws, the constitutions, or customary usage.

*Judex qui contra sacras principum constitutiones, contra
jus publicum quod apud se recitatum est, pronunciat, in
insulam deportatur.* (Paul. Sent. v. 25. 4.)

If the judge gave a sentence manifestly wrong, or if the
sum were fixed in the condemnation by the prætor, and the
judge condemned the defendant in a different sum (see
Tit. 4. 9), the sentence was treated as void without any appeal
being necessary. If the judge was mistaken, as, for instance,
in the mode in which he regarded some fact, an appeal was
allowed, which had to be brought within two days (prolonged
to ten days by Justinian in Nov. 23) after the sentence, or
three days if a procurator, and not the party himself, had
conducted the suit. The appeal lay from the judge back to
the prætor, from the prætor to the senate, or, in later times,
to the council of the emperor with the prætorian præfect as
its head judge, and finally to the emperor himself.

1. Ideoque si noxali judicio addictus est, observare debet, ut si
condemnandus videatur dominus,
ita debeat condemnare: Publium
Mævium Lucio Titio decem aureos
condemno, aut noxam dedere.

1. Consequently, in a noxal action, if he thinks the master ought
to be condemned, he ought thus to
shape the condemnation: 'I condemn Publius Mævius at the suit of
Lucius Titius to pay ten aurei, or to
abandon the cause of the injury.

D. xlii. 1. 6. 1.

2. Et si in rem actum sit, sive
contra petitorem judicaverit, ab-
solvere debet possessorem; sive
contra possessorem, jubere eum
debet ut rem ipsam restituat cum
fructibus. Sed si possessor neget
in præsenti se restituere posse, et
sine frustratione videbitur tempus
restituendi causa petere, indulgen-
dum est ei, si tamen de litis æstimatione caveat cum fidejussore, si
intra tempus quod ei datum est
non restituisset. Et si hereditas
petita sit, eadem circa fructus interveniunt, quæ diximus interven-

2. In a real action, if he determines against the claimant, he ought
to absolve the possessor; if against
the possessor, he ought to order the
possessor to give up the thing itself
together with the fruits. But if the
possessor states that it is out of his
power to give up the thing at once,
and his request for delay seems honestly made, the indulgence should
be accorded him; but he must first
furnish a *fidejussor* to give security
to the amount of the value of the
thing in dispute, in case he should
not restore it within the time al-

lis in singularum rerum petitiono: illorum autem fructuum quos culpa sua possessor non perceperit, in utraque actione eadem ratio pene habetur, si prædo fuerit; si vero bona fide possessor fuerit, non habetur ratio consumptorum, neque non perceptorum.  Post inrhoatam autem petitionem, etiam illorum fructuum ratio habetur qui culpa possessoris percepti non sunt, vel percepti consumpti sunt.

lowed him.  If it is an inheritance that is claimed, the rules with regard to the fruits are the same as those we have laid down in the case of particular things.  Of the fruits not gathered by the fault of the possessor, account is taken almost in the same way in both actions, when the possession is *mala fide*.  The *bona fide* possessor has not to account for fruits, whether consumed or not gathered.  But from the time when the claim is made, the possessor has to account for all fruits not gathered through his fault, or gathered and consumed.

D. vi. 1. 17. 1 ; D. vi. 1. 35. 1 ; D. vi. 1. 62. 1 ; C. iii. 32. 22.

What the words *eadem pene ratio* refer to is not easy to say.  Perhaps they may have reference to the lesser degree of severity with which an account of fruits not gathered was exacted in the case of an inheritance, the possessor not being accountable for all, but only for those which it could be fairly said he ought to have gathered.  (D. v. 3. 25. 4.)

Justinian here says that the position of a *bona fide* possessor was the same in the case of an inheritance and of a particular object ; for that in neither case was he answerable for fruits gathered and consumed.  But this was not the case after a *senatus-consultum* made in the time of Hadrian (D.v. 3. 20. 6.), which made the *bona fide* possessor of an inheritance answerable for all that he had profited by (D. v. 3. 28) ; and he was therefore answerable for the fruits he had consumed.  Perhaps the text may be based on some passage in the writings of a jurist who wrote before the *senatus-consultum* was made.

3. Si ad exhibendum actum fuerit, non sufficit si exhibeat rem is cum quo actum est ; sed opus est ut etiam rei causam debeat exhibere, id est, ut eam causam habeat actor quam habiturus esset, si cum primum ad exhibendum egisset, exhibita res fuisset: ideoque si inter moras usucapta sit res a possessore, nihilominus condemnabitur.  Præterea fructus medii temporis, id est, ejus quod post acceptum ad exhibendum judicium ante rem judicatam intercessit, rationem habere debet judex.  Quod si neget is cum quo ad exhibendum actum est, in præsenti exhibere posse, et tempus exhibendi causa petat, idque

3. In the action *ad exhibendum* it is not sufficient that the defendant exhibits the thing, but he must also exhibit everything derived from the thing, that is, he must place the claimant in the same position as he would have been in, if the thing had been exhibited immediately on the demand being made.  If, therefore, during the delay, the possessor completes the usucapion of the thing, he will still be condemned.  The judge ought also to make him account for the fruits of the intermediate time, that is, of the time elapsed between the granting the action *ad exhibendum* and the sentence.  If the defendant states that it is out of his

sine frustratione postulare videatur, dari ei debet, ut tamen careat ea restituturum. Quod si neque statim jussu judicis rem exhibeat, neque postea exhibiturum se caveat, condemnandus sit in id quod actoris intererat ab initio rem exhibitam esse.

power to make the exhibition immediately, and his request for delay seems honestly made, he should have time given him, but he must first give security that he will give the thing up. But if he neither exhibits the thing at once, upon the order of the judge, nor gives security for exhibiting it afterwards, he must be condemned in an amount equivalent to the interest of the claimant in having it exhibited immediately.

D. x. 4. 0. 5, 8;   D. x. 4. 12. 4, 5.

4. Si familiæ erciscundæ judicio actum sit, singulas res singulis heredibus adjudicare debet; et si in alterius persona prægravare videatur adjudicatio, debet hunc invicem coheredi certa pecunia, sicut jam dictum est, condemnare. Eo quoque nomine coheredi quisque suo condemnandus est, quod solus fructus hereditarii fundi percepit, aut rem hereditariam corruperit aut consumpserit. Quæ quidem similiter inter plures quoque quam duos coheredes subsequuntur.

4. In the action familiæ erciscundæ, he ought to adjudge each object to each heir separately, and, if any one heir has more than his share adjudged him, the judge ought, as we have said above, to condemn him to pay his coheir a fixed sum as an equivalent. So, too, an heir ought to be condemned to make compensation to his coheirs, who has alone enjoyed the fruits of the land of the inheritance, or has damaged, or consumed anything forming part of the inheritance. And these rules apply, whether the coheirs are two or more.

D. x. 2. 51, 52. 2.

As to the office of the judge in the three actions noticed in this and the two succeeding paragraphs, see Introd. sec. 103.

5. Eadem interveniunt, et si communi dividundo de pluribus rebus actum fuerit. Quod si de una re, veluti fundo, si quidem iste fundus commode regionibus dividionem recipiat, partus ejus singulis adjudicare debet, et si unius pars prægravare videbitur, is invicem certa pecunia alteri condemnandus est. Quod si commode dividi non possit, velut homo forte aut mulus erit de quo actum sit, tunc totus uni adjudicandus est, et is invicem alteri certa pecunia condemnandus.

5. It is the same in the action communi dividundo for the division of a number of things. If there is only one object to be divided, for instance, a piece of land, the judge ought, if the land easily admits of division, to adjudge their respective shares to the several co-proprietors. And if one of them receives too large a share, the judge ought to order him to pay a sum of money as compensation to the other. If the thing is one that cannot be advantageously divided, as, for instance, a slave or mule, then the whole must be adjudged to one, and he must be condemned to pay a fixed sum as compensation to the other.

D. x. 3. 55;   C. iii. 37. 3.

6. Si finium regundorum actum fuerit, dispicere debet judex an necessaria sit adjudicatio: quæ sane uno casu necessaria est, si evidentioribus finibus distingui agros communidius sit, quam olim fuissent distincti; nam tunc necesse est ex alterius agro partem aliquam alterius agri domino adjudicari, quo casu conveniens est ut is alteri certa pecunia debeat condemnari. Eo quoque nomine damnandus est quisque hoc judicio, quod forte circa fines aliquid malitiose commisit, verbi gratia, quia lapides finales furatus est, vel arbores finales occidit. Contumaciæ quoque nomine quisque eo judicio condemnator, veluti si quis jubente judice metiri agros passus non fuerit.

6. In the action finium regundorum the judge ought to examine if the adjudication is necessary, and it is so only in one case, viz. if it would be advantageous that the boundaries should be more clearly marked than before. In that case it becomes necessary to adjudge to one party a portion of the field of the other, and consequently the person to whom it is adjudged ought to be condemned to pay a fixed sum as compensation to the other. In this action he ought also to be condemned who has fraudulently interfered with the boundaries, as, for instance, by carrying off the boundary stones, or cutting down the trees that mark the limit. A person may be also condemned by this same action for contumacy, who, in defiance of the order of the judge, opposes the measurement of the fields.

D. x. 1, 2. 1; D. x. 1. 3, 4. 3, 4.

7. Quod autem istis judiciis alicui adjudicatum sit, id statim ejus fit cui adjudicatum est.

7. In these actions, anything adjudged becomes at once the property of the person to whom it is adjudged.

See Introd. sec. 103.

## Tit. XVIII. DE PUBLICIS JUDICIIS.

Publica judicia neque per actiones ordinantur, neque omnino quidquam simile habent cum ceteris judiciis de quibus locuti sumus, magnaque diversitas est eorum et in instituendis et in exercendis.

Public prosecutions are not introduced by actions, and bear no resemblance to the other legal remedies of which we have been speaking. There is a great difference between them, both in the mode in which they are begun and in that in which they are carried on.

The subject of public prosecutions is foreign to a treatise which, like the Institutes, professes to treat only of private law. It is not noticed at all in the Institutes of Gaius, and is treated in a very cursory manner in this Title. For the comprehension of this Title, it will be sufficient to observe that, in the later times of the Republic and in the first years of the Empire, a series of laws was made, fixing the penalty to be attached to particular crimes, and prescribing the procedure to be employed in the trial. Many of these laws are briefly alluded to in this Title; and it was the trials conducted under their provisions that alone received the name of *pub lica judicia.* Under the Empire, most of the crimes not coming under these special laws, and especially those provided against by a *senatus-consultum* or constitution, were judged by the prætor or *præfectus urbi* in a more summary method. The *judicium* was then said to be, not *publicum,* but *extra ordinem;* and gradually the method of procedure prescribed by the law for the different *publica judicia* fall into desuetude, and nothing was retained of the special laws but the penalty they fixed (D. xlviii. 1. 8), the procedure being the same as in the *judicia extraordinaria.*

| | |
|---|---|
| 1. Publica autem dicta sunt, quod cuivis ex populo executio eorum plerumque datur. | 1. They are called public, because generally any citizen may institute them. |

D. xxiii. 2. 43. 10.

There were certain persons excluded from the right of bringing a criminal accusation; for instance, women, unless the injury complained of was done to themselves or their near relations, and persons below the age of puberty, persons made infamous by a judicial sentence, and persons so poor as not to possess fifty *aurei.* (D. xlviii. 2. 2. 8 and 10.) But, generally speaking, it was the right of anyone to make a criminal charge, although he might be totally unconnected by any ties with the person who suffered from the crime.

| | |
|---|---|
| 2. Publicorum judiciorum quædam capitalia sunt, quædam non capitalia. Capitalia dicimus, quæ ultimo supplicio afficiunt, vel aquæ et ignis interdictione, vel deportatione, vel metallo; cetera, si quam infamiam irrogant cum damno pecuniario, hæc publica quidem sunt, non tamen capitalia. | 2. Some public prosecutions are capital, some are not. We term capital those which involve the extreme punishment of the law, or the interdiction from fire and water, or deportation, or the mines. Those which carry with them infamy and a pecuniary penalty are public, but not capital. |

D. xlviii. 1, 2.

| | |
|---|---|
| 3. Publica autem sunt hæc: lex Julia majestatis, quæ in eos qui contra Imperatorem vel rempublicam aliquid moliti sunt, suum vigorem extendit. Hujus pœna animæ amissionem sustinet, et memoria rei etiam post mortem damnatur. | 3. The following laws have reference to public prosecutions. The *lex Julia majestatis,* which subjects to its severe provisions all who attempt anything against the Emperor or State. The penalty it inflicts is the loss of life, and the memory of the guilty is condemned even after his death. |

D. xlviii. 4. 11.

The *lex Julia majestatis* was passed in the time of Julius Cæsar. (D. xliii. 4.)

*Aliquid moliti sunt.* The design, without any overt act,
was enough to sustain the charge.

*Etiam post mortem.* (See Bk. iii. Tit. 1. 5.)

| | |
|---|---|
| 4. Item lex Julia de adulteriis coercendis, quae non solum temeratores alienarum nuptiarum gladio punit, sed et eos qui cum masculis nefandam libidinem exercere audent: sed sad-in lege Julia etiam stupri punitio punitur, cum quis sine vi vel virginem vel viduam honeste viventem stupraverit. Poenam autem eadem lex irrogat peccatoribus, si honesti sunt, publicationem partis dimidiae bonorum; si humiles, corporis coercitionem cum relegatione. | 4. Also the *lex Julia de adulteriis*, which punishes with death not only those who defile the marriage bed, but those also who give themselves up to works of lewdness with their own sex. The same law also punishes the seduction without violence of a virgin, or of a widow of honest character. The penalty upon offenders of honourable condition is the confiscation of half their fortune, upon those of low condition, corporal punishment and relegation. |

D. xlviii. 34, pr. and 1.

The *lex Julia de adulteriis* belongs to the time of Augustus, about B.C. 167.

*Gladio punit.* The *lex Julia* only punished the guilty with confiscation of a portion of their property and relegation. (PAUL. *Sent.* ii. 26. 14.) Constantine affixed the graver penalty. (C. ix. 9. 31.)

| | |
|---|---|
| 5. Item lex Cornelia de sicariis, quae homicidas ultore ferro persequitur, vel eos qui hominis occidendi causa cum telo ambulant. Telum autem, ut Gaius noster in interpretatione legum Duodecim Tabularum scriptum reliquit, vulgo quidem id appellatur, quod ab arcu mittitur; sed et omne significatur quod manu cujusdam mittitur. Sequitur ergo ut lapis et lignum et ferrum hoc nomine contineatur, dictumque ab eo quod in longinquum mittitur, a Graeca voce ἀπὸ τοῦ τηλοῦ. Et hanc significationem invenire possumus et in Graeco nomine: nam quod nos telum appellamus, illi βέλος appellant ἀπὸ τοῦ βάλλειν. Admonet nos Xenophon, nam ita scribit: καὶ τὰ βέλη ὁμοῦ ἐφέρετο, λόγχαι, τοξεύματα, σφενδόναι, πλεῖστοι δὲ καὶ λίθοι. Sicarii autem appellantur a sica, quod significat ferreum cultrum. Eadem lege et venefici capite damnantur, qui artibus odiosis tam venenis quam susurris magicis homines occiderint, vel mala medicamenta publice vendiderint. | 5. Also the *lex Cornelia de sicariis*, which strikes with the sword of vengeance those who for the purpose of killing a man go armed with a *telum*. By *telum*, according to the interpretation given by our Gaius in his commentaries on the Twelve Tables, is ordinarily meant anything that is shot from a bow, but it equally signifies anything sent from the hand. Thus, a stone, a piece of wood, or of iron, is included in the meaning of the term, for it merely implies something impelled to a distance, being derived from the Greek word τηλοῦ. And the corresponding word in Greek has the same signification, for what we call *telum*, they call βέλος, from βάλλειν, as we may learn from Xenophon, who says, 'they carried βέλη, viz. spears, arrows, slings, and a great quantity of stones.' Assassins are called *sicarii* from *sica*, a short sword. By the same law, poisoners are condemned who by hateful arts use poisons or magic charms to kill men, or publicly sell hurtful drugs. |

D. xlviii. 8. 1; D. 1. 10. 233. 2.

*Lex Cornelia de sicariis* passed during the dictatorship of Sylla, B.C. 80.

6. Alia deinde lex asperrimum crimen nova pœna persequitur, quæ Pompeia de parricidiis vocatur. Qua cavetur, ut si quis parentis aut filii, aut omnino affectionis ejus quæ nuncupatione parricidii continetur, fata properaverit, sive clam sive palam id ausus fuerit, nec non is cujus dolo malo id factum est, vel conscius criminis existit, licet extraneus sit, pœna parricidii punitur. Et neque gladio neque ignibus neque ulla alia solemni pœna subjiciatur, sed insutus culeo cum cane et gallo gallinaceo et vipera et simia, et inter eas femlea angustias comprehensus, secundum quod regionis qualitas tulerit, vel in vicinum mare vel in amnem projiciatur: ut omnium elementorum usu vivus carere incipiat, et ei cœlum superstiti et terra mortuo auferatur. Si quis autem alias cognatione vel affinitate conjunctas personas necaverit, pœnam legis Corneliæ de sicariis sustinebit.

6. Another law, the *lex Pompeia de parricidiis*, inflicts on the most horrible of crimes a singular punishment. It provides, that any one who has hastened the death of a parent or child, or of any other relation whose murder is legally termed parricide, whether he acts openly or secretly, and whoever instigates, or is an accomplice in the commission of the crime, although a stranger, shall undergo the penalty of parricide. He will be punished, not by the sword, nor by fire, nor by any ordinary mode of punishment, but he is to be sewn up in a sack with a dog, a cock, a viper, and an ape, and inclosed in this horrible prison he is to be, according to the nature of the place, thrown into the sea, or into a river, that even in his lifetime he may begin to be deprived of the use of the elements, and that the air may be denied to him while he lives, and the earth when he dies. He who kills other persons allied to him by cognation or alliance, shall undergo the penalty of the *lex Cornelia de sicariis.*

D. xlviii. 9. 1. 9 ; C. ix. 17.

*Lex Pompeia de parricidiis*, passed in the consulship of Pompeius, B.C. 52. The punishment mentioned in the text is borrowed from the legislation of the Twelve Tables. The *lex Pompeia*, under the term *parricidium*, embraced the murder of any ascendant of a husband or wife, of *consobrini*, of a step-father, step-mother, father-in-law, mother-in-law, &c., of a patron, and of a child if killed by the mother or grandfather, but not if killed by the father. (D. xlviii. 9. 1.) If there was no river at hand, the offender was torn to pieces by wild beasts. (D. xlviii. 9. 9.)

7. Item lex Cornelia de falsis, quæ etiam testamentaria vocatur, pœnam irrogat ei qui testamentum vel aliud instrumentum falsum scripserit, signaverit, recitaverit, subjecerit: quive signum adulterinum fecerit, sculpserit, expresserit sciens dolo malo. Ejusque legis

7. Also the *lex Cornelia de falsis*, otherwise called *testamentaria*, punishes any one who shall have written, sealed, read, or substituted a false testament, or any other instrument, or shall have made, cut, or impressed a false seal, knowingly and wilfully. The penalty is, upon a slave, the ex-

pœna in servos ultimum supplicium est (quod etiam in lege de sicariis et veneficis servatur), in liberos vero deportatio.

treme punishment of the law, as is pronounced by the *lex Cornelia* upon assassins and poisoners: that upon freemen is deportation.

D. xlviii. 10. 1. 13. 10. 1.

*Lex Cornelia de falsis,* or *Cornelia testamentaria,* was passed under the dictatorship of Sylla, B.C. 80.

8. Item lex Julia de vi publica seu privata adversus eos exoritur, qui vim vel armatam vel sine armis commiserint: sed si quidem armata vis armatur, deportatio ei ex lege Julia de vi publica irrogatur; si vero sine armis, in tertiam partem bonorum publicatio imponitur. Sin autem per vim raptus virginis vel viduæ vel sanctimonialis vel alterius fuerit perpetratus, tunc et peccatores et ii qui opem flagitio dederunt, capite puniuntur, secundum nostræ constitutionis definitionem ex qua hoc apertius est scire.

8. Also the *lex Julia de vi publica seu privata* punishes those who are guilty of violence, whether with armed force or without. For violence with armed force, the penalty inflicted by the *lex Julia de vi publica* is deportation. For violence without arms, it is the confiscation of a third of the offender's property. But in case of the rape of a virgin, a widow, a person devoted to religion, or any one else, both the ravishers and all who have aided in the commission of the crime are punished capitally, according to the provisions of our constitution, in which may be found fuller information on this head.

D. xlviii. 6. 10. 2; C. ix. 13. 1, pr. and foll.

*Lex Julia de vi,* passed in the time of Julius Cæsar or Augustus, but its exact date is not known.

9. Item lex Julia peculatus eos punit, qui pecuniam vel rem publicam vel sacram vel religiosam furati fuerint. Sed si quidem ipsi judices tempore administrationis publicas pecunias subtraxerint, capitali animadversione puniantur; et non solum hi, sed etiam qui ministerium eis ad hoc exhibuerint, vel qui subtractas ab his scientes susceperint. Alii vero qui in hanc legem inciderint, pœnæ deportationis subjugantur.

9. Also the *lex Julia de peculatu,* punishes those who have stolen public money, or anything sacred or religious. Magistrates, who, during the time of their administration, have stolen the public money, are punishable capitally, as also are all who aid them in their robbery, or who receive their plunder from them. Other persons who offend against this law are subject to the penalty of deportation.

D. xlviii. 13. 1. 3; C. ix. 28.

*Lex Julia peculatus.* The exact date of this law is also unknown. It probably belongs to the same epoch as the *lex Julia de vi.*

10. Est et inter publica judicia lex Fabia de plagiariis, quæ interdum capitis pœnam ex sacris constitutionibus irrogat, interdum leviorem.

10. There is also the *lex Fabia de plagiariis,* which inflicts, in certain cases, capital punishment according to the constitutions, sometimes a lighter punishment.

C. ix. 20. 7.

Cicero refers to this law (pro *Rabirio*, 3), but nothing more is known of it. A *plagiarius* was one who knowingly kept in irons, or confined, sold, gave, or bought a citizen (whether freeborn or a freedman) or the slave of another.

11. Sunt præterea publica judicia, lex Julia ambitus, lex Julia repetundarum, ex lege Julia de annona, et lex Julia de residuis: quæ de certis capitulis loquuntur, et animæ quidem amissionem non irrogant, aliis autem pœnis eos subjiciunt qui præcepta earum neglexerint.

11. The following laws also pertain to public prosecutions: the *lex Julia de ambitu*, the *lex Julia repetundarum*, the *lex Julia de annona*, and the *lex Julia de residuis*. These laws apply to certain special cases, and do not carry with them the punishment of death, but lesser punishments against offenders.

D. xlvii. 11; D. xlviii. 10. 2. 4, 5; D. xlviii. 12. 2, pr. and foll; D. xlviii. 14.

*Lex Julia de ambitu*, made in the time of Augustus, to repress illegal methods of seeking offices. (D. xlviii. 14.)

*Lex Julia repetundarum*, made in the time of Julius Cæsar, to punish magistrates or judges for receiving bribes.

*Lex Julia de annona*, made to repress combinations for heightening the price of provisions.

*Lex Julia de residuis*, made to punish those who gave an incomplete account of, or misappropriated, public moneys committed to their charge. (D. xlviii. 13. 2.)

It is uncertain whether these last two laws belong to the time of Julius Cæsar or of Augustus.

12. Sed de publicis judiciis hæc exposuimus, ut vobis possibile sit summo digito et quasi per indicem ea tetigisse: aliorquin diligentior eorum scientia vobis ex latioribus Digestorum seu Pandectarum libris, Deo propitio, adventura est.

12. This notice of public prosecutions has only been meant to give you the merest sketch that might serve you as a guide to studying them. You may, with the blessing of God, gain a more complete knowledge of them from the fuller account given in the Digest or Pandects.

# INDEX.